DATE DUE

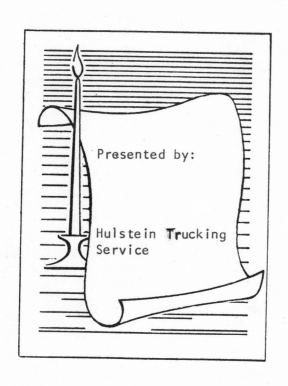

Presented by:

Hulstein Trucking
Service

INVESTMENT POLICIES OF
LIFE INSURANCE COMPANIES

INVESTMENT POLICIES OF

LIFE INSURANCE COMPANIES

LAWRENCE D. JONES

Associate Professor of Business Economics
and Public Policy, Indiana University

Formerly Instructor in Economics,
Harvard University

DIVISION OF RESEARCH
GRADUATE SCHOOL OF BUSINESS ADMINISTRATION
HARVARD UNIVERSITY · Boston, 1968

43297

Library of Congress Catalog Card No. 68-18719

Printed in the United States of America

Foreword

This book is the second in the planned series of publications of the Capital Markets Project. The project was started in 1958 as a joint endeavor of faculty members at the Harvard Business School, the Department of Economics at Harvard, and the School of Industrial Management at the Massachusetts Institute of Technology. The intent of the project was to attempt to explain the way in which the whole set of interactions among households, nonfinancial businesses, governments and their agencies, and financial intermediaries produces a balance between the supplies and demands for securities of various types—in the face of continuous changes in the volume and composition of both supplies and demands. The objective was to bridge the gap between the formal theoretical literature and the statistical and descriptive literature of capital markets with an analysis of the process by which investment flows are actually brought into balance in the capital markets.

In organizing the Capital Markets Project, we have attempted to delineate the "anatomy" of the markets for capital funds in the American economy by studying the activities of major participants in those markets. The project has sponsored studies of the investment and financing decisions of business firms, of saving and investment practices of households, and of the financial portfolio choices of financial institutions. The authors of these studies have generally drawn on their own field work to frame hypotheses about the responses of households and businesses to changes in interest rates and other potentially significant variables, and then gone on to test those hypotheses with statistical and econometric techniques.

In this book Professor Jones has written an outstanding study of the performance of life insurance companies as financial intermediaries. How responsive have life companies been to movements in interest rates in making decisions which affected the composition of assets and the allocation of newly acquired funds to business and household and government borrowers? This is the central question which runs through the entire study.

To clear the way for a realistic examination of the question, Professor Jones first describes the basic investment objectives of life companies and the legal and tax and technical considerations which restrict and condition their investment practices. He then turns to the difficult problem of dealing with expectations—of future investment opportunities and interest levels and investible cash inflows—and analyzes the types of decisions which were deliberately made to affect the time pattern of investment allocations. The study concludes with a specific investigation of the composition of life company commitments and an attempt to isolate the most important determinants of investment decisions.

The primary support of the Capital Markets Project came from a generous grant of the Merrill Foundation for the Advancement of Financial Knowledge. The grant was made to the Business School for the three cooperating institutions, and the project has been administered at this School. Support for the completion stages of the project has come from a grant to this School from the Ford Foundation in support of a broad research program in business finance. We would like to express for ourselves and our co-director, Professor Duesenberry, Department of Economics, Harvard University, as well as for Harvard and M.I.T., our gratitude to the Merrill Foundation and the Ford Foundation for their support of this work.

ELI SHAPIRO   LAWRENCE E. THOMPSON
Professor of Finance   Professor of Business Administration

Boston, Massachusetts
March 1968

Acknowledgments

This study was prepared under the auspices of the Merrill Foundation Capital Markets Project, and was designed in accordance
with the project's overall objectives.   I am grateful to the Merrill
Foundation for financial support received, and to the project directors, James S. Duesenberry, Lawrence E. Thompson, and Eli
Shapiro and to Bertrand Fox, Director of Research, Harvard
Business School, for encouragement and support.

The ideas which led to this book had their beginnings in my
Ph.D. dissertation, *Portfolio Objectives, External Constraints, and
the Postwar Investment Behavior of Life Insurance Companies*,
which was written under the direction of Professor Duesenberry
and submitted to Harvard University in 1959.   Work on the present study began in 1960 with intensive field work including interviews with over fifty investment officers representing fourteen
major life insurance companies.   Investment data were collected
from interviewed companies and from the major trade associations,
particularly the Life Insurance Association of America.   James J.
O'Leary, then Director of Economic Research of the Life Insurance Association of America, and Eli Shapiro, then Deputy Research Director of the Commission on Money and Credit staff,
were especially helpful at this stage.

Most of the basic research was carried out while the author was
Instructor of Economics at Harvard and had access to the Harvard
libraries.   Major computations were carried out at the Harvard
Littauer Statistical Laboratory and the Wesleyan University Com-
puter Center.   I am particularly indebted to Gary Fromm for
extensive programming assistance at an early stage and to my
Wesleyan student assistants, Charles Jacob and John Lapp.

Most of the book was written while I was Assistant Professor
of Economics at Wesleyan University.   My wife handled all the

typing chores and provided biting editorial comment and encouragement in many forms. The manuscript was completed while I was a Brookings Research Professor and guest of the Center for Real Estate and Urban Economics at the University of California, Berkeley. I am appreciative of support provided by the Brookings Institution and grateful for the excellent facilities and secretarial assistance provided by the Real Estate Center.

In addition to the project directors, several friends and colleagues read portions of the manuscript and contributed helpful comments and criticism. In particular, I thank John Cornwall, Burton C. Hallowell, Ira Horowitz, Stanley Lebergott, Basil Moore, and Thompson Whitin. Eli Shapiro read the complete manuscript with great care and made many useful comments. Bertrand Fox supplied invaluable guidance in the final stages of preparing the manuscript for publication. Miss Ruth Norton skillfully directed the editing, oversaw the preparation of the charts and index, and guided the study through the complex publication process.

My original interest in capital markets and financial institutions was sparked by James Duesenberry, and his ideas and methodological inclinations permeate this book. Only those who have enjoyed the privilege of working closely with Professor Duesenberry over a period of time can appreciate the extent of the debt which I owe to his stimulating suggestions, unlimited ideas, and persistent prodding.

Unfortunately, none of the above have consented to accept responsibility for errors, omissions, or the conclusions of this study. This is the responsibility of the author.

LAWRENCE D. JONES

Bloomington, Indiana
April 1968

Contents

List of Tables

List of Charts

ABSTRACT

Investment Policies of Life Insurance Companies

In this book Professor Jones has written an outstanding study of the performance of life insurance companies as financial intermediaries. The central question running through the entire study is: How responsive have life insurance companies been to movements in interest rates in making decisions which affected the composition of assets and the allocation of newly acquired funds to business and household and government borrowers? The author's investigations in his search for an answer to this question are described below.

This volume is the second of a series of publications of the results of studies under a broad research program entitled the Capital Markets Project. The author, Lawrence D. Jones, was Instructor in Economics at Harvard University when he undertook this research. He is presently Associate Professor of Business Economics and Public Policy, Indiana University.

This study is concerned with the process by which U.S. life insurance companies make their portfolio selections. The life insurance industry is of special significance because of its size and because life companies have invested in a wider range of financial and real assets than most other financial intermediaries.

The investigation deals with both the application of portfolio selection ideas and public policy problems. Its primary objective, however, is to systematically explore the role that life insurance companies have played in the capital markets. This objective dictated the limits of the study, the specific problems chosen for investigation, the methodology employed, and the data utilized. As one consequence life companies are treated as an essentially homogeneous group of lenders and the empirical analysis is performed upon aggregative industry data and evidence representative of the larger companies in the industry.

Underlying this study is a desire to clarify the function that interest rates perform in influencing the volume and allocation of funds supplied to the capital markets. Applied to life insurance companies, the central questions are: Do asset yields play the primary role in determining life companies' investment decisions? If not, why not? And, if not, what are the primary considerations governing their portfolio choices? The investigation is carried out in three stages. First, the setting in which life company portfolio decisions are made is described in terms of (1) life companies' internal investment goals and (2) the features of the external environment which impinge upon life company asset selections. In the second part, the focus is upon portfolio decisions which determine the intertemporal allocation of life insurance industry investment funds. The study concludes with an analysis of the factors determining the composition of portfolio choices.

With respect to internal investment goals, it is difficult to demonstrate that success in the insurance industry is closely linked over time to the rate of investment return. Competing portfolio objectives are primarily concerned with insuring financial solvency. The solvency objective has been responsible for most of life companies' interest in non-yield asset and portfolio characteristics such as liquidity, maturity, credit quality, and diversification. This concern has been reinforced, and redefined, by state investment statutes and asset valuation rules. These internal goals, and state regulations, together with the federal income tax laws, have had the effect of restricting life companies' asset acquisitions primarily to medium-term to long-term, private, investment grade, debt obligations.

The study concludes, however, that life companies pay relatively little attention to portfolio proportions and that non-return asset and portfolio considerations have had a very limited impact on investment choice decisions at the margin. Various problems associated with the mechanics of the investment process appeared to be more significant in restraining life companies from basing portfolio selections upon a yield-maximization objective. The volume and composition of asset choices appeared to depend primarily upon:

(1) relative yields among alternative assets,
(2) the desire of life companies to invest funds quickly and "permanently" as they become available, and
(3) the desire of life companies to maintain good customer, brokerage, and agency relations.

The relative weight of these three factors varied substantially among the various portfolio problems examined. This study finds the pattern of life companies' liquidation of Treasury obligations after World War II to be broadly consistent with an assumption of yield responsiveness on the part of life companies. In contrast to conclusions reached by other observers, an abrupt slackening in the Government securities disposal rate after 1951 is found to be consistent with yield responsiveness. Non-yield considerations became more relevant to an explanation of the disposal patterns as liquidation continued during the 1950s and 1960s.

The level of interest rates or expectations about interest rates did not appear to play a significant role in life company decisions with respect to the maturity distribution of assets, optimal liquidity holdings, or borrowing activity. Except for life company insistence on reasonably strong call protection on corporate bond investments during periods of cyclically high interest rates, maturity characteristics of assets did not seem to influence portfolio choices within the predetermined set of eligible investments.

There seems to be no evidence that life companies have borrowed funds as part of a cyclical interest rate strategy. A clear, but quantitatively modest, cyclical pattern in life companies' liquid asset holdings is apparent from the data, but this pattern also cannot be explained as a response to the cyclical pattern of interest rates. Both the borrowing and liquidity patterns seem to be the product of systematic errors in forecasting cash flows and loan commitment takedown dates together with inadequate controls over new commitments.

Extensive use of the forward commitment device makes it possible to separate in time most investment decisions from the actual delivery of funds. Conceivably forward commitments could be an effective means of speculating on future interest rate movements while maintaining a "loaned up" position. Analysis of this possibility, however, produced the conclusion that the potential for using loan commitments for interest rate speculation was quite limited, and, in any case, that commitments have not been employed successfully by life companies for this purpose. It appeared that the time path of new commitments authorized by life companies was best explained by (1) the normal inflow of investible funds anticipated over the upcoming six months or so, and (2) the demand for long-term forward commitments by corporate borrowers. The first factor reflects use of the commitment device to achieve a "fully invested" position and the second, use of forward commitments as a service offered to corporate borrowers as an inducement to negotiate debt issues privately with life companies.

Variation in yield spreads among alternative assets did seem to have an impact upon the asset composition of forward commitment authorizations. The impact on the mortgage loan/corporate bond mix was reduced, however, by life companies' special use of mortgage commitments as a means of keeping asset acquisitions in line with available cash inflow, their willingness to make long-term commitments to corporate customers, and their aversion to substantial price discounts on federally underwritten loans. Commitments to acquire state and local government debt issues appeared to be made almost entirely on the basis of yield attractiveness. Choices of equity investments, including corporate preferred and common shares and real property, seemed to be based on anticipated income yield—not on prospective capital gains.

On balance, the study concludes that over the long run life companies achieve a satisfactory rate-of-return performance more by keeping fully invested and maintaining close contacts with brokers and potential customers than by speculating in their liquidity, borrowing, and forward commitment decisions or "reaching for yield" in their asset mix selections. This policy does tend to restrain life company temporal and investment composition responses and consequently serves to make capital market adjustments more sluggish than would be the case if life companies were more aggressive and yield conscious in the short run. Nonetheless, life companies are not locked-in to any sector of the capital markets, portfolio choice responses are clearly observable, and some responses are due to variation in asset yields.

In its concluding chapter, the study examines the impact of life company portfolio policy upon some important public policy questions. Four areas receive special attention: (1) the extent to which life companies have contributed to a mechanism creating cyclical instability, (2) the impact of monetary policy upon nonbank financial intermediaries, particularly life insurance companies, (3) the significance of ongoing structural changes in the mortgage markets (including the proposed removal of administratively imposed ceiling contract rates on federally underwritten loans) to life company participation in mortgage markets, and (4) the extent to which life insurance company investment policy is over-regulated by state laws and state insurance commissioners.

(Published by Division of Research, Harvard Business School, Soldiers Field, Boston, Massachusetts 02163. xxi + 555 pages, $10.00. 1968)

INTRODUCTION

This study is concerned with the manner in which a group of major financial intermediaries in the United States — legal reserve life insurance companies — make their portfolio selections. The life insurance industry provides abundant sources of empirical material for examination of ideas emanating from the theory of portfolio choice alone. In addition, however, the investment behavior of life insurance companies has important public policy implications, and some knowledge of their practices is indispensable to an understanding of the process of equilibrium determination in the capital markets. In this study we shall be concerned with each of these areas: portfolio choice ideas, public policy problems, and the role of life insurance companies in the capital markets. But our ultimate objective concerns the last, i.e., to identify the elements of life insurance company investment decisions which are relevant to the analysis of the process by which supplies and demands are balanced in the capital markets. This objective leads us to treat life insurance companies as an essentially homogeneous group of lenders and to concentrate attention particularly on the larger companies that hold most of the industry's assets.

The central thread running throughout this study is the question of whether market interest rates in fact play a primary role in directing the actions of capital market participants. During the past 30 years, this question has been the subject of numerous investigations of the determinants of real capital expenditures and the demand for external financing. Much less study has been devoted to the function of interest rates in influencing the volume and direction of funds supplied to the capital markets. Life insurance companies are of especial importance for this sort of analysis because of the substantial volume of financial assets they control and because they lend in a wider range of assets than most other financial intermediaries. Our attention will be focused, then, on the extent to which life insurance company investment decisions have been responsive to movements in market interest rates.

Responsiveness can take a number of forms. These include willingness of life companies to adjust the composition of their portfolio stocks through trading existing assets as well as through allocation of the current cash flow generated by the insurance business and by regular portfolio repayments. Responsiveness includes the temporal reactions of investment decisions to interest rate changes or expectations about interest rate movements; it covers decisions governing the total volume of funds supplied from period to period as well as the mix of assets disposed of and acquired over time. We shall be concerned with interest rate responses in all these dimensions.

Failure to observe elastic life insurance company supply responses to interest rate variations could result from several diverse causes. It may be, for instance, that life companies are not even proximately yield maximizers. Other portfolio objectives may compete with, and perhaps swamp, the rate of return goal. Investment decisions may often depend upon other attributes of portfolio assets and other goals may determine investment timing. Stability of capital value, security of income, and various liquidity needs are commonly suggested as alternative portfolio goals of life insurance companies. On the other hand, life companies may be essentially yield motivated; but various constraints, including external regulations governing investment decisions, tax considerations, limited marketability of assets, or organizational inflexibilities inherent in the mechanics of investing a large volume of funds, may inhibit their ability to respond strongly and quickly to changes in the level and structure of market yields. Interest rate inelasticity on the demand for funds side of the market may force the equilibrating process to take place through variables other than interest rates. Yield responsiveness on the supply side may be very difficult to observe where it does exist. Differences among lenders in time horizons and expectations held can produce a variety of responses among lenders, all of whom are strongly yield oriented. Finally, available interest rate series may inadequately represent expected returns available on alternative broad categories of assets.

In this study we shall assume that existing interest rate series are tolerable proxies for anticipated yields available on the various asset categories. We also assume that it is reasonable to examine portfolio selectors' decisions in terms of a few broad asset alternatives. If these assumptions are unreasonable, then the construction of workable capital market models that can be integrated into real expenditures models will be very difficult indeed.

The objectives of this study are carried out in three distinguishable parts. Chapters I and II provide some background on life company portfolio policy and the environment in which it is carried out. Specifically, in Chapter I we briefly describe the role life companies have adopted within the capital markets and examine the relative importance of the various internal investment goals on which portfolio policy is based. In Chapter II we investigate the extent to which external regulations imposed upon the life insurance industry alter companies' investment objectives or restrict their ability to achieve internally formulated goals. With these objectives and environmental constraints set out, the remainder of the study deals specifically with the life insurance industry's portfolio allocation decisions during recent years. The empirical analysis focuses primarily upon the period from the end of the Korean War to 1960, but some attention is necessarily devoted to the earlier postwar years in order to place the later period in perspective.

Chapters III through VI deal with features of the time pattern of allocation decisions. Attention is directed first at the dramatic postwar liquidation of U.S. Government securities from life company portfolios. The determinants of the time rate of this adjustment process are investigated in detail in Chapters III and IV. Chapter V examines the extent to which life companies have responded to cyclical movements in interest rates through their borrowing policy or management of their liquid asset holdings. Chapter VI deals with the role of forward investment commitments in the timing of portfolio decisions. In analyzing all these time sequence decision patterns attention is focused upon whether the behavior is consistent with a yield maximization objective, and if not, what specific competing goals, mechanical inflexibilities, or external constraints were responsible for shaping the time patterns observed.

Finally, in Chapters VII and VIII, the influence of relative yields upon the mix of asset selections is analyzed. Again, alternative determinants of investment decisions are also considered. Some of these derive from temporal objectives uncovered in the analysis of the preceding chapters. Some broad conclusions and specific implications emanating from the study are summarized in Chapter IX.

Chapter I | PORTFOLIO OBJECTIVES OF LIFE

INSURANCE COMPANIES

In Chapters I and II we explore the determinants of life insurance company investment policy and the problems which confront companies as they seek to implement policies in making specific portfolio decisions. In this chapter we attempt to isolate the overriding investment goals which life companies pursue in common and examine the role of these goals in shaping life company preferences for particular characteristics of assets and portfolios. Specifically, we wish to know whether it is reasonable as a working hypothesis to describe life insurance companies as rate-of-return maximizers. Following this appraisal, Chapter II is devoted to an analysis of the impact of government regulatory and tax policy on the portfolio behavior of life companies.

We begin this chapter with a brief description of the life insurance industry and the position it occupies in the U.S. capital markets. This will be followed by the main business of the chapter, i.e., an analysis of the primary forces determining life insurance company portfolio decisions.

The Industry and Its Role

The Life Insurance Industry

For purposes of this study, the life insurance industry is defined as the set of legal reserve life insurance companies domiciled in the United States. At the end of 1945 there were 473 institutions considered legal reserve by their chartering agencies; the number of active companies had increased to 1,585 by year-end, 1964.[1] Home offices of these companies are spread throughout the 50 states and the District of Columbia. Life insurance companies in this country are chartered and have been almost exclusively regulated by the states.

As of 1964 about 90% of the operating life insurance companies were owned by stockholders; the remainder were mutual organizations. Mutual companies however, accounted for 70% of the industry's nearly $150 billion of assets. As these figures suggest, there is a fairly high concentration of industry assets in a relatively few, predominantly mutual, companies. Although concentration ratios have declined throughout the post-World War II years, the industry's 10 largest companies in 1964 held 60% of industry assets and the 50 largest held 86% of the assets.[2]

Life Insurance Companies as Financial Intermediaries

Life insurance companies can be analyzed from a number of perspectives. In the view of most life insurance company managements, the primary business of life companies is the sale of insurance and annuity protection. Of primary interest to us, however, is the fact that many life company policyholders accumulate a considerable equity interest in the process of purchasing this protection, and this equity constitutes a significant financial asset in policyholder balance sheets. In turn, life companies are provided with large sums to invest. Our focus is upon life insurance companies in their role as financial intermediaries.

Financial intermediaries are business institutions which issue financial liabilities and own (principally) financial assets. In the process of conducting their business they perform various intermediary or brokerage functions in financial markets. A subset of this institutional species specifically intermediates in the transfer of loanable funds from surplus to deficit sectors. In the U.S. economy this subset, sometimes called "savings intermediaries," consists principally of the various savings depositories, life insurance companies, noninsured pension funds, and open-end invest-

---

[1] Institute of Life Insurance (ILI), *Life Insurance Fact Book*, 1965.
[2] Eight of the 10 largest and 26 of the 50 largest were mutuals. Compiled from company data in *The Fortune Directory*, 1965.

ment companies.[3] These institutions intervene in the borrowing-lending process by offering ultimate wealthholders obligations which are in some respects more attractive than the direct debt and equity issues emitted by the ultimate borrowers. Among the features savings intermediaries can offer wealthholders are liquidity, reduced portfolio risk, lower investment costs, and ancillary services such as insurance protection. Judging from the growth of savings intermediaries in recent decades, such attributes have attracted the surplus sectors.

A rough impression of the post-World War II growth in savings through intermediaries can be gained from inspection of Table I-1, where estimates of accumulated household savings in selected intermediaries are presented. The household sector's holdings of savings accounts, private life insurance and pension reserves, and mutual fund shares accounted for about one-third of household financial assets at the end of the war. Ten years later this proportion was essentially unchanged, but growth of the savings intermediaries accelerated during the second postwar decade, and the share of household financial assets in these intermediaries rose to about 45% by 1964.[4]

Nearly the entire increase in household ownership of credit and equity instruments issued by primary borrowers since 1945 has taken the form of corporate stocks. Since common stock prices rose approximately eightfold between World War II and 1964, most of the increase in corporate share ownership reflected gains in market value.[5] Consequently over four-fifths of net household saving in financial assets (excluding capital gains) during the two postwar decades is accounted for by savings deposits, life insurance and pension reserves, and mutual fund shares.[6] Thus

---

[3] In this study we will use the term "savings depositories" to refer to mutual savings banks, savings and loan associations, credit unions, and time deposit activity of commercial banks. By "savings intermediaries" we mean these institutions plus life insurance companies and noninsured pension funds.

[4] Based on Federal Reserve Board *Flow of Funds Accounts* data for the consumer and nonprofit and various savings intermediary sectors. Household inventories of demand deposits and currency are excluded from these estimates.

[5] Based on Standard and Poor's index.

[6] Based on FRB, *Flow of Funds Accounts,* for the consumer and nonprofit sector. Life insurance and pension reserves include those in government programs in this estimate.

the savings intermediaries have played a major role in allocating household saving flows among the primary borrowers in the postwar years, and life insurance companies have exercised control over a significant share of the savings channeled through intermediaries.

TABLE I-1.   Savings Held by Households in Selected Savings Intermediaries: 1945, 1955, and 1964

(billions of dollars)

	1945	1955	1964	Net Change 1945–64
Life Insurance Companies	40.6	77.1	123.5	82.9
Savings and Loan Associations	7.4	32.2	102.0	94.6
Mutual Savings Banks	15.4	28.2	49.2	33.8
Commercial Banks	28.7	44.6	97.9	69.2
Private Pension Funds	2.3	16.7	51.2	48.9
Investment Companies	1.3	7.8	29.1	27.8
Credit Unions	0.4	2.4	8.2	7.8
Totals	96.1	209.0	461.1	365.0

NOTES: Data for life insurance companies are policy reserves; for savings and loan associations, outstanding savings shares; for mutual savings banks, outstanding savings accounts; for commercial banks, time deposits of the consumer and nonprofit organization sector; noninsured pension funds, pension fund reserves; open-end investment companies, total financial assets; credit unions, total savings shares. All data represent asset holdings of the consumer and nonprofit sector.

SOURCE: Federal Reserve Board, *Flow of Funds Accounts*.

In evaluating the impact of financial intermediaries, traditionally a sharp distinction has been made between commercial banks in their role as issuers of and transfer agents for demand deposit liabilities, and other financial intermediaries. The distinction has rested upon the conception of demand deposits as the primary component of the money stock, and the existence of a generally accepted monetary theory which allotted a significant causal role to the stock of money as a determinant of the level of general economic activity. In contrast, the activities of other financial intermediaries were regarded as part of the market mechanics that underlay and made plausible a macro-equilibrium theory of saving and investment. Assumptions that the asset-mix desires of saver-lenders and investor-borrowers could be matched successfully through the price mechanism presupposed an efficient set of market mechanics to facilitate the matching process. The certification, endorsing, and brokerage activities of financial intermediaries were viewed as a significant part of those market mechanics.

More recently, it has been argued that this view of the function of intermediaries was too limited. Gurley and Shaw, among others, have contended that the actions of nonbank intermediaries have expansionary and deflationary repercussions on economic activity no different in kind or degree from those of commercial banks.[7] Both through their competition for funds and their investment activity, nonbank intermediaries exercise influence on the level of economic activity by affecting the public's demand for money. It is a controversial empirical question whether this impact is so systematic and quantitatively important as to require substantial modification of the theoretical and policy approaches to monetary and financial problems.[8] In approaching this study of life insurance companies in their role as financial intermediaries, we shall be interested in the implications of life company portfolio behavior both for the allocative efficiency of capital markets and for the level and stability of the aggregate demand for goods and services.

Life Insurance Companies in the Capital Markets

The life insurance industry owned assets amounting to $44.8 billion at the end of 1945. By the end of 1964 total industry assets had increased to $149.5 billion. A small share of these assets was invested in tangible properties, primarily real estate and equipment of various sorts. Better than 95% of life company assets, however, have been invested in financial instruments. In selecting financial investments during the period since World War II, life companies have concentrated their acquisitions in

---

[7] The Gurley-Shaw view has been expressed in a book, *Money in a Theory of Finance,* and a number of articles and monographs including particularly Gurley and Shaw, "Financial Intermediaries and the Saving-Investment Process"; Gurley, "Financial Institutions in the Saving-Investment Process"; and Gurley, *Liquidity and Financial Institutions in the Postwar Economy.*

[8] For a survey of the major theoretical and policy issues, see Johnson, "Monetary Theory and Policy."

TABLE I-2. *Percentage Composition of All Life Insurance Companies' Invested Assets: 1945, 1955, and 1964*

	1945	1955	1964
Bonds:			
U. S. Government	45.9%	9.5%	3.7%
State and Local Government	2.3	3.0	3.8
Foreign Government	2.1	.4	.6
Corporate	22.5	39.9	37.4
Mortgages:			
1–4 Family Properties	5.2	19.5	19.6
Other Properties	9.6	13.1	17.2
Corporate Stocks	2.2	4.0	5.3
Policy Loans	4.4	3.6	4.8
Real Estate	1.9	2.9	3.0
Miscellaneous	3.9	4.1	4.5
Total	100.0%	100.0%	100.0%

SOURCES: Institute of Life Insurance and Federal Reserve Board.

intermediate- and long-term private sector, taxable, interest-bearing debt obligations.   An overview of the distribution of life company investments among the broad categories of assets is shown in Table I-2.

As can be seen from inspection of this table, life company funds have been predominantly invested in bonds and mortgage loans. During the early postwar years particularly, life companies effected a major adjustment in the composition of their portfolios by disposing of a large portion of their U.S. Treasury security holdings and reinvesting the proceeds primarily in corporate bonds and loans on various types of mortgaged properties.   Consequently the share of corporate bonds and mortgage loans in the industry's assets rose from three-eighths of the total in 1945 to nearly three-quarters a decade later.   The increase in the share of life company assets held in corporate bonds is attributable largely to the success of life companies in negotiating direct placement debt contracts with industrial and commercial enterprises.[9]   Changes in the mix

[9] Life company holdings of "industrial and miscellaneous" bonds increased from 4.3% of assets in 1945 to 23.7% in 1964, while the percentage share of public utility bond holdings was about the same in both years, and holdings of railroad bonds declined as a proportion of total assets.   About $30 billion of the $35.3 billion of "industrial and miscellaneous bonds" held by life companies in 1964 were estimated to have been private placements.   See ILI, *Life Insurance Fact Book*, 1965, p. 78.

of mortgaged properties on which life companies held loans reflected broad changes in the composition of new construction among single-family homes, apartments, and commercial buildings.

Otherwise there has been a modest increase in life company experimentation with equity investments in the form of both corporate shares and real property. The "miscellaneous" category in Table I-2 includes small amounts of leased equipment and oil, mineral, and timber rights, as well as cash holdings and due and deferred premiums. Life company acquisitions of state and local government debt issues are limited by the impact of the tax-exempt feature on municipal bond yields. Policy loans are initiated by policyholders, not life company investment departments.

Most investors in financial assets tend to confine themselves to a relatively narrow segment of the spectrum of available instruments. For many financial institutions, legal restrictions on portfolio choice have contributed to limiting the range of their investments. For some investors, tax considerations are primarily responsible for restricting the variety of assets selected. Specialization by institutional investors derives also from the nature of their liabilities, their size, history, geographical location, and problems of investment organization created by the diversity of market mechanics prevailing in the various asset submarkets. During the postwar years there has existed a modest but observable trend toward less specialization and more points of contact among competing lenders. This trend has been produced in part by some relaxation in the statutory and administrative constraints on institutional investment policy.[10]

Despite a tendency toward less specialization, very considerable market segmentation remains. This is illustrated in Table I-3 where a matrix of net investments in credit and equity instruments by major lenders is shown for the period 1953–1960. This is essentially the period on which this study's analysis of life insurance company investment behavior will concentrate.

An examination of Table I-3 reveals lender specialization to a significant degree. For example, the net flow of investible funds through savings and loan associations and mutual savings banks

---

[10] For a summary of the regulatory situation, see U.S. Congress, House, Subcommittee on Domestic Finance, *Comparative Regulations of Financial Institutions*, 1963.

TABLE I-3. Net Flow of Funds into Credit and Equity Instruments, by Sector and Asset: 1953–1960
(billions of dollars)

Sector/Asset	Treasury Obligations	State and Local Debt	Corporate Bonds	Corporate Stock	Mortgages 1-4 Family	Mortgages Other	Consumer Credit	Other Loans	Total Net Flows by Sector
Consumer and Nonprofit	2.8	10.9	1.9	10.2	3.9	10.2	—	—	40.1
Business	-.3	1.7	—	—	—	—	4.5	1.6	7.5
U.S. Government	—	—	—	—	4.6	2.7	—	6.2	13.3
State and Local Government	7.4	3.2	8.2	—	1.1	—	—	—	19.9
Monetary Authorities	2.7	—	—	—	—	—	—	—	2.7
Commercial Bank	-2.2	7.4	-1.1	—	8.1	4.9	11.2	28.6	57.0
Mutual Savings Bank	-2.8	.4	1.3	.5	12.2	3.4	.1	—	15.2
Savings and Loan Association	3.4	—	—	—	37.8	3.9	.7	—	45.7
Credit Union	—	—	—	—	—	—	3.4*	—	3.4
Life Insurance	-3.8	2.4	17.6	1.2	13.1	7.4	—	2.9	40.8
Private Pension Fund	.3	—	10.5	8.5	.9	—	—	—	20.1
Nonlife Insurance	.1	6.4	1.2	1.3	—	.3	—	—	9.3
Finance Nec.	1.2	.2	.7	5.3	1.0	—	8.9	5.8	23.0
Rest of World	6.6	—	.3	1.2	—	—	—	.6	8.6
Total Net Issues	16.6	32.5	40.7	27.8	82.8	32.9	28.5	45.8	306.6/307.6

* Includes a small amount of real estate loans.
NOTE: Components do not add to total in some cases due to rounding errors and statistical discrepancy. The large discrepancy in the net issues of Treasury obligations arises from sector differences in valuation. U.S. Government liabilities (total net issues) are valued at par; consumer and nonprofit sector holdings of U.S. Government obligations are also valued at par, but other sector holdings are recorded at book value.

The sectors are Flow of Funds sectors, except that the farm, noncorporate, nonfinancial, and corporate nonfinancial sectors have been consolidated into one ("business") sector. Asset categories are also Flow of Funds transaction categories, except that "other loans" includes bank loans nec.
SOURCE: Federal Reserve Board, Flow of Funds Accounts, 1945–1962. 1963 Supplement.

is channeled almost entirely into mortgage loans, predominantly loans on 1–4 family residential properties. Noninsured pension funds invested almost exclusively in corporate securities, and state and local governments invested their assets (largely retirement funds) mostly in government and corporate securities. Life insurance companies, as we have seen, allocate loanable funds primarily to corporate bonds and mortgage loans, and nonlife insurance organizations invest a substantial portion of their assets in municipal debt obligations.

As a consequence of lender specialization, the credit and equity submarkets often tend to be dominated by two or three investor types. Thus funds supplied to the corporate bond market have come primarily from life insurance companies and private and public retirement funds. Life companies and the savings depositories have dominated the lending side of the residential mortgage loan market. Wealthy individuals, commercial banks, and nonlife insurance companies acquired about three-quarters of the net debt issues of state and local governments during the period, 1953–1960. Commercial banks and finance companies did most of the lending in the consumer credit sector.

Two things are particularly worth noting about the life insurance industry's role in supplying funds to credit and equity markets. One is the significant influence life companies' portfolio choices must have given them in the corporate bond market[11] and to a lesser extent in the mortgage markets. The other is that life companies have been investing in a wider variety of capital markets than the other nonbank financial institutions. Life companies invest in all the broad categories shown in Table I-3 except the consumer credit sector and, indeed, are probably represented in the consumer loan market in a limited way through their loans

---

[11] Table I-3 is perhaps deficient in not showing commercial bank term loans as competitive with bond issues. We know of no existing time series data which sorts out that portion of bank term loan activity which is significantly competitive with bond issues as a source of funds. During the 1950s, term loans appear to have accounted for less than 10% of the net increase in corporate long-term debt. (See Robinson, *Money and Capital Markets*, p. 191, and Bankers Trust Company, *The Investment Outlook*, annual.) The "10%" share was exceeded in 1955–1956 (*The Investment Outlook*, 1961, Table 6). More recently (1963–1966) there does appear to have been a significant increase in the use of term loans as a source of long-term funds for nonfinancial corporations (*The Investment Outlook*, 1967, Tables 10 and 25).

to policyholders. It is this demonstrated ability of life companies to lend in a wide variety of markets that makes analysis of life company investment responsiveness to changing market yields particularly important to an appraisal of the allocative efficiency of U.S. capital markets. Having sketched broadly the character and role of life companies' investment activities, we turn now to the main purpose of this chapter; namely, an analysis of the determinants of life insurance company portfolio behavior.

The Determinants of Life Insurance Company Portfolio Decisions

The Theory of Portfolio Choice

Broadly viewed, the changes in the mix of portfolio assets held by life insurance companies during the years since World War II were the joint product of changes in the investment opportunities available and changes in life company investment requirements or in their attitudes regarding the investment strategy best suited for fulfilling portfolio objectives. Implicit in any study of portfolio decisions is the belief that lenders' portfolio objectives and strategies are relatively stable over time and that it is change in the composition of the demand for external financing and changes in the shares of funds flowing into the various types of lenders which are primarily responsible for observable year-to-year changes in an investor's portfolio selections.

Investment choices are made in an atmosphere of uncertainty about what consequences will flow from the decisions made. Theories of portfolio selection under conditions of risk generally assume that investors formulate subjective beliefs about investment outcomes in terms of characteristics of probability distributions of investment returns for each potential asset opportunity.[12] Information concerning the probable outcomes associated with each investment possibility is used to describe the characteristics of probability distributions for combinations of assets. Using the techniques of portfolio analysis, it is possible to derive the set of what Markowitz calls "efficient" portfolios,

---

[12] The most influential work on this subject since World War II has been that of Markowitz. See, in particular, Markowitz, *Portfolio Selection.*

that is, portfolios which satisfy the requirement that no combination of assets can produce a higher expected return without also incurring greater variability of return.[13] Assuming that investors desire high expected return and low variability of return, they will select a portfolio from among the set of efficient combinations.

The specific portfolio chosen is determined by each investor's needs and preferences. Sometimes it is postulated that these needs and preferences can be formalized in terms of a utility function and, further, that the investor can be assumed to select portfolios which will maximize his expected utility.[14] In what follows we shall be investigating, albeit in a crude fashion, the nature of life insurance companies' "utility functions," i.e., their preferences toward portfolio return and portfolio risk.

Portfolio Policy of Life Insurance Companies

Life insurance company preferences between "return" and "risk" are reflected in their "portfolio policy," that is, a set of principles governing specific decisions to acquire or dispose of portfolio assets. Preferences and policies are formulated from consideration of a company's portfolio objectives. Portfolio objectives in turn derive from firm and industry characteristics, including the nature of a company's liabilities, its size, geographical location, organizational structure, history and tradition, competitive position, and the subjective attitudes held by the particular investment officers and directors who are making portfolio decisions.

The specific manner in which a company seeks to implement its policy and achieve its goals depends upon most of the same factors, and in addition upon the particular set of investment opportunities (or prospective opportunities) which it faces, and upon the externally imposed constraints which limit its freedom of choice. We shall comment upon the determination of the opportunity set below, and we shall examine at some length the significance of the primary external restraints in Chapter II. Our immediate task is to identify the principal internally formulated portfolio objectives that shape life insurance company investment policy.

---

[13] *Ibid.*, Part III.

[14] The expected utility rule is controversial, however. See Markowitz's discussion in Chapter X.

Portfolio Objectives of Life Insurance Companies

There are basically two ways of determining the dominant portfolio goals of life insurance companies. One method is to ascertain, and rely upon, what life company executives say their objectives are; the other is to infer from observation of the relevant industry characteristics what their objectives are. We shall make use of both procedures.

ULTIMATE GOALS

Any life insurance company must determine its specific portfolio goals in light of its desire to fulfill two ultimate objectives: (1) to maintain its solvency; and (2) to be competitive. The desire to avoid insolvency has often led life companies to emphasize capital certainty and/or investment income certainty as primary portfolio objectives. These objectives are considered achievable through selection of individual assets possessing low default risk and market risk attributes, portfolio diversification, and pursuit of conscious asset maturity objectives. It is generally assumed that these specific portfolio characteristics can be bought only at some cost in terms of foregone investment return. Thus, although in the long run a high rate of portfolio return may contribute to providing a margin of protection against the insolvency risk, the risks inherent in aiming at maximization of the rate of return are considered unacceptable. Companies then have to balance competitive pressure for high investment yields against the security requirements of solvency. We shall examine the importance of the solvency objective in some detail and then briefly discuss the significance of investment return as a portfolio goal.

THE SOLVENCY OBJECTIVE

The obligations issued by life insurance companies are priced on the basis of assumptions about mortality experience, operating costs, and investment returns over the life of the policies. Insolvency threatens whenever substantial losses are produced by adverse mortality, expense, and investment experience. Up to a point, losses can be absorbed by net positive cash flows generated by margins incorporated into the pricing of insurance and annuity policies, and by a company's initial balance sheet cushion between total assets and total liabilities. The cash flow protection built into an insurance company's liabilities include loading allowances in the mortality and operating expense estimates. Also a margin exists between the return assumed to be realizable on invested policy reserves and the true expected value of investment return. The latter cushion is, of course, particularly significant in "participating" policies. The balance sheet margin consists primarily of capital (in a stock company) and various surplus accounts.

In principle, a life insurance company is solvent at any point in time as long as it possesses invested assets which are adequate, allowing for the assumed future rate of return on them, to meet net claims which will arise over time from currently outstanding liabilities. Net claims consist of benefit and surrender payments plus operating expenses less the premium inflow from outstanding policies. The present value of this future stream, discounted at the interest rate guaranteed in existing policies, is known as the legal reserve and represents the current value of a life company's liabilities. A life company is legally solvent if its admitted assets (i.e., assets accepted by and valued under rules established by the state insurance commissioners) exceed its legal reserve.

Legal solvency is the primary concern for most life companies. Companies have considerable latitude in computing policy reserves and establishing premiums, although the states have imposed minimum standards with respect to the mortality and interest rate assumptions used in calculating the reserve position. But most significantly, the states have limited the size of surplus accounts life companies may carry, and the National Association of Insurance Commissioners regulates the valuation of assets and the establishment of asset valuation reserves. In particular, the asset valuation rules have created problems for life companies largely because historically valuation policy has placed considerable emphasis upon the liquidation value of life insurance company assets. The impact of these regulations on portfolio policy will be examined in Chapter II.

In addition to being solvent in the basic balance sheet and long-term cash-flow senses, life insurance companies also have to be in a short-term position to meet extraordinary cash demands in the form of benefits, surrenders, and policy loans. If the normal net cash inflow is inadequate, companies must be able to liquidate portfolio assets or borrow quickly. A general liquidity crisis affecting the life insurance industry as a whole is likely to be handled by legislative action permitting life companies to postpone payment of claims.[15]

THE NATURE OF LIFE INSURANCE COMPANY LIABILITIES

The full implications of life insurance company concern with solvency can be made clearer by considering the specific characteristics attached to the industry's liabilities. Life insurance and annuity contracts are characterized by the following attributes:

(1) They are very long term. The average maturity of life insurance company policies depends upon many factors including the mix of various types of contracts issued, the age composition of policyholders, and the variety of benefit and cash value options. Nonetheless we know contracts are commonly issued which will run 30, 40, 50 years or more to maturity.

(2) Policies are contractual. They obligate policyholders to pay specified premiums at regular dates in the future in return for a life insurance company promise to deliver specified amounts of cash in the event of certain contingencies or on demand. Since normally the major portions of future cash flows produced from existing policies are determined by mortality, these flows are highly predictable in advance. However, the incorporation of demand features and a wide variety of settlement options into policies has tended to reduce the predictability of the net premiums-benefits flow.

(3) Life insurance companies enter into contracts that promise to pay fixed dollar amounts. While there has been some dent in the tradition of issuing only fixed dollar liabilities in recent years,[16]

---

[15] The moratorium legislation enacted in 1933 affecting surrenders and policy loans was passed to deal with the liquidity problem, not because life companies were threatened with insolvency in a more basic sense. See Bell, "Asset Reserves of Life Insurance Companies," p. 9. Details of the moratorium legislation are reported in Temporary National Economic Committee, *Study of Legal Reserve Life Insurance Companies*, pp. 135–140.

[16] For a summary of recent trends in the industry's pension business in the direction of variable dollar contracts, see Hart, "Life Insurance Companies and the Equity Capital Markets."

the life insurance industry's basic product continues to be protection guaranteed in dollar amounts.

(4) Contracts guarantee a minimum rate of return on policyholder equity; in recent years the assumed interest rate on insurance policy reserves has been 2.5% to 3%. The interest rate assumption differs strikingly from mortality and operating cost assumptions incorporated in policy contracts because portfolio earnings are far more difficult to predict years in advance.

(5) Insurance and annuity contracts are not generally considered liquid assets by policyholders. Thus liquidity features of these assets are utilized only when cash needs exceed amounts available from primary liquidity sources.

(6) Life insurance companies, state insurance commissioners, and state legislatures have regarded policy reserves as having the essential character of trust funds. This attitude results from the fact that life company contracts have long been the primary source of financial protection to many families.

IMPLICATIONS OF THE LIABILITY CHARACTERISTICS

It is this last characteristic, the quasi-trustee role adopted as a public relations image by life insurance companies themselves, and repeatedly emphasized by statutory and administrative regulations, that is particularly responsible for the insistence upon a portfolio policy protecting individual companies and the industry from any suspicion of inability to meet claims as they arise. As indicated above, the concern with investment safety has taken two primary forms: (1) security of principal, and (2) security of income.

Capital security

Traditionally, both the industry and its public overseers seem to have been concerned first with preservation of the value of invested capital in line with a famous dictum attributed to J. M. Keynes: "Capital depreciation is the great enemy of insurance companies." [17] This attitude toward risk clearly dominated in-

---

[17] See Nerlove, "Common Stocks as Investments of American Life Insurance Companies," p. 42.

dustry thinking prior to World War II.[18]   Most people associated with the life insurance industry would have agreed that ". . . safety of principal is the first law of life insurance investing." [19] Since companies do guarantee a minimum rate of return on policy reserves, however, portfolio policy cannot be formulated with only the capital security objective in mind.   The objective must be to earn a rate of return in excess of the assumed rate while reducing default risk as far as possible consistent with the expected return target.   Default risk is reduced through selection of individual assets possessing only limited risk of loss and through portfolio diversification.   The possibility that cash demands may force liquidation of some assets before maturity can be handled by setting aside a portion of the portfolio for assets which can be quickly liquidated without significant loss.   Thus a life company emphasizing capital security will select a diversified portfolio of high investment quality debt instruments, some of which possess strong liquidity attributes.

Capital certainty appears to have remained the primary investment goal for some life insurance companies in recent years.   The past president of the industry's largest company once asserted that, "In choosing investments, Metropolitan's prime objective is safety of principal commensurate with a reasonable return. . . ." [20] On balance, however, there has been a noticeable trend in the industry's rhetoric away from quite such strong insistence upon capital security, a change accompanied by the industry's lobbying for liberalization of both statutory investment restrictions and administered asset valuation rules.[21]   One life insurance company financial vice president has observed with respect to liquidity

---

[18] For a brief summary of views expressed in articles appearing in actuarial journals, see Wehrle, "Life Insurance Investment — The Experience of Four Companies," pp. 71–77.   A similar emphasis on capital security can be found in the Canadian life insurance industry; see Hood, "The Financing of Economic Activity in Canada," p. 358 f.

[19] M. J. Cleary, "The Response of Life Insurance Funds to American Needs," p. 61.   For other examples of the primacy in which the safety of principal goal was held, see Rydgren, "An Investment Policy for a Life Insurance Company"; Penman, "A Review of Investment Principles and Practices"; and the testimony of life company investment officers in the TNEC *Hearings*, Part 28, "Life Insurance, Operating Results and Investments."   (Hereafter referred to as TNEC *Hearings*.)

[20] Frederick W. Ecker, quoted in *The Wall Street Journal*, August 7, 1957.

[21] See Chapter II.

needs, "Life insurance investment as contrasted to most other institutional investment is strikingly characterized by its ability to take the long look — to invest for the long term with minimum economic consideration necessary for liquidity and marketability." [22]

Taking the long view, acceptance of some default risk also seemed less horrifying to industry officers. Indeed life companies found that some debt instruments that went into default in the 1930's eventually worked out so well that over the long run the rates of return realized on these issues were quite favorable. [23] Many life insurance companies' investment departments became aware of the growing evidence that over the long run "blue chip" debt obligations produce a significantly lower overall rate of return than lower quality issues. [24] Growing confidence in government full employment policy has lessened the fear of capital depletion through large-scale defaults. Unemployment compensation and other income stabilization measures have further reduced the likelihood of massive policyholder liquidity demands.

Income security

If it is true that many life insurance companies have gradually re-evaluated the importance of capital security as a portfolio objective, there remain differences in the implications drawn from this re-evaluation. For some, downgrading of the capital security goal implies upgrading of the rate-of-return objective. Many life company spokesmen continue to regard (1) safety of principal and (2) rate of return as the prime portfolio objectives and have simply adjusted the weights a little toward more emphasis on yield. A life insurance trade association monograph prepared for the Commission on Money and Credit study states the portfolio objective this way:

---

[22] Conklin, "Some Fundamental Considerations of Investment Policy."

[23] For example, see Sherwin Badger's discussion of the New England Mutual Life Insurance Company's experience with railroad debt issues: "Unusual Features of Life Insurance Investing."

[24] Several officers we interviewed reported they were aware of and impressed by the results of the National Bureau's corporate bond study. See Hickman, *Corporate Bond Quality and Investor Experience.*

In placing policy reserves into various investment outlets within the limits of the safety of the principal, the objective of life insurance investment officers is to obtain the maximum rate of return available for these funds.[25]

Other observers and life company investment officers, however, reached the conclusion that capital certainty was an overrated objective because it failed to deal adequately with the nature of the risk assumed by life insurance companies in investing policy reserves. In their view, the unique risk assumed by life insurance companies derives from two other attributes of policy contracts: (1) their long term and (2) the guarantee of a minimum rate of return on invested reserves. These characteristics expose life companies to the risk of loss resulting from substantial reduction in market yields in the future. This risk can only be hedged by a conscious asset maturity policy. In growing funds, the usual case in United States life insurance companies, this "income risk" is offset by choosing portfolio assets with maturities longer than those of life company liabilities.[26] Adopting such a maturity policy may require accepting more default risk and/or lower portfolio return.

Summary

Capital certainty and income certainty objectives may render implausible the hypothesis that life insurance companies seek to maximize the average rate of portfolio return over time by selecting from the set of available opportunities assets with the highest expected yields. Protection against insolvency seems to demand concern with other characteristics of individual assets and portfolios: namely, liquidity, marketability, credit quality, diversification, and maturity composition. We shall, therefore, proceed to an evaluation of the significance of these nonreturn, risk-reducing attributes.

---

[25] Life Insurance Association of America–Commission on Money and Credit Monograph, *Life Insurance Companies as Financial Institutions*, pp. 60–61. (Hereafter referred to as LIAA–CMC Monograph.) Very similar statements appeared in the replies of life insurance companies to a 1950 Congressional inquiry. See U.S. Congress, Joint Committee on the Economic Report, *Monetary Policy and the Management of the Public Debt, Replies to Questions and Other Material*. (Hereafter referred to as the Patman *Replies*.)

[26] See the discussion of income risk below.

The Importance of Nonreturn Portfolio Characteristics

LIQUIDITY AND MARKETABILITY

Potential liquidity needs

As we have seen, life insurance company concern with capital certainty has been expressed as a desire to avoid market risk as well as default risk in making portfolio choices. Avoidance of market risk is a relevant objective if the cash flow experience of life insurance companies is such that they are sometimes forced to liquidate assets prior to maturity in order to meet cash demands for which they are liable. Market risk can be hedged by placing some portion of the portfolio in liquid assets, i.e., assets which are readily marketable and experience little variation over time in market price. The particular types of assets suitable for meeting liquidity requirements depend upon the nature of the need. It is convenient to distinguish among three potential kinds of liquidity needs, that is liquidity desired to provide for:

(1) normal transactions,
(2) emergency cash demands, and
(3) portfolio flexibility.

Transactions needs derive from the failure of cash inflows to mesh exactly with cash outflows. Unless low-cost overdraft banking services are available, a life company will necessarily hold some currency, deposits, and near-due marketable securities as a cash inventory. Additional liquidity provision may be regarded as necessary to protect against abnormal cash demands rising out of possible natural or economic catastrophes (for example, epidemics or severe general economic depression). Finally, portfolio liquidity may be desired in order that a company may be prepared to take advantage of investment opportunities as they become available.

Portfolio flexibility and "rare-event" needs may be met by some mix of short-dated securities and longer-term, high-quality, readily marketable assets. Given the institutional environment in which life companies operate, this primary liquidity protection is provided by cash, short-term commercial and industrial paper, and Treasury obligations of all maturities. In some circumstances other assets, such as marketable corporate and municipal securities, may serve liquidity functions, but the market value risk assumed in these asset categories is often substantial. In rare-event crises which affect the industry as a whole, the government is likely to arrange additional liquidity sources, and if necessary, enact moratorium legislation with regard to cash payments. In this circumstance the individual company assumes risk when it is significantly less liquid than the average company in the industry.

Evaluating liquidity requirements

An examination of life companies' portfolio composition indicates that their basic liquidity needs can be satisfied by holding only a modest portion of assets in liquid form. Although cash and U.S. Government securities accounted for about half the life insurance industry's assets at the end of World War II, these holdings were obviously far in excess of liquidity requirements and have since been pared down to well under 5% of total assets. By the mid-1960s life insurance company holdings of Treasury bonds and notes amounted to only about 3% of industry assets. Cash and short-term obligations (Treasury bills and certificates plus private sector paper due to mature within one year) accounted for only about 1% of assets.[27]

(i) The cash flow record

Liquidity needs are modest because most life companies have experienced a growth rate adequate to generate a regular and substantial net cash inflow. Industry assets increased at a rate of approximately 7% per annum during the first postwar decade and 6% in the second decade. For the life insurance industry as a whole the cash inflow from premiums and other considerations has continued to exceed annually the outflow from benefit and other contractual payments, insurance expenses, and taxes. This net savings flow is augmented by the net earnings inflow from invested reserves. Consequently the total net savings flow through the life insurance industry during the 1950s averaged

---

[27] Based on data from the Life Insurance Association of America, 49 company monthly tabulation. These companies represent about 82% of industry assets (1965). Smaller companies tend to have slightly greater liquid asset holdings.

better than $5 billion annually.[28] The flow of gross investment funds is further augmented by normal portfolio turnover from scheduled principal repayments. By the end of the 1950s this source was adding another $5 billion cash inflow per annum to the industry.

Not only do most life companies experience a regular, substantial net positive cash inflow, but the net flow generated by the insurance business, in particular, is normally highly predictable twelve months in advance.[29] This means that, excepting companies with unusually low growth rates, the cash inventory required to conduct insurance business transactions is quite minimal. Cash flows generated by investment activity are somewhat unpredictable, and depending upon the degree of flexibility desired, additional liquid asset provision may appear necessary. This problem is further complicated by the increasing use made of the forward commitment device by life companies. Use of this procedure reduces the available flow of uncommitted funds in any period and could necessitate either additional liquidity provision or borrowing authority to accommodate temporal bunching in the demand for delivery of committed funds.

(ii) Cash-flow experience and rare-event needs

The favorable cash-flow experience of most life companies raises the question of whether any portfolio provision for emergency cash needs is required. Extraordinary cash demands on life companies could arise, in principle, from either an exceptional increase in life insurance and annuity policy benefit claims or from a massive exercise of cash surrender and policy loan rights by policyholders. Historical experience is helpful for gauging the significance of these possibilities.

(a) *An epidemic.* The greatest mortality crisis life insurance companies have had to face in this century was produced by the

---

[28] See the LIAA-CMC Monograph, p. 24. The LIAA data are on an accrual, not cash, basis, but nonetheless provide an approximate measure of the cash savings flow. Net savings is defined as the change in admitted assets less net policy loan extensions less net capital gains. In the late 1950s the growth rate of net savings was somewhat under the rate of total asset growth due to an increase in policy loan demand and, in some years, to capital gains.

[29] See W. M. Anderson, "The Long View of Life Insurance Investment."

1918–1919 influenza epidemic. Prior to the epidemic, life companies' cash and near-due earning asset holdings amounted to approximately the same proportion of assets they do in the 1960s; yet the normal cash-flow margin appears to have covered claims adequately, and forced asset liquidations occurred rarely if at all. Cash-flow estimates computed by Keir for each of the 14 largest companies showed that premium inflows were sufficient to cover the sharply increased benefit claims over the period as a whole.[30] Nine of the 14 did engage in modest short-term bank borrowing to meet unusual concentration of claims, but the loans were quickly repaid and no asset sales were required.[31]

(b) *A depression.* The historical experience with policyholder premium payments and cash withdrawals during periods of general economic stress is also quite reassuring. Most life company policy liabilities are subject to cash demands in the form of surrender benefits or policy loans, liquidity characteristics introduced by life companies to make policy contracts more attractive. The nature of the policy has some effect on the likelihood of liquidation. For example, individual policies possessing a high savings element such as single payment annuity and endowment contracts are more susceptible to withdrawal. Also, liabilities with no life contingency provisions at all (policy dividends left with the company to earn interest or settlement options based on interest earning assumptions) are particularly unstable generators of cash flow.

The general "liquidity crisis" associated with the 1929–1933 depression, however, did not create a liquidity crisis within the life insurance industry. Sharp increases in cash demands did occur and did significantly narrow the margin between the premium and investment income inflow and the benefits and expenses outflow. Nonetheless all the major companies maintained a positive net cash inflow from these sources.[32]

Additional cash flow was available from normal portfolio turn-

---

[30] Keir, "The Liquidity Structure of Life Insurance Companies," Chapter IV and Appendix B.

[31] *Ibid.*, p. 82.

[32] Evidence of this is presented in Keir for 14 companies. Also see A. D. Wood, "The Permanence of Life Insurance," and Loewy, "Net Cash Money Flows Through Life Insurance Companies," p. 446.

over and voluntary asset liquidation. While government action helped avert a liquidity crisis, life companies possessed impressive internal financial strength, unique among financial intermediaries.[33] In particular, remarkable stability in the renewal premium flow demonstrated the strength of the contractual characteristics of life insurance policies. Renewal premiums scarcely declined at all in 1932 and 1933.[34]

Curiously, the strength displayed by life companies during the worst of the depression had consequences that led to some genuine concern regarding portfolio liquidity needs later in the decade. This concern was prompted by heavy purchases of single payment annuity, pure endowment, and endowment insurance policies. Industry officials interpreted these sales as evidence that individuals were using life insurance companies as savings depositories and concluded that life companies should prudently expect much higher cash withdrawal rates than normal on these contracts.[35] To deal with this hazard many life companies apparently discouraged or suspended sales of single premium annuities and adjusted upward their minimum portfolio liquidity goals.[36]

(c) *Postwar developments.* Over the postwar years the importance of savings-oriented individual policies has diminished substantially as individual term insurance has become increasingly popular. Group annuity pension reserves, however, have become an increasing proportion of life insurance company obligations. On the whole these reserves are probably less susceptible to withdrawal than ordinary life insurance policy reserves. Conditional vesting provisions make it unprofitable for the employee to withdraw his contribution in the event of termination of his employment. In deposit administration plans, the employer usually has the privilege of cashing out his account, but this right

---

[33] Many states enacted moratorium legislation for a few months in 1933 limiting cash outgo for surrender benefits and policy loans, and some companies did borrow from the Reconstruction Finance Corporation.

[34] Loewy, p. 446, and Keir, p. 118. The first-year premium flow did decline somewhat, but the volume of new policies issued has little impact on cash flows for a year or two after the sale.

[35] Expression of this concern can be found annually in the American Life Convention *Proceedings* from 1933 to the end of the decade.

[36] Hubbell, "Investment Indicators," and the testimony of life insurance company officers in TNEC *Hearings* (e.g., T. Buchner, p. 14752 ff.).

is well hedged with reservation devices protecting the life company from mass withdrawals.[37] There is perhaps some risk of mass employee retirements resulting from a severe general economic depression and leading to a sharp increase in cash payments.[38]

Throughout the 1930s and 1940s some types of life insurance company "demand obligations," namely, dividends left on deposit and supplementary contracts without life contingency, did increase in importance. Only a little more than 3% of the industry's liabilities were represented by these two categories in 1930, but their share increased to nearly 8% in 1940, and to over 11% in the early 1950s.[39] If, in fact, the cash flow generated by these options is vulnerable, then an increasing proportion of these obligations among all life company liabilities may at least marginally increase the liquidity concern of investment officers. Indeed, some of the cash-flow squeeze that did affect life companies in the middle and late 1950s appears to have been a product of the negative effect of rising interest rates on the attractiveness of life insurance settlement options not involving life contingency.[40] There is some evidence then that while mortality rates among policyholders are highly predictable, the impact of the mortality rates on cash flows is made less predictable by the variety of settlement options offered.

Similarly, the existence of cash surrender and policy loan privileges is responsible for some uncertainty with regard to cash demands. Normally these demands are easily met out of the regular cash inflow. During the 1950s gross cash outflow due to

---

[37] The hedging provisions generally include a "contractual liquidation charge" and the insurer reserves the right to spread the payout over a period of years (usually ten). See McGill, *Fundamentals of Private Pensions*, pp. 169–171. This book is a useful reference source for detailed accounts of various types of pension plans. Also see Melone and Allen, *Pension Planning*; Biegel et al., *Pensions and Profit Sharing*; Bernstein, *The Future of Private Pensions*; and Marples, *Actuarial Aspects of Pension Security*.

[38] This possibility results from the incorporation of optional retirement ages in pension programs. Often group plans permit retirement as early as 55. This is suggested as a potential liquidity hazard in Federal Reserve Bank of New York, "Private Pension Plans," *Monthly Review*, December 1953, p. 187.

[39] Estimates from data for companies licensed in New York State reported in the *New York Insurance Report*, Volume I, *Life*, 1955, Table 1-B, p. 989.

[40] See Wright, "Gross Flow of Funds Through Life Insurance Companies." These two types of "demand obligations" had been reduced to less than 7.5% of industry liabilities by 1964. (ILI, *Life Insurance Fact Book*.)

surrenders and loans averaged about 10% of the gross inflow of funds from premiums, other considerations, and net investment income, with a range from about 8% to 12% per annum. Surrenders and loans increased faster than cash inflow during the 1950s and contributed significantly to a reduction in the growth rate of net savings through life companies.[41]

In sum, upon examination not all life insurance obligations appear quite as illiquid as is sometimes suggested. Nonetheless a company with a good growth rate should not need to be concerned with liquidity and marketability attributes in making portfolio choices. For the industry as a whole the annual net funds inflow from premiums, net investment income, and scheduled portfolio turnover has amounted to about 10% of industry assets in recent years. Barring liquidity needs generated by the portfolio selection process, this makes it possible to liquidate a significant portion of the portfolio without loss in a short period of time. Only aging companies would seem to need additional protection against emergencies in the form of permanent holdings of liquid assets.[42]

To check this conclusion directly, we asked officers from 12 leading life insurance companies whether they felt it was necessary to provide portfolio liquidity beyond nominal amounts of cash and short-term securities. Four of the 12 indicated they thought it prudent to hold some additional amounts in intermediate or long-term Treasury bonds for emergency liquidity purposes. For three of the companies, this meant minimum holdings of Treasury obligations of about 3% to 5% of assets. The fourth company's goal was significantly higher. Several of the other eight companies replied in reference to Government bond holdings that, although it was not necessary to hold Government bonds for liquidity, they probably would continue to hold some Treasury securities[43] for "window dressing"[44] or to "help the Treasury."

[41] Wright, *ibid.*

[42] For a demonstration of the effect of aging on a company's ability to withstand emergency cash demands, see Linton, "Panics and Cash Values."

[43] No company we interviewed had completely liquidated its Treasury bond holdings accumulated largely during World War II. We shall examine the determinants of the time path of liquidation in Chapters III and IV.

[44] In this connection, at least one observer suggested in the 1930s that reasonable portfolio liquidity is necessary to maintain confidence of the policyholders and asserted that the incidence of surrenders and policy loans was

Conclusions

The inclusion of liquidity options in liabilities issued by life insurance companies does hinder accurate forecasting of future cash flows and does make possible a crisis should policyholders attempt to cash out their insurance and annuity contracts on a large scale. However, the size and relative predictability of net cash inflows into life companies makes extremely unlikely the occurrence of cash demands that force asset liquidation. This a priori judgment has been corroborated historically by the strength which life companies displayed during general economic and mortality crises. Thus it seems unlikely that most life insurance companies would require more than a limited quantity of reasonably liquid assets, limited to less than 5% of their total assets, to help meet the possibility of massive cash demands.

In order to meet the normal cash inventory needs required to handle insurance business transactions, a portion of these liquid asset holdings will be held in cash or near-due marketable obligations. Companies that conclude emergency liquid asset holdings are unnecessary may nonetheless wish to provide some liquidity for purposes of insuring flexibility in portfolio operations. The uses of liquid assets in investment strategy are examined in Chapter V.

We conclude, then, that any transactions and precautionary liquidity needs of life insurance companies can be met for most companies by placing a nominal portion of total assets in liquid form. Therefore, for the bulk of investment decisions, liquidity and marketability attributes are immaterial. Portfolio selections can be made on yield or other criteria.

ASSET QUALITY

The question here is whether life insurance companies are willing to trade off risk for return throughout the range of markets in which they participate, or whether they typically restrict themselves to a subset of investment opportunities selected on quality criteria. In fact, life companies are restricted to some such subset

---

higher during the depression in companies with relatively little portfolio liquidity. See Rydgren, "An Investment Policy for a Life Insurance Company."

by statutory investment regulations and perhaps by state insurance department rules governing the valuation of portfolio assets. The operative question then is whether companies set asset quality constraints independent of, and more stringent than, those which are externally imposed upon the industry. Companies do not so restrict themselves if in effect they compute "risk equivalent" yields on alternative prospective assets and then choose assets with the highest expected discounted rate of return.[45] They do so restrict themselves if they refuse to accept some prospective "risky" investments regardless of how attractively they are priced.

In this section we shall simply summarize the limited evidence available on (1) life company attitudes toward individual asset quality, and (2) the quality ranges in which life companies, in fact, have been active. In subsequent chapters we shall examine the extent to which external regulations have involuntarily forced life companies into higher quality investments and the degree to which companies consciously alter quality standards cyclically.

Securities portfolios

(i) Company attitudes toward quality

In his exhaustive study of the performance of corporate bond issues by quality grade during 1900–1943, W. Braddock Hickman found that lower quality issues (based on rating agency grades): (1) carried higher promised yields; (2) had higher default rates; (3) experienced higher loss rates (net of gains); but (4) realized higher life span yields than higher rated issues.[46] Hickman suggested that these findings were consistent with two alternative explanations of the determination of promised yields. One of these, the neoclassical theory, he observed distinguishes three elements of the promised bond yield: (1) the basic yield; (2) the pure risk premium; and (3) the risk-bearing component.[47] Given probability beliefs about future outcomes, the pure risk premium

---

[45] Conceptually, risk may be taken into account in the estimate of expected return per annum over the life of available assets or in the choice of capitalization rates used in calculating discounted rates of return on prospective investments.

[46] Hickman, *Corporate Bond Quality and Investor Experience*, p. 14.

[47] *Ibid.*, p. 15.

is conceived as just adequate to offset expected net default losses over a numerically large, randomly selected set of similar corporate obligations. An additional risk-bearing component may be required by small investors who are unable to diversify sufficiently to reduce risk to the point where net losses can be expected to be covered by the pure risk component. Thus the neoclassical version explains higher realized yields on lower grade issues by the existence of a proximately atomistic corporate bond market dominated by investors too small to diversify their bond holdings fully.[48]

Hickman's alternative thesis is applicable to a bond market dominated by large institutional investors, large enough to obtain essentially full mileage from diversification. Nonetheless, this thesis holds that because financial intermediaries are closely regulated and sensitive to public opinion, they are embarrassed about holding defaulted obligations even though no portfolio losses result.[49] Thus conservative financial giants place a premium on bond quality even though their size provides them with a strong risk-taking potential. They bid down yields on higher quality obligations and thereby permit lower grade issues to realize significantly higher returns.

As we have seen, the post-World War II corporate bond market has been dominated by sizable institutional investors, primarily life insurance companies and various types of retirement funds. Thus the continuation of the earlier pattern of higher realized yields on lower rated issues would support the view that this result is largely produced by the actions of quality-oriented financial intermediaries.[50] In connection with this study we interviewed investment officers representing 14 major life insurance companies. In discussions with representatives of 10 of these companies we talked specifically about company attitudes toward

---

[48] Strictly, some additional yield margin on lower grade issues may be required by any investor to cover the additional real investment costs associated with servicing a high risk, default-prone portfolio. Furthermore, the power of diversification is reduced to the extent that the outcomes of various bond issues are highly intercorrelated. Normally, diversification cannot be expected to totally eliminate risk. See the discussion of diversification below.

[49] *Ibid.*

[50] The Hickman study is being continued for the postwar period by T. Atkinson, but no results are available at this writing.

quality. These officers echoed the trade association statement of objectives (see footnote 25 above) in asserting in one manner or another that their company's goal was maximization of the discounted expected rate of return provided that the invested principal was adequately protected. This latter concern did seem to be interpreted as placing absolute limits on the degree of risk acceptable in individual investments.

Thus the most common responses to questioning about the reasons for rejecting specific loan and investment opportunities were that:

(1) The promised yield was inadequate in the context of going market yields for the risk characteristics of the loan proposal; or,
(2) The proposal contained a degree of risk unacceptable at any price.

In discussion of specific examples, the risk appraisal was usually based on the potential borrower's financial statements or the cyclical vulnerability of the borrower's industry. In some cases, however, it was apparently income risk, not default risk, considerations that prompted rejection of the investment. Lack of adequate protection against refunding was cited in a number of instances as the reason for rejecting a bond issue.

Among life insurance companies interviewed there appeared to be a rather wide range of quality standards applied to portfolio selections. Two of the companies possessed bond portfolios in which the median of the quality distribution was apparently Aa on Moody's scale.[51] The median quality bond holding of the other companies seemed to be distributed in the range from A-Baa to Baa-Ba. Excepting the two highly quality-oriented companies, the investment officers interviewed acknowledged they acquired some corporate and municipal debt issues which the rating agencies would likely grade below Baa. In some instances this was explained as representing a disagreement between the rating services and the investment officers over the rating of the securi-

---

[51] Because of the concentration of life company activity in privately negotiated issues, most life company corporate bond acquisitions are not rated by any of the agencies at the time of purchase. Most, but not all, of the companies interviewed did rate their bond holdings on criteria roughly corresponding to those employed by rating services. For most of the companies interviewed, we did not have access to internal bond ratings so we are reporting impressions derived from interview responses and a review of bond portfolios held by each of the companies.

ties; i.e., the investment officers felt the securities were of "sound investment quality." Often, however, the companies were admittedly and consciously acquiring more speculative issues in order to improve yield performance.[52] Nearly all the officers had a reasonably clear-cut notion concerning the existence of restraints on investment activity in lower quality issues, either in terms of an absolute quality floor the company would not dip below on any individual investment or in terms of limits on the proportion of the portfolio that could be devoted to bonds below Baa quality, or both. Several officers indicated that they never consciously accepted an issue below Ba quality. Most of those who had any quantitative notions of overall limits indicated that the dollar investment in debt obligations below Baa rating was limited to 10% or 15% of the bond portfolio.

(ii) Quality of securities held by life companies

At the time we conducted most of these interviews (1960), the Life Insurance Association of America was just beginning to collect yield data on corporate debt obligations privately placed with life insurance companies. Yield data were collected by quality rating and industrial classification by means of a monthly survey of life companies holding about two-thirds of the industry's assets. Four quality classes are distinguished. The responding companies were requested to use grading criteria which ". . . correspond roughly to the standards used by Moody's for rating as Aaa, Aa, A, or Baa, respectively." [53] A fifth category of "unclassified" placements includes all convertible obligations, issues of Canadian and foreign obligors, oil and gas production loans, and other corporate debt issues not reported in the first four classes. Since some of the issues in the fifth category are no doubt of equivalent quality to issues in the first four grades, the unclassified category does not represent a clean "below 4th quality" collection of placements.

These survey data for 1960–1964 are summarized in Table I-4. Both the percentage distribution of placements by quality class

---

[52] Sometimes these issues were "sweetened" with equity options. This practice is discussed further in Chapter II.

[53] LIAA, *Instructions and Definitions*, "Report on Direct Placement Yields."

TABLE I-4. Distribution of New Commitments for Directly Placed Corporate Bonds by Quality Class and Average Yield by Class Annually: 1960–1964

Quality Class	1960		1961		1962		1963		1964	
	%	Yield	%	Yield	%	Yield	%	Yield	%	Yield
1	0.7	5.73	1.1	4.88	0.2	5.22	0.5	4.81	1.5	4.81
2	4.8	5.66	5.9	5.18	6.0	4.91	6.5	4.78	6.4	4.88
3	26.1	5.70	25.0	5.47	18.2	5.25	19.8	5.04	16.3	5.05
4	42.8	6.03	46.6	5.71	52.4	5.59	50.3	5.39	53.1	5.37
Unclassified	25.5	6.18	21.3	6.03	23.2	5.74	22.8	5.64	22.7	5.70

NOTE: Data from monthly survey reports filed by 35 to 41 life companies, accounting for about two-thirds of industry assets. Percentage distribution based on dollar amount of new commitments. Yield data are averages weighted by dollar amount committed.

SOURCE: Life Insurance Association of America.

and the (weighted) average yield by class are presented. Only corporate obligations with initial maturity of more than one year are included. The data reported are new commitments, not acquisitions, so the yield series should reflect current market yields.

From the distribution data in Table I-4, it appears that, during this period at least, the median quality of life company corporate bond investments was in the Baa class. Yields reported by the surveyed life companies appear to run significantly higher (typically about 50 basis points) than yields on newly issued publicly offered corporate bonds.[54] In our interviews, life company investment officers expressed the view that directly placed bonds typically carried yields of about 25 to 50 basis points more than similar public issues of the same obligors. In three of the five years, yields on the few first-quality selections were higher than second-quality bond yields, perhaps indicating that life companies invest only in blue chip issues which carry exceptional yields. Since the fifth category contains issues of varying quality, the 1960 interview responses to the effect that life companies

[54] Based on a comparison of the yields in Table I-4 with the best-known new issue yield series available: Moody's; First National City Bank Aaa Corporate Bonds; Bankers Trust Grade 2 Utility Bonds, and a series covering recently distributed issues compiled by Kaplan (see "Yields on Recently Issued Corporate Bonds: A New Index").

limit bond investments of below Baa quality to no more than 10% or 15% of their bond portfolios are neither confirmed nor denied by these data.

(iii) An overview of the role of quality in securities selection

Our overall impressions with regard to life company securities portfolios can be summarized as follows. Considerable variance among life companies exists in their attitudes toward investment quality. A few significant companies continue to pursue a strong quality-oriented policy. Most companies, however, invest in only those high-quality corporate bonds (Aaa-A public utility and Aaa-Aa industrial issues) that offer exceptional yields, call protection, attractive maturities, or other desired attributes. Most life companies concentrate their corporate bond selections in A-Baa rated industrials and Baa-Ba public utility obligations where skilled and knowledgeable investment staffs are an advantage and there is considerable room for trade-offs between yield and quality. Investment in lower grade issues is limited by some combination of company attitudes toward default and regulatory restraints.

In the municipal bond market the tax environment limits life company investment primarily to lower quality issues (Baa-Ba general obligation issues and revenue bonds) which require more sophisticated appraisal than many individuals and commercial bankers are capable of performing. Life company activity in equities has been restrained by internal attitudes and external restrictions. An attempt to separate these two causal elements will be deferred to Chapter II.

Mortgage loans

(i) Company attitudes toward quality

Most life insurance companies seem to believe that their mortgage loan portfolios are of essentially the same quality as their bond portfolios. There are varying opinions, however, with regard to what "equivalent quality" means in terms of the descriptive loan, property, and borrower characteristics associated with mortgage loans.

In part, disagreements relate to differences in attitudes about the quality of federally underwritten mortgage loans. Some officers feel VA-guaranteed and FHA-insured loans have been close to "riskless" investments. Many, however, are of the opinion that liberal terms on government underwritten loans are likely to produce more default problems than companies experience with their conventional loan holdings.

A life insurance company officer once suggested that the most attractive mortgage loans to a yield-conscious investor should be federally underwritten loans selling at a price discount with a high probability of defaulting in the near future.[55] This is an unrepresentative opinion, however, judging from our interviews with life company investment officers. Life companies more typically feel that loan defaults are bad for business regardless of whether the principal and interest payments and all costs are fully recovered or more than recovered. One large company, which has had one of the most aggressive and adventurous corporate bond investment policies and one of the highest realized portfolio rates of return in the industry, turned out to have the most quality-oriented mortgage lending policy we encountered. The mortgage loan officers felt that with an efficient mortgage organization they were able to select residential loans from among the top 2% of the quality distribution, and due to the imperfections inherent in a market composed of thousands of largely independent local markets they sacrificed relatively little in yield with the purchase of quality. Only conventional loans were being acquired.

(ii) Evidence on the quality of mortgage portfolios

Within mortgage markets life insurance companies have had the reputation of being quality-focused lenders particularly as compared to the dominant lenders in postwar residential mortgage markets, the savings and loan associations. Specific evidence relevant to this proposition is scarce but what evidence is available seems to support the contention. Table I-5 presents data comparing single-family residential loan portfolios of the major mortgage lenders by various characteristics commonly assumed to be indicators of loan quality. These data were produced by a census sample survey conducted early in 1960. Summary char-

---

[55] Conklin, "Some Fundamental Considerations of Investment Policy."

TABLE I-5. Summary Characteristics of Single-Family Residential First-Mortgage Loans Outstanding, by Selected Holders: 1960

	Commercial Banks	Mutual Savings Banks	Savings and Loan Associations	Life Insurance Companies	All First-Mortgage Loans
A. Conventional Loans					
Mortgage Characteristics:					
Loan Size (dollars)	5,600	8,300	7,800	11,300	7,300
Loan Term (years)	9	19	16	20	15
Interest Rate (%)	6.0	5.1	6.0	5.0	5.6
Monthly Payments (dollars)	60	56	62	73	61
Delinquent Loans (% of loan amount outstanding)	3.71	2.80	9.29	2.51	8.49
Loan as % of Purchase Price (%)	58	63	66	62	68
Total Outstanding Debt as % of value (%)	33	38	46	41	44
Property Characteristics:					
Value (dollars)	13,000	17,200	15,000	22,200	13,900
Owner Characteristics:					
Annual Housing Costs as % of Income (%)	19	20	20	18	20
Income (dollars)	6,400	7,400	6,600	9,700	6,500
Purchase Price-Income Ratio	1.9	2.1	2.2	2.1	2.0
Regular Mortgage Payments as % of Income (%)	12	9	12	9	12
B. FHA Loans					
Mortgage Characteristics:					
Loan Size (dollars)	9,100	10,100	8,800	9,500	9,500
Loan Term (years)	23	26	24	24	24

Interest Rate (%)	4.6	4.6	4.6	4.6	4.6
Monthly Payments (dollars)	57	57	55	59	56
Delinquent Loans (% of loan amount outstanding)	3.22	1.89	1.13	5.04	3.52
Loan as % of Purchase Price (%)	83	82	84	86	80
Total Outstanding Debt as % of value (%)	64	62	65	69	57
Property Characteristics:					
Value (dollars)	13,700	13,900	12,000	14,300	14,200
Owner Characteristics:					
Annual Housing Costs as % of Income (%)	18	18	17	20	18
Income (dollars)	6,900	7,300	6,200	7,100	7,100
Purchase Price-Income Ratio	2.0	2.0	2.0	1.9	2.0
Regular Monthly Payments as % of Income (%)	10	10	10	10	11
C. *VA Loans*					
Mortgage Characteristics:					
Loan Size (dollars)	10,200	10,800	9,900	10,800	9,100
Loan Term (years)	25	25	25	27	22
Interest Rate (%)	4.5	4.5	4.5	4.5	4.1
Monthly Payments (dollars)	58	61	57	58	59
Delinquent Loans (% of loan amount outstanding)	4.98	3.95	7.04	3.11	3.49
Loan as % of Purchase Price/(%)	91	91	92	91	83
Total Outstanding Debt as % of Income (%)	91	92	93	92	84

TABLE 1-5 (continued)

	Commercial Banks	Mutual Savings Banks	Savings and Loan Associations	Life Insurance Companies	All First-Mortgage Loans
Property Characteristics:					
Value (Dollars)	14,700	15,000	13,900	13,900	13,800
Owner Characteristics:					
Annual Housing Costs as % of Income (%)	19	20	19	18	19
Income (Dollars)	6,900	7,000	6,800	6,900	6,800
Purchase Price-Income Ratio	1.8	2.1	1.9	1.8	2.0
Regular Monthly Payments as % of Income (%)	10	11	11	10	10

NOTE: Excepting for the delinquent loan ratio, all entries are median values. Data for loans outstanding at the time the sample survey was conducted: January–February 1960.

DEFINITIONS:

Loan size refers to the loan amount at the time it was obtained by the current owner. Loan term is the total time required to repay the loan principal in regular periodic payments as stated in the loan contract.

Interest rate is the contract rate on an annual basis. No fees, charges, or insurance premiums are included. FHA and VA rates are not adjusted for price discounts or premiums.

Monthly payments consist of the amount of principal and interest required to be paid regularly, shown on a monthly basis. Loans with no required regular payments are excluded.

Delinquent loans are loans for which required payments are past due 30 days or more.

Mortgage loan-purchase price ratio computed at the time the loan was made or assumed. Properties not acquired by purchase are excluded.

Property value is the amount the owner estimated the property would sell for on the market in early 1960.

Annual housing costs include real estate taxes, and expenses for property insurance, utilities, mortgage principal and interest payments, and other mortgage payments (FHA insurance premium, servicing fees, life insurance premium and ground rent). Repair and maintenance costs are not included. Costs were estimated by owners for the previous 12 months. Properties acquired after 1958 are excluded.

Income is the total 1959 income received by the owner, the spouse, and relatives 14 years old and over who live with the owner.

Purchase price-income ratio relates purchase price to owner's family income for 1959. Data are limited to properties purchased after 1956.

Monthly payments-income ratio is limited to loans where regular interest and/or principal payments are required.

SOURCE: U.S. Census of Housing, 1960. Volume V, *Residential Finance*, Part 1, *Homeowner Properties*, Washington, 1963.

acteristics are shown separately for conventional, FHA-insured, and VA-guaranteed loans. As would be expected, differences among the loan portfolios of the major lenders are greatest in the conventional loan sector. As compared to all other lenders in general, and savings and loan associations in particular, life company conventional, single-family, first-mortgage loans are typically larger loans on more valuable properties with lower loan/value ratios, longer maturities, and lower interest rates. Home owners borrowing from life companies on a conventional basis tend to have higher incomes and allot a smaller portion of their annual incomes to housing costs in general, and to regular mortgage payments in particular. A smaller proportion of life companies' loans compared to those of other lenders were, in fact, delinquent at the time the survey was conducted.

Because of secular liberalization of loan terms and rising interest rates during the postwar years, comparisons of portfolio stocks have to be treated with caution. There are significant differences among the major lenders in the growth rates of their mortgage portfolios and, as seen in Table I-5, in loan maturities. Consequently there are significant differences in the age distribution of loans outstanding in the survey period. Of all conventional, single-family, first-mortgage loans outstanding in early 1960, 74% had been made in the previous five years (since 1954). Some 82% of commercial bank conventional loans, 76% of savings and loan association loans, 62% of mutual savings bank loans, and 62% of life insurance company portfolios had been originated since 1954.[56] Therefore the interest rate data reported in Table I-5 exaggerate the differential between rates obtained on loans made by commercial banks and savings and loan associations, on the one hand, and savings banks and life insurance companies, on the other. Some distortion in comparing other characteristics may also occur as a result of differences in the age of loans held in early 1960.

In 1963 the Federal Home Loan Bank Board began collecting and publishing monthly survey data on conventional first-

[56] For all first-mortgage loans outstanding on single-family residences, the proportion made since 1954 was 69%, and for the particular lenders: savings and loan associations, 74%; commercial banks, 69%; savings banks, 62%; and life companies, 60%. Computed from the 1960 Census of Housing data cited in Table I-5.

mortgage loans on single-family residences. Loans originated by the five major types of residential mortgage lenders are canvassed, and information is collected on loan characteristics. These data are illustrated in Table I-6, where average loan characteristics are reported by lenders for selected dates.

The data reported there are derived from loans made for the purpose of purchasing a newly constructed home. Similar data are also available for loans designed to enable the borrower to acquire an existing house. Loan information is collected as of the date of loan approval so the summary characteristics reported should reflect current market activity consistently for all lender types.

Since the data shown in Table I-6 are classified by the loan originator, the results displayed for life insurance companies are limited to loans originated by home office or branch office personnel of life companies. Most of the larger life companies depend primarily upon outside correspondents to produce mortgage loan opportunities. Thus many of the loans classified under "mortgage companies" were, no doubt, originated for life company portfolios. While there is no apparent reason to think loans originated directly by life companies are systematically different from loans originated for them by agents, nonetheless the reported data may not be wholly representative of life company lending activity.

Assuming, however, that the relative position of life companies in the residential mortgage market is fairly depicted in Table I-6, it then appears that some market segmentation does exist and that life companies tend to make loans on more expensive properties with lower loan-purchase price ratios, longer maturities, and lower interest rates than other lenders as a group. Again, life company loans are particularly distinguishable from those of savings and loan associations in the purchase price, loan/price ratio, term, and interest rate characteristics.[57]

A priori, it seems plausible that the relative loan, property, and borrower characteristics displayed in Tables I-5 and I-6 indicate that life insurance companies tend to make relatively safe loans. In fact, not much is known about the relationships between these

---

[57] Relative loan characteristics for loans on existing properties are quite similar, and for that reason are not displayed in Table I-6.

TABLE I-6. *Average Loan Characteristics of Newly Approved Conventional First-Mortgage Loans for Purchase of New Single-Family Houses, by Lender: Selected Dates, 1963–1965*

Characteristic and Lender	Jan. 1963	July 1963	Jan. 1964	July 1964	Jan. 1965	July 1965
Loan Term (years)						
Commercial Banks	16.0	17.4	17.9	18.0	19.4	19.7
Mutual Savings Banks	23.5	24.7	24.7	24.5	25.2	25.0
Savings and Loan Assns.	22.9	23.9	24.4	24.6	24.7	25.0
Life Insurance Companies	26.4	25.4	26.1	27.0	26.4	26.5
Mortgage Companies	26.2	27.0	28.2	26.9	27.2	27.7
All Loans	23.1	24.1	24.7	24.5	24.7	25.0
Loan/Purchase Price Ratio (%)						
Commercial Banks	60.4	61.9	61.5	61.6	65.1	64.5
Mutual Savings Banks	69.3	69.1	71.4	69.0	70.8	72.5
Savings and Loan Assns.	75.2	75.9	76.4	77.0	76.9	77.5
Life Insurance Companies	68.5	68.3	68.7	69.7	70.0	68.9
Mortgage Companies	71.1	73.6	78.3	72.8	72.8	77.0
All Loans	72.3	73.3	74.7	73.9	74.0	75.0
Purchase Price (dollars)						
Commercial Banks	24,300	23,300	26,100	27,900	25,200	27,800
Mutual Savings Banks	21,200	23,800	21,600	24,100	23,500	24,200
Savings and Loan Assns.	20,100	21,200	21,500	22,300	22,900	22,700
Life Insurance Companies	28,700	27,500	27,200	27,700	31,000	30,400
Mortgage Companies	24,300	25,700	23,200	26,100	24,300	26,700
All Loans	21,900	22,800	25,600	23,800	23,900	24,700
Contract Interest Rate (%)						
Commercial Banks	5.80	5.71	5.67	5.60	5.67	5.64
Mutual Savings Banks	5.66	5.56	5.61	5.50	5.56	5.57
Savings and Loan Assns.	6.05	5.93	5.92	5.88	5.90	5.88
Life Insurance Companies	5.59	5.55	5.53	5.49	5.49	5.47
Mortgage Companies	5.75	5.70	5.78	5.61	5.69	5.72
All Loans	5.92	5.82	5.83	5.76	5.79	5.77
Fees and Charges (%)						
Commercial Banks	.14	.11	.15	.13	.09	.08
Mutual Savings Banks	.19	.23	.05	.05	.03	.04
Savings and Loan Assns.	.84	.72	.67	.65	.69	.63
Life Insurance Companies	.16	.18	.15	.16	.19	.12
Mortgage Companies	.98	.83	1.03	.64	.89	.91
All Loans	.68	.61	.64	.52	.59	.55

NOTE: Data are the result of a monthly sample survey of the five types of lending institutions shown. The "All Loans" category refers only to loans made by these lenders. Loans are reported as of the date of approval, by the originating lender.

Loan characteristics are averages weighted by the estimated number of loans in the group.

Fees and charges include only nonreimbursable discounts and initial payments that provide additional income to the lender.

SOURCE: Federal Home Loan Bank Board, monthly releases.

characteristics and the probability of default. However, a study by Leon Kendall of savings and loan associations' loans revealed delinquencies were highly (positively) correlated with loan/price ratios and interest rates.[58] The positive relation between interest rates and delinquencies existed within each geographic region as well as for the country as a whole. Loan size and loan maturities, and the borrower's income distribution, did not differ significantly in the sample of loan delinquencies from the sample of current loans.[59] No information on the burden of housing costs or mortgage payments to owner-borrowers was reported.

In sum, the available evidence does corroborate the belief that life insurance company conventional loan portfolios are of relatively high quality and some yield sacrifice is involved in the purchase of quality. An overall appraisal of the quality of life company residential mortgage loan portfolios depends upon how one evaluates the risk characteristics of federally underwritten loans as well. Our interview responses suggest that many companies have acquired high-quality loan portfolios by choice. Defaults are considered undesirable *per se*. It is possible, however, that some companies have higher quality loan portfolios than they would choose if freed of confining regulatory rules.

DIVERSIFICATION

Purpose of diversification

Limiting asset selections to high-quality debt issues does not by itself insure a lender against portfolio loss. Indeed, concen-

---

[58] Kendall, *Anatomy of the Residential Mortgage.* The study is based on a sample of conventional single-family loans selected from the portfolios of 38 large savings and loan associations located in major metropolitan areas throughout the United States. Separate samples were drawn from the populations of current and delinquent loans. Loans were considered delinquent if payments were 60 days or more past due.

[59] It was generally presumed that larger loans and higher income borrowers were less likely to default. There was probably a presumption that longer maturities are more risky, but evaluating this attribute is complicated. Other things being equal, longer maturities reduce monthly payments and ease the payments burden. Also, unrealistically short-term loans are obviously not safer. There may be significant interrelationships among characteristics with which only a systematic multivariate analysis could hope to deal. For example, lenders may make long-term loans only to borrowers who qualify as particularly safe in other attributes.

tration of invested funds in a few highly regarded economic sectors places an investor in a vulnerable position should changes in technology or tastes affect one or more of those sectors adversely. History does not support an attitude which considers investment in certain select areas of the economy essentially riskless.[60]

Consequently, a conservative investment policy reduces portfolio risk by dispersing funds among a variety of assets whose (uncertain) returns are thought not to be highly correlated with each other. Portfolio diversification is clearly a sensible and desirable policy objective for investors who, like life insurance companies, abhor risk. The policy question is whether the benefits of diversification are obtainable without significant sacrifice of investment return or other portfolio objectives. It is usually contended that a portfolio selected to maximize the discounted value of future expected returns will be a portfolio with little or no diversification.[61] In this view, reduction of capital and income uncertainty can be achieved by a policy of conscious diversification, but only at the cost of accepting a portfolio with lower expected return.

Diversification exacts a price in anticipated return for two reasons. First, funds are spread among a number of different assets instead of being concentrated in the single asset or handful of assets with highest expected return. Second, costs associated with the mechanics of the lending process (i.e., transactions, search, analysis, and review costs) rise per dollar invested as portfolio funds are dispersed among a larger number of assets. The cost of reducing the variability of returns to some specified target depends upon the degree of interdependence existing among the probability distributions of returns for the assets in the opportunity set.

Power of diversification

Diversification is very powerful when returns are uncorrelated (or negatively correlated). Using variance as the measure of risk

---

[60] Earlier in this century some investors regarded securities issued by railroad and street railway corporations as unquestionably safe. In fact, this particular appraisal was written into some states' statutory regulations governing life insurance company investment activity. See Chapter II.

[61] See Markowitz, "Portfolio Selection," esp. pp. 77–79.

and assuming the variances associated with the distribution of returns for each asset in the set are bounded, then as the number of assets included in the portfolio is increased, the variance of the average of the uncorrelated random returns approaches zero.[62] In this case, it does not take a very large number of independent assets to reduce the uncertainty of portfolio return to a quite modest level.[63]

The case of random uncorrelated variables, however, is more relevant to an understanding of a life insurance company's mortality risks than its portfolio risks, for the returns on portfolio assets tend to be positively intercorrelated. Positive intercorrelation of outcomes means that there is a limit to the reduction in variance obtainable by adding more assets to the portfolio. This limiting value is equal to the average co-variance.[64] Given the average co-variance, little ordinarily is gained by investing in more than 50 or 100 different items. Additional assets are helpful only if they reduce the average co-variance.

Portfolio asset returns tend to be particularly intercorrelated in part because income statement and balance sheet performances of most enterprises and households are related to the general level of economic activity. Considerable diversification is obtainable, however, by spreading portfolio funds among industries and geographical regions which are otherwise loosely linked at most and by avoiding the placement of very large sums in obligations of a few borrowers. The optimal amount of diversification is determined by a lender's preference for return as against security of

---

[62] Bounded means that there exists an upper limit to the individual variances. The expected value of the portfolio returns equals the average of the expected returns on the individual assets (weighted by the proportion of portfolio dollars placed in each asset). See Markowitz, *Portfolio Selection*, Chapter V. The standard deviation (variance) is commonly used as a measure of the dispersion of returns although other measures exist, and some (e.g., semi-variance) may, in principle, be preferable. (See *ibid.*, pp. 193–194, 294–297.) For some investors higher moments may be relevant.

[63] For example, see *ibid.*, p. 112, Table 1. Also an earlier and interesting recognition of this property of portfolio selection among assets with uncorrelated returns can be found in Meader, "Diversification: A Sound Principle Often Carried to Unwarranted Extremes."

[64] Defined as the ratio of the sum of all distinct co-variances to the number of distinct co-variances. (If unequal amounts are invested in the various assets, a weighted average, where amounts invested determine the weights, is necessary). See Markowitz, *Portfolio Selection*, pp. 109–115.

return and by the nature of the existing trade-off function between the two objectives. In this connection theoretical formulations of the trade-off relation usually do not deal explicitly with the role of the real costs incurred in the investment process. These costs, however, are very much in the minds of insurance company investment officers[65] and are no doubt a significant limitation on the extent to which it is profitable for life insurance companies to disperse their funds among many borrowers.[66]

Life insurance company behavior

Life insurance companies are typically quite large investors. Life companies with total assets of $500 million or more accounted for about 84% of industry assets during the late 1950s. Typically, each company held several hundred different security issues and those active in the residential mortgage market held many thousands of separate mortgage loans. The number of different assets owned by each large company seems to exceed the number that it might be expected to hold on diversification grounds alone. There are apparently other reasons for spreading portfolio funds among a substantial number of loans and securities.

Several forces compel life insurance companies to disperse funds among many investments. Consider the following:

(1) In rejecting the hypothesis that investors act so as to maximize the discounted value of expected returns, Markowitz contended, *"If we ignore market imperfections* the foregoing rule (maximize discounted returns) never implies that there is a diversified portfolio which is preferable to all nondiversified portfolios."* [67] However, life insurance company portfolios are very large compared to the size of individual loans and security issues in their opportunity set. Due to this "market imperfection," life companies must necessarily invest in more than a single asset

---

[65] For example, see Patrick, "Management of the Life Insurance Investment Portfolio," esp. p. 75.

[66] This is Patrick's view. Indeed, he suggests life insurance companies have overdiversified, in light of the real cost of dispersal. Also, Meader's theoretical formulation of the optimum diversification problem did focus on lending costs and emphasized the importance of this constraint on diversification. See Meader, "Diversification."

[67] Markowitz, "Portfolio Selection," p. 77. Italics added.

or handful of assets. For this reason alone, the observation that life company funds are dispersed among many assets is not evidence that the maximization of discounted returns hypothesis is inapplicable as an explanation of their behavior.

(2) The opportunity set of available investments is not given to life insurance companies. Active search techniques must be implemented to develop a satisfactory variety of opportunities. This involves staffing costs and the development and maintenance of contacts with securities brokers; past, present, and potential borrowers; real estate developers; mortgage bankers; and builders, among others. Success in these endeavors may involve the creation of high-overhead internal organizations and require a willingness to allocate some funds to important market contacts regardless of the existing yield structure. One of the costs of being able to generate attractive investment opportunities in the future is that the current flow of available funds may have to be invested in ways inconsistent with maximizing portfolio returns on this year's selections.

(3) It is sometimes suggested by insurance company officers that it is important to direct investment funds back into areas from which premiums are produced. Some geographic dispersal of funds may be motivated by considerations of the insurance business. Although they do not seem to be a major factor in investment policy, tie-ins between insurance sales and loans are not unknown.

(4) Although life insurance companies do trade in outstanding assets more often than their statements of policy sometimes suggest, portfolio trading is nonetheless quite limited. This is due in part to the fact that secondary market facilities and certification procedures have been slow to develop in mortgage markets, and many corporate investments are difficult to market because they have been negotiated directly with the borrower. The significance of limited asset turnover prior to maturity is that a life company's portfolio at any point of time reflects investment decisions made over a number of years in the past. In a dynamic, ever-changing economy, this means that even a company following a returns maximization goal is likely to have a rather widely diversified portfolio.

It does not necessarily follow that because portfolio funds are spread out over numerous assets for nondiversification reasons, they are spread out efficiently from a diversification standpoint. However, the extent to which a yield oriented investment policy seems likely to produce a portfolio with wide geographical and industrial representation indicates that significant reduction in variability of return must be a by-product of funds dispersion motivated by other goals. The amount of reduction in variance obtained "free" may not be sufficient, of course, to attain target, yield-certainty objectives. Therefore we shall examine further (Chapter VII) the extent to which diversification may seriously compete with investment return in determining asset choices.

ASSET MATURITY

Reasons for concern with asset maturities

Several considerations may prompt life insurance companies to be concerned with the maturity composition of their portfolios. For example, maturity attributes are relevant for an investment policy derived from liquidity and rate of return objectives. A company with liquidity objectives decides to set aside a portion of its portfolio for investment in short-term assets and/or consciously schedules asset maturities so that the cash flow generated by maturing assets will be stable over time. A simple yield-maximization policy may focus on maturity characteristics by directing investment departments to select assets from the peak of the yield to maturity curve. Alternatively, the yield to maturity schedule may be used as an interest rate forecasting device, and the company may follow a policy of investing long when the level of yields are "high" (downsweeping yield curve) and investing short when yields are "low" (upsweeping yield curve).

Beyond this tangential involvement of asset maturities in the portfolio choice problem, it has been asserted that ". . . it is not possible to satisfactorily explain the investment decision of life insurance companies without recourse to the explanatory variable, demand for maturity *qua* maturity." [68] In particular, industry spokesmen have often observed that life insurance companies tend to favor long-term investments because their liability con-

---

[68] Wehrle, "Life Insurance Investment—The Experience of Four Companies," p. 126.

tracts are typically long term.[69] Among the advantages cited for long maturities are: (1) yields usually have been higher on longer maturities; and (2) investing long significantly reduces the cost of running the investment operation. The most outspoken advocates of a conscious maturity policy, however, have urged upon life companies the necessity of investing long in order to obtain adequate investment income security.[70]

The income certainty objective

In this view, life insurance companies should be willing to sacrifice something in the expected value of investment returns, capital certainty, etc., in order to assure that the realized return will exceed the contractually guaranteed return. The realized rate of return of investment funds could potentially fall short of the assumed rate for several reasons:

(1) Assets may have to be sold prior to maturity at a capital loss.
(2) Debt obligations may default with respect to interest or principal payments; equities may return less in dividends and capital appreciation than anticipated.
(3) Savings generated from policy contracts currently in force may have to be invested in the future at lower than the contractually assumed interest rates.

Investment policy deals with possibilities (1) and (2) in the attention given to liquidity, asset quality, and diversification. Maturity attributes may enter into these considerations in an incidental way; e.g., investment officers seem to feel that, other

---

[69] For example, see the LIAA-CMC Monograph, pp. 58–59. Also the Patman *Replies*, pp. 1227 ff.; O'Leary, "The Institutional Savings-Investment Process and Current Economic Theory"; S. C. Badger, "Unusual Features of Life Insurance Investing"; J. H. Wood, "What the Life Insurance Underwriter Should Know About Investments"; Cleary, "The Response of Life Insurance Funds to American Needs," p. 61.

[70] In addition to Wehrle's previously cited work, concern that income risk is the primary investment problem facing life companies can be found in W. M. Anderson, "The Long View of Life Insurance Investment," pp. 359–362; Nerlove, "Common Stocks as Investments for American Life Insurance Companies: A Non-Academic View"; Winn, "Factors Influencing Life Insurance Company Investments"; Conklin, "Factors Determining the Investment Policy of Life Insurance Companies"; Hood and Main, "The Role of Canadian Life Insurance Companies in the Postwar Capital Market"; and Hood, *The Financing of Economic Activity in Canada*.

things equal, longer maturities carry with them greater risk of default. But the primary income security risk develops from the possibility that interest rates may decline to substantially lower levels in the future.

Funds available for investment in the future, but identifiable with currently outstanding contracts, derive from two sources:

(1) Interest and dividend income flows from current investments plus turnover of current assets.
(2) Future premium inflow generated by current policy contracts.

Abstracting from any relations between maturity and default risk, maturity policy determines what risks life insurance companies assume in the event of future changes in interest rate levels. In general, a short-term maturity position endangers the policy reserve fund if interest rates fall in the future, and a long-term maturity position costs a company the opportunity to take advantage of future increases in the interest rate level. On the assumption that the solvency risk associated with a short position is of more concern than the opportunities foregone in assuming a long position, life insurance companies have often been urged to invest long.

Means of insuring income security

The formal properties of an investment policy designed to reduce or eliminate income risk have been quite thoroughly investigated. Suggested procedures take two principal forms: (1) "matching" and (2) "immunization." [71] A matching policy marries assets and liabilities with the objective of guaranteeing both income security and capital security. Discussion of matching procedures assume that mortality, operating expenses, asset maturities, and liability maturities are all precisely predictable. The availability of readily marketable compound interest securities is also assumed.[72] Under these circumstances, capital certainty is achieved at the relevant time by matching the maturity dates

---

[71] For a thorough review of the literature and exposition of the various hedging techniques, see Wehrle, *A Theory of Life Insurance Company Portfolio Selection.*

[72] *Ibid.*, p. 8. See Wehrle also for additional references dealing with the matching problem.

of assets with liabilities. Income certainty is insured by purchasing an asset with interest and maturity features identical to those on liabilities each time a policy is issued. Unfortunately, matching inception and maturity dates is possible only if the company has funds at the time policies are issued sufficient to cover the present value of all existing liabilities. For growing companies this is not generally the case; i.e., existing policies will generate a positive cash flow (premiums less benefits) for some years to come. In this case, matching of asset and liability inception dates is possible only if borrowing and/or sales policy can appropriately alter the time shape of the life company's liability flow.[73] This is not likely to be practicable.[74]

The immunization technique drops the capital-certainty half of the twin matching objectives and deliberately accepts some capital value risk in order to guarantee income security. Stability of capital value is considered a lesser problem for reasons we have indicated above. Immunization, therefore, does not match the maturity rates of assets and liabilities, but rather directs the selection of assets whose maturities are longer than those of liabilities being insured. The object is to hedge the impact of future changes in interest rates with offsetting changes in capital value. If implemented successfully, this policy guarantees equality through time of the discounted values of the asset flow and liability flow.[75]

Implications of income-risk hedging policies

In any case, complete hedging of income risk seems to require life companies to purchase assets with maturities as long or longer than the maturities on liabilities issued. Actually since asset maturity dates, liability maturity dates, and operating expenses

---

[73] The problem is to convert a "humped fund" into a "declining fund." This might be accomplished by borrowing, and through the sale of single premium immediate annuities and acceptance of advance premiums. See Wehrle, *ibid.*, pp. 11–15; and W. M. Anderson, *op. cit.*, for a discussion of these possibilities.

[74] See Wehrle, p. 15.

[75] Because future interest rate changes are automatically offset, the previous assumption of compound interest securities can be dropped. The other assumptions listed above, including marketability, remain in force. Immunization is discussed thoroughly in Wehrle, pp. 15–26.

are not exactly predictable, even full implementation of the rec-ommended maturity policy will not absolutely hedge income risk.[76] Call features on debt obligations produce uncertainty regarding the maturity of such issues. As we have observed, liquidity options and the multiplicity of settlement options incorporated in life insurance policies have reduced the ability of companies to forecast cash outflows from maturing liabilities. While operating expenses are highly predictable over twelve months or so, the forecasting precision declines with time. The asset marketability assumption also is not completely fulfilled in life insurance com-pany portfolios, but so long as insurance sales are experiencing substantial growth, this does not seriously affect a company's ability to immunize.

Since liability maturities are not so easy to predict, and since there exist substantial variations in the liability mix outstanding among companies, it is not possible to generalize with any pre-cision about the maturity distribution which ought to exist in companies concerned with income risk. A reasonably educated guess, however, is that matching asset and liability maturities will typically produce life company portfolios with maturities distributed through the 20 to 40 year range.[77] It is clear that life company funds are generally invested for a significantly shorter time than this. Mortgage loans seem to have average maturities of about 10 years and corporate bond investments typically an effective life of less than 20 years.[78] Consideration of other portfolio assets (equities, municipal obligations, liquid assets) would probably lengthen the overall average asset ma-turity slightly for most companies. Nevertheless, for one reason

---

[76] See *ibid.*, pp. 26–29.

[77] See W. M. Anderson, *op. cit.*, p. 361.

[78] Judging from various pieces of evidence including inspection of listed maturities of bond holdings and bond acquisitions for a number of companies, and Life Insurance Association of America survey data contained in the LIAA-ALC cash flow reports and bulletins dealing with income and costs from mortgage loans. Because of the frequency of prepayments, realized maturities are on the average shorter than "promised" maturities for both corporate bond and mortgage loan investments. The variance among com-panies in average maturities appears significantly greater for their corporate bonds than their mortgage instruments. Some companies have made cor-porate bond investments with shorter average maturities than their mortgage loan acquisitions. See the article by Wehrle, "Life Insurance Investment — The Experience of Four Companies," for an example of this.

or another, life companies have been accepting income risk in significant amounts.

Reasons companies do not completely hedge income risk

There are two fundamental sets of reasons why life companies have been, in practice, quite willing to accept some income risk. First, achievement of income security is accomplished only at some price in rate of return, capital certainty, and possibly other company objectives. Second, there exist significant stock and flow cushions which insulate life companies from the effects of considerable declines in interest rate levels. Since companies do have the capacity to absorb income risk to a substantial degree, there are limits to what they are willing to pay for income security.

Because the yield-to-maturity curve is often characterized by a hump in intermediate maturities, a policy of always investing long in such circumstances will be inconsistent with investing near the peak of the yield schedule. A commitment to long maturities also calls for sacrificing returns when a company's investment officers have reasonably firm expectations of an upward trend in future interest rate levels.[79] In addition, our interviews with life insurance company officers disclosed strong feelings on their part that credit risk is significantly positively correlated with maturity for most debt obligations.[80] Indeed, the trend toward incorporation of amortization features in mortgage loan and corporate bond issues since the 1929–1933 depression reflects a general market preoccupation with this relationship. Consequently there has in fact been a scarcity of available debt obligations for investors who desire effective maturities of more than 20 to 25 years. In general, to invest long in debt issues a life company would have to concentrate in Treasury bonds, blue chip industrial bonds, or public utility bonds. Investing in Treasury and high grade industrial issues involves sacrificing expected returns. Many public utility obligations have lacked adequate protection

---

[79] There is, of course, room for companies to respond to shorter-run (and perhaps cyclical) forecasts of interest rate movements within an essentially long-term investment policy.

[80] This attitude was also found by Wehrle in the four companies he analyzed. See his "Life Insurance Investment," esp. pp. 125–126.

against refundings, so that nominally long-maturity issues by this sector have often been refunded well in advance of the maturity date. This suggests long-term investors ought to look to equity markets as primary outlets for their funds, but the capital-certainty, fixed dollar asset, trustee traditions apparently have inhibited life companies from seriously exploring this possibility. Life companies, however, have been explicitly constrained by statutory and regulatory rules from equity investments; hence it is possible that income security and rate of return considerations would induce them to invest actively in equities were they free to do so. This is an important but complex question, so we will defer its examination to Chapter II.

There are other life company objectives which may be compromised by the sort of long-term investment policy required to eliminate income risk. One problem dealt with in the immunization literature is that of implementing an equitable insurance dividend policy. It is commonly held that equity among generations of policyholders requires policy dividend rates on all contracts to be responsive to changes in the level of interest rates. The absolute immunization solution does not meet this kind of equity criterion. Rather, it freezes the dividend rate at the time of issuance of the policy; in effect, it treats all policies as if they were nonparticipating. Dividend responsiveness to changes in the time pattern of interest rates requires investment in shorter-term assets and consequently acceptance of less income security.[81]

Discussions of immunization with dividend policy constraints explicitly recognize the fact that participating policies provide a built-in cushion which permits life companies to absorb income risk. Dividend loading is very substantial. Life companies have written policies incorporating earning guarantees of 2.5% or 3% while investing the current funds flow at yields, net of investment costs, of better than 5%. Even if funds are invested for only 10 or 15 years at (say) 5%, life companies would be in a position to reinvest these funds a decade or more hence at much lower rates and meet their policy guarantees, so long as their dividend policy

---

[81] See Wehrle, *A Theory of Life Insurance Company Portfolio Selection*, pp. 29–32, for a discussion of modified immunization procedures which allow for partial or full dividend responsiveness to changes in interest rates, at some cost in income security.

and the terms quoted on new policies are reasonably responsive to changes in the level of interest rates. In addition, the companies' surplus accounts are able to absorb transitional losses which might occur as the result of a large and sustained decline in market yields.

There is a dramatic piece of historical evidence relevant to this problem. The increased emphasis on income risk relative to capital risk, which appeared in the decade after World War II, resulted from the recent behavior of interest rates. The decline in rates which began in 1929 was far greater than anybody could have reasonably anticipated in the 1920s, and still more sobering, interest rates remained at very low levels for an extended period of time. Yet life companies survived two decades (1931–1950) in which long-term yields on eligible investments were below rates guaranteed on policies written in the 1920s. During the 1930s and 1940s policy dividends were cut, premium rates were raised, and the life insurance industry achieved a unique record of solvency among financial institutions.[82]

Impact of income risk on portfolio policy

The primary impact of income risk considerations on actual life insurance company investment policy can be summarized as follows:

(1) Broadly conceived, life insurance companies' concern with income security causes them to prefer longer-term investments. This is perhaps most accurately expressed as a negative proposition; that is, companies avoid placing funds in assets with maturities of less than ten years unless there are strong overriding considerations (e.g., in the form of liquidity needs, yield expectations).

(2) Life companies are particularly open to opportunities to invest in quite long-term debt obligations of high credit quality so long as little or no cost in yield is involved. Indeed, the highly publicized large long-term loans made by life insurance companies during the 1950s were priced at yields somewhat higher than rates the same borrowers would have had to pay for loans with more

---

[82] See Nerlove, "Common Stocks as Investments for American Life Insurance Companies." The average industry net earnings rate remained above the rate required to maintain policy reserves until 1947, and then dropped slightly below the required rate for only a short time.

common maturities.[83]   There is no evidence that life companies are interested in insulating themselves against future interest rate declines by acquiring long-term Treasury bonds.[84]

(3) Life insurance companies do seem to have a strong aversion to bond issues which are not well protected against refunding. This attitude appeared very strongly in our interviews and has been frequently expressed or recognized in the literature.[85]   Aversion to callable bonds exists not just because maturities will, on the average, turn out to be shorter than stated maturities, but also because the timing of calls tends to operate systematically against life company interests.   Life company earnings rates suffered substantially from unscheduled portfolio turnover during the period 1935–1945.[86]   Our interview responses indicated that

---

[83] Prudential Life initiated six "100-year" direct placement commitments with large corporate borrowers during 1951–1954. The loans ranged in amount from $50 million to $300 million.   Prudential made the entire loan in four cases and participated in the other two loans. No repayment of principal was required prior to the maturity date, but after eight years (10 years for two of the loans) either the borrower or lender may opt to convert the 100-year notes into 20-year sinking fund notes in three cases (25 years in the other three loans).   The rate on all six issues was 3.75%, about 25 basis points above what the borrowers would have to pay on a more conventional 25- to 30-year private placement according to R. M. Soldofsky. For further discussion of the terms of these loans, see Soldofsky, "The Size and Maturity of Direct Placement Loans," esp. pp. 37–42.   In the same article Soldofsky reports that a compilation of all direct placement loans made in 1955 disclosed four loans with final maturity of more than 40 years.   One of the four is one of the six 100-year loans previously committed.   The other three ranged in amount from $25 million to $75 million.   Two carried rates of 3.75%, the third, 4.0%.   All were made by large life insurance companies (*ibid.*, pp. 36–37).

[84] Life companies did purchase about $400–$500 million (estimated from holdings data in the *Treasury Bulletin*) of two long maturity Treasury issues offered in the mid-1950s [the 3¼'s (1978–83) offered in 1953 and the 3's (1995) offered in 1955].   However, our interviews with investment officers of companies which had acquired these issues disclosed they had made the purchases to "help the Treasury" in the short term and had no intention of holding these bonds to maturity.   Substantial disposals were, in fact, effected.

[85] See, for example, Gerard, "More Call Price Protection Is Vital"; Burnett, "Some Aspects of Portfolio Management" p. 411; and articles by W. M. Anderson, Conklin, Hood and Main, Nerlove, and Winn, cited previously.

[86] See the American Life Convention, *General Proceedings*, Report of the Manager, annually during these years.   During 1938–1943 there were also many complaints in this source of raiding of policy loans by commercial banks and "widespread raiding" (1942 *Report*) of life company mortgage portfolios by other lenders.

the decline in the life insurance industry's share of public utility financing (and the proportion of life company funds going into public utility sectors) since 1950 was attributable principally to the lack of satisfactory call protection on many utility company debentures.[87]

(4) Concern about income risk provides a strong rationale for life company investment in equities, but some combination of traditional views with respect to the inappropriateness of equities for life company portfolios and externally imposed restrictions on equity investment has resulted in only limited life company exploration of this area.

In sum, income risk considerations explain why the life insurance industry has not attempted to compete with commercial banks and others in short-term business loan and consumer credit markets. Short-term loans are not considered in the eligibility set, except for limited liquidity purposes. Corporate sector loan opportunities without at least five to ten year call protection (and usually a penalty redemption price) are also eliminated from the eligibility set unless they possess unusual offsetting features. Within the eligible opportunity set that remains, there is no reason to believe that maturity attributes will distract life companies from making selections on a rate-of-return basis.

A Summary of the Impact of the Solvency Objective Upon Portfolio Selection

Historically, the life insurance company concern with insuring solvency has appeared to compete significantly with their desire to earn a high rate of investment return. Maintenance of solvency is thought to demand portfolio choice decisions which pre-

---

[87] As a check on whether public utility bond refundings were still in fact a real problem in the 1950s, we made a partial compilation of calls of bonds offered during the cyclical interest rate peak period in 1953. We listed all 1953 public offerings of Aaa, Aa, and A rated utility bonds reported in the weekly Moody's *Bond Survey* and followed their history thereafter. Seventy issues, amounting to $1,853 million, were offered in 1953; 35% of the dollar volume of these issues were redeemed within two years; about two-thirds of the dollar amount in three years. Of 39 issues offered during the peak months of the interest rate cycle (April–September), 28 were redeemed within two years. These accounted for 78% of the dollar amount of April–September 1953 offerings. Thus life companies' reluctance to acquire unprotected issues offered in high interest rate periods appears to have been well founded.

serve both capital values and the stability and certainty of investment income flows. This means that portfolio selections must be
made on the basis of such portfolio attributes as (1) liquidity and
marketability, (2) quality, (3) diversification, and (4) maturity.
Our examination of these portfolio attributes in the context of the
life insurance company investment problem has been conducted
with a view to ascertaining: (1) how important these nonreturn
characteristics are to life companies, and (2) in what specific ways
they impinge upon investment choices.

Our tentative conclusion is that the solvency objective has had
a profound effect upon the composition of life insurance company
portfolio decisions. The main thrust of this effect, however, has
been to restrict the set of investment opportunities which life
company investment departments seriously consider as potential
portfolio additions. Within this restricted set, it does not appear
that there are significant marginal decisions involving trade-off
of expected returns against the various nonreturn asset characteristics. Thus, within the eligible opportunity set, the assumption
that portfolio choices are made so as to maximize the expected
discounted portfolio rate of return may be an acceptable working
hypothesis.

Specifically, the universe of potential investment opportunities
is reduced to a relatively narrow set of acceptable assets in the
following ways. Most life companies apparently regard it necessary to hold a small portion of their assets in a highly liquid form
as a cushion against the possible, though unlikely, event of concentrated cash demands on the part of policyholders and benefi-
ciaries. Normally, the portion of the portfolio allocated to this
purpose is probably less than 5% of total assets. It is not necessary for solvency protection to be concerned about liquidity and
marketability characteristics in selecting the remaining 95% of
the portfolio.

Loan and investment defaults and capital losses appear to be
considered undesirable by life companies independent of their
impact on rate of return. Consequently, concern with the investment quality of individual assets limits the range of eligible assets.
This concern eliminates most debt obligations below Ba quality,
most corporate equities, and probably a significant volume of

potential mortgage loan opportunities from the eligibility set. Many companies have specifically restricted the amount of federally underwritten mortgage loan financing they were willing to undertake, and some have refused to consider FHA and VA loan opportunities at all, because the anticipated default rate is higher on these loans than on conventional loans which meet companies' credit standards.

The desire to achieve a degree of income certainty restricts the maturity range from which life insurance companies are willing to select portfolio assets. Excepting their modest liquidity requirements, this objective keeps life companies out of the short-term loan business and limits the eligibility set to intermediate and long maturities. It also seems to eliminate most securities with little or no call protection from serious consideration.

Portfolio theory singles out diversification as the primary objective which competes with expected return. This goal differs in its impact from the other nonreturn objectives we have been discussing in that pursuit of diversification does not restrict the range of alternative assets from which life companies choose their investments. Rather, its impact is felt at the margin in selecting among portfolios with different mixes of return and variability of return. A plausible case however can be made that diversification, in the pure sense of dispersing funds among a variety of assets whose probabilistic outcomes are not highly correlated, is obtained by the larger life companies at little, if any, cost in expected return. Other forces do cause life companies to spread funds among a variety of assets, but most of these forces are subsumable under the general objective of maximizing portfolio returns. If diversification is essentially costless, then its contribution to company solvency can be achieved within a return maximization policy.

The above conclusions have been stated boldly, without the qualifications discussed previously. Also, the conclusions are tentative because to this point we have made only a sweeping survey of the content of life company investment objectives and because for some types of assets and for some companies, it may be externally imposed constraints, not competing internally formulated goals, which are primarily responsible for restricting the coverage of the effective opportunity set. In any case, our analysis of the solvency objective permits the conclusion that a maximization of expected return objective remains a plausible working hypothesis within the eligible range of investments. We turn finally to an examination of the desirability and achievability of the rate-of-return goal.

The Rate-of-Return Goal

DESIRABILITY OF PORTFOLIO RETURN

All investors presumably regard a "high" rate of return on portfolio assets as a good thing. In publicly owned corporations, benefits from realization of a high return are ordinarily received by stockholders in the form of current or future dividends or capital gains. This applies to life insurance company stockholders. Many life companies, however, are mutualized, and defining corporate interests and goals for mutual organizations is more difficult. Nonetheless a higher investment return does lower the net cost of a company's policies, improves its competitive position, thereby enabling it to grow faster and to reward its managerial personnel more handsomely.

The value of investment yield performance, then, depends upon (1) the relation between portfolio earnings and the net cost of insurance and annuity policies, and (2) the importance of net cost to business success. The impact of investment return upon net cost varies widely with the type of policy offered. It is strongest for policies with a high savings element (e.g., endowment insurance, single payment annuities, pension funds) and weakest for the individual term and group life insurance business. It has been estimated that, within the range of life companies' realized return on invested assets, an additional 100 basis points in the net average rate of return will reduce the net cost of ordinary life insurance policies about 10%.[88] Since considerable variance does exist in the net rate of return realized among life companies, there

---

[88] Estimated from a regression analysis of net cost on operating expense, mortality, and rate-of-return variables performed by the Life Insurance Association of America. The estimation is based on an ordinary life policy issued at age 35. It was assumed that all gains are returned in policy dividends, mortality rates were those assumed in the 1941 Standard Ordinary Table, and expenses were pegged at $3.65 per $1,000 of insurance. This result is reported by Brimmer in *Life Insurance Companies in the Capital Market*, pp. 26–27.

are presumably significant differences in the net cost of policies offered.[89]

It is not easy to evaluate the importance of net cost of insurance and annuity policies in determining the competitive success of a life company within the insurance industry, or among financial institutions generally. Life insurance companies offer insurance and annuity services in peculiarly complex contracts through aggressive sales organizations. It is extremely difficult for the most well-informed consumer to compare the costs of a variety of policies offered by a number of companies. The difficulty is compounded by the issuance of participating policies in which the actual cost of the protection is dependent upon uncertain future experience. In these circumstances it is not clear that net cost is necessarily an important element in the competitive environment.

Crude comparisons between available portfolio rate-of-return estimates and company success indicators (size, growth rates of sales, and assets) do not corroborate the hypothesis that investment return is a crucial factor in determining relative performance.[90] In our background visits to a number of large life insurance companies we were impressed by the wide divergence among companies in the effort and attention devoted to portfolio decisions. This was reflected in the variance observed in the size of investment departments, the procedures used for locating investment

---

[89] Barring any reason to expect systematic offsets in mortality experience or operating costs. During the 1950s the range of net rates of return on invested assets (before taxes) apparently exceeded 200 basis points. (See Walter, *The Investment Process*, p. 66, Table II-A-3). Among the larger companies the range was considerably narrower, but still amounted to around 80 basis points, judging from rates of return reported by the 25 largest companies. (Estimated from company data reported in annual statements and Best Life Insurance *Reports*.)

[90] See, for example, Walter, *op. cit.*, Chapter III. Also, we experimented with a variety of relationships between company investment return, size, and growth rates for various periods and found no significant positive or negative correlations. Rate of return data do leave much to be desired, however. Capital gains and losses are omitted, common stocks are included in the admitted asset base at market value, and there is reason to doubt that the allocation of investment costs is accomplished on either a rational or uniform basis. Nonetheless the reported rate of return estimates are the best indicators of comparative investment performance available. The problem deserves more serious treatment than the objectives of this study permit. Clearly there are many potential causal relationships between investment return and asset growth.

opportunities, the attention paid to controlling the cash position and forecasting future cash flow, and the general awareness of returns to be obtained from pursuing a rational and aggressive investment policy.

INVESTOR RESPONSES TO VARIATIONS IN YIELDS

The strength and speed of life company portfolio responses to changes in the level or structure of investment yields depends upon a number of factors which we can conveniently summarize as follows:

    (1) The strength of competitive pressures to earn a high return.
    (2) The significance of competing portfolio objectives.
    (3) The importance of impediments to response produced by the mechanics of the investment process.

As we have just seen, competitive pressures unquestionably induce life companies to pay attention to portfolio earnings, but there remain questions with respect to the strength of these pressures. The primary competing objective is maintenance of solvency, and this concern does force life companies to consider asset and portfolio attributes other than yield. As a broad generalization, these considerations restrict the eligible opportunity set from which portfolio selections are made, but leave companies free to pick on a yield basis within the remaining set.[91]

Assuming that life companies do aspire to maximization of portfolio return over the long period, there are many aspects of the mechanical process of investing continuously a large volume of funds which impede life company responses to changes in the pattern of asset yields and/or impair our ability to observe and measure such responses. At this point, we shall simply indicate the nature of some of these problems. We consider obstacles to portfolio adjustment through asset sales, the sequential nature of investment decisions, and costs of the lending operation.

Portfolio trading

The theory of portfolio selection ordinarily assumes that it is possible to specify: (1) an opportunity set of available investments;

---

[91] We ignore for the present the impact of externally imposed restrictions upon investment choice.

(2) the investor's portfolio goals (utility function); and (3) the investor's budget constraint. The investor provides subjective estimates of return and risk for each asset in the opportunity set and for combinations of assets. Ignoring investment cost complications it is then possible, in principal, to identify the optimum (utility maximizing) portfolio.

Available investment funds derive from several sources, including (1) net new cash inflow, (2) drawing down of the cash position, and (3) turnover of existing portfolio assets. For a growing life insurance company new cash flow is generated by the excess of premiums and investment income inflow over the benefits, operating expenses, policyholder and stockholder dividend outflow. This net inflow of funds is approximately equivalent to the net increase in an insurer's assets.[92]

The insurance company is free to invest this newly generated cash inflow plus any portion of its liquid position as it wishes. In order to select its entire portfolio in any decision period, however, the company must be able to dispose of assets it inherits from previous decisions. Some portion of these outstanding assets will be liquidated automatically through scheduled repayments of principal. Another portion will be liquidated by the triggering of contingency provisions or at the option of the borrower.[93] Due to the maturity composition of life company portfolios, however, most of the portfolio will not be liquidated in these ways during a normal decision period (e.g., month, quarter, or year). Disposal of the rest of the portfolio can be accomplished only by the lender's decision to liquidate, normally by selling assets in secondary markets.

A lender's ability to select the optimum portfolio then depends upon its ability to trade existing assets for other assets efficiently and cheaply. Portfolio assets vary widely in their marketability characteristics. Thus, while most U.S. Treasury obligations are salable quickly at the going market price, bank loans are essentially nonmarketable. Most life insurance company investments are more like bank loans than Treasury securities. In recent years, probably more than four-fifths of the dollar volume of the larger life insurance company portfolios have been composed of

---

[92] Net increase in assets equals net funds inflow plus net capital gains.
[93] For example, security calls or prepayment of mortgage loans.

assets of very limited marketability at best. Most privately negotiated corporate debt issues, mortgage loans, policy loans, real property, and municipal revenue bonds fall into this category. Outside their modest liquidity positions, active trading has been possible only in Governments, corporate share issues, and a very limited portion of life company corporate and municipal debt holdings.

Corroboration of this view is found in the cash flow data displayed in Table I-7. In this table, gross investment funds are shown by source for the four-year period, 1959–1962. The period was chosen because an independent estimate of life company sales of corporate shares was available for these years. The cash flow data were collected by a quarterly survey of a sample of companies accounting for about 62% of industry assets. For these companies, net asset gain, scheduled repayments, and principal repayments made at borrower's option accounted for more than 90% of available investment funds during the period. Asset sales accounted for less than 10% of funds. As expected, most asset sales were made from securities portfolios.

Although the cash flow survey distinguishes only sales of U.S. Governments (excluding short-term issues) from all other security sales, we report a separate estimate of corporate share sales by the whole industry. This evidence suggests that something like 60% of security sales, and at least half of all asset sales, were made from life company holdings of Governments and corporate stock issues, categories accounting for less than 10% of all life company assets.[94] This evidence is consistent with the a priori impression that better than four-fifths of life company assets are essentially not marketable.

It is not, then, reasonable to assume that life companies have complete control over portfolio acquisitions and disposals in each decision period. A large portion of each company's portfolio is frozen from period to period. Portfolio adjustment takes place presumably through investment of the cash flow generated by the

---

[94] Earlier in the postwar period U.S. Treasury obligations accounted for a much higher proportion of assets, and the sale of these securities dominated life company portfolio management decisions for some years. Life company portfolio behavior in these circumstances is examined at length in Chapters III and IV.

TABLE I-7. Sources of Investment Funds of Life Insurance Companies Reporting
in the LIAA Cash Flow Survey: 1959–1962
(millions of dollars)

Source	Amount
Net Change in:	
Ledger Assets	14,108
Cash position	−137
Subtotal	13,971
Repayments:	
Mortgages	9,313
Securities	
Maturities	2,858
Contingency sinking funds and other calls	1,126
Subtotal	13,297
Asset Sales:	
Mortgages	82
Securities	
U. S. Governments	702
Other	1,831
Real Estate	127
Sales and repayments, other assets	230
Subtotal	2,972
All Other Sources:	23
Grand Total	30,263
Less: Net Increase in Policy Loans	1,540
Total: Free Investment Funds	28,723
Memo: Sales of Common and Preferred Stock (all life insurance companies)	1,415

NOTES: Cash position includes cash and deposits, short-term Treasury
securities and commercial paper. Turnover of these items is then not
included under "securities" below.

Only cash flows are reported. Substitution of one asset for another
is not included.

SOURCES: Except for the memo item, all data are from the LIAA
Cash Flow Survey. Data are summed from reports of companies accounting for about 62% of life insurance industry assets.

The memo item is from ILI, *Tally of Life Insurance Statistics*.

insurance business and repayment of principal. The important question in this situation is whether the composition of the frozen stock of assets influences asset selections made from the normal flow of available investment funds. Our investigation of liquidity, diversification, maturity, and quality characteristics above supports the assumption that within the eligible opportunity set, stock composition along these dimensions is not very important within a considerable range. Therefore it is reasonable to assume that portfolio choices can be made with the normal cash flow independent of the distribution of attributes characterizing the existing portfolio. We shall proceed upon such an assumption in this study. Explicit stock adjustment decisions, however, will be recognized and dealt with in Chapters III and IV where we examine the postwar liquidation of Governments from life company portfolios and in Chapter V where the cyclical pattern of adjustments in company liquidity and borrowing positions are analyzed.

The rate-of-return goal and the investment process

Assuming that earning a high return on invested assets is an important objective of life insurance companies, and assuming that the primary effect of competing objectives is to narrow the range of acceptable assets, and that active trading is normally limited to a small proportion of life company portfolios, two questions remain. They are:

(1) How should the rate-of-return goal be formulated?, and
(2) What problems arise in the implementation of a rate-of-return objective?

The nature of the problems associated with the general proposition that life insurance companies aim at maximizing the average rate of return on portfolio investments over time can be illustrated by stating the objective more specifically and then examining the statement. Maximization of portfolio return over time may be viewed as achieved by an investment policy which ranks the members of a predetermined eligible opportunity set by their expected return, and allocates the current period's normal flow of investment funds among the available opportunities by selecting the investment with the highest expected return and proceeding down the list until the investment budget is exhausted.

Either as a normative principle or as a hypothesis about life company behavior, this statement of policy is open to several kinds of objections. In particular, this sort of formulation depicts life companies as quite passive investors in accepting a predetermined opportunity set and a predetermined budget. It may be doubted that passivity in these regards is characteristic of investors seeking the highest achievable rate of portfolio return. As we have observed previously, locating attractive portfolio opportunities requires an active organization geared to the task, particularly in those markets in which life companies tend to concentrate. Search and analysis are companion activities of life company investment departments and the results of both sorts of efforts are to a considerable extent dependent upon the costs expended in implementing these activities.

Furthermore, investment is a continuous sequential process, and consequently only a portion of the relevant set of investment opportunities is visible to life company investment officers when decisions are made on specific prospective investments. The practice of committing investment funds for future delivery makes it all the more clear that any opportunity set concept must be not only not predetermined, but itself probabilistic. Just as some current portfolio decisions will not commit current funds, so commitments made in the past will absorb part of the current period's available investment funds. Recognition of the temporal open-endedness of the investment process suggests that specific account must be taken of the role of life company expectations about future opportunities in explaining their current portfolio decisions. This involves not only forward commitment policy, but also activity in the trading accounts which we have previously admitted as potentially active, namely, short-term liquid assets, U.S. Government bonds, and corporate shares, and life companies' ability and willingness to borrow.

Expected return in the above tentative formulation of a life company's investment policy must be understood, of course, to refer to returns net of appropriately allocated lending costs. This is not a simple task. Some investment costs are incurred over the life of a loan and are probabilistic in nature. In some sectors the life company organizational requirements seem to involve high overhead operations. This means that lending costs per dollar invested are sensitive to the volume of loan activity in the sector, and marginal investment costs are a function of the time horizon considered and of the relation between general organizational efficiency and the level of operation. Many investment costs may be implicit, i.e., paid by altering the allocation of loanable funds in ways which maintain market contacts, improve organizational morale, and service customers or public projects. All these concerns with expectations and investment mechanics suggest that companies act on the assumption that selecting assets which maximize this period's net discounted expected rate of return is not the way to earn the highest realized return over a longer span of time.

A primary objective of this study is to identify and analyze what appear to be the major expectational and institutional influences on life company portfolio policy in a manner that permits evaluation of the yield responsiveness of life company investment policy. We deal with expectations in our analysis of the temporal allocation of funds and investment decisions in Chapters III-VI. In Chapters VII and VIII we examine the impact of policies derived from temporal considerations on the yield responsiveness of investment decisions among broad asset categories.

Summary

This chapter has been concerned with identifying the types of investments from which life insurance company portfolio choices are made, determining at least tentatively the nature and relative importance of life company portfolio objectives and establishing the ways in which these goals shape portfolio decisions. We found that while life companies have invested in a somewhat wider range of assets than other nonbank financial intermediaries, their selections nonetheless have tended to be concentrated in assets which can be briefly characterized as intermediate- and long-term, private sector, investment grade debt obligations. During the post-World War II period, life companies' investment activity has been directed primarily to the corporate bond and mortgage loan markets.

In discussing the particular characteristics of individual assets and portfolios which enter strongly into life company investment preferences, we related their tastes back to two primary objectives. First, life companies must make portfolio choices which are consistent with maintenance of a strong financially solvent position; and second, each company needs to earn a return on its invested assets which will maintain its competitive position in the industry. These are likely to be viewed as competing objectives by investment officers in the process of making judgments about the desirability of alternative combinations of assets. Broadly stated, we found that life company concern with both the fact and appearance of solvency, together with the restraint of governmental regulations we have yet to examine, was responsible for limiting life company investments in equities and shorter maturities. In some companies, at least, the distaste for defaults was so strong as to significantly limit or even prohibit investment in federally underwritten mortgage loans. During the postwar years desire for portfolio return seems to have prevented life companies from allocating much of their portfolios to liabilities of governmental bodies.

It is ultimately the solvency objective that causes life companies to consider favorably nonreturn portfolio attributes such as liquidity, maturity, credit quality, and diversification. Liquidity needs appear to be satisfactorily met in normal times by allocating a quite small portion of the portfolio to highly-liquid, marketable investments. Purchase of maturity and quality attributes has the effect of limiting the range of portfolio selections in the ways outlined above. For the larger life companies, which own most of the industry's assets, it was not clear that expected return had to be sacrificed in order to reduce the variability of return through diversification. Consequently, within the narrowed set of investment opportunities considered relevant by life companies, it seemed reasonable to accept as a working hypothesis the proposition that life companies select portfolios which maximize the expected discounted rate of return.

Rate-of-return maximization proved to be quite a complex goal, however. It is wrapped up in temporal problems having to do with the long time horizon of insurance companies, the sequential nature of the investment process, and the significance of the wide use by life companies of the forward commitment investment technique which permits separation in time of the decision to invest from the actual outlay of funds. All this raises serious questions regarding the role of expectations in life company decisions. The significance of the rate-of-return objective is further obscured by the difficulty of demonstrating that high marks in investment performance are, in fact, a requisite for success in the industry. A number of aspects of the investment process itself complicate the implementation of a rate-of-return objective and cloud our ability to observe yield responsiveness. The ability of life companies to adjust portfolio holdings quickly is limited by the fact that probably 80% of life company portfolios have been composed of essentially nonmarketable assets. Also the need to operate from an investment organization capable of locating as well as analyzing investment opportunities complicates the response mechanics of life companies to changes in yields. Nonetheless statements of life company officers concerning investment return and their decisions with regard to assets they choose not to select as well as those they do acquire, indicates a strong, if not overriding, interest in rate of return as a portfolio goal. Therefore it does appear reasonable to approach the analysis of life insurance company portfolio behavior as if high return was a major concern and to look deeply into the investment process itself for clues to the ways in which the search for investment return is conducted.

In order to complete our description of the range of capital markets and asset types in which life companies can find realistic opportunities to invest, it remains necessary to evaluate the impact of government regulations and tax policy in narrowing the set of potential assets appropriate to life company portfolio needs. This is our task in Chapter II.

Chapter II | EXTERNAL INFLUENCES ON LIFE INSURANCE COMPANY PORTFOLIO POLICY

Life insurance company portfolio policy is not shaped by internally generated goals alone. A number of facets of the external environment also play a determining role. The purpose of this chapter is to examine and evaluate the importance of the externally created constraints and inducements affecting life insurance company portfolio selection. The primary external influences on investment policy consist of:

(1) statutory regulation of investments;
(2) rules governing the valuation of portfolio assets; and
(3) taxation of investment income.

We shall consider the role of each of these determinants in turn. In each case, we shall provide a brief historical review of the relevant legislation and rulings, summarize the regulations in force since World War II, and evaluate the degree to which these aspects of the environment have influenced life company investment policy. The factors to be considered here largely impinge upon portfolio composition decisions. The broad question to be considered is the extent to which external influences have been responsible for the specialization of life company investments in relatively high quality long-term private sector debt issues. To make it easier for readers who so desire to skip the regulatory details, we have segregated our analysis of the influence of each of these external constraints on life insurance company portfolio policy into three sections. The impact of investment statutes is explored in pp. 94–121; the effect of asset valuation rules in pp. 143–145; and the significance of federal income taxation in pp. 157–168.

Statutory Regulation of Investment Policy

Sources of Regulation

Regulation of life insurance companies has traditionally been left to the states, although a 1944 court decision[1] clearly established federal government prerogatives in this area. Congress has spurned legislative action to date and has reaffirmed state authority in insurance regulation.[2] Although the National Association of Insurance Commissioners has succeeded in bringing about some uniformity in the state investment laws, substantial variance among the states remains. A few states are dominant, however, in that their laws influence the bulk of invested assets of all legal reserve insurance companies. New York state occupies an especially influential position; it has been relatively severe in erecting investment restraints, has a number of major companies domiciled within the state, and requires all companies licensed to do business in New York to "comply in substance"[3] with New York investment law. New York's regulations have often been imitated by other states.

During the 1950s, companies chartered by New York state held about 35% of the assets of all life insurance companies, and companies doing business in the state accounted for over 80% of the industry's assets.[4] The latter included the 15 largest companies

---

[1] *United States* vs. *Southeastern Underwriters Association*, 322 U.S. 533 (1944), brought the life insurance industry under the interstate commerce clause.

[2] In response to the 1944 court decision, Congress specifically affirmed the authority of the states to regulate insurance companies, Public Law 15, 79th Congress (1945). However, in 1957 the Securities and Exchange Commission became involved in regulation of life insurance companies by asserting authority to regulate variable annuities, contending such contracts were a form of security. The authority of the SEC was validated by the Supreme Court in 1959. See Brimmer, *Life Insurance Companies in the Capital Market*, pp. 72–77.

[3] New York Insurance Law, Laws 1939 as amended, c. 882 90(1). This provision was interpreted to mean "complete compliance" by Attorney General Javits in 1956, but the Superintendent of Insurance has not insisted on literal completeness.

[4] See *New York Insurance Report*, Volume I, *Life*, annual. In these terms, New York has become somewhat less dominant over time. At the time of

in the industry which together held over 70% of industry assets in the mid-1950s. These facts make New York of paramount importance from the regulatory standpoint, although some other states, notably Connecticut, Massachusetts, New Jersey, Pennsylvania, and Wisconsin, are not without influence.[5]

Purpose of Investment Regulation

Protection of policyholders' equity from management incompetence, dishonesty, and/or speculative excess seems to have been the primary motivation behind the state-imposed constraints on life insurance company investment policy. Some limitations placed on life companies, however, reflect fear of their ability to become powerful "money trusts" if left uncontrolled. In addition, some states have experimented with statutes designed to induce or force life companies to invest funds within the state.

As a means of protecting policyholders, state laws have urged "safety of principal" upon life companies as their primary investment objective. This has been achieved through legislation by limiting the proportion of assets life companies can place in specified types of assets and, in some cases, prohibiting particular kinds of investments altogether. The "safety" objective is also enforced by statutes regulating the quality standards of assets permissible for life insurance company portfolios, usually through the establishment of earnings and balance sheet tests. Both the quantitative limits and qualitative standards are apparently designed to limit the absolute risk of loss associated with any given portfolio investment of life companies. However, the requirements also have the effect of guaranteeing a minimum amount of portfolio diversification.

The diversification principle is also fostered by limits placed on the amount of funds a life company can invest in the security issues of a given borrower (usually as a percentage of the life insurance company's assets). Some states also limit a life company with respect to the percentage of a given security issue or the percentage

the Armstrong investigation (1907) companies domiciled in New York held nearly 60% of the industry's assets. This proportion was reduced to about one-third by 1960.

[5] Companies domiciled in these six states accounted for over four-fifths of industry assets in 1950; about three-quarters ten years later.

of all outstanding security issues of a given obligor the life company may hold. This sort of constraint seems more often directed at restricting the financial power and control exercised by life companies.

Finally, some states have attempted to increase life insurance company investment within their borders by offering tax abatements or requiring that a given proportion of the policy reserves, generated from life insurance policies sold to residents of the state, be invested within the state. Continuance of a life company's license to conduct insurance business within the state depends upon fulfillment of such requirements.[6]

History of Investment Regulation

EARLY HISTORY, 1794–1928

State regulation of the investment policy of life insurance companies has a long history. Pennsylvania restricted investments of its chartered life companies as far back as 1794.[7] During the 19th century, regulation was formalized by the establishment of state insurance departments to which life insurance companies doing business in the state were required to file annual statements as well as submit to periodic examinations. By and large, however, life insurance companies had considerable leeway in their choice of assets until the first decade of this century. Modern investment restriction dates to the flurry of legislation induced by the Armstrong Committee *Report* of 1906.[8] The New York state legislature responded to the *Report*'s exposure of management abuses by passing stringent restrictions on life insurance companies' investment freedom. As a result, life companies doing business in New York state were limited to investments in debt obligations of federal, state, and local governments; adequately

---

[6] These attempts are examined in Beard, *The Effect of State Investment Requirements for Life Insurance Companies.* See especially pp. 9–20.

[7] *Ibid.*, p. 4.

[8] *Report* of the Joint Committee of the Senate and Assembly of the State of New York Appointed to Investigate the Affairs of Life Insurance Companies, 1906. (Hereafter referred to as the Armstrong Committee *Report*.) This report was the result of probably the most thorough public investigation of life insurance companies ever conducted. Numerous management malpractices were uncovered, and the influence of this report upon the regulation and internal practices of life insurance companies remains significant to this day.

secured corporate debt issues; first mortgage loans on real property (limited in amount to 50% of the property's appraised value), and loans to policyholders not to exceed the value of the policy reserve. Investments in real estate,[9] unsecured corporate obligations, and preferred and common stock issues were prohibited altogether by the New York state law. Other states passed similar legislation although some important states, notably Pennsylvania, New Jersey, Massachusetts, and Connecticut, did continue to permit limited amounts of investment in equities. Exemplifying the fallibility of rigid investment regulation (in the light of later events) was the Wisconsin law which limited life companies' holdings of corporate securities to debt obligations of railroads and street railways.[10]

No significant modifications were made in New York law until 1928, at which time life companies were authorized to invest in unsecured corporate obligations and preferred and guaranteed stock.[11] This amendment opened an investment field which later became a major outlet for life insurance funds; namely, debentures and notes of industrial and commercial corporations. Such authorization was clearly a prerequisite to any significant life insurance contribution to the financing of manufacturing firms. Investment in equities, whether in the form of common stock or real estate (other than the home office), remained prohibited to New York companies.

A SUMMARY OF STATE LAWS AS OF 1928–1930

Some other state laws, however, were even more restrictive than New York's. As of 1929, nine states forbade investment in railroad debt and twelve specifically prohibited public utility bonds, while eight disallowed purchase of any corporate bonds what-

---

[9] Real estate acquired through foreclosure was required to be disposed of within five years. Companies could also own property used for their own business.

[10] See Zartman, *The Investments of Life Insurance Companies*, p. 167. Zartman observes that this law ". . . is regarded in many quarters as possessing exceptional merits." For other summaries of early state investment regulation see Bell and Fraine, "Legal Framework, Trends and Developments in Investment Practices of Life Insurance Companies"; and McDiarmid, *Investments of Life Insurance Companies in the United States and Canada*, Chapter XI.

[11] New York Insurance Law, 1928, c. 539. Eligibility depended, however, on the security's passing rather stringent earnings tests.

soever.[12]   Railroad equipment trust indebtedness were permissible investments for life company funds in only six states.

All states did authorize investment in federal government obligations, and generally in debt of states and other political subdivisions in the United States, though permission in the latter was hedged in some states with restrictions involving the obligor's default record, size (population) and debt ratio (debt as a percentage of assessed valuation), and the market value of issues in question.   Dominion of Canada bonds were allowable investments for companies in only 21 states, and Canadian provincial obligations in 17 states.   Fourteen states permitted acquisition of debt issues of governments other than the United States and Canada. New York forbade investment in Canadian provincial debt but permitted acquisition of bonds of central governments of countries in which a life company transacted business, up to the amount necessary to meet its obligations there.

Investment in income-producing real estate was generally prohibited.   Mortgage loans were permitted in all states — usually limited to first mortgages on "improved and unencumbered property." [13]   Most states restricted loans to 50% of appraised value, though several, including New York and New Jersey, authorized loan/value ratios of 67%.   Mortgage loans on leaseholds were allowed in only 14 states (not including New York).   Some 25 states authorized investment in preferred and/or common stock but generally with severe restraints as to amount and characteristics of the securities.

PRINCIPAL STATUTORY AMENDMENTS, 1931–1951

On the whole, changes in state investment law during the period 1931–1951 were in the direction of increased liberality.   By the end

---

[12] See the digest of state investment laws in Arnold, "The Investment of Policyholders' Legal Reserve Funds."   This along with a 1930 Committee Report, "A Study in Life Insurance Company Investments," appearing in the 1930 ALC *Proceedings* form the basis for this summary of state investment laws.   Both papers are reprinted in Life Office Management Association, *Readings in Life Insurance, A Compendium,* Vol. II.

[13] Permitted encumbrances generally include taxes and assessments (if not delinquent), mineral, oil, or timber rights, rights of way, sewer rights, rights in walls, building restrictions, etc.   See New York Insurance Law, Section 81(6)(a).

of the war most states permitted conventional mortgage loans in amounts up to two-thirds of appraised value, although amortization provisions also had become required. Generally, states were quick to amend statutes during 1934 and 1935 to legalize the new 80% FHA-insured loans for life insurance investment. With the inauguration of the Veterans' Administration's guaranteed loan programs (1945), G.I. loans for purchase or construction of homes, farms, farm equipment, and business property were legalized by the states for life companies.

A series of amendments were passed in the late 1930s to stimulate construction of low- and medium-income housing and to redevelop certain urban areas. These amendments authorized life company investment in obligations of public housing authorities and in high percentage mortgage bonds or stock of urban redevelopment corporations. New York and New Jersey permitted one or more insurance companies to organize a redevelopment company. In 1939 New York authorized direct investment (construction and ownership) in housing projects for "persons of low and moderate income." [14] Granted temporarily at first, extensions were granted in 1941, 1943, and 1946 before authorization was made permanent in 1949.

Some states relaxed earnings requirements on corporate securities during the late 1930s, but a general recodification of the New York Insurance Code in 1939 actually made earnings coverage tests used to determine corporate bond eligibility more stringent.[15] Municipal revenue bonds were expressly authorized as life company investments by New York in 1940.

The most significant trend toward greater portfolio choice in the postwar period has been some small steps in the direction of permitting life insurance companies greater opportunity to invest in equities. Limited investments in income-producing real estate

[14] See Section 84 of New York Insurance Law. For further discussion of these amendments, see Shands, "Investment Laws — Changes During the Last Decade." Also see Bell and Fraine, *op. cit.*

[15] However, previously eliminated was a section which had required an obligor to earn at least 4% on outstanding capital in order that his unsecured obligations be eligible for life company acquisition. This had made issues of oil companies generally ineligible in the early 1930s though later in the decade oil company indebtedness became for many life companies their leading industrial investment.

(usually up to 3% to 5% of assets) became generally authorized by the states during the early postwar years (1946 in New York). New York finally relented in 1951 to the extent of permitting life companies to invest in common stocks meeting various quality and earnings requirements, and in amounts limited in several dimensions. Many states have further liberalized their investment restrictions through introduction of "basket" or "leeway" clauses, which allow life company management to invest some (usually small) portion of their assets in areas not otherwise expressly permitted. Leeway provisions vary with respect to the degree of discretion granted company investment officers and finance committees.

Despite an observable trend in state investment laws toward liberalization, it is clear that these statutes have continued to restrict the portfolio choices of life companies in significant ways. In the remainder of this section, we shall first survey the important statutory constraints operating during the period since World War II, and then evaluate their impact on life insurance company investment decisions.

Principal Provisions of the State Laws

In order to isolate the investment restrictions which are of primary importance as constraints on life company asset choices, we shall summarize the key statutory provisions in existence during the period 1945–1960. A much more complete compendium of the statutory provisions of 19 states as of 1960 is available in a recently published monograph.[16] For convenience of exposition, this survey is organized by type of asset. We cover in order: (1) government obligations, (2) corporate securities, (3) mortgage loans, and (4) income producing real estate. This review will largely ignore the additional freedom of choice provided in leeway provisions. Therefore we shall conclude with a brief examination of the scope of leeway clauses.

---

[16] LIAA-CMC Monograph, pp. 97–159. For other recent discussions of the state laws regulating investment policy, see Brimmer, *Life Insurance Companies in the Capital Market*, pp. 51–77, and the author's unpublished doctoral dissertation, "Portfolio Objectives, External Constraints and the Postwar Investment Behavior of Life Insurance Companies," Chapter II.

GOVERNMENT OBLIGATIONS

Central Governments

Debt obligations issued, assumed, or guaranteed by the United States government and not in default as to principal or interest are legal investments for life companies in all states. Similarly, obligations of the Dominion of Canada are generally authorized investments, although the aggregate amount held by any company may come under a general limitation of foreign securities as a proportion of assets. Life insurance company acquisition of indebtedness of other governments is rather strictly limited. Until 1956 New York law limited investment in foreign (non-Canadian) securities to companies doing business in the country in question and then such investments were limited to one and one-half times a company's liabilities in that country, or the amount the country required the insurer to invest, whichever was greater.[17] A 1956 amendment authorized any domestic company to invest in foreign securities in addition to the above, up to 1% of admitted assets.[18] The New York law limiting investment in foreign countries seems to be reasonably typical of other state restrictions.

State, provincial, and local Governments

Both general and revenue obligations of states and political subdivisions thereof in the United States are legal investments for life insurance companies. Some states, New York included, do not permit acquisition of special assessment bonds, however. Limitations on the amount of municipals which companies can hold are rare and inconsequential. Although New York puts no restriction on characteristics of issues of obligors, other than that issues acquired be not in default, some states do exclude debt of small municipalities and/or prescribe limits on tax-supported

---

[17] New York Insurance Law, Section 81(8)(b). The limit on all securities and investments in Canada is stated in the same terms, except that up to 10% of a company's assets may be invested in Canada, if this is greater than the amount permitted under the other two clauses.

[18] New York Insurance Law, Section 81(8)(c).

general obligation debt as a percentage of assessed valuation of the municipality.

Canadian provincial debt obligations are eligible investments under New York law, although the aggregate amount so invested is constrained by the ceiling on all Canadian investments (10% of an insurer's assets). During the war and postwar years, Canadian provincial and municipal bonds became increasingly popular among life companies.[19] Canadian provincial debt is a much larger proportion of public debt than is state indebtedness in this country, and Canadian provincial and municipal issues enjoy no tax-exempt status, making their yields more attractive to life companies. Investments in debt issues of political subdivisions of other countries come under the general limitation on foreign securities noted in the previous section.

CORPORATE SECURITIES

Debt obligations

(i) Qualitative constraints

Corporate debt issues "not in default as to principal or interest" are authorized investments for life insurance companies in practically all states. Among the more influential states, Connecticut and New Jersey demand only that issues acquired be free from default. Many other states, including New York, hedge the above authorization with qualifying provisions. The most important qualifications have to do with the investment quality of corporate bonds acquired. As a test of quality, many states have required bonds to pass established earnings coverage requirements to be eligible investments for life insurance funds. In application of such tests, some states have discriminated by industry, the requirements for railroad and utility bonds being less stringent than for other corporate debt issues. New York makes the distinction rest on mortgage security, secured bonds facing less difficult earnings tests than debentures. Further distinctions are made between fixed interest bearing obligations and contingent interest obligations in applying earnings coverage tests. Typically, earnings coverage tests require that for its bonds to be eligible for life insurance company purchase, the obligor's net

---

[19] See McDiarmid, *op. cit.*, p. 78.

earnings must have covered fixed charges about $1\frac{1}{4}$ to 2 times (depending on the state in question and class of the bond) over some stipulated period in the past. Net earnings are taken after depreciation but before income taxes and interest charges in the calculation.

For example, the New York law has three earnings tests for bonds, one for each of three classes of bonds. In order for "adequately secured" [20] fixed interest bearing obligations to be eligible for life companies, the issuer must have earned $1\frac{1}{4}$ times fixed charges during any three, including one of the last two, of the five preceding years. For obligations not "adequately secured" to be eligible investments, the obligor must show net earnings averaging not less than $1\frac{1}{2}$ times annual fixed charges for the past five years, and $1\frac{1}{2}$ times coverage one of the last two years. Eligibility of "adjustment, income or other contingent interest obligations" depends on the issuer's net earnings covering fixed charges (plus the maximum contingent interest applicable) at least $1\frac{1}{2}$ times on the average over the preceding five years and during one of the last two years.[21] However, a 1951 amendment eliminated the earnings coverage requirement for "adequately secured" fixed interest bearing obligations "with investment qualities in which speculative elements are not predominant." [22] This provision permits investment in debt issues of corporations without past earnings records and has facilitated the extensive life insurance financing of construction of oil and natural gas pipe lines. A 1957 amendment permits investment in corporate debt obligations not otherwise eligible to the extent of 0.5% of the issuer's admitted assets.[23]

New York law does not permit life companies to make unsecured loans to unincorporated businesses. Indeed, only one state does.[24] Therefore unincorporated enterprises can ordinarily obtain life company funds only through mortgage loans and, perhaps to some

[20] The New York law stipulates that not more than one-third of the required collateral may consist of stock other than preferred stock eligible for life company portfolios. This limitation is found in several other states as well. Some states have additional collateral requirements.

[21] See Section 81(2)(a)(b)(c). The earnings tests were somewhat stiffer before 1951.

[22] New York Insurance Law, Section 81(2)(a).

[23] New York Insurance Law, Section 81(2)(c).

[24] LIAA-CMC Monograph, p. 89.

degree, through policy loans. Limited life company investments in unincorporated businesses may be made directly under leeway provisions, of course, and indirectly through life company investments in development credit corporations.

(ii) Quantitative limits

A few restrictions on the proportion of its assets a life company can invest in corporate bonds, or in particular types of corporate bonds, remain in some state laws,[25] but they are relatively insignificant. None of the six major states (see above) any longer have significant constraints of this type.

Limitations on the amount a life company can invest in the obligations of a single corporation are somewhat more common. Prior to 1949 the only restriction in New York law was a general limitation providing that "no insurance company shall have more than 10% of its admitted assets invested in or loaned on securities of any one institution." [26] In 1949 this limit was reduced to 5%. New Jersey limits investment in a single issuer's bonds to 10% of capital and surplus for a stock company; 10% of surplus for a mutual life company. Limits are occasionally specified with regard to a single bond issue. Wisconsin has a discriminatory provision of this sort, placing a limit of 10% of a life company's assets in securities of railroad, public utility, and "other" corporations, but restricting investments in a single issue of other firms to 2% of the life company's assets where the issue is a secured bond, and 1% if it is a debenture.

As noted above, New York's general quantitative limitation on investment in foreign securities has been an aggregate ceiling of 1½ times the insurer's policy reserves and other obligations in any foreign country, or the amount the country in question requires the insurer to invest there, whichever is greater. Although Canadian government and provincial obligations were excepted from this limit, Canadian corporate obligations were not until a 1956 amendment made all eligible Canadian securities permissible

---

[25] For example, Illinois permits no more than 33.3% of a company's admitted assets to be held in debt of corporations in any one of the following three categories: railroads; public utilities; other corporations. LIAA-CMC Monograph, pp. 130–131.

[26] New York Insurance Law, Section 87.

investments up to 10% of the insurer's admitted assets. Also in 1956, New York authorized additional investment in qualifying foreign securities up to 1% of the life company's admitted assets.

Preferred and common stock

Some of the most stringent statutory constraints upon life insurance companies' investment choices are in the rules restricting investments in preferred and common shares. The relevant restrictions are both qualitative and quantitative. Qualitative requirements include earnings coverage, dividend payment, and yield tests. Some states exclude shares of specific types of corporations from the authorized list. Quantitative restrictions exist which limit an insurer's aggregate investment in stock issues and limit the amount which can be invested in stock of a single corporation, both as a percentage of the insurer's assets (or surplus) and as a proportion of the insurer's outstanding shares.

In applying these restrictions many states make no distinctions between preferred and common shares. New York, however, has a very elaborate law which distinguishes among preferred, guaranteed, and common stock issues. Preferred and guaranteed stocks are treated similarly to unsecured debt issues in the New York statutes. Like debentures, preferred and guaranteed shares first became eligible investments for companies regulated by the New York law in 1928. Restrictions on common shares have been much more stringent.

(i) Qualitative restrictions

The variation in qualitative standards for stocks to be classified as eligible for life insurance company portfolios ranges from California's simple provision that the stock "must qualify as a sound investment," to New York's earnings and dividend tests, and other special provisions. Some states expressly prohibit certain types of stocks. Preferred issues of mining companies and common shares of "mining and manufacturing other than gas and electric" corporations are prohibited to life companies by Connecticut law. A number of states prohibit investments in stocks of insurance companies, banks, and/or real estate corporations. Texas law expressly prohibits life company investments in the preferred or common shares of small manufacturing and oil corporations.[27] Wisconsin prohibits investment in the preferred or common shares of holding companies. New York eliminated a stricture forbidding investment in the common stock of insurance, bank, and trust companies in 1957. In order for preferred or common stock issues to be eligible investments in New York, all the issuer's senior securities must be eligible investments. Several other states have similar provisions. Under New York law, only common shares listed on a national securities exchange are eligible investments. Separate provision in the New York law is made for investment in the stock issues of housing and redevelopment companies,[28] as well as capital stock of federal home loan banks and shares of savings and loan associations.

Dividend and earnings requirements are fairly common. New Jersey requires that dividends must have been paid the last five years prior to the insurance company's acquisition. This applies to both preferred and common shares. Connecticut has required a five-year record of cash dividends for all stocks, at a rate of at least 3.25% per annum on the par or stated value. New York requires that all stocks must be dividend paying. Common stocks must have paid cash dividends in each of the prior ten years.

Earnings requirements for preferred and guaranteed stocks under New York law are quite similar to those for unsecured debt obligations. Eligibility of preferred shares is based upon the issuer's net earnings over the preceding five years averaging $1\frac{1}{2}$ times fixed charges (including the maximum contingent interest and preferred dividends applicable) and specifically covering fixed charges $1\frac{1}{2}$ times in one of the last two years. Guaranteed shares are qualified if they meet the earnings requirements applicable to unsecured debt obligations.[29] Common stocks are qualified investments only if the issuing corporation has earnings during the

---

[27] Manufacturing corporations with less than $25,000 capital stock and oil corporations with less than $500,000 capital stock.

[28] Permission was originally granted for investment in this field in 1940. See New York Insurance Law, Section 81(9). Total investment in all forms in such projects is limited by Section 84 to 10% of an insurer's assets.

[29] That is, net earnings must cover fixed charges at least $1\frac{1}{2}$ times on the average over the preceding five years, and specifically either of the past two years; fixed charges being construed to include the amount of the guaranteed dividend.

past ten years of at least 4% of the par or stated value of its outstanding common stock.

(ii) Quantitative limits

Several states have limits on the total holdings of preferred and/or common stocks a life insurance company can carry in its portfolio. Wisconsin restricts preferred stock holdings of life companies to 5% of a company's assets; common stock investments are also limited to 5% of the insurer's assets. Illinois limits preferred stock holdings to 10% of an insurer's assets; common stock investments are restricted to one-half of capital and/or surplus.

Total holdings of common stock under Pennsylvania law are limited to 5% of an insurer's assets. Authorization to purchase stocks under Connecticut, Massachusetts, and Wisconsin laws is embodied in their leeway provisions. California and New Jersey have no limits on total holdings of preferred and/or common shares.

New York has no overall limit on life company investment in preferred and guaranteed stocks. Common stocks, however, were absolutely prohibited by New York prior to 1951. A 1951 amendment permitted investment in common shares up to the lesser of 3% of the insurer's admitted assets or one-third of surplus. This authorization ceiling was raised to 5% of assets or one-half of surplus in 1957. Since New York was a latecomer in adoption of a leeway provision (1958), it is clear that New York's restriction on aggregate common stock holdings of life companies was the most stringent among the major states during the 1940s and 1950s.

A number of states limit the amount a life company can invest in a single stock issue, or in all securities of a single corporation. When New York authorized common shares in 1951, the statutes limited holdings of the common stock of a single corporation to one-tenth of 1% of an insurer's admitted assets. This ceiling was later raised to one-fifth of 1%. No other important state has so restrictive a limit.

Finally, some states limit the amount of a single issuer's stock an insurance company can hold as a proportion of the issuer's outstanding stock. New York limits an insurer's holdings of a corporation's preferred stock issues to 20% (10% prior to 1951) of the issuer's preferred stock outstanding. Common stock holdings are restricted to 2% of a corporation's outstanding common shares. This sort of restriction apparently reflects a continuing apprehension on the part of the regulators that life companies might gain control of a number of noninsurance businesses if left unregulated in this respect.[30] The New York law again seems particularly stringent in comparison with other states.

MORTGAGE LOANS

New York law authorizes life insurance companies to make first mortgage loans ". . . upon improved and unencumbered real property located in the United States." [31] Many other states extend this permission expressly to Canada. Mortgage lending is not permitted in other countries. Many state laws distinguish between mortgages on properties held outright by the borrower and mortgages on leased property. Loans with leaseholds as security are often authorized only under additional qualifying provisions. Leaseholds were unacceptable as security for loans by New York law prior to 1951. A 1951 amendment authorized loans on leased property where the lease has an unexpired term of at least 21 years. The loan is required to be fully amortized within the lesser of the unexpired term of leasehold or 35 years. Some other states have similar qualifications. Some states specify lower loan/value ratios for loans on leasehold property than on owned property.

All states limit the loan amount as a proportion of the appraised value of the securing property. The most common maximum loan/value ratio prevailing during the first postwar decade was two-thirds. More recently, a number of states have amended their statutes to permit up to 75% loans on some types of property.[32] Where a distinction is made among types of property,

---

[30] Indeed, this kind of concern seemed to be the primary motivation behind the exclusion of common stocks from life company portfolios following the Armstrong Committee *Report*. The Committee's *Report* was quite explicit on this point. See Vol. 10, p. 382.

[31] New York Insurance Law, Section 81(6)(a).

[32] As of June 1960, 13 of the 19 states covered by the LIAA summary of state regulations permitted 75% loans on at least some types of property. See the LIAA-CMC Monograph, pp. 110–112.

the higher loan/value ceiling generally applies to single family homes. New York restricted all mortgage loans to two-thirds of the appraised value of the security during the 1950s but has since increased the loan limit to 75% on single family home loans under $30,000 and fully amortized in 30 years. Mortgage loans insured by the FHA or guaranteed by the VA have been under no statutory restrictions.

Only a few states have established limits on the total mortgage holdings of a life insurance company. New York state, however, is one of those that has enacted such a limit, and its law has become a significant constraint in investment choice for some companies. New York law has long limited mortgage loans to 40% of a life company's admitted assets.[33] FHA and VA loans are excluded from this provision.

Somewhat more common are provisions limiting the amount a life company can invest on the security of a single parcel of property. The New York state limit is $30,000 or 2% of the insurer's admitted assets, whichever is greater. These restrictions also apply only to conventional loans.

Finally, although state insurance laws do not restrict the geographic location of mortgaged property within the United States, general state regulations governing real estate financing may sometimes affect the willingness of life companies to conduct an active mortgage loan business within the state.[34] In particular, states with costly and complicated foreclosure procedures may be avoided or receive smaller allocations of funds, other things being equal.[35]

INVESTMENT REAL ESTATE

The most severe statutory restraints on life insurance company investment choice have been those limiting investment in equities. These restrictions have applied to income-producing real estate investments as well as to stock issues. As with shares, the strin-

---

[33] New York Insurance Law, Section 81(6)(a).
[34] See Colean, *Impact of Government on Real Estate Finance in the United States*, Chapters 3, 4.
[35] This point was made by several life insurance company officers whom we interviewed. Also see *ibid.*, p. 46.

gent regulations date to the Armstrong Committee *Report*. Actually, the New York law prior to the Armstrong investigation limited real estate ownership essentially to property necessary for the conduct of the insurance business. Nevertheless the Committee reported that:

Despite these restrictions the testimony taken by the Committee discloses flagrant abuses in connection with investment in real estate. Under the guise of procuring suitable accommodations for the transaction of business, excessive amounts have been expended in the acquisition of land and buildings not necessary in any proper sense for the uses of the corporation, which yield a poor return upon the amount expended.[36]

The Committee felt that real estate investments should be prohibited to life insurance companies because they were (1) illiquid, and (2) risky.[37] During the 1930s and 1940s many states gradually liberalized their prohibitive statutes to permit investment in some types of real estate. By 1953, all but three states authorized some forms of real estate as investments.[38]

Contemporary regulations governing real estate investments include restrictions with respect to the type of property, amortization period and quantitative limits on total holdings, and the amount invested in a single parcel. The New York Insurance Law (Section 81(7)) permits life companies to invest in the following categories of real estate:

(1) Land and buildings in which a company has its principal office, and other such property required for "convenient accommodation in the transaction of its business."
(2) Property acquired in the satisfaction of debt or in part payment from the sale of real property, provided the transaction effected a net reduction in the company's investment in real property.
(3) Real property and equipment necessary or convenient for enhancing the sale value of property already held.
(4) Income-producing property.

The limitation on property held for business purposes is 10% of admitted assets. There exists no quantitative limit on property obtained through foreclosure, but such property must be disposed of within five years of acquisition unless the Superintendent of

---

[36] Armstrong Committee *Report*, p. 383.
[37] Risky with regard to the likelihood of loss of principal and income. See the Committee *Report*, p. 383.
[38] Jewett, "Real Estate and Other Property," p. 181.

Insurance certifies the company would "suffer materially," in which case a time extension may be permitted.[39]   Approval of the Superintendent is required on real estate acquired for business use, through the sale of property, or to enhance the sale value of property owned.   The permission to invest directly in housing projects was granted in the late 1930s by New York and other states on a temporary basis, extended through the war to stimulate construction of "emergency war housing," and made permanent in 1949.   Under this authorization, companies may undertake housing projects in any city of population exceeding 75,000 in any state in which the company does business.   Aggregate investment in housing projects including stock and debt issues of housing companies is limited to 10% of the insurer's admitted assets. New York law further permits one or more insurance companies to organize a redevelopment company under the Redevelopment Companies Law.   Redevelopment companies are usually of the limited dividend type, having power of eminent domain, and are closely regulated.

New York originally granted permission for investment in general income-producing real estate in 1946.[40]   That law limited the aggregate of such investment to 3% of the insurer's invested assets, and single parcels to 0.5% of the insurer's admitted assets up to $250 million, plus 0.25% of assets in excess thereof.   The aggregate limit was raised to 5% of assets in 1957, and the $250 million cutoff was increased to $500 million at the same time.   The law further provides for a minimum write-down of cost of property acquired under this section, including improvement and development costs, of 2% per annum plus any excess of net income before depreciation (less previous write-downs) of over 4% of book value of the property.   Specifically excluded from the authorization is property used primarily for "agricultural, horticultural, ranch, mining, recreational, amusement, or club purposes."

Most states do limit the overall investment insurance companies may make in income-producing real estate.   Typically the maximum appears to be 5% to 10% of admitted assets (usually exclusive of investment in housing).   New Jersey permits 5% of assets

---

[39] Foreclosed property qualifying as income-producing real estate may be held under the latter provision.

[40] New York Insurance Law, Section 81(7)(h).

to be invested in housing property in New Jersey cities and an additional 5% in other income-producing property if approved by the state insurance department. Massachusetts permits overall real estate ownership of 20% of assets, but no more than 5% in income-producing property other than housing. In addition, Massachusetts permits a substantial portion of an insurer's assets to be invested largely at its discretion. Connecticut does not authorize holding of investment real estate specifically, but companies are free to invest in real estate under the leeway provision.

Limitations on the size of individual parcels of real estate acquired are less common. New York's 0.5% of assets[41] is relatively stringent. The only other major states that appear to have such restrictions, Massachusetts and California, have 1% limits. A number of states like New York, require write-downs of the book value of income-producing property of at least 2% per year. Companies which invest in real estate under leeway provisions usually are free from any restrictions other than limits on their total real estate investment.

On the whole, life insurance companies have avoided managerial responsibility in connection with their real estate investments. Over 80% of investment real estate held by life companies at the end of 1957 consisted of commercial and industrial properties, mostly acquired through purchase and leaseback arrangements.[42] These transactions are treated in the same manner as any other real estate investments under the statutory regulations. The extent of life insurance companies' activity was also affected during the 1950s by uncertainty regarding the federal income tax status of life companies with respect to these contracts. This problem will be discussed below.

LEEWAY PROVISIONS

The impact of the statutory restrictions upon portfolio choice has been blunted somewhat during the postwar years by the adoption by many states of "leeway" or "basket" provisions. In general, these provisions allow some limited portion of a life insurance company's assets to be invested in forms not permitted or

---

[41] See above. The limit is somewhat lower for large companies.
[42] ILI, *Life Insurance Fact Book*, 1958, p. 85.

not eligible under the established statutory regulations. The degree of management discretion permitted under these clauses varies among the states.

Connecticut allows 8% of an insurance company's assets to be invested in forms not qualifying or permitted under their charter or other statutory provisions. No limits to this freedom are expressed. The Massachusetts clause allows all funds in excess of three-quarters of an insurer's reserve to be invested in any manner the directors determine. This freedom is qualified only by the statutory limits on holdings of stocks. No investment in stock of insurance companies is permitted. Also, the single issuer limits of 10% of the capital and surplus in the stock of one corporation and 10% of the capital stock of a single corporation, remain in effect. New Jersey permits 2% of an insurer's assets to be held in forms not otherwise qualifying or permitted. Pennsylvania and Wisconsin extend similar leeway permission to 5% of an insurer's assets. None of these three states otherwise qualifies its discriminatory clauses.

New York state resisted for many years the pressure applied by the life insurance industry for enactment of a leeway provision. Finally, in 1957 the legislature amended the insurance law to permit life companies to invest up to 0.5% of their admitted assets in corporate debt obligations not otherwise qualifying. A general leeway provision, permitting up to 2% of an insurer's assets to be invested in forms not qualifying under other statutory provisions was enacted in 1958. All the quantitative limits on holdings of specific types of authorized assets remain in force, however, except the just noted limit on investments in corporate bonds not meeting eligibility standards. An additional 1.5% of assets may be invested in such corporate debt issues.[43] On balance, then, the leeway granted by New York has been quite limited in comparison with the other important states.

---

[43] The legislature's attitude was reflected in the legislative committee's reaction in 1950 to a proposal that 3% of a life company's admitted assets be allowed to be invested free of statutory restrictions, except common stock and real estate. The committee regarded this proposal as ". . . a radical departure from the established and traditional policy of the state of New York in the control and regulation of investments of domestic insurers," and recommended "further consideration and study." See the New York Joint Legislative Committee on Insurance Rates and Regulations, *Report*, 1950, pp. 39–44.

Impact of the Statutory Regulations on Investment Policy

To what extent has the mix of life insurance company portfolio acquisitions during the postwar years differed from what it would have been in the absence of state laws regulating investment policy? We find this a very difficult question to answer with accuracy and confidence. In an attempt to estimate the direction and relative magnitude of the restrictive effects of these regulations, we shall rely on various scraps of evidence. These include comparison of life company portfolio proportions with the specific quantitative legal ceilings, the historical record of changes in the statutes and the record of industry pressure for amendments to the insurance laws, the public testimony of life insurance officers, our interviews with company officers, and direct inferences drawn from the laws themselves. We shall proceed by evaluating the impact of the provisions governing each asset category. Then we shall summarize the principal impact of these externally imposed regulations on the allocation of life company funds.

GOVERNMENT AND FOREIGN SECURITIES

To be eligible for life company portfolios, securities must be in "good standing." Quantitative limits have also been imposed on investments in foreign securities. Although the "not in default" requirement may well have constrained life companies from acquiring attractive state, local, and Canadian provincial obligations during the depression and war years, we have found no evidence that this requirement served as a deterrent in the post-World War II period. Some life companies may have found the restriction on foreign investments a deterrent. In response to a 1963 Life Insurance Association of America survey, several companies indicated that they would like to see liberalization of the New York statute limiting investment in foreign countries (other than Canada) and countries where the company conducts insurance business to 1% of assets.[44]

---

[44] In September 1963 the LIAA-ALC, at the request of the Superintendent of Insurance, sent a letter to all life companies domiciled in New York state or licensed to do business there requesting the companies' opinions respecting desirable modifications of the New York Insurance Law. The responses are

CORPORATE SECURITIES

Debt obligations

In many states, corporate bonds in good standing must qualify under earnings coverage tests to be eligible for life insurance company portfolios. As we have seen, the severity of the earnings tests depends upon the industrial classification of the obligor in some states, and on the existence of collateral security in others. It is probably true that for most debt issues the state qualifying tests are less strict than those most life companies apply internally.[45] However, some companies replying to the 1963 LIAA survey suggested that the industry should urge liberalization of the corporate bond earnings tests.[46] Although O'Leary's summary of these suggestions does not indicate specifically what reforms were advocated, or what kinds of opportunities life companies were being forced to pass up due to the corporate debt investment regulations, it is possible to infer something about these matters from the rules themselves.

Earnings tests tend to discriminate against newly incorporated enterprises. This is a consequence of requiring a potential borrower to possess a satisfactory earnings record for five years in the past. Even for companies that have survived incorporation the requisite time, the earnings coverage requirement may well be unduly restrictive for young, growing companies. In some in-

---

summarized in an interim report prepared by James J. O'Leary and sent to the Superintendent in February 1964. See O'Leary, *A Review of the New York Law Governing Life Insurance Investments*, pp. 1–3. The survey responses and O'Leary's conclusions are also summarized in the New York State, Joint Legislative Committee on Insurance Rates and Regulations, *Report*, 1964, pp. 47–70.

[45] From testimony of investment officers in the 1930s, this was apparently true at that time. See the TNEC *Hearings*, Part 28, especially pp. 14753; 15278–9. For a similar conclusion made following the 1951 revision in the earnings tests, see McDiarmid, *op. cit.*, p. 129. For some evidence on the balance sheet ratio and income tests used by life companies in screening corporate debt opportunities, see Walter's interview results in *The Investment Process*, pp. 431–436.

[46] O'Leary, *op. cit.*, and the New York Joint Legislative Committee, *Report*, 1964, *op. cit.*, p. 48.

dustries, at least, a more appropriate measure of risk might relate coverage of fixed charges to cash inflow produced from depreciation and depletion allowances as well as from earnings. To the extent that the existing eligibility requirements do restrict life company choices, they prevent insurers from lending to corporate enterprises during the point in their life cycle when their demand for external funds is normally greatest.

Perhaps the strongest evidence that these provisions have been restrictive for some life companies is to be found in the liberalizing statutory amendments that were enacted during the 1950s. As we have noted, bonds "adequately secured" with "investment qualities" have become eligible investments under New York law without being put to the earnings tests. A second amendment permitted use of the last three years of a predecessor's earnings record in the case of a recently incorporated enterprise. Since 1957 life companies have been allowed to invest 0.5% of admitted assets, plus another 1.5% of assets under the 1958 leeway provision, in corporate debt obligations not otherwise qualifying.

Part of the original motivation behind industry pressure for a leeway provision was to facilitate life company loans to small business, incorporated and unincorporated. Metropolitan Life proposed experimentation in this area in a 1950 report.[47] The plan envisaged partnership loans with commercial banks. Also, an industry committee made a specific proposal in a 1951 report that would have permitted life companies to experiment in small business lending.[48]

Until the leeway provision came into effect, life insurance company lending to unincorporated enterprises was essentially confined to mortgage instruments. Mortgage debt, however, is not always a possible or practical means of financing. Three companies we interviewed indicated that they had been unable to make some oil and gas production loans they found attractive

---

[47] *A Study on the Necessity and Desirability of Amending Section 81 of the New York State Insurance Law to Provide More Adequately for Loans to Small Business*, Metropolitan Life Insurance Company, 1950.

[48] American Life Convention-Life Insurance Association of America, *Report of the Joint Industry Committee*, 1951. This report recommended a five-year trial period during which life companies be permitted to make small business loans not otherwise authorized, and not to exceed 0.25% of the company's assets or 1% of surplus.

because they lacked statutory authorization to make unsecured loans to unincorporated firms.[49]

Finally, some evidence of life company interest in exploring loans to young and growing firms with some considerable "speculative element" is present in the increased use of "equity sweeteners" in direct placements, most often in the form of common stock options. Warrants and similar forms of sweetening came into significant use during the "tight funds" period of 1956–1957, presumably because traditional 6% usury ceiling rates otherwise rationed out the lower grade corporate debt issues.[50] For most life companies the amount of such activity is not large. From interview evidence, Williams and Williams suggest the total amount of this sort of financing by life companies "is limited to several hundred million dollars," [51] that is, presumably less than 0.5% of industry assets. They found one company, however, which had equity incentives incorporated into about half (number and dollar amount) of its industrial bond direct placements during 1959. More common among companies considered active in this field was a proportion of 10% to 15%.[52] Many companies, however, have not entered into any contracts of this sort. It would seem likely that the more aggressive life companies found that earnings coverage requirements restricted their opportunities. The limited New York leeway provisions do not provide much flexibility for a company that wishes to cultivate this area. Increased pressure from the industry, directed at further liberalizing

---

[49] Oil and gas in the ground is not eligible mortgage collateral in many states. Bell and Fraine, *op. cit.*, make the same point. O. M. Whipple of the Mutual Life Insurance Company testified in 1949 that his company would expand lending to individuals and partnerships in general, and specifically oil and gas production loans if the statutory constraints were relaxed. See his testimony before the U.S. Congress, Joint Committee on the Economic Report, *Hearings on the Volume and Stability of Private Investment.* A bill introduced in the New York legislature in 1944 would have authorized oil production loans to individuals but failed to be enacted. The life insurance industry recommended a similar amendment to the New York Joint Legislative Committee on Insurance Rates and Regulations in 1950. No action was taken.

[50] See C. M. Williams and H. A. Williams, "Incentive Financing—A New Opportunity."

[51] *Ibid.*, p. 133. They suggest that adding publicly acquired convertible debentures would not raise the total to more than 2% or 3% of industry assets (p. 134).

[52] *Ibid.*, p. 134.

leeway provisions, has been developing. From the compilation of results of the 1963 LIAA company survey, O'Leary listed an increase in the leeway percentage as one of four urgently needed amendments to the New York law.[53] Industry witnesses, in testimony to the New York State Joint Legislative Committee in November 1963,[54] recommended that the general leeway proportion be raised from 2% to 5% of a company's assets.

We have found no evidence that the existing quantitative restrictions on the amount of assets insurers may invest in particular classes of corporate debt obligations or in a single corporation's issues have been significant restraints on life companies' investment choices.

Preferred and common stock

Life insurance company holdings of preferred and common shares have been quite modest in amount. Despite the very substantial rise in common stock prices during the 1950s, the market value of life company investments in all stocks never rose above 4% of admitted assets during the decade.[55] This performance contrasts with that of noninsured corporate pension funds which held about one-fourth of their assets in share issues in the mid-1950s and one-third by the end of the decade.[56] It also contrasts with British life insurance companies which increased their stock holdings to well over 20% of their assets during the 1950s.[57]

---

[53] The other three dealt with real estate mortgage loans and are noted below. See O'Leary, *A Review of the New York Law*, p. 2.

[54] The testimony of R. Manning Brown, Jr., Executive Vice President, New York Life Insurance Company, is summarized in the 1964 Joint Legislative Committee *Report, op. cit.*, pp. 55–58. Mr. Brown testified that New York Life had made use of the 2% leeway provision to invest in (1) loans against developed oil and gas reserves; (2) loans to new, financially sound corporations with less than the required five years' history of earnings; and (3) loans to educational and religious institutions.

[55] ILI, *Life Insurance Fact Book*, annual.

[56] Securities and Exchange Commission, *Statistical Bulletin*, June issues.

[57] British life companies increased the proportion of their assets in share issues from 18.7% in 1950 to 22.2% in 1955 and 26.3% in 1960. Ordinary share issues alone as a percentage of assets increased from 11.1% to 15.3% to 21.2% over the same periods; the proportionate holdings of preference stock declined somewhat. See Clayton and Osborn, *Insurance Company Investment: Principles and Policy*, Appendix Table 2, p. 254.

The small proportion of stocks in life company portfolios obviously is not due to a lack of available issues. Although equity financing has accounted for only about 5% of external financing during the postwar period,[58] life companies' net acquisitions of corporate stock amounted to only about 4% of the funds raised through this medium.[59] In terms of outstanding issues as of 1958, life insurance companies held less than 0.6% of all corporate common shares outstanding and about 8.5% of outstanding preferred issues.[60]

(i) Alternative explanations of corporate equity investment practice

Considering what we know of the statutory restrictions limiting the ability of life insurance companies to undertake significant preferred, and particularly common stock investment programs, it might seem reasonable to explain their modest share holdings as primarily a consequence of these externally imposed restrictions. Some observers, however, have expressed doubt that the state laws have made much difference; instead they suggest that restraint in equity investment is deeply ingrained in the investment philosophy of U.S. life companies.[61] This element of investment philosophy derives from a long-standing interpretation of the nature of life companies' trustee function. In this view, life companies should invest policyholder reserves in accordance with a set of objectives which establish safety of principal as the primary and overriding investment principle.[62] Compliance with this

---

[58] Computed for the period 1946–1958 from data in Goldsmith, *The Flow of Capital Funds in the Postwar Economy*, Table 21, p. 104.

[59] Computed from data for 1946–1958, in *ibid.*, Table 81, p. 241. Life companies' net flow of funds into common stock accounted for less than 3% of the total net financing through common stock issues; they acquired about 15% of the net preferred stock issues.

[60] *Ibid.*

[61] For a recent observation to this effect from a prominent life insurance company officer and economist, see Hart, "Life Insurance Companies and the Equity Capital Markets," p. 359.

[62] The subordination of income and other investment objectives to safety of principal as a statement of priority appropriate for life insurance companies is usually traced back to a famous paper by A. H. Bailey, Esq., "On the Principles on Which Funds of Life Assurance Societies Should Be Invested" (1862), pp. 142–147. For a recent industry statement of basic investment principles, see the LIAA-CMC Monograph, Chapter 4. Also, see our discussion of portfolio objectives in Chapter I.

priority has been understood as meaning an emphasis on investments in senior securities with an equity cushion. Uncertainty with respect to dividend return and market value renders extensive investment in corporate shares incompatible with the fixed dollar liabilities issued by life insurance companies and the legally imposed limits on their surplus positions.[63] Hart summarizes the pervasiveness of this attitude:

> For since the time of the Armstrong Investigation in 1905, and actually pretty much the history of the life insurance business in this country, American life insurance companies have been predominantly fixed income investors, seeking certainty in investment return and safety of principal over potential appreciation through stock market profits.

and concludes,

> A half century or more of successful accommodation to the present investment philosophy would cause all managements to think twice before venturing strongly into common stocks, whatever the laws might permit, with their general investment accounts.[64]

Some empirical support for this position is provided by the performance of Canadian life insurance companies. Canadian companies have had considerably more freedom to purchase common stocks than American companies, but have in fact held only a slightly larger proportion of their assets in common shares.[65] Hood attributes this primarily to the security of principal tradition which is also prevalent in Canada and honored by most Canadian companies, although he also cites the deterrent effect

---

[63] Many states, including New York, limit surplus of mutual companies to 10% of their assets.

[64] Hart, *op. cit.*, pp. 359 and 360. In a 1962 action, the New York state legislature authorized life insurance companies to establish a separate investment account for their pension business. Hart's conclusions apply to the investment of funds generated by the insurance business (80% to 85% of life companies' assets), not necessarily to insured pension funds. For his views on the latter, see pp. 362–367.

[65] There was no overall quantitative limit in Canadian life company common stock holdings until 1932, when a ceiling of 15% of a company's ledger assets was imposed. There are also dividend record requirements and a limitation of 30% of the shares of any single issuer. See Hood, *The Financing of Economic Activity in Canada*, pp. 348–349. In 1956 Canadian companies had 3.6% of their assets invested in common shares and 5.3% in all stocks (*ibid.*, p. 357 and p. 333 respectively). The largest Canadian insurer (Sun Life Company) did have 50% of its assets invested in common stock in 1930, but other companies had very modest holdings (*ibid.*, p. 333).

of asset valuation rules which require common stock to be carried on life company books at market value.[66]

Since the New York state law has been so restrictive and influential, it is difficult to appraise the significance of its effect on life company portfolio decisions with respect to corporate shares. In particular, the gap between the New York overall limit on the proportion of assets a life company is permitted to hold in common stocks and the actual industry holdings is necessarily narrow. It has been pointed out that no substantial response to the 1951 liberalization of the New York law was observable.[67] Brimmer also reported that most life companies responding to his 1959 questionnaire survey displayed little interest in undertaking significantly greater common stock programs.[68] Nearly one-third of the companies responding to his survey indicated that they did not purchase common stocks at all. Furthermore, almost three-quarters of the respondents did not favor liberalization of the statutes in their home states which restrict common stock investments. However, nearly half of the responding companies did favor liberalization of the New York law.[69] The respondents strongly approved of statutory limits on the amount life companies could invest in common stocks and expressed specific disapproval of a proposal to substitute a "prudent man rule" for statutory restrictions. The typical, overall limit recommended was 10% of an insurer's assets (or 100% of surplus).[70]

---

[66] *Ibid.*, p. 357. Similar security valuation rules have been also a problem for U.S. companies. The nature and significance of these regulations are discussed below.

[67] Brimmer, *op. cit.*, p. 341. Total stock holdings of life companies remained unchanged as a proportion of assets (3.3%) from 1950 through 1953. Investments in common shares did rise somewhat from 1.01% of assets in 1950 to 1.31% in 1953 (*Life Insurance Fact Book*). The response following the further liberalization in 1957 was stronger.

[68] See Brimmer, pp. 347–357.

[69] Brimmer received a large nonresponse to this question. Of those answering, 9 of 15 companies in Brimmer's largest size group of life companies (over $359 million in assets as of end-1957) favored liberalization of the New York statutes. *Ibid.*, Table IX-13, p. 354.

[70] Some inconsistency is apparent between the answer to this question and the question of liberalizing the New York statutes. Brimmer reports 31 of 41 companies which specified a desirable ceiling selected one of 10% or higher, but only 23 of 48 companies were reported as favoring the liberalization of New York's statute which limited common stock holdings to 5% of assets (50% of surplus). See his Table IX-13.

Presumably life companies' approval of statutory regulation is based in part on its usefulness as a device to restrict competition. Also, some companies no doubt genuinely fear management discretion with respect to investment policy would lead to speculative abuses by some small life companies, resulting in losses to their policyholders and bad public relations for the industry.[71] This mix of motives is often present in regulated industries and it is difficult to gauge their relative importance.

Public relations sensitivity is also involved in the resistance to significant investments in equities for fear that such activity would compromise life companies' traditional emphasis on the soundness of fixed dollar insurance and annuity contracts,[72] and weaken the industry's resolve to carry on the political fight against inflation. To some life company officers the anti-inflation fight and the limitation of portfolio investments essentially to fixed dollar assets is viewed not as the act of a paternalistic trustee but as a direct response to policyholder directives. Hart sums up this view:

> The fact is there is little demand from our policyholders, other than employees setting up retirement systems, to invest their reserves in common stocks. Our policyholders may seek appreciation with their own funds by investing them in common stocks. They may even neglect their real insurance needs to provide funds for common stock investment in periods when common stock prices are rising. But when it comes to their life insurance they want what they have to be safe beyond question. Safety is the paramount consideration. Policyholders do not regard their insurance as a vehicle of possible profit through fortunate equity investment. Even in periods when the price level seems to be indicating a sustained rise they do not ask us to move into common stocks, but rather that we oppose easy money government spending, or other developments they believe are responsible for the inflation.[73]

Finally, there is little doubt that most life companies desire to avoid gaining influence or control over corporate activity through

---

[71] See *ibid.*, p. 356. The small companies in Brimmer's survey were more strongly against the adoption of a prudent man rule than the larger life companies.

[72] Concern for this image of guaranteed dollars motivated companies who opposed modification of state laws to permit life companies to invest in variable annuities. For an account of this intra-industry feud, see *ibid.*, pp. 72–77.

[73] *Op. cit.*, p. 360.

their equity investments, and would limit their ownership of the common share issues of any corporation with this in mind, regardless of whether or not they were required to do so by statute.[74] Given the amount of outstanding corporate shares, however, this sort of restraint has been no barrier to common shares playing a much larger role in life companies' portfolios.

On the other side of the question of compatibility between life insurance company portfolio goals and the statutory regulations governing investment in preferred and common shares, there is some evidence which suggests that life companies might hold substantially more corporate shares were they free to do so. Possibly the most persuasive evidence that the New York statutes have been a constraint on life company portfolio selection in this area is the fact that the New York legislature was moved twice during the 1950s to enact liberalizing amendments to the law.[75] Legislative amendments of this sort are the product of years of industry pressure for more freedom.

Although life companies generally were not restricted with respect to the amount which they might invest in preferred shares, there is evidence that many life companies felt the New York earnings and dividend requirements, as well as the limits on holdings of the preferred shares of a single issuer, were overrestrictive. Testimony to this effect on the part of life company officers appeared in the TNEC *Hearings*.[76] Ten years later the President of the New York Life Insurance Company testified that although on the whole he found "no serious obstacle to the making of desired investments" in state insurance laws, the restrictions on preferred stocks did prevent his company from acquiring as many issues as the officers would if "left to our own judgment." [77] A

---

[74] In this as in other areas, the British have no legally imposed limitations, but life companies observe an unwritten law and restrict their share holdings of a single issuer. Clayton and Osborn report that in most cases the limit is 2%, although one or two of the larger life companies will acquire up to 5% of a single issuer's voting shares (Clayton and Osborn, "Insurance Companies and the Finance of Industry," p. 93). These conventional limits are well within the statutory ceilings established by most states in the United States.

[75] 1951 and 1957. See the account of the legal provisions above.

[76] For example, see the testimony of T. Buchner of the New York Life Insurance Company, TNEC *Hearings*, Part 28, pp. 14726 ff.

[77] Joint Committee on the Economic Report, *Hearings*, December 1949, pp. 305 ff.

1951 Life Insurance Association of America publication refers specifically to the New York statutory restrictions on preferred stocks as "high." [78] In 1950 an industry committee recommended raising the 10% limit on holdings of the preferred shares of a single corporation to 25%.[79] As we have seen, the legislature responded in 1951 by increasing this limit to 20%. Also, some slight easing of the earnings coverage requirements for preferred issues was enacted. In general, earnings tests for preferred stocks present the same sort of problems as discussed above with regard to bonds. There is no evidence of increased life company activity in preferred issues following the 1951 amendments. The extent of the liberalization involved, however, was very modest, and the statement valuation rules for preferreds (discussed below) also restrained life company interest in them.

The primary restriction on life company investment in common stock issues prior to 1951 was, of course, the New York state law prohibiting them to life companies. Not surprisingly, the degree to which the industry lobbied for freedom to invest in corporate equities appears at least broadly related to the availability of attractive alternative outlets. The drive to amend the New York law appeared to accelerate during the 1940s. It seems not unreasonable to explain this desire for wider investment choice by the scarcity of traditional fixed-income debt instruments relative to the volume of life company funds seeking outlets. Associated with this market demand/supply situation were, of course, exceptionally low yields on bonds and mortgage loans. From the mid-1930s on, current investments of life companies were being made at yields less than the return guaranteed on policies issued. By the end of the war, life companies on the average were earning somewhat less on their outstanding assets than the minimum return written into their outstanding policies. In the early 1940s, this circumstance had led a New York state legislative committee to review thoroughly the advisability of permitting life companies to acquire common stocks but no recommendations to this effect were made. Concern about the availability of eligible assets

[78] LIAA, *Record of Life Insurance Investments*, p. 35.
[79] ALC-LIAA, *Report* of the Joint Industry Committee, 1950.

continued during the early postwar years,[80] and no doubt contributed significantly to the eventual enactment of the amendment permitting New York companies to invest a limited amount in common shares.

The postwar inflation experience added further to the attractiveness of common stocks for life insurance company portfolios. As we indicated above, some life companies feared that failure to offer alternatives to fixed dollar insurance and annuity contracts would have serious consequences for the industry's future growth. Life companies did in fact find they were losing ground in the individual annuity and group pension plan business during the 1950s. Changes in their product mix significantly reduced the growth rate of saving through life insurance companies. This seemed to be primarily a consequence of inflationary expectations.[81] In order to improve their competitive position, a number of life companies lobbied for greater statutory freedom to offer variable annuity contracts and to invest more heavily in equities. The success of the initial experiment in variable annuities, the College Retirement Equities Fund,[82] spurred other life companies to explore the possibilities in this field.[83] The desire to improve their position in the pension business was a significant part of the reason companies pushed New York state, in particular, for more liberal common stock and general leeway investment regulations.[84]

---

[80] Abundant evidence of this concern appeared in print during the early postwar years. For some examples see Edmunds, "Outlets for Life Insurance Investments," 1947; McDiarmid, "Life Insurance Company Investments and the Capital Markets," 1948; McLean, "Present Day Problems in Investment of Life Insurance Funds," 1948; Federal Reserve Bank of Boston, *Monthly Review*, "Broader Investment Channels for Life Insurance Companies," November 1949.

[81] For some estimates and analysis of the trend in the savings flow and the gross flow of funds through life companies during the 1950s, see Wright, "Gross Flow of Funds Through Life Insurance Companies."

[82] This is the fund administered by the Teachers Insurance and Annuity Association. It began operation in 1952 under special authorization of the New York state legislature.

[83] For examples of the discussion generated see the American Life Convention *Proceedings*, 1954, and the "Symposium on Changing Conditions" in the Life Insurance Association of America, *Proceedings*, 1954.

[84] Companies also sought authorization to sell separate group pension accounts independently of their general investment account, with the pension reserves free to be invested in common stock without limit. With the enactment of a permissive amendment in 1962 by New York, all the important states now allow separate accounts. See Hart, *op. cit.*, pp. 360–365.

Over 80% of life insurance company assets have been generated by the insurance—as distinguished from the pension — business. Substantial investment in equities of funds originating from insurance sales would presumably necessitate some changes in the fixed dollar contracts life companies have customarily issued.[85] Even with fixed dollar liabilities, life companies, it has been argued, ought to invest in equities as a means of hedging the general inflationary pressure on operating costs. Accomplishing this may itself require common stock holdings amounting to 7% or 8% of assets.[86]

In sum, low yields, a scarcity of eligible assets, inflation, and a changing mix of liabilities prompted the desire for greater investment freedom. Life companies also contended during the early postwar years that permission to invest in common stock need not result in increased portfolio risk. This argument was mounted both on a priori grounds[87] and through presentation of empirical evidence demonstrating the stability of income return from common stock portfolios despite substantial fluctuation in market values.[88] Market value risk, it was argued, can be sufficiently

---

[85] This need for modifications in policy contracts resulting from portfolio choice decisions depends upon the going asset valuation rules which are discussed below. It has been suggested that abandonment of the guaranteed rate of return on policy reserves and the linking of cash surrender values to the market value of assets are contract changes which would moderate the impact of market fluctuations in common stock prices. See Souvain, "Some Economic Considerations Affecting Investment Policy," p. 308. Also Clayton, "Role of the British Life Assurance Companies in the Capital Market," p. 83.

[86] See W. M. Anderson, "The Long View of Life Insurance Investment."

[87] For example, see Hoffman, "Preferred and Common Stocks," esp. pp. 193–200. In particular, Hoffman points out that prohibiting common stock investments eliminated security issues of any strong corporations having little or no funded debt or long-term notes from representation in life company portfolios. Investment in these companies, it was stated, would increase portfolio diversification and provide life companies with individual investment opportunities whose risk of loss is no greater than that of many corporate debt obligations.

[88] One impressive source of empirical evidence used by the industry was tabulations of the investment return since 1929 on securities investments of 18 large life companies. See *The Investment Experience of Eighteen Major United States Life Insurance Companies in Bonds and Stocks*, an annual ALC-LIAA *Joint Investment Bulletin*. Also, see Hoffman's summary of the experience of seven New England life companies, *op. cit.*, pp. 204–207, and the evidence summarized in two reports used to support the proposed amendments to the New York law in 1951: viz. ALC-LIAA, *A Report in Support*

moderated through the adoption of security valuation rules which take the long view and permit asset valuation on a going concern basis.[89]

Rates of return on common stock holdings over the long run do look very good by comparison with bond yields.[90] The spread between the return on common stocks and that on corporate bonds appeared particularly wide during the late 1940s and early 1950s when some life companies were agitating for more investment freedom.[91] Some observers outside the life insurance industry contended that life companies needed freedom to invest in common stocks in order to lengthen the maturity of their portfolios and bring them closer in line with the maturity of their liabilities. Equity investment appeared to be the only way life companies could obtain assets of sufficient term and avoid assuming undue income risk.[92] American life companies, themselves, do not seem to have put much emphasis on this problem in making their case for greater statutory freedom to invest in corporate stock.[93]

---

of *Proposed Amendments to Article 5, Section 81, of the New York Insurance Law*, 1951, and *Report of the Trust Investment and Study Committee* (Trust Division, New York State Bankers Convention), 1950, pp. 54, 62. Also, see Eleanor Daniel's review of the existing studies on comparative investment results, "Some Observations on Recent Studies of Investment Risk," *Journal of Finance*, May 1953, pp. 99–112.

[89] Security valuation rules are discussed later in this chapter.

[90] Total return, including realized gains and losses, computed on a base of actual cost, for the 18 company ALC-LIAA sample from 1929 to 1955 was about 3.5% on corporate bonds, 4.7% on preferred and guaranteed stocks and 6.5% on common stocks. ALC-LIAA *Joint Investment Bulletin*, No. 293. Comprehensive estimates of rates of return on common stocks have been produced recently by the University of Chicago Stock Market Study. See especially Fisher and Lorie, "Rates of Return on Investments in Common Stocks."

[91] This spread appeared even larger in Britain, and although British life companies have increased their holdings of common shares very considerably during the postwar period, some observers have viewed their portfolio adjustment in this direction as extraordinarily sluggish. See Farrell, "On the Structure of the Capital Market."

[92] See our discussion of income risk in Chapter I.

[93] British life companies apparently have been more conscious of income risk. Much of the literature emphasizing maturity as a crucial asset characteristic has evolved in the British actuarial journals. Clayton and Osborn suggest that the postwar increase in equity holdings by British life companies is a consequence of inflation and a change in product mix toward longer-term liabilities (particularly group pension plans). See their 1958 *Three Banks Review* article, p. 27.

(ii) The restrictive influence of investment laws or corporate equity acquisitions: Some additional evidence

To ascertain life company attitudes with respect to common stock investments following the 1957 liberalization of the New York insurance law, we included questions on this subject in interviews with several life insurance company officers in 1958 and again in 1960. Officers from 11 life companies were asked whether the New York law restricted their acquisition of common (and preferred) stock. Included were nine large companies (over $1 billion in assets) and two medium-sized companies (with assets of about $400 million and $500 million, respectively).

Four of the 11 company representatives indicated that they did not find the New York law restrictive with respect to their decision to acquire preferred and common stock. One of these companies was basically opposed to common stocks as outlets for life insurance companies' funds. Investigation of its annual statement showed this company's common stock holdings limited to some AT&T shares. Two of the other three companies, unconstrained by the New York law, had a tradition of emphasizing quality in their securities portfolio and were disinclined to include common shares to any significant extent in their portfolio. Both these companies had an abnormally high proportion of Aaa and Aa grade corporate bonds in their securities portfolio by comparison with other large life companies. The fourth company in this group had a regular common stock purchase program, but it was quite modest in magnitude and was not likely to bring it in conflict with the New York state overall ceiling on common shares for some years. The officer interviewed indicated that the company was satisfied with its program and would not be likely to increase its rate of common stock acquisitions if the New York law were further liberalized.

The spokesmen for seven companies, including the two medium-sized companies, testified that their companies found the New York limits restrictive in some degree. We asked these officers what sort of internal ceiling on common stock holdings existed independent of the statutory limits. This is a complex question since the requirement of state insurance departments that common stocks be valued on annual statements at market value also dampens companies' interest in corporate equities. Assuming satisfactory valuation rules, one officer suggested that his company would consider holding as much as 25% or 30% of its assets in common stocks if this seemed advisable on a yield basis. Three others felt that their companies would hold from 10% to 20% of assets in common shares if yield spreads were sufficiently attractive. Officers of three other companies responded that they had no idea how far they might go into common stocks if there were no external constraints. One of these companies, not domiciled in New York, already held about 8% of its assets in common shares, so presumably it would be in the 10% to 20% range if uninhibited by statutory limits. The representatives of the other two companies focused the discussion more on the restrictive nature of other elements of the investment statutes, that is, the earnings and dividend payment requirements and particularly the limits on investment in the shares of a single corporation. Both companies regarded the latter limits restrictive with respect to common and preferred issues. One officer indicated that his department had an interest on several occasions in taking the entire preferred issue of a corporation, but were restricted by New York law to 20% of the issue.

Curiously, there appeared to be no observable correlation between the degree of restriction the New York overall limit on common stock holdings imposed on a company and the company's common stock portfolio as a proportion of its assets. Indeed, the company which reported the highest internal ceiling (25%–30% of assets) held only a negligible amount of common stocks. The officer interviewed indicated that this was due to one strong-willed and influential member of the board of directors who long had adamantly opposed common stocks as investments for a life insurance company. At the time of our interview this director had recently left the board, and the officer felt the directors were now convinced of the wisdom of including common stocks within the set of eligible assets. One of the companies reporting a willingness to hold 10% to 20% of assets in corporate equities, under the right circumstances, held less than 2% of its assets in common shares at the time of the interview although the New York ceiling was 5% of assets (50% of surplus). This gap was attributed to the fact that the company did not deem it profitable to assign analysts to a regular stock purchase program when the overall limits were so restrictive. But if they were free to hold 10% or more of their assets in common stocks, they would be willing to reallocate duties in the securities department and actively acquire equity shares.

A number of companies replying to the aforementioned 1963 LIAA survey were reported as desirous of further loosening of New York's statutory restrictions on common stock holdings. In particular, the overall ceiling on common stock holdings was pinpointed as overrestrictive although apparently a number of suggestions were made with respect to reducing constraints dealing with eligibility of particular issues.[94]

Some feeling for the restrictive character of the New York law is obtainable from comparing the proportion of assets New York domiciled life companies hold in common shares with the proportion held by companies chartered by states with the most liberal statutes. A compilation made by Brimmer from end-1957 balance sheets showed that the 150 largest life companies held 1.7% of their assets in common stock. Companies domiciled in New York, however, had common stock holdings amounting to only 0.6% of their assets as compared to 7.1% for Massachusetts companies and 7.9% for Texas companies.[95] Among the more important states, Texas and Massachusetts have the most liberal regulations governing common stock investments.[96] Thus, although the balance sheets of the New York companies by themselves might be taken to indicate that the New York law is not constraining, the interstate comparison suggests the severity of governing statutes does make a difference.[97]

---

[94] O'Leary, *A Review of the New York Law Governing Life Insurance Company Investments*, p. 2.

[95] Brimmer, *op. cit.*, Tables IX-11, p. 350, and IX-12, p. 351.

[96] The overall limit specified by Texas law is 100% of capital and/or surplus. Common stocks are legal investments for Massachusetts companies under that state's general leeway provision.

[97] The overall New York limit on common stock holdings relevant for this period was 3% of the insurer's assets or one-third of surplus. The New York data are dominated by the large mutual companies which are domiciled there. However, if anything, large companies seem to hold a higher proportion of their assets in stocks than smaller companies. There is also some evidence that stock companies are somewhat more attracted by common stock than mutual companies. See Brimmer, Table IX-11, p. 350.

(iii) The magnitude of the regulatory impact upon investments
in corporate equities

As the summary of our interview results indicates, life insurance
companies seem interested in corporate shares as portfolio investments largely for yield considerations. Assuming that the statutory regulations prevailing in recent years have constrained life
companies from investment in corporate equities, the degree to
which their portfolio choices would have been different if unre-
strained depends upon the existing yield spreads, and the manner
in which life companies calculate expected yields on common stock
issues. In commenting in December 1964 on yield differentials,
Orson Hart observed that, "At the present time, bonds and mortgages have rate advantages of considerably more than 1% over
common stocks." [98] Although he does not specify how he computes the rate of return on common stock for this comparison,
judging from his estimate of the spread he was representing the
common stock return by the current dividend yield. This is how
life companies generally report yields on currently acquired shares
as illustrated in Table II-1.

More importantly, life companies seem to focus on the going
dividend yield in evaluating the relative attractiveness of common
stocks. We found this approach quite pervasive among the life
insurance company officers we interviewed.[99] This attitude is
apparently derived from the fixed-interest bearing debt issue tradition. The emphasis upon looking for return from regular stable
dividend payments rather than anticipated capital appreciation
is often rationalized in terms of equity among the various generations of policyholders. While it is difficult to find any merit in
this rationalization, it does appear to be taken seriously by many
life company officers.

Yields reported by a dozen leading life companies in their 1958
securities acquisitions are displayed in Table II-1. This comparison suggests life companies do not literally consider only the

---

[98] Hart, *op. cit.*, p. 358.
[99] Others have commented on the emphasis of life companies on dividend
return. For example, see McDiarmid, *Investments of Life Insurance Companies in the United States and Canada*, p. 112.

TABLE II-1. *Yields Obtained on Securities Acquired by 12 Large Life Insurance Companies During 1958*

Company	Industrial Bonds	Preferred Stock	Common Stock
Metropolitan	4.89%	—%	6.06%
Prudential	5.26	—	3.44
Equitable (N.Y.)	5.03	4.91	4.35
New York Life	4.91	5.44	4.03
John Hancock	4.94	4.69	4.70
Northwestern	5.02	5.55	3.90
Mutual Life	5.18	5.45	4.27
Mass Mutual	5.24	5.80	5.47
New England Life	5.14	5.38	3.51
Penn Mutual	4.67	—	3.70
Conn Mutual	5.27	4.87	5.07
National Life	4.97	—	3.06

NOTE: Yields on stocks are current dividend yields based on cost.

SOURCE: Data compiled by the Northwestern Mutual Life Insurance Company from annual statements.

current dividend yield in making decisions on common stock purchases. In the majority of cases, the dividend yield on newly acquired common shares is less than the bond and preferred stock yields.[100] But for most companies the amounts invested are quite small and the reported yields are consistent with emphasis on paying regular, stable dividends and an aversion to "growth stocks." [101] To the extent that this attitude governs investment selection by life company investment officers, their activity in stocks may have been dampened in recent years by relatively low dividend yields even if otherwise unconstrained.[102]

[100] At the time of these acquisitions life insurance companies were not allowed the 85% intercorporate dividend credit on their federal income tax liabilities.

[101] Brimmer reported from his survey responses that industry officials emphasized that "present or prospective income should be the fundamental objective" governing common stock selection and, "furthermore, it should not be subordinated to any desire to achieve capital appreciation and make capital profits." Brimmer, *op. cit.*, p. 360. The theory of stock valuation underlying this particular distinction between "prospective income" and "capital appreciation" is obscure, but, again from Brimmer's discussion, the operating principle still seems to be: "Stick to stocks with substantial current dividend yields."

[102] For comparison, the dividend/price ratio based on Standard and Poor's 500 stocks averaged 3.97% for 1958. The earnings/price ratio was 5.92%.

On balance, it seems unlikely that removal of the legal barriers to common stock investments at any point in the past 20 years would have triggered a rush into common shares by life companies. Nonetheless we would have expected a perceptible adjustment in the composition of their portfolios in the direction of greater common stock holdings. No doubt old and oft-repeated investment principles die very hard. Life company attitudes with regard to proper investment outlets were shaped to a substantial degree by the Armstrong Committee investigation and the subsequent record of statutory regulations. Despite these restraining influences, a number of substantial companies seem to have been prepared to accept common stocks into their portfolios in significant amount if free to do so. If the law had been greatly liberalized, their example and the act of statutory liberalization itself would undoubtedly have induced a number of other, more conservative, tradition-oriented companies to consider corporate equities as competitive portfolio assets.

The extent of life insurance company activity in the equity market, of course, would depend upon what point in time permissive statutory amendments had been enacted. If, for example, common shares had been opened to life companies at the end of the war (1945), the excess liquidity in life company portfolios, the scarcity of traditional outlets, the wide spread prevailing between dividend yields and bond and mortgage rates, and expectations of price inflation would have led life companies into substantial exploration of equity markets. Under these circumstances, it does not seem unreasonable to expect that by 1960 the industry would have held 10% to 15% instead of less than 3% of its assets in common stock.[103] The later in the postwar era the postulated

---

The decline in these measures of yield has been dramatic; the dividends/price ratio fell from 6.51% in 1950 to 2.97% in 1961, and the earnings/price ratio from 14.61% to 4.79% over the same period. Data from various *Federal Reserve Bulletins*. The 1950 ratios are based on Moody's 125 stock issues. Capital appreciation was the dominant form of return to investors in common stock during these years.

[103] This assumes common stocks valued at market prices in life company balance sheets. Assuming the statement value of total life insurance industry assets to be unaffected by portfolio composition, 15% of 1960 assets would imply common stock holdings of $17.9 billion as opposed to the $3.2 billion life companies in fact held in 1960. To reach this proportion of common stock holdings, the net increase in the market value of common shares

liberalization occurred, the less dramatic would we expect life company portfolio adjustment to have been in the light of trends in interest rates, yield spreads, and the general inflationary pressure.

MORTGAGE LOANS

Evidence that the mortgage lending restrictions in the New York Insurance Law have had some restraining effect on life insurance company portfolio choices is available in the replies to the 1963 LIAA Survey.[104] Three of the four amendments urged upon the New York State Joint Legislative Committee in November 1963, as a result of this survey, dealt with mortgage loan restrictions.[105] Two of these proposals are relevant to a consideration of the external restraints under which life insurance company investment policy operated during the 1950s.[106] One requested that the overall limit on conventional mortgage loan holdings established

---

held by life companies would have to amount to about 27% of the net increase in life company assets over the 15-year period. However, an additional $14.2 billion of investible funds were made available by life companies' liquidation of Treasury security holdings over this period. If this amount is added to the net gain in assets, the net increase in common shares must amount to 22% of net investible funds. Since the statement value of life company assets in 1960 would have been higher, other things being equal, had life companies been so active in common stocks, the net increase in equity share holdings as a percentage of the net gain in total assets would have been still less. Thus, common stock holdings amounting to 15% of life company assets does not imply an implausible composition of investment flows during 1945–1960. This magnitude of life company common stock investments would still leave them holding less than 4% of outstanding common shares in 1960. Holdings amounting to 10% of assets are, of course, all the more credible.

[104] O'Leary, *A Review of the New York Law Governing Life Insurance Company Investments.* Also see the testimony of O'Leary, J. F. Oates, Jr., G. T. Conklin, and R. E. Pille before the New York State Joint Legislative Committee on Insurance Rates and Regulations as summarized in the Committee'. 1964 *Report, op. cit.*

[105] See *ibid.*, pp. 1–2. The fourth urgently proposed amendment was the request for a more liberal leeway provision. See the discussion of corporate securities above.

[106] The third amendment dealt with a provision of the New York law enacted in 1962 restricting joint participation in a mortgage loan to loans of $5 million or more. Combined with the single property loan limit of 2% of an insurer's assets, this provision does discriminate against smaller life companies. See Pille's comments recorded in the 1964 Joint Committee *Report*, p. 60.

at 40% of an insurer's assets be raised to 50%. The other urged an increase in the maximum loan/value ratio to 75% on all conventional loans.[107]

In the early postwar years the New York 40% limit on conventional mortgage holdings did not act as a constraint on life companies. During the 1950s, however, mortgage debt was a major outlet for life insurance company funds, and some companies, which for one reason or another confined their mortgage lending activity largely to conventional loans, found themselves closing in on the 40% ceiling. Two of the dozen companies we interviewed in 1960 reported that they had altered their funds allocation policy because of this statutory barrier. Several other companies were not yet affected but would be within five years if they continued to acquire conventional mortgage loans at the same rate as in their recent past. It is probable that some companies, active in mortgage lending, cultivated the VA and FHA loan markets somewhat more energetically because of New York's conventional mortgage limit.[108]

Judging from our interview response, the two-thirds loan/value limit was more generally an impediment to life company investment policy during the 1940s and 1950s than the overall ceiling on conventional loan portfolios.[109] Nearly all the mortgage officers we interviewed, whose departments were active in single family

---

[107] This ratio, which had been two-thirds for all loans, was raised in 1959 to 75% for loans up to $30,000 on single family homes amortized within 30 years. See Conklin's remarks in *ibid.*, p. 58.

[108] New Jersey also had a similar 40% ceiling. Other significant states have no provision or a more liberal one. Some other states do have limits on the amount of funds a life company can invest in leasehold mortgages.

[109] There was a general movement toward liberalization of statutory loan/value maxima during the 1950s. By June 1960, 9 of the 19 states whose statutory regulations have been summarized by the LIAA-CMC Monograph (pp. 110–113) generally permitted 75% loans. Some state laws excepted leaseholds and/or placed limits on loan maturity for 75% loans. New York and three other states (Ohio, Virginia, Vermont) permitted 75% loans (80% in Vermont) on single family (or 1–2 family) residences, but restricted loans on multifamily and commercial property to two-thirds of appraised value. The other six states, including Connecticut, Wisconsin, and Indiana, retained a general two-thirds ceiling, although Wisconsin expressly permitted larger loans with the amount exceeding two-thirds of value to be allowed under the leeway provision. However, during the 1940s and 1950s most of the larger life companies were operating under a two-thirds rule for all conventional loans.

residence loans, indicated that a two-thirds loan/value ceiling prevented them from meeting the competition in a significant proportion of the loan opportunities falling within their acceptance standards. All these officers suggested that a 75% ceiling would allow them to make practically all the loans they desired.

Generally life companies have adhered to more conservative loan/value standards in their mortgage lending on multifamily, commercial, and industrial properties. Actually the majority of companies we interviewed in 1960 seemed not to feel constrained by a two-thirds loan/value ceiling on income-producing properties. A few, more aggressive officers did list this regulation among the more serious statutory obstacles to their exploitation of loan opportunities. In the early 1960s, life company activity in mortgages on income-producing property had sharply increased. Judging from the 1963 LIAA survey results, this increased activity induced more companies to seek freedom to make larger loans on given properties.[110] Among the life companies in our interview sample active in farm mortgages, we did not find any desirous of making loans greater than two-thirds of the appraised value of the farm property.

These restraints on life company conventional mortgage lending have placed life companies at somewhat of a competitive disadvantage vis-à-vis their major competitors in the home loan market, i.e., savings and loan associations, commercial banks, and mutual savings banks. The S & Ls have been unrestricted with respect to the proportion of assets they may hold in conventional mortgage loans. There are some limitations on holdings of commercial and savings banks.[111] But all these institutions have been free to make loans of 75% of the securing property value; in some cases

[110] See O'Leary's comments summarized in the Joint Legislative Committee's 1964 *Report, op. cit.*, p. 50. It is also clear that some life insurance company real estate ownership on a net lease basis has resulted from a desire to avoid the mortgage loan size limitation. This is also true in the case of some so-called real estate bonds.

[111] National banks have been limited to total mortgage holdings of 100% of capital and unimpaired surplus or 60% of time and savings deposits, whichever is greater. The limit for commercial banks chartered by New York state is 60% of time and savings deposits. New York mutual savings banks may invest up to 65% of their assets in conventional mortgage loans and real estate. See U.S. House, Subcommittee on Domestic Finance, *Comparative Regulations of Financial Institutions*, 1963, Chapters 1, 3, and the New York Joint Legislative Committee *Report*, 1964, p. 53.

higher loan/value ratios are permitted.[112]   Thus the generally prevailing two-thirds loan/value limit did seem to accentuate the competitive disadvantage life companies have had in competing with local lenders in what remain essentially local markets.   Several companies have ceased active participation in the single family loan market.   Others indicated to us that the rapid growth of the S & Ls relative to the growth rate of demand for mortgage financing during the 1950s, together with the relative severity of the insurance law — particularly the loan/value ceiling — had made them aware of the possible desirability of reducing or dissolving the portion of their mortgage organization responsible for generating single family home loans.   Although it is difficult to estimate the magnitude of the effect involved, the two-thirds loan/value limit unquestionably diverted some life company funds into the VA and FHA loan programs during the 1950s.

INVESTMENT REAL ESTATE

As we have seen, life insurance company freedom to invest in investment real estate has been controlled by statutory provisions to about the same degree as their freedom to acquire common stocks.   Investment in commercial and industrial property was first authorized by New York state in 1946.   These holdings were limited in the aggregate to 3% of the insurer's assets; this ceiling was raised to 5% in 1957.   The law also established a single parcel size limit and provided for a minimum rate of writedown of property acquired for investment purposes.   Certain types of commercial and industrial properties were excluded from the general authorization.   Separate provisions govern life company investment in residential properties, buildings used by the life company for its own business, and property acquired through foreclosure. The total holdings of a life company in property used for its own business are limited to 10% of the insurer's admitted assets. Investment in housing projects is also permitted up to 10% of a life company's assets.   No quantitative limits are imposed on property acquired via foreclosure, but an insurer is expected to dispose of such property within a stipulated period.

[112] *Comparative Regulations of Financial Institutions*, pp. 37, 90, 120.   Also, the Federal Savings and Loan Associations are permitted to make 75% loans on multifamily properties.   *Ibid.*, p. 126.

Some observers have expressed surprise that life companies have not taken more complete advantage of the latitude that postwar statutory amendments have offered them in the purchase of real estate for investment purposes.[113] Holdings of the relevant types of real estate, expressed as a proportion of industry assets, are presented in Table II-2. It is clear that overall life insurance

TABLE II-2. *Real Estate Holdings of U.S. Life Insurance Companies as a Percentage of Total Industry Assets: 1947–1963*
(by type of property)

		Investment			
Year	*Company Used*	*Residential*	*Commercial*	*Other*	*Total*
1947	0.49%	0.39%	0.42%	0.33%	1.63%
1948	0.54	0.43	0.69	0.24	1.90
1949	0.57	0.51	0.88	0.17	2.12
1950	0.57	0.56	1.05	0.14	2.31
1951	0.58	0.53	1.24	0.10	2.45
1952	0.59	0.65	1.38	0.06	2.67
1953	0.59	0.58	1.42	0.04	2.63
1954	0.62	0.55	1.56	0.03	2.76
1955	0.66	0.50	1.65	0.03	2.84
1956	0.68	0.44	1.68	0.02	2.82
1957	0.79	0.44	1.87	0.02	3.12
1958	0.77	0.38	1.86	0.02	3.03
1959	0.87	0.37	2.02	0.03	3.29
1960	0.84	0.32	1.82	0.03	3.01
1961	0.91	0.33	1.93	0.04	3.21
1962	0.99	0.33	1.90	0.06	3.29
1963	0.88	0.29	1.81	0.05	3.02

SOURCE: ILI, *Life Insurance Fact Book*.

company investments in real estate have fallen considerably short of statutory authorization.

[113] For example, see Badger and Guthman, *Investment Principles and Practices*, 4th ed., Chapter 26.

In particular, life company activity in housing projects has been negligible in comparison to the amount of investment permitted. After some early postwar experimentation in this field life companies have largely ignored it. The greatest dollar amount life companies have held in residential real estate was $461 million in 1952. Experience proved that housing project investments usually had to be undertaken on a large scale in order to control the environment, and life companies were reluctant to undertake the considerable management duties which were almost always involved.[114] Risks associated with rapid increases in building costs, competition from public housing projects, rent control, and short-term loans also may have dampened life company enthusiasm for this form of investment.

Although the postwar record of New York's control over total life company holdings of nonresidential investment real estate is similar to the controls established for common stock investment, there does not seem to have been the same degree of pressure behind the drive to liberalize the real estate provisions. As with common stocks, the initial postwar authorization approving investment in commercial and industrial properties limited total holdings to 3% of an insurer's assets. Within three or four years of the 1946 amendment authorizing these real estate holdings, pressure developed to raise the overall holdings ceiling to 5% of assets.[115] The New York State Joint Legislative Committee considered this proposal but refused in a 1951 report to recommend its adoption. The rejection was based in part on the fact that, "Only one large company has availed itself of the opportunity of making investments of this type to the extent that it has approached the statutory limit of 3 per cent." [116] The industry persisted in pushing for liberalization of both the aggregate

---

[114] See McDiarmid, *op. cit.*, p. 107, and Jewett, *op. cit.*, p. 175.

[115] The desire for more freedom to invest in real estate was not limited to New York companies or directed exclusively at the New York law. As early as 1949, J. M. Bryan of the Jefferson Standard Life Insurance Company stated that a North Carolina law limiting a company's purchase and leaseback investment to 4% of assets had prevented his company from going as far in this field as desired. See Bryan's testimony before the Joint Committee on the Economic Report, *Hearings*, p. 276.

[116] New York Joint Legislative Committee on Insurance Rates and Regulations, *Report*, 1951, p. 63.

holdings and single parcel limits,[117] and, as we have seen, modest increases in both limits were achieved in 1957.

As with common stocks, it is difficult to tell from the actual record of portfolio holdings whether the 3% overall limit prevailing from 1946 to 1957 was much of a constraint. Life company holdings of nonhousing investment property remained under 2% of assets throughout this period (Table II-2). But within that aggregate experience, it is possible that a significant number of companies felt constrained by the ceiling although the New York legislative committee found this not to be the case. As with stocks, some companies may have been awaiting more positive liberal authorization before exploring investment in real estate seriously.

With a 5% overall limit and a somewhat higher single parcel ceiling since 1957, there is little evidence that many companies have been constrained. The aggregate holdings of investment real estate as a proportion of assets remained unchanged (1.8%) from 1957 to 1963. Only one large company we interviewed in 1960 reported that it was up against the 5% ceiling and was desirous of obtaining permission to expand its holdings further. O'Leary's review of the responses from the LIAA's 1963 survey of opinion on the New York law does not mention any specific grievance companies held against the real estate restrictions. Real estate is only noted as one of a number of investment areas about which "several suggestions" were made by responding companies.

In formulating investment policy in the commercial and industrial real estate field, the primary limitation on life company acquisitions has been (as with residential properties) aversion to undertaking managerial responsibilities. Thus, nearly all life company real estate investments in this sector — excluding some properties occupied by the life company in question — have taken the form of long-term absolute net leases. In the most well-known of these arrangements, the insurance company purchases

---

[117] For example, industry representatives returned to the Joint Legislative Committee in 1952 with a proposal which accepted the overall limit on investment real estate holdings at 13% (10% in housing projects and 3% in other income-producing real estate) but would permit up to 5% to be invested in nonhousing property. This proposal was rejected at the time. See the Joint Legislative Committee on Insurance Rates and Regulations, *Report*, 1952, p. 92.

a property, and as prearranged, executes a lease with the former owner as lessee. The life company receives rental payments while the tenant assumes all operating costs and manages the property.[118] This type of sale and leaseback deal developed partly out of tax advantages accruing to the lessee from obtaining funds by this means rather than incurring debt. The attractiveness of these investments from the perspective of life companies has been strongly influenced by their tax position. Therefore we shall defer further discussion of real estate investment to the section on tax considerations below.

Summary

Life insurance company portfolio selections are made within the framework of a complex, varied, and detailed set of state statutory regulations. The primary purpose of investment statutes seems to have been protection of policyholders' interests. Most state legislation in this area appears founded on the assumption that this objective is best carried out by imposing investment restrictions designed to preserve safety of principal. This goal is accomplished by the imposition of quantitative restraints which prohibit or limit life company investment in specific types of assets. Eligibility tests of the quality of individual loans and investments are also employed. Less consistently, some of the quantitative restrictions legislated appear designed to guarantee a minimum degree of portfolio diversification.

The strictest controls over life companies have been those dealing with investment in equities. The New York state law has been particularly restrictive and influential in this area, as in many others. From the Armstrong Committee investigation (1906) to the end of World War II, equity investments were essentially prohibited to life companies by New York law and prohibited or severely limited by most other major states. New York extended to life companies permission to invest in commercial and industrial

---

[118] Not all life company investment officers have agreed that these net lease arrangements are the most profitable way for insurers to invest in real estate. For a view that yields on leasebacks have not been attractive relative to bond and mortgage yields, and that life companies would do better to accept managerial responsibilities in real estate, see Burnett, "Some Aspects of Portfolio Management."

real estate properties in 1946 and in common stocks in 1951. Each of these classes of assets was limited in amount to 3% of assets, however, and only common stocks passing stringent earnings and dividend tests qualified for life company portfolios. The aggregate limit was raised to 5% of assets for each of these asset types in 1957.

Given the severity of the statutory rules, it may seem natural to conclude that these controls have been responsible for the very limited participation of life companies in the equity markets. We found, however, that some observers have concluded that deeply ingrained in the minds of most life insurance company officers is the principle that equities are unsuitable investments for the trust funds held by life companies for policyholders. There were several corroborating pieces of evidence that made this position credible. On the other hand, there were strong reasons why life companies should have been interested in equity investment during the postwar years and there existed evidence that the industry had lobbied hard for liberalization of the more restrictive statutes.

On balance, we concluded that life companies' primary preference for debt issues existed independently of state investment laws, but that nonetheless the statutory controls were significant constraints in some areas. In particular, these statutes seemed to restrict investment in common stock to well below what it otherwise would have been. The interview evidence indicated that a dual set of restraints was operative here, however, i.e., not only legislative regulations but also rules established by the state commissioners governing the valuation of assets. The latter rules are discussed in the next section. As a rough estimate of the significance of these sets of constraints we concluded that, had life companies been free of the statutory and asset valuation restrictions during the entire postwar period, they might have held, in the aggregate, 10% to 15% of their assets in common stocks by 1960 instead of only 3%.

We did not find that the statutory rules contributed as much to the explanation of limited life company acquisitions of real estate. Life companies did not use fully the authority they had to invest in residential properties. Although a few companies did find the 3% of assets limit on nonresidential property holdings restrictive, this constraint was clearly much less widespread than the constraints on common stock investments. Rather, their limited activity in real estate seemed a consequence of the usual doubts about the propriety of significant real estate holdings and a strong reluctance to get into the business of managing properties. Life companies have engaged in some long-term net lease transactions which avoid managerial responsibilities, but uncertainty about their tax situation may have limited their willingness to invest larger amounts in this sort of contract. The impact of taxation on portfolio policy is discussed below.

Within the private debt markets, it is not clear whether state statutory regulations influenced the corporate bond/mortgage loan composition of life company acquisitions. Within the mortgage sector, however, qualitative restrictions on conventional mortgage loans may have significantly impeded life companies' ability to compete with the other major lenders, particularly with savings and loan associations for conventional home loans. The restriction of most relevance in this connection was the two-thirds loan/value ratio maximum which the various states only gradually raised during the 1950s. The loan/value limit seemed less of a constraint in loans on nonfarm, nonresidential properties and hardly a constraint at all in the farm mortgage loan market. In the residential market, however, the loan/value restriction probably contributed to increasing life company activity in the federally underwritten mortgage loan market during the 1950s. It may also, of course, have increased life company investments in other sectors, particularly in the commercial mortgage loan and corporate debt markets. The New York law restricting holdings of conventional mortgage loans to 40% of a company's assets had affected at least a few companies by the end of the 1950s. For the companies affected, this constraint most likely resulted in the diversion of additional funds to corporate securities.

Statutory regulations of life company corporate debt investments seem to have been generally less influential during the postwar era. Their primary effect has probably been to limit the ability of life companies to finance newly incorporated enterprises. Similarly, life companies have been restricted from making unsecured loans to unincorporated firms. Generally, quality standards have prevented some more adventurous life companies from experimenting as much as they might wish with lower quality corporate debt issues, particularly those with equity options designed to compensate lenders for taking risks. These and most of the other restraints summarized here have been relaxed in some states by general "basket" or leeway provisions. New York state, however, has given companies in its jurisdiction very limited leeway authority.

Rules Governing the Valuation of Life Insurance Company Assets

In addition to statutory restrictions on life insurance company portfolio choice, investment policy has been influenced and constrained by the complex set of rules governing the valuation of securities in companies' annual statements. In this section we shall discuss the nature and background of the established security valuation procedures and attempt to evaluate their impact on life insurance company investment decisions.

The solvency of a corporation at any point in time depends, among other things, upon the value of its assets relative to the value of its liabilities. A life company's liabilities are its obligations defined in the insurance and annuity contracts it has outstanding. The statement value of its liabilities are a function of the basis on which policy reserves are built up. Life companies in this country have had substantial freedom in choosing the actuarial assumptions from which the valuation of their liabilities is determined.[119] Solvency of a company depends on its ability to meet its policy claims as they come due or as payment is demanded under terms of the contract. The difference between the value of an insurer's assets and his liabilities represents capital (in a stock company) and surplus, which serves as a cushion to absorb changes in the value of assets or liabilities. The size and

---

[119] State laws establish minimum bases upon which policy reserves may be accumulated. Adhering to these minima, companies still have considerable freedom in choosing premium rates and the basis on which reserves are calculated. The value of an insurer's liabilities derives from the basis on which policy reserves have been set up from past premium payments. Thus management discretion in valuation of liabilities is substantial, although, as will be seen, its choice is highly restricted in valuing assets and in determining the size of surplus.

maintenance of this cushion and an accurate appraisal of the state of the business depends on sound valuation of a company's assets. For protection of the policyholder, therefore, the state insurance supervisory authorities have declared that asset valuation is not to be left to the discretion of management but to be constrained within an established set of procedures. Substantial uniformity among the states has been achieved through the efforts of the National Association of Insurance Commissioners (NAIC).

Throughout the post-World War II years, life insurance companies have been governed by a complex and ever-changing system of asset valuation procedures established by the NAIC's Committee on Valuation of Securities. In addition to defining values at which securities can be carried in life insurance company balance sheets, the NAIC Committee has required life companies to establish a securities valuation reserve to cushion the impact on surplus of realized and unrealized capital losses in the security portfolio. The Committee has rigidly defined the amount to be credited to this reserve each year and the required reserve balance outstanding each year. The distinctions made in these statement value and valuation reserve rules between different types of portfolio assets, together with statutory rules limiting life insurance company surplus positions,[120] influence the portfolio selection of life companies by relating the legal solvency of companies to their portfolio composition. In order to evaluate the significance of these rules as a constraint on life company investment policy, we shall briefly outline the evolution of the valuation rules, summarize the problems they create, and indicate the direction of impact they must have on portfolio choices.

Evolution of the Valuation Standards

Prior to 1907 securities owned by life insurance companies were valued at market prices.[121] However, there apparently was substantial variation among life insurance companies with regard to

---

[120] The New York Insurance Law (Article IX-A, Section 207) limits any domestic company, other than stock companies doing exclusively nonparticipating insurance business, to a surplus of no more than 10% of policy reserves and policy liabilities. Other states have similar limitations. See LIAA-CMC Monograph, p. 160.

[121] Tatlock, "On the Proper Method of Valuation of Fixed Term Securities Owned by Life Insurance Companies," pp. 69–72.

the market prices used in valuing the same securities for statement purposes.[122] Furthermore the sharp decline in market values associated with the 1907 financial panic dramatized the inadequacy of market prices as an asset valuation measure for long-term investors.[123] Concern over these problems prompted the state insurance commissioners to take action directed toward standardizing and stabilizing security valuation. In 1910 the National Convention[124] of Insurance Commissioners created a permanent committee, the Committee on Valuation of Securities, and endowed it with responsibility for achieving and maintaining the desired standardization. Since that time, securities owned by life insurance companies have been subjected to a complex variety of statement valuation rules. However, investment real estate and real estate mortgage loans, not in default, have been accepted in annual statements on a cost basis.[125] Stabilization of security values was furthered by the introduction of the "amortized cost" principle as a valuation standard for "amply secured" fixed maturity bonds by New York state in 1909.[126] "Ample security" was left undefined by the legislation, but responsibility for its determination was vested in the state's Superintendent of Insurance.

During subsequent years, with the recommendation and support of the National Convention of Insurance Commissioners, most other states adopted amortization value principles for all "amply secured" bonds with fixed maturities and fixed interest rate. It is not clear from the record what standards of "ample security" were used by insurance commissioners until the explicit adoption of agency rating tests by some insurance departments in the early 1930s. It is clear that many securities did not qualify for valua-

---

[122] LIAA-CMC Monograph, p. 161.

[123] This decline led the New York Superintendent of Insurance to permit use of the "rule of thirteen" (average of market prices on the first day of each month and December 31) rather than the end-year quotations for 1907 statement purposes. Even with this degree of averaging, the value losses for New York insurance companies were very substantial proportions of their surplus. See Bell, "Asset Reserves of Life Insurance Companies."

[124] "Convention" was changed to "Association" in 1935.

[125] Some states, including New York, do establish a minimum rate of write-down of the cost of investment property owned, most commonly of 2% of cost per annum.

[126] New York Insurance Law, 1909, Section 18.

tion at amortized cost. In fact, during 19 of the 28 years following the general adoption of the amortization provision (1917), it was necessary for the state insurance commissioners meeting in convention to give relief to some classes of securities from year-end market valuation by establishing special "Convention Values." [127]

For a definition of "ample security" the states eventually came to depend upon the bond ratings of the various rating services. Use of bond ratings for this purpose was approved by the NAIC in 1940.[128] After an insurance department ruling in 1938, however, passing the established rating test was not even sufficient for bonds with low market prices in the portfolios of New York companies to qualify for valuation on an amortized cost basis.[129]

In 1942 the NAIC added a market yield test to its rating test, bonds passing either test qualifying for amortization. Under the market yield criterion, a bond was qualified for amortization if its current yield exceeded the yield on fully taxable United States Government bonds of comparable maturity by less than a pre-established differential. The magic differential would be set each year by the NAIC in accordance with the commissioners' appraisal of market conditions. The differentials established by the com-

---

[127] During the years 1917–1921 and 1931–1944 inclusive, "Convention Values" were adopted for some classes of securities. See Bell, *op. cit.*, p. 17. The specific convention rules adopted each year are published in the annual *Proceedings* of the National Convention (Association) of Insurance Commissioners. Also the TNEC Monograph 28-A, Section III, has an account of these rules through 1938.

[128] The New York Insurance Department informed companies that bond ratings were being used as a guide to "amply secured" bonds as early as 1932. Generally, bonds in the first four (or five in New York) grades of one or more of the three (four) recognized rating services were regarded as eligible for valuation on an amortized basis. Differences among states accounted for wide variations in the value at which the companies carried bonds during the thirties. As late as 1938 the TNEC found bonds in the fifth grade of the rating services being carried by some companies at market value and by others at amortized value, depending upon the rules of their respective states. For examples of the variation in the valuation of some railroad bonds held by various companies, see TNEC Monograph 28, p. 362.

[129] The ruling involved declared that for bonds carrying "quotations or sale prices (under) fifty during the three months immediately preceding the date of the statement, satisfactory proof of value . . . must be furnished . . . if such a bond is to be amortized for statement purposes." *New York Insurance Report*, Volume I, *Life*, 1940, p. 36a. The minimum price was raised later to fifty-five and then to sixty (1941).

missioners for purposes of the test, until its abandonment in 1953, were as follows:[130]

| | Maximum Allowable Yield Differential |
Year	(basis points)
1942	390
1944	290
1945	210
1946	180
1949	170
1950–52	150

Neither the rating nor the yield test answered the problem of determining statement values for bonds directly placed with insurance companies and consequently having neither service ratings nor market yields. Initially, direct placements were allowed to be carried at issue price, but as their volume grew, valuation of private placements was undertaken on an individual basis by a Subcommittee of the NAIC's Committee on the Valuation of Securities, their decisions being based on criteria unknown to the companies. This fact, together with the frequent necessity of the commissioners to abandon market values and adopt expedient substitutes, hindered the formulation of investment policy by leaving companies uncertain as to what the valuation rules were this year or would be next year.

Dissatisfaction with the system led to a concerted attempt by the industry to place valuation standards on a more rational and predictable basis. In 1951 an industry committee report proposed valuing all but bonds in default on an amortized basis and establishing contingency asset reserves to absorb losses.[131] A modified version of these recommendations was adopted subsequently by the NAIC. The rules and procedures governing statement values and the accumulation and use of a securities reserve that prevailed during the 1950s are based largely on the 1951 plan.

---

[130] Hickman, *Corporate Bond Quality and Investor Experience*, p. 285.

[131] ALC-LIAA, Joint Committee on the Valuation of Assets, *Report*, April 10, 1951. Bonds in default, preferred stocks, and common stocks would continue to be carried at market value.

Summary of the Prevailing Rules

ASSET VALUATION RULES

As of the end of World War II, the security valuation rules had evolved to the point that bonds eligible for valuation at amortized cost included:

(1) United States and Dominion of Canada Government obligations.
(2) Obligations "secured by the full faith and credit" of political subdivisions of the United States and Canada, not in default.
(3) Bonds rated in the first four grades by any two of the three recognized bond rating agencies (Moody's, Fitch, Standard Statistics).
(4) Bonds with market yields exceeding yields on unrestricted fully taxable U.S. Treasury bonds of comparable maturity by less than a designated differential.
(5) Bonds without ratings or market quotations deemed equivalent to bonds in any of the above categories by the NAIC Sub-Committee of the Committee on Valuation of Securities.
(6) Obligations of foreign governmental bodies deemed "amply secured" by the NAIC Sub-Committee.

Bonds not covered in any of the above categories were required to be carried at market value, or, lacking market quotations, at values set by the NAIC Sub-Committee. All stocks other than privately placed preferred stocks had to be valued at market price on the statement date. Privately acquired preferred stock could be valued at cost providing the dividend yield on cost valuation exceeded an NAIC specified figure derived as an average of yields on high grade publicly held preferred stocks. Otherwise, the stock was to be written down to that price at which the dividend yield matched the required yield. Mortgage loans not in default were permitted to be valued at amortized cost.

The NAIC did not adopt the 1951 industry committee recommendation that all bonds not in default be valued on an amortized cost basis. In June 1953, however, the Commissioners did adopt somewhat more liberal valuation tests for bonds. Under the new rules, bonds included in the first four grades of *any* of the three rating services automatically qualified for valuation on an amortized cost basis. Other bonds were subjected to further earnings and balance sheet tests to determine their eligibility. Corporate bonds not qualifying under the ratings tests could be valued at amortized cost provided the obligor's net earnings before taxes covered fixed charges at least 1½ times on the average over the preceding five years, and actually in either of the last two fiscal years. In addition, the bonds had to meet a balance sheet requirement limiting the ratio of funded debt to total capitalization.[132] The service rating, earnings, and balance sheet tests summarized in this paragraph are listed under Test No. 1 in the NAIC *Instructions*.

Corporate bonds failing to qualify under Test No. 1 could still be valued at amortized cost under the 1953 rule changes if they passed Test No. 2. This test includes an earnings test similar to the one above, but requiring only one-times coverage of fixed charges. It probes more deeply into other earnings and balance sheet characteristics of the obligor.[133] Separate standards are set forth for railroad equipment trust, leased line and terminal obligations, and religious institutional obligations not qualifying under the rating agency grades (NAIC *Instructions*, Section IV). Oil and gas production loans are treated in a separate classification (NAIC *Instructions*, Section V). Municipal revenue bonds included in the four highest grades by any of the rating agencies or, alternatively, passing a yield spread test or otherwise judged by the Committee on Valuation of Securities as "amply secured," [134] are eligible for valuation at amortized cost.

---

[132] The maximum acceptable ratio under this test is 50% to 75%, the specific figure depending on the industry. For bonds issued by "new enterprises" the NAIC computes projected net earnings and fixed charges to which the earnings test is applied [NAIC *Instructions*, Section II, C]. The above summary is derived from changes in instructions reported in the 1953 NAIC *Proceedings*. The complete set of asset valuation instructions for statements of December 31, 1961 (for bonds essentially unchanged since 1953) has been reproduced in Fraine, *Valuation of Securities Holdings of Life Insurance Companies*, Appendix A.

[133] Test No. 2 requires that the current assets/current liabilities ratio of railroad obligors be not less than 125%. For public utility and industrial and miscellaneous obligors it requires either that "adjusted earnings" (net income before depreciation, depletion, and extraordinary nonrecurring items of income or expense) be equal to mandatory principal payments and sinking fund requirements in each year, or working capital equal to 100% of long-term debt. NAIC *Instructions*, Procedures for Valuing Bonds, Section III.

[134] The Committee has authority under Section V (Discretionary Authority) to permit a security failing the tests to be carried at amortized cost. It also has the authority to require securities passing the amortization tests to be valued at market price. The industry understood the latter power to be a

The rules governing the statement valuation of preferred stock holdings of life insurance companies were somewhat liberalized by the NAIC in 1957. Publicly traded preferred stocks qualifying under specified tests became eligible for valuation under the "one-fifth" rule; that is, this year's statement value plus (or minus) one-fifth of the difference between last year's statement value and this year's December 31 market price. Preferred stock purchased during the year could be valued at cost. To qualify for valuation under the one-fifth procedure, cumulative preferred stocks must:

(1) have net earnings after income taxes for the most recently completed fiscal year period equal to at least $1\frac{1}{4}$ times the issue's fixed charges, full contingent interest, and preferred dividend requirements; and
(2) not be in arrears as to dividends.

Noncumulative preferreds are required to meet the same earnings standard and to have paid full dividends in each of the last three years.[135] Qualified directly placed preferreds are also eligible for valuation under the one-fifth rule.[136] Common stocks continued to be valued at "Association Value," i.e., year-end market quotations.

THE MANDATORY SECURITIES VALUATION RESERVE

The 1951 life insurance industry Joint Committee *Report* recommended to the NAIC the adoption of a securities reserve. In December 1951 the NAIC responded by adopting the reserve principle and outlined initial rules which followed, with some modifications, the Joint Committee's proposal.

A series of industry committees considering asset valuation

---

reservation authority to be used only in extreme cases. See LIAA, *Record of Life Insurance Investments*, 1953, p. 44.

[135] *Final Report to Insurance Companies, Societies and Associations re: Annual Statements as of December 31, 1957*. Published by the NAIC Committee on Valuation of Securities, June 17, 1957.

[136] For details of qualification, see the NAIC *Instructions*, Procedures for Valuing Preferred Stocks, Section II. The "Association Value" for a privately placed preferred stock is defined as the lesser of the current call price or an amount computed by dividing its dollar dividend yield by the yield of a comparable publicly traded preferred stock of the same issuer. If no comparable issue exists, the average yield of a published "selected group" of high grade preferreds is substituted in the above computation.

procedures concluded that a provision for a securities reserve was an essential part of a rational solution to the valuation problem. As has been observed above, most life insurance companies are limited by legislative statute in the amount of surplus they can accumulate. During the early 1950s the average ratio of surplus to total assets for the industry was about 7%. Under these circumstances, life companies could not absorb wide fluctuations in the value of their assets independent of their liabilities without serious threat to their solvency. This fact was the force behind efforts to find ways of stabilizing statement values of life insurance company assets; in particular, to adopt rules which do not subject "going concerns" to asset valuation on a liquidation basis. However, regulatory concern with the quality of life insurance company assets has prevented the commissioners from being willing to accept valuation of all securities — or even all securities not in default — on an original or amortized cost basis.[137] Therefore prudence seemed to dictate establishment of an asset reserve capable of absorbing realized losses and some fluctuations in the market value of security holdings.

In offering its asset valuation and contingency reserve proposals, the 1951 Joint Committee was armed with results obtained from the National Bureau of Economic Research's Corporate Bond Research Project which demonstrated clearly that the NAIC valuation rules forced writedowns of assets greatly in excess of ultimate actual losses.[138] This project also provided a body of raw material from which predictions of losses on corporate bond portfolios could be made. Fraine has summarized the conventional accounting distinctions between valuation reserves and surplus as follows: ". . . the valuation reserve is regarded as a reserve for the calculable while surplus is regarded as an additional reserve against the incalculable." [139]

In authorizing a securities valuation reserve in 1951, the insurance commissioners set out rules specifying the size of the reserve to be established, the manner in which reserves would be accumu-

---

[137] No doubt the existence of market price quotations has had a peculiar psychological effect on the commissioners. As we have seen, all mortgage loans not in default have long qualified for reporting at amortized cost.

[138] The evidence relevant for life companies is summarized by Bell, *op. cit.*, pp. 21–22.

[139] Fraine, *op. cit.*, p. 26.

lated, and the extent to which various losses could be charged against the reserve. Under the valuation reserve proposal that finally took effect, the maximum reserve was established at 1% of the statement value of all bonds amortizable under prevailing NAIC rules plus 20% of the statement value of all other securities.[140] As we have seen, the NAIC in 1953 revised the amortization standards for bonds. Under the 1953 procedures, bonds qualifying under Test No. 1 (see above) for amortization also qualified as "Class One" securities in the reserve formula; i.e., they were to carry an ultimate reserve of 1% of their statement value. Bonds failing Test No. 1 but amortizable under Test No. 2 were treated as "Class Two" securities requiring a maximum reserve of 20% of statement value. A mandatory rate of accumulation of the reserve was established at 0.05% of statement value for Class One securities and at 1% for securities in Class Two. All net capital gains (realized and unrealized) were also to be added to the reserves and net capital losses (realized and unrealized) charged against the reserve.[141]

In addition to establishing a maximum reserve and a mandatory rate of additions to the reserve, the NAIC has required a minimum reserve. Originally the rule stated that the reserve could not be reduced below 20% of the statement value of Class Two securities plus 0.05% of the value of Class One securities. Each subsequent year another one-twentieth of the statement value of Class One securities has been added to this definition of the floor balance. Among resolutions adopted by the NAIC in December 1956 was one which amended the minimum reserve provision so that it now required companies to carry the stated minimum. This modification took on some significance the following year when the commissioners adopted a valuation stabilization formula for preferred stock. In its 1957 resolution permitting life companies to carry

[140] On the basis of portfolio data for 60 companies, this formula would have permitted a maximum composite reserve for all securities of 2.4% of statement value as of December 31, 1951. Bell, *op. cit.*, p. 33.

[141] During the initial period of accumulation, only 50% of net capital losses were to be deducted from the reserve. This was amended to the rule in the text in 1954. During the accumulation period limited additions to the reserve above the mandatory figure could be made. After passage of the Life Insurance Company Income Tax Act of 1959, taxes incurred on net long-term capital gains were to be deducted from capital gains in computing the mandatory reserve addition.

qualified preferred stocks on an "adjusted value" (one-fifth rule) basis, the NAIC also increased the required minimum reserve balance by 7% of the statement value of preferred stocks carried at "adjusted value." Thus for companies with valuation reserves only slightly above the previously defined minimum reserve this meant significant immediate additions to the reserve with its accompanying impact on policy holder dividends.[142]

Problems Created by the Valuation System

A thorough analysis of the NAIC valuation system has recently been completed by a research team operating under a grant made by the Life Insurance Association of America to the University of Wisconsin.[143] They reported finding it impossible to appraise the success of the valuation rules in terms of purposes and goals set forth by the NAIC because a thorough search ". . . failed to yield comprehensive official statements as to purpose, function, and goals." [144] Nor did the history of the development of the regulations or an examination of the current rules reveal qualities of consistency and stability which would permit valid inferences about a set of objectives. Therefore the appraisal undertaken by the Wisconsin task force was conducted against a set of desirable criteria established by the research team itself. They held that a valuation system should be clear, certain, workable, equitable among companies and generations of policyholders, and above all should promote, not interfere with, solvency.[145]

Simplicity, clarity, certainty, and stability have not been obvious virtues of the NAIC valuation regulations. As we have seen, the rules prevailing in recent years include many different methods for valuing securities depending upon the type of security in question and the ability of its issues to pass a battery of financial

---

[142] Evidence of industry concern over this portion of the minimum reserve rule can be found in LIAA, *Record of Life Insurance Investments*, 1957, pp. 19–21, and in Travis, "Life Insurance Company Investments in Preferred Stocks," pp. 25–30. Mr. Travis had been chairman of the ALC-LIAA Joint Committee on the Valuation of Assets.

[143] Published as Fraine, *Valuation of Securities Holdings of Life Insurance Companies*.

[144] *Ibid.*, p. 128.

[145] These criteria are set forth and discussed in *ibid.*, Chapter 5.

tests.[146] Regulations governing the securities reserve are also quite complex, uncertain, and in addition have raised many questions regarding the reserve's sufficiency and equity.

Our brief review of the history of asset valuation rules provided examples of the system's uncertainty and unworkability. In particular, these deficiencies were dramatized by continual changes in the commissioners' valuation *Instructions*, and their frequent necessity to abandon the official rules and adopt expedient substitutes.[147] Moreover, until the explicit adoption of classification standards in 1953, decisions on the eligibility of privately placed securities for valuation at amortized cost were made by an NAIC subcommittee whose criteria were not made known to life companies. This lack of explicit knowledge of the valuation rules, together with the frequently demonstrated unworkability of the system, must have hindered the formulation of investment and dividend policy and have directed portfolio choices away from those assets whose current or future statement values were most in doubt.[148] While this situation was somewhat improved by the 1953 and subsequent NAIC resolutions, many unresolved doubts regarding the workability, stability, and equity of the current system remain.

Promotion of solvency would seem an obvious objective of a valuation system. A good case, however, can be made that the

---

[146] The Fraine report counts at least ten different methods. *Ibid.*, pp. 16–17.

[147] The need to adopt temporary measures did not cease after World War II. For an example produced by the valuation reserve rules, see the discussion below.

[148] The uncertainty created by the proven unworkability of the valuation rules and the erratic nature of the changes made by the NAIC over time in the basic regulations was underscored by a prominent life insurance company official in the early 1950s. See Sherwin C. Badger, "The Valuation of Assets." The prevailing concern over and dissatisfaction with the valuation system during the late 1940s and early 1950s was frequently expressed. In addition to Badger, critical appraisal appears in the public testimony of life insurance company officers (see the testimony of Clarke, Josephs, Whipple, and Bryan before the Joint Committee on the Economic Report, *Hearings*, 1949). Also, see Bell, "Asset Reserves of Life Insurance Companies"; Fraine, "The Valuation of Security Holdings of Life Insurance Companies"; McDiarmid, *Life Insurance Investments in the United States and Canada*, Chapter 12; and the annual *Proceedings* of both the Life Insurance Association of America and the American Life Convention during this period.

NAIC regulations, together with statutory surplus limitations, have had the effect of reducing the real solvency of life insurance companies.[149] This result derives from over-attention to fluctuations in market price quotations, inappropriate for an industry with stable, predictable, long-term liabilities, and establishment of an insufficient and unusable reserve which fails to preserve companies' limited surplus for unpredictable needs. We can briefly highlight the specific weaknesses inherent in the prevailing NAIC rules.

The primary problem with respect to statement value rules is simply that the movement toward more stabilized values proved only partially successful. Common stocks remain valued on life company books at December 31 market quotations. Until 1957 publicly traded preferred stocks were also valued at year-end market. Since 1957, preferred issues meeting earnings and dividend requirements have been allotted partial value stabilization under the one-fifth rule. In recent years nearly all bonds in life insurance company portfolios that are not in default have been eligible for statement reporting at amortized cost. However, it is conceivable that a significant number of corporate bond issues could fall out of the amortized cost category under prevailing rules in a severe economic recession.

It seems clear that, measured by ultimate workout values, the prevailing rules for valuing nonamortizable bonds, preferred stocks, and common stocks lead to overvaluation in some periods and undervaluation in others. Overvaluation is undesirable since, when combined with surplus and reserve limitations, it can force companies to pay out dividends to policyholders in excess of their payments over the true net cost of insurance. Undervaluation means large statement losses, especially following statement overvaluation, which are chargeable against the loss reserve or surplus, and may reduce current policy dividends and increase the risk of insolvency. Firms in the insurance business are

---

[149] Curiously enough, it would be difficult to make a case that sound asset valuation procedures are much of a protection for policyholders against failure of life companies. Historically, failures seem to have resulted most often from management improprieties, dishonesty, or incompetence; these are not weaknesses preventable by exercising close control over the statement value of a company's assets. See Fraine, pp. 20–21, and Walter, *The Investment Process*, pp. 46–49.

apparently unique in being required to write up above cost investments held for the long term. Indeed, cost valuation seems to prevail in most other fields even for secondary cash assets.[150]

It is sometimes argued that write-ups to market value — particularly of common stock holdings — are necessary to preserve equity among the generations of policyholders. Waiting for gains to be realized is not feasible because life companies tend not to be traders, so that the gains are never realized or are realized only after a very long time. The evidence with respect to life company activity in their limited common stock portfolios, however, shows that they do trade enough to completely turn over a portfolio in 20 years.[151] In addition, even without trading sustainable market value increases are realized to some extent in dividend receipts.[152] Furthermore, as indicated above, valuation on a market price basis risks distorting the time pattern of payments of dividends to policyholders and thereby creates temporal inequities.

None of this evidence suggests that sound common stock valuation procedures would ignore market price changes. It simply means that the choice lies between stabilization through a valuation formula which smooths market price fluctuations or through crediting valuation gains and debiting valuation losses to an asset reserve. It does seem clear that the common stock reserve created under current NAIC rules is inadequate if stocks are to be valued at year-end market price. Since an adequate reserve would be quite large, the most rational solution would seem to be a combination of a market price smoothing formula and a valuation reserve consistent with the valuation rule.[153]

Actually, the commissioners learned very quickly after the adoption of the security reserve that the combination of rigid limitations on the loss reserve (and surplus) and required valuation of common stocks at market price can easily create problems.

[150] Fraine, p. 26.

[151] This was true for the 20 years, 1929–1949, for the average company among 18 companies whose experience is reported annually by the ALC-LIAA. See Fraine, p. 153.

[152] Data for the 18 life companies from 1929 to 1958 showed an increase in dividend receipts at least as great as the rise in market value of their common stock holdings; Fraine, p. 107. For stocks as a whole, the long-term growth in dividends has been about the same as that of market prices, although in the short run, of course, dividends lag somewhat.

[153] See Fraine's discussion, pp. 151–155.

Substantial appreciation of the modest common stock holdings of some life companies during 1954 resulted in their reaching the maximum securities reserve permissible while approaching the statutory surplus ceiling.[154] Rather than permit further market gains to force increased dividend payments to policyholders, the NAIC granted an additional allowance of 10% of the statement value of common stocks to the securities reserve for 1955. In 1956 the excess allowance over the maximum reserve (as established by the 1953 resolution) was limited to the lesser of the sum of net capital gains on common stock during 1955 and 1956 or 10 times the mandatory annual reserve increment of 1% of the value of common stocks held.[155]

We have alluded above to the questionable sufficiency, usability, and equity features of the securities reserve system devised by the NAIC. The soundness of the reserve has to be evaluated, of course, in the context of the prevailing securities valuation criteria. The specific criticisms of the reserve system made in the Fraine report focus on the definitions of the maximum and minimum reserve balances permitted and the classification of securities for purposes of assigning required reserve balances and accumulation rates.

Since the sufficiency of an asset reserve is dependent upon its usability, we begin with a comment on NAIC rules affecting the ability of life companies, in fact, to use the reserve to absorb valuation losses. The difficulty is with the phrasing of the minimum reserve balance rule. As we have seen, the minimum reserve was originally defined as the sum of 20% of the statement value of bonds eligible for amortization under Test No. 2 (Class 2 bonds) and 0.05% of the statement value of bonds passing Test No. 1, or otherwise deemed equivalent to Test No. 1 bonds. Another 0.05% of the amortized cost value of Test No. 1 bonds is added to the minimum balance each succeeding year. Presumably after 20 years (1970) the minimum balance will be simply 20 times the annual credits to the reserve. As a result of the 1957 action to partially stabilize statement values of preferred stocks, the definition of the minimum reserve balance was expanded to include a

---

[154] See ALC-LIAA, Joint Committee on the Valuation of Assets, *Report*, 1954, p. 111; and the LIAA *Record of Life Insurance Investment*, 1955, p. 67.
[155] LIAA *Record of Life Insurance Investments*, 1956, p. 86.

third item: 10% of the statement value of preferred stocks carried at "adjusted value." [156]

The stated maximum permissible securities reserve balance was originally 1% of the stated value of all Test No. 1 bonds plus 20% of all other securities. As we have noted, an additional allowance to the maximum reserve was permitted in 1955 because of the appreciation in common stock portfolios. This was made permanent so the common stock component of the maximum reserve balance in the 1961 rules could amount to 30 times the annual reserve credit (1% of statement value) required for common stocks. The 1956 rule limiting the additional 10% to valuation gains in common stocks remained effective, however.

These definitions mean that, once the ultimate reserve goal is obtained (depending on a company's portfolio mix), the gap between the maximum and minimum reserve balance is likely to be quite small and can be nonexistent. During the reserve accumulation period, modest additions in excess of the minimum required rate are possible. The effect of wording the minimum balance in the same terms as the maximum is that valuation losses typically force companies to make additional credits to the reserve, offsetting a significant part of the debiting of the valuation losses against the reserve. It is not difficult to construct plausible circumstances in which only a negligible portion of a valuation loss can be charged against the reserve accumulated for that purpose.[157] The problem occurs both with valuation losses on bonds and on preferred stocks. The unusability of the reserve means, of course, that the impact of losses is felt on current earnings and surplus. In these cases the net effect of the valuation reserve system is to generate, ". . . a double impact on income and surplus; first when reservation is made; and secondly, when the loss is incurred." [158]

---

[156] The 10% is the 1961 rule. It had been introduced at 7% in 1957. Actually, according to the 1961 rule, it is the lesser of this 10% item and the sum of 7% of the December 31, 1957 statement value of adjusted value preferreds plus 1% of the statement value of qualified preferred issues in each subsequent year plus 1% of the net increase in statement value of qualified preferreds for each subsequent year over the December 31, 1957, value. See the NAIC *Instructions*.

[157] For some examples, see Fraine, pp. 133–135 and 146–147.

[158] *Ibid.*, p. 131. Since this was written the NAIC has modified the reserve system so as to unfreeze the reserve. See the NAIC *Instructions*, 1965.

It is difficult to say much about the adequacy of a reserve formula if the reserve cannot, in fact, be used in many circumstances to absorb more than a negligible portion of valuation losses. For this reason the Fraine monograph discusses the securities reserve sufficiency under the assumption that the minimum reserve balance requirements will be modified to permit the reserve to fulfill its function. We can briefly summarize Fraine's conclusions with regard to the reserve's adequacy.

From the past record of losses on investment grade corporate bonds, Fraine judges that both the annual formula credits rate and the ultimate maximum reserve balance are insufficient to average out and absorb predictable valuation losses.[159] Specifically with respect to the accumulation rate of 0.05% of the statement value of Class 1 bonds, Fraine concludes that ". . . the present formula rate is probably equal to no more than a quarter to a half of reasonably expectable future average annual bond losses." [p. 139] The reserve balance of 1% of statement value of these minimum reserve bonds is judged as ". . . probably only a fourth to a half as much as might easily be required in future depressions." [p. 140] The study further is critical of the lumping together of bonds varying widely in quality in the same reserve class. In these circumstances it becomes a practical impossibility to have both an adequate and equitable reserve.[160]

This latter criticism also applies to the single reserve accumulation rate for preferred stocks. Even though preferred issues, which qualify for "adjusted value" reporting, may have earnings averages greater than bonds in the minimum reserve category, all preferreds are Class 2 securities in determining the required reservation rate. Since both real losses and losses generated by the valuation system differ significantly by the quality grade of preferred issues, a single rate cannot be both adequate and equitable among companies with portfolios of differing quality.[161]

As observed above, the requirement that the statement value of preferreds be linked to market price quotations creates a need for a larger loss reserve to absorb predictable losses on preferreds even though the record of undefaulted preferreds has been as good or better than medium grade bonds, i.e. no larger reserve is required

[159] *Ibid.*, pp. 137–140.
[160] *Ibid.*, p. 141.   [161] *Ibid.*, p. 150.

to cover real losses, only system-generated statement value losses.[162]
With regard to the reserve balance, there is a gap between the
preferred stock component in the minimum reserve required and
that in the maximum permitted, the minimum component being
10% of statement value and the maximum 20%. Given the
performance record of preferred issues (see the evidence in Fraine,
Chapter 3), the minimum reserve requirement seems higher than
necessary to cover real losses. At the same time the maximum
limit may well be inadequate to absorb losses generated from
fluctuations in statement values. The reserve problem is a system-
generated problem. It results from market valuation rules for
securities with no maturity dates, and therefore a high variance
of price quotations associated with fluctuations in interest rates.
Fraine suggests that, if the statement value of preferreds was
stabilized, a reserve accumulation rate of 0.5% per year would
be more than adequate.[163]

The maximum permissible common stock component of the
securities reserve is set at 30 times the annual formula credit for
common stock. The Fraine study finds this component inadequate for valuation losses which are likely to occur given a year-
end market value system.[164] It would take a very large reserve
to average out losses on a market value system. This is what
makes a market price smoothing formula essential for common
stock valuation. Fraine predicts that, in the absence of some
such stabilizing improvements, the commissioners will very likely
again find it necessary to adopt temporary substitute rules for
year-end market valuation.[165]

A final odd consequence of the securities reserve accumulation
rate should be noted. It will be recalled that the annual formula
credit for any security is defined as a percentage of the statement
value of the security. For nonamortizable securities this means
that the reserve credit is a function of market value. If the
financial prospects of the issues of such a security improve, the
market quotations on the security are likely to rise. Consequently

[162] *Ibid.*, p. 149.
[163] *Ibid.*, p. 150. This is the rate Roger F. Murray suggested for the
preferred stock component of the reserve for savings banks. Murray's study
is reproduced as Appendix B of Fraine's book.
[164] *Ibid.*, p. 155.
[165] *Ibid.*

the securities reserve will have to receive a larger credit. Thus the rules require that as a nonamortizable security becomes less risky, the loss reserve rate on it becomes higher. Conversely, when a security deteriorates and its market price declines, a lesser reserve credit is required to be accumulated.[166]

In this section we have been highlighting some of the problems created by the specific rendering of the NAIC securities valuation and valuation reserve regulations. In addition to their security portfolio, most life insurance companies hold significant amounts of other assets, particularly various types of mortgage loans. In contrast to the detailed valuation rules which have been set down for securities during most of this century, very little attention has been directed toward the valuation of mortgage loans. Since the Armstrong Committee *Report*, all mortgage loans not in default have been accepted in life companies' annual statements at amortized cost. At times, particularly during the 1930s, many mortgage loans have been written down to the appraised value of the property securing the loan or to some percentage of the appraised value. In some cases the establishment of a reserve, representing the spread between the loan principal and the appraised value of the property, was either required or permitted by the regulatory authorities. But these cases were handled *ad hoc* and no overall valuation standards or procedures for setting up valuation reserves have been formulated.[167]

The logic, however, of averaging out predictable losses in the portfolio over time through establishment of a valuation reserve seems as valid for mortgage loans as it is for securities. If unsuitable statement valuation rules or an inadequate loss reserve can produce an undesirable impact on earnings and surplus, then the failure to provide for any standardized valuation procedures for assets not in good standing or for a valuation reserve can generate similar problems. The retrospective capital loss rate on securities and on real estate and mortgage loans combined was not so very

---

[166] Excepting the case of a bond moving all the way from the nonamortizable category to the minimum reserve class, or a bond dropping from Class 1 status. This peculiarity could be corrected by basing the reserve credit on a cost basis, regardless of whether or not cost is acceptable as the statement value. See Fraine's discussion, p. 172.

[167] See Bell, *op. cit.*, p. 40.

different in the 1930s.[168] Thus the failure to include mortgage loans and real estate in the valuation reserve system constitutes another, possibly serious, failing of the prevailing NAIC valuation system.[169]

Impact of the Valuation System on Portfolio Policy

In outlining a set of desirable criteria for a securities valuation system, the Fraine report observes that valuation requirements, ". . . should be responsive to variation in investment policies among companies, rather than the reverse." [170] One of the consequences of a badly designed valuation system is that life companies will have to formulate portfolio policy with the "system risks," as well as "real risks" in mind. As we have seen, there is abundant evidence of serious weaknesses in the asset valuation regulations governing life companies. Therefore this part of the external environment can be expected to have had an impact upon portfolio selections.

Life companies have had to contend with a set of valuation rules which are overdependent on market prices and based on unstable and uncertain criteria, combined with a mandatory reserve which is inequitable, insufficient, and unusable in some circumstances, and inconsistent in its treatment of various types of assets. A curious consequence of the ubiquitous problems created by this patchwork system is that almost no portfolio choices can escape the risks which it creates. As we have seen above, even a conservative, high quality corporate bond portfolio is not immune from valuation risks associated with the mandatory reserve accumulation rules. Nor are mortgage loan portfolios safe, even though all loans not in default are eligible for valuation on an amortized basis and mortgages are unencumbered by a mandatory reserve requirement. The lack of any reserve provision means

---

[168] See *ibid.*, pp. 41–42.

[169] Bell (pp. 42–43) notes Lintner's conclusion that the lack of a valuation reserve, out of which savings banks could absorb losses in their mortgage portfolios during the 1930s, led the banks to adopt undesirable investment practices in order to delay the recording of losses and thereby protect their surplus positions. Lintner, *Mutual Savings Banks in the Savings and Mortgage Markets.*

[170] Fraine, *op. cit.*, p. 115.

losses from loan defaults have to be absorbed out of current earnings or a surplus account limited by state statutes.

The primary effect of the valuation system, however, seems to be that by adding to portfolio risks it reinforces life company tastes for investment quality and safety. The failure of the system to be responsive to variations in portfolios tends to discourage a life company management from adopting an atypical portfolio policy, particularly one which is much more risky than the average. In terms of portfolio composition this means that the valuation procedures have tended to discourage investment in common and preferred stocks and lower quality debt issues.

Our summary of the interview responses of life company investment officers reported in the previous section indicated that the impact of the valuation rules on common stock investments was quite strong. Officers who expressed willingness to hold anywhere from 10% to 30% of their assets in common stocks if unencumbered by statutory and asset valuation restraints reported that they would not want to invest more than the amount of their surplus accounts (about 7% of assets typically) under the prevailing valuation rules regardless of the freedom otherwise granted them. The rules governing valuation of preferred stocks were modified in 1957 to allow for partial stabilization, but the reserve accumulation provisions are inconsistent with the valuation rules and an irritant to life companies. The problem created by requirements imposed on corporate bonds may have been largely resolved by the 1953 revision which included a statement of valuation criteria for bonds without agency quality ratings. It is true that since then most directly placed issues have been eligible for amortization. Our interview evidence indicates that as of the late 1950s, no more than 2% to 3% of privately placed bond holdings of life companies were ineligible for valuation on an amortized cost basis. At a lower general level of economic activity, however, a number of these issues might drop from this valuation class, bringing into play weaknesses inherent in the securities reserve system.

In sum, it appears that the state legislatures and insurance commissioners have created a set of external influences which have significantly restrained life companies from greater investment activity in corporate equity shares and lower quality debt issues.

Many companies have been moved, as a result of these restrictions, to emphasize investment quality and safety more than they otherwise would. More liberal investment statutes and a more liberal and rational valuation system would contribute to creating an atmosphere in which life companies could take more suitable risks and concentrate more completely upon portfolio yield.

Taxation of Life Insurance Companies

Life insurance companies have been subject to taxation at both the state and federal levels. State taxation has largely taken the form of premium taxes. With the exception of a few cases where states offer tax abatements to life companies investing specified amounts of funds within the state,[171] these taxes have had no impact on the investment behavior of life companies. However, the federal income tax law as applied to life insurance companies has exerted some influence upon portfolio selections, particularly since investment income has served as the tax base during most of the history of life insurance company income taxation. In this section we shall briefly review that history, examine the tax legislation applicable to life companies during the years since World War II, and assess the impact of federal income taxation upon life insurance company investment policy.

History of Federal Income Taxation of Life Insurance Companies

1913–1941

From the inception of the federal income tax in 1913 until 1921, life companies were taxed under the general corporate provisions. The taxable base included premiums as well as investment income. Capital gains were also taxed. In addition to the regular corporate deductions, life companies were granted two special deductions:

(1) sums, other than dividends, paid on policy and annuity contracts;
(2) legally required net additions to policy reserves.

---

[171] A 1958 study lists 10 states using this approach. In most of these cases the premium tax rate is varied according to the percentage of assets a life company has invested within the state. See Beard, *op. cit.*, pp. 11–15. It is doubtful whether these laws have more than a negligible impact on the geographic distribution of life insurance funds.

In addition, cash dividends paid to policyholders were eventually ruled a legitimate deduction, although dividends left with the company for application against future premiums were not allowed.[172]

Both the policy-dividends and reserve-additions deductions proved difficult to administer, however, and were the subject of "continual litigation." [173] In order to escape these difficulties, the Treasury recommended amending the relevant legislation so as to tax only the investment income of life insurance companies. This recommendation was carried out in the Revenue Act of 1921. Premium income, capital gains and losses, and underwriting gains and losses were excluded from the new tax formula. Deductions were permitted for expenses properly allocable to the investment operation and for investment income "required by law" to be added to policy reserves. The latter deduction was computed by applying an arbitrary interest rate to the *mean* of a company's policy reserves for the taxable year. Up to 1931 the assumed rate was 4% for all companies.[174]

The 1921 tax law was based on the proposition that the "only true basis of income of a life insurance company is its investment income." [175] This formula at least had the virtue of simplicity. However, the deduction for investment income necessary to maintain policy reserves, together with declining investment income during the 1930s, operated to reduce the life insurance industry's income tax payments to practically nothing in the latter half of the decade. This situation and the coming mobilization effort induced Treasury action to insure that the industry contributed its "fair share" to the federal revenues.

---

[172] U.S. House, Subcommittee on the Taxation of Life Insurance Companies, *A Preliminary Statement of the Facts and Issues,* November 1954, p. 18.

[173] See the testimony of a Treasury official, T. S. Adams, *Hearings* Before the Senate Finance Committee on H.R. 8245, 1921, p. 83. Dr. Adams asserted that because of these "special and highly unscientific deductions . . . the taxation of life insurance companies is one of the faultiest parts of the income tax act."

[174] House, Subcommittee, *A Preliminary Statement.* The rate used for this deduction was reduced to 3.75% in 1932 for life companies computing reserves with a rate less than 4%. Both the 4% and 3.75% rates were higher than those guaranteed in most policies.

[175] Testimony of Adams, *Hearings,* p. 83.

1942-1957

The Revenue Act of 1942 contained a new procedure for taxing life companies. This formula, which was a joint product of extensive negotiation between the Treasury and a joint Life Insurance Association of America-American Life Convention industry committee, preserved the investment income approach but modified the calculation of the reserve interest allowance. Under this plan the Treasury computed for each taxable year, on the basis of the previous year's experience, the ratio of the required reserve allowance to net investment income.[176] This was calculated on the basis of aggregate industry experience,[177] and the ratio so derived was applied to each company's net investment income to determine the amount of that income which was deductible. Thus, for example, as calculated on 1941 industry operating experience, this "Secretary's Ratio" was .93, which meant that the taxable base for each company consisted of 7% of its investment income. To this tax base the regular corporate rates were applied. Thus, contrary to the previous law, each company paid tax regardless of its individual experience so long as the industry as a whole had investment earnings in excess of the (assumed) reserve allowance, and no company paid the tax if aggregate earnings fell short of required additions to reserves.

As constructed, the formula made tax collections highly sensitive to changes in the industry's net earnings rate. Since interest rates remained low, the net earnings rate on life company assets continued to decline until by 1947 the Secretary's Ratio exceeded 100% and as a consequence companies paid no tax on their life business. Once again the Treasury was stimulated to search for a more suitable plan for taxation of life companies. During the next decade, numerous meetings were held between the Treasury and industry groups, and the Subcommittee on Internal Revenue Taxation of the House Ways and Means Committee annually conducted hearings designed to produce a permanent tax formula.

---

[176] Net of allowable investment expenses. Provision for deduction of tax-free interest and dividends was also made.

[177] The computation assumes an arbitrary minimum guaranteed interest return on all policy liabilities.

Satisfactory solutions to this problem proved elusive because of the difficulty of meaningfully defining an insurer's net income over any period less than a span of several decades. In addition, complications arose in attempting to avoid inequities between tax treatment of new and old, small and large, mutual and stock companies, and companies selling different kinds of products. These problems were less serious in the early days of income taxation, partly because companies were more homogeneous then, but particularly because tax rates were so low that inequities inherent in the tax provisions were of little consequence. Because these difficulties proved so intractable, a permanent formula was not enacted until 1959. In the meantime companies were taxed on the basis of annual stopgap measures.

The first such measure, adopted in 1950, eliminated the arbitrary guaranteed interest assumption in the calculation of the reserve allowance under the 1942 law and substituted an actual average reserve requirement still determined on an industrywide basis. This simply had the effect of reducing the percentage of investment income deductible as a reserve allowance[178] and thereby increased the tax base. This procedure was applied retroactively to 1949 as well as to 1950 income. It yielded the Treasury about $42 million on 1949 income and $72 million in 1950.[179]

The Revenue Act of 1951 adopted a new approach, eliminating the calculation of the Secretary's Ratio and simply taxing all net investment income at the flat rate of 6.5%.[180] The rate was selected so as to yield revenue approximately equivalent to what would have been forthcoming under the 1950 plan. Intended as a one-year stopgap measure to apply only to the taxable year 1951, the law nonetheless was extended one year at a time through 1954 as Congress failed to enact a permanent plan.

On March 13, 1956, Congress enacted the Mills Bill into law (Public Law 429, 84th Congress) which maintained the approach of the 1951 Act but increased the rates for most companies. In addition, there was some tightening of the definition of an insurer's

---

[178] For example, the Secretary's Ratio of 100.99% applicable to the 1949 taxable year under the 1942 Act was reduced to 93.55% by the 1950 amendment.

[179] ALC *General Proceedings*, 1957, "Report of the Actuary," p. 131.

[180] Actually 3.25% on the first $200,000 of investment income and 6.5% on income in excess of $200,000.

investment income.[181]   The new rate was 7.8% of taxable income
(3.75% on the first $1 million).   This rate was the equivalent
of taxation at the regular corporate rate on investment income
remaining after an 85% deduction for the reserve allowance.   This
figure corresponded approximately to the Secretary's Ratio as
computed under the 1942 law on the basis of 1954 data.   Although
again this stopgap measure was designed to apply only to 1955
income, failure to agree on a permanent solution resulted in extension of the Mills formula to the 1956 and 1957 taxable years.
Throughout this period the 1942 law applying to taxation of life
companies was never repealed so that, although in fact companies
were taxed under special stopgap measures from 1948 to 1957,
failure of the Congress to enact specific measures in any of these
years would have meant automatic reversion to the 1942 formula
for the taxable year in question.   During most of this period
application of the 1942 tax law would have resulted in higher tax
liabilities.   Generally the Congress succeeded in achieving the
maximum dramatic effect by postponing until a matter of hours
before the tax-filing deadline the passage of some stopgap
amendment.

1958–

The search for permanent federal income tax legislation applicable to life companies finally ended in March 1959 with the passage of the Life Insurance Company Tax Act of 1959.   With the
enactment of this legislation, the basis of life insurance company
taxation reverted to the pre-1921 "total income" approach.   The
1959 law, first applied to 1958 income, provides for a levy on
underwriting gains as well as on investment income.   Also, in
contrast to the preceding tax laws, life companies now incur tax
liabilities based largely on their individual experience rather than
the overall industry performance.

Briefly, the 1959 Act provides for a three-phase tax.[182]   In

---

[181] Net income was now to include royalties, commitment fees, mortgage
prepayment penalties, and income from noninsurance business.   Further, the
85% dividend deductions granted most taxpayers were denied life companies
in the 1956 act.

[182] This summary of the 1959 Act benefits from work done for a senior honors
thesis by a student of the author.   The student, Stephen M. Kaufman, submitted his thesis entitled, "The Life Insurance Company Income Tax Act

Phase I, taxable investment income is computed in a manner similar to previous legislation except that the deduction for required additions to policy reserves is determined more on the basis of each company's record, and short-term capital gains are included as part of gross investment income. The effective tax rate on investment income differs widely among companies, but for most companies is higher than under earlier acts. Also the average and marginal rates are no longer identical, the tax structure being progressive for most companies.

Life companies are taxed on 50% of the excess of their mortality and "loading" gains over taxable investment income in Phase II of the 1959 Act. If underwriting gain is less than taxable investment income, the company's liability is based only on investment income.

Phase III of the formula is applicable only to stock companies. The purpose of this phase is to tax the remaining 50% of underwriting gain at the time it is distributed to stockholders.

Finally the Act provides for a 25% tax on long-term capital gains net of short-term capital losses. Net capital losses are not deductible but there is a five-year carryover provision.

Federal Income Tax Rates Applicable to Life Insurance Companies Since 1945

Summarizing the historical survey, we have seen that from the Revenue Act of 1921 to the Life Insurance Company Tax Act of 1959, life insurance companies were taxed only on their investment income. Prior to the introduction of the 1951 stopgap legislation, the tax code called for ordinary corporate rates to be applied to "free" investment income. Free investment income was calculated as gross investment income less allowable expenses and less a large deduction intended to allow for a life company's obligation to credit investment returns to insurance policy reserves and other obligations to pay or credit interest to policyholders. Under the temporary codes applying to taxable years 1951–1957, the compu-

---

of 1959," to Harvard University in 1962. A condensed version of this work has subsequently been published; see Kaufman, "The Life Insurance Company Income Tax Act of 1959," *National Tax Journal*. Also see Nash, *Federal Taxation of Life Insurance Companies*.

tation of this deduction was dispensed with and a flat rate was applied to total investment income.[183]

Because the reserve additions deduction was computed on the basis of industry data, all life companies were taxed at essentially the same rates on their investment income during the period 1946–1957. Under the Revenue Act of 1942 life companies incurred a federal income tax amounting to less than 2% of investment income in 1946 and, as we have seen, paid no tax at all on earnings for the taxable years 1947 and 1948. The tax rates produced by the 1950 stopgap formula seem to have been about 2.5% of net investment income in 1949 and nearly 4% in 1950.[184] The Revenue Act of 1951, which was in force for four years (1951–1954), provided for a flat rate on investment income of 6.5% (3.25% on the first $200,000). Enactment of the Mills Bill in 1956 raised the rate to 7.8% (3.75% on the first $1 million) and enlarged somewhat the definition of investment income.

Passage of the 1959 Tax Act clearly resulted in a significant increase in the federal income tax burden carried by life insurance companies. Unfortunately, however, because of the complexity of the 1959 Act and because calculation of the tax base is now based on each individual company's experience, it is not possible to state simply the tax rates prevailing on investment income since 1957. Not all of the increased tax liability is incurred on portfolio earnings. Indeed, a primary purpose of the long search for a permanent insurance company tax code was to design a law that would include underwriting income in the tax base.[185]

Since the Act was designed to capture income earned on "non-

---

[183] See the applicable definition of investment income above. Tax-exempt interest income from obligations issued by state and local governments was excluded from taxable income. The 85% intercorporate dividend deduction was allowed under the 1942 Act but denied by the stopgap codes of the 1950s.

[184] Tax rates approximate. Estimated from data on net investment income and federal income taxes paid by life companies belonging to the American Life Convention or Life Insurance Association of America. ALC *Proceedings*, 1957, p. 131.

[185] See the statement of Fred C. Scribner, Jr., Undersecretary of the Treasury, in U.S. House, Subcommittee on Internal Revenue Taxation, *Hearings-1958*. The rapid growth of nonreserve life insurance and of specialty companies in this field during the postwar years made inclusion of underwriting profit in the tax base imperative. See Kaufman, *op. cit.*, Part I, p. 344.

reserve" and specialty life insurance policies, the impact of higher tax rates generally impinged more on stock than on mutual companies. It was estimated that the tax burden on mutual companies would be raised about 45% as a consequence of the 1959 legislation, while the tax liability of stock companies would be increased about 90% on the average over what it would have been under the preceding law.[186] Nearly all the taxes incurred on underwriting gains would be paid by stock companies; mutuals, for the most part, would continue to be taxable only on investment income.

The tax rate applicable to investment income can vary from zero to nearly the full corporate rate. In general, the level of the rate varies with the ratio of interest required to maintain policy reserves to total interest earned.[187] One estimate of the tax base suggests that in the aggregate about 25% of investment income is taxed under the 1959 law.[188] Applying the 52% corporate rate in existence prior to the 1964 general federal income tax revision, this means that the 1959 Tax Act raised the average tax rate on life companies' investment income from 7.8% to 13%. Moreover, in its operation the tax structure in the 1959 Act is progressive. According to an estimate by Matz, an average company paying a 13% average rate might expect to be paying a marginal rate of about 26%.[189]

Estimates of tax rates applicable to new investments for a number of life companies during 1960 have been reported by Walter.[190] These estimates for new corporate bond and mortgage loan acquisitions varied from 11% to 23% for six mutual companies; the rate for one of two stock companies was reported at 39%, the other at 12%. Not only do the rates vary widely among com-

---

[186] See Guertin, "Life Insurance Company Income Tax Act of 1959," p. 52.

[187] See Kaufman, *op. cit.*, Part II, pp. 49–50.

[188] Ernst and Ernst, *Guide to the Life Insurance Income Tax Act of 1959*, Cleveland, 1960, pp. 10–13.

[189] Matz, *Transactions*, p. 159.

[190] Walter, *op. cit.*, Table VIII-5, p. 285. Walter also reproduces a chart comparing the before-tax yield on various types of securities with the yield net of federal income taxes obtained from each, based on the relevant data for one large company. This comparison indicates that the company must obtain 6.3% on a newly acquired taxable bond in order to earn 5% net of the federal income tax, implying an incremental rate of nearly 21% on *gross* investment income for this company.

panies, but the effective rates themselves are sensitive to variations in a given company's experience from year to year. Thus the typical rates reported are quite tenuous and it is difficult to make valid generalizations about the quantitative impact of the 1959 Act.

Uncertainty and the Tax Environment, 1946–1958

Although reliable estimates of tax rates applicable to life company portfolio selections are much more difficult to make after passage of the 1959 Act, the relevant tax burden was not as simply measured during the preceding years as the above summary of rates suggests. The 1946–1958 period was clouded by the knowledge that the tax rates applied to each year's investment income were temporary. Indeed, throughout most of this period life companies did not know during any taxable year what tax legislation applied to their current year's activities. Generally this decision was not made by Congress until March of the following year. Portfolio choices, therefore, had to be made in an atmosphere of exceptional uncertainty about what tax rates would apply to investments acquired. In reacting to this situation, the president of one life company complained of the ". . . frustrating difficulties of managing our individual life insurance companies amid the uncertainties and apprehensions which result from the inability to know from day to day what our tax liabilities are. . . . These uncertainties affect nearly all phases of our planning." [191]

Amid the uncertainties, however, it was quite clear that the permanent tax formula, when achieved, would impose higher tax rates on life companies. This was evident from the tenor and substance of the annual Congressional hearings dealing with life insurance company taxation, and from the fact that Congress never repealed the 1942 Revenue Act. Life companies would have been taxed under the 1942 law any year Congress failed to pass substitute legislation. The Act also proved useful as a guide to the level of taxation life companies in the aggregate might expect to pay under a permanent tax formula. Thus the 1942 law remained relevant for life company decisions beyond 1948, the last year, it turned out, that it actually was applied.

---

[191] U.S. Senate, Committee on Finance, *Hearings*, testimony of Deane C. Davis, President of National Life Insurance Company (Vermont), pp. 25–48.

In order to gauge the expectations the life insurance industry might have reasonably held during the 1950s about forthcoming tax rates, we shall briefly review the operation of the 1942 Act and the tax rates its application would have produced during the 1950s. As we have seen, the 1942 law continued in the investment income tradition of life insurance company taxation. Neither underwriting profits nor capital gains were included in the tax base. Under the 1942 Act taxable income for life companies consisted of the excess of investment income, net of expenses allocable to the investment operation, over required additions to reserves for policies or other liabilities.

As always, the primary difficulty in formulating the tax base involved determination of "required additions to reserves, etc." For their own accounting purposes life companies have been free, within broad limits set by state laws, to establish the value of their liabilities and so to allocate retained income among "reserves," "capital," or "surplus" in accordance with the assumptions they make about operating expenses, mortality losses, and rate of return on invested assets. For tax purposes, however, equity considerations have led to the imposition of uniform rules for calculating reserve additions.

The 1921 Act arbitrarily assumed a uniform rate of return for all life companies which was applied to the *mean* of each company's reserves for the taxable year, and the resulting product was deducted from net investment income to determine the tax base. The 1942 Act substituted the industry's *mean* reserves for the individual insurer's. Essentially the 1942 formula provides that this aggregate mean reserves figure is multiplied by an assumed reserves earnings rate and the resulting product is deducted from net investment income to yield the tax base.[192] The actual summary formula for computation of the tax base is slightly more complex due to the manner in which the 1942 Act treats tax-

---

[192] This summation of the reserve allowance calculation is oversimplified in several respects. For details of the computation, see Huston, "Actuarial Developments of 1942." The calculation of the reserve deduction continued to vex framers of a new life company tax code during the 1950s. The resolution of this problem in the 1959 Act does revert to each company's individual experience and method of computation but there is also an adjustment built into the calculation designed to equalize variations among company reserve allowance procedures. See Kaufman, *op. cit.*, Part I, pp. 346–347.

exempt forms of investment income. To avoid a double deduction for tax-exempt income the Act recognizes that this income is available for addition to policy reserves, and therefore in computing the industry reserve credit, prorates tax-exempt interest and dividend receipts to (a) policy reserves and (b) surplus in proportion to the allocation of total investment income to these accounts. Therefore the resulting taxable income base for any company under the 1942 Act was:

$$TIB = (i - e)(1 - R/I)^{193} \text{ where,}$$

TIB = Taxable Income Base for the company
i = the company's investment income net of allowable expenses
e = the portion of the company's investment income which is tax-exempt
R = the industry reserve credit
I = the industry net investment income
R/I = the Secretary's Ratio.

To this base the regular corporate tax rate is applied. This produces a flat tax rate on investment income identical for all companies.[194] Although each company pays a flat rate independent of its portfolio return, the rate applied is quite sensitive to changes in aggregate investment income for the industry. The formula in effect taxes the margin between the earned rate of return and the rate of return required to maintain policy reserves. An increase in industry earnings, given the reserve credit require-

---

[193] The logic of this can be seen more clearly if the equation is written as if all variables were computed from the individual company's experience. Then the taxable income base is $TIB = i - e - r(1 - e/i)$, where r is the individual company's reserve credit. Since tax-exempt income is available for assignment to reserves, the r deduction is reduced by the proportion of tax-exempt to total investment income. Rewriting the equation $TIB = (i - e)(1 - r/i)$. Now the 1942 Act computes the reserve credit/investment income ratio on the basis of industry experience. Thus, when R/I is substituted for r/i, we have the formula in the text.

[194] For example, the Secretary's Ratio applied to the 1942 tax year was .93, computed from industry data for the previous year (1941). Since the normal tax plus surtax rate for 1942 was .40, the (approximate) tax liability of life companies was $.40(i - e)(1 - .93)$, or a flat rate on taxable net investment income of 2.8% for all companies. Life companies were essentially unaffected by the excess profits tax because of their low earnings rate.

ment, is taxed at an implicit marginal rate equal to the full corporate rate. Actual changes in the required rate of return have a lesser impact on the effective tax rate because the reserve allowance contains items other than credits to policy reserves and because changes in required rates receive only a fractional weight in the computation of the assumed industrywide rate.[195] As a result of this sensitivity of the industry's tax liability to changing experience, federal income taxes incurred by life companies fell to zero a few years after passage of the 1942 Act and then would have increased substantially during the 1950s had the Act been in force. It was possible for life companies to estimate during the 1950s what their tax liability would be if the 1942 law were in effect. The variations in the tax base produced by changes in the earnings rate and the assumed required rate of return are shown in Table II-3. The taxable income base, as computed under the 1942 Act, fell from 7% of net investment income in 1942 to zero by 1947 and rose steadily after 1949.

The Secretary's Ratio, as computed under the revised procedure provided for in the 1950 stopgap law, is also displayed in Table II-3. Each piece of tax legislation during the 1950s was related to the tax liability as computed under the 1942 Act. The 1950 formula, applied to taxable years 1949 and 1950, used a lower (more realistic) assumed required rate of return. This arbitrary rate was chosen so that the Secretary's Ratio for 1949 was about the same as the original Secretary's Ratio computed under the 1942 law and actually applied to determine 1942 tax liabilities. The Revenue Act of 1951 established a flat rate of 6.5% which produced about the same tax liability for 1951 as application of the 1950 formula would have done. The 6.5% rate was in force for four taxable years. But by 1954 it produced a smaller tax liability than the 1942 formula. The 1956 amendment raised the tax rate (second step) to 7.8% which is about the rate the 1942 formula would have produced in taxable year 1954. The 7.8% rate applied for three years, 1955–1957. We have seen that the 1959 Act provides for a tax base on portfolio return of about 25% of net investment income on the average. This is about the base that the 1942 formula would have produced for the industry if applied to 1958 experience. Thus the 1942 Act had a pervasive

[195] See Huston, *op. cit.*, for a detailed discussion.

influence throughout the 1950s since Congress and the Treasury apparently based their estimates of desired revenue production from the life insurance industry on computations of what reactivation of the 1942 formula would produce.

TABLE II-3. Factors Determining the Life Insurance Industry's Tax Base under 1942 and 1950 Tax Legislation

Year	Rate of Return on Invested Assets*	Rate of Return to Maintain Reserves†	Secretary's Ratio	
			1942 Law	1950 Law
1942	3.44%	3.24%	93.00%	93.00%
1943	3.33	3.21	91.98	91.40
1944	3.23	3.16	92.61	92.55
1945	3.11	3.09	95.39	92.83
1946	2.93	3.04	95.95	92.11
1947	2.88	3.00	100.66	94.36
1948	2.96	2.97	102.43	95.20
1949	3.06	2.95	100.99	93.55
1950	3.13	2.92	96.87	90.63
1951	3.18	2.90	94.03	87.88
1952	3.28	2.88	91.93	85.57
1953	3.36	2.86	88.07	81.71
1954	3.46	2.83	85.16	78.73
1955	3.51	2.82	82.38	76.00
1956	3.63	2.80	79.99	73.49
1957	3.74	n.a.	77.66	70.81

* Before federal income tax.

† Assumed rate calculated under 1942 formula. Excludes supplementary contracts, dividend accumulations, and cancellable accident and health policies.

SOURCE: ALC General Proceedings, "Report of the Actuary," 1957.

In sum, portfolio managers for life insurance companies had grounds for expecting that investment acquisitions during the 1950s would be taxed over at least a portion of their lives at rates higher than those prevailing at the time funds were committed. Furthermore, from projections of the industry's portfolio earnings rate and the rate required to maintain policy reserves, it was possible to make a reasonable guess about the extent of the increase in at least the average rate of the investment income tax. In general such expectations would have made tax-exempt income seem somewhat more valuable than the current tax rates during the 1950s would indicate, and presumably would have made investment officers more cautious about certain types of investments (particularly net lease real estate investments) which are based upon life companies' relatively favorable tax position. We conclude this section with a summary evaluation of the effect of the federal income tax environment on life company portfolio choices since World War II.

Impact of Federal Income Taxation on Portfolio Policy

Federal income taxation can potentially impinge upon portfolio policies of institutional investors in several ways. The most important of these include:

(1) Trading policy.
(2) Tax-exemption of certain types of investment income.
(3) The relative tax position of financial intermediaries competing for savings of surplus sectors.
(4) The tax position of financial intermediaries relative to deficit sectors.

We shall briefly summarize the tax position of life insurance companies under these four headings and indicate the potential influence of the tax environment upon life company investment decisions.

TRADING

As is well known, taxpayer decisions to sell or exchange portfolio assets are often influenced in an important way by the federal income tax provisions covering capital gains and losses. Prior to 1959 life companies were not taxed on capital gains and were not permitted to offset capital losses against income. Therefore trading decisions involving realized gains or losses were unaffected by tax considerations. In particular, this was true for the major postwar adjustment which occupied life companies' portfolio decisions, the liquidation of Government securities.

Under the 1959 Act, short-term capital gains are included in the definition of investment income. Short-term gains may be offset with long-term capital losses. An ordinary capital gains tax is also imposed. Long-term gains, net of short-term losses, are taxed at the 25% rate.[196] Net losses can be carried over up to five years and used to offset gains within this period.

It does not seem likely that these changes in the tax legislation would have greatly affected life company trading policy. Some increased trading may result in an attempt to offset losses against gains. Most companies, however, have no reason to prefer portfolio return in the form of realized gains rather than in interest or dividends since the marginal rate on capital gains is, for the typical company, in the same neighborhood as the incremental rate on ordinary investment income. Realized gains are preferable only if losses exist to offset the gains. Since the disposal of low-yield bonds acquired during the 1930s and 1940s had been largely completed by 1959, there was no longer a consistent stream of losses emanating from this source. It is difficult to measure the impact of the imposition of capital gains taxation upon life company security sales because many factors affect trading decisions. However, no obvious changes are apparent in the sales data reported in Table II-4. Sales of other assets have always been negligible in amount and continued to be after enactment of the 1959 Act.

ATTRACTIVENESS OF TAX-EXEMPT INCOME

Some buyers of financial assets find certain types of assets particularly attractive on a relative yield comparison because the income received from these assets is wholly or partly exempt from taxation. During the postwar years obligations of state and local governments and common and preferred stocks have possessed this asset characteristic for most taxpayers.

Municipal bonds attract life companies essentially only on a yield basis. There seem to be no other portfolio objectives, political considerations, or internal organizational constraints which induce life companies to buy municipals.[197] However, since life company portfolio earnings were taxed at a relatively

[196] A 1962 amendment permits an alternative computation which takes into account losses in other phases of the tax formula. Thus, the effective incremental rate on long-term gains could be somewhat less than 25% in certain instances. See Kaufman's *Addendum, op. cit.*, Part II, p. 56.

[197] See Chapters VII and VIII for a discussion of the composition of investment choices.

TABLE II-4. Life Insurance Company Security Sales as a Proportion of Gross
Investible Funds: 1957–1964

(billions of dollars)

	(1)	(2)	(3)	(4)	(5)
	Security Sales*				
Year	Treasury Obligations	Other Securities	Total Investment Funds†	(1)/(3)	(2)/(3)
1957	$254.4	$ 420.4	$ 5,796.3	4.39%	7.25%
1958	375.8	502.4	6,663.1	5.64	7.54
1959	238.5	414.4	6,795.5	3.51	6.10
1960	119.8	441.2	6,310.5	1.90	6.99
1961	123.0	536.0	7,395.5	1.66	7.25
1962	220.4	439.4	8,221.9	2.68	5.34
1963	398.1	820.1	9,586.4	4.15	8.55
1964	151.0	1,031.1	10,183.3	1.48	10.13

* Excludes sales of short-term "temporary" investments.

† Net increase in ledger assets plus (minus) net decrease (increase) in liquid asset position plus (minus) net decrease (increase) in policy loans plus all other asset turnover.

Data are based on reports of 52 to 56 companies holding 61% to 62% of all U.S. life insurance company assets.

Source: Life Insurance Association of America.

low rate during the 1940s and 1950s, the tax-exemption feature of municipal bond income had little attraction for them.   Instead it led financial asset buyers in relatively high tax brackets (primarily commercial banks and high income individuals) to bid yields on most municipal debt issues below levels at which they attracted life company purchases.[198]   Indeed, the sharp increase in individual and corporate tax rates in the Revenue Act of 1942, together with the removal of the tax-exemption feature from Treasury issues after March 1, 1941, resulted in a bidding down of municipal bond yields well below market yields on comparable maturity Treasury obligations.   As a result, life companies sold a substantial portion of their state and local government security holdings and bought U.S. Governments.[199]

---

[198] See Robinson, *Postwar Market for State and Local Securities*, esp. Chapter 3.

[199] Life companies' holdings of U.S. state and local issues declined from $1,995 million in 1941 to $614 million in 1946.

During the late 1940s life companies paid very little in federal income taxes, as we have seen. From 1951–1954 their marginal tax rate on investment income was 6.5%; from 1955–1957 it was about 7.8%. Given prevailing market interest rates, this meant that the tax-exempt characteristic was worth about 15 to 35 basis points[200] during the period from 1951 to 1957. Since the market was dominated by buyers facing much higher incremental tax rates, life company acquisitions in this market were modest in amount and confined largely to selective buying in lower grade general obligation issues, revenue bonds, and taxable Canadian provincial and local government debt issues. The 1959 Tax Act, in increasing substantially the marginal tax on investment income for most life insurance companies, necessarily improved the after-tax yield position of municipals relative to taxable bonds from the perspective of life company portfolio managers. On the basis of market yields prevailing on Baa municipal bond issues in the early 1960s, the 1959 Act increased the tax-exempt advantage of municipals from about 30 basis points to around 100 basis points.[201] This order of increase does not allow for the influence of tax expectations in the years preceding 1959; recognition of anticipated higher rates would reduce the immediate impact of the 1959 Act by admitting a higher value to tax-exemption during the mid-1950s than is suggested in the above calculation.

Nonetheless the adoption of the 1959 Act must have had a significant impact on the value of tax-exempt interest to life companies. This result, however, is not reflected in increased life company activity in the municipal securities market since

---

[200] Disregarding expectations about future rates. See below.

[201] Taking the pre-1959 incremental tax rate as 7.8% and assuming the post-1959 marginal rate is typically about 25%, the yield advantage of municipals over fully taxed corporate bonds would seem to be 120 to 140 basis points depending upon the level of yields, i.e., a 4.00% municipal issue is equivalent to the after-tax yield of a 5.33% corporate bond. However, the 1959 Act reintroduced the "proration principle" in the treatment of tax-exempt income in the calculation of the policy reserve deduction (see the discussion of the 1942 Act above). Thus, the tax rate on municipal bonds is not really zero under the 1959 Act, but more on the order of 5% to 7%. The 1959 Act also resulted in some stock companies' realizing an additional benefit from tax-exempt interest and dividends received. This is because all tax-exempt income is credited to the shareholder's account; in some circumstances this can reduce a stock company's Phase III tax liability. See Kaufman, *op. cit.*, Part II, p. 53.

1958. The acquisition data in Table II-5 do suggest that the tax code revision may have increased the volume of life company funds allocated to municipal bonds during 1958–1960. But since then the flow of municipal obligations into life company portfolios

TABLE II-5. Net Acquisitions of Municipal Bonds by Life Insurance Companies: 1951–1964

(billions of dollars)

	(1)	(2)	(3)	(4)	(5)	(6)
	Net Acquisitions			Net Funds to Private		
Year	U.S.	Foreign	Net Gain in Assets	Sector*	(1)/(3)	(1)/(4)
1951–54	$694	$308	$20,466	$24,855	3.39%	2.79%
1955	192	−45	5,946	6,440	3.10	2.98
1956	235	80	5,579	6,600	4.21	3.56
1957	103	49	5,298	5,824	1.94	1.77
1958	305	42	6,271	6,117	4.86	4.99
1959	519	106	6,070	6,385	8.55	8.13
1960	388	53	5,926	6,367	6.55	6.09
1961	300	163	7,240	7,533	4.14	3.98
1962	138	172	6,475	6,439	2.13	2.14
1963	−174	378	7,830	8,187	—	—

* Net gain in assets plus net decline in holdings of U.S. Government securities.

SOURCE: Institute of Life Insurance.

has been greatly reduced. The explanation of this response appears to be found in other influences upon relative yields. Market yields on Baa corporate and municipal obligations are shown in Table II-6. From these data it is apparent that, although the 1959 Act increased the value of municipal bonds to life companies by up to 70 basis points (depending upon the allowance for anticipation of the tax revision), the movement in before-tax yield spreads between the mid-1950s and the early 1960s wholly offset the tax effect. The widening corporate/municipals yield differential does not reflect a lessened demand for funds from state and local governments during the early 1960s. On the contrary, net debt issues by this sector increased quite sharply. However, the rapid growth of commercial bank assets during the early 1960s

TABLE II-6.   Yields on Baa Corporate and Municipal Bonds: 1952–1964

Year	(1) Corporate	(2) Municipals	(3) Differentials (1)–(2)
1952	3.52%	2.70%	.82%
1953	3.74	3.41	.33
1954	3.51	3.09	.42
1955	3.53	3.14	.39
1956	3.88	3.50	.38
1957	4.71	4.20	.51
1958	4.73	3.95	.78
1959	5.05	4.24	.81
1960	5.19	4.22	.97
1961	5.08	4.01	1.07
1962	5.02	3.67	1.35
1963	4.86	3.58	1.28
1964	4.83	3.54	1.29

SOURCE: *Federal Reserve Bulletins.*

has generated an increase in bank demand for municipals well in excess of the increase of net municipal debt issues.[202]   Apparently bank appetite for municipals has been so strong as to bid down Baa yields as well as higher grade municipal bond yields.

During the late 1940s and most of the 1950s the tax law had only a very modest effect in directing life company funds toward common and preferred stock.   This again reflects the relatively low tax rates imposed on life companies during this period.   During the mid-1950s expectations of higher taxes might have made dividend income more attractive, but the stopgap legislation which applied to taxable years 1955–1957 denied the normal 85% intercorporate dividend credit to life companies.   Therefore there was little tax incentive for life companies to acquire equity shares during the postwar years up to the enactment of the 1959 Act.   By restoring the dividend credit and raising tax rates on most life companies, the 1959 Act should have increased life company interest in common and preferred shares.   But imposition

---

[202] During 1961–1964, net state and local government debt increased $23.1 billion as compared to $17.8 billion during the preceding four years.   However, the commercial bank net acquisitions of municipal debt increased from $4.6 billion during 1957–1960 to $15.7 billion in 1961–1964.

of a capital gains tax in the 1959 law may have acted as a deterrent to life company investment in equities, or at least reinforced their tastes for dividend yield as opposed to capital appreciation in selection of shares. If the tax-exempt interest on municipals is valued at about 100 basis points by life companies since the 1959 Act, the tax value of dividends is about 85 basis points.[203] If life companies took the dividend/price ratio as a literal measure of corporate stock yields, there was enough of a tax advantage to make preferred shares, but not common shares, competitive with corporate bonds during the early 1960s.[204]

Net life company acquisitions of corporate stock (both common and preferred) have increased somewhat during the 1960s,[205] but many factors could be responsible. Nonetheless the tax environment since 1958 has been somewhat more favorable to life company purchase of equity shares.

COMPETITION FOR SAVINGS

Life insurance companies compete with a number of other intermediaries for the current savings flow. However, their most direct competition in recent years has been with trusteed pension funds. The relative tax position of these two institutional forms has influenced the relative rate of growth of insured and non-insured pension plans.

Life insurance companies played a primary role in the development of group pension plans in the 1920s and 1930s. Since World War II, however, noninsured pension plans have grown at a substantially higher rate than insured funds.[206] The explanation of these disparate growth rates is commonly based on two

---

[203] It should be recalled that the proration principle, applied to computation of the reserve credit, refers to tax-exempt dividends as well as interest.

[204] Based on a comparison of Baa bond yields and Standard and Poor's stock yield series as reported in the *Federal Reserve Bulletin*.

[205] Net acquisition during 1960–1964 amounted to about $2 billion as compared to only about $400 million in the previous five years. (Market appreciation of outstanding holdings excluded.)

[206] At the end of 1950 the insured plans and the noninsured corporate pension funds had approximately equal shares of the private pension business (about $5.5 billion each). But by the end of the decade (1960), insured pension reserves amounted to only $18.8 billion as compared to trusteed corporate pension fund assets of $28.7 billion. Data from the Securities and Exchange Commission, *Statistical Bulletin*.

burdens borne by life insurance companies: (1) life companies earnings from invested pension plan assets were taxable while the investment income of noninsured corporate funds was exempt from the federal income tax; and (2) life companies were seriously constrained by statutory limits on investments in equities while the corporate funds were able to take advantage of opportunities in the equity markets.[207]

We have discussed developments in the realm of statutory investment constraints above. As tax rates on investment income increased during the 1950s, life companies' relative tax disadvantage in the pension business increased. Particularly costly was the fact that in the temporary tax legislation preceding the 1959 Act, earnings credits to pension plan reserves were not allowed as part of the policy reserve additions deduction. This was remedied in the 1959 Act.[208]

The impact of this part of the federal income tax environment upon portfolio policy is indirect. From our discussion of life company interest in common stocks above, however, it is clear that the rate at which they have explored the equities markets and lobbied for greater investment freedom in this area has been related to their interest in developing the pension and annuity fields. To the extent the federal tax code held back insured pension funds growth, it probably also slowed the movement of life companies into the equity markets.[209]

THE INFLUENCE OF TAXATION ON FINANCING AGREEMENTS

Life insurance companies have long been taxed on investment income at quite modest rates; most of their corporate customers at the same time have been taxed at the full corporate rate. This difference in tax incidence has induced borrowers and lenders to work out financing arrangements which take advantage of the differential. The clearest examples of this sort of consideration

---

[207] See Hart, "Life Insurance Companies and the Equity Capital Markets," p. 360.

[208] See Kaufman, *The Life Insurance Company Income Tax Act of 1959*, Thesis, p. 103.

[209] Hart, *op. cit.*, represents an extreme position on this point; he argues that the diversion of life company funds to common stocks depends entirely upon developments in their pension business.

have developed in life insurance company acquisitions of real estate.

As we have seen, life insurance companies' real estate investments have largely taken the form of lease arrangements which allow the lender to avoid any managerial responsibilities. The life company purchases the property and receives rental payments. The tenant manages the property and assumes the maintenance expenses, real estate taxes, and insurance payments. The most discussed form of these arrangements are the "purchase lease" or "sale-leaseback" deals, where the lender purchases the property and by prearrangement executes a lease with the former owner. Similar long-term net leases are contracted in other circumstances, however.

As usually drawn, the lease is noncancellable for the primary term during which the rental payments fully amortize the investment. At the end of this term the lessee will often have options which include renewing the lease at a reduced rental (sometimes nominal) or repurchasing the property. The sale-leaseback form developed originally as a means of financing retailers, but the device spread to the industrial sector and has been used with many types of properties.

The purchase-lease arrangement can provide a number of advantages to the lessee compared to the alternative of borrowing on the property. In effect, the lessee is able to borrow a larger amount with more liberal prepayment provisions than statutory restraints would permit on a mortgage loan. In addition, no debt appears on the balance sheet so that the lessee's future access to credit is not diminished by this form of financing. Furthermore the full rental payments are deductible for tax purposes whereas only the interest payments on a mortgage loan are deductible. However, since the lessee loses a depreciation deduction by selling the property, the extent of the gain depends upon the depreciable characteristics of the property. Tax benefits are also sometimes realized by the taking of a capital loss or gain in the original sale transaction.[210]

---

[210] A detailed discussion of the tax position and other considerations involving both principals in purchase-lease deals is available in Cary, "Corporate Financing Through the Sale and Leaseback of Property: Business Tax and Policy Considerations."

The life insurance company is induced into this type of investment by being offered a share of the (eventual) tenant's benefits. Life companies have an investment which they treat like a debt instrument, but they receive a rate of return in excess of going bond yields.[211]   On its tax accounting the life company depreciates the property and deducts a portion of rental payments as return to principal.   The remainder of the rental receipts are taxable as investment income.   Depending upon the Internal Revenue ruling on the specific transaction, the taxable portion may often exceed the taxable interest income that would accrue had the financing been carried out on a debt basis.   So long as low tax rates were imposed on life companies, they could absorb the tax and still obtain a favorable net after-tax return.

Profitability of lease arrangements to life insurance companies has, however, depended upon favorable tax rulings and low tax rates.   Tax rulings have not always been so favorable as anticipated, and during the 1950s a substantial increase in life company tax liabilities became more and more probable.   These circumstances undoubtedly inhibited life companies from developing the investment real estate field more fully.   They did explore various alternative forms which offered more protection.   One device is to have a third party (possessing limited tax exposure) purchase the property and borrow approximately the full cost of the property from an insurance company with the lease serving as collateral.[212]   Investments of this type show up in a life company portfolio as bond holdings.   There is some risk that such deals will not be sanctioned by the state insurance commissioner.

The 1959 Tax Act seems to have had a considerable impact upon real estate lease deals.   Substantially higher tax rates, including a capital gains tax, and tighter rules governing the portion of rental payments chargeable as amortization, the depreciation deduction, and the valuation of the property forced a general reevaluation by life companies of their real estate investment programs.   It is clear that some forms of leaseback arrangements were rendered

---

[211] Estimated in the late 1940s at anywhere from $3/8\%$ to 1% over the identical financing in debenture form.   See Bell and Fraine, *op. cit.*, and Cary, *op. cit.*

[212] See Winn, "Factors Influencing Life Insurance Company Investments," p. 115.

unprofitable by the 1959 Act.[213] In particular, leases with renewal and/or repurchase options at a token rental or sale price were effectively quashed. Life companies stand to take losses on some outstanding leases of this type when the options are exercised.

Thus the tax environment played an important role in determining the extent to which and the form in which life insurance companies engaged in real estate investment during the period since World War II. The differential between the full corporate incremental tax rate and the rate applied to life insurance companies allowed insurers to make attractive real estate investments without undertaking managerial responsibility and without assuming a risk position essentially different from debt financing. At the same time, uncertainty about the portion of rental income on which the life company would have to pay taxes and fear of a substantial increase in their marginal tax rate inhibited life companies from investing more than a modest proportion of their portfolio assets in real estate. During the postwar years life company investment in commercial and industrial real estate (not company occupied) has never amounted to more than 2% of the industry's assets.[214] Passage of the 1959 Tax Act rendered unprofitable to life companies some of the popular forms of lease contracts they had been making. Investment in commercial and industrial real estate has continued to expand since 1959 but at a very modest pace. Net acquisitions of investment real estate in these forms by life companies amounted to $427 million during 1960–1964, or slightly better than 1% of the increase in life insurance industry assets over the period.

Concluding Remarks

During the years since World War II American life insurance companies have invested their cash flow largely in private sector, medium- to long-term, investment quality debt instruments. New acquisitions of corporate bonds and mortgage loans by life companies amounted to 90% of the net gain in the industry's assets

---

[213] See Matz, *op. cit.*, pp. 158–165.
[214] See Table II-2 above.

during the period 1946–1964, and nearly 80% of the net asset gain plus funds obtained from the liquidation of life companies' U. S. Treasury securities portfolios. Probably about 90% of life company corporate bond holdings are of Baa quality or better. Mortgage loan acquisitions are regarded as of comparable quality. In addition to these dominant investment forms, life companies have lent small amounts without mortgage security to unincorporated enterprises. Also, life companies have invested positive amounts since 1945 in policy loans, debt issues of state, local, and foreign governments, corporate preferred and common shares, and real property. Activity in policy loans is largely beyond the control of life company investment departments. In this chapter we have attempted to estimate the extent to which the modest life company activity in areas other than investment grade corporate debt and mortgage loans is due to the pressure of external constraints.

The primary external influences to which life companies have been subject have been examined under three headings:

(1) State statutory constraints on investment policy;

(2) Asset valuation rules; and

(3) The federal income tax law.

Together these factors affect estimates of net yield and risk attached to specific assets and to alternative portfolios. In addition, they restrict the range of choices available to life company investment officers.

In particular, we have found that these external features of the environment have significantly limited life companies' exploration of equity markets. There are some good reasons (e.g., yield, inflation, reduction of income risk) for greater life company interest in equity investments. On the other hand, the traditional emphasis on stability of capital value and asset quality has restrained investment officers from placing more than quite modest proportions of their portfolios in equities. Historically, statutory restrictions on portfolio selection and the system of rules governing valuation of portfolio assets have partly created and partly reinforced the "safety of principal" priority. Life companies' freedom to invest in corporate common shares has been especially restricted by the prevailing investment statutes and valuation rules. Statutory limits upon life company ownership of nonresidential real

property have also provided very little freedom for experimentation in this sector, although most life companies have displayed
little interest in holding as much real estate as the more influential
statutes have permitted.

The federal income tax code has also affected life companies'
appetite for equity investments. Relevant features of the tax
environment include the tax position of stock dividends relative
to other forms of income, the treatment of capital gains and losses
and of depreciation allowances on owned property, the definition
of the tax base and the relation between effective rates imposed
upon life companies and rates incurred by their competitors and
by potential borrowers. Low tax rates, applied to life companies
during the postwar years, and the denial of the intercorporate
dividend deduction during the mid-1950s produced little tax incentive for life companies to invest in corporate shares prior to
passage of the 1959 Tax Act. Higher tax rates and reintroduction
of the 85% intercorporate dividend deduction were products of
the 1959 Act which should have increased life companies' interest
in corporate stock issues. However, this tendency may have been
dampened by introduction of a capital gains tax and reimposition
of the "proration principle" in treating tax-exempt income in computation of the tax base.

It has been argued that a disadvantageous tax position of life
companies as against trusteed corporate pension funds hindered
life companies' ability to compete effectively for pension fund
business. To the extent that the tax code did retard the growth
of the life insurance industry's pension accounts during the 1950s
(the problem is alleviated in the 1959 Act), it presumably also
retarded the rate at which companies moved into equity markets
in search of investment outlets.

Few life companies have appeared interested in undertaking
managerial responsibilities in connection with real estate investments. Consequently, the most popular form of life company
investment in commercial property has been prearranged purchase
and lease-back transactions. Tax considerations have had an influential role in promoting these arrangements. Life companies'
interest in this form of investment has been dependent, however,
upon favorable IRS rulings with regard to cost deductions and low
tax rates. Sufficiently favorable rulings have not always been

forthcoming, and the depreciation rules and higher tax rates written into the 1959 Act have adversely affected the return on some types of lease-back investments.

Aside from specifically discouraging equity investments by life companies, the statutory and asset valuation regulations have generally restrained experimentation by investment departments with lower quality assets. The investment legislation does this by prohibitions or quantitative limitations on certain categories of assets and by establishing measures of debt quality which must be satisfied for assets to be eligible for life company portfolios. Some states grant freedom for life companies to invest a modest proportion of their funds in assets not qualifying under the prevailing tests, but the influential New York law has been quite stringent in this respect. No assets are completely insulated from the peculiar risks created by the valuation systems, but lesser quality assets are most vulnerable to capital value risk generated by the valuation rules. In general, the statutory and valuation regulations inhibit any individual company from deviating too far from the aggregate industry portfolio composition.

The ability of life insurance companies to compete in the conventional residential mortgage loan market was restricted somewhat during the 1950s by a relatively stringent maximum loan/value ceiling and for some companies by New York state's 40% limit on conventional loans as a proportion of assets. To the extent that these regulations were effective constraints, they directed life company funds away from conventional home loans and toward federally underwritten loans and corporate securities.

Life insurance companies have not played a major role in the market for state and local government debt issues. The tax-exempt interest income on these issues has resulted in this market's being dominated by investors (commercial banks, individuals, nonlife insurance companies) who incur relatively high marginal federal income tax rates. Life company investment in municipal bonds has, therefore, been confined largely to issues falling outside the tastes or analytical abilities of the dominant investors, i.e., lower quality or special situation general obligation issues, revenue bonds, and taxable obligations of Canadian political subdivisions.

Thus, the existing statutory regulations, asset valuation rules, and federal income tax legislation have contributed significantly to limiting the range and variety of life insurance company port-folio selections. In particular, legislated investment restrictions and administered valuation rules have limited the ability of life companies to respond to changing subjective estimates of risk, to relative yields, and to capital market innovations as fully as they would have in a more liberal environment. This is both because established rules and regulations act as an effective constraint and because they affect attitudes held by life company investment officers and finance committees regarding the appropriate range of outlets for life insurance company funds.

The effect of the existing combinations of internally formulated portfolio goals and externally imposed restrictions has been to confine life company investment activity predominantly to the corporate bond and mortgage markets. In the remainder of this study we shall focus upon the allocation of life insurance company loanable funds in both time and asset mix dimensions. We shall limit the investigations largely to the period 1946–1960. Also, since for reasons we have been discussing, life company investment ventures outside the corporate bond and mortgage markets have been quite restricted during this period, we shall conduct most of the analysis on the assumption that the range of investment choice was essentially limited to these markets. We turn in the following three chapters to an analysis of the allocation of life company funds over time to the corporate bond and mortgage markets.

| Chapter III | POSTWAR LIQUIDATION OF

GOVERNMENT SECURITIES BY LIFE INSURANCE

COMPANIES: *I. The Time Pattern of Portfolio Disposal*

In this chapter we take a broad look at the investment problem facing life insurance companies following World War II. Our perspective for viewing life company portfolio policy in the postwar period is an examination of the time pattern of the industry's disposal of its portfolio of Government securities accumulated during the depression and war years. By the end of 1945, life companies held United States Treasury obligations amounting to $20.6 billion, or 46% of their admitted assets.[1] Judged by historic proportions, or by consideration of basic liquidity needs, life company portfolios were in extreme imbalance.[2] Consequently, during the postwar years life companies concentrated on the transference of their assets from Government securities to obligations of the private sector.

During the early postwar years this portfolio switching operation was facilitated by the existence of a Government bond market supported by the monetary authorities. In this environment life companies did not really face a portfolio allocation problem. Endowed with an excessive abundance of riskless assets and a painless means of liquidating them, companies were able to ac-

---

[1] ILI, *Life Insurance Fact Book*, annual.

[2] At the end of the war fully half the industry's assets were in highly liquid, riskless, low-earning forms: cash, Treasury obligations, and Canadian central government obligations. At the end of 1940 these types of assets amounted to 24.7% of the industry's assets, a historic high at the time. Ten years earlier the proportion was only 5%. These data, for 49 companies (accounting for 92% of the industry's assets), are reported in the LIAA, *Record of Life Insurance Investments*, annual.

quire all private sector assets that passed credit analysis and offered a rate of return containing a minimum risk premium over the Government bond yields. In these circumstances, explaining life company investment policy is largely a matter of explaining the time sequence of conversion of Treasury obligations into risk assets. This is the task we undertake in this chapter.

There are several reasons for bothering to conduct this examination. First, our overall concern in Chapters III and IV of this study is estimating the extent to which life companies make intertemporal allocations of funds in response to actual or forecast movements in the level and structure of market yields. Second, we would like to get the historical record straight. As of now there are several alternative and not altogether consistent propositions in the literature which purport to explain the broad pattern of life companies' disposal of Government securities. Third, this investigation is necessary in order to pinpoint reasonably well the timing of the transition from a flush funds environment to one in which portfolio choice reappears as a major problem. Many writers have found this point of time easy to select; namely, March 1951, the date of the Treasury-Federal Reserve "Accord." However, we do not find the dating problem so simple. Finally, this piece of history proves quite instructive for the student interested in the mechanics and efficacy of monetary policy.

We proceed in this chapter to examine the pattern of Government securities liquidation by life companies and the existing explanations of this phenomenon. Following this, we introduce an additional hypothesis in Chapter IV.

Disposal of Government Securities by Life Insurance Companies, 1946–1964

The broad pattern of the life insurance industry's postwar disposal of Government securities is visible from inspection of Table III-1. Life companies made net purchases of Treasury obligations in 1946, but liquidation was under way in earnest in 1947. There are two interesting features of the time sequence of disposals:

(1) the extended duration of the liquidation program, and
(2) the rather abrupt and substantial reduction in the rate of liquidation after 1951.

These two characteristics may be interrelated, of course.[3]

TABLE III-1. *Holdings and Net Change in Holdings of U.S. Government Securities by Life Insurance Companies: Annual, 1946–1964*
(millions of dollars)

Year	Holdings*	Ratio of Holdings to Assets	Net Change†
1946	$20,583	45.9%	+$1,046
1947	21,639	44.9	−1,608
1948	20,021	38.7	−3,275
1949	16,746	30.2	−1,456
1950	15,290	25.6	−1,831
1951	13,459	21.0	−2,450
1952	11,009	16.1	−757
1953	10,252	14.1	−423
1954	9,829	12.5	−759
1955	9,070	10.7	−494
1956	8,576	9.5	−1,021
1957	7,555	7.9	−526
1958	7,029	6.9	+154
1959	7,183	6.7	−315
1960	6,868	6.0	−441
1961	6,427	5.4	−293
1962	6,134	4.9	+ 36
1963	6,170	4.6	−357
1964	5,813	4.1	—

* As of January 1, each year.
† During year indicated.
SOURCE: ILI, *Life Insurance Fact Book*, annual.

---

[3] The pattern of liquidation, stretched out over a long period of years, contrasts sharply with savings and loan association behavior. These institutions completed disposal of their excessive holdings of Treasury obligations during the 1940s and have since been adding to their Governments' portfolio. The SLAs had, however, emerged from the war with a smaller proportion of their assets tied up in Governments than life companies, and have experienced a postwar growth rate well in excess of life companies. Furthermore, the Spence Act, passed June 27, 1950, imposed formal reserve requirements on

Some Explanations

The pattern of a sharply reduced liquidation rate after 1951 has not escaped other observers, and explanations of this phenomenon are available in the literature. Most of these explanations focus on the change in monetary policy following the Treasury-Federal Reserve Accord of March 1951. The reduced rate of disposals following 1951 is attributed to "locking in" effects of the revival of monetary restraint. The lines of argument follow from the main proposition of the "credit availability" doctrine, which held a central place in discussions about the efficacy of monetary policy during the 1950s.[4] The significance of the Accord for life insurance company mortgage loan activity has been described by Saul Klaman in these terms:

> Regardless of asset size or type of mortgage operation all life insurance companies alike were faced with the need for basic changes in investment policy after March 1951. Before the Federal Reserve-Treasury Accord there was no need to allocate funds for mortgage investment. The general policy was to invest as much money in mortgages as the market would take. Maximum flexibility was permitted by unlimited access to the government securities market, supported by Federal Reserve. The change in monetary and fiscal policy required companies to allocate their funds carefully among alternative investments in accordance with their anticipated income. The large companies, therefore, adopted the allocation technique for acquiring mortgages. The day of pouring funds into markets for mortgages and corporate securities closed with the

---

members of the Federal Home Loan Bank System. Since Treasury obligations were the only earning assets which qualified as reserves under this requirement, S & Ls have consistently added to their Governments' portfolio since 1950. Mutual savings banks have a pattern of Government securities liquidation stretched out in time much like that of life companies.

[4] The theory was apparently conceived in the minds of central bankers associated with the Federal Reserve Bank of New York. For a discussion of its origins, see Roosa, "Interest Rates and the Central Bank." Also see Roosa's contribution to the 1952 Oxford Symposium on Monetary Policy. The doctrine was discussed extensively in the Patman Investigation of 1952; see Tobin, "Monetary Policy and the Management of the Public Debt: The Patman Inquiry." The clearest official statement of the thesis as the rational basis of Federal Reserve policy is to be found in the *Federal Reserve Bulletin*, March 1953, pp. 219–234. Critical evaluations of the theory are to be found in Smith, "On the Effectiveness of Monetary Policy"; Hansen, *The American Economy*, Chapter 3; Karaken, "Lenders' Preferences, Credit Rationing and the Effectiveness of Monetary Policy"; and Lindbeck, *The "New" Theory of Credit Control in the United States*.

"accord." Almost without exception life insurance companies, and other institutional investors too, consider March 1951 to be the turning point of investment policy and operating techniques in postwar mortgage markets.[5]

In the same vein, Andrew Brimmer has argued that:

. . . the unpegging of government securities prices and the subsequent decline in these prices had a strong effect on life insurance companies' investment behavior. The realization that Governments were no longer the equivalent of cash and could not be sold in the future at known fixed prices had the effect, in most cases, of causing life insurance companies to restrict current investment commitments more nearly to the flow of funds which would develop from sources other than further disposals of Governments.[6]

An alternative explanation of the liquidation pattern has been offered by some who have doubted the significance of the "locked-in" arguments. Warren Smith has found the return of life company holdings of Governments, as a proportion of assets, to prewar levels by end-1951 a more plausible explanation of the reduced rate of disposals thereafter.[7] Government security holdings had been reduced to 16.1% of assets by end-1951, as compared with 18.7% at the end of 1940. The argument presumably is that having reached familiar portfolio proportions, life companies no longer felt the same sort of urgency about reducing their holdings to the level of minimum secondary reserve needs.[8] Some explanations, including some offered by life company officers, have contained both credit availability and portfolio balance

---

[5] Klaman, *The Postwar Residential Mortgage Market*, p. 147.

[6] *Life Insurance Companies in the Capital Market*, pp. 158–159. Brimmer goes on in this passage to attribute the reduced salability of Governments following the Accord to "the potential loss in sales." He argues that realized capital losses impinge on life companies' limited surplus positions and that companies "are reluctant to show large fluctuations in surplus." A few paragraphs later he also associates locking-in effects with changes in yield spreads between Government bonds and alternative private investments. Both these lines of argument appear among the credit availability propositions. Klaman is not explicit with regard to the reason the Accord deterred future sales of Treasury obligations by life companies, but he appears to be thinking in credit availability terms. We shall list and discuss the main elements of the credit availability doctrine in the next section.

[7] Smith, *op. cit.*, p. 592.

[8] This proposition can be given a more formalized statement, and we shall do that in a later section of this chapter.

arguments.[9] We shall now turn to an examination of the validity of these explanations of the Government securities disposal pattern.

Relevance of the Credit Availability Thesis to Life Insurance Company Behavior

Review of the Doctrine

The essence of the credit availability doctrine is that Central Bank credit control operates more by affecting the supply of funds than by influencing demand through the price (interest rate) mechanism. Operating primarily through imperfections in the money and capital markets, the Central Bank is allegedly able to control lenders' willingness to extend credit. Imperfections associated with these markets are of several varieties: lagged adjustments (of yields), monopoly, and knowledge imperfections.[10] To some extent, adjustment lags may be a result of monopoly imperfection and imperfect knowledge. Effectiveness of Federal Reserve credit control is also alleged to depend on ownership of substantial amounts of Government securities by the major lenders. Given widespread holdings of Governments, skillful application of open market purchases and sales is said to allow the System to alleviate or accentuate market imperfections and so to induce an increase or contraction in credit extensions.

Prior to 1951, through its support operations the Federal Reserve maintained a floor on prices of marketable Government securities. During most of this period market participants had near-certain knowledge regarding minimum current and future

---

[9] See the LIAA, *Proceedings* of the Annual Meeting, 1951, p. 38. The replies prepared by life company executives to a Patman Committee Questionnaire in late 1951 emphasized the role of both portfolio balance and capital loss considerations in determining sales of Governments. Joint Committee on the Economic Report, the Patman *Replies*, replies to Questions 1 and 2, pp. 1228–1244.

[10] The dependence of the credit availability thesis on market imperfections was apparently first pointed out by Paul Samuelson in testimony before the Patman Subcommittee, see Joint Committee on the Economic Report, *Hearings on Monetary Policy and Management of the Public Debt, Their Role in Achieving Price Stability and High Level Employment*, pp. 691–710 (hereafter referred to as the Patman *Hearings*); also see the Tobin and Karaken articles referred to above.

prices and even the largest investors were able to liquidate essentially unlimited blocs of Governments on the market without significantly depressing prices. Following the Accord, the Federal Reserve was free to practice a more restrictive credit policy and, by applying pressure to increase interest rates, was able to create uncertainty in the minds of lenders with regard to (1) future market prices, (2) yield differentials between Governments and risk assets, and (3) the "depth, breadth, and resiliency" of the market. This uncertainty induced by rising yields is what makes "an *increasing* yield on government bonds an extremely good substitute for a high yield." [11]

Implications for the Behavior of Life Insurance Companies

Rising interest rates are supposed to have the effect of "locking in" Governments in the portfolios of long-term lenders[12] for several reasons:

(1) The decline in the market value of assets reduces portfolio liquidity. Lenders therefore attempt to recoup lost liquidity by shifting funds from the private sector to purchase of Governments, or at least by refraining from further sales of Governments.

(2) The declining value of fixed, interest-bearing assets also leads lenders to a reappraisal of future economic conditions. Thus "as interest rates increase, investors become less optimistic about the business outlook and therefore change their appraisals of risk position."[13] Consequently, lenders shift their emphasis toward prime quality assets. This action leads to a relatively greater decline in the value of lower grade assets, which leads investors to "become more restrictive and selective."

(3) Institutional investors are typically conservative and prefer low-risk investments when such "quality" assets carry yields adequate to allow them to earn the minimum rate of return required to meet their liabilities. An absolute rise in yield on Governments, independent of yield spreads, allows such investors to safely carry more "riskless" assets in their portfolios.

[11] Tobin, *op. cit.*, p. 122. Italics in original.
[12] The Federal Reserve's statement of the thesis in the *Federal Reserve Bulletin*, March 1953, is especially valuable as it makes clear which effects are meant to apply to long-term lenders (including insurance companies). See pp. 222–224.
[13] *Ibid.*, p. 223.

(4) Yield spreads are affected. Government bonds are more attractive due to the lag in adjustment of yields on private securities following the rise in yields on Governments.

(5) Market uncertainty results in market "thinness." Large institutional lenders (insurance companies) find they are no longer able to liquidate long-term Governments in "chunks of five, ten, fifteen, twenty millions, or more, on short notice," [14] without "breaking the market." Thus technical market difficulties are supposed to constrain the large investors if they still desire to liquidate Governments.

(6) As market prices of Governments decline more investors find that sales out of their Government securities portfolio can be made only at prices below original cost or book value. Reluctance of many institutional investors to realize capital losses on Governments restrains them from further sales.

In addition to the immediate direct effects of slowly rising rates are the effects resulting from expectations engendered. Rising rates generate expectations (fears) of further increases with consequent increased yield-attractiveness of Governments, and further loss of liquidity, value-impairment of lower quality assets, and larger capital losses on sales. Life insurance companies are particularly susceptible to *potential* capital losses because of their extensive use of forward commitments.

> Nonbank lenders will hesitate to commit themselves beyond the funds they expect to have coming in if they fear that interest rates may rise in the near future and that they may therefore have to sell securities at a loss to meet future commitments.[15]

In sum, then, it is argued that conditions of credit restraint and market uncertainty characterized most of the years following the Accord and, through the process outlined above, resulted in substantially smaller disposals of Governments by life companies than during the pre-Accord years. Rising interest rates restrict sales of Governments by: (1) affecting life company liquidity positions adversely; (2) creating conditions which make investment officers more quality conscious in their asset selections; (3) causing yield spreads between Governments and risk assets to

---

[14] See Sproul, "Central Banking and the Private Economy."
[15] *Federal Reserve Bulletin*, March 1953, p. 223.

narrow; (4) producing market conditions unfavorable for disposal of substantial blocs of Treasury bonds; and (5) forcing life companies to absorb capital losses on security sales. We turn now to an examination of each of these propositions.

Evaluation of the Credit Availability Doctrine as Applied to Life Insurance Companies

We can take care of the liquidity, quality, and sticky yield contentions quickly. The market thinness and capital loss arguments require more serious consideration.

EFFECTS ON PORTFOLIO LIQUIDITY

It is argued that

> . . . in a period of tightening credit, long-term lenders and investors . . . become more interested in retaining or in adding to their portfolios the more liquid types of assets, because of concern about the decline in the market value of their entire investment portfolio and the general uncertainty about future developments.[16]

It is difficult to see how this argument can make any contribution toward explaining the reduced rate of Government securities liquidation by life companies following the Accord. The bulk of life company assets, including all their Government security holdings, are valued for statement purposes on an amortized cost basis. Therefore fluctuations in market prices do not threaten any company's solvency, and it is not necessary to hedge the risk of additional market price decline by purchase of additional short-term prime quality assets.[17]

Furthermore, in the specific context of the immediate post-Accord years, it is clear that life companies were endowed with portfolio liquidity well in excess of their needs. Evidence of this fact is found in life companies' disposal of nearly $5 billion of Governments (net) in the decade of secularly rising interest rates following 1951 (Table III-1). In addition, the absolute holdings of cash and temporary investments by life companies remained stable in dollar terms over the decade cited, even though their total assets nearly doubled (see Chapter V). A rise in interest

---

[16] *Ibid.*

[17] Realized losses through sales will, of course, affect the surplus position, but this is a different argument and is considered below.

rates might, of course, lead to expectations of further increases, which might in turn induce the accumulation of short-term assets in order to be able to take advantage of future opportunities, but this sort of speculative action would imply greater, not smaller, sales of Government bonds currently.

QUALITY OF LOANS

The credit availability doctrine alleges that rising interest rates lead to pessimism, caution, and increased aversion to risk-taking on the part of long-term lenders. Consequently, as interest rates rise, credit standards are tightened. "They will become less willing to make any but the best grade loans and investments." [18] As the highest quality earning asset available, Treasury bonds become a more attractive investment to life companies. It is not at all clear a priori why long-term lenders should react so perversely to economic expansion, and no evidence is offered in support of this contention. What little ex post empirical evidence there is available suggests the contrary conclusion. [19]

There is a related and somewhat more sophisticated argument that underlies many discussions of credit rationing. Without any presumptions about changes in lenders' subjective risk evaluation, it is argued that higher interest rates permit lenders to purchase more portfolio "safety" and maintain an optimum balance between portfolio risk, which is assumed to have nega-

---

[18] *Ibid.*, p. 222.

[19] For a review of work in this area, see Moore, "The Quality of Credit in Booms and Depressions." For evidence of deterioration of the quality of corporate bonds during booms, see Hickman, *Corporate Bond Quality and Investor Experience*, pp. 100–110. Most of the NBER evidence refers to "major cycle" boom and construction phases. Hickman, for example, found no relation between the quality of corporate bond credit and business cycle phases for the National Bureau's cycle. Furthermore it is not clear to what extent, if at all, deterioration of the quality of credit in major cycles reflects changes in investors' subjective risk estimates. However, Saulnier's investigation of mortgage lending practices of life insurance companies suggests quality standards weakened in the 1925–1929 boom. See Saulnier, *Urban Mortgage Lending by Life Insurance Companies*, Chapter VI. Life insurance company officers have judged the industry guilty of "reaching for yield" during the "prosperity phase of the cycle." See Burnett, "Some Aspects of Portfolio Management," p. 412 ff. Burnett supports the basic contention of the argument being considered; viz., the longer the prosperity phase lasts, the more risky lower quality debt issues become; but he warns that life company investment officers have been ignoring this fact since World War II in the search for yield.

tive utility, and expected yield, which has positive utility.[20] It is quite possible that lenders do tighten their standards of credit eligibility in a period of monetary restraint.[21] This does not mean, however, that lenders are likely to push the search for quality investments to the extreme of investing in Treasury obligations. Barring any other reasons for holding Governments, lenders could improve the quality of their private sector portfolios by liquidating Governments and investing in high quality private obligations.

It is sometimes argued, however, that Governments become more attractive to life companies when interest rates rise because investment officers have rate of return goals defined in terms of the guaranteed return written into outstanding insurance policies.

In addition, the higher interest rates on these more liquid assets in a period of tightening credit come closer to providing the average interest rate which institutional lenders must obtain on their earning assets in order to meet contracts with their own creditors.[22]

It is true that life company executives have often told the Treasury, Congressmen, and themselves that they would (should) buy (hold) Government bonds if yields were high enough to meet policy reserve requirements.[23] Their affirmations, however, occurred in periods when Government bond yields were low and served as rationalizations for life companies' not buying or holding Treasury obligations. The argument is also inconsistent with the more prevalent position that "life companies are keenly competitive with one another with respect to the rate of investment re-

---

[20] For a discussion of this kind of rationing within a credit availability context, see Lindbeck, *op. cit.*, pp. 29–35.

[21] There is not much evidence on this. It appears that inferences have been made about insurance company behavior in this respect from observation of credit rationing by commercial banks. Even with respect to bank practice, however, it is not clear that loan rationing is used as a device to upgrade quality. Explanations of bank rationing more often run in terms of serving priority customers. See, for example, Robinson, *The Management of Bank Funds*, pp. 11–18, and Hodgman, "The Deposit Relationship and Commercial Bank Investment Behavior."

[22] *Federal Reserve Bulletin*, March 1953, p. 223.

[23] See, for example, the annual ALC-LIAA *Report* of the Joint Committee on Economic Policy, for reports of meetings with Treasury officials during 1954 (published in the American Life Convention *Proceedings*, 1954, p. 88); and replies of life insurance executives, the Patman *Replies*, Part 2, Chapter XII, pp. 1227–48.

turn" because "the higher the rate of investment return, the greater the possibilities for reducing the cost of life insurance to policyholders, and thus the more favorable competitive position of a company." [24] In any case, the experience of continued disposals in recent years is hardly consistent with the position that high yields, relative to the rate of return guaranteed on policy reserves, are sufficient in themselves to make Government bonds attractive investments for life companies.

YIELD DIFFERENTIALS

The credit availability doctrine asserts that Central Bank action, which places upward pressure on Government bond yields, makes Governments relatively more attractive than alternative private investments. This occurs as a result of stickiness in yields on most obligations issued by the private sector. Market uncertainty in an oligopolistic market structure results in a substantial time lag in adjusting yields on private loans to the new higher market-clearing levels. So long as this lag can be maintained by exerting continued pressure on Government bond yields, the spread between yields on risk assets and Governments is narrowed.

Samuelson suggested in 1952, however, that playing on market uncertainty with rising yields was likely to be a one-shot affair and continuing changes of yields in the same direction would result in shortening or eliminating the yield adjustment lag. [25] This prediction appears to have been confirmed by experience in subsequent years. In Chart III-1 two bond yield series are plotted for the period 1951–1960; the lower of the two series shown is the yield on Treasury bonds and the upper, yields on new issue Grade 2 public utility bonds. [26] Two periods of cyclical

---

[24] LIAA-CMC Monograph, pp. 192–193. The passage quoted goes on to emphasize that the search for a higher rate of investment return is also crucial for meeting the competition of other institutions, e.g., mutual funds and uninsured pension funds. It is, however, debatable whether the competitive pressure for rate of return is as strong as this quotation suggests. See our discussion of the rate of return objective in Chapter I.

[25] Samuelson's testimony in the Patman *Hearings*, pp. 696–697; also see Tobin, *op. cit.*, p. 124.

[26] The utility bond yield series is compiled by Bankers Trust Company, New York. Grade 2 is approximately equivalent to Moody's Aa. Since the bulk of life company bond acquisitions are new issues, this series is a closer

recession followed by recovery, monetary restraint, and rising bond yields are depicted within the time span covered in this chart. It is true that as bond yields rose from their 1954 recession low, some narrowing of the corporate bond-Governments yield spread took place. This proved to be a temporary phenomenon, however, and after mid-1956, spreads were much larger than they

CHART III-1. *Market Yields on Long-Term Treasury Bonds and New Issue Grade 2 Public Utility Bonds: Quarterly, 1951/I–1960/IV*

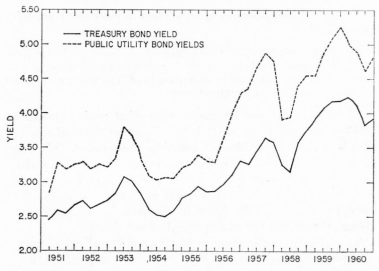

SOURCES: *Federal Reserve Bulletin;* Bankers Trust Company.

had been during the previous recession. Yield spreads declined in the 1957–1958 recession but widened with very little lag as inter-

representation of yields obtainable on private securities of interest to life companies than seasoned bond yields would be. We have also made a comparison between Treasury bond yields and yields obtained by three different life companies on authorizations to purchase corporate bonds and on bond acquisitions. The magnitude of changes in yield spread and the length of the adjustment lag vary somewhat according to which corporate bond yield series is used, but the qualitative conclusion reached below is not affected by the choice.

est rates subsequently recovered.[27]   Therefore during periods of
buoyant demand and high interest rates it appears that yield differentials are more likely to "pull-out" than "lock-in" Government
security holdings.[28]   The magnitude of the increase in yield differentials is so large that this conclusion holds even if, because
of their attitude toward portfolio risk, lenders require somewhat
larger spreads to choose private obligations when interest rates
rise.[29]

MARKET THINNESS AND CAPITAL LOSSES

The two arguments most often applied to insurance companies
are:

(1) The alleged inability of large investors to liquidate sizable blocs
    of long-term bonds in markets characterized by uncertainty;
(2) The alleged reluctance of companies to sell Governments at prices
    below original (or amortized) cost.

The market thinness argument asserts that market quotations
in times of rising yields are "phantom" in that the market is unable to digest sizable blocs of bonds at going prices.   Thus the
technical difficulty of marketing Governments has a differentially
strong impact on large investors — in particular, on the larger life
companies.   It follows that disposal rates must be expected to
have been substantially lower in the post-Accord years, even
though the desired rate of disposals had not changed.

Capital losses on Government bonds are only realized, of course,
if bonds are sold prior to maturity.   Conventional portfolio theory

---

[27] A comparison between mortgage loan yields and Governments would be
somewhat more favorable for the thesis we are criticizing.   However, most of
the expansion of the demand for credit in cyclical upswings seems to derive
from the corporate sector, and it is corporate obligations therefore which must
be the primary competition for scarce investible funds.

[28] The more conventional institutional beliefs seem to be consistent with
these empirical observations.   In general, the accepted principle seems to be
that increased demand for funds is accompanied by rising yields and rising
yield spreads among quality grades of assets.   This belief is associated with
the assumption that lenders upgrade eligibility standards when interest rates
are high.   For a statement of principle on the relation between the state of
corporate demand and yield spreads, see *Moody's Bond Survey*, June 10, 1957.

[29] It is also true that the arithmetic of the present value computation works
out so that "higher" interest rates require slightly larger yield spreads given
the same subjective risk evaluation.   See Smith, "On the Effectiveness of
Monetary Policy," p. 591.   This is of little quantitative significance, however.

offers no reasons for rational yield-maximizing investors to refrain from absorbing book losses so long as the risk differential in yield is adequate. However, in addition to the possibility that life insurance company officers "irrationally" dislike showing book losses, they may objectively hesitate to sell bonds below book value because of:

(1) The effect on limited surplus positions and the risk, therefore, of technical insolvency;
(2) The effect on insurance sales;
(3) The asymmetrical risk position of an investment officer in which mistakes of commission may weigh more heavily than those of omission.

The market thinness argument

The market thinness argument carries the implication that large investors, large life insurance companies in particular, were especially affected by the withdrawal of the Federal Reserve from full support of the Government securities market. Since 1951 and particularly in periods of credit restraint, rising interest rates, and market uncertainty, it is alleged that large companies could no longer regard market quotations as given. Attempts by these companies to dispose of large chunks of Government bonds as in the pre-Accord days, would now "break the market." Thus the "monopoly" imperfections associated with uncertain markets constrained the larger investors to lower rates of liquidation. To the extent that post-Accord markets were characteristically "uncertain," resulting market thinness[30] is supposed to explain the reduced level of disposals after 1951.

A priori, this argument is not very convincing. Considering that the Government securities market is "made" by a handful of specialists[31] who are accustomed to dealing in sizable transactions, it is not clear why it is feasible for the market to absorb

---

[30] Presumably the "bills only" policy adopted by the Federal Reserve in 1952 is not supposed to have strengthened the long-term market sufficiently to allow pre-Accord size disposals by large investors, at least not during periods of credit restraint.

[31] For a description of the trading mechanics of the Government securities market, see Roosa, "Federal Reserve Operations in the Money and Government Securities Markets," Piser, *Government Bond Market Analysis*, or Scott, *Government Securities Market*.

$20 millions of bonds placed on the market by a number of commercial banks but impossible for it to digest a similar amount placed by one or two life insurance companies. Commercial banks appear to have been able to liquidate long-term Governments at will since the Accord.[32] Since the argument appears to occupy an important place in the credit availability theory, however,[33] it seems best to test its impact on life company disposals directly.

If this argument is correct, then the sales by large life insurance companies should have been restricted much more than those of smaller companies. In Table III-2 net disposals of Governments are displayed for 55 life companies classified into four size groups. The companies represented include all but one (see Note to Table III-2) of the life companies reporting continuously to the New York State Superintendent of Insurance from 1947 to 1956. The 15 largest companies in the country make up Groups I and II. Groups III and IV represent companies licensed in New York with assets of $300 million to $1 billion and less than $300 million respectively.[34] Group bounds were selected on the basis of natural breaks in the rank list of companies by asset size.

Several conclusions seem to follow directly from this table:

(1) Reduced disposals of Governments are observed for all size groups in the second five-year period relative to the first.
(2) There is no indication of a significantly greater decline in disposals for the largest companies.
(3) The initial impact of the Accord and market uncertainty appears to have had the least effect on Group I companies, as judged by 1952 disposals.
(4) It was *not* Group I companies that took advantage of conditions of market strength in 1954. Rather, companies in Groups II–IV increased their liquidation during this year.

---

[32] For example, commercial banks included in the "Treasury Survey of Ownership" liquidated net $750 million of Treasury bonds during the "hard money" period of January–June 1953. Again, during the resumption of credit restraint following the 1954 recession, banks disposed (net) of nearly $3 billion of bonds in eight months (November 1954 to July 1955). Figures computed from ownership data in the *Treasury Bulletin*.

[33] It is this oligopolistic element that Roosa appeared to have in mind as the "kind of 'uncertainty' that has been of key importance in United States credit control." See his "Monetary Policy Again: Comments," p. 257.

[34] Asset ranges as of 1956.

TABLE III-2.   Net Disposals of Government Securities by 55 Life Insurance
Companies Grouped by Asset Size: 1947–1956
(millions of dollars)

Year	Group:	I	II	III	IV
1947		$1,183	$ 302	$115	*
1948		1,953	795	189	$16
1949		1,063	286	66	14
1950		1,228	361	142	8
1951		1,712	446	151	16
1947–1951		7,139	2,190	663	54
1952		711	95	33	−4
1953		305	51	61	4
1954		303	276	119	9
1955		352	159	10	4
1956		741	146	38	8
1952–1956		2,412	827	261	21

* Less than $500,000.

NOTE: A minus sign means a net increase in holdings of Governments for the year. Companies represented include all but one of the life insurance companies licensed to conduct business in New York state continuously from 1947 to 1956. The excluded company is a small re-insurance company which held over 80% of its assets in Government securities at end–1951 and was excluded for this reason. Its inclusion would only strengthen conclusions drawn from this and succeeding tables.

Group I consists of the industry's 5 largest companies.

Group II consists of the industry's next 10 largest companies, each with assets in excess of $1 billion (1956).

Group III consists of 12 companies with assets between $300 million and $1 billion (1956).

Group IV consists of 28 companies with assets less than $200 million (1956).

SOURCE: New York Insurance Report, Volume I, Life, annual.

The weight of this evidence seems inconsistent with the market thinness contention. In addition, Table III-3 shows that the larger companies succeeded in reducing their stock of Governments as a share of total assets more dramatically than smaller companies in the post-Accord years.[35] This again is not what the market

[35] The averages in Table III-3 are weighted; that is, they represent the total stock of Governments held by the group divided by total assets of the

TABLE III-3. Holdings of Government Securities as a Percentage of Admitted Assets for Life Insurance Companies Classified by Size: 1946, 1951, and 1956
(weighted averages in percents)

End Year Group:	I	II	III	IV
1946	50.91%	39.51% (36.52)	37.67%	34.32%
1951	16.21	15.34 (12.83)	14.56	16.59
1956	6.80	7.94 (6.03)	7.02	9.34

NOTE: For group composition see Note to Table III-2. The figures in parentheses under Group II represent average ratios for Group II *excluding* Travelers Insurance Company. Travelers has had a peculiarly strong preference for Government securities.

SOURCE: *New York Insurance Report*, Volume I, *Life*, annual.

thinness argument would lead us to expect.[36] It seems clear, then, that whatever forces operated to reduce the disposal rate of Government securities after 1951 affected companies in all size groups. No differential effect on larger companies is observable. The market thinness thesis must, therefore, be rejected.

The capital loss thesis

(i) The magnitude of capital losses during the post-Accord period

At the end of 1951 life insurance company holdings of Treasury bonds were concentrated in the marketable war loan issues carrying coupons of 2.25% and 2.50% and in several nonmarketable issues of which the Investment Series B bonds were most important. It is from these issues, then, that most subsequent sales

group. For 1956, we also computed an unweighted average of the Governments/Assets ratio for 101 companies classified into the same size groups. The results were: Group I, 6.60%; II, 7.91% (6.30% excluding Travelers); III, 8.54%; and IV, 10.03%. The source for this computation was data prepared by Shelby Cullom Davis and Co., New York.

[36] It might be argued that small companies have higher desired Governments/Assets ratios and were closer to minimum desired holdings in 1952 than were large companies. However, it is difficult to give much credence to this proposition since all groups continued to dispose of Governments throughout the 1952–1956 period, and all groups liquidated more Treasury obligations in 1956 than they had in 1952.

were made. A summary of the composition of securities liquidated during the 1950s can be made from data on life company Government securities holdings presented in Table III-4. Most of the war $2\frac{1}{4}$'s and $2\frac{1}{2}$'s were not eligible for commercial bank ownership in December 1951. Over time, this restriction was lifted from all the securities in question. The $2\frac{1}{4}$ coupon issues were due to mature in 1962 (callable in 1959). The $2\frac{1}{2}$'s had final maturity dates from 1967 to 1972, and became eligible for call five years in advance of their maturity dates. Most sales during the first five years of reduced disposals, 1952–1956, were made from this essentially homogeneous collection of marketable obligations.

The $2\frac{3}{4}$ percent Investment Series B issue represented a Treasury attempt to lock-in part of the Government bond portfolios of institutional lenders at the time of the Accord. This nonmarketable issue was offered in 1951 and again in 1952 in exchange for some series of the marketable $2\frac{1}{2}$'s.[37] The new issue was eligible for call in 1975 and had a final maturity date in 1980. The issue was only nominally nonmarketable, however, since the $2\frac{3}{4}$'s were convertible at the option of the holder into special issue five-year marketable notes carrying $1\frac{1}{2}$ percent coupons. During the latter half of the 1950's, these holdings were liquidated in substantial amounts through the process of conversion to the note issue and subsequent sale of the notes. The internal shifts in the composition of life company holdings which are evident in Table III-4 toward the end of the decade reflect the first of a series of Treasury experiments with advance refunding techniques.

The nonmarketable issues were acquired by life companies at par. Marketable Government bonds are carried by life companies at amortized cost for statement purposes. Most of the marketable war issues were purchased by life companies at par or a slight premium. Potential capital losses can, therefore, be measured from par.

Monthly observations of price discounts below par on mar-

---

[37] Therefore, part of the approximately $900 million decline in life company holdings of the $2\frac{1}{2}$'s, during 1952, represents bonds exchanged for the nonmarketable $2\frac{3}{4}$'s rather than outright sales. The subscriptions for the exchange issue were closed on May 29. During the following month life company holdings of Investment Series B bonds rose by $235 million. Therefore this must be about the magnitude of the 1952 exchange.

TABLE III-4. Life Insurance Company Holdings of Treasury Obligations: End-Year 1951–1959

(millions of dollars)

Type of Obligation	1951	1952	1953	1954	1955	1956	1957	1958	1959
Bills	$ 428	$ 464	$ 410	$ 537	$ 396	$ 222	$ 131	$ 456	$ 191
Certificates	217	56	37	4	3	34	102	53	54
Notes	1	8	52	67	50	55	55	61	219
Marketable Bonds									
Bank Restricted									
2¼'s	709	708	633	325	239	206	186	93	97
2½'s	5,752	4,855	4,717	4,223	3,927	3,444	3,378	3,140	3,065
Bank Eligible									
Old	259	185	119	80	65	63	20	16	13
New	—	59	217	269	533	427	429	875	1,065
Nonmarketable Bonds									
Investment Series B	2,923	3,179	2,935	2,865	2,669	2,433	2,160	1,898	1,692
Other	603	613	567	552	533	495	358	325	185
Total	10,892	10,127	9,687	8,922	8,415	7,379	6,819	6,917	6,531

NOTE: Data from the *Treasury Bulletin*. Total holdings are somewhat lower than those reported in Table III-1 because the Treasury survey does not provide complete coverage of all domestic life insurance companies. The "Bank Restricted" designation applies to the situation as of December 31, 1951. Subsequently all these issues became eligible for bank purchase. "Old" Bank Eligible issues refer to issues outstanding on December 31, 1951. "New" bonds are those issued after 1951.

CHART III-2. *Market Price Discounts Measured from Par on Treasury Bonds Held by Life Insurance Companies: Monthly, April 1951–December 1959*

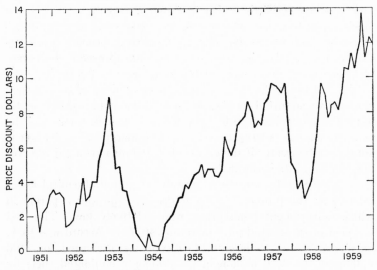

SOURCE: *Treasury Bulletin.*

ketable Treasury obligations are plotted in Chart III-2. The series is made up of prices recorded in the particular issues life companies held and liquidated. Investment Series B bonds are treated as marketable at the price quoted on the most recent issue of the special issue five-year notes.[38] Measuring losses from par, it is clear from inspection of Chart III-2 that sales of Treasury bonds from life company portfolios involved capital losses of less than five price points during most of the period between the Accord and the second quarter of 1956. Potential losses have ranged higher in subsequent years.

(ii) Effect of realized losses on solvency

Is it possible that book losses of the magnitude observed would have threatened the solvency position of life companies if bond sales had not been curtailed substantially below the pre-Accord

---

[38] There were two issues of these notes per year. Since life companies have never held much of an inventory of these notes, it appears sales were normally made shortly after conversion.

volume? An insurance company's primary protection against technical insolvency is the margin between its admitted assets and required reserves. This margin consists of capital (for a stock company), surplus, contingency reserves, and the differential between stated and required reserves. Secondary protection is provided by the investment earnings in excess of the rate of return guaranteed on outstanding policies.[39] Walter has estimated that the median values for ratios of surplus and contingency reserves to admitted assets, for mutual companies classified by asset size, range between 6% and 9%. For stock companies the estimated range is 11% to 15%.[40] The margin of protection is substantially greater if the excess of stated over required reserves is also taken into account.[41]

In order to estimate the magnitude of potential capital losses relative to the protective surplus cushion, consider a period in which Government bond prices were relatively low. The first full year of substantial price discounts after the Accord was 1957. During 1957 the 15 largest life companies accounted for $396 million of the $526 million in Governments liquidated (net) by the industry. Is it possible that during this year these companies would have liked to dispose of Governments at a much greater rate, say $2 billion, but that the impact of the capital losses on their surplus positions caused a curtailment of selling activity?

[39] For mutual companies, surplus is restricted by state law. The contingency reserves consist of various special surplus funds and security valuation reserves. For further discussion of the margin of protection and estimates of the magnitudes involved, see Walter, *The Investment Process*, pp. 49–55.

[40] *Ibid.*, p. 51.

[41] Policy reserves depend upon the rate of interest assumed as well as upon the mortality table used and the method of valuation. Maximum rates which may be used in computing reserves are established by state laws. Typically, these maximum rates have been 3% or 3.5%. These legal maxima substantially exceed the average interest rates actually assumed by life companies in determining required reserves. Therefore the excess of legal statement reserves over required reserves provides an additional cushion to absorb portfolio losses. Assuming typical ratios of surplus to admitted assets are on the order of 7.5% for mutual companies, the addition of excess reserves increases this ratio to 10.1% if a 3% legal interest rate is assumed, or to 14.7% under the assumption of a 3.5% ceiling. If 13% is assumed to be the typical surplus/admitted assets ratio for stock companies, adding excess reserves to the cushion raises the ratio to 13.1% under the 3% ceiling or to 17.5% given a 3.5% maximum. See *ibid.*, pp. 52–53.

Assets of these companies amounted to about $73 billion at the end of 1957. If we take a narrow interpretation of the surplus cushion and use the 7.5% surplus/assets ratio cited for mutual companies above, then the primary protective margin for the 15 companies would have amounted to about $5.5 billion. If capital losses on sales during 1957 averaged 10% of book value, disposals of $2 billion would have implied a book loss of $200 million to be absorbed by the protective cushion.[42] It is difficult to believe that temporary book losses amounting to 3% to 4% of the surplus margin could be regarded as constituting a serious threat to the legal solvency of life companies, thereby causing them to reduce bond sales well below the otherwise desired volume. Therefore we conclude that the objective impact of capital losses on the surplus position and solvency of life companies was not great enough to have deterred bonds sales during 1957. This conclusion is reinforced by the knowledge that the calculation we made exaggerated the extent of capital loss at going bond prices and underestimated the size of the protective margin. The solvency argument would be still less applicable to the 1952–1956 period since loss rates realized on sales were significantly less during these years than in 1957. During the pre-1957 period, losses would generally have run less than $50 million per billion dollars of sales.[43] Therefore, no real threat to life company solvency can explain the post-Accord reduction in bond sales.

---

[42] This assumption may also exaggerate the worst, for prices averaged well above 90 during the year for bonds held by life companies (Chart III-2). A calculation made for 11 companies for 1957 showed losses of $5.7 million on sales of $88.1 million of marketable bonds, or an average loss of 6.5%. Loss is computed as the difference between sales price and original cost. Data was obtained from Schedule D, Part 4 of the companies' Annual Statements. Disposals of Investment Series B bonds were not included in this calculation. Loss rates would have been greater, however, if companies had, in fact, sold $2 billion of Governments, both because of any impact additional life company sales would have had on market prices and because they would have had to dip into lower priced bonds.

[43] However, Brimmer has argued that a book loss of $24 million on sales of $1,047 million (the record of six companies' disposals during 1952–53) was "clearly a significant amount of loss." Brimmer, "Monetary Policy, Interest Rates and Life Insurance Company Investment Behavior," dissertation, p. 184. It is not indicated in what sense the loss is judged to be significant.

(iii) Capital losses, insurance sales and the risk position of investment officers

(a) *The argument.* From the perspective of this study, life insurance companies are financial intermediaries, allocating a savings flow drawn from current surplus sectors among various deficit sectors. In this view lending policy is not conceived as a device for influencing insurance sales. From the perspective of most life insurance companies' managements, however, selling life insurance is their primary business and the savings flow through life companies is a by-product of a device developed for the purpose of increasing sales, i.e., the level premium plan.[44] Given this orientation, yield maximization and other investment criteria will very likely be subordinated when they conflict with the company's interests in the insurance business. In the present context, life companies may dislike to show "excessive" book losses in their annual reports for fear they may be misunderstood by policyholders, or misrepresented by competitors' agents, to the detriment of insurance sales. For this reason the consequence of depressed bond prices may be a reduction in the disposal rate of Governments.[45]

It is also possible to believe that investment officers themselves occupy an asymmetrical risk position with regard to sales of Governments. Losses on Government bonds are realized only if an investment officer makes a positive decision to sell at a loss. If the investment officer chooses to make the sale and absorb the loss, investing the proceeds in a "private" asset, he risks the possibility of not recovering the expected return from the new investment. On the other hand, choosing not to make the sale involves the risk of missing an attractive alternative.[46] If, as

---

[44] This point, and the argument that follows, was suggested to this writer from the interviews with life company officers.

[45] It will be recalled that, prior to the 1959 revision in federal income tax legislation applicable to life companies, no tax benefits were associated with realization of capital losses (or gains). See Chapter II.

[46] Involved in the estimation of the return from switching out of Governments are expectations with respect to future movements in bond prices and changes in the yield spread between private assets and Treasury securities. The problem could be posed in terms of choosing the "right" volume of forward commitments to contract at current levels and anticipated future levels of Treasury bond prices. The extent to which decisions to make advance loan

seems plausible, the risk of an "actual loss" is subjectively weighed more heavily by cautious investment officers than the risk of "opportunity loss," then declining bond prices may lead *ceteris paribus* to reduced disposals of Governments.[47]

It is finally possible, of course, that life company portfolio managers have an "irrational" distaste for book losses that cannot be explained by reference to concerns over insurance sales or their personal job security. In the interviews with life company investment officers, we attempted to appraise their attitude toward book losses from security sales.

(b) *The evidence.* In interviews with 12 companies, the question of capital losses on Treasury bond sales was raised. Eleven of the respondents indicated that book losses were a deterrent to sales in some degree. One "economic man" claimed that such losses were irrelevant. All 11 who considered book losses a deterrent were still willing to absorb the losses as long as alternative investments were sufficiently attractive. They seemed to be saying implicitly that a larger yield differential between private securities and Governments was required to induce sales of Treasury bonds when the market price of these bonds were depressed below their book value. In most cases the primary consideration was stated in terms of the period of time it would take to "recover" the capital loss. Bond sales were made if the loss involved could be made up in x years. For the officers interviewed, x was placed somewhere between two and six. In four responses the rule of thumb was phrased in terms of the first call date in the private obligation acquired with the sale proceeds. That is, for the sale to be made, the loss must be made up "before the first call date

---

commitments are in fact based on expectations about future rates is discussed in Chapter VI.

[47] If the problem is viewed strictly in a cyclical context, then optimum behavior over the cycle may call for sales of Governments in excess of current needs when bond prices are cyclically high, the proceeds being stored in cash assets for use in periods of low bond prices. An investment officer may be reluctant to sell bonds and realize book losses because such action would constitute an admission that the sales should have been concluded earlier in the cycle, before the decline in bond prices took place. This sort of reaction on the part of portfolio managers is suggested as a possibility by Lindbeck, *op. cit.*, pp. 24–25. We will examine the cyclical sensitivity of life company liquid asset holdings in Chapter V. In the thesis under consideration, however, life company officers are depicted as reluctant to realize losses regardless of future price expectations.

on the alternative investment," or, for two respondents, *"twice before the first call date."* Even the officer to whom book losses were irrelevant seemed to feel that call protection was of more than normal importance where funds were obtained from bond sales involving a capital loss.

It was difficult to pin down precisely what was meant by making up the loss in *x* years. Most officers interviewed appeared to be thinking simply in terms of the sum of interest receipts anticipated over *x* years on the new investment over and above interest receipts which would have been earned on the disposed Treasury bond. No time or risk discounting seems to be performed in this sort of calculation. Some officers, however, in quoting a loss recovery range (e.g., two to four years) apparently had in mind adapting the specific period required to the quality of the private loan alternative, thus indirectly allowing for risk. This strikes one as a rather crude and peculiar decision rule to use.[48] Whatever the rationale, however, its use does reflect a reluctance on the part of life companies to absorb substantial book losses on bond sales.

Assuming that we have correctly interpreted the most typical version of the loss recovery rule, its effect can be illustrated in an arithmetic example. Suppose a life insurance company holds a portfolio of Government securities purchased at par and yielding $2.50 per $100 face value in interest receipts per year. Suppose, further, that when Governments are selling in the market at par,

---

[48] This rule implicitly assumes that the private sector investment is acquired at par and expected to be held for some time, presumably to maturity. Since most of the officers interviewed were associated with large companies, this may simply reflect their attitude that the most attractive investments for them during a period of high interest rates are normally corporate direct placements, which generally satisfy the assumption.

We were not successful in attempts to extract from those interviewed a conscious rationale for using this sort of loss recovery decision rule. The use of this device may mean, as suggested above, that it takes a wider yield spread to induce life companies to opt for private sector loans when interest rates are high and bond prices depressed. Both the kind of considerations discussed above, i.e., the ability to buy more portfolio safety when returns are high, and the arithmetic effect of losses (potential gains) reflected in Warren Smith's approach (note 29 above) may be involved in determining the required yield spread. However, no such attitude is necessarily implied. The rule may simply be a convenient means of restricting sales at a loss in order to limit the impact on surplus and/or the risk exposure of investment officers.

the minimum return on private sector investments which will induce the life company to switch from Governments to private securities is $3.50 per $100.[49] Now we assume that the life company makes a gross comparison of (undiscounted) interest receipts anticipated over future years from the alternatives before it. This permits us to calculate how far prices of Governments can fall before the company is disturbed; i.e., before it will need additional yield inducement to make the switch from Governments to private loans. This critical price can be computed from the relation:

$$(r_p P_g - 2.50)x = 100 - P_g \text{ where,}$$

P_g = market price of Government bonds on $100 face value,
r_p = going yield on new private loans,
x = required loss recovery period in years.

Assuming, then, that new private loans return $3.50 per year per $100 invested, and that the book loss $(100 - P_g)$ must be made up in five years, the critical price is $P_g = 95.74. Losses of less than $4.26 per $100 book value will not affect bond sales, but wider yield spreads (a higher r_p, other things being equal) will be required to induce sales at lower prices (larger losses). Examples

TABLE III-5. *Critical Values of P_g for Various Loss Recovery Periods (x) and Yields on Private Loans (r_p)*

x	r_p: 3.50%	4.00%	4.50%	5.00%	5.50%
2	98.13	97.22	96.33	95.45	94.59
3	97.29	95.98	94.71	93.48	92.28
4	96.49	94.83	93.22	91.67	90.16
5	95.74	93.75	91.84	90.00	88.24
6	95.04	92.74	90.55	88.46	86.48
10	92.60	89.29	86.21	83.33	80.65

NOTE: Prices quoted in hundredths. Computed using formula in text assuming 2.5% Treasury bonds with book value of $100.

of critical prices computed in this way for various r_p and x are displayed in Table III-5. Thus, if r_p rises to 4% in the illustration

---

[49] We assume that private debt issues are purchased at par. Presumably this is the same yield differential that applies to the decision respecting the allocation of a new dollar of income to either Treasury or privately issued securities, although this need not be the case.

at hand, the critical price can fall as low as $93.75 before book losses lead companies to restrict bond sales.

Given observations on r_p and P_g for the post-Accord years, it is then possible to make a rough evaluation of how effective depressed bond prices were in locking in life company holdings of Governments. The appropriate measure of r_p must be yields on loans of the type and quality which life companies, in fact, were making during the period. However, since life companies have been active in contracting future delivery loans, yields on their portfolio acquisitions tend to be a distributed average of past yields rather than an accurate reflection of current market conditions and, therefore, of current investment alternatives. Ideally we would like to use for r_p a series of yields obtained by life companies on current loan authorizations rather than acquisitions. We do not have much yield information in this form, but we were able to collect monthly yield data on bond and mortgage authorizations for one large company over the period of interest. Comparison of this series with fragmentary evidence from several other companies led to the conclusion that this series was reasonably representative of yields obtainable by other large companies.[50] An average of the bond and mortgage loan yields for this company is displayed in Table III-6 along with a series of typical prices of the Treasury 2½ issues that dominated the marketable Treasury bonds held by life companies during the 1950s. Using the rule-of-thumb formula presented above, we can estimate the degree of restriction implied by these bond prices.

One such measure is presented in column (3) of Table III-6. On the assumptions underlying Table III-5, we have recorded the approximate loss recovery requirements for which the indicated bond prices would have some locking-in effect. Thus a 4 in column (3) means that for any life company that insists on making up a capital loss in four years or less, the going market yield in column (1) is insufficient to offset the current market price for Treasury bonds (column (2)). A life company with a less strin-

---

[50] The yields in question also were compared with annual average yields on loan and investment authorizations made during 1953–1956 by 67 life companies reporting in an LIAA survey. The individual company yields on authorizations matched very closely the LIAA data in all major categories. The LIAA results were published in the ALC-LIAA *Joint Investment Bulletin*, No. 321, December 13, 1957.

TABLE III-6. *Estimation of the Restrictive Effect of Book Losses on Bond Sales: 1951/II–1959/IV*

	(1) Yield on Private Loans (r_p)	(2) Price of Treasury 2½'s	(3) Losses Restrictive for a Minimally Acceptable x of:
1951/II	3.69%	$ 97.10	2
III	3.86	97.94	—
IV	3.75	96.91	2
1952/I	4.04	96.72	2
II	3.94	98.41	—
III	3.86	96.78	2
IV	4.09	96.63	2
1953/I	3.98	94.93	4
II	4.39	92.18	5
III	4.37	94.15	4
IV	4.39	96.35	2
1954/I	4.24	99.45	—
II	4.32	100.01	—
III	4.23	100.22	—
IV	4.04	99.24	—
1955/I	3.97	96.87	2
II	4.08	96.26	3
III	4.00	94.92	4
IV	4.17	95.70	3
1956/I	4.19	95.42	3
II	4.39	94.68	3
III	4.38	92.05	5
IV	4.70	89.92	6
1957/I	5.05	91.50	4
II	5.21	88.29	6
III	5.36	87.04	6
IV	5.47	91.27	4
1958/I	5.58	95.25	—
II	5.49	95.79	—
III	5.22	90.08	5
IV	5.28	87.83	6
1959/I	5.44	86.89	6
II	5.44	84.19	7
III	5.44	82.79	8
IV	5.72	82.35	8

See p. 202 for sources.

gent loss recovery requirement than four years would not be inhibited from selling bonds at the going price to acquire private loans at the stated yield.

Our interview evidence suggests that the locking-in effect would be negligible in periods represented by a blank in column (3) of Table III-6. Some companies would likely reduce bond sales (compared to a no-loss situation) in periods where a 2 or 3 is recorded. More companies would feel some selling constraint in periods with a 4 or 5, and the inhibition would be widespread and of substantial magnitude in periods characterized by 6 or higher. If this decision rule is a reasonable approximation of life company behavior in the aggregate, then we must conclude that during the first four post-Accord years the locking-in effect could have been a significant explanation of reduced sales only during three of the twelve quarters (1953/I-III). Some constraining effect may have been present during the period 1955/II through 1956/II. After 1956, excepting the 1958 recession period, the locking-in phenomenon could have been very strong.

EXPECTATIONS AND THE CREDIT AVAILABILITY THESIS

This evaluation has been based on an analysis of the direct impact of the credit availability propositions upon the willingness of life companies to liquidate Treasury bonds. As we have seen, however, a central tenet of the credit availability doctrine was that monetary tightness produced slowly rising interest rates which, in turn, generated expectations about future yield spreads, liquidity protection, risk, and capital losses, and these expecta-

---

Table III-6 continued

SOURCES: The yield on private loans represents the experience of one large life insurance company. The series is derived from a monthly summary of yields obtained on corporate bond and mortgage loans authorized during the month. The recorded yield is an average of the reported yield on bond authorizations and the reported yield on mortgage loans net of an estimate of origination and servicing costs. The Treasury bond price series is an average of monthly observations of bid prices on the marketable Treasury $2\frac{1}{2}$'s held in largest amounts by life companies. Column (2) is from the *Treasury Bulletin*. Column (3) is derived from the formula underlying Table III-5. The loss recovery period is measured in years. A blank means that the book losses do not restrict sales given loss recovery periods of two or more years.

tions acted as a deterrent to bond sales. The expectations phenomenon does not seem relevant to the market thinness strand of
the credit availability thesis.

Does a consideration of the uncertainty produced by the Accord
and subsequent upward pressure on interest rates revive the credit
availability hypothesis? If we are correct that the liquidity,
portfolio quality, and yield-spread propositions turn out to be
specious upon direct examination (i.e., assuming sharp increases
in interest rates), then there is nothing for life companies to fear
from the expectation that substantial increases in interest rates
may occur. With regard to capital losses, however, we have
found that substantial book losses do inhibit security sales. If
this is so, cannot expectations of future capital losses lead life
companies to act currently to avoid those potential losses? Imagine that current bond prices are at or only slightly below book
value and therefore do not deter current sales of Treasury bonds
from life company portfolios. However, suppose there is a reasonable expectation of increasing monetary tightness over the upcoming months, so there is reason to *fear* potential losses on
sales of Governments in a few months. Suppose life companies
react to this situation by reducing their current forward loan
commitments in line with the expected normal cash flow for future
months, exclusive of funds obtainable from security sales. By
cutting back on loan authorizations today, life companies will very
likely reduce future sales of Governments regardless of whether,
in fact, expectations of lower bond prices are realized. Thus,
with a lag, expectations about probable future capital losses can
slow the rate of Government security disposals independent of
actual losses.

There is, however, one serious flaw in this version of the capital
loss — locking-in thesis. Given the above assumptions about life
company expectations, the argument fails to explain why companies ration out attractive loan commitments rather than switch
from long-term Government bonds into short-term earning assets.
The latter adjustment seems a much more plausible reaction to
the postulated situation. Indeed it is precisely what life companies did during the period around the Accord. In addition to
heavy net disposals of Governments during this period, life companies added over a billion dollars to their short-term holdings of

Treasury obligations between October 1950 and June 1951.[51] The uncertainty about future prices of Governments which characterized this period fits very closely the circumstances assumed by the expectations thesis.[52] The failure of life companies to engage in this sort of internal adjustment within their Governments portfolio during the mid-1951 to mid-1956 period[53] indicates either that they did not expect a substantial decline in future bond prices or that this possibility was not of much concern to them. Thus the uncertainty-expectations argument does not contribute additional explanatory power to the direct capital loss hypothesis.

SUMMARY EVALUATION OF THE CREDIT AVAILABILITY PROPOSITIONS

We have rejected four of the five dimensions of the credit availability thesis as applied to the post-Accord reduction in life insurance company Treasury bond sales. There seemed to be nothing in the (1) liquidity, (2) asset quality, (3) sticky private asset yields, or (4) market thinness strands of the credit availability doctrine. Furthermore, we found the actual impact of book losses on life company surplus and solvency positions to be too quantitatively insignificant to produce much of a locking-in effect.

However, there did exist other considerations which might

---

[51] Bills, certificates, and notes. (*Treasury Bulletin* ownership data.)

[52] For some confirming testimony, see the answers of life insurance company officers to Patman Committee questions in the Patman *Replies*, pp. 1227–33. Also, see the discussion by B. C. Hallowell of the article by O'Leary, "The Institutional Savings-Investment Process and Current Economic Theory," pp. 483–484. It is true that the specific responses by life company investment officers to the Patman questionnaire in late 1951 seem to support the uncertainty-expectations thesis. See the Patman *Replies*, answers to question 2, pp. 1234–44. Also, C. M. Shanks' testimony in the Patman *Hearings*, especially pp. 457–462. However, many of the respondents admitted that they had not been put to the test since they had liquidated bonds very heavily prior to the Accord and, therefore, were supplied with sufficient short-term assets to live some months without being forced to consider whether to sell bonds at a loss. Furthermore since life companies had some degree of self-interest in higher interest rates and reduced inflationary pressure, their positive statements regarding the efficacy of tighter monetary policy upon their portfolio behavior should perhaps be treated with caution.

[53] There is a modest cyclical buildup of short-term Governments in 1954 and 1955. (See Chapter V.) But this accumulation is quite small compared to the sort of adjustment implied here.

conceivably discourage security sales involving a book loss. These other considerations included real or imagined effects on insurance sales and the general desire of investment officers to limit their personal risk exposure. At any rate, although the rationale remained vague, interviews with life insurance company officers did clearly establish the existence of widespread inhibitions respecting decisions to sell bonds at a time when market prices are substantially below book value. Thus the evidence did not warrant total rejection of the capital loss portion of the locking-in doctrine.

The use of such a rule suggests that investment funds obtained from bond sales at a loss are treated differently (i.e., higher private loan yields are required to induce commitment of such funds) than more normal sources of funds, including portfolio sales *not* involving book losses. Interview responses also emphasized the importance of redemption risk to life companies. When the source of funds is proceeds of bonds liquidated at a loss, investment officers are particularly sensitive to the need for protecting new investments against early call.

Using the loss recovery decision rule and evidence on yields obtainable by life companies on private sector investments during the post-Accord years, we concluded the locking-in effect of book losses could have been strong during the first three quarters of 1953 and most of the mid-1956 to 1960 period. During the remaining time segments, it would appear that the impact of capital losses would have been modest at most. This means, in particular, that the capital loss hypothesis appears unable to explain the sharp decline in Treasury bond sales after 1951.

Taking the five years 1952–1956 as a unit, however, the capital loss effect seemed to be of significance in 5 of the 16 quarters. The evidence suggested that some companies would reduce their sales of Governments with market prices at the levels that existed in those quarters. Since the capital loss thesis explains little or nothing of the reduced Treasury security sales during 11 of the 16 quarters, it is doubtful whether book losses alone explain all the sluggish disposal rate during the few quarters in which they are relevant. Therefore concluding that the capital loss–locking-in effect explains five-sixteenths of the reduced liquidation rate during 1952–1956 (using 1947–1951 as the norm) would exaggerate the importance of capital losses. But it is conceivable that the capital loss impact explains something like 20% of the slowdown in this portfolio adjustment process.

Clearly, though, something else was at work. We continue our analysis of the time pattern of Government securities liquidation with an examination of the portfolio balance hypothesis.

The Portfolio Balance Hypothesis

We have suggested a portfolio balance hypothesis as a possible alternative (or complement) to the credit availability doctrine. It is argued that by 1951 life insurance companies "had reduced governments to something like a normal proportion of their portfolios" [54] if normalcy is judged by the 1940 portfolio composition. Consequently life companies might be expected to display some caution with regard to further liquidation of their Treasury security holdings. On the other hand, life company holdings of Governments in 1951 (and for that matter in 1940) [55] were well in excess of minimum liquidity needs, as demonstrated by the continued liquidation of these securities over the subsequent decade. The latter experience would seem to cast doubt on the explanatory value of a portfolio proportions hypothesis. However, the disposal rate was substantially reduced after 1951, and portfolio balance advocates suggest that the *approach* to portfolio equilibrium leads to a "spreading out" of further liquidation. [56] We turn to an examination of this possibility.

The Problem

Let us recall what has to be explained. Government security holdings of life companies amounted to $11.0 billion (16.1% of

[54] Tobin, *op. cit.*, p. 124.

[55] The consensus of life company executives testifying in the TNEC *Hearings*, during the liquidity-conscious late 1930s, was that liquidity needs would be amply met with Treasury security holdings amounting to 10% of assets. (See, for example, the opinions of J. W. Stedman, p. 15260, and D. S. Beebe, p. 15295.) Government security holdings of life companies amounted to 18.7% of assets at year-end 1940, and 16.1% at the end of 1951.

[56] Some support for this view is found in the 1951 testimony of Carroll Shanks, President of the Prudential Insurance Company of America. He expressed the belief that most companies were "reaching the minimum holdings of Governments," and that in these circumstances companies tend to "spread it out." Patman *Hearings*, p. 461.

assets) at the end of 1951, $7.6 billion (7.9% of assets) five years later, and $6.1 billion (4.9% of assets) after a decade (1961). Thus, in the first five years (1952–1956), life companies liquidated (net) $3.4 billion of Governments; in the second five years (1957–1961), $1.5 billion.[57]   At the 1947–1951 disposal rate, $4.9 billion of Governments would have been liquidated in two and one-half years, rather than ten.   We have seen that the locking-in effect of capital losses may have contributed significantly to a slowdown in disposals after mid-1956.   However, the credit availability doctrine seemed of limited assistance in explaining the immediate post-1951 decline.

Suppose that the ultimate objective of life companies, taking into account the diversity of individual company tastes, was to reduce industry holdings of Government securities to $5 billion.[58] Taking the beginning of 1952 as a starting point, this means that about $6 billion in Governments remained to be liquidated.   Now net disposals averaged $2,125 million per annum during the 1947–1951 period.   If this rate had continued, life companies would have reached the postulated target in less than three years.   However, we already know that the capital loss–locking-in effect might have reduced the disposal rate by as much as 20% after 1951. If in fact the capital loss impact was of this order of magnitude, the typical annual liquidation rate after 1951 would have been only about $1,700 million on this account.   At this rate it would have taken three and one-half years to dispose of $6 billion of Government securities.   But the actual 1952–1956 disposal rate was not $2,100 million or even $1,700 million per annum, but less than $700 million per annum.   At this rate it would have taken nearly nine years to reach the assumed target.   If the portfolio balance hypothesis is to rationalize the 1952–1956 experience, this is the degree of spreading out which must be explained.

---

[57] Liquidation has continued since 1961.   As of the end of 1964, life companies held $5.5 billion in Governments, a decline of $600 million in three years.

[58] Depending on when the goal was expected to be reached, this implies a leveling off at an industry Governments/assets ratio of 4% to 5%.   Taking into account the historical record, interview evidence we have obtained, and public testimony of life company officers, this seems to be a plausible assumption.

The Hypothesis

Although it seems intuitively plausible that a slowing down of disposals might occur in the final stages of liquidation, apparently no one has laid out the logic of such behavior. The common-sense notion seems to be that once life company portfolio proportions returned to a familiar neighborhood, there was no sense of urgency about completing the liquidation process. Indeed the portfolio managers may have decided to become more selective in considering alternative ways of utilizing proceeds obtained from the last batches of Governments disposed. This may mean spreading out disposals over time to obtain a larger selection of alternatives.[59] The situation we are being asked to explain stretches this sort of commonsense approach beyond the realm of plausibility. We are attempting to explain the stretching out of liquidation of a three or three and one-half years' stock of Governments (measured by the pre-Accord disposal rate) over nearly nine years. This is not the sort of closeness to equilibrium that is implied by commonsense considerations.[60]

In the absence of any more formal formulation of a portfolio balance hypothesis, we shall have to supply the logic of such a thesis. Two possible interpretations of the spreading-out phenomena occur to us. One depends upon the existence of a substantial degree of conscious oligopolistic interdependence among life companies in formulating decisions respecting the liquidation rate of Governments. The other interpretation is consistent with independent decisions in a competitive market framework.

In either case, the background of the problem may be summarized as follows:

At the end of the war life companies held, as one investment

---

[59] Referring again to Mr. Shanks' testimony, he observed specifically that, "if you have only $50 million to go, you will spread it out." Patman *Hearings*, p. 461.

[60] To continue with the Prudential case, it is clear that the Prudential was not down to its last $50 million when Mr. Shanks was testifying. During the following six years (1952–1957), the Prudential liquidated $643 million (net) of its Governments portfolio. It is possible, of course, that Prudential, and life companies in general, annually readjusted downward their desired Governments/assets ratio after 1951. There may be a little merit in this proposition, but in order to support an explanation of the extended disposal pattern there would have to be a lot in it.

officer put it to this writer, a "bottomless bag" of Government securities. Under these conditions, rational behavior dictated swapping "riskless" Governments for "risk" assets so long as the yield spread was sufficient to cover the investor's subjective evaluation of risk[61] plus transactions costs. Formally, in a world with two assets, Governments and private securities, the life insurance industry's supply of funds schedule to the private sector under the assumed circumstances would be perfectly elastic[62] at the yield:

$$r_p = r_g + d, \text{ where}$$

r_p = yield on private securities
r_g = yield on Governments
d = minimum risk differential.

Given r_g and d, actual sales of Governments are determined by the demand for life insurance funds.[63]

It may now be argued that by end-1951 the circumstances had changed. Industry holdings of Governments (relative to total assets) had been reduced to historically familiar levels. The bag was no longer bottomless and the desired Governments/assets ratio was within the horizon. Under these circumstances, higher yields on currently invested funds could be obtained if the time rate of transfer from Governments to private obligations were slowed down.

Consider Figure III-1. In this figure, the life insurance industry supply schedule of funds offered to the private sector is perfectly elastic at the yield r_m, where $r_m = r_g + d$. Two sources of funds are distinguished. The amount ON represents the "normal flow" of investible funds[64] through life companies in the period under consideration. Beyond ON, funds are obtained from liquidation of Treasury obligations. This portion of the supply sched-

---

[61] For large investors able to obtain adequate diversification only the pure risk differential is relevant. See Chapter I.

[62] That is, over a long range covering any conceivable supply/demand equilibrium. We ignore here the possibility that the risk differential should increase with a rise in the level of r_g.

[63] Assumed to be represented by a Chamberlinian *ceteris paribus* demand schedule, with the aggregate demand for funds from the private sector given as well as the supply schedules of competing lenders.

[64] Net gain in ledger assets adjusted to a cash basis plus portfolio rollover exclusive of sales of assets.

FIGURE III-1. Hypothetical Supply of and Demand for Life Insurance Company Funds: Private Sector

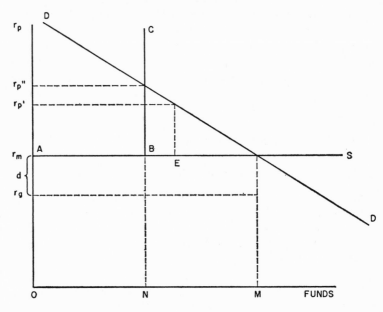

ule is drawn in accordance with the open-to-buy environment which it is agreed characterized the postwar, pre-Accord period. With an essentially limitless stock of Governments, the equilibrium yield obtained on private securities is always r_m; the total amount of life company funds invested in private obligations during any period depends upon the position of the net demand for life insurance funds, represented by the schedule, DD. We assume that life companies always invest their "normal" cash flow during the period in which it is generated.[65] Thus, this portion of the supply schedule is always of the form ABC in Figure III-1.

Now, given r_g, d, ON, and DD, suppose the stock of Governments in excess of the desired stock is reduced to (say) 3NM dollars, that is, three years' worth of disposals given the current position of the relevant functions. In this situation, would it make sense for life companies in the aggregate to reduce the

---

[65] The extent to which companies have, in fact, deviated from this "fully invested" principle is examined in Chapter V.

liquidation rate of Governments and spread the disposal of the 3NM dollars worth of holdings over (say) nine years? This is approximately the decision the industry faced in 1951.[66]

The advantage to the life insurance industry of restricting sales is that higher yields can be obtained on current investments in private obligations. In our example, restriction of sales to $\frac{1}{3}$NM = BE (Figure III-1) has the result of raising the yield obtained on current investment to r_p'.

The cost associated with this action is that $\frac{2}{3}$NM of the portfolio remains in low yielding Government securities. In terms of yield spreads, the loss on this portion of the portfolio is, of course, $r_m - r_g$.

Whether or not a decision to hold back part of the Government securities portfolio earmarked for sale in any time period will result in a net benefit for the industry depends on the elasticity of DD. It seems intuitively clear that when the stock of Governments is very large (e.g., 50% of assets), the carrying costs of holding Government securities over an extended period would exceed the benefits from restricted disposals over any plausible range of demand elasticity. At some point in the liquidation process, however, the stock of Governments may become sufficiently reduced to shift the balance in favor of reducing the disposal rate. If this thesis has explanatory value, it must be argued that the life insurance industry reached this position about 1951.[67]

The question arises as to whether the decision to restrict sales

[66] To keep the illustration simple, we assume a three years' stock of Governments. Allowing for the capital loss effect, a three and one-half years' assumption could be used.

[67] This argument obviously assumed that life companies treat investible funds obtained through sales of Governments differently from funds generated through "normal" channels. That is, we have assumed that the normal cash inflow is always invested during the period in which it originates in private obligations so long as the demand/supply equilibrium occurs in the perfectly inelastic portion of the supply curve (BC in Figure III-1). Analogous behavior with respect to liquidation of Governments would mean always transferring the amount indicated by NM in Figure III-1 from Governments to private obligations. But the portfolio balance thesis being investigated seems to assume that companies may choose to restrict the supply of funds obtained from sales of Governments. Some may regard this presumption of inconsistent behavior as sufficient reason to dismiss the portfolio balance hypothesis (assuming acceptance of the fully invested principle) out of hand. However, we do not find the postulated behavior inconceivable on these grounds. (See Chapter V for an examination of the fully invested principle.)

of Governments was a plausible option open to the life insurance industry. Deliberate exercise of this option by the industry depends upon the existence of a strong and conscious feeling of oligopolistic interdependence among life companies, and the absence of comparable competitive imperfections among competing lenders. On this ground, the above interpretation of the portfolio balance thesis appears highly improbable to us. Even if private security yields, and yield spreads, were temporarily raised through concerted action, the degree of oligopolistic cooperation required to prevent individual companies from reacting to wider yield spreads with increased sales of Governments is far beyond that which seems compatible with the structure of the life insurance industry. The latter response makes it unlikely that the two or three largest companies could successfully carry out a restrictive sales policy unless their actions produced expectations of further widening in the yield differential between private and Treasury obligations.

It might simply be argued, however, that as the industry Governments/assets ratio returned to a historically familiar neighborhood, with the desired portfolio balance in sight, expectations of rising yields *and* widening yield spreads were generated. Such expectations might have been reinforced by the Accord. Given such expectations, it might pay companies to delay liquidation of part of their Governments portfolio in order to be able to take advantage of potentially more attractive opportunities. In this case the spreading-out response is compatible with independent life company decisions in an essentially competitive atmosphere.[68]

Given that life companies act like competitive firms and that their individual and independently made decisions have an inconsequential influence on market yields, the terms obtained on investment of the normal funds flow is expected by them to be independent of their disposal rate. Under these circumstances the problem can be visualized as follows:

Given: (1) A stock of governments to be liquidated
(2) A horizon or cutoff date, $t = m$, by which time under any

---

[68] Again if the fully invested principle is presumed to apply to life company treatment of their normal cash inflow, this hypothesis assumes a differential response to funds obtained from Government security sales. Interest rate forecasts affect supply of funds generated from the latter source but do not influence the supply of normal funds flow.

circumstances the stock of Governments will have been disposed of

(3) Normal funds available for new investment in each period, i.e., the inflow of investible funds excluding proceeds from security sales

(4) Demand for life insurance funds, each period

(5) The market yield on Government securities $r_g(t)$ for each t

Determine: The optimum (i.e., yield-maximizing) time path of liquidation of the stock of Governments.

The horizon date could be defined in terms of the maturity date of new private security acquisitions as well as the final maturity dates on the stock of Governments. In the case at hand, taking 1952 as $t = 0$, the bulk of Governments in life company portfolios had final maturity dates 15 to 20 years distant (1967 to 1971). Since the effective life of private obligations generally purchased by life companies is probably around 15 years, not too much violence will be done by assuming a fixed horizon date around $t = 15$ to $t = 20$. As before, the demand for insurance funds is thought of in terms of a *ceteris paribus* demand schedule. For simplicity of statement the market yield on Governments is assumed to be constant for all t.

Suppose the givens are known with certainty. Then it is possible to derive the optimum time path of disposals. The problem can be viewed as one of balancing,

(1) the carrying cost of holding Governments, against

(2) the opportunity cost of disposing of Governments.

The cost of holding a dollar of Governments is measured by the difference between the return on Governments and the alternative return on private securities over the holding period. Continued disposals of Governments for the alternative yield, $r_p = r_g + d$, involves sacrifice of higher yielding future opportunities.[69] Given the yield on private securities at $t = 0$, $r_p(0)$, we can compute the equilibrium yield, $r_p(k)$, for any $t = k$. The equilibrium yield for $t = k$ is defined as that yield at which the investor is indifferent between disposing of a dollar of Governments[70] at $t = 0$ and holding that sum for disposal at $t = k$. Under the assumption of

---

[69] On the assumption that companies expect wider yield spreads in the future.

[70] And placing the proceeds in private securities carrying a yield $r_p(0)$.

certain expectations, the difference in yield, $r_p(k) - r_p(0)$ is just adequate to cover the carrying costs of Governments.[71]

It is to be expected that the transition from an open-to-buy environment to one in which hard portfolio choices have to be made would produce an increase in the yield spread between private obligations and Governments. In Figure III-1, in the absence of sales of Governments as a source of funds, the yield differential rises from $r_m - r_g$ to $r_p'' - r_g$. Whether yield spreads can be reasonably expected to rise sufficiently to explain the magnitude of spreading out of Governments sales after 1951 is open to question. A partial check on the plausibility of this sort of explanation can be made by computing the future equilibrium yields necessary to cover the costs of holding back Governments.

The alternatives for disposal of a dollar of Governments are as follows:

(1) Disposal at $t = 0$ and investment of proceeds in private securities carrying a yield of $r_p(0) = r_m$;
(2) Retaining the Governments for disposal in some future $t = k$, and investing the proceeds in private securities with yields $r_p(k)$.

In order to determine the minimum $r_p(k)$ for any k that is necessary to induce retention of Governments until $t = k$, it is necessary to have a procedure for comparing alternative streams of receipts. There are any number of possibilities depending on investors' objectives, but two conventional comparisons suggest themselves:

(1) the present value comparison;
(2) the "number of dollars" at horizon date, $t = m$, comparison.

Under the present value method an investor is indifferent between immediate disposal and disposal at some $t = k$, where the present value (at $t = 0$) of the two alternative streams of returns from $t = 0$ to $t = m$ (horizon) are identical. In this calculation future dollars are discounted at an appropriate marginal rate of return. In the calculations below we use the "riskless" rate, r_g. It is possible, however, that an investor with long-term, fixed dollar liabilities is more interested in the number of dollars a dollar

---

[71] Given a procedure for comparing alternative streams of receipts. This question is discussed below.

in $t = 0$ can earn by some distant horizon date, and less concerned with the time path of receipts.

Table III-7 displays the equilibrium private security yields, $r_p(t)$, at which investors would be "indifferent" between immediate transfers and holding Governments, for $r_p(0) = 4\%$, $\bar{r}_g = 3\%$, and horizon dates, in line with our previous estimates of 15 and 20 years. Computations are made by both present value and horizon sum methods. Securities are assumed to be compound-interest obligations with interest compounded semiannually. They are assumed to be redeemable at par on the horizon date. Governments are assumed to be marketable at par at any time, i.e., r_g is fixed through time. Private issues acquired are held until the horizon date; we assume there is no trading of private securities. Now, looking at Table III-7, imagine that life companies in 1952 were at $t = 0$. The portfolio balance thesis asserts

TABLE III-7. Time Path of Indifference Yields Computed on the Assumption of $r_g = 3\%$, $r_p(0) = 4\%$, for Two Horizon Dates

Year	Present Value Method Years to Horizon		Horizon Sum Method Years to Horizon	
	20	15	20	15
0	4.00%	4.00%	4.00%	4.00%
1	4.07	4.09	4.05	4.07
2	4.15	4.19	4.11	4.15
3	4.24	4.31	4.18	4.25
4	4.33	4.45	4.25	4.37
5	4.44	4.62	4.33	4.50
6	4.57	4.83	4.43	4.67
7	4.72	5.09	4.54	4.88
8	4.90	5.43	4.67	5.15
9	5.10	5.89	4.83	5.51
10	5.35	6.51	5.01	6.01
11	5.65	7.45	5.24	6.78
12	6.03	9.02	5.52	8.05
13	6.51	12.18	5.87	10.62
14	7.16	21.63	6.35	18.53
15	8.07	—	7.04	—

NOTE: Computation assumes compound-interest securities with interest compounded semiannually. All bonds assumed to be redeemable at par on horizon date. r_g is the yield on government bonds assumed constant over time; $r_p(0)$ is the yield on private securities in year 0.

Table III-7 continued

Computational Procedure:

1. Present Value Method
   Step 1: Computation of Present Value of future returns from $100 placed in 4% security at $t = 0$, redeemable at par at horizon.

$$PV = 2\left(\frac{1 - V^{2m}}{.015}\right) + 100V^{2m}$$

   Step 2: Substitution of above figure in formula below

$$\overline{PV} = 1.50\left(\frac{1 - V^{2k}}{.015}\right) + p\left(\frac{1 - V^{2m}}{.015}\right) - p\left(\frac{1 - V^{2k}}{.015}\right) + 100V^{2m}$$

   solve for p, $(k = 1 \ldots m)$, where m = horizon date; k = disposal (of Governments) date; p = yield in dollars on $100 placed in private securities on disposal date $(t = k)$;

$$V = \frac{1}{1 + r_g}.$$

2. Horizon Sum Method
   Step 1: Computation of sum at horizon date from $100 placed in 4% security at $t = 0$, redeemable at par at horizon; interest compounded semiannually.

$$S = 100(1.02)^{2m}$$

   Step 2: Substitute S in formula below and solve for $r_p(k)$ where $P_k = 100(1.015)^{2k}$

$$\overline{S} = P_k\left(1 + \frac{r_p(k)}{2}\right)^{2m-2k}$$

   Other symbols same as above.

that life companies held back Government securities they would have sold in the same circumstances in previous years because their expectations about future yields had changed. In particular, companies expected the corporate bond-Treasury bond yield spread to widen more than is indicated in the table. This is the hypothesis. We proceed now to test its plausibility.

Evaluation of the Hypothesis

We do not know what expectations were in the minds of life company executives during 1951 and 1952. We do know, however, that life insurance company investment officers consistently deny they make long-range interest rate forecasts (i.e., beyond a few months) in the process of formulating portfolio decisions.[72] From a casual examination of historical movements in yield spreads, it seems unlikely that holding back Governments for four or five years (let alone six to nine years) would often be profitable. To assume that life companies did refrain from liquidation of Governments on the basis of forecasts of yield spreads widening more than shown in Table III-7 strikes us as incompatible with the intuitive and qualitative knowledge we have of life company operations.

However, we are investigating a rather special period. The Federal Reserve System had been pegging Treasury bond rates for a long time, and it appears a reasonable first approximation to assert that life companies had been effectively pegging the Treasury security-risk asset yield spread. Under these peculiar circumstances a combination of the Accord and the approach of life companies to their long-run target Government security holdings might have been enough to create strong expectations about future interest rate patterns. Although we cannot know what specific expectations were created, it may be helpful to look at what in fact happened to yield spreads.

In order to simplify the comparison of actual movements in yields with the theoretical indifference yields presented above, we have recorded annual average yields for several bond series in Table III-8. Three comparable bond yield series are presented: (1) new issue yields on Grade 2 public utility bond issues successfully placed in the public market, (2) new issue yields on corporate bonds directly placed, and (3) the weighted average of yields obtained on all corporate bond commitments authorized by one, aggressive, large life insurance company. We also show the average market yield on seasoned long-term Treasury bonds, and

---

[72] See O'Leary, "The Institutional Savings-Investment Process," pp. 460–461. Also, to anticipate the results of chapters to come, in Chapter V we examine the cycle in liquid asset holdings of life insurance companies and find: (1) that usually it has been of modest amplitude, and (2) that variations in the level of interest rates play a secondary role, at best, in explaining the cyclical pattern. Then in Chapter VI we investigate the extent to which the volume of forward commitments life companies make is determined by their forecasts of interest rate movements. The evidence presented there suggests that interest rate expectations also play no more than a secondary role in life company forward commitment decisions.

TABLE III-8. Bond Yields and Yield Spreads: 1950–1961

Year	(1) Treasury Long-Term Bonds	(2) New Issue Direct Placement Corporate Bonds	(3) Life Insurance Company Corporate Bond Authorizations	(4) Bankers Trust Grade 2 Public Utility Bonds	(5) Theoretical Indifference Yield	(6) (2)−(1)	(7) (3)−(1)	(8) (4)−(1)	(9) (5)−3.00
1950	2.32%	3.38%	3.50%	2.72%	—	1.06%	1.18%	.40%	—
1951	2.57	3.61	3.65	3.14	—	1.04	1.08	.57	—
1952	2.68	3.82	4.08	3.24	4.00%	1.14	1.40	.56	1.00%
1953	2.93	4.14	4.34	3.54	4.09	1.21	1.41	.61	1.09
1954	2.53	3.86	4.20	3.06	4.19	1.33	1.67	.53	1.19
1955	2.80	3.96	3.83	3.28	4.31	1.16	1.03	.48	1.31
1956	3.08	4.30	4.31	3.79	4.45	1.22	1.23	.71	1.45
1957	3.47	5.07	5.48	4.66	4.62	1.60	2.01	1.19	1.62
1958	3.43	5.26	5.67	4.19	4.83	1.83	1.80	.76	1.83
1959	4.07	n.a.	5.68	4.93	5.09	n.a.	1.61	.86	2.09
1960	4.01	n.a.	n.a.	4.83	5.43	n.a.	n.a.	.82	2.43
1961	3.90	n.a.	n.a.	4.59	5.89	n.a.	n.a.	.69	2.89

SOURCES:
Col. (1): *Federal Reserve Bulletin.*
Col. (2): Series obtained from Eli Shapiro, prepared for National Bureau Capital Markets Study.
Col. (3): Yields on all corporate bond authorizations of one large life insurance company.
Col. (4): Bankers Trust Company.
Col. (5): Table III-7. Present Value calculation, 15 years to horizon.

finally, the theoretical indifference yield on corporate bonds calculated by the present value (15-year) method. It will be recalled that the computation of the latter series assumes a fixed Government bond yield of 3% and a beginning corporate bond yield of 4%.

We make a comparison of the relative movements in these yield series over time using 1952 as the base year for the theoretical series. The actual yields for the corporate bond yield series are approximately in line at this point in time with those assumed for $t = 0$ in the theoretical computation, i.e., they are about at 4%. These series should be reasonable approximations of yields life companies were obtaining on corporate investments in 1952. The Treasury yield series is somewhat below 3%, but not too far below for our purposes. The Bankers Trust series represents bonds of higher grade than median life company takings, but has the advantage of being standardized for quality and reflective of general corporate bond market pressures.

Comparison between the actual corporate bond-Treasury bond yield differentials and the spread required by the portfolio balance thesis suggests it generally did not pay life companies to reduce the disposal rate of Governments during 1952 and subsequent years by as much as they did in the expectation of substantially wider yield spreads in the future. Recalling that excessive Government security holdings would have been disposed of in three to three and one-half years at pre-1952 liquidation rates,[73] these rough comparisons indicate it may have paid life companies to divert some funds obtainable from sales of Governments to take advantage of the yield spreads that prevailed in 1957.[74] But,

---

[73] Three and one-half years allows for some capital loss–locking-in effect.

[74] Even this is doubtful. The calculations in Table III-7 are made under the assumption that no capital losses are incurred on Government bonds held in anticipation of wider yield spreads. Also, it might be argued that $r_p(0) = 4\%$, not $r_g = 3\%$, is the appropriate discount rate to use in computing present value. Taking account of these factors would increase the amount of future yield spread widening required to induce companies to hold off sales of Governments. If the capital loss–locking-in impact is assumed to be at work, then a direct conflict between it and the portfolio balance thesis is avoidable only if life companies react by selling Treasury bonds in advance of the rise in yields. Holding the proceeds in cash or short-term assets would increase the carrying costs and would narrow, if not eliminate, the profit margin obtainable from postponing the liquidation of Governments. Also, as we have indicated

aside from this particular intertemporal allocation, it does not appear that holding back Governments from disposal during 1952–1954 for sale and reinvestment at later points in time would have benefited life companies' investment returns. In particular, an even spreading out of sales over nine years would not have been justified on a yield basis. Therefore, the explanatory power of the portfolio balance thesis depends upon life companies' having forecast in 1952 and subsequently substantially wider yield spreads than in fact we know developed. This assumption seems to us quite uncharacteristic of life company behavior and therefore we find the portfolio balance hypothesis unconvincing.

Before completely dismissing the spreading-out thesis, however, we should point out that this examination of its merits has been conducted on a highly aggregative level. It is conceivable that a more disaggregative approach might show the portfolio balance thesis to have more explanatory significance. We therefore conclude this chapter with a brief investigation of this possibility.

A Disaggregated View of the Portfolio Balance Hypothesis

The analysis of the portfolio balance thesis we have just completed was based on the assumption that life companies as a group were strongly yield conscious in their decisions to transfer investments from U.S. Government obligations to private debt instruments. The only exception admitted to this presumption was the possibility that some companies may have compromised the yield objective in order to restrict the amount of book losses they realized on sales out of their Treasury bond portfolios. In particular, it was assumed that life company supply of funds schedules during the early postwar years were very highly elastic with respect to the private security-Treasury security yield spread (Figure III-1). It might be, of course, that some life companies were not very yield sensitive and rather passively adjusted their holdings of Governments downward at a pace which defies rational explanation. If passivity, irrationality, or inertia in forms not specifiable dominated life company behavior in disposing of Governments; then, of course, our entire investigation of this piece of

---

above, life companies were not in fact switching from long-term to short-term Governments during most of the 1952–1954 period.

history will only be able to establish that no rational explanation of the time path of liquidation is observable.

However, let us assume matters are not completely intractable. It is still possible that some companies that aggressively sold Governments during the 1947–1951 period had essentially completed this task by end-1951. If substantially all life companies behaved consistently with the open-to-buy description, i.e., transferred funds from Governments to private sector obligations so long as the minimum required yield spread was available, then the fact that some companies reach their long-run target poses no difficulty for the aggregative analysis. Other companies step up their disposal rates and yield spreads continue to be effectively pegged by life companies.

If, however, a significant number of life companies do not have investment motivations which fit under the open-to-buy rubric, a problem does arise. Suppose, for example, two sets of companies exist: one consisting of rational, yield-conscious firms whose liquidation of Governments fits the open-to-buy mold, and a second, relatively inert set of firms, who are not responsive to yield spreads and do not consistently take advantage of opportunities to convert Governments into private debt issues. Suppose the aggressive set of companies liquidated Governments during the early postwar years at a rate consistent with an industry open-to-buy hypothesis, but that these companies had essentially finished their disposal job by 1951. The slow attrition of Governments beyond 1951 would be due to the continued disposal of Governments by the second, passive group of companies, selling Governments at no apparently rational (predictable) pace.

To check this possibility, we shall examine the time path of Government security holdings of each of the 15 largest life companies. We are interested in knowing how many companies who actively sold Governments during the early postwar years had completed the process by end-1951. These 15 companies held nearly three-quarters of the Government securities in life company portfolios at the end of 1951. Government security holdings of these companies are reported in Table III-9 for three selected points of time, end-year 1946, 1951, and 1957. Most companies which sold Governments heavily during the 1947–1951 period continued to sell substantial amounts after 1951. An examination

TABLE III-9. *Government Security Holdings of the Fifteen Largest Life Insurance Companies at Selected Dates*

(millions of dollars)

| Company | End-Year | | | Net Change During | |
	1946	1951	1957	1947–51	1952–57
Metropolitan	$4,001	$2,290	$1,185	$1,711	$1,105
Prudential	3,939	1,555	912	1,384	643
Equitable (N.Y.)	1,640	599	384	1,041	215
New York Life	1,477	747	226	730	521
John Hancock	733	460	307	273	153
Northwestern	595	285	177	310	108
Aetna	560	279	224	281	55
MONY	894	211	86	683	125
Travelers	846	618	521	228	97
Mass Mutual	300	182	69	118	113
Mutual Benefit	502	247	88	255	159
New England Life	251	116	69	135	47
Penn Mutual	427	286	121	141	165
Conn General	128	137	133	−9*	4
Conn Mutual	108	60	35	48	25

* Negative sign indicates an increase in the portfolio stock over the period.

Source: *New York Insurance Report*, Volume I, *Life*, annual.

of Table III-9 discloses, however, that a few companies were reasonably close to completing their sales by the end of 1951 — close enough, at least, so they could not have been expected to continue to liquidate Governments very long at the 1947–1951 rate.

In order to obtain some quantitative notion of how much reduction in the pace of disposals might have resulted from these companies approaching equilibrium, we arbitrarily assigned a target to each company and computed the difference between the actual 1951 holdings and the target Government securities portfolio. The target assigned for each company was 4% of its realized total assets at the end of 1957. From interview evidence, it seemed a reasonable presumption that the industry's holdings of Governments would eventually level off at around 4% of assets. The industry had not reached this position by end-1957, of course, but we know there had been other factors restricting the rate of liquidation in the meantime; in particular, the locking-in effect of

TABLE III-10. Computation of Target Government Securities Holdings for the Fifteen Largest Life Insurance Companies

(millions of dollars)

Company	(1) Total Assets (end-1957)	(2) 4% of Total Assets, 1957	(3) Holdings of Government Securities, (end-1951)	(4) Actual Less Target Holdings, end-1951 [(3)-(2)]	(5) Average Annual Disposal Rate 1947-1951
Metropolitan	$15,536	$621	$2,290	$1,669	$342
Prudential	14,732	589	1,555	966	277
Equitable (N.Y.)	8,876	355	599	244	208*
New York Life	6,425	257	747	490	146
John Hancock	5,163	207	460	253	55
Northwestern	3,727	149	285	136	62*
Aetna	3,275	131	279	148	56*
MONY	2,959	118	211	93	137*
Travelers	2,574	103	618	515	46
Mass Mutual	2,075	83	182	99	24
Mutual Benefit	1,726	69	247	178	51
New England Life	1,876	75	116	41	27*
Penn Mutual	1,676	67	286	119	28
Conn General	1,754	70	137	67	−2†
Conn Mutual	1,329	53	60	7	10*

* Average annual disposal rate for 1947–1951 exceeds three times excess Government security holdings at end 1951.

† Negative sign indicates a positive increase in Government security holdings during 1947–1951.

SOURCE: Annual Reports and New York Insurance Report, Volume I, Life, annual.

capital losses.[75]   This assumption is unsatisfactory in presuming negligible variance among final Government securities targets of life companies, but it is perhaps more plausible than assuming that few companies deviate from a yield-conscious, open-to-buy behavioral pattern.

Given this target assumption, we compute the differences between actual and target holdings of Governments as of end-1951. These results are displayed in Table III-10.   We now need a criterion for selecting the companies which are close to their assumed targets.   Suppose we call a company close if its holdings of Governments in excess of the target amount as of the end of

---

[75] Additional factors are examined in Chapter IV.

1951 is less than three times its average annual net disposals during 1947–1951; i.e., a company is assumed to be near completion of the liquidation process if it could reach the target in less than three years by continuing to dispose of Governments at its 1947–1951 pace. On this basis six of the fifteen largest companies were close to equilibrium as of end-1951; these are marked with an asterisk in Table III-10. Suppose these companies spread out their remaining disposals over three years. The difference between their average disposal rates during 1952–1953 and their 1947–1951 liquidation rates, summed for the six companies amount to $277 million annually. If this figure is extrapolated to the remainder of the industry, we obtain a reduction in the disposal rate for companies close to equilibrium as of 1951 of about $350 million annually for the immediate post-1951 years. This compares with the actual average reduction of about $1,400 million annually.

It is, of course, possible that these companies decided it would pay to spread out their final liquidation even longer,[76] although the aggregative analysis above suggests such a decision would not have been consistent with a yield maximization goal. On the other hand, the $277 million figure is too high if some of the other companies approximated the open-to-buy behavior pattern and stepped up their own disposal rate to at least partially offset the reduced sales by the six companies. Even if only six-fifteenths of the industry was yield-conscious, the approach of these companies to their target portfolio composition explains only 25% of the reduced liquidation rate after 1951. Assuming some degree of yield spread sensitivity for the rest of the industry reduces the explanatory power of this possibility further. Nonetheless, from a disaggregated view of the portfolio balance argument it appears that the approach to the target by some companies can, like the capital loss effect, contribute something to the overall explanation of the post-1951 reduction in Government bond sales by life companies. Both arguments may be more relevant to an explanation of the very long stretch-out of liquidation well into the 1960s.

---

[76] A comparison of Tables III-9 and III-10 indicates at least three of the six companies did spread out sales over a longer period, assuming they had targets set at 4% of assets. But we have no reason to think this reflected expectations on their part of gaining by waiting for wider yield spreads.

Concluding Remarks

In this chapter, we have proceeded from the proposition that life companies have no liquidity, diversification, or other non-yield portfolio objectives which have compelled them to hold more than a very modest amount of Treasury obligations since World War II. Therefore we assumed that in adjusting their Government securities portfolios following the war life companies acted upon the yield objective alone. Indeed there seemed to be general agreement in the literature that this was an accurate generalization about life company interests and behavior in the immediate postwar years. Under these conditions life companies were characterized as willing to acquire eligible private (nonfederal government) sector assets without limit so long as they could obtain yields which compensated their subjective risk differential between the private obligations and Treasury securities. In effect, companies with their virtually limitless Government security holdings were pegging the yield differential between risk assets eligible for their portfolios and Government bonds. The rate at which life company Government securities portfolios were emptied, then, was determined by the relative position of the schedules depicting the "normal" supply of funds (excluding sales from their portfolios) available to life companies and the *ceteris paribus* demand for life company funds.

We have characterized the above posture of life companies as an open-to-buy position. It seems generally agreed that this is a fair representation of the industry's position from the war through 1951. However, although liquidation of Governments by life companies proceeded apace from 1946 through 1951, sales of Treasury securities declined sharply after 1951, and the liquidation continued in a slow and stretched-out manner through the remainder of the 1950s and into the 1960s.

Not surprisingly this abrupt change in the time configuration of disposals caused many students interested in this phenomenon to assume that life companies had altered their objectives and that their actions could no longer be characterized under the open-to-buy rubric. We have classified the existing explanations of the liquidation pattern under two broad headings: (1) credit availability, and (2) portfolio balance propositions. Most rationalizations of the slowdown in the liquidation process seem to fall under the credit availability label. In these explanations, emphasis is placed upon the March 1951 Treasury-Federal Reserve Accord and the subsequent increase in monetary restraint as the critical events causing life companies to adjust portfolio policy.

Monetary restraint is viewed as operating through many channels in affecting life insurance companies' decisions. Actually not all these channels carry the implication that life companies deserted an open-to-buy position. For example, it is sometimes contended that rising Government security yields can be counted upon to narrow the differential between yields on risk assets and those on Governments. The empirical evidence contradicts this assertion, however. A second strand of the credit availability doctrine suggests that, while life companies may have wished to continue selling Government securities at pre-Accord rates, rising interest rates created "thin" markets which were unable to absorb such a heavy volume of transactions. We found this contention not sustainable on a priori or empirical grounds.

These two rejected propositions were consistent in their formulation with an assumption that life companies continued in an open-to-buy posture after the Accord. However, the remaining elements of the credit availability hypothesis seem to be based upon the presumption that rising interest rates diverted life companies from a single-minded concern with relative yields. Instead, it is argued, life companies became more concerned about the adequacy of their liquidity position, the quality of their portfolio assets, and the book losses now incurred when bonds were sold. To accommodate these problems life companies moved to reduce Government security sales and accepted some cost in lost opportunities to improve portfolio yield.

We found the contentions about liquidity and asset quality totally unconvincing. Most life companies, however, do seem to have been deterred from heavy bond sales when market prices on Governments fell substantially below book value. We could only supply tentative explanations of this aversion, but from the interview evidence we were able to make a rough estimate of the magnitude of the capital loss impact upon disposals. In terms of time periods we found that capital losses had some significant restraining effect on sales during three (1953/I-III) of the twelve quarters immediately following the Accord. The capital loss effect could also have been quite restrictive during much of the period from mid-1956 on. As a maximum estimate of the impact of capital losses on life company sales during 1952–1956, we concluded that aversion to losses might explain as much as 20% of the reduced disposal rate, using 1947–1951 as the norm. Although much of the credit availability argument is couched in terms of the effect of rising interest rates on life insurance company market expectations, we found the expectations thesis inconsistent with life company behavior after 1951.

Thus the lone strand of the credit availability thesis worthy of some credence was the capital loss–locking-in effect, and its contribution to explaining the time pattern of disposals is modest. In particular it does not account for the abrupt and sharp reduction in sales after 1951, and as just noted explains at best a relatively small proportion of the reduced rate of sales over the several years following 1951. The capital loss effect may have more of a role in accounting for the extended duration of disposals into the 1960s.

References in the literature to portfolio balance are rather vague in terms of the mechanics by which the liquidation rate was affected. Generally it is contended that the liquidation of Governments from life company portfolios had been largely completed by 1951, and either it paid to spread out the remaining disposals, or at least there was no particular urgency about finishing the task. We attempted to formulate these feelings more explicitly and to examine the plausibility of the formal propositions.

In contrast to the implication of the capital loss thesis, the most straightforward formulation of the portfolio balance argument presumes that life companies continued to focus on the yield objective after 1951. It is argued that when life companies came within sight of their minimum desired holdings of Government securities, it paid them, in terms of portfolio yield, to spread out the final stages of the liquidation process, i.e., no longer sell enough Governments to keep the yield differential between risk assets and Governments pegged at the minimally acceptable spread. With the end of Government securities sales as a source of funds to the private sector in sight, expectations of widening yield spreads were generated. The Accord, contrary to the credit availability argument, may have reinforced these expectations. Thus although the optimal time path of disposals continued to be determined by the yield maximization goal, this path no longer implied an open-to-buy position for life companies. Upon investigating the logic of this thesis, however, we found the set of expectations it implied life companies held in 1952 and subsequently to be implausible.

We also examined the possibility that a significant number of life insurance companies were not strongly yield oriented, or at least not very aggressive about improving investment yield in their decisions to sell Treasury obligations. This could be relevant to understanding the duration of liquidation if most of the aggressive, yield-conscious companies had nearly completed their disposal program by end-1951. If this were true, then as time went on beyond 1951, sales behavior would be more and more dominated by companies whose disposal rates could not be explained in the framework of a simple, yield maximization model. To test this we examined the progress made by each of the fifteen largest life companies in liquidating their Government securities portfolios by end-1951. Six of the fifteen appeared close enough to completing liquidation that their disposals could not have been maintained at the 1947–1951 rate. Thus part of the explanation of the reduced 1951 disposal rates could lie here. At best, however, assuming that all other companies were quite inert or irrational, this explanation could not reasonably be expected to account for more than 25% of the reduced sales in the years immediately following 1951.

In sum, although the capital loss strand of the credit availability doctrine and a disaggregated view of portfolio composition do contribute to an explanation of the time path of Government security disposals, their overall performance is disappointing. The most generous estimate of their explanatory power leaves well over half the reduced post-1951 liquidation rate to be explained. Both of these hypotheses do agree that the open-to-buy period of flush funds ended in 1951. Both potentially contribute more toward understanding the long-drawn-out period of liquidation running well into the 1960s than toward rationalizing the 1952–1956 experience.

With respect to the latter problem, perhaps this analysis implies that we have been searching hard for an explanation of a shift in life insurance company portfolio policy that never occurred to the extent that has been generally assumed. Is it possible that the open-to-buy period did not end abruptly with the March 1951 Accord but slowly phased out over a period of years? This is possible, but only if an abrupt outward shift in the life insurance industry's normal supply of funds schedule and/or backward shift in the demand for life insurance funds occurred in 1952. We move to an examination of this possibility in Chapter IV.

Chapter IV | POSTWAR LIQUIDATION OF

GOVERNMENT SECURITIES BY LIFE INSURANCE

COMPANIES: *II. The Open-to-Buy Hypothesis*

In Chapter III we examined several conventional explanations of the time pattern of life insurance companies' postwar Government securities liquidation. The most striking characteristic of this pattern was the sharp reduction in the rate of disposals after 1951. The per annum net disposal rate declined from an average of $2.1 billion during the five-year period, 1947–1951, to less than $700 million annually during 1952–1956. Net disposals amounted to about $300 million annually in the period 1957–1961, and about $200 million per annum during 1962–1964. Although elements of the credit availability and portfolio balance hypotheses examined in Chapter III contributed toward explaining the extended duration of disposals, they are not very convincing rationalizations of the abrupt post-1951 reduction. We continue the analysis of the latter experience by investigating further the applicability of what we have called an open-to-buy portfolio policy.

On the assumption that life companies aim at fully investing the current inflow of loanable funds, we have postulated the existence of a perfectly elastic supply of normal funds schedule for the life insurance industry up to the limit of current gross cash inflow (ABC in Figure III-1). This schedule reflects the willingness of life companies to supply funds to private (nonfederal government) borrowers. The level of the schedule is determined by the going rate on long-term Federal Government obligations plus a pure risk differential. Government securities are a residual investment, i.e., acquired only when the demand curve intersects the elastic portion of the normal funds supply schedule.

It has been further assumed that during the early postwar years life companies were willing to supply essentially unlimited amounts of additional funds to the private market on the same terms as the normal flow, i.e., $r_g + d = r_m$ in Figure III-1. These additional funds were obtained from sales of Treasury obligations with which their portfolios were well stocked. Given r_m, the amount of funds supplied from this extraordinary source is determined by: (1) the normal cash flow (ON in Figure III-1), and (2) the demand for life insurance funds. In Figure III-1, NM is the amount of Government security sales determined in this manner. Both the capital loss and portfolio balance hypotheses explain the post-1951 reduction in sales as a result of deliberate and conscious restriction of disposals by life companies to amounts substantially less than NM.

An alternative possibility is that life companies' willingness to supply funds from liquidation of Treasury obligations remained unaltered during the period in question. In this case, shifts in the normal cash inflow and/or the demand for life insurance company funds would have to be called on to explain variations in the disposal rate. In particular, the sharp reduction in liquidation after 1951 would have to be explained by a substantial increase in normal cash flow and/or decline in the demand for life company funds. This possibility seems worth investigating. To perform this task, however, we need some elaboration and clarification of the concept "demand for life insurance company funds." For this purpose, we shall construct a rudimentary model of the capital markets' allocation mechanism in the next section. Following this exposition, we shall examine whether this hypothesis is consistent with the evidence.

A Partial Capital Markets Model

Is the reduced rate of life companies' Government security liquidation after 1951 explainable only in terms of decisions to terminate open-to-buy portfolio policies, or would sales have been reduced anyway as a consequence of changes in the demand for and "normal" supply of life insurance funds?

The model presented below is designed to supply the theoretical framework needed to answer this question. In particular, it attempts to formulate the manner in which lending competition affects the demand for insurance funds. In order to keep the focus on the essentials, we make some extremely simplifying assumptions. We shall assume that investors' portfolio choice is made from a limited selection of assets, each asset type being treated as if all its members were homogeneous. It is also assumed that the allocation of funds and determination of market yields is made as if the market functioned through a competitive bidding mechanism. We also rigidly limit the number of competitors explicitly recognized. The model is designed to depict as simply but as accurately as possible relevant characteristics of capital markets during the early 1950s.

In particular, it is assumed that life companies choose among four kinds of assets: Government bonds, corporate bonds, conventional mortgage loans, and federally underwritten mortgage loans. We assume that the corporate bond market is dominated by life companies and self-administered pension funds.[1] Like life companies, trusteed pension funds are long-term lenders with minimal liquidity needs. Their investments are concentrated in common stocks and corporate bonds. It appears that during the first postwar decade pension funds had a strong diversification demand for corporate bonds; some substantial proportion of investible funds were apparently allocated to bonds regardless of yield spreads.[2] Given this emphasis on portfolio proportions, it

---

[1] This is a reasonable first approximation for the period 1951–1956, with which we are primarily concerned. During the early postwar years life companies were the sole lenders of note in this market. (For an investment banker's view of that market, see Smutney, "Investments of Retirement Funds.") Corporate trusteed pension funds began offering significant lending competition around 1950 or 1951. Life companies' and pension funds' acquisitions accounted for most of the net increase in corporate bonds outstanding during the next few years. Since the mid-1950s, some attrition in the almost exclusive dominance of these lenders has taken place.

[2] Presumably to Government bonds if the corporate-Government yield spread did not cover the minimum risk premium. For a discussion of pension fund portfolio policy during the 1950s, see Natrella, "Implications of Pension Fund Accumulations," esp. pp. 142–143; Haines, "Pension Fund Investing"

seems reasonable to regard pension funds as willing and able to bid away a substantial bloc of bonds from competing investors, including life companies.[3] In the early 1950s this competition was most strongly apparent in the public new issue market.[4] Pension funds did not share life companies' aversion to lack of call protection in public utility bonds. Therefore, we shall assume that pension funds have a strong preference for investing a minimum proportion of their funds flow in corporate bonds, and that this insures their acquisition of such amount.

In the residential mortgage loan market, we treat federally underwritten (FHA and VA) loans as a distinct asset type. These instruments have played an important role in increasing the geographic mobility of mortgage funds. The Government guarantee (insurance) feature and the existence of secondary market facilities provided by FNMA distinguish these obligations in some degree from conventionally originated loans. The most significant distinguishing characteristic for our purposes, however, is the administrative regulation of contract interest rates on FHA-VA lending. In the model presented below, we shall assume that effective yields on federally underwritten loans are rigidly constrained by administratively imposed ceiling rates.[5] The first

---

p. 1057; Howell, "A Re-examination of Pension Fund Investment Policies"; V. Andrews, "Pension Funds in the Securities Markets," and Andrews, "Noninsured Corporate and State and Local Government Retirement Funds in the Financial Structure," CMC Monograph, esp. pp. 404–408; 482–485.

[3] See Howell, *op. cit.*, for a strong criticism of inflexible pension fund investment policies.

[4] See Andrews, CMC Monograph, pp. 493–500, for a discussion of the slow emergence of pension funds into the private placement market for corporate securities.

[5] This assumption, of course, is an exaggeration of the facts. Legal maximum rates on FHA-VA loans apply to contract rates. These loans have been acquired and traded at prices below par. Therefore, effective yields on FHA and VA loans have significantly exceeded legal maximum contract rates at times. Congressional frowns directed toward discounting have constrained the extent to which it has been practiced. On two occasions the Congress has written discount controls into housing legislation. Restrictions imposed in the Housing Act of 1950 remained in force until August 1954. During this period, there was apparently considerable uncertainty with regard to the legality of discounts on federally underwritten loans. For this period, at least, assumption of a rigid ceiling on FHA and VA loan yields is not too wide of the mark. Since we wish to focus primarily on the 1951–1952 reduction in Government securities disposals, we shall accept this rigid interpretation of mortgage loan ceiling rates for the time being. We shall return to the

postwar decade was characterized by a strong demand for mortgage funds by borrowers entitled to incur federally underwritten mortgage debt. Under these conditions the demand for underwritten loan funds must have been highly elastic at the ceiling yield over a considerable range.

Four groups of lenders have dominated the postwar residential mortgage loan market: savings and loan associations, commercial banks, life insurance companies, and mutual savings banks. The savings and loan associations are most firmly entrenched in the conventional home loan market. By law and tradition these institutions are home mortgage loan specialists.[6] Further, by statutory restriction, they were strictly local lenders during the 1950s. In their capacity as local lenders, the S & Ls exercised a competitive advantage over life insurance companies (and mutual savings banks) because they were able to establish direct personal contact with the borrower. This advantage is realized in terms of being better able to seek out and originate loans, in adjusting loan terms to the credit worthiness of the borrower, and in providing faster service. Life company mortgage officers interviewed by this writer agreed that neither correspondents nor branch office personnel were able to compete effectively in loan search and service with aggressive S & Ls.

Statutory restrictions on loan terms have been generally more liberal for the S & Ls than for other lenders, giving the S & Ls added flexibility. These advantages and the strong preference associations have for home mortgage loans assured that a large portion of the annual savings flow through these institutions found its way into conventional home loans. Additional funds were obtained by the associations through exercise of their privilege to borrow from the Federal Home Loan Banks. In the model

---

discounting question in Chapter VII. For a brief summary of the significance of mortgage discounts and Congressional action in the matter, see Grebler, *Housing Issues in Economic Stabilization Policy*, Appendix A, pp. 121–127.

[6] Federally chartered association portfolios were limited to first mortgage loans, property improvement loans, Government securities, and stock of the Federal Home Loan Banks. State-chartered associations came under similar restrictions. See "Savings and Loan Associations in the Mortgage Market," Federal Reserve Bank of New York, *Monthly Review*, July 1956, p. 95, and Kendall, *The Savings and Loan Business: Its Purposes, Functions, and Justification*, CMC Monograph, Chapter 3 and Chapter 6, pp. 96–99.

below, we assume that the savings and loan associations will underbid life companies in order to obtain the minimum amount of conventional residential mortgage loans they wish to add to their portfolios.

Commercial banks share the savings and loan associations' on-the-spot lending advantage to a considerable degree.[7] They have been, however, much less wed to mortgage loans as permanent investments.[8] The cyclical variance in mortgage loan activity has been substantially greater for commercial banks than other major mortgage lenders. In periods of monetary ease, commercial banks may be very strong bidders for conventional home mortgage loans.

Life companies and mutual savings banks suffered competitively in the conventional loan market because of their geographic displacement from local markets. Mutual savings banks, which are concentrated particularly in the New England-Middle Atlantic financial surplus region, have been hampered by geographic restrictions governing their conventional loan activity.[9] Since 1950 they have been able to lend nationwide under the FHA-VA programs. Life companies are dependent upon mortgage correspondents or branch office systems to generate a flow of mortgage loans. This, and the somewhat more stringent statutory restrictions on loan terms under which they operate, have placed them at a competitive disadvantage vis-à-vis the savings and loan associations, particularly in the conventional loan market.

In sum, the savings and loan associations had strong portfolio preferences and competitive advantages which we expect allowed them to underbid (in yield or other contract terms) the other major mortgage lenders. Commercial banks may underbid life

---

[7] Branches of commercial banks may lack the full measure of personal contact and speed in closing loans that a unit S & L possesses.

[8] See, for example, "Commercial Banks in the Mortgage Market," Federal Reserve Bank of New York, *Monthly Review*, April 1956, pp. 45–50; Klaman, "Effects of Credit and Monetary Policy on Real Estate Markets: 1952–1954," pp. 244–245; and American Bankers Association, *The Commercial Banking Industry*, CMC Monograph, Chapter 7.

[9] See Klaman, *The Postwar Residential Mortgage Market*, pp. 147–156, and National Association of Mutual Savings Banks, *Mutual Savings Banking: Basic Characteristics and Role in the National Economy*, CMC Monograph, pp. 152–158.

companies for substantial blocs of conventional loans in periods when their higher priority loan demand is slack.[10] Mutual savings bank conventional lending activity has been highly restricted geographically. Although a good case might be made for including commercial banks, if not savings banks, the model presented below explicitly recognizes only life companies and savings and loan associations as suppliers of mortgage funds.

To keep matters simple, therefore, we limit the number of actors in our model to those whose activity clearly has a very substantial impact on the demand for life insurance funds. Only pension funds and savings and loan associations are explicitly recognized as competitors to life companies. Five types of portfolio assets are admitted, Governments, corporate bonds, common stock, and the two types of residential mortgage loans. Life companies are presumed to supply funds to four of these sectors, common stocks being excluded. Savings and loan associations are limited to Governments and mortgage loans; pension funds to Governments and corporate bonds and stocks. Each lender has a supply of funds schedule for each market in which it is willing to lend. The nature of these supply schedules depends upon asset preferences, relative yields and the sources of investible funds. Three sources of funds are distinguished:

(1) the normal gross savings inflow
(2) sales of Government securities
(3) borrowing

Borrowing is excluded as a choice for life insurance companies and pension funds, but is admitted as a source of funds to savings and loan associations. Cash balances are not considered as a source of funds for any lender.

Lenders are assumed to purchase only new issues of private borrowers' debt obligations. No trading is admitted in any outstanding assets other than federal obligations.[11] The volume of

---

[10] The notion of priorities in commercial bank portfolio choices appears in a number of works. For example, see Robinson, *The Management of Bank Funds*, pp. 11–18, and *The Commercial Banking Industry*, CMC Monograph, p. 107.

[11] The market for corporate equities is not "explained" in the model. We are assuming that pension fund trading activity in corporate stocks has little relation to the minimum amount they desire each period to allocate to new corporate debt issues.

corporate bonds and conventional mortgages acquired by the lenders each period is assumed to be determined by borrowers; the demand for funds via these instruments is assumed to be perfectly inelastic with respect to interest rates. The demand for funds through issuance of guaranteed mortgages, as noted, is assumed to be perfectly elastic so that the volume of guaranteed mortgage loans made is determined by lenders.[12] The market yield on federal obligations is assumed to be established by the monetary authorities and yields on guaranteed mortgages by the FHA-VA administrators.

The Model

Lenders:

Life Insurance Companies (L)
Pension Funds (P)
Savings and Loan Associations (A)

Assets:

Federal Obligations (F)
Corporate Bonds (B)
Conventional Home Mortgage Loans (C)
Guaranteed Mortgages (G)
Common Stocks (S)

Variables:

(1) Exogenous or Predetermined

Flow variables: (i) $\bar{l}, \bar{p}, \bar{a}$ represent gross savings flows into life insurance companies, pension funds, and savings and loan associations, respectively. $\bar{p}_s$ is the net amount pension funds invest in corporate stock issues per period.

(ii) $\bar{b}, \bar{c}$ represent new funds raised through corporate bond and conventional mortgage instruments respectively.

---

[12] The distinction between the two categories of mortgage demand is admittedly rather strained. Lenders, obviously, have considerable influence in determining whether a given loan is made in "conventional" or "guaranteed" form. However, because of administratively imposed stickiness in yields on federally underwritten loans, the distinction is useful for market analysis from the lender's perspective.

Stock Variables:

$\overline{T}$ represents total assets held by the specified lender.

$\overline{F}$ the stock of Governments held and

$\overline{D}$ the lender's total outstanding debt.

Subscripts identify the lending institutions to which these stock items are attached.

Interest Rates:

$\overline{r}_g$, $\overline{r}_f$ represent yields on guaranteed mortgages and federal obligations, respectively.

(2) Endogenous

Flow variables: (i) l_b, l_c, l_g, l_f represent flows of life insurance funds into various asset categories (identified by subscripts).

(ii) p_b, p_f — flows of pension fund funds into various assets.

(iii) a_c, a_g, a_f — flows of savings and loan association funds into various asset categories. a_d represents debt repayment.

(iv) g represents the volume of new guaranteed mortgage issues.

Interest Rates:

r_b, r_c — yields on corporate bonds and conventional mortgage loans, respectively.

All flow and stock variables refer to the same time period, stocks being measured at the beginning of the period.

Equations:

Budget Equations:

$$(1) \quad l_b + l_c + l_g + l_f \equiv \bar{l}$$
$$(2) \quad a_c + a_g + a_f + a_d \equiv \bar{a}$$
$$(3) \quad p_b + p_f + p_s \equiv \bar{p}$$

Corporate Bond Market:

$$(4) \quad l_b = f_1(r_b, \overline{r}_f, \bar{l}, \overline{F}_L/\overline{T}_L)$$
$$(5) \quad p_b = f_2(r_b, \overline{r}_f, \bar{p}, \overline{F}_P/\overline{T}_P)$$
$$(6) \quad l_b + p_b \equiv \bar{b}$$

Conventional Home Mortgage Market:

$$(7) \quad l_c = f_3(r_c, \overline{r}_f, \bar{l}, \overline{F}_L/\overline{T}_L)$$

(8) $a_c = f_4(r_c, \bar{r}_f, \bar{a}, \overline{F}_A/\overline{T}_A, \overline{D}_A/\overline{T}_A)$

(9) $l_c + a_c \equiv \bar{c}$

Guaranteed Mortgage Market:

(10) $l_g = f_5(\bar{r}_g, \bar{r}_f, \bar{l})$

(11) $a_g = f_6(\bar{r}_g, \bar{r}_f, \bar{a})$

(12) $l_g + a_g \equiv g$

These twelve equations, six behavioral and six identity relations, are sufficient to determine values for the following twelve endogenous variables: l_b, l_c, l_g, l_f, a_c, a_g, $(a_f + a_d)$,[13] p_b, p_f, r_b, r_c, and g. The model makes some highly simplifying assumptions. For example, the gross savings funds flow into each institution is treated as predetermined, i.e., independent of portfolio acquisition and asset yields which are determined during the period; the amount raised through corporate bond issues and conventional home mortgage loans is assumed to be independent of the cost and availability of credit; it is hypothesized that the demand for funds via federally underwritten mortgage loans is perfectly elastic, and finally we postulate that the yields on federally underwritten mortgage loans and on Treasury obligations are determined exclusively by the FHA-VA administrations and by the monetary authorities, respectively. Since the model is being formulated for a very limited and very specific purpose, i.e., to clarify the nature of the private sector's net demand for life insurance funds, we have elected not to include enough lender and asset types to close the model.

The behavioral pattern assumed for each of the lender types included can be briefly summarized. The model incorporates quite literally the notion that private pension fund allocations between debt and equity issues were (prior to the mid 1950s) traditionally rigid, the aim being to preserve fixed portfolio proportions. Thus we assume that the predetermined savings inflow ($\bar{p}$) is

---

[13] We have not supplied sufficient specification of savings and loan associations' behavior to separate sale of Treasury obligations from Federal Home Loan Bank borrowings as a source of funds (or Treasuries as against debt repayment as a use of funds). In fact, perhaps as a result of the liquidity requirements imposed upon insured S & Ls by the Spence Act (H.R. 6743, enacted June 27, 1950), the associations, in the aggregate, have made net purchases of Governments each year since 1950 (indeed, since 1948) and have relied increasingly upon the Home Loan Banks for operating liquidity.

allocated in fixed proportion between bonds (corporate and Treasury) and common shares. Consequently, the model only has to determine the division of a given sum between federal and corporate debt obligations. This division is a function of yields on the two types of assets, the size of the portion of the savings flow available for bonds $(\bar{p} - \bar{p}_s)$ and the inherited stock of Treasury obligations as a proportion of total portfolio assets. Normally we expect the pension funds' supply of funds schedule for corporate bonds to be essentially perfectly elastic over a considerable range, at a yield which underbids life insurance companies, and then rising as the amount supplied approaches $\bar{p} - \bar{p}_s$. Since pension funds have generally pursued a fully invested policy and have not required a very sizeable liquidity reserve,[14] the amount supplied to the corporate bond market at the equilibrium yield is not normally expected to deviate very much from the amount $\bar{p} - \bar{p}_s$.[15]

Savings and loan associations are home mortgage loan specialists. In particular, they have been specialists in the conventional residential loan market. The S & Ls resisted enactment of the FHA mortgage insurance program in the 1930s and the industry, until the late 1950s, invested only nominal amounts in FHA insured loans. During the first postwar decade their allocation of funds to VA guaranteed loans was more significant, perhaps in part reflecting a public service motivation. However, conventional loans have been the primary outlet for S & L funds throughout the postwar period.[16] S & Ls have purchased small amounts of Government securities each year in order to satisfy the minimum legal reserve requirements.

We assume that the S & L supply schedule of funds to the conventional residential mortgage loan market is highly elastic over a considerable range with respect to the spread between yields on

[14] See Andrews, CMC Monograph, p. 404.

[15] That is, pension funds have not carried a very large stock of Government securities on which to draw for liquidity, and usually feel only modest additions to their secondary reserve holdings are required. It is assumed however, that some flexibility exists and that the precise allocation of funds between corporate and Treasury bonds depends upon the yield differential between these asset categories.

[16] For example during five years, 1950–1954, on which we are focusing attention, the S & Ls made net conventional loan acquisitions of $11.9 billion as compared with $2.6 billion (net) placed in FHA-VA loans.

hese loans and yields on Treasury bonds. Further, the schedule s positioned so that the associations normally "underbid" life nsurance companies on a substantial bloc of conventional loans n order to achieve their specialized investment objectives. The schedule is also shaped by the known (or forecasted) gross savings low and the availability of extraordinary funds as measured by the ratios of Treasury security holdings and of outstanding bor-owings to total assets. As noted above, holdings of Governments nust be adequate to meet liquidity requirements. Availability of funds through borrowing is assumed to be inversely related to the D_A/T_A ratio both because of internal preferences and because of credit policies of the Home Loan Bank System. Borrowings are induced by a strong demand for conventional loan funds and/or by retarded savings flows produced usually by increased with-drawals.

The S & L supply of funds schedule to the federally underwritten mortgage loan market is assumed to be considerably less elastic with respect to the mortgage loan–Treasury bond yield spread than the conventional loan supply schedule. S & Ls are assumed to want normally to allocate some modest proportion of funds generated by the savings flow to guaranteed loans but that be-ond this amount, guaranteed loans are a second-order priority. The shape and position of this schedule will thus depend upon the "normal" or anticipated investment in conventional loans. Errors n the anticipated savings flows and conventional loan acquisitions re absorbed by S & L borrowings, adjustment in their Govern-nents portfolio, and perhaps to a limited extent in their purchases f guaranteed mortgage loans.

The model implicitly presumes that life insurance companies ave more flexibility in allocating funds among various asset ategories than do their chief competitors. The description of fe companies' supply of funds schedules to the corporate bond nd conventional loan market is somewhat different depending n whether or not a pure open-to-buy environment is assumed. f life companies are in an open-to-buy posture, then their supply chedules are perfectly elastic at yield spreads over Treasury onds $(r_b - r_f,\ r_c - r_f)$ which express life companies' minimum isk differential requirements. In this situation, with r_f being

determined by the monetary authorities, life companies as a grou[
determine r_b and r_c. In this case the $\bar{l}$ and $\bar{F}_L/\bar{T}_L$, variables ca[
be dropped from these two supply of funds equations.

If there are some constraints on the amount of funds life com[
panies are willing or able to supply because their Treasury securit[
holdings are limited (the portfolio balance hypothesis) or becaus[
capital losses must be incurred (the locking-in hypothesis), the[
the two schedules are presumably highly elastic over some co[
siderable range but then begin to rise more sharply at a poir[
dependent upon the values of $\bar{l}$, $\bar{F}_L/\bar{T}_L$, and $\bar{r}_f$, the absolute valu[
of the latter reflecting roughly the degree to which book loss[
will be sustained when Treasury bonds are sold.

In the funds constraint case, the corporate bond market supp[
schedule also implicitly depends upon "normal" or forecasted est[
mates of amounts to be invested in conventional mortgage loar[
as well as amounts to be placed in guaranteed mortgage loan[
Similarly the supply schedule for conventional loans depends upo[
assumed investments in corporate bonds and guaranteed loan[
Regardless of whether or not life companies are open-to-buy an[
amount of corporate bond and conventional loan instruments, w[
assume that they limit the amount of funds they will invest i[
guaranteed loans. Thus, although the life company supply [
funds schedule to the guaranteed loan market may be high[
elastic over some range, it then rises due to the existing limits o[
the amount of these loans life companies are willing to hold. Th[
variable $\bar{l}$ is included in this equation to indicate the existence [
such a constraint. In the *non*-open-to-buy case, the supply [
funds to guaranteed loans also must depend upon normal or antic[
pated amounts to be placed in the corporate bond and convention[
loan markets. In this case, errors in forecasting acquisitions b[
sector are expected to be absorbed by the Treasury securit[
portfolio.

The model is solved very easily when the open-to-buy assum[
tion prevails for life insurance companies. With r_f determine[
by the monetary authorities and r_b and r_c then determined by li[
insurance companies, the amount of conventional mortgage loar[
taken by savings and loan associations and the amount investe[
in corporate bonds by pension funds are known. Life compani[
acquire conventional loans in the amount, $\bar{c} - a_c$ and corpora[

bonds amounting to $\bar{b} - p_b$. With r_g set by the federal mortgage guarantee authorities, all variables affecting S & L and life insurance company investment in these loans are exogenous or predetermined and therefore a_g, l_g, and g can be calculated. Values for the variables l_f, $(a_f + a_d)$ and p_f are derived residually from the budget equations.

If life companies are assumed not to be in an open-to-buy position, then the variables l_c, a_c, and r_c are solved for jointly given the two supply of funds schedules for conventional loans and the demand for funds schedule $(D_c = \bar{c})$. Similarly, the two supply of funds schedules for corporate bonds together with the demand schedule $(D_b = \bar{b})$ are sufficient to determine the values for l_b, p_b, and r_b. Values for the other variables are determined in the same manner as they were in the open-to-buy case.

As the model stands it is not closed with respect to many markets. In particular, the Treasury securities market is not specified. Given plausible values for the variables in the environment of the early 1950s, the model may very well call for life insurance companies to liquidate substantial amounts of Governments. Given the stock of outstanding Treasury obligations, the model would be closed if life companies, pension funds, and S & Ls were the only significant traders. Since this is obviously not a plausible assumption, we need to consider the implications of assuming that investors outside the model absorb Governments marketed by life insurance companies.

The mix of buyers of Treasury obligations in the secondary market depends to a significant degree upon monetary policy. If, for example, the monetary authorities in setting r_f are determined to keep it below some policy ceiling, then the monetary authorities may have to absorb substantial quantities of Treasury issues sold by life companies and others. If, however, the monetary authorities limit the amount of Governments they are willing to purchase, and accept (controlled) rising market yields on Treasury obligations, then other investors must be induced, by the higher yields, to purchase Governments. Under some circumstances this mechanism could cause some difficulty with our assumption that savings flows into the several lending institutions are predetermined. Probably the most serious cause for concern would occur if rising yields on Governments generated by heavy life company sales induced households to liquidate S & L share accounts to purchase Treasury bonds. We would have little cause for concern if those induced to add Governments to their portfolios represented a wide variety of investors, with households playing a small role. Fortunately the latter situation appears to have prevailed in the early 1950s. Purchases of Treasury bonds were spread among the monetary authorities, nonfinancial corporations, state and local governments, nonlife insurance companies, pension funds, and S & Ls. Households were modest net sellers during this period. Thus, it appears that we can postulate the existence of a mechanism for absorbing life company Government security sales which does not invalidate the underlying assumptions of our model.

Application of the Model

The problem at hand is to show what the time profile of life company Government security disposals would look like if the influences discussed under the credit availability and portfolio balance headings had been inoperative. That is, we are asking whether the time pattern of liquidation observed is consistent with the continuance of a life company open-to-buy posture through 1951 and beyond. As we have just seen, in an open-to-buy world, corporate bond and conventional mortgage loans acquired by life companies each period would amount to the difference between the total (inelastic) demand for funds through these channels and the dollar volume other lenders are willing to acquire at the going yield differential. Under the open-to-buy assumptions, life companies establish and maintain the yield spread between private debt issues (i.e., corporate bonds and conventional mortgage loans) and Treasury bonds. Thus, while the monetary authorities may peg the Treasury bond yield, life companies are viewed as pegging the yield spread.

In terms of Figure III-1, as we have seen, the open-to-buy assumptions mean that life company sales of Government securities would amount to NM dollars each period. The post-1951 reduction in disposals must then be explained as a consequence of either an increase in the normal flow of investible funds through life companies (ON) or a decline in the demand for life insurance funds (DD). A leftward shift of DD could occur as a result of either a decline in the total demand for funds through the relevant private debt issues or an increase in the amount competing lenders are willing to supply at the established yield spread. If either ON expands or the *ceteris paribus* demand for life company funds declines, NM will be squeezed.

In the model just presented, we have made some highly simplifying but reasonably plausible assumptions about the "normal" supply of life company funds, the total demand for funds by private borrowers in the form of corporate bonds and conventional residential mortgage loans, and the supply responses of nonlife company lenders. The logic of the model suggests two kinds of tests of the proposition that an open-to-buy environment was maintained for some time beyond the Accord (or the end of 1951).

First, assuming no change in life companies' evaluation of the risk differential, the open-to-buy version implies maintenance of an essentially constant yield spread between the relevant private investments and Treasury bonds. This contrasts with the credit availability and portfolio balance explanations which view life companies as backing up along the DD schedule (Figure III-1) to wider yield spreads between private sector asset acquisitions and Governments. On either of the latter hypotheses a sharp cutback in sales of Governments ought to be accompanied by observable increases in yield differentials.

In addition, consistency of the extended open-to-buy thesis can be tested by direct estimation of the above-mentioned gap between the total demand for funds and the amount competing lenders were willing to supply at the pegged yield spread. If life companies in fact pegged the yield spread and maintained it over the period in question, then their sales of Treasury obligations each period would have equaled the total (inelastic) demand for funds less the amount other lenders are willing to lend at the going yield spread and less the normal supply of life company funds. This proposition cannot be tested precisely because we cannot hope to estimate satisfactorily the supply of funds schedules for all competitors of life companies in every investment market. However, a rough sort of consistency test can be performed by estimating (1) the funds supplied by the principal competitors isolated in the foregoing model and (2) the normal supply of life company funds. Using the heroic assumption that issues of corporate bonds and conventional mortgage loans were determined solely by borrowers, independently of interest costs, we can rank the relevant years according to the net demand for life insurance funds. By deducting corporate bond acquisition by pension funds and conventional loans made by S & Ls from the total funds raised through these instruments, we can then test for a relationship between the net demand for life company funds less the "normal" supply of life insurance investible funds and life company Government security sales. Lack of a positive relationship over the years of interest would be damaging to the open-to-buy thesis.

The Yield Spread Test

The yield spread between private sector debts and Treasury bonds is plotted in Chart IV-1. Two measures are shown in this chart, using two previously encountered private debt yield series. The upper line represents the difference between the yields obtained on corporate bond authorizations for one large life insurance company (this is the same series used in Table III-8) and long-term Treasury bond yields. The spread between the Bankers Trust Grade 2 Public Utility Bond series (plotted above in Chart III-1) and Treasury bond yields is the other set of points plotted in Chart IV-1. The behavior of these two estimates of the private-government debt yield spread is consistent with the thesis that the open-to-buy environment continued some time beyond 1951.[17] As we have seen, the discontinuance of an open-to-buy policy by life insurance companies implies widening yield spreads. However, no obvious widening of the spread seems to have been associated with the sharp reduction in life company Government bond

---

[17] The yield series representing one life company's corporate bond authorization was not available for the years prior to 1950. The Bankers Trust series was, however, available back to the beginning of 1946. The spread between yields on Grade 2 Public Utility obligations and long-term Treasury bonds ranged between 27 and 73 basis points on a quarterly average basis between 1946/I and 1951/I inclusive. No trend in the size of this spread was observable over the period. As can be seen in Chart IV-1, the spread remained within this range through 1956/II.

CHART IV-1. *Spread Between Yields on Corporate Bonds Authorized for Purchase by a Large Life Insurance Company and Bankers Trust Grade 2 New Issue Public Utility Bond Yields, and Yields on Long-Term Treasury Obligations: 1950/I–1959/IV*

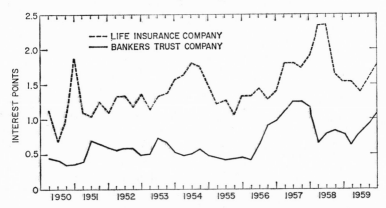

SOURCES: Authorizations of a large life insurance company; Bankers Trust Company; *Federal Reserve Bulletin.*

sales after 1951. There is a sharp rise in yield differentials recorded in 1956,[18] which is a clear indication that the open-to-buy proposition is devoid of explanatory value from 1956 on. This is not surprising, given our earlier conclusion that the credit availability (and probably the portfolio balance) explanation took on significance during 1956. The continuance of an essentially unchanged private-government debt yield differential for five years beyond the Accord suggests again that the credit availability-portfolio balance hypotheses are of limited value in explaining the post-1951 reduction in Government security sales.

This evidence on yield spreads is consistent with our alternative hypothesis to the effect that the time pattern of life company Government security sales has to be explained by shifts in the demand for, or normal supply of, life insurance funds within the context of a life company open-to-buy portfolio policy. This alternative explanation would be more convincing if we could identify the

---

[18] A rather sharp, but temporary, widening of the differential occurred during the first half of 1953. This is, however, consistent with our finding above that the locking-in effect could have been quantitatively significant during the first three quarters of 1953.

schedule shifts that produced the observed pattern of sales and thereby test the proposition more directly. If the simplifying assumptions enumerated in the above model are accepted, it is possible to make rough estimates of the normal supply of life insurance funds and the demand for those funds.

The Demand — Normal Supply Test

Conceptually, it seems most appropriate to define the normal flow of loanable funds through life companies in terms of the gross inflow of investible funds on a cash basis less the proceeds obtained from sales of Government securites.[19] However, due to the absence of reliable cash flow data prior to 1957, the estimates of normal supply reported below are based on the net change in life company assets. We limited life company portfolio choices in the above model to three types of private assets: corporate bonds, conventional home mortgage loans, and federally underwritten mortgage loans. Therefore, in computing our estimate of the "normal" net supply of life company funds, we shall deduct net gains in the residual types of assets (other than Treasury obligations), treating them as special purpose loans which absorb funds in amounts independent of the current inflow of investment funds. In addition, in the above model, we have distinguished life companies' attitudes toward FHA and VA loans from their policy with respect to the other two asset categories. We assumed that life companies did not adopt an open-to-buy policy with regard to FHA-VA loans, but rather that the supply schedule, $l_g = f(r_g - r_f)$ [Equation 10 above], had a finite elasticity. This assumption, together with the assumption of a perfectly elastic demand for funds schedule through the FHA-VA loan medium (at the ceiling contract interest rate), permits us to estimate net life company FHA-VA loan acquisitions separately. This amount can then be deducted from the net normal supply of life insurance funds to yield the volume of normal inflow available for investment in corporate bonds and conventional mortgages. The difference between this figure and demand for life company funds by corporate

---

[19] See Chapter V for a description of alternative measures of gross cash inflow.

and conventional home mortgage borrowers is covered by sales of Governments in an open-to-buy environment.

A defense of our special treatment of FHA-VA loans is in order. There is no unanimity in life companies' views regarding the desirability of federally underwritten loans. Some life company officers seem to feel that FHA and VA loans are essentially riskless obligations and therefore would be highly attractive in unlimited amounts in an open-to-buy environment so long as they provide yields above Treasury bonds of comparable maturities. A more commonly expressed opinion, however, holds that FHA-VA loans carry some nonnegligible elements of risk. In part, such attitudes reflect doubts respecting the value of the federal insurance and guarantee features.[20] The programs do not protect lenders fully against loss. Apparently more important than the protection details, however, is the uneasiness which derives from the belief that federally underwritten loans are of lower quality than conventional loans in life company portfolios, and consequently more susceptible to wholesale default in a future economic depression. FHA and VA loans are thought to be of lower quality because their loan terms are relatively liberal and because the basic credit standing of FHA-VA borrowers is assumed to be weaker than that of their conventional loan counterparts.[21]

The expense of defaults is, of course, greater than the direct loss on specific loans defaulting. Substantial costs may be involved in personnel time utilized in attempting to secure settlements or complete the foreclosure procedures. Correspondents handling mortgage servicing may themselves be vulnerable in a period of widespread loan defaults, necessitating additional insertion of life companies' salaried personnel into mortgage portfolio housekeeping activities. Recovered funds must be invested in a depressed market. Finally, life companies are sensitive to the

---

[20] A more thorough review of life company attitudes toward federally underwritten loans is undertaken in Chapter VII.

[21] This is not an obviously correct assumption. In fact, on the basis of evidence from the beginning of the VA program through 1956, Break finds FHA and VA borrowers to have been somewhat better credit risks on the average than conventional loan borrowers. Break, *The Economic Impact of Federal Loan Insurance*, pp. 58–59. However, life companies have offered less liberal loan terms on conventional loans than most of their competitors, particularly the S & Ls, and quite probably have enforced tighter acceptable credit standards. See Chapter I, Table I-5.

public relations repercussions of being associated with many foreclosures.

Thus, from this point of view, FHA-VA loans appear potentially more risky than conventional mortgages and corporate bonds, let alone Treasury obligations. As a consequence, many life companies seem to have placed limits on the proportion of their portfolios they are willing to have in federally underwritten loans. It is these considerations that have led us to postulate an eventually upward rising supply schedule of life company funds for FHA-VA loans.

The demand schedule for life insurance funds depends upon the aggregate demand for funds by potential borrowers whose proffered debt issues fall within life company preference and eligibility standards, and also upon the supply schedules of competing lenders. For purposes of making a rough computation, we have assumed the relevant aggregate demand schedules to be perfectly inelastic. With regard to competitors' supply schedules, we have assumed their portfolio preferences are characterized by a high degree of specialization. As a consequence of their concentration in specific loan areas and concern over portfolio proportions, we assumed that savings and loan associations will underbid life companies to satisfy their tastes for conventional home mortgage loans,[22] and similarly that corporate pension funds underbid life companies in the corporate bond market to obtain the volume of bonds necessary to maintain their desired portfolio balance. Consequently we can obtain a first approximation of the net demand for life company funds by deducting the net acquisitions of corporate bonds by pension funds and conventional home mortgage loans made by the S & Ls from the aggregate increase in these categories of debt issues. By combining these estimates with

---

[22] The term "underbid" is employed because, for convenience of exposition, we have formulated the argument in terms of a market operating through a competitive bidding mechanism. The kind of underbidding performed by the S & Ls may involve advantages usually associated with market imperfection. For example, unit S & Ls seem to possess tactical advantages derived from their location and specialization which in many cases may quite possibly permit the S & Ls to fulfill their loan requirements without sacrifice in loan terms compared to life companies. Thus, the underbid rubric is meant to cover a mixed bag of genuine underbidding — acceptance of more liberal loan terms than life companies — and competitive advantages in loan search and service.

the normal life insurance supply of funds estimates, we are able to rank the postwar years in terms of the relationship between the net demand for life company funds and their normal supply.

The computations we have been describing are reported in Table IV-1 for the period 1946–1960. In column 7 of this table, we have the net additions to corporate bonds and conventional home mortgage loans after deduction of pension fund and savings and loan association acquisitions. The "normal" net supply of life company funds, computed in the manner described above, appears in column 8. Columns 9 and 10 display two measures of the relationship between available investment opportunities and life companies' normal supply flow. The dollar gap between available investment and normal life company supply is recorded in column 9 and the ratio of life companies' normal supply of funds to available investment opportunities appears in column 10. If an open-to-buy policy were maintained, we would expect to observe an inverse relationship between the amount of Government securities liquidated and the normal funds-available investments ratio and a positive correlation between net disposal of Governments and the available assets-normal funds gap.

In support of the open-to-buy hypothesis, it does appear that the correlation between each of the two supply-demand measures and the annual volume of Government bond disposals occurs as predicted. In Chart IV-2 net disposals of Governments are plotted against each of the investment opportunity–normal supply flow measures for the 1946–1951 period generally characterized as open-to-buy. The general relationship seems to be preserved beyond 1951, although the fit is less tight.[23]

If the behavior of all lenders other than life companies was correctly specified and measurable, then we could derive for each year the volume of extraordinary funds life companies would have had to supply to maintain market yield spreads. We have, in a rough way, taken account of pension fund and S & L competition.[24] Any estimate of what life company Government security

---

[23] The rank correlation coefficient between net Government securities liquidated and the normal supply/available assets ratio for 1946–1957 is .882, significant at the 1% level.

[24] We have also computed the normal life insurance funds/available investments ratio, with commercial bank acquisitions of conventional mortgage loans also deducted from the total net increase in conventional loans. This, of

TABLE IV-1. Estimates of Normal Life Insurance Funds, Available Corporate Bonds and Conventional Home Mortgage Loans: 1946–1960

(millions of dollars)

Year	(1) Total Corporate Bonds	(2) Net Flow into Pension Funds	(3) Available Corporate Bonds	(4) Total Conv. 1–4 Family Mortgages	(5) Flow into S & Ls	(6) Available Conv. Home Mortgages	(7) Total Available Investments (3) + (6)	(8) Normal LI Funds	(9) Gap: Investments Less Funds (7)–(8)	(10) Ratio of Funds to Available Investments (8)/(7)
1946	$1,096	$ 150	$ 946	$2,629	$ 838	$1,791	$2,737	$2,853	$ – 116	104.2%
1947	3,004	150	2,854	1,976	583	1,393	4,247	1,561	2,686	36.8
1948	4,655	240	4,415	1,892	868	1,024	5,439	1,288	4,151	23.7
1949	3,284	300	2,984	1,805	947	858	3,842	1,399	2,443	36.4
1950	2,004	450	1,554	3,697	1,485	2,212	3,766	693	3,073	18.4
1951	3,577	800	2,909	2,529	1,540	989	3,898	823	3,075	21.1
1952	4,940	1,017	3,923	4,297	2,495	1,802	5,725	3,146	2,579	55.0
1953	4,755	1,039	3,716	4,874	2,634	2,240	5,956	3,291	2,665	55.3
1954	3,799	1,178	2,621	5,586	3,132	2,454	5,075	2,284	2,791	45.0
1955	4,188	866	3,322	5,714	3,587	2,127	5,449	2,146	2,303	39.4
1956	4,752	1,479	3,273	5,739	3,206	2,533	5,806	2,066	3,740	35.6
1957	7,053	1,688	5,365	5,300	3,500	1,800	7,165	3,022	4,143	42.2
1958	5,856	1,339	4,517	7,200	4,200	3,000	7,517	3,142	4,375	41.6
1959	4,076	1,066	3,010	9,400	5,800	3,600	6,610	2,599	4,011	39.3
1960	5,034	1,342	3,692	7,800	5,700	2,100	5,792	2,140	3,652	36.9

NOTES AND SOURCES:

Col. (1): Net change in corporate bonds and notes outstanding, Securities and Exchange Commission.

Col. (2): Net change in holdings of corporate bonds by corporate pension funds. Figures for 1946–1951 are estimates based on asset growth of pension funds. The 1948 and 1951 figures are 60% of the net gain in assets; for other years figures shown represent 50% of asset increase. 1952–1960 figures are computed from year-end corporate bond holdings of pension funds. SOURCE: SEC, *Survey of Corporate Pension Funds*, 1951–1954, pp. 25–26, and SEC, *Statistical Bulletin*, various.

Col. (3): Col. (1) minus Col. (2).

Col. (4): Net flow of conventional 1–4 family mortgage loans, data for 1946–1956 from Klaman, *The Volume of Mortgage Debt in the Postwar Decade*, Table 35, p. 126; 1957–1960 data from mortgage debt data in the Housing and Home Finance Agency's *Housing Statistics*, monthly.

Col. (5): Net flow of conventional 1–4 family mortgage funds through savings and loan associations. Data for 1946–1956 from Klaman, *ibid.*, p. 126. Remainder from HHFA, *Housing Statistics.*

Col. (6): Col. (4) minus Col. (5).

Col. (7): Sum of Col. (3) and Col. (6).

Col. (8): Estimate of normal life insurance funds. Computed as net change in assets minus net flow into all asset categories except corporate bonds, 1–4 family conventional mortgage loans, and U.S. Government securities. Data from ILI, *Life Insurance Fact Book*; Klaman, *ibid.*; and HHFA, *Housing Statistics.*

Col. (9): Col. (7) minus Col. (8).

Col. (10): Col. (8) divided by Col. (7) times 100.

sales would have been in an open-to-buy world carries in it some implication regarding the behavior of the remaining suppliers of funds to the conventional residential mortgage loan and corporate bond markets. To obtain some notion of what volume of Government bond sales might have been reasonably expected in an open-to-buy environment beyond 1951, we made three crude estimates based on widely varying assumptions about the behavior of the residual lenders in these markets.

We are primarily interested in explaining why such a sharp drop in the rate of life company Treasury security sales occurred after 1951. We suppose that the extent of the decline is measured by the difference between average net sales in the period of heavy Government security liquidation, 1947–1951, and actual liquidation in the years beyond 1951. Average net sales during 1947–1951, as we have seen, amounted to $2,126 million annually. To be explained is the gap between the $2,126 million average figure and actual net sales in the post-1951 years. Estimates of net liquidation that could have been expected in an open-to-buy environment then would show whether the decline in sales was consistent with life companies' open-to-buy policy or whether the sharp decline does, in fact, signal the end of the open-to-buy period as the credit availability and portfolio balance hypotheses assert.

We made estimates of expected net Government security sales in three ways:

(1) Absolute gap measure. Using six observations, 1946–1951, we fit a least squares line to net Government bond sales as a function of the dollar gap between investments available to life com-

---

course, increases the value of the ratio for all years, but only slightly modifies the pattern. Its main effect is to increase the difference between 1951 and 1952; the 1951 ratio is 22.3% using this method and the 1952 ratio, 60.2%. This compares with the 21.1% and 55.0% for these years reported in Table IV-1. If anything, assuming that commercial banks underbid life companies on conventional mortgage loans, would therefore "explain" somewhat more of reduced life company Government bond sales after 1951, than does the method used in Table IV-1. Perhaps it should be argued that banks also underbid life companies on intermediate term corporate financing through the use of term loans, but we are unable to justify any particular method for deducting a portion of commercial bank loans to corporations. It does not appear that within a wide range of assumptions the pattern depicted in Table IV-1 would be significantly altered.

panies (column 7 in Table IV-1), and the net normal supply of life company funds (column 9 in Table IV-1). The result

$$\text{Net Sales} = -973.69 + 1.0068\ (A - F_N)^{25}$$
$$(.0722)$$

is plotted in Chart IV-2.

If this regression line is then used to predict Government bond sales during the post-1951 years, it provides the estimates reported in Table IV-2. The constant term in this regression is interpreted as the amount supplied by residual lenders in an open-to-buy pegged yield world. Using this relation to project future life company bond sales means assuming that the absolute dollar contribution of residual lenders at the pegged spread would continue unchanged at the typical 1946–1951 level. Therefore, whenever the available investment — normal funds gap widens, life companies must sell Governments dollar for dollar to maintain fixed yield spreads. In a world of growing investment opportunities, this implies heavy bond sales out of life company portfolios as is reflected in the estimates reported in Table IV-2.

(2) The funds/available assets measure. We also fit a least square regression line to the observations of Government security disposals against the normal funds/available investments ratio (column 10 in Table IV-1). These points and the fitted line are plotted in the lower panel of Chart IV-2. The regression line is:

$$\text{Net Sales} = 3263.75 - 4159.8\ (F_N/A)^{26}$$
$$(859.4)$$

The constant term can be interpreted as the volume of Govern-

---

[25] A represents available investments and F_N the normal supply of funds. The standard error of the 'b' coefficient is shown in the parenthesis. For this equation $R^2 = .98$ and the standard error of estimate (S) equaled 231.19. The same equation estimated over annual observations from 1946 to 1960, inclusive, yielded the following results:

$$\text{Net Sales} = 149.97 + .360\ (A - F_N)$$
$$(.244)$$

$$R^2 = .14,\ S = 1017.9$$

[26] For this equation, $R^2 = .85$, $S = 621.7$. When this equation is estimated from annual observations for 1946–1960, the results are:

$$\text{Net Sales} = 2641.68 - 40.3696\ (F_N/A)$$
$$(16.3633)$$

$$R^2 = .59,\ S = 1234.53$$

ments life companies would sell if the normal funds flow were zero. At higher normal funds/available investments ratios, Government bond liquidation would be less. The regression line passes

CHART IV-2. *Net Sales of Treasury Obligations by Life Insurance Companies and the Relation Between Normal Funds Inflow and Available Investments (Scatter Diagrams): Annually, 1946–1960*

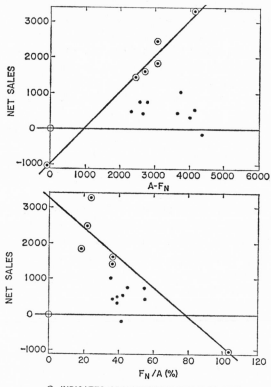

⊙ - INDICATES OBSERVATIONS FOR 1946 - 1951

SOURCES: Net Sales, Table III-1.
$A - F_N$, Table IV-1, Col. 9.
F_N/A, Table IV-1, Col. 10.

through the x axis at a F_N/A ratio of about .78, meaning that at this ratio life company net sales of Governments would be zero. The residual lenders, by implication, supply funds amounting to

22% of available assets at this point. The .78 life company share at zero Government bond sales is consistent with the observation that during 1946–1951 life companies supplied funds (from the normal flow and sales of Governments) to the residential mortgage and corporate bond markets in amounts averaging about 75% of available investments.

Use of this functional relationship means assuming that life company Government security sales are unaffected by scale changes, e.g., secular growth in F_N and A that leave the proportion F_N/A unchanged. This means assuming that the residual lenders expand and contract activity in line with scale changes. In a steady growth world with F_N and A growing at the same percentage rate (F_N/A a constant), residual lenders must grow sufficiently fast to absorb the gap between available investments and funds supplied by life companies (F_N plus a constant amount of proceeds from Government sales). In a world where $A - F_N$ grows rapidly, this measure probably underestimates the volume of Government security sales life companies would have to make to maintain yield spreads. In fact, however, the gap declined after 1951 and did not rise significantly again until 1956.

(3) The constant-share measure. The absolute gap measure implies that if net available investment opportunities grew over time, the life insurance industry's share of acquisitions also would have increased. We should expect life companies' share of available investments to decline if their Government security disposals were functionally related to their normal funds as a proportion of available investments. In both cases we are assuming life companies persevere in an open-to-buy policy at unchanging yield spreads.

A third basis for calculation that suggests itself is to compute the volume of Government security sales life companies would have made if they could have preserved yield spreads by maintaining net investment acquisition at the same proportion of available investments that prevailed during 1946–1951. Their share of available assets during this period averaged about 75% (annual shares ranging from about 66% to 84%). In column (4) of Table IV-2, we show the amount of Government security sales life companies would have had to make each year to absorb 75% of available investments.

These three sets of predictions cover a wide range of alternative assumptions with regard to the magnitude of extraordinary funds

TABLE IV-2. *Estimates of Net Disposals of Government Securities by Life Insurance Companies Consistent with an Open-to-Buy Policy under Various Assumptions Respecting Funds Supplied by Residual Lenders: 1952–1960*
(millions of dollars)

Year	(1) Average Sales 1947–51	(2) Absolute Gap Measure	(3) Ratio Measure	(4) Constant Share Measure	(5) Actual
1952	$2,126	$1,623	$1,076	$1,148	$ 757
1953	2,126	1,709	1,063	1,176	423
1954	2,126	1,836	1,492	1,522	759
1955	2,126	2,352	1,725	1,941	494
1956	2,126	2,792	1,883	2,289	1,021
1957	2,126	3,197	1,608	2,352	526
1958	2,126	3,431	1,633	2,496	−154
1959	2,126	3,065	1,729	2,359	315
1960	2,126	2,703	1,829	2,204	441

NOTES:

Col. (1): Arithmetic average of annual net liquidation of Government securities by all life insurance companies, 1947–1951.

Col. (2): Estimates obtained from using the least squares regression line: Net disposals = $-973.69 + 1.0068 (A - F_N)$. Annual observations, 1946–1951, where A = available investments and F_N = normal supply of life insurance funds (see Table IV-1).

Col. (3): Estimates obtained from using the least squares regression line: Net disposals = $326.76 - 4,159.82 (F_N/A)$, fitted to annual observations, 1946–1951.

Col. (4): Estimates obtained from assuming that life companies acquired a constant share of available investments (A) each year. Net disposals = $.75A - F_N$. The constant share = .75 is the arithmetic average of life companies' F_N + net disposals/A, annually, 1946–1951.

Col. (5): Actual net disposals of Government securities by life insurance companies. Negative sign (−) means positive net acquisitions.

life companies would have had to supply to maintain yield spreads. Most interestingly, we find from these computations that a substantial decline in Government security disposals in the immediate post-1951 years is consistent with continuance of an open-to-buy policy. Conservatively, it seems fair to attribute about half of the reduced disposals in 1952–1953 to shifts in demand and supply within a continuing open-to-buy framework.

To sum up, our analysis of yield spreads between private investment opportunities and Treasury long-term bonds led us to the conclusion that no dramatic end to the open-to-buy period took place in 1951. To confirm this judgment, we wanted to identify the shifts in the supply of and/or demand for life insurance funds which were therefore responsible for the sharp decline in sales of Governments after 1951. Inspection of Table IV-1 shows that the increase in the demand for funds through the corporate bond — conventional home mortgage loan media outpaced the growth in pension fund — S & L supply in 1952–1953, resulting in a large increase in net investments to be allocated among life companies and the residual lenders. However, the normal supply of funds flowing through life companies also increased sharply after 1951, more than offsetting the gain in investment opportunities. The net result, therefore, was a reduction in the available investments — normal supply gap, or, using the ratio measure, an increase in normal funds/available investments proportion. Because of the gain in normal supply, therefore, it was possible for life companies to maintain an open-to-buy posture and reduce their sales of Governments.

A breakdown of the normal funds flow into major categories is provided in Table IV-3. This breakdown indicates the post-1951 increase in normal supply derived principally from two broad sources: (1) a gain in the rate of asset growth (roughly speaking, an increase in the net savings flow through life companies), and (2) diversion of funds out of federally underwritten mortgage loans. The step-up in asset growth resulted from favorable experience in the insurance business. However, the gain in normal supply deriving from a reduction in FHA-VA loan activity has to be attributed in large part to the revival of monetary policy. We have postulated above that the supply of funds by life companies to the FHA-VA markets was a function of the spread between the administratively imposed ceiling contract rates on these loans and the market yield on long-term Government bonds. It is clear

TABLE IV-3. Composition of the Normal Supply of Life Insurance Funds:
1947–1957

(millions of dollars)

Period	Net Change in Total Assets	Net Change in FHA-VA Loans	Net Change in Misc. Assets	Net Normal Supply
1947–51*	$4,017	$1,405	$1,459	$1,153
1952	5,097	640	1,311	3,146
1953	5,158	544	1,323	3,291
1954	5,953	987	2,682	2,284
1955	5,946	1,845	1,955	2,146
1956	5,579	1,513	2,000	2,066
1957	5,298	568	1,708	3,022

* Annual average.

NOTE: Miscellaneous assets include all assets except corporate bonds,
1–4 family conventional residential mortgage loans, FHA and VA mortgage loans and U.S. Government securities. Data are from ILI, *Life
Insurance Fact Book.*

in Chart IV-3 that rising Treasury bond yields following the Accord narrowed this yield differential significantly.[27]

Real estate credit and construction material restrictions imposed
during the Korean conflict may have had some dampening impact
on life company FHA-VA loan acquisitions. However, the impact
of these selective controls appears to have been marginal; note the
expansion in total conventional 1–4 family mortgage loans in
1952 (column 4 of Table IV-1). The net reduction in all life
company mortgage lending activity in 1952 compared with 1951
was just $296 million, compared with a net decline in FHA-VA
lending of $1,071 million. It appears, then, that the Accord
and subsequent restrictive monetary actions do sneak in the back
door and contribute here to explaining the reduced Government
security sales. However, their functioning here is due largely to
the special accident of controlled contract lending rates and the
discounting constraints and does not constitute a demonstration
of the truth of the generalized credit availability thesis. Nonetheless, it should be noted that in this environment of selective
constraints, monetary restriction was potentially quite effective.

---

[27] See note 5, p. 223, for the justification of employing the legal ceiling rates
imposed by the Federal Housing Administration and the Veterans Administration.

This is especially true in a world in which life companies maintained an open-to-buy position, for in this situation each dollar discouraged by narrowed yield spreads from investment in the controlled market represented a full dollar reduction in life company credit extensions. In an open-to-buy world there is no offsetting increase in funds allocated to other private sector markets.

CHART IV-3. *Yields on Long-Term Treasury Bonds and Ceiling Contract Rates Permitted on FHA and VA Loans: Quarterly, 1946/IV–1959/IV*

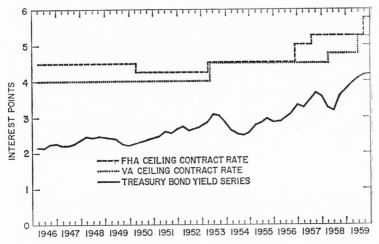

SOURCES: *Federal Reserve Bulletin;* Federal Housing Administration; Veterans Administration.

At this point in our excursion we have accumulated a mixed bag of explanations of the time pattern of life companies' postwar Government securities liquidation. Before attempting a summary evaluation of this aspect of life company behavior, we shall briefly add one more item to the mix. Throughout this analysis we have treated the Government security disposal problem under the implicit assumption that all Treasury obligations held by life companies were identical assets. However, the debt issues in life company Government security portfolios in fact differed substantially in one primary investment characteristic — maturity dates — as well as in some attributes of secondary importance.

In the next section we ask whether the mix of these characteristics could have influenced the overall disposal rate.

Effect of the Composition of Life Company Government Security Holdings on Their Disposal Rate

In conducting the examination of their postwar pattern of Government securities' liquidation we have implicitly assumed that life companies emerged from the war with a homogeneous collection of Treasury obligations essentially identical in coupon rates, maturity dates, and other characteristics. In particular we have assumed that the long-term market yield on Treasury bonds was the relevant base from which to compare returns available from private sector debt issues. Had life companies during the war been able to predict with a high degree of certainty that the Fed would commit itself to par support of the Government bond market for some years after the war, it is probable that life companies would have elected to concentrate their wartime purchases of Governments in the long-term sector and have entered the postwar liquidation period with a portfolio consisting almost exclusively of the bank restricted $2\frac{1}{2}$'s.

In fact, however, some hedging of bets on the postwar market environment is reflected in the significant amounts of shorter-term Treasury obligations that life companies actually acquired during the war. Aggregate life company holdings of Governments continued to rise for about a year after the end of the war, peaking in the third quarter of 1946. The composition of their holdings at this time is displayed in the first column of Table IV-4. About $5 billions of certificates, notes, and bank eligible bonds were represented among the $21.7 billion Governments portfolio. These issues had quite low market yields relative to the bank restricted bonds. For the most part they had low yields because they were relatively short-term obligations[28] — the prevailing yield curve was strongly upsweeping. In addition the bank eligible bonds carried

[28] As of September 1946, $1,464 million of the bank eligible bonds reported in Table IV-4 had maturity or call dates within five years. Most of the rest were due or callable in less than ten years.

TABLE IV-4. *Treasury Obligations Held by Life Insurance Companies by Type, Selected Dates (End of month)*

(millions of dollars)

	Sept. 46	Dec. 47	Dec. 48	Dec. 49	Dec. 50	Mar. 51	Dec. 51
Bills	*	$ 138	$ 42	$ 27	$ 391	$ 652	$ 428
Certificates	$ 420	57	86	137	1	*	217
Notes	456	24	8	38	165	295	1
Marketable Bonds:							
Bank Restricted	16,543	16,425	13,802	12,958	11,529	10,406	6,461
Bank Eligible	4,129	2,825	2,174	1,459	650	639	259
Nonmarketable Bonds	119	432	535	552	604	610	3,526
Total	$21,667	$19,901	$16,647	$15,171	$13,341	$12,602	$10,892

* Less than $500,000.

SOURCE: *Treasury Bulletin.*

somewhat lower yields because they were eligible for commercial bank portfolios[29] and, for some issues, because their interest payments were partially tax exempt (i.e., exempt from the normal tax and partially exempt from the surtax).

It is not surprising to observe in Table IV-4 that the first wave of liquidation (1946–1947) was concentrated in this collection of low yield obligations. But does this fact and the Governments portfolio mix in existence at the beginning of liquidation have any relevance for the explanation of the time rate of disposals? In principle it should not. If some companies felt in retrospect that, given the Fed's apparent post-war commitment to market support, they were overstocked in shorter-term, low yielding Treasury obligations, they could easily perform the appropriate shuffling within their Governments portfolio. It seems the correct formulation of the portfolio problem during the open-to-buy era was in terms of choosing between long-term Governments and eligible private debt of roughly comparable maturity.

There is, however, some reason to believe that the maturity structure of Government securities portfolios held by life companies did have some impact on the net liquidation rate during the early postwar years. This suspicion is based primarily on the experience of one large company, The Equitable Life Assurance Society (New York). The Equitable made a firm wartime bet on the postwar environment and the monetary authorities' reaction to it. The company expected a postwar boom accompanied

---

[29] During 1946–1947, for 2½s of the same maturity, the differential between bank restricted and bank eligible bonds was about 15 or 20 basis points.

by rising interest rates. Therefore, Equitable concentrated its purchases in the short end of the Government securities market.[30] Unfortunately for the company, its forecast proved to be only half correct. The boom occurred but the monetary authorities successfully resisted the upward pressure on long-term market yields. Equitable's reaction apparently was to place the proceeds of its maturing Treasury obligations into private sector issues. Additional amounts of Governments were sold and the funds reinvested in private debt. The magnitude of Equitable's disposals is compared with those of the rest of the industry in Table IV-5. Through a concentrated disposal program Equitable re-

TABLE IV-5. Net Change in Government Security Holdings: Equitable Life and the Remainder of the Industry
(millions of dollars)

	Equitable	Rest of Industry
Holdings: End 1945	$1,924	$18,659
Net Disposals 1946	−284	+1,330
Net Disposals 1947	−341	−1,267
Net Disposals 1948	−522	−2,753
Holdings: End 1948	777	15,969

SOURCE: Equitable Life data from *New York Insurance Report*, Vol. I, *Life*, annual. Industry data from ILI, *Life Insurance Fact Book*.

duced its Government holdings by about 60% in the first three postwar years as compared with a 14% reduction in the rest of the industry's holdings.

There is little doubt from our interview evidence that the peculiar maturity structure of Equitable's portfolio accounts almost entirely for its extraordinary liquidation performance. During 1946–1947 the Equitable added $1,069 million (net) to its corporate bond holdings. This amounted to about 25% of the net increase in corporate bonds outstanding. To accomplish this the company must have been very active in the secondary market and/or offered extremely liberal terms on new loans.[31]

---

[30] This account is based on interview evidence.

[31] For example, the Equitable reported receiving $200 million in cash from maturing Treasury notes in March 1947. Since Treasury refunding offers during this period consisted exclusively of short-term, low yield obligations,

It is difficult to rationalize this behavior. Apparently it reflected a feeling on the part of the company's officers that shifting from short-term to long-term Governments would only serve to dramatize an unfortunate wartime decision. If this response was repeated in less dramatic fashion elsewhere in the industry, then part of the post-1951 reduction in disposals was a consequence of the lack of additional certificates, notes, and bank eligible bonds to be sold.[32] Even if Equitable's behavior was unique, the magnitude of its action alone was sufficient to account for part of the early postwar disposals in excess of what can be explained by the more normal and neater rationality hypothesis.

Summary

In Chapters III and IV we have been examining the allocation of life insurance company funds over time. We have focused on one extraordinary source of funds supplied by life companies to private sector capital markets, namely, funds obtained from the sale of U.S. Treasury obligations. The postwar liquidation of life companies' Government security holdings permitted the industry to supply the private sector with funds well in excess of their normal cash flow. We have been concerned with explaining the time sequence of the conversion of life companies' Treasury securities portfolio into risk assets.

Liquidation of Government securities by life companies proceeded apace during the period 1946–1951. The disposal rate was reduced sharply after 1951, however. Nonetheless sales continued throughout the remainder of the decade of the 1950s

---

the company had to accept cash and choose between long-term Governments or private sector issues. Usually the choice was to invest in private obligations. At the time in question part of the proceeds were apparently invested in a private placement concluded with Gulf Oil, at a yield of $2\frac{1}{8}\%$ (average maturity of 15 years). Long-term Governments were yielding about $2\frac{1}{4}\%$ at this time. This is open-to-buy with a vengeance.

[32] As Table IV-4 shows, life companies had run off nearly all of their bank eligible bond holdings by the end of 1951. Except for the bills and certificates accumulated because of market uncertainty surrounding the Accord, life company holdings were made up of the war bank restricted bonds and some nonmarketable series, primarily the $2\frac{3}{4}$s Investment Series B issued in exchange for some issues of the war $2\frac{1}{2}$s in connection with the Accord.

and well into the 1960s. This, then, was the broad time configuration of disposals we had to explain.

We found general agreement that in the early postwar years life companies faced no real portfolio choice problem in selecting private sector assets. Because of its large holdings of Governments the life insurance industry was able to provide an effectively unlimited supply of funds to the purchase of risk assets. Under these conditions life companies were open-to-buy all eligible private debt issues that carried an effective yield exceeding the yield on comparable maturity Governments by their minimum subjective risk differential.

Most observers have concluded that this open-to-buy condition ended during 1951. This dating seemed obvious from the abrupt decline in disposals after 1951. Conventional explanations of this decline and the subsequent extended duration of liquidation attribute the time pattern to either the locking-in effects of monetary restriction or to the fact that a number of companies had largely completed liquidation by 1951. The latter argument has to assume that the remaining companies were less yield conscious and therefore more sluggish in liquidating their Governments than the companies which essentially finished this task by 1951. We examined both these explanations in Chapter III and found there was some merit in them, but that together they could not explain as much as half the reduction in the 1952–1956 as compared with the 1947–1951 disposal rates.

Therefore, in this chapter we turned to an investigation of the possibility that the time path of disposals was consistent with the maintenance of an open-to-buy policy well beyond 1951. Consistency would imply that the post-1951 period was characterized by an increase in the normal cash flow through life companies and/or a decline in the demand for life company funds. Closer examination also indicated that while it was plausible to think of life companies adopting an open-to-buy policy in allocating funds to corporate debt and conventional mortgage loans, it was doubtful that in the aggregate they were prepared to acquire unlimited amounts of federally underwritten loans. One means of testing the open-to-buy proposition was to examine the behavior of yield spreads. Since preservation of an open-to-buy position implied maintenance of the differential between yields on corporate bonds and Treasuries, an abrupt end to an open-to-buy environment should be reflected in significantly wider yield spreads. Movements in yield differentials do not confirm the assertion that the open-to-buy period ended in 1951. Except for the first half of 1953, the relevant yield spreads remained at pre-Accord levels until mid-1956. The 1953 exception matched the time period for which a significant capital loss locking-in effect was predicted.

We also ran a consistency test of the proposition that the open-to-buy period was essentially maintained beyond 1951. This was done by making rough estimates of the demand for life insurance company funds and the normal supply of funds (excluding Government security sales as a source) through life companies. Some highly simplifying assumptions were made regarding the "normal" supply of life company funds, the total demand by private sector borrowers for funds through issuance of corporate bond and conventional residential mortgage instruments, and the supply responses of competing lenders. Applying these assumptions to the data, we found a decline in life company Government securities disposals after 1951 to be consistent with maintenance of an open-to-buy policy.

Although the estimates derived did not support the position that the entire post-1951 decline in disposals was consistent with a continued open-to-buy environment, shifts in demand and supply in an open-to-buy framework appeared capable of explaining about half the reduction in sales. The primary shift that accounted for this result appeared to be an increase in the normal supply of the funds flow through life companies available for corporate bonds and conventional residential mortgage loans, derived in part from an increase in the savings flow through life companies and in part from a diversion of funds away from federally underwritten mortgage loans. The latter experience was a consequence of a more restrictive monetary policy following the Accord, which resulted in a narrowing of the difference between the administered ceiling rates on FHA-VA loans and market yields on Treasury bonds. During the Korean War period considerable doubt existed regarding the legality of discounts on FHA and VA loans. By this indirect means, then, monetary policy did have some influence on the time path of life company Government security sales.

Finally, it appeared that the maturity composition of Government security holdings may have had an influence on the early postwar liquidation rate. Early disposals (1946–1947) were concentrated in low yielding — largely short-term — issues. It appeared that Equitable Life, in particular, converted large amounts of its short-term Government security holdings into private sector obligations in preference to longer maturity Governments. This had the effect of making disposals in the 1940s somewhat higher than they would have been if all Government holdings had been in bonds and exaggerating in some degree the difference between 1946–1951 and post-1951 disposal records.

In sum, the concept of life companies maintaining an open-to-buy policy proves to be a useful handle for explaining life company investment behavior further into the postwar period than most writers have previously assumed. It appears to us to be incorrect to assume an abrupt transition from an open-to-buy to a portfolio choice environment during 1951. We find instead that it is more appropriate to regard the 1952–1956 period as one of transition between an open-to-buy and a portfolio choice world.

Aggregate life company behavior in the transfer of funds from Government securities to risk assets was, then, broadly consistent with the hypothesis that yield maximization was the principal goal of companies. However, certain evidences of inertia and irrationality are present which compromise to a degree the pursuit of portfolio return. The specific forms which we found these qualifications to take were:

(1) aversion to capital losses;
(2) passivity of some companies in responding to widening risk asset-Government bond yield spreads with greater sales of Governments; and
(3) irrational dependence of the sales volume upon the maturity distribution of the Governments portfolio.

Depending upon one's objective view of the risk characteristics of FHA-VA loans, the apparent unwillingness of life companies to accept unlimited amounts of these loans may or may not be regarded as a qualification to pursuance of the yield objective.

If these pieces of the explanation of life companies' time path of Government securities liquidation were additive, it appears that they would account for 100% of the reduction in sales during the years following 1951 and the extended duration of the disposal process thereafter. They are not necessarily additive, however. Nonetheless, we do seem to have caught the principal elements which must explain this part of life companies' intertemporal allocation of funds to the private sector.

The conclusion that the open-to-buy period did not end abruptly in 1951 is not a particularly happy finding, for it stretches the liquidity disequilibrium position further into the 1950s than had previously seemed warranted. Thus in analyzing the sequential and investment composition choices of life companies during the 1950s, we shall have to keep in mind that the 1952–1956 transition period may possess different characteristics and portfolio responses from those of the later 1950s.

Chapter V | ALLOCATION OF INVESTMENT

FUNDS OVER TIME: *Liquidity and Bank Credit*

In this chapter we continue the analysis of life insurance companies' intertemporal allocation of funds. Previously we have examined the willingness of life companies to acquire risk assets in amounts exceeding normal cash flow by trading Government securities for private sector debt issues. Now abstracting from the exceptional liquidation of Government securities which took place following World War II, we shall investigate the extent to which the time sequence of life company portfolio acquisitions deviates from the time sequence of cash flow available for "permanent" investment. In balance sheet terms there are two ways such a deviation can show up in companies' accounts: as a change in liquid asset holdings, or as a change in the companies' outstanding debt.

Intertemporal reallocation of cash flow may be desirable for several reasons. Short-run reallocations may be prompted by bunching either in the inflow of loanable funds or in the availability of eligible investments. In the life insurance company context, for example, there is predictable seasonal bunching in the receipt of some types of insurance premium payments and portfolio repayments. There is also some seasonal pattern in the availability of certain types of investments, e.g., residential mortgage loans. Both deliberate and accidental nonseasonal bunching of loan acquisitions also may occur within any year.

Longer-run expectations may affect the trend level of liquid asset choices with respect to the maturity distribution of current investments. The longer-run aspects of liquidity and maturity decisions have been discussed in Chapter I. Our objective in this chapter will be confined to an analysis of the time rate of portfolio acquisitions by life companies over the business cycle. In particular, we wish to examine the possibility that life companies have altered the timing of portfolio investment to take advantage of cyclical swings in interest rate levels. Shifting funds over the cycle from "low" to "high" interest rate periods may be a feasible means of improving life companies' investment return over time. Such action may also be regarded by the monetary authorities as destabilizing, and therefore a matter of serious policy concern.

We proceed by considering the extent to which life companies' bank indebtedness and temporary cash investment holdings display a cyclical pattern. To the degree such a pattern is observable, we shall inquire whether it is consistent with the hypothesis that intertemporal funds shifts are designed to increase portfolio yield by shifting investment to the "high" interest rate phase of the business cycle. Finally, we investigate the possibility that other factors may be responsible for variations in life companies' liquid asset holdings and bank indebtedness. Since the analysis of life companies' use of bank credit during the 1950s can be dealt with relatively quickly, we shall handle this portion of the problem first and then proceed to an analysis of the cyclical play in liquidity holdings.

Bank Credit as a Source of Funds

Attitudes Toward the Use of Bank Credit

The stability of the inflow of funds to life companies and the predictability of outflow on insurance claims places these companies in a peculiarly good position to make substantial use of bank credit with minimal incurrence of risk. There is, however, a strong tradition in the industry against borrowing for investment purposes.[1] Outstanding bank debt rarely shows up in the year-end financial statements submitted to the various state insurance

---

[1] This is no doubt one of the legacies of the long past, but not forgotten, Armstrong investigation. For a discussion of the accepted doctrine regarding the use of bank credit see Burnett, "Some Aspects of Portfolio Management," p. 411.

departments. Net additions to bank credit as a source of investible funds is reported in a residual "other sources" item in the
LIAA *Cash Flow Survey*.[2] This item, which may contain miscellaneous sources other than net new borrowing, is of negligible
significance in the total sources of funds, generally accounting for
less than 1% of the gross flow.[3] The magnitude of swings between
net repayments and net borrowings is quite modest, the largest
movements being of the order of $25 million. This magnitude of
play is negligible in the context of the swings in total sources of
funds.

Mortgage Warehousing

There is an additional use of bank credit, however, which has
attracted considerable attention and which is probably not reported as a funds source in the *Cash Flow Survey*.[4] This is the
practice of mortgage warehousing. The term refers to the extension of short-term commercial bank credit to nonbank real estate
lenders. For the most part these loans have been made to mortgage brokers in order to finance their loan inventory between the
time of delivery of funds to the builder (home purchaser) and the
delivery of the completed mortgage instrument to the permanent
lender. In the most commonly used procedure, the mortgage is
pledged as collateral for the loan.[5] Much of the interest in ware-

---

[2] This is a quarterly survey of the gross flow of investible funds through life
insurance companies. Forecasts of funds flows two quarters in advance are
also made. Reporting companies account for about 62% of industry assets.

[3] The largest positive sum reported for this item for the period for which
the survey data was available, 1957/I to 1960/II, was $17.4 million (1958/II)
or slightly better than 1% of the total investible funds reported for that
quarter. This observation was the largest as a percentage of total funds as
well as in absolute value. We do not possess these data for recent years, but
it appears that a sharp increase in policy loans during 1966 (about a $1 billion
rise) may have sent some life companies to the banks in search of short-term
credits.

[4] There is no way of knowing with certainty what companies report in the
"other sources" item, but, in general, they do not appear to count warehousing
loans as bank debt in their financial statement. In any case, as we shall see
below, most warehousing has not been undertaken by insurance companies
directly but by their mortgage brokers.

[5] For a discussion of the loan mechanics and various functions of warehousing, see two Guttentag articles: "Commercial Banks in the Mortgage Market,"
and "Mortgage Warehousing." Also Klaman, *The Postwar Residential Mortgage Market*, pp. 182–190.

housing expressed by the monetary authorities[6] derived from a concern about the use of the warehousing technique as a means of achieving relatively long-run transfers of funds among time periods by the permanent institutional lenders. One large warehousing loan of $350 million granted by a syndicate of 150 banks to the Prudential Insurance Company in 1955[7] focused attention on this means of increasing the current volume of insurance company mortgage loan commitments. Indeed, this loan was apparently instrumental in prompting the Federal Reserve System to undertake a survey of bank credit extended to real estate mortgage lenders. The data for insurance companies from the surveys taken is summarized in Table V-1. The evidence suggests that outside of the one-shot Prudential loan life companies have made little direct use of mortgage warehousing.

It is possible for life companies to accomplish similar results, however, by pushing the financing problem back on their mortgage correspondents. This can be done by requesting postponement of delivery of completed mortgage loans. The mortgage broker may then warehouse the loans until the insurance company is ready to accept delivery. Since the loan is presumably backed by a written commitment from the insurance company to purchase the loan, this is a perfectly attractive transaction from the bank's viewpoint. As in the Prudential loan, this practice goes beyond the short-term technical functions of warehousing and permits additional funds to be currently placed by permanent lenders.[8]

Data on the volume of bank credit outstanding to mortgage companies is also available from the Federal Reserve surveys. Mortgage company bank indebtedness, however, is not classified by purpose of the loan. In particular, there are no data on the number of completed loans being warehoused. In addition, of course, there is no way of knowing what proportion of loans being warehoused are designated for eventual placement in life company

---

[6] U.S. House, Subcommittee on Housing, *Investigation of Housing, Hearings, 1955*, Part I, and the Subcommittee's report, *Mortgage Credit and FHA Multifamily Housing*, Report No. 2, January 31, 1956.

[7] Like most such loans to insurance companies, this one took the form of a mortgage purchase and resale agreement. The banking syndicate was headed by Irving Trust.

[8] This device was not open to Prudential since its home mortgage loans are generated through a large salaried branch office system rather than through independent correspondents.

TABLE V-1. Volume of Loans Outstanding from Credit Extended to Insurance Companies by Weekly Reporting Member Banks: August 1954–February 1959
(millions of dollars)

	Loan Type			
	(1)	(2)	(3)	
			Not	
	Under	*Secured*	*Secured*	
	Resale	*by*	*by*	
Survey Date	*Agreement*	*Mortgage*	*Mortgage*	*Total*
11 August 1954	$ 4	$12	$ 4	$ 20
10 August 1955	235	11	4	250
16 November 1955	265	20	2	287
15 February 1956	116	11	3	130
16 May 1956	113	10	4	127
8 August 1956	104	9	8	121
14 November 1956	102	7	5	114
13 February 1957	62	5	3	70
15 May 1957	47	4	3	54
14 August 1957	33	3	11	47
12 February 1958	39	4	6	49
13 August 1958	22	3	14	39
11 February 1959	28	9	11	48

NOTES:

Col. (1): Real estate mortgage loans purchased from real estate mortgage lender (insurance company) under resale agreement.

Col. (2): Loans to real estate mortgage lenders (insurance companies) secured by pledge of real estate mortgage loans owned by the borrower.

Col. (3): Loans to real estate mortgage lenders not secured or secured other than by pledge of mortgage loans owned by borrowers.

SOURCE: *Federal Reserve Bulletin,* various issues.

portfolios. We can, however, make a reasonable guess at the order of magnitude involved.

The Federal Reserve surveys were conducted periodically between August 1954 and February 1959. The mortgage company bank credit data are displayed in Table V-2. Three additional observations are included from Klaman's study of mortgage companies.[9] The data provide coverage of the 1954–1955 residential

[9] Klaman, *The Postwar Rise of Mortgage Companies,* Table A-12, p. 98. Klaman's study is particularly helpful because it provides an earlier observation (December 1953) in the 1953–1955 housing upswing than does the Federal

construction boom and most of the 1958–1959 expansion phase. The estimates recorded in Table V-2 are plotted on Chart V-1 along with life insurance companies' stock of outstanding commitments to take residential mortgage loans and the gross acquisitions of these loans by life companies. There is no direct evidence on whether life companies deferred takedowns of mortgage commitments during either period of high residential construction and mortgage loan activity. However, the substantial increase in mortgage company warehousing during 1955–1956 is consistent with the hypothesis that life companies stretched out loan takedowns in this manner.

The expansion in mortgage company bank debt between December 1953 and December 1955 is seen from Table V-2 to have amounted to $649 million. There is little question that this borrowing was undertaken to finance an increased inventory of mortgage loans. There is practically a dollar-for-dollar expansion of mortgage company bank indebtedness and loan holdings over the period.[10] We would like to know what proportion of this increased loan inventory and bank debt reflects normal expansion in a period of increased activity and what proportion represents extraordinary carrying of completed loans awaiting takedown by permanent lenders.

Klaman has made estimates of loans closed during the year relative to year-end mortgage holdings for 66 surveyed mortgage companies. He reports a decline in the ratio of loan closings to loan inventory, for this group of companies, from 4.2 in 1953 to 3.2 in 1955.[11] We have no grounds for knowing what would happen to this ratio during a period of increased activity if permanent lenders did not backlog completed loans in mortgage company inventories. However, the reported 31% increase in loan holdings relative to closings suggests that mortgage companies were holding abnormal quantities of completed loans by 1955. If there had been no change in the closings/inventory ratio between 1953 and 1955, loans held by these companies would have been

---

Reserve survey. As can be seen from Table V-2 and Chart V-1, Klaman's other two estimates of mortgage company bank indebtedness are consistent with the neighboring Federal Reserve estimates.

[10] See Klaman's balance sheet data for 66 surveyed mortgage companies, *ibid.*, Table 27, p. 63.

[11] *Ibid.*, Table 11, p. 37.

CHART V-1. *Outstanding Residential Mortgage Commitments of Life Insurance Companies, Acquisitions of Residential Mortgage Loans by Life Insurance Companies, and Outstanding Bank Indebtedness of Mortgage Companies: Quarterly, 1952/III–1960/II*

(millions of dollars)

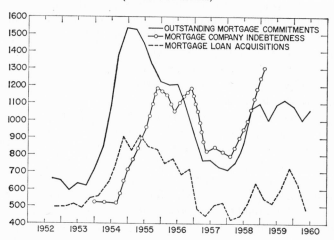

SOURCES: Insurance company loan commitments and acquisitions from the Life Insurance Association of America. These data are for reporting companies which account for about two-thirds of life insurance industry assets. Mortgage company indebtedness from Table V-2.

about $63 million less in December 1955 than they in fact were.[12]

The companies in question held about 25% of the industry's loan inventory during the period 1953–1955.[13] Assuming that the 66 respondents were reasonably representative of the industry's experience, this implies an extraordinary inventory increase of $252 million for the industry.[14] Life companies were probably

[12] Mortgage loan inventories for the 66 companies combined totaled $128.4 million in December 1953 and $265.7 million in December 1955. Applying the loan closing/inventory ratios reported above, this implies loan closings of $539.3 million in 1953 and $850.2 million in 1955. If the 1953 closings/ holdings ratio of 4.2 had also existed in 1955, the 1955 inventory would have been $202.4 million (i.e., 850.2/4.2) or $63.3 million less than the actual inventory of $265.7 million. Data from Klaman's Table 27, p. 63.

[13] The year-end figures were: 1953 — 23.5%; 1954 — 28.7%; 1955—23.8%. Computed from Klaman's Table 19, p. 48, and Table 27, p. 63.

[14] Actually, Klaman reports a disproportionate number of large companies in the sample of respondents, compared to the universe of all mortgage com-

TABLE V-2. Volume of Loans Outstanding from Credit Extended by Weekly Reporting Member Banks to Mortgage Companies: December 1953–February 1959

(millions of dollars)

Loan Type

	Survey Date	(1) Under Resale Agreement	(2) Secured by Mortgage	(3) Not Secured by Mortgage	Total
*	December 1953	—	—	—	$ 522*
11	August 1954	$ 44	$ 460	$13	517
*	December 1954	—	—	—	712*
10	August 1955	90	911	24	1,025
16	November 1955	109	1,035	38	1,182
*	December 1955	—	—	—	1,171*
15	February 1956	107	1,001	40	1,148
16	May 1956	107	899	45	1,051
8	August 1956	103	974	60	1,137
14	November 1956	113	1,011	57	1,181
13	February 1957	98	845	43	986
15	May 1957	92	690	37	819
14	August 1957	88	715	38	841
12	February 1958	84	673	37	794
13	August 1958	92	852	53	997
11	February 1959	129	1,118	58	1,305

NOTE: For further description of loan types, see Table V-1.

SOURCE: * Observations from Klaman, *The Postwar Rise of Mortgage Companies*, Table A-12, p. 98. Other data from the *Federal Reserve Bulletin*, various issues.

taking about four-fifths of the loans originated by mortgage companies in this period.[15] If this proportion is applicable to the

panies (p. 29). Since we are interested here in companies that carry significant amounts of loans in inventory, however, the concentration on larger companies may not be a drawback. Klaman indicates that many small companies operate with little or no mortgage inventory, and that their loan closings/loan holdings ratios are particularly sensitive to changes in the rate of mortgage originations (p. 36).

[15] See Klaman, Table 16, p. 43. Taking the median proportion of loans delivered to life companies by the asset size groups reported in this table and weighting them by the dollar volume of assets by size group for the industry (Klaman, Table 3, p. 20), the median percentage of total loans which went to life companies was 81.4%. This figure was used in the calculation in the text. The estimates apply to the year 1955.

mortgage company inventory expansion, we could conclude that about $205 million (see footnote 15) of the inventory increase was accounted for by completed loans awaiting delivery to life companies. This is obviously a very crude estimate, but sufficient for the sort of qualitative judgment we are trying to make. Adding this amount to the direct warehousing credit extended to life companies, it appears that directly and indirectly life companies borrowed about $450 to $500 million dollars between August 1954 and the end of 1955 to assist financing of their mortgage loan activity.

There is even less evidence available for the 1958–1959 housing expansion. It is clear, however, that life insurance company involvement in mortgage warehousing was quantitatively less in this period than during 1954–1956. There was no increase in direct warehousing debt for life companies in the second boom (cf. Table V-1). Since, by the estimate above, direct warehousing accounted for better than half of the total increase in life company warehousing loans in 1954–1956, this represents a substantial difference between the two periods.

No doubt there was some indirect warehousing through mortgage companies in 1958–1959. We do not have a count on the total expansion of commercial bank credit extended to mortgage companies during this period, since the Federal Reserve survey was discontinued after the February 1959 survey.[16] The expansion of mortgage company bank debt amounted to $511 million in the year, February 1958–February 1959, about the same magnitude as the August 1954–August 1955 increase.[17] Since the February 1959 date precedes the peak of the housing cycle by only a few months, it is unlikely that the total expansion of mortgage company bank indebtedness exceeded the 1954–1955 increase.[18] We have no conclusive evidence on the relative volume of mortgage company loan origination activity in the two periods.

---

[16] The elimination of this survey by the Fed is of some significance since this action presumably reflected a conclusion by the monetary authorities that extension of bank credit to permanent real estate lenders was no longer quantitatively important enough to warrant their concern.

[17] The beginning dates in this comparison are not exactly comparable in terms of business cycle dating but are close enough to make the comparison valid.

[18] By midyear 1959, housing starts had begun to decline.

However, it appears that mortgage company loan production in 1958–1959 exceeded the volume they originated in 1954–1955, despite the fact that their most important customers, life companies and mutual savings banks, placed smaller amounts in mortgage loans during 1958–1959 than they had in 1954–1955.[19]

The expanded volume of mortgage company loan originations in the second period suggests that a larger proportion of mortgage warehousing was of the technical variety. Moreover, the reduced level of life company mortgage activity as well as the lack of any increase in direct warehousing on their part suggests that indirect warehousing credit extensions to life companies would have been less important in 1958–1959.[20] Corroborating evidence on the liquidity position of life companies and the relation of their forward commitment activity to cash flow indicates the 1954–1956 squeeze was not repeated in 1958–1960.[21] In sum, then, it is reasonable to believe that indirect warehousing credit extensions to life companies during 1958–1959 did not exceed, and were probably smaller in magnitude than, the comparable use of bank credit in 1954–1955. Thus, if life companies borrowed $450 to $500 million through warehousing activity during the 1954–1955 housing expansion, their comparable borrowing activity in 1958–1959 probably amounted to substantially less than $200 million.

---

[19] Total mortgage company originations of FHA and VA loans amounted to $7,150 million during 1954–1955 and $7,601 million in 1958–1959. Comparable data are not available for conventional loans and mortgage companies are not included separately in mortgage recordings data. The nonfarm mortgage recordings data, however, do seem to corroborate the FHA-VA originations evidence. Miscellaneous mortgage investors (other than the permanent institutional lenders and individuals), a category dominated by mortgage companies, recorded $11,192 millions of loans under $20,000 in 1958–1959 as compared with $9,537 million in 1954–1955. Life companies and savings banks recorded about $1.4 billion less in home loans under $20,000 during 1958–1959 than they had in 1954–1955, and the net increase in 1–4 family home loans held by these two lenders amounted to only $5.3 billion in 1958–1959 compared with $8.2 billion in 1954–1955. Their reduced activity was only partially offset by increased FNMA participation. Data are from the Federal Housing Administration, Veterans Administration, Federal Home Loan Bank Board, and Housing and Home Finance Agency.

[20] The expansion of mortgage company lending activity in the late 1950s in the face of reduced life company loan commitments suggests mortgage companies were becoming less dependent on life companies. This decline in the importance of life companies to mortgage companies apparently had been going on for some time. See Klaman, *op. cit.*, pp. 40–41.

[21] See the remainder of this chapter and Chapter VI.

Mortgage Warehousing and the Interest Rate Cycle

Unless very substantial forecasting errors are assumed, the life insurance borrowing pattern during the one business cycle for which we have evidence of significant borrowing activity is not explainable as an attempt to play the interest rate cycle. Interest rates in the 1954–1957 expansion rose slowly during 1955 and early 1956 and then sharply to postwar high levels in the middle of 1956. Rates continued to rise through the third quarter of 1957. Thus the high interest rate period of this cycle can be placed in the latter part of 1956 through 1957. Warehousing activity, however, had the effect of shifting funds from the latter part of the cyclical expansion to an earlier period. Therefore, in terms of the goal of altering the temporal investment pattern to concentrate investment in the high interest rate phase of the business cycle, life company warehousing decisions were perverse. Barring extreme errors in forecasting interest rates, this behavior may be attributable to life company desires to service market contacts (e.g., mortgage brokers, tract developers) or to problems in maintaining internal control over the rate at which loan commitments are made relative to anticipated cash flow. We shall defer analysis of these possibilities until after an examination of the pattern of life companies' liquid asset movements during this same period.

The Liquidity Position of Life Insurance Companies

As we have seen (Chapter I), liquidity needs of life companies can be conveniently distinguished in three categories:

(1) transaction needs;
(2) "rare event" emergency needs; and
(3) opportunity needs.

The first two liquidity functions have been discussed previously. Here we are primarily interested in swings in life company liquid asset positions which may be motivated by companies' desire to take advantage of investment opportunities. The elements of liquidity relevant to this analysis are life company holdings of cash (including deposits), short-term Treasury obligations and commercial paper, and longer-term Treasury securities. Since the available information on holdings of commercial paper is meager,[22] the discussion will have to run in terms of cash and Treasuries.

Cash Holdings

As we have observed, there is no compelling transactions need for life companies to have positive cash holdings on the average over any year. The other liquidity needs could presumably be met with interest-bearing short-term marketable obligations. Life companies have, however, always maintained part of their liquidity in nonearning cash form. In periods of general prosperity and relatively high interest rates, such as the decades of the 1920s and the 1950s, aggregate currency and demand deposit holdings for the industry have amounted to 1.00% to 1.50% of admitted assets. During the liquidity oriented 1930s, cash accounted for well over 3% of assets in some years. There has been a general secular decline in the cash/assets ratio during the postwar years, from around 2% at the end of the war to about 1% by 1962.[23]

In absolute dollar terms there has been some secular increase in cash holdings during the postwar years. Actually there was a decline in cash held by life companies between 1947 and 1951, but the subsequent trend is positive. Aggregate life company cash holdings are displayed quarterly in Chart V-2 for the 1952–1960 period. A significant seasonal pattern in life company own-

---

[22] The Life Insurance Association of America reports "commercial paper, etc." as a separate item in the cash position of companies covered in the *Cash Flow Survey*. These data are available beginning in 1957. The Institute of Life Insurance began in 1959 to segregate "industrial and miscellaneous obligations; one year or less at issue," in its monthly asset composition data. (See its *Tally of Life Insurance Statistics*.) Limited evidence we obtained from individual companies suggests that while for a few large companies private sector short-term paper was a significant portion of their temporary cash investments during the 1950s, it became a dominant short-term asset for the industry as a whole only in the 1960s.

[23] Computed from aggregate cash and admitted asset figures in ILI, *Tally of Life Insurance Statistics*, monthly. Data in the New York Insurance *Reports*, Vol. I, *Life*, annual, for companies licensed to do business in New York state show somewhat lower ratios for the immediate postwar period. This simply reflects the tendency for small companies to carry higher cash/asset ratios than large companies.

ership of cash exists. The months of above-average holdings are November, December, and January, particularly December. This is apparently due to the fact that there is a concentration of cash inflow from the insurance business toward the end of the year.[24]

CHART V-2. *Cash Holdings of Life Insurance Companies: Quarterly, 1952/I–1960/IV*

(millions of dollars)

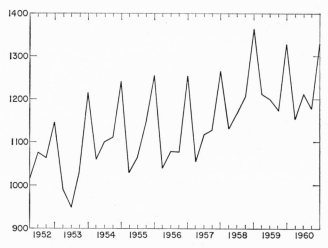

SOURCE: ILI, *Tally of Life Insurance Statistics.*

The trend in life company cash ownership during the 1952–1960 period is best represented by a linear function of cash against time, indicating a secular decline in the growth rate of cash assets.[25]

---

[24] At least, in part, this seems to be caused by annual or semiannual premium payments and adjustments made on some kinds of policies (particularly group insurance). This seasonal pattern of cash inflow makes it relatively painless for companies who borrow during the year to have their books free of bank debt in the year-end statement.

[25] Least squares trend estimates were fitted to seasonally adjusted monthly cash holdings data utilizing seasonal adjustment and smoothing techniques developed at the Bureau of the Census and the National Bureau of Economic Research. (See Shiskin, "Electronic Computers and Business Indicators.") The linear equation provided a better fit and forecasts than second and third degree equations. Using the linear equation (Cash Holdings = 1031.58 + 1.82367 (time)), cash measured in millions of dollars and time in months elapsed from the January 1952 origin), the growth rate in cash assets declined from 2.12% in 1952 to 1.67% ten years later.

A modest cyclical response in cash ownership is suggested by the concentration of the 1952–1960 increase in (seasonally adjusted) cash holdings during the cyclical recession phases of 1953–1954 and 1957–1958. To a limited degree life companies may have accomplished some shifting of funds from low interest rate recession periods to more buoyant portions of the business cycle. Since substantial substitution between cash and short-term earning assets can occur, the analysis of cyclical movements in liquid asset holdings is better made for both forms of liquidity combined.

Cash Plus Short-Term Treasury Obligations

Aggregate life company holdings of cash plus short-term Treasuries[26] are plotted in Chart V-3. The most striking build-up of these assets occurred in 1950–1951, as about a billion dollars was shifted from Treasury bonds to short-term Treasury obligations. This, of course, was a move dictated by the market uncertainties generated by Treasury-Federal Reserve disagreement over supporting operations in the Government bond market. From 1951 through 1960 the trend level of the life company liquid asset position was essentially constant (no growth), the modest secular increase in cash holdings being offset by a comparable decline in ownership of short-term Treasuries.

There is, however, a pronounced cyclical swing about the stable secular level. The magnitude of these cyclical movements is summarized in Table V-3. This table shows the net change in life company liquid asset holdings during cyclical expansions and contractions. The data utilized are a three-month moving average of the seasonally adjusted liquid asset holdings series.[27] Two expansion and two contraction phases are available in the post-Accord portion of the 1950s.[28] The beginning date, April 1952, is

---

[26] Short-term Treasuries here refers to Treasury obligations due or callable in less than one year.

[27] This computation utilizes Shiskin's MCD (Months for Cyclical Dominance) index. The additional moving average is intended to smooth the irregular movements in the series. The MCD measure is a device for determining the number of months it takes for the cyclical element in the series to dominate the random element. For this series it took three months, and consequently a three-month moving average is employed.

[28] A third contraction phase appears to have taken twelve months. Liquidation from June 1959 through June 1960 amounted to $343 million (raw data unadjusted). If short-term commercial paper is included, the figure is $379 million.

CHART V-3. Life Insurance Company Holdings of Cash and Short-Term Treasury Obligations: Quarterly, 1952/I–1960/IV

(millions of dollars)

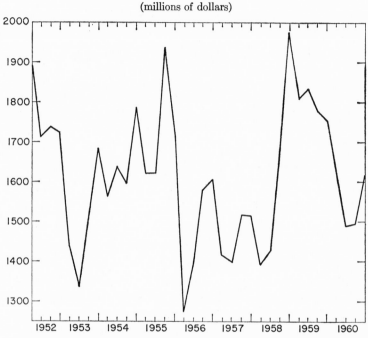

SOURCES: Institute of Life Insurance and *Treasury Bulletin*.

somewhat arbitrary, being in the nature of a local peak rather than a true cyclical peak. This selection was made to remove the rather special circumstances of the accumulation and decumulation of liquidity associated with the Accord. It should also be observed that the 27 months listed as the duration for the second contraction is somewhat misleading. As can be seen in Chart V-3, the entire decumulation of liquidity in this phase took place in six months following the peak holdings of liquid assets. This action apparently reduced aggregate life company liquidity to something like the minimum desired level, which was maintained throughout the remainder of the boom phase of the cycle.

For the two cyclical movements displayed in Table V-3, then, the size of the swing is nearly $500 million. Cyclical swings of this magnitude are not particularly large relative to commercial

TABLE V-3. *Magnitude and Length of Expansion and Contraction Phases of the Cycle in Liquid Asset Holdings of Life Insurance Companies: April 1952–June 1959*

Cycle Phase	Dating	Number of Months	Net Change in Liquid Assets (millions)
Contraction	4/52– 5/53	13	−$484.6
Expansion	6/53–10/55	29	+ 481.8
Contraction	11/55– 1/58*	27	− 482.8
Expansion	2/58– 6/59	17	+ 468.9

* This contraction phase actually took place in only six months, and was followed by a long relatively stable trough before the next expansion (see Chart V-3).

SOURCE: Three-month moving average of the seasonally adjusted series on aggregate life insurance company cash and short-term Treasury securities held. Data on cash came from ILI, *Tally of Life Insurance Statistics*, monthly; holdings of short-term Treasuries are from the *Treasury Bulletin*, monthly.

bank or even savings and loan association shifts via liquid asset play and borrowing during the same period. Curiously, the liquidity build-up of $482 million between June 1953 and October 1955 is of about the same magnitude as the estimated warehousing credit obtained directly and indirectly by life companies over about the same period.[29] Thus for the industry as a whole it appears that the bank borrowing in effect financed the liquidity accumulation. Verification of this requires knowing whether this was true for individual decision units; that is, whether the companies that engaged in mortgage warehousing, directly or indirectly, were at the same time augmenting their liquid positions. In the short run, it is to be expected that liquid assets will rise as soon as a bank loan is completed. If, however, a strong reluctance to borrow exists, one might expect to observe, over a period of several months following delivery of the bank loan, the original liquidity position being depleted along with the loan proceeds. A reluctant borrower resorts to the money lenders only

---

[29] See above. The increase in direct bank credit to life companies was $267 million between August 1954 and November 1955. We guessed that about $200 million more credit might have been obtained indirectly by life companies through having mortgage correspondents carry part of their loan inventory. The warehousing expansion began about midway in the liquidity accumulation, and outstanding bank credit remained at a high level beyond the subsequent decumulation of liquid assets.

when his liquidity holdings are inadequate to meet upcoming drains from insurance benefits and investment commitments.

As we know, only one company, the Prudential, was directly engaged in warehousing. The evidence for the Prudential is mixed. There was a substantial rise in liquid asset holdings (cash and short-term Treasury obligations)[30] associated with the large warehousing loan. The warehousing agreement was concluded in December 1954. The increase in holdings of liquid assets during the first quarter 1955 amounted to $120 million, about a 50% rise. More significantly, although fluctuating widely from quarter to quarter, Prudential's liquidity position generally remained above its preloan level until the fourth quarter 1956. Corroborating evidence for the position that the Prudential was not forced to the bank syndicate for lack of alternatives is found in the stock of longer-term Government securities held by the Prudential. There was no change in the stock of this source of extraordinary funds between the end of 1954 and the middle of 1956. Not until the latter half of 1956 did Prudential dip into this secondary reserve. Net liquidation of Treasury note and bond obligations amounted to $127 million during the latter half of 1956 and $99 million in 1957. This is rather curious behavior since it meant that sales of longer-term Governments were delayed to the point where price discounts below par had become significant (see Chart III-2). Briefly, then, the warehousing operation of early 1955 enabled Prudential to postpone liquidation of its short-term Treasury position and use of its longer-term Government security portfolio until the latter half of 1956.[31]

---

[30] It appears that the Prudential held little or no commercial paper at this time.

[31] Prudential was obligated by terms of the loan agreement to complete repurchasing the mortgages involved by June 30, 1956. It may be helpful if the magnitudes involved are kept in mind. As would be expected, the variance over time in cash held by the Prudential was quite small. Practically all the variance in liquidity holdings over time is attributable to the short-term Treasury portfolio. At the end of 1954 the Prudential held only $80 million in short-term Treasuries. Given the magnitude of the warehousing loan made ($350 million), the stock of short Treasuries was an inadequate substitute for the loan. The logical alternative would have been to liquidate the necessary amount of longer-term Treasury securities. Prudential held about $1,135 million in Governments with maturity and call dates more than a year away. It does not appear that the Prudential drew on the entire $350 million credit. The expansion in bank credit extended to insurance

The industry's liquidity accumulation was expended in a brief period, November 1955–April 1956. We have, in effect, a displacement of about $500 million in investible funds from mid-1953 through three quarters of 1955 to a five- or six-month period in late 1955 — early 1956. Not all of this amount represented a diversion of the "normal" inflow of investible funds, of course. Part of the short-term asset accumulation derived from liquidation of portfolio investments, particularly Treasury bonds. In a broader context, however, we ought to regard Treasury bond sales as a normal source of funds during the decade of the 1950s. If one takes the view that Government bonds became part of the investible funds flow at the time of liquidation, then that portion of the proceeds reinvested in short-term assets is diverted from the period in which funds became available in the same way as is any part of the regular inflow when it is placed in cash or short-term assets.

It is not possible to pinpoint in time the placement into the long-term market of funds obtained from warehousing credits. In general, however, this borrowing activity tended to transfer funds forward from 1956–1957 into 1955. The investment of funds from these two extraordinary sources was concentrated in the period from mid-1955 to mid-1956.

Overlapping these sources of additional funds were net sales of longer-term Treasury obligations amounting to a little over a billion dollars during the four quarters, 1955/IV to 1956/III. Consistent with the argument above, part of this liquidation should be regarded as a normal source of funds. The mean quarterly run-off of the longer term Governments portfolio was $114 million

---

companies under mortgage resale agreements amounted to $231 million from August 1954 to August 1955. Probably not all of this is attributable to Prudential, but even this amount could certainly have been obtained at the time by marketing Government securities, and rather painlessly since Government bond prices were still close to par in first quarter 1955. It is possible that Prudential investment officers at the time foresaw a strong possibility of lower interest rates on the horizon. This seems to be Brimmer's explanation of Prudential's behavior. (Brimmer, *Life Insurance Companies in the Capital Market*, pp. 265–266.)

Klaman indicates that the price of the highest quality repurchase agreements was generally 50 basis points above the prime loan rate (*The Postwar Residential Mortgage Market*, p. 188). This implies Prudential paid 3.5% for the December 1954 arrangement. This was nearly a hundred basis points in excess of the Treasury bond rate.

TABLE V-4. *Investible Funds Obtained by Life Insurance Companies from Liquidation of Cash, Short-Term Treasury Obligations, and Longer-Term Treasury Securities: Quarterly, 1951/III–1960/II*

(millions of dollars)

Source of Funds: Year and Quarter	(1) Cash	(2) Short-Term Governments	(3) Other Governments	(4) Total
1951/III	$ 11	$ 170	$ 279	$ 460
IV	−153	254	154	255
1952/I	82	−96	289	275
II	−62	136	319	393
III	12	−34	−58	−80
IV	−81	105	98	122
1953/I	156	127	5	288
II	42	60	−30	72
III	−82	−79	182	21
IV	−185	1	157	−27
1954/I	155	−33	142	264
II	−41	−36	357	280
III	−10	51	210	251
IV	−129	−60	128	−61
1955/I	211	−44	23	190
II	−35	26	19	10
III	−78	−131	48	−161
IV	−112	339	244	471
1956/I	114	223	278	615
II	−38	−84	208	86
III	1	−187	303	117
IV	−196	171	102	77
1957/I	217	−27	132	322
II	−62	79	78	95
III	−10	−107	153	36
IV	−136	137	137	138
1958/I	132	−9	−43	80
II	−33	—	23	−10
III	−44	−217	−111	−372
IV	−156	−145	247	−54
1959/I	154	15	−39	130
II	11	−36	19	−6
III	27	31	46	104
IV	−154	175	146	167
1960/I	174	−40	80	214
II	−60	190	50	180

for the period 1952–1960. If this is used as a standard of normality, then net sales of Governments during the four-quarter period cited provided extraordinary funds amounting to $578 million. It is clear, then, that life companies invested well over a billion dollars in the private capital market during portions of 1955 and 1956 at the expense of preceding and succeeding time periods. This expenditure of abnormal funds was particularly concentrated in 1955/IV and 1956/I. The quarterly record of funds obtained from the cash and Treasury security holdings is displayed for 1951/III to 1960/II in Table V-4.

The second expansion in cash and short-term Treasury obligations (1958–1959) was shorter than the first by twelve months (Table V-3), but of about the same dollar magnitude. The succeeding liquidity run-off was somewhat smaller than the accumulation. Mortgage warehousing was of much less significance than in the preceding boom, and sales of longer term Treasury securities were quite modest throughout the cyclical recession and expansion phases. Only in the fourth quarter 1958 did sales of Treasury bonds appear to be a significant source of liquid asset expansion. In sum, life companies supplied much less in extraordinary funds to the 1958–1960 cyclical expansion than they had in 1955–1957. There was, however, a repetition of the cyclical movement in cash and short-term Treasury obligations. As before, liquid assets were accumulated in the recession and recovery phases of the business cycle and expended in later stages of the expansion.

After mid-1960 life companies again built up their liquid asset position although at a somewhat slower rate. The quarterly record is reported in Table V-5. During the 30 months from July 1960 through December 1962, life company holdings of cash and short-term Treasury securities expanded by $266 million ($429

Table V-4 continued

NOTE: A positive sign (no sign) represents a net reduction in the given sector of the portfolio; a negative sign means a net increase in holdings of that asset.

SOURCES:

Col. (1): ILI, *Tally of Life Insurance Statistics.*

Col. (2): *Treasury Bulletin.*

Col. (3): Total holdings of Treasury obligations from the *Federal Reserve Bulletin,* less Col. (2).

Col. (4): Col. (1) + Col. (2) + Col. (3).

million, if short-term corporate paper is included). Liquidation of the longer-term Government securities portfolio continued to provide a steady, though reduced, volume of investible funds. There is, of course, no information on warehousing activity after 1959.

The period mid-1960–1962 covers the 1960–1961 recession and subsequent recovery. Interest rates varied relatively little in this period. Bond rates declined modestly during the recession and

TABLE V-5. *Investible Funds Obtained by Life Insurance Companies from Their Cash and Security Portfolios: Quarterly, 1960/III–1962/IV*

(millions of dollars)

Source of Funds: Year and Quarter	(1) Cash	(2) Short-Term Industrial and Miscellaneous Obligations	(3) Short-Term Governments	(4) Other Governments	(5) Total
1960/III	$ 35	$ −78	$ −39	$ 261	$ 179
IV	−152	−39	27	115	−49
1961/I	111	−58	−38	−53	−38
II	−51	37	64	70	120
III	−30	−5	−80	91	−24
IV	−92	138	147	108	301
1962/I	190	−319	−183	61	−251
II	7	−11	65	−38	23
III	−73	−122	−70	−37	−302
IV	−143	294	39	109	299
Totals	−198	−163	−68	687	258

NOTE: A positive sign (no sign) represents a net reduction in the given sector of the portfolio; a negative sign means a net increase in holdings of that asset.

SOURCES:

Cols. (1), (2): ILI, *Tally of Life Insurance Statistics.*

Col. (3): *Treasury Bulletin.*

Col. (4): Total holdings of Treasury obligations by life companies reported in the *Federal Reserve Bulletin,* less Col. (3).

Col. (5): Col. (1) + Col. (2) + Col. (3) + Col. (4).

actually softened further during 1962 so that interest rates were lower at the end of 1962 than at any time since the 1958 recession.

Explanations of the Liquidity Cycle

Given that reasonably clear-cut (although modest) cyclical movements in life company holdings of liquid assets do seem to have occurred, the question remains whether this pattern reflects deliberate action to shift funds into periods distinguished by relatively high demand, interest rates, or other inducements. Table V-6 summarizes the relation of the life insurance portfolio liquidity cycles to the National Bureau of Economic Research reference cycle. Troughs in the life insurance liquidity position correspond closely to business cycle peaks, although in the 1954–1957 expansion the liquid asset position "bottomed out" well in advance of the business cycle peak. Peaks in liquidity stocks have occurred roughly midway in the expansion phase of the business cycle. Thus liquidity tends to be accumulated during the recession and early expansion and then run off as the expansion progresses.

TABLE V-6. *Peak and Trough Dates for National Bureau of Economic Research Reference Cycles and Life Insurance Company Liquidity Cycles: Quarterly, 1949/IV–1960/II*

NBER Reference Cycle		Life Insurance Liquid Asset Cycle	
Trough	1949/IV	1951/II	Peak
Peak	1953/II	1953/II	Trough
Trough	1954/III	1955/IV	Peak
Peak	1957/III	1956/II to 1958/I	Trough
Trough	1958/II	1959/II	Peak
Peak	1960/II	1960/II	Trough

SOURCE: NBER Reference Cycle Dates from Moore, *Business Cycle Indicators*; life insurance liquidity data: see Chart V-2.

We shall first examine the proposition that the observed liquidity cycle results from conscious action to shift a part of the cash inflow from the low interest rate phase of the business cycle to the period of high yields. This hypothesis implies some willingness to compromise a frequently stated goal of life insurance company portfolio policy, namely, to maintain a "fully invested" position. This means that it is an objective of investment policy to invest "permanently" funds as they become available and to avoid speculation on interest rate movements or other market variables.[32] Given the relatively modest magnitude of cyclical swings in liquidity which are involved, only a limited compromise of the fully invested objective is implied.

Liquidity and Interest Rates

Charts V-4, V-5, and V-6 present the relation between the life company liquid asset position and the level of bond yields. The seasonally adjusted cash plus short-term Treasury holdings series is graphed along with a new issue public utility bond yield

CHART V-4. Life Insurance Company Liquid Asset Holdings and New Issue Corporate Bond Yields: Quarterly, 1952/I–1960/II

(millions of dollars)

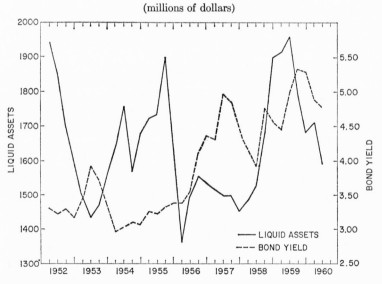

SOURCES: Institute of Life Insurance, *Treasury Bulletin*, and Bankers Trust Company.

---

[32] It is quite common for observers of life insurance company portfolio behavior and investment officers to assert that a primary goal of investment policy is to maintain a fully invested position. See, for example, LIAA-CMC Monograph, p. 185.

CHART V-5. *Life Insurance Company Liquid Asset Holdings and New Issue Corporate Bond Yields (Scatter Diagram): Quarterly, 1952/I–1960/II*

(millions of dollars)

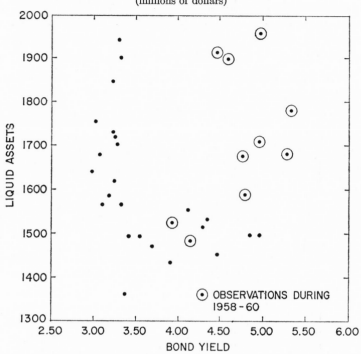

SOURCES: See Chart V-4.

series in Chart V-4.[33] The same data are plotted in a scatter diagram in Chart V-5. Since cyclical movement in interest rates around its trend is presumably most relevant for explaining the liquidity cycle, Chart V-6 presents the liquid asset series plotted against the spread in basis points between the utility bond yield series and a 12-month moving average of the same series.[34]

[33] This series is compiled by Bankers Trust Company. Rates are on "Grade 2" quality issues approximately equivalent to Moody's Aa.

[34] It may be unreasonable to postulate that life companies are able to forecast the mean and variance in the relevant interest rate indices over the forthcoming cycle. More plausibly, their judgments about current interest rate levels may be based on experience with interest rates in the recent past. This is the reason for using the series plotted in Chart V-6, as well as the bond yield series itself.

When observations are limited to the period 1952/III–1957/IV, there is some indication of the expected negative relationship between liquid stocks and interest rates. However, inclusion of the 1958–1960 experience belies this relationship. This is because the

CHART V-6. *Life Insurance Company Liquid Asset Holdings and Current Compared to Past Corporate Bond Yields (Scatter Diagram):* *Quarterly, 1952/I–1960/II*

(millions of dollars)

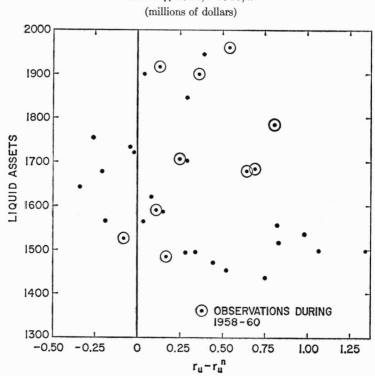

SOURCES: See Chart V-4.

interest rate decline in 1957–1958 was quite shortlived and rates returned within a year to previous high levels. In the meantime, the accumulation of liquidity continued well into the business cycle expansion as before. The similarity among the liquidity stock expansions in 1953–1955, 1958–1959, and 1960–1962 in the face of rather different interest rate behavior suggests that some other factor(s) must have been at work.[35]

Liquidity and Cash Flow

A plausible factor to consider is the relation of liquidity to cash flow. Two possibilities suggest themselves. One is that liquidity is built up when the availability of investible funds over some months in the future are "tight" relative to the loan commitments coming due for takedown. Such tightness might reflect heavy demand and/or high interest rates, but could also presumably have other causes (e.g., unanticipated bunching of funds delivery on outstanding commitments, errors in inflow forecasts, or faulty control over the rate of issuance of forward commitments).[36] If this hypothesis is correct, then we would expect the current level of liquid assets to be negatively related to the volume of investible funds (net of committed funds) expected to be available during the coming months.

---

[35] We have collected some data on bond yields received by insurance companies. This evidence suggests that the 1957–1958 decline in yields on life company authorizations to acquire corporate bonds was more modest than the reduction in comparable public new issue bond series. In addition, mortgage loan rates were clearly "sticky" relative to bond yields during this period. The clear-cut cyclical movement in liquid asset holdings in the face of this highly dampened cyclical response of yields indicates that the level of interest rates could not be the prime cause of the liquidity cycle. As noted above, although the industry's liquidity position peaked in 1962, there was no upward movement of interest rates until much later in the expansion (1965).

[36] Some industry spokesmen seem to take the position that variation in liquid asset holdings from the minimum permanent desired holdings is explained by the need to build up liquidity to meet anticipated takedowns of commitments in coming weeks. See, for example, LIAA-CMC Monograph, p. 63 and p. 183. This is usually presented as a short-run proposition. Brimmer however, has put the argument in a cyclical setting. His position is that life companies sell long-term Government securities to be able to meet commitment deliveries when commitments have been expanded beyond the normal funds flow in response to rising interest rates. In the time interval between sales of Governments and takedown of commitments, short-term earning assets are held. Although the Government bond portfolio is held to be the usual source of funds used to build up short-term assets, exceptions are admitted. For example, with regard to the 1954–1955 accumulation of short-term assets, Brimmer says, "Apparently, life insurance companies were accumulating funds from the normal cash inflow in order to honor a part of the huge backlog of commitments (especially commitments for VA mortgages) accumulated during the 1953–1954 recession" (p. 97). Brimmer, *Life Insurance Companies in the Capital Market*, pp. 95–97.

The second possibility is that the liquid stock position may be positively related to the rate of inflow of investible funds in the current period and recent past. This would be true if there exists a lagged response to changes in the flow of available funds combined with imperfect forecasting of changes in the cash flow. Or an abnormally high rate of cash inflow may make companies less concerned about keeping their liquidity positions to the minimum level desirable and instead induce willingness to hold back part of the funds flow for future use. Since we have observed a cyclical movement in the liquid asset holdings of life companies, this hypothesis would seem to imply the existence of a comparable cycle in cash flow, and the imperfect forecasting version suggests systematic underestimation of the variance in the cash flow.[37]

There are two distinct sources of funds for liquid asset accumulation: (1) the normal inflow of investible funds, and (2) proceeds from security sales. Somewhat different implications for life company behavior flow from the use of one source opposed to the other. Liquidity build-up accomplished from security sales need not imply any compromise with a goal of investing the cash flow as it becomes available. Diversion of the normal inflow of funds into liquid asset holdings does involve some deviation from a "loaned up" objective, although where forecasting errors and sluggish responses to them are involved, the deflection is of a rather passive nature. We have then to investigate whether life company liquidity holdings are either positively associated with past (current) cash flow, or negatively associated with anticipated future cash flow; whether security sales or the normal inflow of investible funds is the primary source of liquid asset accumulation; and whether forecasting errors seem to have played a role in accounting for the variations in liquidity levels.

TESTING THE CASH FLOW HYPOTHESIS

We shall first look to the evidence to see whether a choice can be made between the alternative hypotheses relating cash flow and liquidity. The data available are not adequate to permit us

---

[37] This is not strictly so since it is conceivable that a liquidity cycle might be the consequence of noncyclical fluctuations in the rate of cash inflow, given the appropriate structure of forecasting errors and lagged responses. It makes sense to investigate first the possibility of a cash flow cycle, however.

to draw a very fine decision in this matter. Evidence summarized in Charts V-7 and V-8 is suggestive, however. In Chart V-7 we have related life company holdings of liquid assets to measures of the flow of available funds. The liquid asset series plotted is the seasonally adjusted series of cash and short-term Treasury obliga-

CHART V-7. *Life Insurance Company Liquid Assets and Available Funds (Scatter Diagram): Quarterly, 1952/III–1960/II*

(millions of dollars)

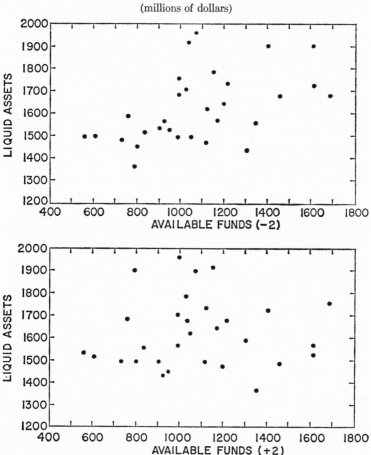

SOURCES: Institute of Life Insurance, *Treasury Bulletin,* and Life Insurance Association of America.

tions held by the industry in toto. The measures of available funds flow are derived from data reported to the Life Insurance Association of America by companies accounting for only about 65% of industry assets. Available funds are estimated for this sample of companies as the gross flow of investible funds during the period indicated less funds obtained through liquidation of Government securities, and net of forward commitments outstanding at the beginning of the period and expected to result in closed loans during the period.[38] Therefore this series reflects the gross flow that was available in fact, not forecasts of cash flow.[39] We shall discuss forecasting errors subsequently. Chart V-7 includes data from 1952 to 1960.

The substantial difference in coverage between the liquid asset data and the available funds measure is obviously a serious deficiency. For a later subperiod the appropriate comparison can be made between series derived from essentially the same sample of companies, but we have no comparable funds flow and liquid asset data prior to 1957. If either of the postulated relationships were essentially correct, however, we would expect it to be reflected even in the crude comparison depicted in Chart V-7. In the upper panel in Chart V-7, liquid asset holdings of life companies at the end of quarter $t = 0$ are plotted against the available funds flow estimated for the preceding two quarters, $t = -2$ to $t = -1$, inclusive. The second hypothesis discussed above predicts a positive relationship between these variables. Liquid asset holdings in $t = 0$ are plotted against the estimated flow of available funds for the succeeding two quarters in the lower panel of Chart V-7. The first hypothesis listed above predicts a negative relationship, liquid assets being built to a high level only when total funds are tight relative to commitments due for takedown. In neither case is the predicted relationship necessarily linear.

---

[38] For further discussion and use of this series, see Chapter VI. The data, except for the estimate of net Government securities liquidated, are drawn from the *Forward Commitment Survey* conducted monthly by the LIAA. The estimate of net sales of Governments is derived from aggregate industry data and deflated. This and other aspects of the series are described more fully in Chapter VI.

[39] Forecasts of expected takedowns from outstanding forward commitments are involved in the net available funds estimate, however.

Inspection of Chart V-7 does not yield any very strong confirmation of either hypothesis. However, the hypothesis that links the current liquidity position to past cash inflow fares a little better. The expected positive relationship does appear whereas there is no evidence of a negative relationship between liquid assets and the upcoming funds flow. As a further check on this, we did estimate the simple linear least squares regression equations from the data displayed in Chart V-7. These results are reported in Table V-7. Equations (1) and (4) regress the stock of short-term liquid assets on future available funds in one case (1) and past available funds in the other (4). As indicated, there is no relation between liquid asset holdings and future funds, and a significant positive relation between liquidity and the cash flow in preceding quarters. We also introduced a measure of the level of interest rates as an independent variable. In the equations reported in Table V-7, the measure is the difference between the current new issue Grade 2 public utility bond yield and an average of yields in the same series over the past twelve months. Even where a significant funds effect has been partialed out, however, bond yields contribute nothing toward explaining life company liquid asset holdings. We also regressed the first difference in liquid asset holdings against the funds and interest rate variables and obtained no relationship regardless of the funds variable used.

A similar comparison, for a more limited period of time but based on data derived from essentially comparable samples of companies, is presented in Chart V-8. The liquid asset series utilized there is obtained from an LIAA cash flow survey that covers approximately the same list of companies which report in the forward commitment survey.[40] This liquid assets series contains holdings of commercial paper as well as cash and short-term

---

[40] There has been some variation in coverage in each survey from month (quarter) to month (quarter). During 1957–1960 the range of coverage in the cash flow survey has been from 45 to 57 companies. The variation in coverage by the proportion of industry assets accounted for has been reasonably small, however, ranging from 58% to 62% of industry assets. Some 65 to 67 companies have been reporting on forward commitments over the same period. These companies account for about two-thirds of industry assets. One large company (with over a billion dollars in assets) has reported to the forward commitment, but not the cash flow, survey.

TABLE V-7. *Liquid Asset Regression Analysis: Quarterly Observations,*
1952/IV–1959/IV

$(n = 29)$

(1) $CT_s = 1485 + .1080 \, AF_{1,2}$
            $(.1188)$

    $R^2 = .029$ $s = 173.8$
    $\overline{R}^2 = -.006$ $\overline{s} = 180.1$

(2) $CT_s = 1539 + .0702 \, AF_{1,2} - 39.3 \, (r_u - r_u{}^n)$
            $(.1590)$ (107.6)

    $R^2 = .034$ $s = 173.4$
    $\overline{R}^2 = -.039$ $\overline{s} = 183.1$

(3) $\triangle CT_s = 238.0 - .1985 \, AF_{1,2} - 69.4 \, (r_u - r_u{}^n)$
            $(.1915)$ (132.2)

    $R^2 = .048$ $s = 170.1$
    $\overline{R}^2 = -.024$ $\overline{s} = 179.6$

Quarterly Observations: $1953/II - 1960/II$ $n = 29$

(4) $CT_s = 1261 + .3108 \, AF_{-2,-1}$
            $(.1026)$

    $R^2 = .253$ $s = 150.1$
    $\overline{R}^2 = .225$ $\overline{s} = 155.5$

(5) $CT_s = 1255 + .3146 \, AF_{-2,-1} + 7.42 \, (r_u - r_u{}^n)$
            $(.1115)$ (75.46)

    $R^2 = .253$ $s = 150.0$
    $\overline{R}^2 = .196$ $\overline{s} = 158.5$

(6) $\triangle CT_s = 11.29 - .0185 \, AF_{-2,-1} + 33.16 \, (r_u - r_u{}^n)$
            $(.1256)$ (84.98)

    $R^2 = .009$ $s = 169.0$
    $\overline{R}^2 = -.066$ $\overline{s} = 178.5$

SYMBOLS: CT_s = stock of cash plus Treasury securities due in less
            than one year, end of quarter $t = 0$.
    $\triangle CT_s$ = first difference of CT_s.
    $AF_{m,n}$ = Gross investible cash flow through life companies
            during quarters m and n, inclusive, less sales of Treas-
            ury obligations, and less the stock of outstanding
            commitments existing at the beginning of m ex-
            pected to result in delivery of funds during $m + n$.
    r_u = Bankers Trust Grade Two Public Utility New Issue
            Bond Yields $(t = 0)$.
    $r_u{}^n$ = average of utility bond yields for the current quarter
            and the four preceding quarters.

CHART V-8. *Liquid Assets of Life Insurance Companies Compared with Their Cash Inflow of Available Investment Funds: Quarterly, Upper Panel 1956/IV–1959/IV and Lower Panel 1957/II–1960/II*

(millions of dollars)

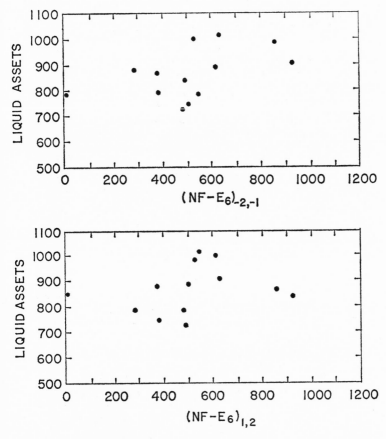

NOTES: Liquid assets include cash and short-term security holdings of life insurance companies reporting to the LIAA *Cash Flow Survey*. Liquid asset data are recorded as of the end of the quarter indicated. Available funds is defined as total cash inflow to reporting life companies (excluding proceeds from security sales), less loan commitments outstanding at the beginning of the period which are due for takedown during the period. This net funds series is presented for six-month periods. The upper panel pairs liquid asset observations with the net cash flow for the six months ending with the observed liquidity position; in the lower panel liquid assets are paired with (actual) net cash flow for the six months immediately following the liquidity observation.

SOURCES: LIAA, *Cash Flow* and *Forward Commitment Surveys*.

Governments.[41] An estimate of the normal inflow of investible funds derived from the cash flow survey is used as the base from which anticipated takedowns of outstanding commitments are subtracted in order to obtain the available funds measures. The normal flow of investible funds is the gross flow on a cash basis less funds obtained from outright security sales and liquidation of the cash position, and less funds absorbed by a net increase in policy loans.[42]

Chart V-8 is analogous to Chart V-7. Quarterly liquid asset holdings (end quarter, 1957/II to 1960/II) are plotted against the net available funds flow for the two preceding quarters in the upper panel. In the lower panel, liquid asset holdings are plotted against the available funds for the succeeding two quarters. In this case the coverage of liquid asset observations is 1956/IV to 1959/IV.[43] As before, the evidence does not lend much support to either hypothesis. Again, however, the notion that the liquidity position should be negatively associated with the future funds position comes off the worst. The chart depicts some positive relationship. In the alternative case, liquid assets are posi-

---

[41] The definitions which pertain to these items are:

Cash — all cash on hand in home and branch offices and bank deposits.

Short-term Government securities — Treasury bills and any other short-term Government securities that are held as temporary investments which roll over several times during the year.

Commercial paper — commercial paper purchased in the open market, directly placed commercial paper, and any other short-term instruments held as temporary investments.

These are the definitions supplied by the LIAA to reporting companies.

[42] Gross inflow consists of the net gain in adjusted ledger assets, and portfolio rollover from all sources (amortization payments, prepayments, maturities, sinking fund payments, calls, and outright sales). Ledger assets are adjusted to a cash basis, therefore representing simply the cash flow from net gains from insurance operations and net investment income. Security maturities and sales exclude obligations which are included in the cash position. This approach of computing the flow of investible funds from the inflow side contrasts with the estimate of available funds used in Chart V-7 in which the investible funds flow is calculated from uses of funds. See Chapter VI for further discussion and use of this measure.

[43] The cash flow survey data were available to us for 1957 to June 1960. This gave us 13 observations for each comparison, given the manner in which available funds are computed. The six-month period for estimates of net funds available is dictated by the survey forecasts of expected takedowns from outstanding commitments. These forecasts are made for two-month and six-month periods.

tively associated with the past funds position as predicted, but the fit is unimpressive.

Actually the test of the relation between liquid assets and future cash flow should be based on forecasted cash flow, not ex post flows. For the 1957–1960 period we did obtain evidence on flow forecasts for those companies reporting to the LIAA cash flow survey. In Chart V-9, liquid earning assets are plotted in a scatter diagram against the difference between the forecasted inflow of investible funds for the upcoming six months less expected

CHART V-9. *Liquid Earning Assets of Life Insurance Companies Compared with Their Net Expected Available Funds Flow over the Succeeding Six Months: Quarterly, 1957/I–1960/II*

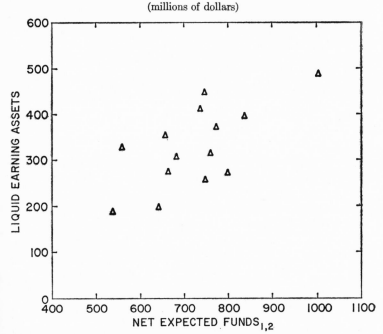

(millions of dollars)

NOTES: Liquid earning assets include short-term Treasury obligations and commercial paper. Available funds are computed on the same basis as the series shown in Chart V-8, except that the series used in Chart V-9 represents cash flow forecasts of the companies reporting to both the LIAA *Cash Flow* and *Forward Commitment Surveys*.

SOURCES: LIAA, *Cash Flow* and *Forward Commitment Surveys*.

takedown from outstanding commitments during the six months. These data are for the sample of companies reporting both cash flow and commitment information to the Life Insurance Association of America. Liquid earning assets include short-term Treasury obligations and commercial paper. The funds variable used in this chart includes anticipated funds to be obtained from security sales and from drawing down the cash position. Whereas the hypothesis being examined postulates a negative relationship between these series, the scatter shown in Chart V-9 is clearly positive.

Several other variants of the liquid asset and available funds variables were compared. Security sales as a source of funds were added to the funds flow series employed in Charts V-7 and V-8. Cash balances were added to the earning liquid assets variable used in Chart V-9. Funds flows were employed without deduction of anticipated takedown of commitments. None of these variations produced results qualitatively different from those we have discussed.[44]

---

[44] It should be noted that there is a curious seasonal aberration in the relation between liquid asset holdings and fund flows. This peculiarity shows up most clearly when the liquid position at the end of the quarter is related to the gross flow of funds in the quarter just completed. When a linear regression is fitted to these observations, it is found that end-year liquidity is consistently quite low relative to the normal funds inflow in the fourth quarter, and the liquid position at the end of the first quarter tends to be consistently high relative to the first quarter's flow of normal funds. Deviations from the regression line are much smaller for second and third quarter observations. This pattern may, in part, reflect a desire on the part of investment officers to clean up outstanding commitments late in the year and produce the smallest feasible liquidity position for year-end statement purposes. Comparable motivations may influence loan originators and some borrowers to complete pending transactions before the year-end, and the seasonal pattern in construction may reinforce these tendencies. However, we have some reason to suspect that the observed phenomenon has part of its explanation in data reporting conventions. It appears that some companies conventionally close their books monthly for reporting purposes several days prior to the end of the calendar month. December is an exception to this convention since a year-end closing is necessitated for annual report and statement purposes. We have no direct evidence on whether this pattern applies to data submitted to the cash flow survey. If it does, however, the result is a reporting fourth quarter substantially longer than the first quarter, perhaps by ten or twelve days. In addition, of course, the calendar fourth quarter is usually two days longer than the first quarter. The consequence of this would be an exaggeration of funds inflow during the fourth quarter at the expense of the first quarter. The liquid stock observations are not similarly affected. The impact of this sort of reporting habit, is dampened somewhat in Charts V-8

In sum, thus far the evidence seems to refute the cyclical form of the commitment hypothesis, *viz.* that the level of liquid assets is negatively related to the volume of funds, net of committed funds, expected to be available in future months. On the other hand, the evidence is roughly consistent with the alternative proposition that the liquid position is positively related to the net inflow of available funds in the recent past. Before proceeding with this investigation, it should be observed that rejection of the cyclical version of the "commitment" hypothesis need not necessarily imply rejection of the shorter-run version of the same hypothesis. That is, within a cyclical pattern determined elsewhere, short-run variation in liquidity holdings may occur to finance temporary bunching of commitment takedowns relative to funds inflow. As we have seen, however, the cyclical element in the liquid asset position is quite strong, leaving little room for significant and systematic short-run swings.

SOURCES OF LIQUIDITY ACCUMULATION

Our next task is to distinguish the sources of liquidity accumulation. There are four broad categories of analytical interest which together make up the available funds measure we have been using. It will be recalled that available funds over any period is defined as the gross inflow of investible funds during the period, less the volume of funds committed for investment prior to the beginning of the period. Thus variation in available funds may reflect variance in the gross inflow of investible funds or variance in the stock of outstanding loan commitments due for takedown within the period, or both. The gross flow itself is composed of three distinct elements, policyholder savings, involuntary portfolio rollover, and outright sales of assets.[45] Policyholder savings through life insurance can be defined approximately as net gain

---

and V-9 above, because funds flows are observed in six-month chunks. The result is still visible, however, and if observations containing fourth quarter and first quarter funds flows were adjusted in the compensating direction, the fit of liquidity on past funds would be better than it appears in these charts. This sort of adjustment does not seem to improve the called-for negative relation between liquid assets and future funds, however.

[45] In some of the available funds measures used above, we treated sales of some or all types of assets as an extraordinary source of funds and excluded such amounts from the estimate of available funds.

CHART V-10. *Estimates of the Normal Flow of Investible Funds Through Life Insurance Companies and the Stock of Outstanding Commitments Expected to Be Closed within Six Months: Quarterly, 1952/IV–1960/I*

(millions of dollars)

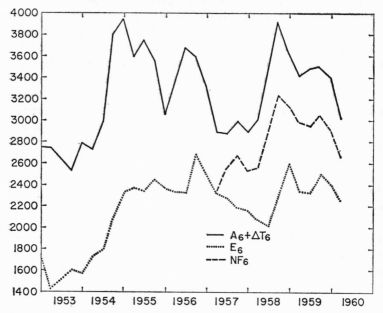

NOTES: A_6 = actual portfolio acquisitions of life insurance companies over a six-month period including the quarter for which the observation is reported and the succeeding quarter. These data cover acquisitions of life insurance companies reporting to the LIAA *Forward Commitment Survey*.

ΔT_6 = an estimate of net Treasury obligations liquidated by surveyed life companies in the same six-month period.

NF_6 = an estimate of gross cash inflow less security sales during the six-month period. This estimate covers life insurance companies reporting to the LIAA *Cash Flow Survey*.

E_6 = outstanding loan and security commitments due to be delivered within six months from the beginning of the quarter for which the observation is reported. These data are for companies reporting to the *Forward Commitment Survey*.

SOURCES: Life Insurance Association of America; *Treasury Bulletin*.

n admitted assets less capital gains less the net increase in policy loans.[46]   Portfolio rollover includes all types of principal repayment on loans and investments.   Sales of assets, of course, reflect conscious voluntary decisions on the part of the portfolio managers.

Chart V-10 is designed to focus on the relative contribution of the gross flow of investible funds and the stock of outstanding loan commitments to the variation over time in available funds. The upper curve on this graph depicts gross acquisitions of portfolio assets during six-month periods less an estimate of the net liquidation of Treasury obligations.   A second estimate of investible funds is available beginning in 1957 from the LIAA cash flow survey.   We have plotted (Chart V-10) the normal funds data utilized in Chart V-8.   It will be recalled that this estimate of investible funds excludes all sales of securities and real estate as well as funds obtained from liquidation of the cash position.[47]   Finally, the stock of outstanding loan commitments expected to be closed within six months is also pictured in Chart V-10.   The difference between the first investible funds measure $(A_6 + T_6)$ and the commitment stock (E_6) represents the available funds measure used in the scatter diagram, Chart V-7.   The available funds estimate utilized in Chart V-8 is simply the difference between the normal cash flow (NF_6) and the commitment stock (E_6).

As we suspected from the examination of the liquid asset — funds

---

[46] This definition is sufficient for our purposes.   Finer conceptual definitions and computations can be made.   See, for example, Goldsmith, *A Study of Savings in the United States*, Volume II, pp. 268–279, and Friend and Natrella, *Individual Savings: Volume and Composition*, pp. 190–196.   Also Loewy, "Net Cash Money Flows Through Life Insurance Companies," and Wright, "Gross Flow of Savings and Investment Funds Through Life Insurance Companies." Asset figures appearing in the annual statements of life companies are reported on an accrual basis.   Therefore further adjustments have to be made to translate these data to a cash basis.

[47] As can be seen, the two investible funds series move in approximately parallel paths.   The difference in level reflects in part a difference in survey coverage; the "acquisitions" series is derived from the LIAA *Forward Commitment Survey* which includes companies accounting for about two-thirds of industry assets, whereas data for the "cash flow" series is collected in the LIAA *Cash Flow Survey* which covers companies accounting for about three-fifths of industry assets.   In addition, the difference in level between the two series reflects differences in computational procedures.   In particular, sales of corporate securities and other non-Treasury obligations are not deducted from gross acquisitions.   Neither are funds obtained from running down the cash position deducted from acquisitions.

flow relationship, there is a clear and rather strong cyclical element in the gross funds flow series. From inspection of Chart V-10 there appears to be a cyclical influence in the time shape of the commitment stock as well. For the most part, cyclical movements in the level of the commitment stock and in the investible funds inflow are in the same direction. However, the absolute dollar variation in funds flow has exceeded changes in the level of outstanding commitments. Therefore, in general, available funds series have tended to have the same cyclical pattern as the gross inflow of investible funds, but the amplitude of available funds fluctuations is dampened by partially offsetting changes in the commitment stock. This pattern provides additional corroboration of the plausibility of the hypothesis that the cyclical pattern in liquidity position is caused by the time sequence of changes in cash flow rather than changes in the rate of commitment authorization.

The composition of the gross inflow of investible funds is displayed in Table V-8 for the period covered by the LIAA *Cash Flow Survey*, 1957–1960. The categories represented correspond approximately to the distinction made above among net policyholder savings, involuntary portfolio turnover, and deliberate sales of portfolio assets. Policyholder savings can be approximately identified as the (algebraic) sum of the net change in ledger assets and the miscellaneous source (Column 4), the latter item representing primarily the net increase in policy loans. Rollover of the mortgage and securities portfolios is recorded in Columns 2 and 3, and security sales in Column 6.

There is a rather strong seasonal element in the flow of investible funds. Nevertheless a significant cyclical influence is also observable. The rate of cash inflow increases substantially during the one cyclical recovery phase included in the 1957–1960 period. During the year beginning July 1, 1958, the normal inflow of investible funds (Column 5 in Table V-8) exceeds the comparable flow for the preceding twelve months by $818 million and the succeeding year's inflow by $555 million.[48] The 1958–1959 inflow

---

[48] As a rough and ready means of eliminating the seasonal effect, one can isolate the highest of the four first-quarter figures, highest of the four second-quarter observations, etc., for each of the four quarters. The four quarters selected in this way occur in a row, 1958/III–1959/II.

TABLE V-8. *Composition of the Inflow of Investible Funds:*
Quarterly, 1957/I–1960/II

(millions of dollars)

	(1) Change in Ledger Assets	(2) Mort-gage Roll-over	(3) Securities Roll-over	(4) Misc. Items	(5) Total Normal Inflow	(6) Sales of Secur-ities	(7) Total Funds
1957/I	$631	$402	$145	$ −38	$1,140	$201	$1,342
II	657	415	150	−34	1,188	162	1,351
III	794	460	159	−48	1,365	181	1,546
IV	784	432	180	−60	1,336	130	1,465
1958/I	723	458	159	−52	1,288	142	1,430
II	757	463	199	−35	1,384	261	1,645
III	819	566	204	−42	1,547	273	1,820
IV	924	556	230	−24	1,686	202	1,888
1959/I	749	564	173	−38	1,450	195	1,646
II	822	552	201	−53	1,522	138	1,660
III	723	553	202	−60	1,418	136	1,554
IV	941	518	230	−70	1,619	184	1,804
1960/I	710	500	169	−105	1,274	138	1,413
II	766	488	198	−106	1,346	176	1,521

NOTES: (Based on instructions given to the surveyed companies.)

Col. (1): Ledger assets are adjusted to eliminate all noncash factors affecting the change in ledger assets.

Col. (2): Consists of all cash repayments of principal and small amounts of sales of mortgages in the secondary market, cash received from foreclosures, liquidation of FHA debentures, and any Farmers Home Administration insured loans assigned to the Government.

Col. (3): Includes all bond maturities (except maturing issues of Treasury bills and short-term commercial paper), contingency sinking funds, and other cash redemptions of securities.

Col. (4): Miscellaneous sources include temporary bank borrowing (net of repayments), and sales of, and repayments from, assets other than mortgages and securities. In addition, the net gain in policy loans is entered with a negative sign. The latter item dominates this series.

Col. (5): Col. (1) + Col. (2) + Col. (3) + Col. (4).

Col. (6): Includes sales of all securities except Treasury bills, commercial paper, and any other temporary investments.

Col. (7): Col. (5) + Col. (6).

SOURCE: LIAA, *Cash Flow Survey*, quarterly. Companies reporting account for 58% to 62% of all life insurance company assets.

exceeds the average of the other two years by about 12%. Examination of Table V-8 shows that all three major components of normal inflow, change in ledger assets, portfolio rollover, and change in policy loans outstanding contribute to this pattern. We can summarize this experience as follows:

Year	Change in Ledger Assets	Portfolio Rollover	Misc.	Total Normal Inflow
1957/III–1958/II	$3,058	$2,510	$−195	$5,373
1958/III–1959/II	3,314	3,048	−157	6,205
1959/III–1960/II	3,140	2,858	−341	5,657

This pattern parallels the build-up in the cash position, which as we have seen was concentrated in the year beginning at mid-1958. Security sales have a very similar pattern except that the period of heaviest sales leads the cash flow increase slightly. Security sales are relatively concentrated in the four quarters beginning with 1958/II.

In Chart V-11 we have plotted both the total normal funds flow and the security sales series from Table V-8 as deviations from their respective arithmetic means for the 14 quarters for which we have ex post observations. Also plotted is the deviation of life companies' cash position[49] from its mean. In general, the cash position is somewhat more closely and positively associated with the normal funds inflow than with security sales.[50] In 12 of the 14 cases a plus (minus) deviation in cash position is associated with a plus (minus) deviation in normal inflow. This coincidence of signs is found in 9 cases when cash position is compared with security sales.

In this period at least, the heaviest security sales appear to have been induced by relatively high security prices rather than borrower demand or high interest rates. This is consistent with the observation others have made[51] to the effect that sales are not planned far in advance but reflect current market opportunities, as well as with our finding in Chapter III that sales are somewhat constrained by capital losses. It is also consistent with the find-

---

[49] This term includes short-term Treasury and commercial obligations as well as currency and bank deposits.

[50] Cash position at the end of the quarter is being compared to cash flow and sales during the same quarter.

[51] See Wright, "Gross Flow of Savings and Investment Funds," p. 155, and Brimmer, *Life Insurance Companies in the Capital Market*, p. 92.

ing below that life company forecasts of security sales have been subject to greater error than forecasts of other major sources of funds. Thus the pattern of security sales does appear to make some contribution to the liquid asset cycle, but a lesser contribution than does the pattern of normal funds flow.

CHART V-11. *The Normal Flow of Investible Funds, Sales of Securities, and Cash Position Plotted as Deviations from Their Respective Means: Quarterly, 1957/I–1960/II*

(millions of dollars)

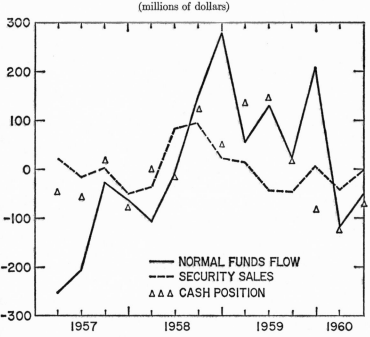

NOTES AND SOURCES: Normal funds flow and security sales are from Table V-8. Cash position includes cash balances, short-term Government securities, and commercial paper. All the raw series are from LIAA, *Cash Flow Survey*.

Explanation of the time rate of the normal flow of investible funds into life companies is beyond the scope of the current study. The life insurance service takes many forms and has numerous attributes and dimensions. Consequently, explaining choices to save through investment in life insurance is a considerably more complicated matter than analysis of choices to invest in savings deposits or securities. The savings flow through life insurance does seem to have a cyclical pattern similar to that experienced by the savings depositories, the highest rate of inflow being concentrated in the recession-early recovery phase. However, the magnitude of this cyclical swing in the savings flow through life companies is very much dampened relative to the cyclical variations in the various forms of savings deposits.

We know very little about the relationship of life insurance sales to cyclical variation in disposable income, interest rates, general price indices, etc. Undoubtedly the most important development in insurance selling in recent years has been the trend toward policies with relatively small savings elements.[52] Thus, a dollar of insurance sales today contributes substantially less to the savings flow and growth of life company assets than it did a decade ago. It is probable that this change in product mix has been accelerated by secularly rising prices and higher interest rates. However, it is not clear whether cyclical variation in prices and interest rates have influenced the composition of policy sales.[53] It is probable, but not proved, that the level of disposable income has some positive effect on insurance sales.[54] However, the response of ledger asset gain to cyclical recovery has appeared too quickly to be a reflection of cyclically induced changes in insurance sales.

Wright has concluded that a business cycle recession has an adverse effect on the savings flow through life companies, through income effects which induce:

(1) increased policy loans, and
(2) increased surrenders of outstanding policies for cash.[55]

---

[52] See ILI, *Life Insurance Fact Book*, 1966, pp. 23–36.

[53] For an analysis of the gross flow of funds into life companies, annually, 1952–1958, see Wright, *op. cit.*

[54] Loewy, "Net Cash Money Flows through Life Insurance Companies," investigated the relation between insurance income flows and disposable personal income for annual data, 1929–1950. Disposable income does not contribute to an explanation of the variation in first-year premiums during this period. This conclusion is not safely transferable to the post-1950 experience, however.

[55] Wright, *op. cit.*, pp. 141, 147–148, 151. Wright found this to be true for both the 1953–1954 and 1957–1958 recessions. Some of the policy surrenders in 1957–1958 may have accompanied the introduction of "family plan"

High interest rates and rising prices, generally characteristic of cyclical boom conditions, seem to have an adverse effect on the savings flow through stimulating:

(1) increased policy loans,
(2) reduced inflow for supplementary contracts, and
(3) increases in the costs of conducting the insurance business.[56]

Table V-8 shows a very substantial percentage increase in policy loans[57] during the 1959–1960 cyclical expansion, presumably a reflection of tighter bank credit. Supplementary contracts originate from settlement options. Reduction of policyholder saving in this form has occurred in supplementary contracts that do not have life contingencies. Wright's data show the net of considerations received over payments made on these policies declining from a plus $37 million in the recession year 1954 to a negative $161 million in 1957.[58]

On the other hand, the net inflow from contracts with life contingency fell much less over the same period, from +$47 million to +$33 million. In the latter contracts the size of periodic policy benefits are related to mortality expectations, whereas in the former contracts the size of payments depend largely on the interest rate assumption. This is Wright's reason for believing that higher market yields were responsible for the decline in policyholder saving through these contracts. Dividends left on deposit net of dividends and interest disbursed were not similarly affected by rising interest rates in the 1952–1958 period, however.[59] Rising interest rates, of course, have a positive effect on the savings flow by increasing investment income but this effect is stretched out over a period of years. There is a fairly marked rise in the rate of increase of general insurance expenses in 1956–1957. Increases in commissions paid, however, also rose by relatively large

---

policies, however (Wright, p. 149). The evidence on policy loans is not very strong. High interest rates seem to induce more policy loans than recession reductions in income.

[56] *Ibid.*, pp. 141, 149–150, 152.

[57] The net change in policy loans dominates the miscellaneous item (Col. 4). The actual reported increase was from a net gain of $49.2 million in 1958/III to $132.9 million in 1960/II, the last quarter for which ex post figures were available.

[58] *Ibid.*, p. 150.

[59] *Ibid.*

amounts in these years so that increased sales may have placed some upward pressure on costs as well as general price inflation.[60] In sum, then, both recession and boom periods have associated with them some economic characteristics which tend to dampen the inflow of policyholder saving. This leaves the early recovery phase characterized by rising incomes and employment but not yet by high interest rates and inflationary pressure as the period of relatively large increases in saving through life insurance companies.

As we have seen, the rate of portfolio rollover has a similar cycle. Inspection of Table V-8 reveals that this cyclical element is strongest in the mortgage loan turnover. There are two types of mortgage principal repayment which are worth distinguishing, amortization payments and cash repayments in full. Amortization payments are contractual. Repayments in full are normally voluntary and made in advance of the contractual schedule usually because of the sale of the mortgaged property by the owner or refinancing of the mortgage with another lender.[61] Segregation of these two items is possible and is presented for 1957–1960 in Table V-9, along with outright sales of mortgage loans, which have not been a significant source of funds. Both forms of repayment have the cyclical pattern we observed in their sum. In particular, the dollar volume of both items is greater in the year July 1958–June 1959 than in the preceding years. The cyclical variance in repayments in full, however, is clearly greater than the variation in the contractual payments. Mortgage repayment is therefore presumably stimulated by increased activity in the real estate market and reductions in interest rates. Most observers think the former to be the stronger influence.[62] Therefore this portion of the gross funds inflow is not completely independent of the use made of investible funds. Increased willingness on the part of life companies to supply mortgage funds may lead to an increased rate of turnover of real estate and consequently a rise in the mortgage repayment flow to life companies. Life companies, however, in no sense dominate the determination of

---

[60] *Ibid.*, p. 152.

[61] *Ibid.*, p. 154.

[62] See *ibid*, p. 154. This conclusion is consistent with the timing of increased repayments recorded in Table V-9.

TABLE V-9. Gross Inflow of Funds from Life Company Mortgage Portfolios: Quarterly, 1957/I–1960/II

(millions of dollars)

Quarter	(1) Amortization Payments	(2) Other Cash Repayments	(3) Outright Sales	(4) Total
1957/I	$285	$115	$1	$402
II	290	120	5	415
III	307	147	6	460
IV	310	117	6	432
1958/I	332	123	3	458
II	309	151	3	463
III	357	206	4	566
IV	342	212	2	556
1959/I	360	201	3	564
II	339	205	8	552
III	337	215	1	553
IV	361	157	1	518
1960/I	331	168	1	500
II	307	177	4	488

NOTES:

Col. (1): Includes all principal repayments of mortgage loans which remain on the company's books. "Privilege" prepayments on account are included as well as scheduled amortization payments.

Col. (2): Cash payments which represent payment in full and result in the removal of the loan from the books.

Col. (3): Sales of loans in the secondary market, sales of FHA debentures, and amounts of Farmers Home Administration Loans assigned to the Government.

Col. (4): Col. (1) + Col. (2) + Col. (3).

SOURCE: LIAA, Cash Flow Survey.

the mortgage lending cycle so that no great violence to the facts is done if the gross inflow of investible funds to life companies is assumed to be determined independently of their current portfolio decisions.

Rollover of the securities portfolio also exhibits a cyclical pattern similar to the other cash flow items we have investigated (Table V-8). The significant distinctions in the turnover of the securities portfolio are among scheduled maturity contingency sinking fund payments and security calls. The breakdown of the securities rollover for 1957–1960 by these categories is presented in Table V-10. Maturity payments (including scheduled cash sinking funds) are largely a function of the size of the securities portfolio and thereby essentially a rise along a trend. Contingency sinking funds are usually based on earnings criteria and consequently produce somewhat larger inflows to life companies in the cyclical boom phase. The greatest cyclical influence is found in security calls, however, which are strongly influenced by the level of interest rates. Calls are responsible for the modest cycle that is observed in the gross inflow of funds from securities rollover during 1957–1960. The short duration of the 1957–1958 recession and the sharp recovery of interest rates from their recession low is undoubtedly primarily responsible for the relatively modest expansion of security redemptions.

If this brief sketch of the pattern of the normal inflow of investible funds into life insurance companies is essentially correct, then we can conclude that this part of cash flow is affected by variables associated with the business cycle. These factors produce a pattern of funds flow in which the greatest rate of inflow occurs during the early recovery phase of the cycle. Overlapping this flow are proceeds from sales of securities which seem to be responsive to the level of bond prices and thereby heaviest in the recession-early recovery phase. Together, these two forms of cash inflow typically produce modest accumulation of liquid assets during the late recession–early recovery period. This liquidity accumulation is run off as the cyclical expansion progresses either because of an increase in the demand for funds or because of a conscious life company objective of adjusting the liquid stock to the minimum desired level. The final strand in this story is the distinction between a deliberate willingness of life companies to divert increased normal flow and proceeds of liquidated assets into larger holdings of temporary investments and the extent to which the liquid asset build-up is an unplanned consequence of errors in forecasting cash flow. To the extent that forecasting errors bear some responsibility, a further distinction should be made between the occurrence of a series of forecasting errors in the same direction and continuous in time, and sluggish response in correcting the liquidity position following a "one-shot" forecasting error. We turn now to consideration of the evidence bearing on this question.

TABLE V-10.   *Gross Inflow of Funds from Life Company Securities Portfolios:*
Quarterly, 1957/I–1960/II
(millions of dollars)

	(1)	(2)	(3)	(4)
		Contingency	*Other*	
	Bond	*Sinking*	*Security*	
Quarter	*Maturities*	*Funds*	*Calls*	*Total*
1957/I	$ 86	$15	$43	$145
II	102	18	31	150
III	116	17	26	159
IV	119	18	44	180
1958/I	122	11	26	159
II	134	16	49	199
III	125	16	63	204
IV	159	16	54	230
1959/I	130	11	34	175
II	143	13	45	201
III	154	16	32	202
IV	172	13	46	230
1960/I	130	11	28	169
II	140	24	34	198

NOTES:
Col. (1): Includes payments from serial maturities, scheduled cash sinking funds and sinking fund redemption of preferred stocks.
Maturing issues of temporary investments are excluded.
Col. (2): All inflow from contingency, as distinguished from scheduled,
sinking funds based on earnings or other criteria.
Col. (3): All security redemption in advance of maturity not coming
under definitions covered in columns (1) and (2). Redemp-
tions associated with new investments involving the same
borrower are not supposed to be included.
Col. (4): Col. (1) + Col. (2) + Col. (3).
SOURCE: LIAA, *Cash Flow Survey.*

Forecasting Errors

We have evidence on cash flow forecasting errors for only a very
limited period covering the 1958–1960 cyclical expansion. Aggregate data pictured in Chart V-12 suggest that life companies generally underestimated their holdings of liquid assets.[63] Forecasts

---

[63] Some observers believe that life companies typically underestimate the
time lag between forward commitment authorization and takedown of the

of cash position (cash, short-term Treasury obligations, and commercial paper) made three months and six months in advance are compared with the level of cash position that in fact resulted. Curiously, three-month forecasts seem to be no more accurate than six-month forecasts for the limited number of observations included. We are interested in whether life companies particularly underestimated their cash position during the recession-early recovery phase of the business cycle. There is some indication in Chart V-12 that this was the case in this particular instance.

**CHART V-12   Life Insurance Companies' Cash Position, Forecast and Actual:
Quarterly, 1958/II–1960/II**

(millions of dollars)

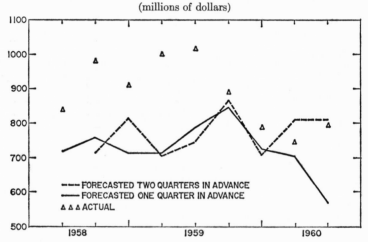

NOTE AND SOURCE: Data for companies reporting to LIAA, *Cash Flow Survey.*

The liquid asset increase in late 1958-early 1959 does not appear to have been planned. For four large life companies, we collected similar data covering 1957 to mid-1960. The magnitude and pattern of errors in cash position forecasts varied considerably among the four companies, but nearly all errors were in the direction of underestimating the level of cash position, and the largest errors

---

loan.   Walter has suggested that this is the case with mortgage commitments; see *The Investment Process*, p. 242. We have no direct evidence on this, but if correct, it may account for the tendency for cash position to exceed expectations.

were concentrated in the sub-period, 1958/II to 1959/II. Again, it appeared in each case that the cyclical accumulation of liquid assets was largely unanticipated.

Errors in forecasting cash position could arise from errors in forecasting any or all components of cash flow, or errors in estimating the time sequence of loan and investment acquisitions from outstanding forward commitments. We have no direct information on the accuracy of loan takedown forecasts. Data on borrower cancellation of commitment agreements show some tendency for this sort of attrition to increase in recessions.[64] This might contribute something to larger errors of underestimation in cash position forecasts during recessions.

TABLE V-11. Errors in Forecasts of Gross Investible Funds and Cash Position Made by Life Insurance Companies Reporting in the LIAA Cash Flow Survey: Quarterly, 1958/II–1960/II

(millions of dollars)

	Error in Two-Quarter Estimates		Error in One-Quarter Estimates	
	Gross Funds Flow	Cash Position	Gross Funds Flow	Cash Position
1958/II	n.a.	n.a.	$-207	$-222
III	$-420	$-269	-198	-223
IV	-370	-95	-15	-197
1959/I	-166	-296	58	-288
II	-309	-268	-6	-227
III	-259	-22	13	-41
IV	-109	-78	-46	-61
1960/I	-75	67	55	-32
II	-132	15	174	-225

NOTE: Cash position consists of the stock of cash, short-term Treasury obligations, and commercial paper. Errors are calculated as the forecast figure *less* the actual figure.

SOURCE: LIAA, *Cash Flow Survey.*

We do have some evidence on forecasts of the gross inflow of investible funds through life companies. Errors in funds forecasts are reported in Table V-11. For comparison, errors in cash posi-

---

[64] These data are summarized in the Appendix to Chapter VI.

tion forecasts are also reported. It appears that life companies had a persistent tendency to underestimate gross funds inflow during the period covered. The errors are somewhat larger during the 1958–1959 recession-early recovery period than subsequently. We are interested in the composition of errors by sources of funds inflow. In particular, we wish to know whether the errors occur in estimating "normal" inflow or in funds obtained from extraordinary sources (security sales). The desired breakdown of the gross funds inflow is provided in Table V-12. It appears from this evidence that unanticipated security sales account for the greatest part of the underestimation of the gross investible funds flow.

TABLE V-12. *Errors in Forecasts of Gross Investible Funds by Life Insurance Companies Reporting to the LIAA Cash Flow Survey: Quarterly, 1958/II–1960/II* (millions of dollars)

I Errors in Two-Quarter Forecasts

Year and Quarter	Net Change in Ledger Assets	Mortgage Portfolio Rollover	Securities Portfolio Rollover	Security Sales	Other
1958/III	$−128	$−112	$−49	$−242	$ 111
IV	−65	−77	−62	8	−172
1959/I	−9	−57	−26	−150	76
II	−107	−46	−27	−107	−22
III	90	−18	−22	−106	−203
IV	−2	32	−35	−155	49
1960/I	65	62	−17	−106	−79
II	−8	46	−15	−133	−22

II Errors in One-Quarter Forecasts

Year and Quarter	Net Change in Ledger Assets	Mortgage Portfolio Rollover	Securities Portfolio Rollover	Security Sales	Other
1958/II	$ −76	$ −4	$−17	$−213	$ 103
III	−124	−100	−30	−141	97
IV	−26	−29	−40	−92	172
1959/I	−9	−35	−33	−119	254
II	−110	−31	−47	−48	230
III	10	+1	−28	−29	61
IV	−18	42	−40	−105	75
1960/I	28	37	−15	−67	72
II	−23	18	−19	−45	243

NOTE: A minus sign means the forecast figure underestimated the actual figure. The "Other" column consists primarily of errors in forecasting the net change in cash position and policy loans.

SOURCE: LIAA, *Cash Flow Survey.*

The extent to which sales seem to be unplanned is suggested by the fact that one-quarter forecasts of sales are little more accurate, if at all, than two-quarter estimates.

Underestimation of funds sources is not limited to security sales, however. Life companies reporting in the survey also apparently underestimated the cash flow from asset growth and portfolio turnover, particularly during the period of recovery from the 1958 recession. Thus, from the very limited data available, it would appear that life companies underestimate the cyclical variance in both normal and extraordinary elements of cash flow, and this contributes to an at least partially unplanned cycle in liquid asset holdings. On the basis of some soft qualitative evidence, there is reason to believe that forecasting errors played a role in the liquidity cycle and the use of extraordinary funds during the 1954–1957 expansion. We will have more to say on this point, however, at the end of Chapter VI.

Summary

In this chapter we have focused on a part of the question of investment timing. We have been concerned with establishing the extent to which life companies have deviated from the principle of investing each dollar of cash flow as it becomes available. In particular, the analysis in this chapter has been directed toward life companies' use of bank credit and their liquidity position as means of altering the time sequence of investment. Emphasis has been placed on timing shifts occurring within a business cycle context. We have found that although life companies seem to adhere to a "loaned-up" investment policy in principle, some modest departures from this rule have systematically occurred. Shifting of investible funds over time has been accomplished through both borrowing and variation in liquid asset holdings.

During the 1950s, life insurance company use of bank credit for this purpose seems to have most often taken the form of mortgage warehousing. Life companies have entered directly into warehousing agreements and made use of this device indirectly by postponing delivery of completed loans from correspondents' inventories. In the latter case, the correspondent (usually a mortgage company) enters into a warehousing arrangement. We estimated that life companies may have used the warehousing device, directly and indirectly, to add something like $450 to $500 million to their mortgage loan activity during a 12- to 16-month period commencing about August 1954. Warehousing was apparently a much less significant source of funds to life companies in the following cyclical expansion, 1958–1960.

There is evidence of a clearly defined cycle in life company liquid asset holdings (cash and short-term obligations) during the period 1952–1962. The amplitude of these cyclical swings was of the order of $400 to $500 million, with liquid asset accumulation tending to be concentrated in the recession-early recovery phase of the business cycle and decumulation occurring during part or all of the remaining portion of the cyclical upswing.

We investigated several alternative hypotheses in seeking an explanation of the liquidity cycle. The evidence failed to confirm the thesis that the liquidity cycle was induced by cyclical variation in interest rates. Also rejected as an explanation of the liquidity cycle was the notion that liquid assets are accumulated in anticipation of heavy takedowns from forward commitments relative to cash inflow. The most plausible explanation considered was that which related the liquidity cycle to a cyclical movement in the gross flow of investible funds. It appeared that liquid asset expansion may reflect, more or less passively, cyclical expansion in the gross inflow of investible funds. All major components of gross inflow, the policyholder savings flow, portfolio rollover, and security sales seemed to contribute to this phenomenon. Evidence covering a limited period, 1958–1960, indicated that the apparent passivity in life company response to changes in the rate of cash flow actually reflected imperfect forecasting of the cyclical element in gross funds inflow. Companies apparently failed to predict the increased cash flow which occurred in 1958–1959, and consequently maintained a larger than planned cash position during this period. It is also possible that variation from the anticipated time lag between forward commitment authorization and loan takedown, and, in particular, the impact of the business cycle on commitment cancellations, also contributed to unplanned liquidity accumulation. Little hard evidence was available to test this proposition, however.

With regard to the dollar magnitude of life insurance funds shifted among time periods during the 1954–1957 expansion, we concluded that life companies may have displaced over a billion dollars into investment during the year 1955–1956 at the expense of preceding and succeeding quarters. This was accomplished through mortgage warehousing, changes in liquidity holdings, and abnormally large sales of long-term Treasury obligations. This sort of shifting over subsequent business cycles appears to have been carried out in much more modest amounts. One possible explanation of this dampening is the relatively slack demand conditions under which the U. S. economy operated during 1958–1962. Apart from this difference, however, there are some reasons to regard the 1955–1957 experience as having some one-shot characteristics. These relate to the substantial, and apparently unpredicted, decline in the rate of cash flow through life insurance companies at this time, the apparent lack of internal control over issuance of new mortgage commitments during 1954–1955, and the relative abundance of secondary reserve holdings in the form of Government bonds which still existed at that time. As we have observed (Chapter IV), this period marks a transition from an open-to-buy environment to a more normal portfolio-choice world. The characteristics listed above are legacies of an open-to-buy situation. Subsequently, more conscious and sophisticated cash flow forecasting procedures have been adopted, mortgage loan commitment activity has been placed under tighter control, and the surplus holdings of Government bonds have been largely dissipated. Consequently we would no longer expect a repeat of 1955–1957 demand conditions to produce as quantitatively large a response by life companies in terms of borrowing, liquidity decumulation, and security sales. This dampened reaction is expected to apply especially to borrowing and bond and common stock sales.

Therefore we have concluded that life company use of bank credit and their liquidity holdings to effect shifts in investment timing over the business cycle exists to only a modest degree. The same portfolio objectives, however, might be attainable through use of the forward commitment device. We turn in Chapter VI to a consideration of the role of forward commitments in determining the timing of investment decisions.

DECISION: *The Role of Forward Commitments*

This chapter continues the examination of the timing element in life insurance company investment decisions. In Chapter V we investigated the extent to which life companies shift funds among periods of time. An alternative device for affecting investment timing is to separate the investment decision from the delivery of funds. This can be done by contracting with the borrower to supply x dollars some y months in the future. This sort of contract is known as a forward commitment. By committing funds today for delivery at various points of time in the future, the lender is able to make loan decisions at a rate which is to a substantial extent independent of both the current rate of inflow of investible funds and the current rate of portfolio acquisitions. Thus it may be possible to use forward commitments as a means of taking advantage of the interest rate cycle by concentrating investment decisions (commitments) in periods of "high" interest rates. In this chapter we examine the extent to which this motive, in fact, determines the timing of life insurance company commitment authorizations. We also examine some alternative explanations of the time sequence of commitment decisions.

The Forward Commitment Contract

Definition

A "commitment" refers to "any firm agreement by a life insurance company, regarded as morally or legally binding by such company whether written or unwritten to purchase or otherwise acquire securities, real estate, mortgages, and real property."[1] A forward commitment is any new commitment which is still outstanding at the end of the month in which the commitment agreement was made. The bulk of life company mortgage loan acquisitions in recent years has involved the use of a written forward commitment. Where new construction is involved, a loan commitment from a permanent lender is commonly a prerequisite for bank provision of construction financing. Most life insurance company corporate security investments are acquired via direct placement and involve a forward commitment of funds.[2] Forward commitments have also been used in acquisitions of real property, and in financing all levels of government.[3]

Function

The forward commitment device is not new or in any sense unique to life insurance companies. Some of the larger life companies have dramatized the commitment contract, however, by engaging in quite long-term commitments of funds — up to two or three years in some cases. As of the middle of 1960 (the last commitment figures we had available), life companies expected that about 40% of their *outstanding* commitments would not be taken down for more than six months. It is the practice of making a substantial volume of commitments involving long-delayed takedowns that makes the study of life company policies with respect to commitment agreements particularly interesting and relevant. In interviews with investment officers of 12 major life companies the writer attempted to determine the role played by forward commitments in fulfilling portfolio objectives. Their responses form the basis for much of the following discussion of commitment contracts.

From the lender's perspective, the rationale of making forward commitments is somewhat different for residential mortgage lending than for security acquisitions. Because of the lack of a well-

---

[1] This is the definition used by the Life Insurance Association of America in its instructions to companies preparing the commitment survey report.

[2] The LIAA commitment data apparently catch some public offerings as well. These presumably involve short-term commitments to underwriters.

[3] For brief discussions of forward commitments by LIAA spokesmen, see O'Leary, "Forward Investment Commitments of Life Insurance Companies," and LIAA-CMC Monograph, pp. 185–188.

developed resale market,[4] an active residential mortgage lender needs a field organization to generate loan opportunities. Mortgage companies which specialize in originating loans for "permanent" lenders do not ordinarily assume underwriting risks and therefore need the commitment of a permanent lender to proceed with the loan operation. For loans on existing structures the commitment will usually be short, rarely more than two or three months. For new construction the commitment may vary in length from four or five months on some single-family homes to a year or more on sizable apartment buildings. Since a commitment from a permanent lender is often required for a developer to obtain bank construction financing, forward commitment agreements are often an inevitable part of mortgage lending on new commercial properties as well. Even if permanent financing is not required for a promoter to obtain interim financing on large projects, the promoter may nevertheless wish to arrange the mortgage loan on the completed property in advance of construction. In this case the forward commitment can be regarded as a service life companies extend at the borrower's convenience.

It is this servicing function which seems to best characterize the use of forward commitments in the corporate debt market. Here the commitment device is more a convenience to borrowers than a part of the inescapable mechanics of the investment process. One of the attractive features to borrowers of placing notes and bonds privately is the opportunity to contract currently for delivery of funds at some point in the future. Life companies participate in issuing forward commitments because they are peculiarly able to do so, and it pays. Their ability stems from the contractual nature of their primary source of funds, and the resulting stability and predictability of this flow. It pays as a servicing advantage life companies offer in competing for corporate note and bond issues; one of the services which resulted in private placements coming to dominate this market. In addition, all life company officers interviewed were convinced that direct placement issues carry interest rates significantly in excesss of yields

---

[4] The reference here is to a true secondary market in which permanent mortgage lenders can trade freely, as distinguished from the transfer of loans from mortgage originators (e.g., mortgage companies) to permanent enders (e.g., life insurance companies).

on public offerings of comparable quality.[5] Estimates of the spread of direct placement over public issue yields in the quality range in which life companies concentrate (roughly A-Baa on Moody's scale) ranged from 25 to 75 basis points.[6]

We found some disagreement among life company investment officers as to whether additional benefits accrued from the forward commitment process. Some felt that forward commitments were a nuisance and made their investment task more difficult. The chief source of difficulty associated with commitments seemed to be the uncertainty attached to the delivery date of funds committed. Construction, legal and other delays, postponements, and changes of plan hinder accurate forecasting of takedowns for any period. Unanticipated bunching of takedowns can squeeze a company's liquidity position, and unanticipated postponements may force abnormal and undesired liquid asset accumulation or exert pressure to find investment outlets quickly. In the extreme case, uncertainty exists as to whether the commitment will be fulfilled at all, for although lenders regard a loan commitment as binding, some borrowers do not. It is a matter of record that borrowers do cancel commitment agreements. An officer of one life company specializing in commercial mortgage loans reported that he would shave 25 to 50 basis points in yield to obtain an immediate delivery loan as opposed to a delayed takedown commitment.

On the other hand, more investment officers felt that forward commitments made the investment task easier. As we have seen, maintenance of a "fully invested" position appears to be a primary goal of life companies. Forward commitment activity may facilitate achievement of this objective since, because of past

---

[5] Forward commitments may sometimes appear in life company agreements to purchase public offerings from underwriters. However, the interesting cases (i.e., involving some time lag between commitment and delivery of funds) occur normally as privately negotiated loans. This is the reason for connecting forward commitments and direct placements in this discussion.

[6] A 1955 SEC report estimated the yield spread on private placement over public issues at about 25 basis points. Securities and Exchange Commission, *Cost of Flotation of Directly Placed Corporate Securities*, 1955. However, a study that appeared while this volume was in galley proof concludes that rates on direct placements have been higher than publicly offered bonds only for issues of large, well-known companies. See Cohan, *Yields on Corporate Debt Directly Placed.*

commitments due for takedown, outlets need be found for only a fraction of the current inflow of available funds. Prospective commitments for future loans can be reviewed and accepted or rejected free from the pressure of investing the current flow of funds. For many officers, this advantage more than offset any increased cash flow forecasting and allocation problems which the commitment process may create.

Pricing

Investment officers commonly reported in the interviews that prospective loans were judged and priced independent of their anticipated delivery date. That is, forward commitment terms, including interest rates, are set on the same basis as loans contracted for current delivery. It is often asserted that life companies do not attempt to forecast the future market in pricing loans for future takedown. At the same time, however, investment officers did concede that they were more willing, or even desired, to make forward commitments when they felt market rates were "high," and were not eager to commit funds very far in advance when rates seemed "low." Some indicated that marginally acceptable loans might be rejected in low rate periods if they involved delayed takedowns. Some marginal concessions were reportedly made in order to swell the company's commitment position in periods of high interest rates. The commitment fee might be reduced or waived altogether to close a loan commitment at such a time. A few officers suggested they might "cheat" a few basis points (up to 25) on rate in some cases to build up their stock of attractively priced commitments. Most of the interviews were conducted during the first half of 1960, a period in which most officers interviewed felt rates were "attractive" and in some danger of softening. Many expressed the wish that they were more heavily stocked with forward commitments, perhaps an indication that concessions were limited.

A possible procedure for hedging the implicit interest rate forecasting problem involved in making forward commitment agreements could be to define the loan rate in terms of some agreed-upon index of market rates at the time of delivery. This kind of hedging operation does not seem to be practiced often, however. We found only two companies which had engaged in this sort of commitment, and these companies reported only three to four cases each. In these cases the loan rate was defined as an agreed-upon spread in basis points over the going rate of an agreed-upon interest rate series (Moody's new issue public utility bond series was mentioned) on the specified delivery date. In sum, then, the consensus of this testimony is that only marginal concessions are made to increase the stock of commitments when interest rates are high,[7] and premium rates and other concessions from borrowers are not generally demanded in forward commitment negotiations during low rate periods.

Terms of a Commitment Agreement

There is some question regarding the point in time at which companies report a new loan commitment as contracted. This is particularly a problem where authority is delegated to branch office personnel or independent correspondents to originate bond or mortgage loan commitments without the specific approval of the home office. The general rule seems to be, however, that commitments are official only when voted favorably by the finance committee, or a comparable body, and most new commitments are undoubtedly recorded as such at that time.

The commitment agreement will normally specify all details of the final loan contract: interest rate, maturity, amortization schedule, constraints on borrowers incurring additional indebtedness, etc. In addition the date of the loan closing and delivery of funds will usually be specified. Some range of time may be set as the delivery date, or simply a terminal date for the commitment may be established. The borrower will ordinarily be required to notify the insurance company some minimum period of time in advance of the desired closing date. If the borrower is not prepared to close the loan by the terminal date, the insurance company usually may choose among several options ranging from cancellation of the loan to a simple extension of the commitment. The lender may grant a commitment extension only under a rewritten loan contract, perhaps raising the price in some respect. The lender may collect any "good faith deposit" pledged by the borrower

---

[7] Indeed many officers reported insisting more strongly on call protection in bond commitments made in high rate periods, possibly discouraging some applicants in this way.

and request another such deposit in return for an extension. Or the lender may impose or increase a nonreturnable commitment fee. Apparently the decision is made on the basis of a judgment as to whether the causes of the delay could reasonably be considered within the control of the borrower. Cash flow considerations may also influence the lender's decision, of course, and lenders have been known to request delays in delivery or staggered takedowns when they have found their cash flow situation tight.

The Commitment Fee

Life companies often charge a commitment fee on forward commitments of more than three months in duration. There does not seem to be much standardization of practice in this regard, however. Reports of rates charged on specific commitments have varied from zero to 2% with rates of 0.5% to 1% reported most commonly. The precise rate seems to depend more on the bargaining power of the lender than any institutionalized rule of thumb. Investment officers typically responded that "we get a fee when we can" when asked how decisions on commitment fees were made.

It is difficult to find any systematic method used in determination of fees but some influences mentioned by officers are:

(1) the level of interest rates;
(2) expectation about changes in rates;
(3) the quality of the loan;
(4) the size of the loan;
(5) the length of the commitment.

Fees were reported to vary positively with interest rates. Officers responding in this fashion usually seemed to be thinking in terms of the secular drift in rates rather than sensitivity of fees to interest rate movements over the cycle. For example: "Five years ago we usually charged a one-half per cent commitment fee; today [1960] we often get one per cent."

Cyclically the pattern may be reversed. If lenders are bullish in their expectations about interest rates, they "will charge the full fee." Thus delayed takedown commitments made in a cyclical recession are very likely to carry a relatively large commitment fee. On the other hand, the fee may be reduced or waived entirely to complete commitment agreements when rates appear high.

A few officers mentioned the quality of the loan as having some effect on the fee charged. Apparently lower quality loans command a larger fee. This may simply reflect the bargaining position of the lender. In some responses there was a suggestion that the fee might bear a rough positive relation to the interest rate on the loan. There is no evidence that this is a common or systematic practice, however. Where the size of the loan is considered, it appears that smaller loans may carry a larger fee. This again may simply reflect bargaining position, or it may also have some rationale in the fact that costs associated with the commitment process may increase less than proportionally with loan size.

The length of the commitment was perhaps most commonly mentioned as an influence on the commitment fee. Size of fee is positively associated with length of commitment. Short commitments (three months or less) often carry no fee. Examples of relatively large fees were always associated with long commitments (twelve months or more).

No uniform or consistent rationale of the commitment fee suggests itself from this discussion. O'Leary suggests that the commitment fee is used to "provide some assurance that the borrower will abide by the agreement." [8] This may indeed be part of the reason, although returnable "good faith" or "stand-by" deposits might seem to serve this objective more directly. Both "commitment" and "good faith deposit" fees sometimes appear simultaneously.

The commitment fee sometimes seems to be thought of as partial remuneration to the lender for holding funds in relatively liquid form in anticipation of the commitment takedown. In its naive form, this notion, which has life companies earmarking liquid assets at the time of the commitment authorization and holding them for the loan closing, has no factual content. To the extent that the commitment process creates additional uncertainty about the available cash flow in future periods, however, the average liquidity holdings over time may be somewhat higher

---

[8] O'Leary, "Forward Investment Commitments of Life Insurance Companies," p. 325.

than would be the case if forward commitments were not made. Thus the commitment process may result in some additional lending costs to insurance companies for which a service fee could be considered a competitive pricing response.

In fact, however, variations in fees do not seem associated with changes in the real costs of commitment contracts. Indeed fees existed during the portion of the postwar period when life companies were endowed with an obvious overabundance of liquid assets and the marginal cost of forward commitments, *per se*, must have been essentially zero. It is likely, then, that commitment fees are best regarded as a noncompetitive return gained from a peculiar servicing and bargaining advantage which life companies possess.

Portfolio Objectives and Forward Commitment Votings

We have seen that the forward commitment contract is an advantageous and sometimes inevitable part of the mechanics of investing in the mortgage loan and corporate bond markets. Our task now is to investigate the timing of life insurance company commitment decisions. The above discussion has yielded three independent portfolio objectives that might influence the time rate of investment decisions. These three goals are:

(1) the "rate of return over time" objective;
(2) the "loaned up" or "fully invested" objective; and
(3) the "servicing" objective.

By the rate of return over time objective, we mean that life companies try to make commitment decisions so as to increase their investment return over time. This means concentrating new commitments in periods of high interest rates. Since most commitments are converted into loans within two years or so, this must be regarded as a cyclical objective. If the rate of return objective does have a significant influence on the timing of commitment authorizations, we should expect to observe a positive relation between commitment votings[9] and interest rate levels.

---

[9] We shall use the term "votings" as shorthand for new commitment authorizations. The term derives from our finding above that a loan commitment is registered officially at the time it is *voted* favorably by the finance committee.

As we have seen in Chapter V, life insurance companies in the aggregate do seem to pursue a loaned-up goal, permitting only relatively modest play in their liquid asset holdings. The question here is whether the forward commitment process is used to assist investment officers in achieving this objective. Forward commitments may ease the fulfillment of the loaned-up objective by requiring investment officers to find outlets for only a fraction of the current period's inflow of investible funds, the remainder being scheduled for takedown under previously issued commitments. In this context the loaned-up goal implies that the time rate of new commitments is tied to forecasts of cash flow in future periods, or, more precisely, that the volume of new commitment votings in any period is positively related to and determined by the size of the gap between the anticipated flow of investible funds in future periods and the volume of existing commitments scheduled for takedown during the same time span. Formally, the commitment decision could be considered as a stock adjustment process, the stock of outstanding commitment due for takedown being adjusted to the anticipated inflow of funds. The desired stock-flow ratio for any period would presumably be less than 100% permitting companies to meet demands for immediate delivery loans.

The final rationale we have found for forward commitments is that they are a service desired by borrowers or others which life companies provide in order to gain some competitive advantage in loan acquisition. In offering this service in mortgage lending, life companies may be catering to any or all of the following: the ultimate homeowner, the builder, the mortgage company, and/or the bank. Benefits, in terms of loan opportunities and insurance sales, may derive from serving these decision units. In corporate bond acquisitions the commitment service is most often utilized in loans made directly to borrowers without the use of intermediaries. For a borrower who has alternative sources of external financing, nonprice service advantages may be quite significant in influencing his choice among these sources. Willingness to make direct placement loans and, in addition, to make forward commitments can substantially increase the range of investment opportunities from which the life company's bond department can choose. Emphasis on using this servicing advantage to improve portfolio quality and return would mean that we ought to expect life companies' new commitments to be influenced by the demand for the forward commitment service. A change in the demand for commitments will not necessarily have an immediate or obvious effect on interest rate levels; therefore this hypothesis is conceptually distinguishable from the rate of return over time objective.

Having distinguished three alternative investment objectives, each of which might influence the time sequence of new commitment authorizations, we now turn to an examination of the time pattern of life insurance company forward commitment votings. Among the explanatory variables to be considered are:

(1) the level of interest rates;
(2) the volume of available funds in future periods;
(3) the demand for forward commitments; and from Chapter V's analysis,
(4) liquid asset holdings.

In the remainder of this chapter we assess the relevance of each of these variables to the explanation of total commitment votings by life companies during the 1950s. We proceed in the next section to a direct examination of the possibility that forward commitment votings have been used as a device to increase the portfolio return over time.

The Forward Commitment Process as a Means for Improving the Portfolio Rate of Return over Time

We know that the time pattern of aggregate life insurance company portfolio acquisitions suggests that they are strongly concerned with getting funds invested in "permanent" form as they become available. For the most part the magnitude of deliberate shifting of investible funds among periods seems to have been modest. As we have suggested, forward commitments could conceivably be a substitute device for the purpose of increasing the volume of high yield investments made over the business cycle. This could be done within a desired time pattern of loan acquisitions (desired liquid asset position), by a judicious selection of investment commitments according to their expected closing dates. Successful operation of this technique would require the same sort of accuracy in forecasting interest rate movements that is involved in altering liquid asset holdings to improve investment return over the business cycle. We ask whether life companies have in fact used the forward commitment process in this way. In this section we attack a piece of this question by examining the record for evidence that life companies have, in fact, improved their average investment return over time through varying the time rate of commitment votings.

Commitment Votings, Loan Acquisitions, and Interest Rates, 1952–1960

Monthly data on new commitments and acquisitions from commitments of life insurance companies were available to the writer for the period October 1952–June 1960. These data are compiled by the Life Insurance Association of America from a monthly survey of companies which account for about two-thirds of the total assets of all U.S. life insurance companies.[10] The ratio of total new commitments to total acquisitions is plotted in Chart VI-1, along with corporate bond yields. The interest rates plotted represent new issue rates on Grade 2 (approximately equivalent to Moody's Aa) public utility bonds. This series is prepared by the Economics Department of the Bankers Trust Company, New York. It is the basic corporate bond interest rate series that we will use in the analysis of life company portfolio policy.[11]

---

[10] The survey covers about 65 or 66 companies (the number has varied slightly over time). The survey was originated in 1951 in connection with the Voluntary Credit Restraint Program. Forty-five companies reported commitment data under this program, including all the largest companies. The monthly aggregates were reported in the *Federal Reserve Bulletin*. When the VCRP was suspended in 1952, the LIAA decided to continue the survey on its own. With the suspension of the VCRP, however, some companies were no longer willing to furnish commitment data. Collection of survey data on the LIAA's initiative began in October 1952. Because of the difference in coverage and some substantive changes in the survey forms, the data from October 1952 forward are not comparable with the previously reported figures. The large companies not reporting in the post-VCRP surveys include Metropolitan, Aetna, and Travelers.

[11] Choice of an interest rate series on which to base primary analytical reliance is always difficult. It seemed important to choose a new issue rate series to reflect terms on which bonds would be available to life companies, since life companies are not active buyers of seasoned bonds. This series had less erratic month-to-month fluctuation than the alternatives we considered. In its broad movements it coincided, especially in regard to timing, with evidence available on yields on bond commitments authorized by life companies.

It would have been preferable to use a direct placement bond yield series,

CHART VI-1. Ratio of New Commitment Votings to Total Acquisitions and Yields on Newly Issued Corporate Bonds: Quarterly, 1952/IV–1960/II

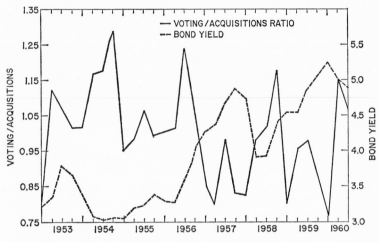

NOTES AND SOURCES: New commitment votings represent all life insurance company finance committee authorizations to make loans and investments during the quarter; data are for the companies reporting to the LIAA *Forward Commitment Survey*. Bond yields are from Bankers Trust Company and represent average yields on new issue Grade 2 public utility bonds.

It is clear from Chart VI-1 that the use of the forward commitment process did result in the dollar volume of loan decisions diverging from the volume of funds placed by as much as ±25%.

but none was available to us. Since 1959 the LIAA has been collecting, from a periodic survey of life companies, yields on new commitments for direct placement of corporate obligations classified by industry and quality categories. This information may become available for future research. Our evidence on life company new commitment yields was too spotty to create a consistent yield series from it.

The Bankers Trust series is also imperfect for our purposes because it includes only public utility bonds. This is particularly a problem because life companies over the period being studied have been moving away from public utility obligations and toward industrials. Examination of yield spreads over time across industry classifications and quality indices convinced us that it was more important to opt for a series that was reasonably consistent over time with respect to the quality grade of issues included. We did attempt to adjust the Bankers Trust series for changes in the public utility-industrial bond yield spread, and this revised series is also used in some of the work that follows. Mortgage interest rates are discussed below.

It is not clear from this chart or the further comparisons of these series in Charts VI-2 and VI-3 that either commitments or acquisitions are positively associated with bond interest rate levels. We are interested here in whether the separation in time of the in-

CHART VI-2. *Total New Commitment Votings by Life Insurance Companies and Yields on Newly Issued Corporate Bonds (Scatter Diagram): Quarterly, 1952/IV–1960/II*

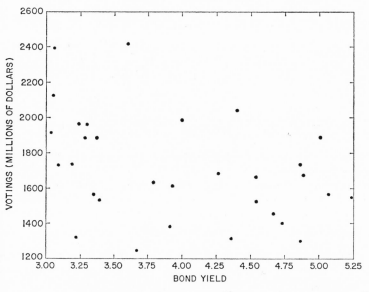

NOTES AND SOURCES: Total new commitment votings represent all finance committee loan and investment authorizations during the quarter. Data are for life insurance companies reporting to the LIAA *Forward Commitment Survey*. Bond yields are the same series used in Chart VI-1.

vestment decision from the investment acquisition has improved the average yield obtained over the business cycle. If it has, the time pattern of new commitments should be more positively correlated with the level of interest rates than is the time sequence of acquisitions.

A Comparison of Votings, Acquisitions, and Interest Rates

In order to ascertain the relation between the votings pattern and interest rates, we shall make a simple calculation. We as-

CHART VI-3.   Total Portfolio Acquisitions by Life Insurance Companies and Yields on Newly Issued Corporate Bonds (Scatter Diagram): Quarterly, 1952/IV–1960/II

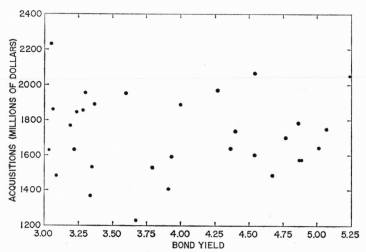

NOTES AND SOURCES: Acquisitions data for life insurance companies reporting to the LIAA *Forward Commitment Survey*.   Bond yields are the same series used in Chart VI-1.

sume that life companies had a specific time rate of acquisitions in mind and, in fact, achieved this desired pattern over the period in question.   We wish to know whether the actual timing of investment decisions (new commitments) resulted in companies obtaining a higher rate of return than they would have recorded if no delayed takedown commitments had been issued.   To make this comparison we will assume that the level of interest rates was unaffected by the time sequence of commitments chosen; that is, that interest rates are influenced only by life company disbursement of current funds and not at all by current decisions to lend at some point in the future.   The plausibility of this assumption is discussed below.

Conceptually, then, we are given for a period of time monthly data on:

(1) loan votings,
(2) loan acquisitions, and
(3) interest rates.

We ask whether the observed pattern of votings resulted in a higher average return on the given volume of funds invested than would have been achieved if:

(1) each loan decision resulted in an immediate outlay (within the month voted) of the funds committed; and
(2) the pattern of loan decisions corresponded to the pattern of acquisitions actually observed.

For each month we obtain the product of the month's loan votings and the current loan interest rate, summed over all months and divided by the total amount of loans voted.[12] This gives the average rate of return obtained on the loans voted in the period in question: $r_v = \dfrac{\Sigma_t(V_t \cdot r_t)}{\Sigma_t V_t}$, where V_t is total commitment votings in period t, and r_t is the going interest rate.

Similarly, the average rate of return that would have been obtained if each loan had been acquired at the loan rate prevailing in the month of acquisition is computed as: $r_a = \dfrac{\Sigma_t(A_t \cdot r_t)}{\Sigma_t A_t}$, where A_t is total investment acquisitions in period t, and r_t is the going interest rate.

This conceptual model assumes investment in a standard homogeneous asset whose interest rate may vary from month to month. In fact, life companies invest in diverse types of assets with different interest rate movements over time. So long as loan rates exist for each type of asset, this adds no conceptual complication to the model. A technical complication which does exist, however, is that loan votings and acquisitions do not match precisely over any period. This is so for two primary reasons:

(1) Some acquisitions will have been made from loans voted in some previous period and some current votings will not lead to acquisitions until a future period.
(2) Some attrition in votings exists, in the sense that some loan commitments voted are canceled by the borrower before any delivery of funds takes place.

If a reasonably long period is taken, the problem of compara-

---

[12] We are assuming that commitments promising the future delivery of funds are made on the same basis (interest rates and other terms) as loans for immediate takedown. With some marginal qualifications this is consistent with the testimony of life company investment officers summarized above.

bility between loan decisions and acquisitions is minimized. There will be some overhang at each end of the period, but for the bulk of loan decisions the corresponding acquisition will occur within the period. The divergence may be reduced further by lagging the acquisitions series a few months behind the votings series.

We do not know a great deal about loan cancellations. There is an asymmetry in this sort of attrition since it is practically always the borrower, not the lender, who cancels the commitment agreement. *A priori* one would expect our calculation of the rate of return on loan votings to be biased upward as a result of loan commitment attrition. That is, borrowers are more likely to cancel loans that turn out to have been agreed to at high interest rates than those with low rates. The evidence that is available is summarized in Appendix A to this chapter. It confirms the reasonableness of this assumption.

With this introduction, we turn to the rate of return calculation. Four investment categories are distinguished: corporate bonds (industrial, public utility, and railroad issues), conventional residential mortgage loans, federally underwritten mortgage loans, and business and commercial mortgage loans. The interest rate series used for each category are described in Appendix B to the chapter. The relevant forward commitment data are available for 93 months, October 1952–June 1960. The average rate of return on commitments for each category is computed as the sum of the new commitments each month times the prevailing loan rate, summed over all months and divided by the total of new commitments. The hypothetical rate of return on acquisitions is computed in a similar manner. The acquisition rate is hypothetical in the sense it is the rate life companies would have earned, given the time pattern of acquisition, if no delayed takedown commitments had been made. If the commitment process was used to increase the portfolio return by altering the time sequence of investment decisions, it should be reflected in higher rates of return on the commitment as opposed to the null, no delayed takedown hypothesis. The results are presented in Table VI-1.

It does not appear from these computations that the particular time sequence of loan votings adopted by life companies over the 1952–1960 period improved the average rate of return achieved over what it would have been if each investment dollar had been placed at interest rates prevailing at *time of acquisition*. The computation of return on loan votings and acquisitions over the period October 1952 to June 1960 shows essentially no difference between the return on votings made and the return on the null

TABLE VI-1. *Average Rates of Return on Investment Commitments and Hypothetical Rates of Return on Portfolio Acquisitions: U.S. Life Insurance Companies, 1952–1960*

Months: *Category*	10/52– 6/60 Commit- ments	10/52– 6/60 Acquisi- tions	10/52– 3/60 Commit- ments	1/53–6/60 Acquisi- tions	10/52– 12/59 Commit- ments	4/53–6/60 Acquisi- tions
Corporate Bonds	3.92%	3.96%	3.89%	3.99%	3.84%	4.01%
Conventional Residential Mortgage Loans	4.72	4.73	4.69	4.74	4.65	4.75
Federally Underwritten Mortgage Loans	4.51	4.50	4.48	4.53	4.45	4.54
Business and Commercial Mortgage Loans	4.65	4.64	4.62	4.65	4.59	4.67
Total Investments	4.36	4.35	4.33	4.38	4.29	4.41

SOURCE: The commitments and acquisitions series are from LIAA *Forward Commitment Survey*. The corporate bond interest rate series used is the Bankers Trust Grade 2 new issue public utility bond series. The mortgage interest rate series are those described in Appendix B. For this calculation 50 basis points were deducted from the raw mortgage yield figures to put them on a net of cost basis, i.e., comparable to the bond yields. Each cell is computed as the sum of monthly interest rates weighted by votings (acquisitions) divided by the sum of the monthly votings (acquisitions) over the period indicated and expressed in percentage terms.

hypothesis (no delayed takedown commitments). In the case where acquisitions are lagged behind votings (three months and six months respectively) in an attempt to pick up more of the votings-acquisitions pairs, life companies appear to have fared worse by playing the forward commitment game. This result reflects the secular increase in interest rates over the period. This secular uptrend would have tended to cancel some of the gains life companies could have made from the cyclical timing of investment decisions and therefore placed an extra premium upon precise timing of new commitments.

The period in question begins toward the end of a cyclical expansion, covers one complete cycle, trough to trough, and the bulk of the subsequent expansion phase. To isolate any peculiar effects that might result from this particular assortment of cyclical phases, we performed the same computation over the 1954–1958 cycle. These results, presented in Table VI-2,[13] strengthen the conclusion that the forward commitment operation has not, in fact, paid off in terms of average realized returns. The higher return on lagged acquisitions again reflects the secularly rising trend in interest rates.

TABLE VI-2. *Average Rates of Return on Investment Commitments and Hypothetical Rates of Return on Portfolio Acquisitions: U.S. Life Insurance Companies over the 1954–1958 Business Cycle*

Category	Commitments	Acquisitions		
	3/54–1/58	3/54–1/58	6/54–4/58	9/54–7/58
Corporate Bonds	3.69%	3.73%	3.77%	3.84%
Conventional Residential Mortgage Loans	4.45	4.47	4.51	4.55
Federally Underwritten Mortgage Loans	4.27	4.29	4.32	4.35
Business and Commercial Mortgage Loans	4.44	4.57	4.52	4.56
Total Investments	4.12	4.17	4.18	4.23

NOTE: The trough months: 3/54 and 1/58 are troughs in the Bankers Trust Grade 2 new issue public utility bond series.
SOURCE: See Table VI-1.

A casual comparison of the time pattern of new commitments and bond yields over the 1954–1958 cycle (Chart VI-4) suggests what happened. From the perspective of a yield maximization goal, life companies committed their funds too early in the expansion phase of this particular cycle. It does not necessarily follow that some other objective was determining the time pattern of new commitments. Rather, it is possible that defective forecasting of interest rate movements explains the difference between

---

[13] The cycle is dated in Table VI-2 by the new issue public utility bond interest rate series. The use of a mortgage yield series or a general business cycle indicator to date the cycle does not affect the conclusion.

the observed votings pattern and the yield maximization ideal.[14] All we have strictly demonstrated here is that life companies did not *successfully* separate investment decisions from acquisitions in order to increase their average return on investments made.

CHART VI-4. Total New Commitment Votings and Total Acquisitions by Life Insurance Companies and Yields on Newly Issued Corporate Bonds: Quarterly, 1952/IV–1960/II

(millions of dollars)

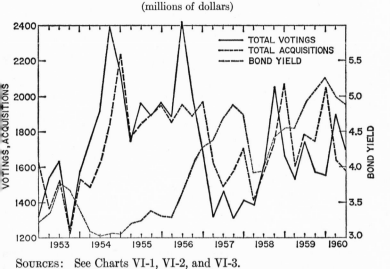

SOURCES: See Charts VI-1, VI-2, and VI-3.

We will comment further on the significance of these results below.

Because some loan commitments are canceled, the dollar volume of loan votings in each category exceeds the comparable volume of acquisitions for each of the periods used in the reported computations. Since cancellation data give no evidence regarding what commitments were canceled (for our purposes, it would be sufficient to know the month the canceled commitment was originally contracted), there is no way to eliminate votings which never resulted in loans from the calculated averages. As noted above,

---

[14] A number of forecasters had anticipated the business cycle peaking out in 1956 and, indeed, the Federal Reserve pursued an "easier" credit policy for a while. "Free reserves" rose from a negative $533 million in April 1956 to a positive $177 million in January 1957.

it is a reasonable presumption that the average rate of return on commitments displayed in Tables VI-1 and VI-2 are higher than the appropriately adjusted averages would be. Therefore it is most unlikely that our conclusion would be changed if the aborted commitments were eliminated from the calculation.

The Impact of Forward Commitment Contracts on the Level of Interest Rates

A critical and questionable assumption, upon which the calculations in Tables VI-1 and VI-2 are based, is that the time pattern of interest rates is independent of the time pattern of new commitments, given the time sequence of the actual outlay of funds. In particular, the above calculations assumed that the observed interest rate series would not have been any different had there been no *forward* commitments, i.e., had loan votings been simultaneously paired with acquisitions. In effect this means that the level of interest rates is determined solely by the supply of and demand for current funds, and that forward commitment activity affects neither of these schedules. Commitment contracts made today have an influence on market price only as the scheduled delivery date of funds draws near. The question naturally arises as to whether this is a defensible assumption, and if not, what difference it makes for our conclusions.

If the rate of issuance of commitment agreements does affect the time path of interest rates, those effects can be thought of as taking place through changes in the supply and/or demand schedules for current funds. Imagine first a world in which delayed takedown commitments do not exist; then impose the forward commitment innovation on this world and consider its consequences on the loanable funds market. It is conceivable that the issuance of forward commitments might reduce the willingness of life companies to supply funds currently. We have seen, however (Chapter V), that this possibility is in fact of negligible, or at least infrequent, significance for life companies. We found that life companies do not as a rule shift current funds into liquid holdings to provide for future takedowns from currently contracted commitments. Thus we expect the introduction of the commitment device to have a negligible effect on the supply of loanable funds in the current period.

It is more likely, however, that the forward commitment process will affect the current demand for funds. Indeed, part of the logic of forward commitments for the borrower is that promises of future loans are in some degree a cheap substitute for current borrowing. Therefore the opportunity to enter into forward commitment agreements may reduce deficit sectors' current demand for funds. The effect on current interest rates is then to make them lower than they would be without the commitment alternative.[15]

The argument can be summarized as follows. Consider a potential borrower who desires external financing for expenditures scheduled some n months in the future. Three alternatives are open to him:

(1) Borrow and hold the funds in some relatively liquid form until needed for the scheduled expenditures.
(2) Postpone action with the intention of borrowing closer to the time the funds are needed. Some credit price and availability risks are assumed if this option is chosen.
(3) Contract for a forward commitment now which promises delivery of funds n months in the future.

It is clear from simply listing the alternatives that a forward commitment is in some degree a substitute for a current loan. Therefore, accepting the assumption that the supply of current funds is affected little by forward commitment votings, the initial effect of introducing forward commitments is that interest rates are reduced below what they otherwise would be. This, of course, may result in a bunching of demand for funds at some later date which may raise interest rates at that time above what they otherwise would be. This would not be a particularly happy consequence for lenders engaged in forward commitment activity, for yields are higher because lenders have previously committed current funds at relatively low yields. This sequence of events may, in fact, essentially represent what has happened in cyclical upswings during the postwar period.

---

[15] Technically, part of the impact of introducing commitments as an alternative may be on the supply side. Future borrowers, having obtained a commitment, might then be willing to operate with a lower level of cash than otherwise, thereby releasing additional funds to the capital market. This is essentially the same phenomenon discussed in the text under the heading of demand effects, however. Also the funds released are likely to be supplied to the short-run market while the committed funds are normally long term.

It is more difficult to speculate in which direction the forward commitment process might distort interest rates during cyclical downswings. Their impact should depend largely on whether new commitments issued offset takedowns from past commitments. New commitments put downward pressure, if any, on current rates and takedowns apply upward pressure. In general, lenders will try to refrain from making many delayed takedown commitments during a recession and hope to gain from past commitments made at high yields. Their latter hope may be somewhat frustrated by an increased rate of commitment cancellations, however.

It is conceivable therefore that we made an unwarranted assumption in presuming that forward commitment activity had no effect on the time path of interest rates. Suppose the commitment process affected interest rates in the way we have just described. Could our original assumption to the contrary have biased the computation against the hypothesis that forward commitments were used to alter the timing of investment decisions so as to improve portfolio return? That is, might not the interest rate pattern have been less favorable to life companies had they not, in fact, extensively utilized the forward commitment contract? The answer to this question must be negative. For as we have seen, if the forward commitment process has any perceptible impact on interest rates, it depresses them at the time when an extraordinarily heavy volume of investment decisions are being contracted.

This discussion has been conducted in a comparative static mode. It is possible that there might be additional, dynamic influences on interest rates as a result of forward commitment activity; e.g., changes in the volume of forward commitment agreements might generate expectations of future changes in interest rates which feed back as pressure on current rates. Therefore, a high rate of commitment activity (relative to the current flow of funds or acquisitions) may generate expectations of higher future rates which place upward pressure on current yields. This kind of effect, however, simply serves to minimize the impact predicted from the static analysis, to the effect that a heavy volume of commitment activity retards the increase in yields. Therefore, we conclude that it may not have been unreasonable to assume that new commitments have no effect on current rates, and in any case the consideration of the plausible commitment impact on interest rates does not in any way strengthen the case for the rejected hypothesis. We conclude then that the forward commitment process has not proved an effective device for improving portfolio yield through choosing a time sequence of investment decisions different from the inflow of investible funds. Indeed, there is some presumptive evidence that on this score, issuance of forward agreements reduced life companies' investment return over the period.

Alternative Explanations of the Time Pattern of New Commitment Authorizations

We return now to an examination of the other plausible hypotheses which might contribute to the explanation of the time sequence of life insurance company commitment votings. We have suggested above two alternatives to the rate of return over time hypothesis. One of these, pursuance of the loaned-up objective, implies that life company votings should be explained by the anticipated flow of available investible funds in the relevant time horizon. The other, the servicing hypothesis, proposes that the principal rationale of investment commitment activity is the servicing of borrowers' desires for assurance of future credit and suggests that commitment votings ought to be sensitive to changes in borrowers' demand for this peculiar service.

We proceed by considering the meaning of the loaned-up goal when applied to forward commitment votings. Appropriate tests will be suggested and some evidence presented. We then show how the servicing hypothesis can contribute to explaining the time rate of votings where the loaned-up relation is weak. In the process of considering these two hypotheses, all major explanatory variables that have been suggested will be evaluated.

The Loaned-up Goal

As we have seen (Chapter V), the loaned-up goal is an institutional hypothesis that has meaning and empirical content when applied to explaining the timing of life company investment acquisitions. Here we are interested in what the loaned-up principle implies for the time pattern of loan authorizations as opposed to acquisitions. We have noted the division of opinion among investment officers with regard to the question of whether forward commitment votings can assist or only impede maintenance of a fully invested position. Realization of the loaned-up objective may be made more difficult to the extent the commitment process increases uncertainty about the timing of loan takedowns. On the other hand, forward commitment votings may ease achievement of the loaned-up goal by reducing the volume of current funds for which immediate outlets must be found.

Loan votings in any period are of two kinds:

(1) votings which result in immediate delivery of funds; and
(2) votings which give birth to acquisitions in some future month.

Most loan authorizations fall into the latter category; i.e., they involve a forward commitment. If immediate delivery is taken to mean within the month of loan authorization, then about 85% of commitments voted by life companies included in the LIAA survey are delayed takedown commitments.[16] Although many delayed takedown commitments do result in closed loans in the two or three months following the voting, well over half of the commitments voted by reporting companies during 1952–1960 seem to have had commitment-to-takedown lags in excess of three months, and perhaps a third were delayed more than six months.[17] Therefore many loan votings cannot be explained by a desire to get currently available funds invested quickly.

It may make sense, however, to conceive of investment officers having in mind some optimal relation between the stock of outstanding commitments and the volume of funds expected to be available for investment in future periods. Then in any period, $t = 0$, life companies could forecast for each future period within their horizon:

---

[16] This is computed from monthly survey data for the period from January 1957 to June 1960. This is the entire period for which we had commitment data distinguishing immediate delivery and delayed takedown commitments.

[17] See the section below dealing with the servicing hypothesis and Chapter VII for evidence on the time lag between commitment authorization and loan closing.

(1) the gross inflow of funds expected to be available for investment; and

(2) the volume of takedowns expected from the currently $(t = 0)$ outstanding stock of commitments.

Suppose investment officers do hold some notions about the appropriate ratio between committed funds and the anticipated inflow of investible funds for each future period. Then loan votings in $t = 0$ can be thought of as being triggered by a smaller than acceptable commitments/investible funds ratio. For most companies the time horizon to which this sort of conscious behavior would apply is probably not much more than a year. This is partly a result of life company hesitancy to engage in the risks associated with long delayed takedown commitments, and partly due to the fact that the market for long delayed takedowns is likely to be thin and specialized. Therefore a supplier of funds may not be able to think realistically in terms of generating more delayed takedown loans through activated investment search or offering marginal concessions on loan terms.

In recent years many life companies have, in fact, begun to make serious attempts at forecasting cash flows.[18] The usual procedure is to make monthly forecasts of investible funds for each month 12 months in advance. Estimates of commitment takedown dates can, of course, be made from knowledge of the commitment agreements and subsequent developments. In interviews with investment officers we found at least some tendency on their part to think in terms of desirable relations between the stock of committed funds and the anticipated flow of investible funds. This tendency was more pronounced for officers located in securities departments than for those in mortgage loan departments. Apparently this difference results from security commitments being more closely and consciously controlled with respect to timing than mortgage loan commitments. This in turn follows from the lending mechanics by which security commitments are originated, processed, and closed by home office personnel, while mortgage loan commitments are generated by branch office employees or independent mortgage correspondents. In addition,

---

[18] See Walter, *The Investment Process*, Chapter VII, and LIAA-CMC Monograph, pp. 180–190.

the mortgage loan business has more of a seasonal rhythm than the bond operation, which makes mortgage commitments less flexible with respect to timing. However, the commitment-take-down time lag for single home mortgage financing has a much smaller variance than the lag distribution associated with other major loan and investment categories. Consequently the short-run timing problem ought to be particularly critical for mortgage loan departments specializing in home loans since these commitments will produce a demand on funds in the near future.

We asked some investment officers interviewed in 1960 what proportion of their 1960 funds were already committed at the beginning of the year. Most of the meaningful responses were obtained from officers connected with securities departments. Estimates obtained from officers of nine companies are presented in Table VI-3, along with some of their relevant supplementary comments. All the companies reported on in Table VI-3 are large; all have assets in excess of one billion dollars. All but one company were making some sort of 12-month cash flow estimates. The differences among companies in effort and precision involved in making their estimates corresponded to inferences one might make from knowledge of differences among companies in growth rates, liquid asset holdings, and average portfolio maturity. In general, a company with a low growth rate, tight liquidity position, and/or low rate of portfolio rollover, has more need for good cash flow estimates than a company in a more advantageous position with respect to the availability of investible funds.

On balance there seems to be enough tendency for investment officers to be conscious of and plan in terms of a commitment stock/anticipated funds ratio to warrant consideration of this relation as a means of explaining the time rate of new commitment votings. The estimates reported in Table VI-3 show a wide variance among companies with regard to the actual proportion of a year's funds that were committed in advance. The supplementary comments, however, suggest that the variance in the desired commitments/funds ratio is not so great. A target ratio in the neighborhood of 50% seems common with some flexibility up or down depending upon the outlook for interest rates and the availability of attractive investment opportunities.

In the sample of nine companies reported in Table VI-3, all

TABLE VI-3. Proportion of 1960 Funds Available to Securities Departments Committed Prior to 1960: Selected Life Insurance Companies

Company	Percentage of Funds Allotted to Securities Departments for 1960, Committed as of 1/1/60	Comments
A	20%	Company more active in public market than in direct placements. Does not make many commitments outstanding for more than six months. Would like to have been more fully committed. By June 1, 50% of July–December funds were committed.
B	35%	Satisfied with this proportion but would have been willing to have it higher. Would not want to go into a year with over 50% of year's funds committed. As of April 30, this company reported 90% of remaining 1960 securities department quota committed. It was anticipated, however, that additional funds would become available through sales of common stock.
C	35%–40%	Would be willing to enter year with higher percentage of the year's funds committed. Indeed, at one point in the past the department had 80%–90% of available funds for the next 18 months committed. This was a period when interest rates were thought to be especially attractive. Probably would not want to commit so heavily again, however. Mortgage department had about 70% of its 1960 quota committed at the beginning of the year.
D	38%	Most commitments were due for takedown in the first half of the year. Has not had many long commitments, i.e., more than six or eight months, but would like to make more. Would definitely like to in-

TABLE VI-3 (continued)

Company	Percentage of Funds Allotted to Securities Departments for 1960, Committed as of 1/1/60	Comments
		crease current stock of commitments, and is actively searching for good investments. Interest is strong enough to make company willing to make some concessions on loan terms and fees.
E	45%	Regard 50% of funds committed at beginning of year as about normal; 70% as maximum would want. Would like a somewhat higher commitment/funds ratio than current 45% since think interest rates are quite attractive. Becoming willing to soften loan terms a little to increase loan commitments.
F	50%	This ratio is an "educated guess" since no formal cash flow estimates are made. The company does not normally make commitments that are expected to be outstanding more than a year. By June 1 this company reported it was in a very tight position with regard to available funds for the following three to four months. It was willing to make some commitments for fourth quarter takedown. Securities department reported it was being squeezed by excessive mortgage loan commitments.
G	60%	This commitment/funds proportion was considered "typical." About the same proportion would apply to the company's commercial mortgage loan commitments. This company is not active in residential loans. It does not make many commitments expected to be outstanding more than a year. As of April 30, 1960,

TABLE VI-3 (continued)

Company	Percentage of Funds Allotted to Securities Departments for 1960, Committed as of 1/1/60	Comments
		about 12% of 1961 funds were committed.
H	60%	Company regards any ratio in the 40%–60% range as normal and acceptable. By mid-1960 expects to have 25% of 1961 funds committed.
I	67%	Regards a 75% ratio as about the maximum would want to have. Willing to be close to this maximum when interest rates look good as they have in recent months (April 1960). Makes long commitments and has maximum commitment/funds ratio in mind for future years. Rule of thumb maxima are 75% for 12 months in advance; 50% for 13–24 months, and 25% for 25–36 months.

SOURCE: Interviews with investment officers of nine life insurance companies conducted between January and June 1960. Confidence with regard to company names was promised to those interviewed.

felt a relatively high proportion of committed future funds was appropriate in early 1960 but only three had reached this goal. The other six were either willing, or strongly desired, to increase their stock of commitments while interest rates were still high. In these attitudes, then, there is some suggestion of a passive willingness to substantially increase forward commitment activity but some inertia in implementing a more intensive search for outlets and making the necessary concessions in loan terms. Finally, it appears that control over the level of commitments is often inadequate for fulfillment of the objective. In particular, excessive commitments by mortgage departments appear to have been a common problem. Increased utilization of dollar volume quotas in planning is aimed at bringing the rate of issuance of forward commitments under control.

Within this rather small sample there is no clear correlation between the ratios reported for 1960 and *a priori,* plausibly related variables such as company size, extent of direct placement activity, bond/mortgage portfolio mix, or the stock of unliquidated Treasury obligations. The two companies at the extremes do contrast sharply. Company A acquires most of its securities in the public market. It originates almost no direct placements on its own, most of its privately placed securities having been obtained from joint participation in loans originated by another lender. By contrast, Company I is one of the industry's leaders in direct placements, and not only had the highest proportion of 1960 funds committed as the year began, but was quite conscious of its commitments/funds ratios for 1961 and 1962. The other companies, however, are not arrayed by this or any other obviously relevant dimension.

To obtain an idea of what order of magnitude might be involved for shorter periods, we computed the ratio of commitments scheduled for takedown to funds available for two-month and six-month periods. This calculation was made from the aggregate LIAA survey data for the period January 1957–December 1959. Expected takedown/available funds ratios were computed for each month of the 36-month period. Unfortunately the survey does not report anticipations with regard to available funds.[19] Therefore an estimate of the actual volume of funds that were available was used in the denominator of the expected takedown/available funds ratio.[20]

The ratios computed were:

(1) E_2/I_2 Ratio of commitments outstanding from which delivery of funds is expected within two months to investible funds available during the two months.

(2) E_6/I_6 Ratio of expected takedowns in six months from commitments outstanding at the beginning of the period to investible funds available over the six months.

The averages of the 36 monthly ratios computed were: $E_2/I_2 = .781$; $E_6/I_6 = .700$.

---

[19] Cash flow estimates are reported in a separate LIAA survey but differences in company coverage are too great to justify pooling aggregate data from the two surveys for this purpose.

[20] Estimated as actual gross asset acquisitions over the period less net disposals of Treasury obligations.

This means that in approaching a "typical" two-month period companies found about 78% of the normal inflow of funds for those two months already committed. About two-thirds of funds available for months 3 to 6 in the future would typically have been committed. The observed ratios for E_2/I_2 ranged from 58.9% to 91.5% and for E_6/I_6 from 58.0% to 83.3%.[21]

Evidence on the Loaned-up Hypothesis

If this sort of commitment stock adjustment theory of life insurance company loan authorizations is relevant, then the current rate of new commitment votings should be functionally related to the anticipated inflow of investible funds over future months, net of that portion of future funds previously committed.[22]

---

[21] Since this was written, the LIAA-CMC Monograph has appeared. A similar calculation appears there, using data from the companies which have consistently reported to both the forward commitment and cash flow surveys over the period 1957–1960. As has been noted, this series was not available to us. The proportion of anticipated cash flow for the ensuing six months committed at the beginning of the period is somewhat higher than in ours. Two sets of calculations are presented (see Table 7-3, p. 189), one based on a cash-flow forecast which includes anticipated security sales and liquidation of the cash position, and the other which does not include these extraordinary sources. The average of 16 quarterly ratios for 1957–1959 are 73% and 80% for the respective cash flow estimates.

As reported above, our computation of a similar ratio using an estimate of the cash flow which turned out to be available averaged 70% for the same period. Our treatment of extraordinary sources of funds excluded funds obtained from sales of Treasury obligations but did not eliminate other security sales or changes in cash holdings. Although there is some difference in company coverage, the LIAA calculations having excluded companies reporting commitments but not reporting expected cash flow, the difference in the ratio estimates are presumably due primarily to errors in funds forecasting. As we have seen (Chapter V), companies tended to underestimate future cash flow in most of the period represented.

[22] This formulation actually differs somewhat from the strict logic of a stock adjustment model. In the stock adjustment formulation it is assumed that investors have a target commitment stock/investible funds ratio,

$$E_{0(K)}/I_K = \gamma \; [\gamma = f(K)]$$

where $E_{0(K)}$ = that part of the stock of commitments existing at the end of the month $t = 0$ expected to be taken down during the following K months,

and I_K = the anticipated inflow of investible funds during months I to K, inclusive.

Given the investible funds forecast, the desired stock of commitments due for takedown in K months is determined as $E_{0(K)} = \gamma I_K$. New commitment

There is a problem with regard to what sort of time horizon is relevant. Presumably the logic of the loaned-up hypothesis should be that as the investor looks further into the future, the availability of funds becomes less and less relevant as an explanation of current votings. Therefore if this is an important objective, available funds for the upcoming six months should be of particular significance in determining the volume of current votings expected to be taken down during the six months. The inducement of funds should be weaker for current votings for which takedown is delayed beyond six months,[23] and indeed for most companies funds available beyond twelve months, while permissive of current delayed takedown votings, are unlikely to be a source of pressure on current decisions. Therefore a regres-

votings in any month are a function of the gap between the desired stock of commitments and the existing stock, i.e.,

$$V_{0(K)} = \alpha(E_{0(K)} - E_{0(K)}^A)$$

$V_{0(K)}$ = new votings in $t = 0$ expected to be taken down during the following K months.

$E_{0(K)}^A$ = the stock of commitments due to be closed within K months that would exist at the end of $t = 0$ if $V_0 = 0$.

Obviously, $E_{0(K)}^A = E_{-1(K)}^A - T_0$, the inherited stock less takedowns (T) from that stock during $t = 0$.

α = the desired rate of adjustment of the gap between the target and actual stock of commitments. If negative new votings (i.e., unilateral cancellations of previous commitments by the lender) are not permitted, α applies only when $E_{0(K)} > E_{0(K)}^A$. If $E_{0(K)} < E_{0(K)}^A$, then $V_{0(K)} = 0$.

In terms of observable variables we have,

$$V_{0(K)} = \alpha(\gamma I_K - E_{0(K)}^A).$$

There are two parameters to be estimated from only one relationship. Therefore, to estimate either parameter, it is necessary to know the value of the other from an independent source. We could simply make an assumption about the desired rate of adjustment, e.g., $\alpha = 1$, and proceed to estimate γ given data on $V_{0(K)}$, I_K and $E_{0(K)}^A$. Alternatively we might use the estimate of a typical γ we have computed above, $\gamma = .70$ for $K = 6$, and estimate α. The formulation in the text appears to be as faithful to the loaned-up hypothesis and avoids the necessity of making those sorts of explicit assumptions.

[23] Some rough estimates of the distribution of votings by number of months to takedown are available below in the section dealing with the servicing hypothesis. It would appear that in a typical month, about two-thirds of total votings can be expected to result in takedowns within six months and about 80% in twelve months.

sion equation of the following type should have explanatory value:

$$V_{0(6)} = \alpha + \beta(I_6 - E_{0(6)}),$$

where $V_{0(6)}$ = forward commitments voted in month $t = 0$ expected to result in loan takedowns during months $t = 1$–6, inclusive.

I_6 = total investible funds anticipated for months $t = 1$–6.

$E_{0(6)}$ = the stock of existing commitments at the beginning of the period $t = 0$ which are expected to lead to loan closings during the period $t = 1$–6.

The current liquid asset position ($t = 0$) is also relevant for determination of the volume of new commitments under the loaned-up objective. For delayed takedown votings (beyond six months) the alternative hypotheses, i.e., the rate-of-return and servicing hypotheses, should have more relevance and might dominate the net cash flow variable. One procedure for attacking the time division problem is to estimate regressions in which the available funds variable is split into several independent variables in this manner:

$$V_{0(12)} = \alpha + \beta_1(I_2 - E_{0(2)}) + \beta_2(I_{3-6} - E_{0(3-6)}) + \beta_3(I_{7-12} - E_{0(7-12)})$$

The appropriate time division depends on how much variance in liquid asset holdings is tolerated over time and on the flexibility life companies actually possess in selecting commitments which will result in takedown at desired points of time in the future. The influence of the anticipated volume of available funds (excluding security liquidation as a source of funds) on commitment votings should, of course, become stronger as life companies moved during the mid-1950s out of an open-to-buy position into an environment where investment acquisitions are approximately constrained to the current inflow of funds from normal channels.

To summarize, the loaned-up hypothesis views life companies as aiming for a time pattern of asset acquisitions which permits the investment of funds as they become available from the normal operation of the insurance business, investment income and portfolio rollover. Variation in liquid asset holdings is assumed to be permissible only within a limited range. Only modest additions to the normal flow of investible funds may be made from sales of excessive holdings of prime quality securities. For commitment authorizations this means that the variance in votings over time should be explained primarily by variation in the level of available funds (net of committed funds) over the upcoming six or eight months. The residual variations in votings may be explained by (1) levels of interest rates, (2) level of demand for the forward commitment service, and (3) excessive holdings of liquid assets.

THE DATA

From the aggregate forward commitment survey data available, it is possible to make at least a rough test of the loaned-up hypothesis as applied to commitment authorizations. As we have seen, the survey does provide monthly data on new commitments. In addition there are available estimates of the volume of outstanding commitments expected to result in acquisitions within six months. The major problem arises in estimating the expected normal flow of investible funds over six months. Unfortunately data on anticipated funds flows were not available prior to 1958 and incomparabilities in coverage between the independent cash flow and commitment surveys make pooling of evidence from the two series inadvisable for the two years where both are available.[24] In the work that follows, therefore, we have fallen back on an estimate of investible funds that actually turned out to be available. Use of this sort of series implicitly assumes absence of forecasting error. Since, as we have seen in Chapter V, there is some evidence of systematic cash flow forecasting errors, we cannot be sure the differences between ex ante and ex post funds estimates are negligible.

The ex post concept is based on actual investment acquisitions. It might have been preferable to use an independent estimate of available funds obtained from cash inflow accounts. To estimate the inflow of normal investible funds, we would want to sum the following sources:

[24] We did not have at our disposal the commitment and cash flow survey data on a comparable basis, i.e., for companies which have reported in both surveys. As will become apparent, our empirical work in this section suffers as a result. Similar investigating procedures could be fruitfully employed should the comparable series become available to researchers at a later date.

(1) net change in ledger assets;
(2) net decrease in policy loans;
(3) principal repayments from mortgage, security, and real estate portfolios.

Again, however, these cash inflow items are not available for the sample of life companies reporting in the forward commitment survey. The estimate of total investible funds used below is simply actual gross acquisitions from commitments over the specified number of months less an estimate of the net sale of Treasury obligations. Policy loans are not included in the commitment or acquisition data. The computation of extraordinary funds obtained from sales of Governments is approximate. It is estimated from the net change in Treasury security holdings monthly for the industry as a whole. This figure is then deflated since companies represented in the commitment survey account for only about 65% of the industry's assets. The deflation coefficient used varies from year to year according to an estimate of the relation of Treasury obligations disposed of by companies included in the survey to total disposals of Governments by the industry. This relation in turn is based on annual net changes in holdings of Treasury obligations by the 12 largest companies included in the commitment survey.[25]

It might be argued, of course, that the loaned-up thesis should apply as strongly to the excess holdings of Government securities in life company portfolios as to the normal cash inflow, and therefore the surplus stock of Treasury obligations should be included as part of the available funds estimate. This, indeed, is the position we have taken in our earlier discussion of life company investment decisions in an open-to-buy environment. However, we are now interested in investigating life insurance company investment commitment policy during a period in which an open-to-buy assumption becomes increasingly tenuous and in the latter part of the period is surely not applicable at all. The decline in relevance of Treasury debt holdings is due both to the shrunken size of the stock of those obligations and to the locking-in effect of high interest rates. In this situation it is appropriate to consider the stock of Government securities, or the ratio of Governments to total

---

[25] These were the companies we were able to identify as respondents to the commitment survey.

assets, as a separate independent variable influencing loan votings positively, but not as a part of the normal volume of available funds. Holdings of short-term obligations might reasonably be treated in either manner. In any case it would have been incorrect to permit funds obtained from sales of Treasuries to appear as part of the available funds flow at the time of liquidation for this procedure would have presumed in advance that the causal relationship flows from anticipated funds to forward commitment votings.

We do make this sort of causal presumption with regard to life companies' cash position by not eliminating funds obtained from cash holdings from the normal flow of available funds. That is, we assume that life companies effectively control their cash position within an objective of maintaining the minimum desired working balances at all times. We found this to be an acceptable hypothesis with only marginal qualifications in Chapter V. As we have seen, variation in life company cash holdings has been of quite modest magnitude.

The most serious deficiency in this part of the available funds calculation results from our inability, for lack of data, to eliminate funds obtained from the sale of non-Treasury securities. We do know that in recent years the volume of these sales has been somewhat greater than the sales of long-term Governments. This would be a problem particularly if sales seemed to be concentrated in periods of high demand for funds suggesting that the forces of causation were running from heavy forward commitments to forced security liquidation. As we have seen (Chapter V), however, there is no evidence in the time pattern of sales for 1957 to mid-1960 that this has been the case. Security sales have been quite regular, and the closest thing to concentration of sales occurred during the 1958 recession when high security prices, not pressure of commitments, must have been the inducement. Some of the recorded security sales may reflect portfolio trading. So long as no forward commitments are involved, trading in securities will not be counted in our available funds data. Thus ordinary trades and swaps will not make any trouble for our commitment analysis. All commitments and acquisitions are for *new* money only; exchanges, refundings, and other noncash forms of portfolio rollover are excluded from the reported data.

Finally, there is always some danger of circularity in causal relations when any gross funds flow concept is used. This is so where portfolio rollover (principal repayment) is generated by votings of loan commitments. Thus, for example, if increased mortgage loan votings stimulates real estate activity (i.e., faster turnover of existing housing resulting in increased mortgage principal repayments), then it may appear that votings were induced by an increase in future funds availability, whereas this is the reverse of the true causal relationship. This would be a serious problem if noncash mortgage transactions inflated both commitment and acquisition figures. Fortunately this is not the case. Since life companies in no sense dominate movements in real estate activity, the causal linkage from easier mortgage credit to increased mortgage loan commitments to a higher rate of housing turnover to a larger volume of mortgage loan repayments becomes tenuous and can be reasonably disregarded.

THE EMPIRICAL RESULTS

With this introduction we turn to an examination of the evidence. Unfortunately the forward commitment data do not classify new commitments by the expected date of loan closing. Therefore we were unable to test the loaned-up hypothesis by relating new votings *due for loan delivery* in K months to the net availability of funds for the same K months. We have proceeded, therefore, with a regression analysis in which total votings are related to the available funds estimates and the other variables we have been considering. If we find confirmation of the loaned-up hypothesis in this broader relationship, we can reasonably assume the relationship would be stronger in its more precise form. We will return to this question below.

Chart VI-5 is a scatter diagram relating total commitment votings to the available funds variable described above. Quarterly observations are plotted for the period from 1952/IV to 1959/IV, inclusive. The available funds variable includes the total normal supply of funds available, net of committed funds, for six months beginning with the first month of the quarter in which the votings observation falls.

Two linear least squares regression lines appear on the chart. The higher of the two is fit to all 29 observations. The lower is fit to the 12, 1957–1959, observations only. The two equations are shown in Table VI-4 along with the coefficient of determination and the standard error of the regression coefficients. The antici-

CHART VI-5. Total New Commitment Votings, Quarterly and Available Investment Funds for Six-Month Periods, 1952/IV–1959/IV
(Scatter Diagram)
(millions of dollars)

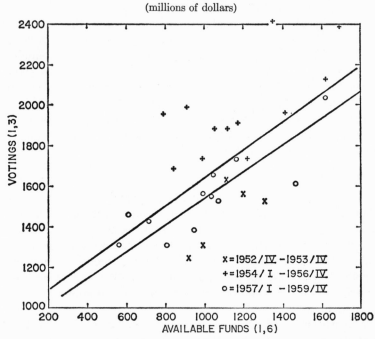

NOTE: Total votings is the same series used in Chart VI-2. Available funds are defined as total acquisitions (reported by companies in the LIAA *Forward Commitment Survey* — see Chart VI-3) less net sales of Treasury obligations less commitments outstanding at the beginning of the period and due for takedown during the period of observation. Available funds are recorded for six-month periods which cover the quarter for which paired votings are reported and the following quarter.

SOURCES: Life Insurance Association of America; *Treasury Bulletin.*

pated positive relationship is found, and the regression coefficients and the R^2 are significant at the 1% level for their respective significance tests. The marginal influence of available funds on votings is not very different in the two regressions.

TABLE VI-4. **Regression Results for Total Commitment Votings Regressed on Available Funds: Quarterly Observations**

I 1952/IV–1959/IV

$$V_{1,3} = 942 + .7029 \, AF_{1,6}$$
   (.1564)

$R^2 = .4282 \quad \overline{R}^2 = .3858$
Standard Error of Estimate = 236.955

II 1957/I–1959/IV

$$V_{1,3} = 893 + .6552 \, AF_{1,6}$$
   (.1112)

$R^2 = .6551 \quad \overline{R}^2 = .5861$
Standard Error of Estimate = 120.995

NOTE: $V_{1,3}$ = *Total Commitment Votings*, quarterly.

    $AF_{1,6}$ = Total investible funds *less* previously committed funds for six months including the quarter to which votings apply and the succeeding quarter.

It is obvious from inspection of Chart VI-5 that substantial positive serial correlation of the residuals exists. Votings during the 1954–1956 segment tend to be high relative to votings in the earlier and subsequent periods. There are several possible reasons for this behavior. It may reflect, in part, a greater willingness of life companies to (a) sell Treasury obligations, and (b) make federally underwritten mortgage loans during the 1954–1956 period. Prices of Governments were more favorable during this time period and the spread between ceiling interest rates on FHA and VA loans and competing market yields was relatively narrow. It is also possible that the demand for the forward commitment service was relatively high in the 1954–1956 period. We shall examine this possibility below. Serial correlation of residuals is absent within the 1957–1959 period. As anticipated, the votings-available funds relationship is somewhat tighter for the latter period.

These two regressions are reproduced in Table VI-5 along with some additional regression results. The regression equations numbered 3, 4, and 5 in this table are computed on the basis of monthly observations. Because there is considerable noise in the monthly data, these fits are less satisfactory than are the regressions based on quarterly observations. However, the relation is consistently positive as the loaned-up thesis predicts, and the regression coefficients and the coefficients of determination are all significant. In regression 4, the available funds observation is lagged three months behind what it is in equation 3. This formulation makes sense if there is typically a lag of about two or three months between a

TABLE VI-5. *Regression Analysis of New Commitment Votings on Available Funds and Other Variables*

I. Influence of Available Funds Flow on Votings

1. Quarterly
   1952/IV–1959/IV
   $n = 29$

   $V_{1,3} = 941.72 + .7029^{**}AF_{1,6}$ $R^2 = .4282^{**}$
             (.1564)
                                  $\overline{R}^2 = .3858$
   Standard Error of Estimate = 236.96

2. Quarterly
   1957/I–1959/IV
   $n = 12$

   $V_{1,3} = 893.10 + .6552^{**}AF_{1,6}$ $R^2 = .6551^{**}$
             (.1112)
                                  $\overline{R}^2 = .5861$
   Standard Error of Estimate = 121.00

3. Monthly
   1953/1–1959/12
   $n = 84$

   $V_0 = 411.11 + .1508^{**}AF_{1,6}$ $R^2 = .1234^{**}$
             (.0444)
                                  $\overline{R}^2 = .1018$
   Standard Error of Estimate = 117.43

4. Monthly
   1953/1–1959/12
   $n = 84$

   $V_0 = 319.78 + .2318^{**}AF_{-2,3}$ $R^2 = .2831^{**}$
             (.0407)
                                  $\overline{R}^2 = .2656$
   Standard Error of Estimate = 106.19

5. Monthly
   1957/2–1959/12
   $n = 35$

   $V_0 = 421.13 + .0963^{*}AF_{0,6}$ $R^2 = .1159^{*}$
             (.0447)
                                  $\overline{R}^2 = .0618$
   Standard Error of Estimate = 34.70

6. Monthly
   1957/2–1959/12
   $n = 35$

   $V_0 = 411.68 + .1490AF_{0,2}$ $R^2 = .1258^{**}$
             (.0984)
          $+ .0758AF_{3,6}$
             (.0576)
                                  $\overline{R}^2 = .0728$
   Standard Error of Estimate = 88.76

II. Liquid Assets Added to the Analysis

7. Quarterly
   1952/IV–1959/IV

   $n = 29$

   $V_{0,2} = 1013.88 + .5582^{**}(AF_{1,6} + XT_{S_0})$
             (.1532)
                                  $R^2 = .3292^{**}$
                                  $\overline{R}^2 = .2795$
   Standard Error of Estimate = 256.28

8. Quarterly
   1957/I–1959/IV
   $n = 12$

   $V_{0,2} = 994.44 + .4893^{**}(AF_{1,6} + XT_{S_0})$
             (.1096)
                                  $R^2 = .6661$
                                  $\overline{R}^2 = .5932$
   Standard Error of Estimate = 124.69

TABLE VI-5 (continued)

III. Level of Interest Rates Added to the Analysis

9. Monthly
    1953/1–1959/12
    $n = 84$

$$V_0 = 544.79 + .0524 AF_{1,6} \qquad R^2 = .1576**$$
$$(.0698)$$
$$- 84.0689 \, (r_u - r_u{}^n)_0$$
$$(46.4009)$$
$$\overline{R}^2 = .1263$$

Standard Error of Estimate = 115.13

10. Monthly
    1953/1–1959/12
    $n = 84$

$$V_0 = 537.67 + .0545 AF_{1,6}$$
$$(.0744)$$
$$- 82.3405 \, (r_u - r_u{}^n)_0 + .0086 T_{s_0}$$
$$(50.7894) \qquad\qquad (.0997)$$
$$R^2 = .1576**$$
$$\overline{R}^2 = .1155$$

Standard Error of Estimate = 115.13

11. Monthly
    1953/1–1959/12
    $n = 84$

$$V_0 = 578.2122 - .0152 AF_{1,6}$$
$$(.0814)$$
$$- 140.7428* \, (r_u - r_u{}^n)_0 - .0199 T_{s_0}$$
$$(55.4371) \qquad\qquad (.0984)$$
$$+ 98.7598* t_2$$
$$(35.7310)$$
$$+ 103.1185** t_3$$
$$(38.6235)$$
$$+ 69.8486 t_4$$
$$(35.5916)$$
$$R^2 = .2529$$
$$\overline{R}^2 = .1850$$

Standard Error of Estimate = 108.45

12. Monthly
    1953/1–1959/12
    $n = 84$

$$V_0 = 632.2099 + .0514 AF_{-2,3}$$
$$(.0584)$$
$$- 168.9359** \, (r_u - r_u{}^n)_{-3} - .1265 T_{s_0}$$
$$(39.2179) \qquad\qquad (.0800)$$
$$R^2 = .4225**$$
$$\overline{R}^2 = .3936$$

Standard Error of Estimate = 95.32

13. Monthly
    1952/10–1960/1
    $n = 88$

$$V_0 = 605.05 = 107.8388** (r_u - r_u{}^n)_0$$
$$(29.3093)$$

$$R^2 = .1360**$$
$$\overline{R}^2 = .1159$$

Standard Error of Estimate = 116.96

TABLE VI-5 (continued)

14. Monthly
     1952/10–1960/1
     $n = 88$

$$V_0 = 345.86 - 9.5817(r_u - r_u{}^n)_0$$
$$(38.5793)$$
$$+ .2096^{**}AF_{1,6}$$
$$(.0579)$$

$$R^2 = .2516$$
$$\overline{R}^2 = .2252$$

Standard Error of Estimate $= 108.86$

15. Monthly
     1952/10–1960/1
     $n = 88$

$$V_0 = 332.44 - 7.0475 (r_u - r_u{}^n)_0$$
$$(40.3137)$$
$$+ .2118^{**}AF_{1,6} + .0206T_{s_0}$$
$$(.0589) \qquad (.0890)$$

$$R^2 = .2521$$
$$\overline{R}^2 = .2165$$

Standard Error of Estimate $= 108.83$

16. Monthly
     1952/10–1960/1
     $n = 88$

$$V_0 = 397.39 - 22.8202 (r_u - r_u{}^n)_0$$
$$(42.0238)$$
$$+ .2101^{**}AF_{1,6}$$
$$(.0587)$$
$$+ .0177T_{s_0} - 659.0196 (T/S)_0$$
$$(.0887) \qquad (516.5785)$$

$$R^2 = .2664^{**}$$
$$\overline{R}^2 = .2222$$

Standard Error of Estimate $= 107.79$

* Significant at the 5% level.
** Significant at the 1% level.
The standard F-ratio test was employed to test the significance of the R^2.
Regression coefficients were tested with the one-tailed 't' test.
$\overline{R}^2$ is R^2 corrected for degrees of freedom.

$V_{m,n}$ = Total new commitments voted during months $t = m$ to n, inclusive, and still outstanding at the end of the month voted. Source: LIAA *Forward Commitment Survey.*

$AF_{m,n}$ = The normal flow of available funds during months $t = m$ to n, inclusive. Computed as total acquisitions from commitments during this period less the stock of commitments outstanding at the beginning of the period and expected to be taken down by the end of $t = n$, less sales of Government securities during the period. Sources: *Forward Commitment Survey* and *Treasury Bulletin.*

XT_{S_M} = Excess holdings of short-term Treasury obligations at the end of the month, $t = m$. Computed as 65% of the difference between the sum of Treasury debt due or callable in decision to change the rate of new votings in response to a change in the availability of future funds, and the completion of loan proposals to the point of a finance committee voting decision. A similar but shorter overlap of voting decisions and funds availability is implicit in regression equations 1 and 2. Comparison of equations 3 and 4 show a somewhat stronger relationship when the lagged version of available funds is used.

In equation 5 a slightly different version of the available funds variable is used. In this case the estimate of available funds covers seven months including the month in which the voting decision is made. The purpose of this version is to facilitate comparison with equation 6, in which the seven months' estimate of available funds is split into two separate variables.[26] In this case, at least, a finer division in time of available funds does not improve the votings/funds relationship. Life companies may, of course, be able to find outlets for immediately available funds in the public market or quickly arranged private loans not involving forward commitments. Therefore it is not possible to conclude

---

[26] Data on takedowns expected to be delayed beyond six months is not subclassified into finer time divisions. Therefore the regression suggested above including available funds for the second six months cannot be run for aggregate data.

---

less than one year held by all life companies and \$300 million. SOURCE: *Treasury Bulletin*.

r_u = New Issue Grade 2 Public Utility Bond interest rate series. SOURCE: Bankers Trust Company.

r_u^n = Moving average of the past twelve monthly observations of r_u.

$(r_u - r_u^n)_m$ = Algebraic difference between r_u and r_u^n during the mth month.

T_{S_M} = The stock of short term Treasury obligations (due or callable in one year) held by life companies at the end of the mth month. SOURCE: *Treasury Bulletin*.

t_2, t_3, t_4 = Quarterly seasonal dummy variables. The first quarter dummy is the constant.

$(T/S)_m$ = Ratio of the stock of Treasury obligations (T) held by all life insurance companies to their total assets (S) at the end of the mth month. SOURCE: Institute of Life Insurance.

n = number of observations.

with certainty that it makes no difference to them whether there are funds available one or two months in the future as opposed to five or six months. The regression result suggests that this sort of difference in the time distribution of future funds does not affect the volume of total forward commitment authorizations.

Regression equations 7 and 8 were fit to investigate the case where short-term Treasury obligations are counted as part of available funds. The values which are added to the normal available funds observations represent the excess of short-term Treasuries held by life companies over an arbitrarily assigned, constant "minimum desired holdings." On an aggregated industry basis, the minimum target figure assigned is $300 million. This amount is not the absolute minimum held by life companies over the 1953–1959 period, but is a level which companies in the aggregate never dipped below more than a month at a time. Since we did not possess liquid asset data on the sample of companies covered in the forward commitment survey, this estimate of short-term Treasury debt was arrived at by deflation of the aggregate life company holdings of Treasuries due or callable in less than one year. On the basis of this estimate we do not find any confirmation of the hypothesis that liquid asset holdings are like anticipated normal cash flow in inducing new commitment votings. Nor do these liquidity observations make a significant contribution to explaining votings when they are included as a separate variable. These tests are deficient, however, because of the crudeness of the liquidity estimate. This crudeness exists not only because the estimate had to be made from aggregate industry data, but also because alternative short-term earning assets are not included. There is evidence that commercial paper became increasingly popular in larger life company portfolios during the late 1950s, as interest rates rose and managers of the cash flow position became more sophisticated. As time elapses and more observations are available from the LIAA *Cash Flow Survey*, a tighter test of this proposition can be made. In the "big picture," however, this is a marginal consideration since life companies have held swings in liquid assets to modest proportions (see Chapter V) so that the quantitative impact of pressure from the liquidity position on votings cannot be very great in any case.

In section III of Table VI-5, regressions are displayed which test the rate-of-return hypothesis, net of the effect of the volume of available future funds on commitment votings. The interest rate variable used in the regression results reported is designed to measure the level of current rates relative to normal interest rate levels. The interest rate series used is the Bankers Trust Grade 2 new issue public utility bond series. The normal rate in any month is computed as an average of the past twelve months' observations. We then use the arithmetic difference between the current month's observation and this normal rate as an independent variable. In regressions run on quarterly data, the value used is a simple average of the three months' observations. Similar regressions were run utilizing the raw observations of the Bankers Trust series themselves (r_u). Qualitatively the results were identical.

The results are quite consistently negative with respect to the rate-of-return hypothesis, even with the influence of available funds netted out. There is substantial negative colinearity between the level of interest rates and the volume of available future funds. This distorts the partial regression coefficients considerably and renders quantitative interpretation of them impossible. The qualitative result that flows from this set of regressions is quite clear, however. The time pattern of new commitment votings is positively associated with the volume of future available funds and negatively with the level of interest rates. The essential usefulness of the approach embodied in the loaned-up thesis is confirmed and the validity of the rate-of-return objective is refuted.

The volume of short-term Treasury obligations held by life companies was also included in some regressions. As above, there is no evidence that the liquidity position exerted positive pressure on votings. The same qualifications made above are also applicable to this conclusion, however. The ratio of total Government securities held in life company portfolios to their total assets was included as an additional independent variable in some equations. This is, of course, a trend variable and its effect, with cash flow and interest rate influences removed, would be expected to be secularly restrictive on votings as the stock of Government security holdings declined over time. This variable did not appear significant, however, and indeed, often (as in regression 16) its coefficient had a negative sign.

Seasonal dummies were employed in some of the regression equations in order to see how much of the residual variation in votings might be due to general seasonal influences. Regression 11 is presented as an example. Quarterly dummies were used; the first quarter being the base. In general, although there is some seasonal variation independent of the primary explanatory variables we have discussed, not much of the residual variation in votings is "explained" by the seasonal.

In sum, although the results leave much to be desired, they do lend credence to the loaned-up thesis; commitment votings are responsive to the portion of the normal inflow of future funds which is uncommitted. We did not find any confirmation of the hypothesis that the level of liquid assets was also a source of influence on new votings. The rate-of-return hypothesis was quite firmly rejected by the analysis.

There are several deficiencies in this analysis. We have assumed away errors in forecasts of cash flow by relating commitment votings to a measure of the flow of investible funds that actually turned out to be available. Our measure of liquid asset holdings is not wholly satisfactory. Finally, we have run the regression analysis over a rather peculiar period, that is, 1952–1959. We have argued that in the early part of this period, life insurance companies were in something closely approximating an open-to-buy situation. In the last three or so years, the open-to-buy characterization clearly does not apply. A transition from one environment to the other occurred in the intervening years. In open-to-buy circumstances, neither the anticipated normal inflow of available funds nor the level of bond yields is expected to be of relevance in explaining the time rate of commitment votings. Thus the hypotheses we are confronting have been asked to overcome the obstacle of being tested over a time period made up of three rather different portions including one portion in which the hypotheses could not be expected to apply and a second in which life companies were struggling with the problem of adapting their commitment behavior to new circumstances. Only the most recent part of the period is normal in the sense of presenting life companies with funds allocation problems similar to what they can expect to continue to face and normal in the sense that some time had elapsed in which they could adjust their lending mechanics to meet this new circumstance. We can and have analyzed the latter period separately, but we are obviously handicapped here by the small number of observations available. We do find added strength in the votings/available funds hypothesis during the 1957–1959 subperiod. And we find, at very best, only marginal support for the rate of return and liquid asset candidates.

We will have a word on the question of cash flow forecasting errors below. But first we must complete the discussion of the regression analysis at hand. There is evidence of substantial positive autocorrelation in the residuals of most of the equations' fit.[27] Since the interest rate and liquid asset variables have been rejected, the most meaningful relationship is the simple votings/available funds formulation. The serial correlation problem is graphically illustrated in Chart VI-6. In the upper panel of this chart, we have plotted the residuals from regression 1 in Table VI-5 ($V_{1,3} = 941 + .70AF_{1,6}$). The simple ratio, $V_{1,3}/AF_{1,6}$, in percentage terms, is displayed in the lower panel.[28] In either case it appears that a strong cyclical influence remains in new commitment votings even after the future available cash flow has been taken into account. This suggests the need to search for another explanatory variable. We have one unused hypothesis remaining — the servicing hypothesis. Let us see whether it can be of assistance here.

The Servicing Hypothesis

The servicing hypothesis, it will be recalled, points to the demand for the forward commitment service as an explanation of the time rate of new commitment votings. We have argued that the time configuration of the demand for loan commitments can

---

[27] There are some exceptions. For example, there is no sign of serial correlation in regressions where several explanatory variables are employed, and where lagged versions of the available funds and interest rate variables are used. These regressions are unsatisfactory from other points of view, however, including the presence of colinearity among the independent variables and wrong signs in some partial regression coefficients. The presence of autocorrelation was tested by calculation of the Durbin-Watson statistic for some representative regressions.

[28] One exact formulation of the loaned-up hypothesis could be $V_0/AF_{m,n} = K$ (a constant).

CHART VI-6. *Residuals from a Total Commitment Votings Regression Equation and the Ratio of Votings to Available Funds: Residuals Quarterly, 1952/IV–1959/IV and Ratio Quarterly, 1952/IV–1960/I*

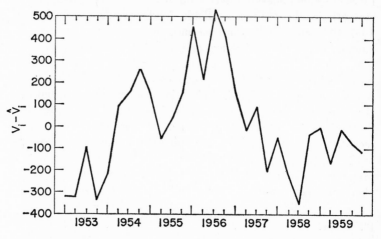

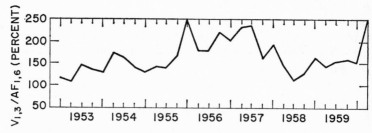

SOURCES AND NOTES:

Upper panel: Residuals [V(actual)-V(estimated)] from regression equation I (1) in Table VI-5.

$$V_{1,3} = 941.7 + .703\ AF_{1,6}$$

Lower panel: Ratio: $V_{1,3}$ to $AF_{1,6}$

be substantially different from the time pattern of interest rates. Therefore our rejection of the rate-of-return hypothesis does not necessarily imply rejection of the servicing hypothesis. Testing the latter hypothesis is difficult, however, because the demand for forward commitments, *per se*, is an elusive concept to measure.

To approach this problem let us re-examine Chart VI-6. We were concerned with the strong suggestion of a cyclical pattern in new votings, net of the influence of available funds. Commitment votings are heavy relative to the available funds regression prediction during 1954, and then again, more dramatically, from about the middle of 1955 to the end of 1956 or perhaps to mid-1957. The major components of total life company new commitment votings are plotted in Chart VI-7. Broadly speaking, it appears

CHART VI-7. New Commitment Votings of Life Insurance Companies by Asset Type: Quarterly, 1952/IV–1960/II

(millions of dollars)

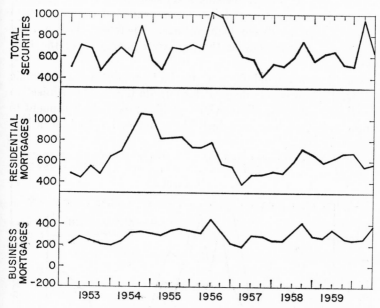

SOURCE: Companies reporting to the LIAA *Forward Commitment Survey*.

that residential mortgage loan votings dominated the 1954 experience, and that votings of corporate bonds were primarily responsible for the 1956 record. Can either of these experiences and the accompanying relatively "low" volume of residual votings at either end of the period be explained by the demand for forward commitments?

To answer this question, we need to anticipate the detailed

discussion of votings by sector in Chapters VII and VIII. There is a strong cycle-like pattern of mortgage loan votings visible in Chart VI-7. As we shall see, however, it is not plausible to consider this configuration as generated by cyclical swings in the demand for housing, mortgage funds, or mortgage commitments. Residential demand tends to change secularly in response to demographic factors, disposable income, population mobility, characteristics of the housing stock, etc., and is relatively impervious to moderate business cycle fluctuations. We shall argue in Chapter VII that one must look to changes in the supply of mortgage funds to explain the residential construction cycle and its reflection in life company mortgage loan votings. Therefore the servicing hypothesis is ruled out as the primary explanation of the 1954 experience.

On the other hand, it is a standard proposition of economic theory that corporate demand for outside financing is subject to relatively volatile cyclical swings. This proposition is thought to apply especially to the industrial, as opposed to public utility,

CHART VI-8. *Residuals from a Total Commitment Votings Equation and Manufacturing Sector Capital Appropriations: Quarterly, 1953/I–1959/IV*
(millions of dollars)

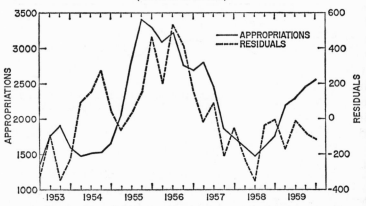

SOURCES AND NOTES: Residuals are the same as those plotted in Chart VI-6. The capital appropriations series is from the National Industrial Conference Board. The capital appropriations series appearing in this chart has been seasonally adjusted by the author using the centered moving average method.

sector.[29] Also, it is here that we conceived of the servicing hypothesis making institutional sense. We have no good proxy variable to represent the industrial sector's demand for outside funds, let alone their demand for forward commitments. This demand schedule is determined by a complex mix of real demand for capital goods and internal financing considerations which are beyond the scope of this study to estimate.

If we are willing to work within the broad classification of time periods discussed above, however, we may at least be able to make a rough and ready test of the plausibility of the servicing thesis. We know that the U.S. economy experienced a substantial capital goods boom during 1956–1957. Somewhere during this cyclical upswing, as the increase in new orders for plant and equipment began to outdistance the growth of internal funds, corporations were forced into the capital markets. One index of the time shape of this capital goods expansion, the National Industrial Conference Board's newly approved capital appropriations series for the manufacturing sector,[30] is plotted in Chart VI-8. This survey series records authorizations by top management for expenditure on new plant and equipment. Authorization, of course, precedes in time the placing of orders for capital goods. This place in the time sequence of the investment decision makes the approval series a likely index to compare with forward commitment votings. We have, therefore, also reproduced in Chart VI-8 the residuals from the votings/available funds regression which was plotted in Chart VI-6. As expected, the capital appropriations series yields no insights into the 1954 votings experience, but is at least roughly consistent with the relatively high level of votings (net of the funds influence) during 1955–1957, and with the subsequent decline in the votings residuals.

In Chart VI-9 we have plotted new commitments for manufacturing sector bonds by life companies along with the NICB series.[31]

---

[29] For a summary of financial sources in manufacturing during 1948–1960, see W. H. Locke Anderson, *Corporate Finance and Fixed Investment*, Chapter 2.

[30] This series is based on a quarterly survey of the largest manufacturing establishments conducted by the NICB. The figures we have used are based on data reported by 353 companies for 1953–1954, 511 companies for 1955–1957, and 602 companies for 1958–1960, adjusted by the NICB to the level of 602 companies currently reporting. Data are courtesy of the National Industrial Conference Board.

[31] For some regression estimates, see Chapter VIII.

There is obviously a great deal of quarter to quarter noise in life company commitments to lend to this sector, but manufacturing commitments are broadly consistent with the capital appropriations data during 1956–1957. To check on whether this sort of demand proxy in fact contributes to the explanation of total investment votings during the 1950s, we ran a few additional regressions on

CHART VI-9. *Manufacturing Sector, Newly Approved Capital Appropriations and New Forward Commitments Made by Life Insurance Companies: Quarterly, 1953/I–1960/I*

(millions of dollars)

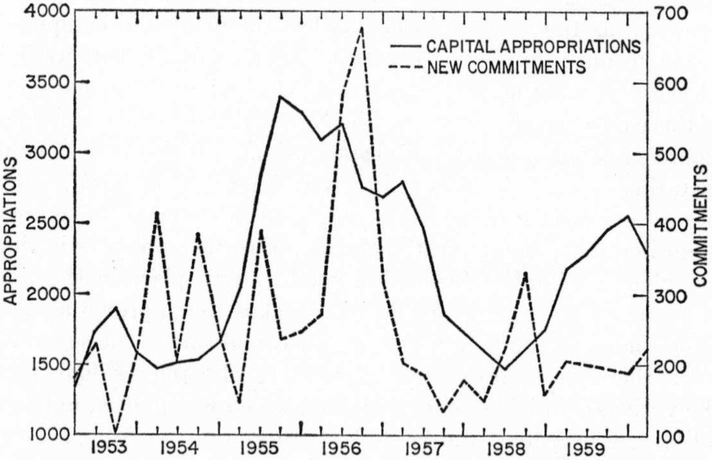

SOURCES AND NOTES: The capital appropriations series is identical to the one plotted in Chart VI-8. Life insurance commitments to the manufacturing sector are from the LIAA *Forward Commitment Survey*.

total votings. The results reported in Table VI-6 indicate that the capital appropriations variable is significant and contributes to at least a modest improvement in R^2. We also reintroduced the level of bond yields as a measure of the influence of the interest rate cycle but found (equation 3) that even with the funds and commitment demand proxy variables partialed out, the level of interest rates had no influence on the time pattern of total votings.

TABLE VI-6. *Further Regression Analysis of Total New Investment Authorizations:*
Quarterly, 1953/I-1959/IV

$$n = 28$$

(1) $V = 968.7 + .6884 AF_{0,1}$
   (.1538)
   $R^2 = .434$ $s = 224.2$
   $\overline{R}^2 = .413$ $\bar{s} = 232.6$

(2) $V = 498.9 + .8298 AF_{0,1} + .1455 CAN$
   (.1528)   (.0601)
   $R^2 = .542$ $s = 201.8$
   $\overline{R}^2 = .505$ $\bar{s} = 213.5$

(3) $V = 531.9 + .8096 AF_{0,1} + .1432 CAN - 18.5 (r_u - r_u^n)$
   (.2136)   (.0636)   (133.7)
   $R^2 = .542$ $s = 201.7$
   $\overline{R}^2 = .485$ $\bar{s} = 217.9$

NOTE: CAN = National Industrial Conference Board series on new capital appropriations. s = standard error of estimate and $\bar{s} = s$ adjusted for degrees of freedom.

Complementarity in the Roles of the Loaned-up and Servicing Hypothesis

We have now reached a point at which we have accepted the loaned-up goal as a portfolio objective which explains a significant part of the variance in life company commitment votings over time. We have further found some presumptive evidence that the servicing hypothesis explains an additional portion of the variance in votings. As things stand, these seem to be competing objectives, which may at times be pulling the life company commitment decision in opposite directions. It is possible, however, that over a considerable range these goals may be essentially complementary. We proceed to investigate this possibility.

We have made a distinction between demand for a forward commitment and demand for current funds. This distinction has little meaning when the lag time between the commitment and delivery of the funds is quite short, but it becomes sharper the longer the commitment-takedown lag. If the increased pace of new commitment votings during a cyclical investment boom, such as the 1955–1957 experience we have been discussing, simply reflects a coinciding time rate of increase in the demand for current funds (i.e., most of the new commitments result in delivered loans within two or three months), then the forward commitment process is a relatively insignificant piece of mechanics from the perspective of understanding the role of the capital markets in financing a capital goods boom. The forward commitment process is most relevant for explanation and forecasting if the cycle is characterized by shifts in the demand for *delayed takedown* forward commitments. Thus we might plausibly have taken the proportion of votings which constituted delayed-takedown commitments as an index of the demand for forward commitments, arguing that an increase in the demand for forward commitments *per se* ought to be reflected in an increase of delayed takedown commitments as a percentage of total votings.

On the other hand, the loaned-up hypothesis seemed to be primarily relevant for explaining loan commitments which involved a relatively short time lag to delivery. Indeed, we suggested that the relevant function to estimate in the regression analysis would be of the form:

$$V_{0(6)} = \alpha + \beta A F_{1,6}$$

where, it will be recalled, $V_{0(6)}$ referred only to votings which were expected to result in delivered loans within six months. Therefore the two hypotheses may be complementary in the sense that the loaned-up hypothesis is critical for explaining votings expected to result in loans within k months, and the servicing hypothesis is especially useful for explaining the volume of votings for which takedowns are anticipated to occur beyond k months. We did not run separate regressions for votings classified by expected takedown dates because the commitment survey does not provide this information.

To obtain some notion regarding the credibility of this argument, we did take the opportunity to work through the files of one of the larger life companies and record expected takedown dates for new commitments made during the relevant time period. In Chart VI-10 we have plotted for this company the percentage of each quarter's security votings for which, at the time of voting,

CHART VI-10. *Percentage of New Security Commitments for Which Takedown Is Expected to Be Delayed More than Six Months: Quarterly, 1951/IV–1954/IV and 1956/I–1959/IV*

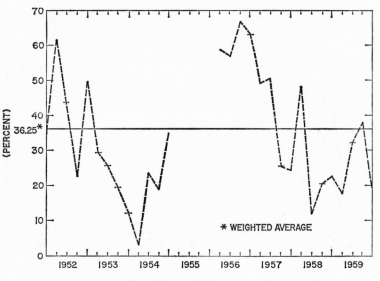

SOURCE: A large life insurance company.

the loan takedown was anticipated to be more than six months away.[32]   This information was compiled from a monthly itemized listing of all security commitments voted on favorably by the finance committee.   Over the period for which these listings were available, October 1951–November 1954, January 1956–December 1959, about 36% of the dollar volume of security commitments involved delayed (over six months) takedowns.   Unfortunately the appropriate records were missing from the files for the period December 1954–December 1955.   Nevertheless it is clear that from some point in 1955 through the second quarter of 1957, the proportion of delayed takedown votings was consistently and substantially higher than the average for the entire period, and quite high relative to preceding and succeeding quarters.   For this one company at least we have dramatic confirmation of the above argument.

---

[32] In this calculation we have included in total votings, commitments which resulted in immediate delivery of funds, i.e., within the voting month.

A somewhat more detailed picture of the same phenomenon for corporate bond votings is graphed in Chart VI-11. Three fre-

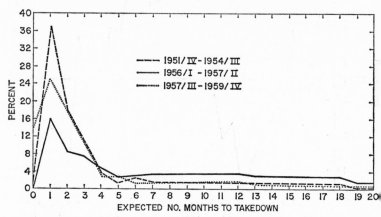

CHART VI-11. Percentage Distribution of New Corporate Bond Commitments Classified by Expected Lag Between Commitment and Acquisition: Selected Periods, 1951/IV–1959/IV

SOURCE: A large life insurance company (same as Chart VI-10).

quency distributions are displayed in this chart, one for each of three time periods. Each graph shows the percentage distribution of corporate bond votings authorized during the period by the number of months expected to elapse between voting and takedown. Here, as above, we have included new commitments which were closed, i.e., funds delivered, before the end of the month. These are represented as having a zero commitment-takedown lag on the chart. We sorted out the heavy votings period we have been considering, 1956 to mid-1957, from the remainder of the period. This middle time period is strikingly different from its predecessor and successor. In the first and third periods, about two-thirds of this company's corporate bond votings had anticipated takedown dates within three months of the voting month. Less than one-third of the middle period's votings were due for closing this soon. The proportion expected to be closed within six months is only 42% during the middle period as against nearly three-quarters for the remaining months. Obviously very little weight can be placed on one company's record. To gain an impression as to what difference it might make to have this sort of information available for all companies, however, we made a bold calculation. On the very heroic assumption that this company's experience was representative of all companies included in the commitment survey, we made quarterly estimates of the proportion of aggregate votings for which takedown was anticipated within six months. The votings series used in the regressions reported in Table VI-5 was divided into two components, security votings and mortgage votings. From the records of the company we have been discussing we computed, for each quarter for which the data were available, the percentage of that quarter's security votings which were anticipated to lead to closed loans by the end of six months. These percentages were then applied to the aggregate security votings to provide an estimate of the dollar volume of security votings for which takedown was expected in six months. We did not possess the analogous data for mortgage loans. Therefore we did not attempt to adjust mortgage votings for quarter-to-quarter variations in the time distribution of voting-takedown lags, but simply assumed that the proportion of mortgage votings for which takedown was anticipated in six months was constant throughout the period. For this constant percentage we used 57%.[33] Having done this, we summed the adjusted security voting and mortgage voting series and used this total as the dependent variable in a regression with six months available funds as the independent variable. This is comparable to regression 1 in Table VI-5, except that the year 1955 for which we had no data to make the adjustment in votings of securities is excluded. The result of this computation is:

---

[33] The 57% figure is derived from a chart by Saul Klaman which depicts the percentage distribution of actual disbursement of mortgage funds over the months following the commitment month for a "large eastern life insurance company." Only loans of less than $50,000 are included. See Klaman, *The Postwar Residential Mortgage Market*, p. 146. In general we would expect variation over time in commitment-takedown lags to be smaller for mortgage commitments than it is for securities. The lag distribution will obviously vary, however, with changes in the mix of new and existing properties, residential and commercial properties, and conventional and federally underwritten loans.

Quarterly $V^4_{1,3(6)} = 363.88 + .5989^*AF_{1,6}$
1952/IV–1954/IV; $(.0830)$
1956/I–1959/IV
$n = 25$ $R^2 = .6937^*$
Standard Error of Estimate = 120.01

* Significant at the 1% level.

This is a substantial improvement in fit. Although this specific equation is not to be taken seriously, it appears that this is a fruitful approach to take in unraveling the mysteries of the time rate of commitment votings. In Chart VI-12 we have plotted

CHART VI-12. *Residuals from Two Regression Equations in Which Total New Commitments Voted Appears as the Dependent Variable: Quarterly, 1952/IV–1959/IV*

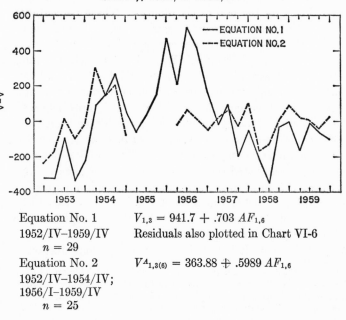

Equation No. 1 $V_{1,3} = 941.7 + .703\ AF_{1,6}$
1952/IV–1959/IV Residuals also plotted in Chart VI-6
$n = 29$

Equation No. 2 $V^4_{1,3(6)} = 363.88 + .5989\ AF_{1,6}$
1952/IV–1954/IV;
1956/I–1959/IV
$n = 25$

the residuals from this regression and, for comparison, the residuals from equation No. I (1), Table VI-5, which we have displayed above in Chart VI-6. The adjustment in the votings series worked in the time period where it was expected to. The residuals from the regression for 1956–1957 are not only much reduced in size but also show no nonrandom characteristics. Also, as expected, this procedure made no contribution to explaining the 1954 experience. Further progress involves proceeding deeper into an investigation of the composition of total votings. This will be the task of Chapters VII and VIII.

We can make a rough check on whether the commitment-take-down lag experience of the company whose records we used was indeed at all representative of the industry's experience. We can compute from the *Forward Commitment Survey* data, monthly ratios of the dollar volume of outstanding commitments for which take-down is anticipated in six months to the total stock of outstanding commitments. The variation in the proportion of new commitments expected to lead to closed loans in six months will, of course, be reflected less dramatically in the proportion of the stock of commitments due for takedown in six months. Comparable stock ratios can be computed for Company X. Summary ratios are presented for the most relevant asset category, business and industrial bonds, in Table VI-7. All months for which the data

TABLE VI-7. Ratio of the Stock of Outstanding Commitments Expected to Be Taken Down Within Six Months to the Total Stock of Commitments: Business and Industrial Bonds

	Industry	Company X
September 1952–November 1954	.480	.627
January 1956–June 1957	.404	.436
July 1957–January 1960	.484	.507
Weighted Average	.458	.527

SOURCES: Industry data are from the LIAA, *Forward Commitment Survey,* and coverage is limited to companies reporting in that survey. Company X data are taken from the company's commitment survey forms submitted monthly to the LIAA. The ratios are weighted averages of monthly ratios for the period indicated; weighted by the stock of business and industrial bond commitments outstanding.

are available from both sources are included. It appears that Company X is not as representative a firm as we should desire. A higher proportion of its industrial bond commitments was expected to be closed in six months than was true for the industry. More importantly, however, the variation in this proportion over time is much less pronounced for the industry than for Company X. Therefore, although the phenomenon of increased delayed takedown bond commitments during the middle time period is clearly present in the industry figures, it appears that we cannot count on the segregation of votings by anticipated takedown dates to do as much for us as the test calculation above suggested. On a qualitative basis we find additional confirmation in Table VI-6 for the premise that the servicing hypothesis has a complementary role to play alongside the loaned-up thesis in explaining the time sequence of total new commitment authorizations. Quantitatively, it appears that the increase in long delayed takedown votings during two years beginning at the middle of 1955 may not be substantial enough to explain all the relatively large volume of total votings during this period.

Problems of Forecasting and Control

We have indicated that the period with which we have been concerned in the preceding empirical analysis, 1952–1959, is a peculiarly difficult one from which to derive useful generalizations about the determinants of investment decisions. This difficulty stems from the changing nature of the life insurance industry's supply of funds schedule over the period. In the early postwar years the enormous holdings of Government securities in life company portfolios gave them an essentially perfectly elastic supply of funds schedule, and therefore no real problems of portfolio choice with regard to the time rate of commitments and acquisitions or among alternative assets. This was still a reasonable approximation of the situation in 1952. During the subsequent years, however, as both life company holdings and the prices of Treasury bonds declined and the demand for funds rose, the environment changed to one in which a very real cash flow constraint emerged, and life companies were faced with difficult problems of timing and asset choice for the first time since the 1920s.

Among the new problems which faced life companies in this situation were the tasks of developing the necessary mechanics to successfully (a) forecast their future cash flow, and (b) control the volume of new commitments voted. In circumstances of this sort, it would not be surprising to find that life companies went through a time-consuming learning process before recognizing the need for new operational mechanics and successfully implementing them. Our qualitative impression is that indeed this was the case. Frequent references were made by investment officers we interviewed to past difficulties arising from having "overcommitted" the cash flow. This problem seemed to be particularly common during the 1955–1957 subperiod.

Two causes of overcommitment situations were most often cited: (a) overestimation of cash flow from the insurance operation, and (b) inadequate control over the rate of issuance of new commitments. If overcommitment problems of this sort were reasonably common and quantitatively significant, then our statistical procedures are bound to fall that much short of explaining the variation in total votings. We have assumed in the empirical analysis in this chapter that life companies correctly forecast their cash flow and that they had effective control over the voting of new commitments so that commitments could be issued at the rate appropriate for meeting the portfolio objectives involved. Perhaps some of the unexplained variation in commitment votings is due to forecasting and control problems.

We have no hard evidence on either possibility. However, we did find some evidence of systematic forecasting errors in cash flow estimation during the years 1958–1960 (see Chapter V). A number of people connected with the industry have suggested that many life companies found themselves overcommitted in 1956–1957 because something unanticipated happened to cash flow. From Table VI-8 it is clear that something did happen to the net flow of funds through insurance companies about this time; it ceased growing in 1956 and declined in 1957. The villains primarily responsible for this turn of events seem to have been the change in the insurance product mix away from policies with a strong savings element and high interest rates.[34] Whether or not this reduction in the net inflow of funds was forecast by life companies, we do not know. Our impression is, however, that not many companies had detailed cash flow estimating procedures in the mid-1950s. As we have seen, they were only beginning to

---

[34] For an examination of this experience, see Wright, "Gross Flow of Savings and Investment Funds Through Life Insurance Companies."

TABLE VI-8. Flow of Savings Through U.S. Life Insurance Companies:
1952–1958

(millions of dollars)

Year	(1) Gross Inflow	(2) Gross Outflow	(3) Net Inflow	(4) Net Change in Total Assets
1952	$13,422	$ 8,625	$4,797	$5,097
1953	14,649	9,649	5,000	5,158
1954	15,727	10,509	5,218	5,953
1955	17,051	11,540	5,511	5,946
1956	18,380	12,811	5,569	5,579
1957	19,899	14,698	5,201	5,298
1958	20,937	15,598	5,339	6,271

Data are on an accrual basis computed from annual statements of all U.S. legal reserve life insurance companies.

Col. (1): Gross inflow from premiums, investment income and miscellaneous sources.

Col. (2): Gross outflow to benefit payments, expenses, taxes, dividends, policy loans and miscellaneous payments.

Col. (3): Column (1) less column (2).

Col. (4): Column (3) plus the net increase in policy loans plus net capital gains.

SOURCE: Wright, "Gross Flow of Savings and Investment Funds Through Life Insurance Companies."

need them. Forecasts based on simple projections would indeed have been overoptimistic. Therefore, it may be that some credence has to be given to forecasting errors as an explanation of the high volume of votings relative to the available funds flow that we observed during the mid-1953 to mid-1957 period.

The problem of control over the rate of votings seems to have been particularly acute in mortgage departments. As we have seen, control difficulties are a consequence of decentralized origination of mortgage loans. We do not know how serious this problem has been. If it was a problem, it most likely applies with particular strength to the 1954–1955 votings experience. We know that the Prudential was faced with an apparently involuntary overcommitment situation in mortgages that forced it to the extraordinary expedient, for life companies, of public borrowing from commercial banks. Our interview information indicated that the Prudential responded to this event by tightening the quota system allocating funds to its branch office originators of mortgage loans. Most of the companies interviewed reported initiating some form of quotas to control the generation of mortgage loan commitments by branch offices and contract correspondents. It is possible therefore that allocation control problems during the transition away from an open-to-buy environment had something to do with the residual variation in votings from our regression analysis.

These particular problems should be much less troublesome as time passes. By the end of the 1950s life companies had reduced their stock of Treasury obligations to a level at which it could no longer be a substantial source of extraordinary funds. In many cases they had instituted relatively detailed cash flow forecasting procedures and finer controls over the process of issuing new commitments. In any case, the existence of improved anticipatory cash flow data will permit a more exact testing of the loaned-up hypothesis than we have been able to perform.

Summary

In this chapter we have dealt with the role of forward commitments in the allocation over time of the life insurance company flow of investible funds. In seeking to explain the time sequence of forward commitment votings three hypotheses were examined. Two of these hypotheses derived from institutional considerations of objectives of portfolio policy and the mechanics of the investment operation in the life insurance context. The third arose naturally from consideration of yield maximization as a general principle governing portfolio decisions.

The loaned-up hypothesis is a logical extension of Chapter V's conclusion that life companies aim at maintaining a fully invested position, i.e., at minimizing fluctuations in liquid asset holdings. In this chapter we have examined the proposition that the forward commitment device is used to facilitate achievement and maintenance of a fully invested position. If this were the case, we would expect to find the time rate of new commitment votings responsive to the volume of uncommitted funds available during the upcoming months. The level of life company liquid asset holdings was also considered relevant in this connection.

The forward commitment seems to make sense to life company investment officers as a nonprice competitive service with which attractive loan and investment opportunities can be exploited. As a competitive device it has particular value in making private placement deals attractive to potential borrowers. To maintain its usefulness in competing for loans, life companies must be ready to meet borrowers' demands for the forward commitment service when they arise. This means that the time rate of forward commitment votings can be expected to be influenced by the demand for forward commitments *per se*. We have labeled this proposition the servicing hypothesis.

Finally, it made sense to think of life companies utilizing the forward commitment procedure as a means of influencing investment timing in order to take advantage of cyclical swings in interest rates. This means concentration of investment decisions (new commitments) in periods of "high" interest rates. In this manner life companies could take advantage of the interest rate cycle without compromising their basic objective to remain fully invested. We have referred to this argument as the rate of return over time hypothesis. If this were a significant concern of life companies, we would expect to observe that life company commitment votings are sensitive to the level of interest rates.

We conducted a partial test of the significance of the rate of return over time objective by calculating whether, in fact, life companies had successfully concentrated commitment votings to take advantage of the interest rate cycle. For the period studied, October 1952 to June 1960, we found that they had not. Given the assumptions under which the computation was made, we found that the time sequence of investment decisions made by life companies over the period did not produce higher yields on the average than would have been obtained had investment decisions been simultaneous in time with acquisitions. It appeared that, if anything, separation in time of the investment decision from acquisitions resulted in some reduction of life company investment return over the period.

The other major piece of empirical work reported in this chapter was a regression analysis of life company votings. Each of the variables suggested by the trinity of alternative hypotheses was tried as an explanatory variable. This analysis led to a rejection of the rate of return over time objective as an explanation of life company voting behavior. The two institutional hypotheses were found to contribute significantly to an understanding of the time pattern of commitment votings. We found no evidence that the liquidity position had any additional influence on votings, however.

We suggested that to some degree the loaned-up and servicing hypotheses play different or complementary roles in their effect on the time rate of new commitment authorizations. The loaned-up hypothesis focuses particularly on explaining voting decisions for new commitments which are expected to result in closed loans within the reasonably near future, say six months. On the other hand, the servicing hypothesis has a more relevant application in explaining votings with a longer commitment to takedown lag. We pointed out a number of deficiencies in the empirical work that led to these conclusions. If the substance of the conclusions is accepted, however, we view life companies as being consistently concerned with the proportion of the anticipated cash flow that is currently committed, and responding in their voting decisions to maintain a desirable stock of commitments relative to cash flow forecasts. Votings are triggered by available funds. On top of this is a desire to service customers or potential customers who wish to make use of the forward commitment service. Satisfaction of this demand may or may not conflict with the loaned-up objective. In short, the behavior of life company investment officers in determining their time rate of commitment votings suggests they prefer the "quiet life" and "keeping the customers happy" to speculating on future interest rates.

Finally we noted some of the peculiar characteristics of the 1952–1959 period which tended to obscure the manner in which the primary determinants of new commitments exercise their influence. These included the relative disappearance over time of the Government securities portfolio as a source of available funds, and difficulties involved in cash flow forecasting and initiating controls over the issuance of new commitments. We have left much unexplained. Further progress seems to depend on probing the determinants of the portfolio mix. We turn to an investigation of this problem in Chapter VII.

APPENDIX VI-A

Cancellations of Commitments

The evidence on cancellations of loan commitments is slim. The LIAA began collecting data on cancellations only in 1957. The dollar figures for major categories are displayed in Table VI-A-1. If there is a tendency on the part of borrowers to cancel commitments made at high interest rates, it should be reflected in increased cancellations during 1958. There is some tendency in this direction visible in the data in Table VI-A-1.

Table VI-A-2 relates cancellations of loan commitments to

TABLE VI-A-1. Cancellations of Loan Commitments Made by Life Insurance Companies: Quarterly, 1957/I–1960/II
(millions of dollars)

Quarter	All Commitments	Corporate Bonds	Business and Industrial	Residential Mortgages
1957/I	$149.1	$ 37.5	$18.5	$77.4
II	190.6	62.9	28.6	80.5
III	129.0	27.2	24.6	56.9
IV	178.6	27.9	55.1	55.0
1958–I	159.7	36.3	26.4	63.3
II	207.5	46.7	72.7	66.2
III	239.5	57.1	86.4	66.3
IV	245.1	57.3	75.3	71.4
1959/I	171.5	40.8	48.9	63.5
II	158.5	39.0	41.0	61.4
III	286.0	156.7	41.7	73.2
IV	169.1	18.2	47.9	81.0
1960/I	153.7	36.3	39.1	58.0
II	201.8	74.6	49.0	62.2

SOURCE: LIAA *Forward Commitment Survey.*

takedown of commitments in the same quarter. Here also there is evidence of some tendency toward a higher rate of cancellations in 1958.

TABLE VI-A-2. *Ratio of Loan Commitments Canceled to Loan Commitments Resulting in Acquisitions Made by Life Insurance Companies: Quarterly, 1957/I–1960/II*

Quarter	Ratio	Quarter	Ratio
1957/I	.108	1959/I	.124
II	.148	II	.104
III	.097	III	.196
IV	.121	IV	.099
1958/I	.133	1960/I	.104
II	.162	II	.144
III	.171		
IV	.136		

SOURCE: LIAA, *Forward Commitment Survey.*

In general, disposition of loan commitments between loans acquired and commitments canceled runs nearly 9 to 1; i.e., about 10% of commitments end up being canceled. For 1957 as a whole, about 89% of commitments disposed of resulted in loan acquisitions; in 1958 the figure was 87%; in 1959, 89%; and the first half of 1960, 89%. This is not a particularly striking swing in the composition. One explanation for the moderate impact may be that the reduction in interest rates was short-lived. Most public market interest rate series turned down sharply in late 1957 but rose again in mid-1958, so that by the end of the third quarter interest rates were back in the neighborhood of previous highs. The brief period of low rates resulted in substantially fewer utility bond calls than had occurred in 1954 and may well have reduced the volume of commitment cancellations also. Yields on private placements seem to be a little sluggish on the turns relative to publicly issued bonds, and interest rates obtained by life insurance companies apparently softened only moderately in 1958. Thus there was not much incentive to cancel a loan commitment in order to enter into a new direct placement loan contract with another lender.

Saul Klaman (*The Postwar Residential Mortgage Market*, p. 144) found that for one large life insurance company on which he had evidence, mortgage commitment attrition was very sensitive to cyclical movements in interest rates. This particular company reported that the proportion of mortgage commitments canceled varied from 10% to 40%, depending on the spread between yields on outstanding commitments and the yields being offered on new commitments. Heavy commitment attrition was observed during the 1953–1954 recession and the attrition rate reportedly declined sharply during 1955–1956.

In summary, there is some evidence, although not overwhelming, which suggests that loan commitment cancellations are more likely to occur on high interest rate loans. Therefore with reference to the problem discussed in Chapter VI, a rate of return calculated on the basis of loan votings is likely to overstate somewhat the rate of return finally achieved.

APPENDIX VI-B

TABLE VI-B-1. *Interest Rate Series Used in the Average Rate of Return Calculations Displayed in Tables VI-1 and VI-2*

Category:	(1) Corporate Bonds	(2) Conventional Residential Mortgage Loans	(3) Federally Underwritten Mortgage Loans	(4) Business and Commercial Mortgage Loans
Month				
1952/10	3.26	4.33	3.85	4.03
11	3.21	4.33	3.85	4.03
12	3.18	4.33	3.86	4.03
1953/ 1	3.23	4.37	3.87	4.09
2	3.36	4.37	3.87	4.09
3	3.42	4.37	3.87	4.09
4	3.62	4.38	3.88	4.16
5	3.83	4.38	3.89	4.16
6	3.92	4.38	3.96	4.16
7	3.68	4.41	4.30	4.23
8	3.64	4.41	4.40	4.23
9	3.70	4.41	4.32	4.23
10	3.42	4.52	4.32	4.26
11	3.30	4.52	4.30	4.26
12	3.33	4.52	4.35	4.26
1954/ 1	3.24	4.40	4.30	4.24
2	3.05	4.40	4.30	4.24
3	2.98	4.40	4.25	4.24
4	3.00	4.22	4.25	4.10
5	3.06	4.22	4.20	4.10
6	3.04	4.22	4.15	4.10
7	3.02	4.17	4.10	4.24
8	3.05	4.17	4.05	4.24
9	3.10	4.17	4.05	4.24
10	3.04	4.16	4.05	4.12
11	3.05	4.16	4.05	4.12
12	3.07	4.16	4.05	4.12

TABLE VI-B-1 (continued)

Category:	(1) Corporate Bonds	(2) Conventional Residential Mortgage Loans	(3) Federally Underwritten Mortgage Loans	(4) Business and Commercial Mortgage Loans
Month				
1955/ 1	3.13	4.17	4.05	4.21
2	3.18	4.17	4.05	4.21
3	3.25	4.17	4.05	4.21
4	3.21	4.20	4.10	4.26
5	3.28	4.20	4.10	4.26
6	3.23	4.20	4.15	4.26
7	3.30	4.26	4.15	4.30
8	3.50	4.26	4.20	4.30
9	3.32	4.26	4.20	4.30
10	3.25	4.33	4.25	4.29
11	3.28	4.33	4.25	4.29
12	3.37	4.33	4.25	4.29
1956/ 1	3.25	4.33	4.25	4.32
2	3.20	4.33	4.25	4.32
3	3.38	4.33	4.25	4.32
4	3.60	4.34	4.25	4.39
5	3.64	4.34	4.25	4.39
6	3.55	4.34	4.25	4.39
7	3.75	4.46	4.35	4.58
8	4.13	4.46	4.35	4.58
9	4.12	4.46	4.40	4.58
10	4.16	4.61	4.50	4.60
11	4.30	4.61	4.53	4.60
12	4.35	4.61	4.62	4.60
1957/ 1	4.51	4.76	4.81	4.76
2	4.25	4.76	4.81	4.76
3	4.31	4.76	4.81	4.76
4	4.40	4.76	4.81	4.71
5	4.65	4.76	4.81	4.71
6	4.96	4.76	4.81	4.71
7	4.85	4.88	4.91	4.95
8	4.91	4.88	5.02	4.95
9	4.84	4.88	5.02	4.95
10	4.92	5.24	5.13	5.18
11	4.85	5.24	5.11	5.18
12	4.43	5.24	5.11	5.18

TABLE VI-B-1 (continued)

Category:	(1) Corporate Bonds	(2) Conventional Residential Mortgage Loans	(3) Federally Underwritten Mortgage Loans	(4) Business and Commercial Mortgage Loans
Month				
1958/ 1	3.75	5.20	5.09	5.12
2	3.83	5.20	5.06	5.12
3	4.14	5.20	5.01	5.12
4	3.89	5.00	4.95	5.13
5	3.97	5.00	4.90	5.13
6	3.94	5.00	4.90	5.13
7	4.03	4.89	4.85	4.98
8	4.42	4.89	4.85	4.98
9	4.75	4.89	4.95	4.98
10	4.54	5.16	5.06	5.15
11	4.50	5.16	5.06	5.15
12	4.57	5.16	5.11	5.15
1959/ 1	4.64	5.21	5.11	4.98
2	4.52	5.21	5.11	4.98
3	4.45	5.21	5.11	4.98
4	4.67	5.22	5.11	5.20
5	4.96	5.22	5.16	5.20
6	4.96	5.22	5.16	5.20
7	4.93	5.42	5.22	5.21
8	4.95	5.42	5.27	5.21
9	5.32	5.42	5.33	5.21
10	5.22	5.63	5.57	5.41
11	5.21	5.63	5.57	5.41
12	5.28	5.63	5.62	5.41
1960/ 1	5.00	5.75	5.68	5.37
2	5.12	5.80	5.68	5.37
3	4.90	5.80	5.68	5.37
4	4.92	5.80	5.65	5.35
5	4.96	5.80	5.65	5.35
6	4.77	5.75	5.65	5.35

NOTES AND SOURCES:

Col. (1): Grade 2 public utility bond new issue yields. SOURCE: Bankers Trust Company.

Col. (2): Composite series which splices yield data from Klaman, *The Postwar Residential Mortgage Market*, Chart 8, p. 81 and survey data on conventional home mortgage loans reported in *House and Home,* monthly. The figures for 1952–1956 are from Klaman. These rates represent a weighted average of contract interest rates reported by four life insurance companies. The post 1956 yields are derived from interest rate data on loans originated by insurance companies in ten metropolitan areas. These data are based on commitments to make loans for future delivery on "houses of typical average local quality with respect to design, location, and construction."

Col. (3): Series is a composite of effective yields reported on FHA-VA loans by respondent originating mortgage lenders in ten metropolitan areas. Yields are based on commitments to acquire loans of 25-year maturities with down payments of 5% or more. Yields are computed on a payments-to-maturity basis. These data are from *House and Home,* monthly, and apply to houses of the same characteristics as indicated in the Col. (2) note.

Col. (4): Series represents interest rates obtained on Manhattan real estate loans of over $10,000. Prepared by James Felt and Co., New York, New York.

The mortgage loan interest rates shown in Table VI-B-1 represent the original mortgage yields less a uniform deduction for lending costs in order to make them roughly comparable to corporate bond yields. Fifty basis points were deducted from the two residential mortgage loan yield series and thirty basis points from the business mortgage loan interest rates.

The average rate of return reported for "total investments" in Tables VI-1 and VI-2 is a weighted average of the yields by category weighted by the dollar volume of new commitments (acquisitions) over the period in question.

Chapter VII

ALLOCATION OF INVESTIBLE

FUNDS AMONG ALTERNATIVE ASSETS

Up to this point we have been concerned with the interperiod allocation of funds by life insurance companies during the postwar years. In particular, we have examined the extent to which life companies have been able and have, in fact, adjusted their sequential investment flow to variations in, and changing expectations regarding, the level of interest rates. This investigation has been concerned with both secular and cyclical responses to rates of return. We have found limited evidence that life companies alter their time pattern of investment activity in response to changes in or expectations about the time path of interest rates.

A Review

In Chapters I, III, and IV, the secular pattern of life company credit extensions to the private sector was investigated. A brief examination of maturity policy in Chapter I led to rejection of the hypothesis that asset maturity selection is related to the level of interest rates. It appeared that statutory constraints, asset valuation regulations, the maturity structure of life company liabilities, and traditional risk preferences narrowed the choice of maturities within the set of eligible assets very considerably, and within the acceptable set other considerations dominated the final portfolio selections.

Most life companies entered the postwar era with a portfolio composition clearly in disequilibrium as a result of depression and wartime acquisitions of U.S. Treasury obligations. The existence of a substantial discrepancy between actual and desired Government security holdings was made dramatically evident by a rapid liquidation of Governments by life companies during the 1947–1951 period. We characterized this period as an open-to-buy environment, emphasizing the willingness of life companies to acquire private sector debt obligations meeting life company eligibility standards in unlimited quantities at a modest risk premium over the going yield on long-term Treasury bonds. After 1951 the trading of Government for private debt obligations in life company portfolios continued but at a much abated pace. The adjustment proceeded at a slowed rate throughout the 1950s and well into the 1960s.

No simple explanation of the time configuration of Government securities was discovered. A substantial decline in the rate of disposals after 1951, however, was shown to be consistent with continuance of an open-to-buy policy on the part of life insurance companies. An abrupt reduction in Treasury bond sales proved explainable in terms of shifts in the normal supply of and demand for life insurance company funds. These schedule shifts were in part a consequence of a tighter monetary policy made potent by reasonably effective government-administered contract rates on federally underwritten mortgage loans. To the extent that life companies' portfolio choice behavior could be accurately characterized by the open-to-buy hypothesis, the time path of this particular stock adjustment was consistent with pursuance of a yield maximization objective. Spreading out the liquidation over time in anticipation of secularly rising interest rates and widening yield spreads did not appear to be a recommended means of improving investment return.

Although there is evidence of yield responsiveness in the intertemporal allocation of funds accomplished by life companies' trading Government securities for private sector debt issues, the open-to-buy proposition is not able to explain much more than half of the post-1951 reduction in sales of Governments. Even within this explanation, life companies were viewed as not adopting an open-to-buy posture with respect to all eligible private loan opportunities; in particular, concern about the quality of federally underwritten loans and a distaste for price discounts on these loans limited their acquisitions in the FHA-VA sector. In addition, we found that reluctance to absorb sizable book losses on bond sales inhibited the liquidation of Governments. Finally, the maturity composition of Treasury debt in life company portfolios and inertia in some companies contributed to explaining the time pattern of portfolio adjustment.

Next we turned to interperiod shifts in life company investment of loanable funds in a cyclical context. In Chapter V, we examined the extent to which life companies divorced investment of funds from cash inflow by making systematic use of bank credit and/or altering their liquid asset holdings. It appeared that life companies essentially adhered to the objective of investing funds as they became available. Modest cyclical patterns in borrowing and liquidity holdings were observable, however. We found no evidence that these cyclical patterns resulted from an attempt of life companies to improve portfolio return by playing the cyclical interest rate pattern. The liquidity cycle seemed to result largely from cash flow and commitment takedown forecasting errors and concentration of security sales in periods of high bond prices due to a distaste for absorbing book losses on sales.

Observable life company borrowing was largely confined to mortgage warehousing. While use of this device did result in substantial shifts in investment timing during the 1954–1956 housing expansion, the relatively extensive use of warehousing as a source of funds had the appearance of being in large part a one-shot event. The pinch that led to use of bank credit as an alternative to Government securities liquidation apparently was the consequence of cash flow forecasting errors and inadequate internal control over the rate of new mortgage loan commitments. In effect, bank credit was employed to tide over the learning process involved in life companies' adjusting to a scarce funds-portfolio choice environment, after living many years in an open-to-buy world.

Finally, in Chapter VI we examined the role of forward commitments in life company investment policy and considered their potential use as a device for playing the interest rate cycle. Here the thesis was that the forward commitment enabled life companies to divorce loan decisions from acquisitions in time and created the possibility of concentrating loan authorization decisions in the high interest rate phase of the business cycle. The evidence on this hypothesis proved negative. It turned out that the pursuance of a loaned-up objective, found in Chapter V to force a close relation between cash inflow and loan acquisitions, also played a significant role in shaping the time path of new loan commitment decisions. Also, long delayed takedown loan commitments seemed to have the characteristic of an important service offered by life companies to certain types of corporate customers who found such a service of value. Thus, rather than being used as a device for playing the cyclical pattern of interest rates, life companies seemed to employ the forward commitment technique as an aid in achieving and maintaining a fully invested objective and as a competitive device in the search for attractive lending opportunities in the corporate, and perhaps income-property, mortgage loan sectors. It appeared that these two functions of advance loan commitments might be more complementary than competitive. This analysis of the rationale of forward commitments brought us face to face with portfolio composition decisions. We turn now to an examination of the determinants of life company portfolio composition choices during the 1950s.

Influence of Yields on Asset Choice

A primary objective of this study is to explore the extent to which the market clearing adjustments in leading financial asset markets take place through variations in observable yields on the relevant assets. We conduct this investigation by focusing on the role of life insurance companies in the capital markets and the responsiveness of life companies' allocation of funds among alternative assets to changes in relative asset yields. Our finding, that life companies' interperiod funds allocation was relatively insensitive to secular and cyclical interest rate patterns, does not necessarily rule out greater sensitivity of intraperiod asset selection to yield spreads.

If we accept the main line of conclusions from our opening discussion of influences on life company portfolio choices (Chapter I) that (1) diversification, (2) income risk, and (3) liquidity considerations have limited impact at the margin on life company asset choices, and if we further accept the existence of a well-defined set of financial assets eligible for life company portfolios, and the assumption that the primary source of investment income for life companies derives from interest earnings on debt obligations; then it seems plausible to postulate that relative yields are a primary force shaping the allocation of life company funds (gross or net) among competing eligible assets. The content of the eligibility set is determined by legal constraints, the nature of a life company's liabilities, and characteristic portfolio tastes ingrained by tradition into the minds of operating officers and finance committee members. The assumption that life companies focus on interest earnings has the effect of denying any appreciable motivation in portfolio policy to look to capital gains from trading as a source of investment return. In our interviews with life company investment officers, we found a strong predisposition to select even common stocks in limited stock purchase programs on the basis of dividend yields rather than prospective capital appreciation.[1]

It might appear that with these assumptions life company portfolio selection principles collapse into a simple decision rule. Given the eligible set of financial assets available for life insurance company purchase during any period, life companies rank assets by their expected yields and select assets from the top of the list until the period's funds, determined according to considerations discussed in previous chapters, have been exhausted. Since relatively high-risk assets have been ruled out of the eligible set (or a small portion of the portfolio is set aside to experiment in higher-risk assets), it is reasonable to expect high correlation between observed promised rates of return and life company expected yields. We could then proceed directly to testing the applicability of this simple decision rule to life company portfolio choices during the 1950s.

Additional complications remain, however. Some of these complications reflect the fact that the investment decision is not accurately characterized by postulating that all the cards to be chosen from are face up on the table when the selections are made.

---

[1] See the summary of our interview evidence on this point in Chapter II. For a view that trading policy is more important than we indicate see Wehrle, "Life Insurance Investment — The Experience of Four Companies." Wehrle found that one of the four companies he analyzed intensively followed a conscious policy of trading for capital gains.

In fact, the number of alternatives available in the eligible set depends upon the ability of life company investment departments to locate prospective loan opportunities. Loan and investment departments exist to generate opportunities as well as to evaluate the risk properties of available assets. Furthermore, investment mix decisions are made sequentially in time. Only a portion of the investment opportunities available during a period are visible at any point in time when a specific go or no-go decision has to be made on a given prospective loan. Such imperfect knowledge is accentuated, of course, where extensive use is made of the forward commitment technique.

Explicit recognition of the costs associated with origination and servicing of portfolio assets raises a number of problems. Obviously, expected yields calculated on alternative assets must be net of investment costs. Unit costs of acquiring types of assets which require substantial overhead expenses will be inversely related to the volume of activity in this sector. This fact may inhibit flexibility in shifting funds allocations among categories. Mortgage lending — especially in residential properties — appears to be an example of a high overhead operation which forces lenders to choose between not lending in this sector or devoting a substantial portion of investible funds to the area. The spread in basis points between gross and net yields is also a function of loan size since many routine costs of loan analysis, origination, and servicing are essentially independent of loan size. For the larger companies that dominate the life insurance industry, the difference in average loan size between corporate bond and residential mortgage loan acquisitions means the unit cost in basis points that must be deducted from the gross yield is many times greater for mortgage lending than for corporate investments. This recognition of the investment cost complexities renders observation of net yields difficult and suggests that responses to variations in yield spreads may be sluggish.

Part of the costs incurred by an investment organization result from the necessity to maintain market contacts with brokers, customers, agents, and other lenders so as to insure a regular flow of prospective investments. Some sacrifice in expected yields may be a short-run cost of cultivating and maintaining contacts. In the mortgage lending illustration, keeping the mortgage correspondents happy may be an additional reason for allocating a minimum flow of funds into the mortgage sector irrespective of prevailing yield spreads.

Further nonreturn considerations appeared in our discussion of life companies' allocation of funds over time in preceding chapters. For example, the time rate of portfolio composition adjustment induced by excessive holdings of Government securities at prevailing yield spreads was slowed in some periods by companies' distaste for showing book losses, and it appeared that life company acquisitions of federally underwritten mortgage loans were constrained at times by companies' dislike of price discounts. Also, as reviewed above, we found the forward commitment technique employed (1) as a competitive servicing device, and (2) as a means of achieving life companies' loaned-up objectives. The former use of the commitment mechanics implies that customers or potential customers may be served to some degree independent of prevailing observable yields, and there was a hint in the analysis of the loaned-up goal that concentration on this objective might have secondary effects on the composition of portfolio decisions. Finally, we found at several points that internal control over commitment decisions was imperfect, and that achievement of control might only be possible by adopting procedures, e.g., dollar quotas, which would almost certainly reduce the speed at which allocation of funds could respond to changing market conditions.

In addition to the inflexibility and inertia that may derive from the mechanics of generating new asset opportunities and servicing the existing portfolio, we are obviously involved in a complex statistical problem in attempting to test and measure the responsiveness of life companies' asset allocation decisions to relative yields. An identification problem plagues us. Life companies' supply decisions must have a role in determining asset yields and terms as well as being responsive to them. This will be true in those sectors in which life company investment activity is concentrated, i.e., the corporate bond and mortgage sectors. Thus we need to review the role of life companies in determining capital market yields before subjecting the yield responsiveness thesis to an empirical test.

In order to assess the significance of loan mechanics and preferences as constraints on life company sensitivity to relative yields we included a number of questions on asset allocation procedures in our interviews with life company investment officers. In the next section we summarize the information received from these interviews. We shall then proceed to formulate a yield spread hypothesis and sort out the primary alternative or complementary determinants of the allocation of life company funds. Following this, in Chapter VIII, we shall present the results of a regression analysis of life company portfolio selection decisions during the 1950s.

Allocation Mechanics and Asset Preferences: Some Interview Evidence

The Questions

In the interviews conducted with life company investment officers, we wished to obtain information on both the institutional mechanics of portfolio choice and the attitudes and tastes which shape the allocation decision. With regard to mechanics we were interested in understanding in a rudimentary way the structure of the investment operation, and the extent to which cash flow forecasts were used to make broad allocation decisions in advance. Specifically we asked whether funds were allocated in advance between securities and mortgages, and, if so, on what basis, and what flexibility of review was retained. Within the securities and mortgage allocations we probed to find how finer allotments were made. Ultimately we wanted to know on what basis it was decided to make loan A and reject loan proposal B, and, in particular, how much the existing investment organization limited the ability of life companies to select assets solely on the basis of portfolio yield and risk preferences.

Specific questions in our mind included: To what extent does the need to maintain working relationships with brokers, customers, agents, builders, and others inhibit the ability of life companies to respond in the short run to changing market conditions? Does investment in most areas require the company to maintain a staff of specialized investment personnel, and, if so, does the existence of such a staff restrict ability to shift the composition of new investment? Are some loans or investments made as a result of direct tie-ins with insurance sales, or because of indirect anticipated benefits for the insurance business? What are companies' attitudes toward specific loan types? Is there a priority ranking of loan categories? Are there limits to the amount a company is willing to invest in a particular asset type for diversification or other reasons? How important are various nonyield attributes of loans within the eligibility set, such as maturities, marketability, call features, equity options? Do companies consciously employ nonprice rationing devices? What attitudes exist toward the government-underwritten mortgage programs? Is there a reluctance to acquire FHA and VA loans at price discounts? Does the company have portfolio composition goals and some reasoned policy governing the rate at which they intend to move toward the desired portfolio mix?

Due to limited time and to variations in the specific competence of officers interviewed, not all areas were covered in individual interviews. Also, the insights and evidence obtained varied considerably among companies and interviewees. To expedite reporting, we shall only summarize here the main lines of the interview evidence obtained. In doing so, we shall be suppressing evidence of substantial diversity in organization and portfolio preferences among the largest life insurance companies.

Summary of the Interview Evidence

AN OVERVIEW OF THE ALLOCATION DECISION

Typically, life insurance company investment operations are carried out in two independently structured organizations existing side by side: a securities department, and a mortgage loan and real estate department. Each department has a vice president at its head. Some, but not all, companies have a financial vice president overseeing the entire lending activity. Coordination of activities and policy is achieved via consultations between the two department heads or in a three-man committee including the financial vice president if one exists. In some companies the financial vice president appears to be quite powerful and makes basic policy decisions unilaterally which are handed down to the department heads for implementation. In principle, the ultimate power of determination of portfolio policy and selection of specific loan and investment proposals rests with the finance committee, which is a subcommittee of the board of directors and contains representation from both operating officers and independent members of the board. The influence of this committee in policy formulation seems to vary widely from company to company.

By the late 1950s most companies employed cash flow and commitment takedown forecasts to estimate the monthly net inflow of funds expected to be available for investment during the upcoming 12 months or more. On the basis of this information, the financial vice president and department chiefs confer late in the calendar year and allocate the succeeding year's loanable funds between the securities and mortgage organizations. In some companies these allocations are meant to be only a rough guide to the respective departments, but in most companies they seem to be reasonably firm and are not exceeded without a prior department request. To facilitate future review of and adjustments in the allocation, some residual portion of the anticipated funds flow may be left unassigned in the original decision.

Ignoring the existence of an unallocated residual, the guiding principle governing the allocation decisions seems to be competitive yields. In principle, given the best information available on market conditions and prospective opportunities, the allocations are meant to be market clearing, at essentially the same terms for each department. This means that the allocating committee also must make a complementary policy decision respecting the minimum return acceptable on loans and investments during the coming year. For companies interviewed during 1960 the standard minimum yield, net of costs, was almost universally 6%. It is understood that this minimum translates into higher net yields for certain categories of riskier or otherwise less desirable assets. If the available funds or market conditions forecasts appear to be faulty as operations proceed into the year in question, the allocation is reviewed and appropriate changes in minimum required returns made.

Although the above summary appears to state the broad principles on which life insurance companies mean to base their funds allocation decisions, a number of nonreturn considerations modify the operation of the net yield decision rule. These may call for compromises at the basic mortgage/securities decision level or at the various suballocation decisions within each department. It is these qualifications to a net yield rule which occupy our attention here. It will be easier to see what sort of considerations are involved by examining the investment process in each of the two departments separately.

THE SECURITIES DEPARTMENT

Responsibilities

The primary task of a securities department is to generate, select, and review corporate debt issues. However, the department is also likely to be responsible for selection and trading decisions in the common and preferred stock, and state and local government portfolios. It may also have the assignment of managing the federal government securities portfolio, although often this task is delegated to the treasurer's or cashier's office. The securities department may be responsible for analyzing prospective purchase and leaseback deals and reviewing existing property, buildings, equipment, etc., owned by the insurance company and under lease.

As we have seen, life companies ordinarily hold corporate bond issues acquired until they mature or are called. During the postwar years most, but not all, large life insurance companies have obtained the bulk of their corporate bond investments via the direct placement route.[2] An investment banker or other intermediary is often responsible for bringing the prospective loan to the life insurance company when a borrower new to the life company is involved. Some loan opportunities come into a company from other lenders seeking to spread a prospective private placement among several lenders. A substantial portion of a securities department's investments in any period seem to go to existing customers. Data assembled by Walter indicate that for large companies about a third to a half of bond issues acquired represent loans to old customers.[3]

---

[2] The 28 companies in the LIAA *Direct Placement Survey* acquired over 90% of their industrial and over 70% of their public utility obligations via the direct placement route during the 1950s. The 28 respondents include the 18 largest life companies. Direct placements are rather broadly defined in these data. See ALC-LIAA *Joint Investment Bulletin*, No. 381.

[3] Walter, *The Investment Process*, p. 333.

Specialization

There exist surprising variations among life companies in the size, depth, degree of specialization, and complexity of their securities departments. It is common for senior staff members' responsibilities to be defined in terms of industrial specialities. Junior members usually perform the routine analytical work on borrowers' financial statements.[4] Some large companies retain on the payroll various technical specialists, such as engineers, scientists, and marketing experts. Others rely largely on outside consultant services for provision of needed technical data and interpretation. Obviously, even in large companies considerable staff flexibility is needed since the variation over time in the composition of incoming prospective loans must be substantial. Flexibility is attained largely by moving junior men around to accommodate changing work loads in the various sectors, but some companies make a policy of rotating assignments of senior men as well. The investment officers interviewed did not seem to feel that staff inflexibilities were a significant constraint in changing the composition of new investments as market conditions warranted.

Staff personnel, however, may well develop particular tastes and preferences, especially if their assignments are not periodically rotated, which have the effect of retarding portfolio adjustments. One officer of a conservative, blue-chip-oriented company with a small investment staff conceded that "the boys in the back room," i.e., the security analysts, probably had more influence on portfolio composition than the chief investment officers charged explicitly with allocation policy. Also, life companies apparently become typed by investment bankers, brokers, agents, and borrowers themselves with regard to their investment tastes. Another officer of a company typed as conservative reported that they were finding it takes a lot of time to move into new sectors and riskier securities for this reason.

[4] For a detailed discussion of staff activity and organization of investment departments, see *ibid.*, Chapter IV.

Customer relationships

One advantage of joint participation loans is that they facilitate increasing contacts with other lenders, intermediaries, and borrowers. Some life companies seem to invest substantial proportions of their funds in pieces of a loan originated by other lenders simply because it is easy. They depend on someone else to perform the background work in financial analysis and to conduct negotiations with respect to terms. Apparently a strong positive advantage of joint participation loans is that they enable any individual company to spread its funds over more borrowers. In the case of some quite large loans this may reflect a diversification concern, but the more controlling reason seems to be that it creates more customer contacts. Most companies do, moreover, operate under statutory or self-imposed limits on the amount of loans outstanding to an individual borrower, usually defined as a percentage of surplus.[5]

Rationing

Customer considerations do lead to some conscious nonprice rationing on the part of life companies particularly in "tight money" periods. An existing or former customer is likely to receive some preference over a new face. Customer relations are not nearly so strong as commerical banking deposit customer relationships, however. In general customers are existing or former borrowers, not policyholders. Nevertheless a borrower with a large group policy might well expect and receive priority treatment from the securities department. Some companies consciously try to keep everybody happy in a tight funds period by reducing the average and maximum loan size so as to spread out the invested funds. Most officers were able to come up with a list of areas and industries which rank high as desirable investments and those which are regarded as only marginally acceptable. Some of the latter are likely to be rationed out in a tight money period.

There is little evidence of diversification objectives compromising life companies' focus on expected return. Companies do

---

[5] For an account of statutory limitations see Chapter II.

limit the amount of credit that can be extended to an individual borrower, but generally statutory limits seem to be more confining than self-imposed rules. It was very difficult to elicit any examples from investment officers of industries or geographical areas in which they limited investment or increased yield requirements out of a concern for diversification. The one standard answer we often received was that "we sometimes cut off finance companies." Here the motivation is usually that finance companies are vaguely regarded as competitors in the lending business, and in addition are regarded as engaging in somewhat unsavory activities. Therefore, even though finance company issues are profitable investments, it is felt that the amount of credit outstanding to them should be restricted. Sometimes finance committee directives for "no more finance companies" seem to be meant as a challenge to investment officers to bring in proposals which take more work to generate but are more attractive. As for diversification, in securities departments it really does seem to take care of itself.

The decision flow

Typically, each prospective loan passes through several stages of evaluation and review within a life insurance company before a final commitment can be made to the borrower. Opportunities flow in directly from borrowers and from various service agencies, commerical banks, brokers, investment bankers, underwriters, and other long-term lenders. Investment officers are also expected to scan all public offerings in their area of responsibility and select the more promising issues for review by the security analysts. Propositions are allocated by an investment officer to a team of security analysts for appraisal. The security analysts report back on the acceptability of the loan proposal within the existing guidelines with respect to eligibility and loan terms. The investment officer reviews their report and concludes that the loan is acceptable as is, acceptable with certain modifications, or not acceptable. Normally, his rejection will end consideration of the proposal. Acceptances are passed on to the vice president in charge of the securities department. If he and the financial vice president find the proposal acceptable, he notifies the prospective borrower, verifies an agreement on loan terms and the desired delivery date, and recommends acquisition of the issue at the next meeting of the finance committee. Ultimate power of acceptance or rejection rests with this committee. When it has voted favorably, the commitment agreement is signed, and the company considers itself bound to deliver the funds as scheduled.[6] As we have seen, borrowers feel less bound by a commitment agreement and sometimes cancel.

The finance committee

It is difficult to evaluate the influence of the finance committee in shaping portfolio policy, but it seems to vary considerably among companies. Interview responses indicated that the finance committee infrequently rejects proposals recommended to it, but this may simply indicate that the committee has communicated its standards for acceptance clearly and effectively to the chief investment officers. To expedite the investment operation finance committees do commonly delegate authority to investment officers, and sometimes even to branch office personnel, to commit the company to loan proposals that meet required specifications.

Typically, board members outside the company constitute a majority on the finance committee.[7] This obviously raises the possibility of serious conflicts of views between the finance committee and chief investment officers. In interviews investment officers often talked as if they felt considerably constrained by the finance committee and blamed committee members for unimaginative investment policies.[8] Whatever the merit of a generalization that types finance committees as obstructionists, it does appear that the allocation process within life company securities departments results from a complex interaction of finance committees, financial vice presidents, chief investment officers, and "the boys in the back room."

---

[6] For a much more detailed discussion of communication flows within the securities department and between investment officers and the finance committee, see Walter, *op. cit.*, Chapter VI.

[7] See Walter, Table VI-1, p. 199, for the composition of finance committees in 24 life companies.

[8] For some examples of finance committees' opposition to specific types of investments, see Walter, p. 201.

It would be most helpful in understanding the results of this decision process to have records of life company investment rejections as well as of their commitments and acquisitions. Unfortunately few companies keep records of rejections. What little evidence is available is very difficult to interpret since there are no standard definitions of what constitutes a rejection. The companies we interviewed indicated that outright finance committee rejections were rare. (Less rare are finance committee directions to the effect: "Don't bring us any more of this type of proposal.") Most officers who had any quantitative feeling estimated that within the department they accepted half to three-quarters of the proposals that came to them. Such a figure must, however, include only rejected proposals that passed preliminary screening. Walter reported that, for industrial bond proposals that reached an intermediate stage in the decision process, New England Life had a rejection/closures rate in 1957 of 1.2/1.[9] For Mutual Life Insurance Company of New York, his data for 1958 indicate an acquisitions/rejection ratio of about *one* for direct placement industrial and public utility securities propositions.[10] These include "all issues analyzed." Rejection rates on public offerings run much higher; rejection/acquisition ratios of 10/1 or more. This apparently reflected a practice of routine examination of all public offerings which seem to fall within Mutual of New York's sphere of interest.

Summary

In sum, within the set of propositions that come into life insurance companies' securities departments and meet the companies' absolute eligibility standards, the simple rule which commands decision makers to select those with the highest expected yields does not fare too badly as a description of life insurance company investment policy. Allowance must be made for the time sequence problem by establishing the minimum acceptable yield in advance at a level which is estimated to just clear the market. Nonyield considerations of greatest importance seem to be maintenance of good relations and contacts with existing and former

[9] *Ibid.*, p. 135. Few rejections were reported in other areas.
[10] *Ibid.*, Table VI-9, p. 140.

customers, investment bankers, and others who supply investment opportunities. In general, companies aim at achieving these objectives with a minimum of yield sacrifice.

While many life companies do have some investment specialities they have built up over time, most active investment departments lend in a wide variety of industries. There does not seem to be anything inherent in the organization and mechanics of the securities operation that locks companies into certain areas and makes it difficult for them to respond to changing market conditions with substantial shifts in the composition of investments. However, some securities departments have permitted inflexibilities to develop by becoming typed as highly specialized or very conservative by brokers and/or borrowers. There is a tendency for security analysts to develop well-formed tastes and biases and to habitually shun unfamiliar types of issues if department heads do not devise means of keeping the organization flexible and fluid.

There was little indication that concern over diversification competes with the expected return objective. Some nonprice rationing does take place, however. Customers obtain preferential treatment when funds are tight, and borrowers unfamiliar to a life company are more likely to find their proposals rejected. Certain types of public service loans may receive favored treatment as will large policyholders. Life companies may offer to lend less than the prospective borrower requested, or to spread out delivery of funds over a longer period. More joint participation loans may be made. To the extent this is so, many borrowers may find they are not rationed out of life company funds, but simply more companies have a share of their new bond issue. Most companies denied any conscious attempts to upgrade portfolios during tight funds periods. However, many officers indicated that they would be especially insistent on strong call protection in such periods. It is difficult to estimate whether the quantitative impact of these rationing devices is of a magnitude to alter investment composition significantly from that consistent with pursuing a maximization of expected yield goal.

THE MORTGAGE DEPARTMENT

Responsibilities

Generally, mortgage departments are subdivided into separate organizations for production and servicing of:

(1) residential property loans;
(2) loans on commercial, industrial, and institutional income producing property;
(3) agricultural loans.

The mortgage department often also has the responsibility of acquiring and managing real estate investments.

Organizational requirements

Given the significance of residential mortgage loans in the life insurance industry's aggregate portfolio, it is surprising to observe that several of the larger life companies are essentially not in the home loan market at all. Three of the companies we interviewed are in this category. This circumstance apparently is a consequence of the organizational requirements for operation in the residential mortgage market. The residential loan market remains essentially a local market. Thus, a life company needs personnel, representatives, or agents in each local area in which it wishes to lend in order to originate loans and service the existing portfolio. Although the federally underwritten mortgage loan programs and FNMA's trading operations have created something of a secondary market in FHA and VA loans, life companies do not regard bloc purchases of FHA and VA loans in this market as a feasible and satisfactory way of building a residential mortgage loan portfolio.[11] Servicing would remain a problem even if loans were acquired through secondary market facilities.

---

[11] One company we interviewed experimented with acquiring loans in this manner and found it unworkable. The problem is partly one of establishing the quality of loans purchased in this fashion. Offers to sell in a secondary market may often be offers to sell loans closest to default status. Life company and mortgage banking representatives we talked to insisted that FNMA automatically purchased the lowest quality FHA-VA loans. [However, FNMA has also been accused of conservatism and "second guessing" the FHA and VA in the quality standards it imposes on loan purchases. See Guttentag's discussion in "The Federal National Mortgage Association,"

Field organizations come in two basic types: (1) branch offices and (2) independent correspondents. Correspondents are most often mortgage companies, but sometimes real estate concerns, banks, and savings and loan associations act as correspondents for life companies. Correspondents, like branch offices, perform two functions: (1) the origination of loans and (2) the servicing of existing loan portfolios. Most correspondents perform both functions for a life insurance company, but some life companies maintain contracts with correspondents who only originate loans or only service existing loans. Ordinarily, separate field organizations are necessary for each of the three principal areas of mortgage lending (residential, city income property, and farm) since the appraisal skills and lending techniques required are quite different.

Only the largest life companies generate and service a significant volume of loans through branch office operations.[12] Most depend on outside correspondents. Some companies do originate and service a significant portion of their income-property loans through the home office. Loans of all types are also sometimes acquired from independent brokers. In the residential market, large tracts are often acquired in this manner.

---

pp. 127–129.] If the FHA-VA foreclosure procedures are fast and essentially costless to life companies, then loan quality should be largely immaterial. Indeed, a real economic man ought to buy up all the deep discount FHA-VA loans with a high probability of default that he can locate. But as we observe below, most life companies view defaults and foreclosures as expensive even if no loss is incurred directly.

[12] In the LIAA 1958 *City Mortgage Lending Income and Cost Survey*, three of 90 companies reporting are listed as branch office organizations. This classification includes companies which originated or serviced over two-thirds of their city loans in branch offices. City loans included all residential and nonfarm income property loans. Another five companies were reported as having combination correspondent-branch office organizations (neither correspondents nor branch offices alone accounting for two-thirds of the loans). Of the large companies we interviewed, two depended almost exclusively on salaried branch office personnel for generating and servicing residential loans, one operated with about a 50-50 branch office-correspondent combination, one depended about 80% on correspondents, otherwise on branch offices and independent brokers; one was beginning to move toward making mortgage servicing a branch office operation. Generally, a higher proportion of income-property than residential loans seemed to be originated and serviced by salaried personnel (branch office and home office). Farm mortgage organizations we interviewed ranged from almost exclusively branch office to exclusively correspondent.

Correspondents on originating and servicing contracts with life companies normally earn their income from such contracts through service fees.[13] The standard fee for residential loans during the postwar period has been 0.5% of the loan outstanding per annum. It is lower and less standardized for nonresidential loans and generally on a sliding scale with respect to loan size. During the late 1950s lenders appeared to be pressing for a reduction in servicing costs. Some life companies reported they had reduced servicing fees. The impetus toward fee reduction arose from the accumulation of postwar experience of few defaults or even delinquents requiring more than routine collection costs on the part of servicing agents. Two of the large companies we interviewed, both having been almost completely dependent on correspondents, were moving toward a salaried personnel servicing organization in order to reduce costs.[14] Finders fees, which were quite prevalent during the early postwar period, gradually disappeared for ordinary loans, though life companies often were still willing to pay brokerage fees for loans carrying yields of one-quarter or one-half an interest point above their minimum requirement.

Organizational rigidity

One consequence of the need for large field organizations in mortgage lending does seem to be reduction in investment flexi-

---

[13] Klaman reported for the early 1950s that service fees from lenders accounted for one-third to two-fifths of gross income to mortgage companies. Mortgage generators also sometimes charge borrowers an origination fee, particularly on federally underwritten loans. Maximum origination fees for FHA and VA loans are fixed by the respective agencies. See Klaman, *The Postwar Rise of Mortgage Companies*, pp. 10–11.

[14] The 1958 LIAA *Income and Cost Survey* results suggest that branch office systems incur lower operating costs than correspondent organizations. Reporting on 34 companies with city mortgage portfolios in excess of $100,000,000, the survey showed that predominantly correspondent operations had an average operating cost ratio of 0.55% of their portfolio while the analogous cost ratio for primarily branch office organizations was only 0.40%. Combination branch office, correspondent operations reported an average cost ratio of 0.45%. If there exist significant operating economies between a $100 million portfolio and a $1 or $2 billion portfolio, these results may be somewhat biased in favor of branch office systems since the branch office organizations exist only in very large companies. Building a branch office organization may also reduce investment flexibility, but the interview responses are mixed on this question.

bility. Most investment officers interviewed emphasized the need to maintain steady flows of funds into mortgage loans in order to maintain a strong, loyal field organization.[15] This applied to both branch office and correspondent organizations. All officers of the large companies interviewed indicated that, over and above funds obtained from mortgage loan turnover, it was necessary to provide the mortgage department with a minimum portion of the net funds flow.[16] The preciseness with which this minimum was formulated varied among companies, apparently reflecting some diversity with respect to the seriousness of this consideration.[17] Nonetheless the overall impression obtained from the interviews was that life companies believe serious and expensive damage to their field organizations would result from severely cutting back on funds allotted to the mortgage department for a year. Thus life companies seemed willing to sacrifice short-run or even intermediate-run yield advantage for maintenance of the mortgage organization.[18]

Since residential lending constitutes the most local of mortgage markets, the need for a proliferated field organization seems to be greatest there. Thus large life companies may have several hundred home loan correspondents under contract or a similar number of branch office sites, but only 40 or 50 correspondents or offices to produce income-property loans. This seemed to be the reason some life companies were not in the residential market at

---

[15] Officers of life companies which commonly finance large tracts also emphasized the need to maintain good relations with tract builders.

[16] One financial vice president in a medium-sized life company denied he would pay any price in yield to keep correspondents loyal. This was the same officer who claimed that book losses on Government securities did not affect the company's decision to liquidate (Chapter III, p. 197).

[17] In talking to a mortgage company officer, we found that he distinguished quite sharply between life companies that were considerate and maintained steady funds allotments and those companies that could not be counted upon. However, it was not clear that the latter companies suffered at the hands of their correspondents for not maintaining a stable flow of available funds.

[18] During most of the postwar period up to 1960, it is doubtful whether life companies faced this decision due to the continued strength of demand for mortgage funds. But after 1956, there may well have been some periods where a pure yield maximization objective would have led companies to cut back mortgage operations further than they did. When we interviewed companies in 1960, they seemed to be obtaining gross yields on mortgage loans little, if any, better than going yields on corporate bond commitments, implying lower realized net yields on mortgages.

all. In general it appears that the half-dozen largest life companies are in the residential market with large field organizations because they hesitate to do without such a major outlet for funds.[19] Small life companies are in residential loans because, like most savings banks, they are not large enough to handle the technically more complex problems associated with corporate bond investment. Intermediate-sized companies (say, with assets of $400 million to $4 billion) may be able to do without home loan organizations provided they are staffed to produce competitively attractive corporate direct placements and income-property mortgage loans.

Allocation procedure

Within the mortgage department the guiding allocation principle is the same as in the securities department, *viz.*, allocate on a competitive yield basis. However, the exceptions to the rule appear more significant in the mortgage operation than they did with securities investments. Allocation of the mortgage departments' annual allotment is often made among the major mortgage categories (residential, income-property, and farm) for planning purposes, but in many companies these allotments appeared less firm than the original securities-mortgage decision. (In some companies, two or three separate mortgage departments coexist on the same organizational level with the securities department, resulting in a single allocation decision.) In general the net yield requirements will be the same for each mortgage category, and minimum acceptable terms will be established by the vice president in charge of mortgages in consultation with the chiefs of each mortgage loan subdivision. Consultations, of course, precede the mortgage-securities allocation decision so in principle the same yield and quality requirements apply to all sectors of the portfolio. Allotments may deviate from this principle if it is deemed necessary to maintain an efficient field organization or good relations with builders or independent brokers. In several cases we found temporary deviations resulting from a

---

[19] However, one of these companies only entered the residential market during the 1930s and then, according to the interview response, only as a negative reaction to the initiation of the FHA program.

desire to build up a particular mortgage category to an efficient scale. This happened particularly to life companies in the agricultural mortgage loan market. Most companies in this market found it necessary during the 1950s to review their position. Out of these reviews came a decision to stay in and build up the portfolio or to phase out the operation. We found examples of both decisions in the set of companies interviewed. Actually either decision seemed to result in a transition period during which uncompetitive loans were made.

The next problem is allocation of funds to the field organization. The basic method is to send out periodic schedules to the field indicating the minimum interest rate and other terms acceptable to the company and any changes in the schedule of fees payable to correspondents or outside brokers. The inflow of mortgage proposals to the home office is controlled by making appropriate changes in acceptable rates or terms. In most cases the field representatives, whether branch office personnel or correspondents, do not have the authority to make commitments in the life company's name but must submit them to the home office where they are reviewed by mortgage department personnel and then voted by the finance committee. Efficient life companies seem to be able to give one week's service on home loan commitment proposals from the field. Other types of loans generally take longer to process.

In principle, the same minimum rate should apply nationwide. Some exceptions exist, however. A number of companies had explicitly higher minimum rates for residential loans in California than elsewhere. (In 1960 this meant 6.25% or 6.5% in California; 6% elsewhere.) Others placed dollar volume limits on California loans but not elsewhere. Some companies reported accepting lower yields in some areas, if it seemed worth maintaining the branch office or correspondent relation in the longer run. (Two companies reported taking 5.75% loans in specific areas during 1960 although they were on a 6% minimum standard.) In nonresidential mortgage loan operations, exceptions to standard minimum terms seemed to be much less common.

Although we did not succeed in obtaining sets of the rate and term schedules sent out to field organizations, the interview respondents indicated that in residential financing terms were changed more frequently than interest rate requirements. Terms that were altered to adjust inflows of loan proposals were, apparently in order of importance: (1) downpayment minimum, (2) maturity maximum, and (3) credit standing of borrowers, the latter most often expressed in debt/income ratio requirements.

Several life companies in the residential mortgage loan business had found it necessary to supplement rate and terms schedules with dollar quotas. In one instance involving a branch office system, the quota allotment was quite formal and made for the upcoming year as soon as possible after the mortgage department had received its twelve-month allocation. In other cases twelve-month quotas were given to field representatives as rough guidelines with firmer six-month or three-month quotas given as the year progressed. Quotas to the field serve at least two functions. In some cases they are meant as firm minimum guarantees the correspondent or branch office can count on so long as it is able to generate acceptable loans. However, the increasing use of quotas in the latter half of the 1950s apparently resulted from companies finding they were not able to maintain adequate control over the rate of residential loan commitments generated from the field simply by varying acceptable rate and terms. Thus dollar quotas were instituted as limiting controls on field organizations. It will be recalled from our previous discussion that a primary reason for companies' adopting annual firm fund allocation procedures between securities and mortgage departments was that they felt a need to place controls on mortgage departments. The need to institute quotas as a control device suggests that dispersed field organizations are likely to be a source of company sluggishness in responding to variations in relative yields.

Diversification

A number of mortgage officers interviewed reported that their companies had established portfolio composition goals by way of setting a target mortgage loan/total assets ratio. These replies came both from companies exclusively in nonresidential mortgage markets and from companies in residential lending as well. In general the goals had been established in the early 1950s. In most cases they had been reached or were on the verge of being reached at the time we conducted the interviews (1960). All but one of the reported targets were in the range of a mortgage/assets ratio of .33 to .38. It happens that the industry ratio fell within this range in 1960. The one exception was a large company which reported having a target ratio of .50.[20]

Although the mortgage/asset objectives were formulated in most cases at a time when the existing ratios were quite low, no officer explained their existence in portfolio balance or diversification terms. The primary rationale for such goals was yield in all cases. Mortgage yields did appear relatively attractive during the early and mid-1950s. (See the yield data in Table VI-B-1.) Apparently target objectives served as an internal device to cut back on allocations to the securities departments. A secondary reason, given by three companies, for the desire to increase mortgage loans as a proportion of the total portfolio was to increase portfolio rollover. More rollover seemed most desirable to companies with low growth rates (contrary to the income risk principle). It also seemed desirable to one company, with a securities portfolio dominated by long-term, low coupon, blue-chip corporate bonds. In all these cases the companies seemed quite bullish about long-term interest rate trends.

Explicit portfolio balance–diversification considerations did appear to enter into decisions to limit residential loan activity in California, either through use of explicit quotas or higher standards on California loans.[21] Other considerations restrict companies from overconcentrating loan activity in high growth, high yield areas, however. One is the need to maintain field organizations in other parts of the country. Unless a company feels confident it will pay to confine mortgage lending to the current high growth areas for the next ten, fifteen, or twenty years, it will not feel justified in dismantling its field organization elsewhere.

Another principle influencing geographic distribution of funds is the rule commanding a company to put its money back where it collected the premiums. Some officers did explicitly state

---

[20] It should be noted that in some companies investment officers in securities departments expressed skepticism at the suggestion that such targets existed as a matter of company policy.

[21] The diversification concern did not come through very strongly in the interviews. Typical of attitudes found was the comment of one officer: "Diversification isn't very important, but you have to pay some homage to it."

that mortgage lending operations were expected to generate some insurance sales. The classic case of this connection was the well-known Equitable Life (New York) "Assured Home Ownership Plan" in which all loans on residences were required to have life insurance protection attached. A preferential rate on residential mortgages was a part of this plan. The plan was abandoned in the late 1950s, apparently largely because of questions about the legality of tie-in loan-insurance policy packages, although internal pressure resulting from the low return on home mortgage loans may also have been a factor. Although other companies have not pushed the relation this far, many companies apparently do provide their insurance agents with lists of mortgage loans made.

A marginal influence on California lending, justifying somewhat higher yields in the view of some officers, are the greater risks associated with climatic conditions (earthquakes, landslides) and, in some areas, dependence on defense industries. Thus a combination of diversification, field organization, insurance sales, and risk considerations have kept the large eastern life insurance companies from acting to eliminate geographic mortgage yield differentials.

Attitudes toward federally underwritten loans

Another significant source of life company deviation from a net yield criterion in allocating residential mortgage funds derives from their attitudes toward the federally underwritten mortgage programs. In our interviews we found various degrees of antipathy toward the FHA insurance and VA guarantee programs. Attitudes expressed fell roughly into three types:

(1) dislike of the ceiling contract rates on FHA-VA loans imposed by Congress and the administrative agencies;
(2) simple ideological dislike of government intervention in the market system;
(3) doubts about the low risk characteristics of FHA and VA loans.

Antipathy toward the ceiling rates came through most often and most strongly. Acquiring loans at a price discount does not seem to most life companies as an adequate substitute for acquiring loans at par at a free market contract rate. This is not a result of concern for builders, although large discounts may lead builders to reduce their activity. (This will be the case when they are unable profitably to absorb deep price discounts as a selling cost or to pass them on to the borrower in financing charges or the price of the house.) Rather, it is simply that many life companies are very reluctant to take many deep discount loans.

The reasons for this reluctance are less than clear. It is apparently considered bad public relations. Discounts may not be understood and may be resented by households in a way that higher market determined interest rate quotations would not be. Life companies wishing to sell insurance policies are solicitous of such feeling, and prefer not to make such loans rather than make them at the going market price when deep discounts are involved. A partial alternative is to make conventional loans at as liberal terms as statutory regulations permit.[22]

Life companies' public relations sensitivity toward discounting has been periodically reinforced by critical comments from Congressmen. Congress has twice experimented with legislating discount controls in the Housing Acts of 1950 and 1957. In both cases controls were later withdrawn.[23] However, these Congressional responses to discounting cast an aura of questionable legality and morality over the discounting practices which seem to have affected life insurance companies particularly among the major mortgage lenders.[24] The emotional reaction of life company investment officers seemed stronger here than in any other phases of business we discussed. Purchase of deep discount loans was characterized as "unethical," "unconscionable," and "pawn-brokers' business" respectively by three officers interviewed. All three, of course, favored elimination of ceiling rates

---

[22] It appears that deepening discounts on federally underwritten loans had something to do with life companies' decision to press during the late 1950s for statutory amendments to permit acquisition of conventional loans with more liberal terms. See Chapter II.

[23] For a brief but cogent discussion of lender attitudes, Congressional attitudes, and the legislative experiments with discount controls, see Grebler, *Housing Issues in Economic Stabilization Policy*, Appendix A.

[24] Mutual savings banks and commercial banks which have been active in the federal programs acquire most of their FHA and VA loans from areas where they have few potential depositors. Savings and loan associations have always been oriented to conventional loans because they are freer to make liberal conventional loans, because they have a competitive advantage, and because they have natural distaste for government programs that reduce the local nature of mortgage markets.

so that the same, or higher, effective yields could be obtained by acquiring loans at par.

Obviously there are imbedded in life companies' adverse reactions to discounting a general ideological distaste for federal government intervention in the capital markets. Federally underwritten loans would no doubt be assigned a relatively low priority position by many life companies even without the technical complications of discounting. Despite the government guarantee and insurance protection, a number of mortgage department officers reported that they regarded FHA and VA loans as relatively risky assets. A low quality rating is given to FHA-VA loans generally because of their liberal downpayment and maturity terms. Delinquent loans result in higher servicing costs for branch office operations. Defaults are considered a nuisance and expensive because of the work load they place on branch office or home office personnel, even though the full value of the outstanding loan principal is recovered. Payment for foreclosed FHA loans is in the form of FHA debentures. Some companies expressed doubt as to the value of these issues since the interest return is low, and in a period of numerous foreclosures the market price might be depressed. There are some doubts as to whether government administrative allowances cover total foreclosure costs. And, perhaps most important to a number of companies, defaults and foreclosures are bad public relations.

All this means that life companies' preference for conventional over federally underwritten loans is likely to produce nonyield rationing of the latter at times. From the interview responses, this should be most evident in periods of deep discounts. We interviewed seven large companies active in residential lending. All testified to the inhibiting effect of deep discounts, though to different degrees. Two had been engaged in practically no FHA or VA lending in recent years. Two others were currently (1960) totally out of the VA market because of high discounts (FHAs had a higher ceiling rate and prevailing discounts were only 3 or 4 points). Three others were still in VAs but to a limited extent because of the discounts.[25] Two of the companies also reported

---

[25] All officers seemed to feel that correspondents could originate VA loans if funds were made available. This was also the position of a mortgage banker interviewed. He felt that builders had been quite successful in getting VA

having placed dollar quotas on FHA loans at the field level although they had none on conventional loans.

There was also an indication that life companies provided funds for FHA and VA loans as a means of generating quality conventional loans. One of the industry's most active residential mortgage investors reported taking some FHA and VA loans in large tract financing that they would not accept on an individual loan basis in order to acquire conventional loans from the tract. Other companies have provided correspondents with funds for FHA and VA loan activity on the condition that the correspondents originate designated amounts of conventional loans meeting required standards.

Priorities and rationing

This review of typical mortgage department organizational requirements, funds allocation procedures, and lending objectives has raised a number of warning signs with respect to the reliability of a loan selection model based upon an expected yield maximization goal. The mechanics of the lending process, as well as the existence of objectives other than investment return, may produce situations in which the yield objective is significantly compromised. Substantial and steady flows of funds into the mortgage sector may be required (1) because unit lending costs are quite sensitive to volume and (2) to maintain the loyalty and efficiency of the field organization and the usefulness of its market contacts. Difficulties with regard to maintaining internal control over the mortgage departments' use of funds appear responsible for the establishment of overall target portfolio composition objectives and advance funds allocation procedures including dollar quota mechanisms for allocating funds to the mortgage loan field organizations. These procedures may make quick responses to changes in relative asset yields impossible. Mortgage investments seem to be less concentrated geographically than they would be if a simple expected yield goal dominated this decision. Both organizational mechanics and competing loan objectives seem to contribute to this result. Finally, dislike of substantial price dis-

---

appraisals adjusted so that even large discounts (10 points or so) could be passed on to the borrower.

counts on federally underwritten loans appears to lead life companies to ration out VA and FHA loans which are competitive with going market discounts on a yield basis.

As a consequence of these problems of lending mechanics and attitudes, loan priority notions often appeared in interview discussions. In general, high priority areas exist wherever a company feels most deeply committed, or where organizational requirements demand minimum levels of activity. For companies active in residential lending, this means preservation of the residential field organization has highest priority. Typical of responses to the rationing question was an ordering of loan priorities as follows:

(1) single family conventional residential loans;
(2) income-property loans;
(3) federally underwritten loans.

Thus, in a tight funds period, federally underwritten activity is rationed first and income-property loans next. This ordering prevailed even though the net yields received on income-property loans had been exceeding conventional home loan yields.

Implications of the Interview Evidence

We undertook the interviews in order to evaluate the applicability of the yield maximization hypothesis and to pinpoint any organization and asset preference constraints which compromise the expected yield decision rule or render it unproductive as a starting hypothesis.

The principal findings from the interview discussions dealing with asset choice decisions were:

(1) Most large life insurance companies have adopted the practice of allocating funds in advance between their securities and mortgage departments. Normally this is done on a twelve-month basis with provision for review. The adoption of such procedures reflects problems of inadequate control over investment flows under a system in which flows are simply guided by a schedule of minimally acceptable yields, terms, credit, and property standards. Dollar allocation procedures are likely to be a source of sluggishness in response to changes in relative market yields. Department heads become conscious of allocation decisions and fight to maintain or increase their allotted proportion of the net available

cash flow. The fairly common practice of mortgage departments allocating their allotments as quotas to branch offices and/or correspondents produces similar results.

(2) Some companies have formulated portfolio mix objectives. During the 1950s these were expressed in mortgage/asset targets. Although the primary motivation for adopting such targets was reported to be responsiveness to attractive mortgage yields, the formulation of even informal objectives of this sort implies that companies may be slow to respond to changes in the structure of asset yields.

(3) The reason for making the crude, long-run forecasts of relative yields implied in mortgage/asset targets is that success in generating prospective loans depends upon the size and efficiency of investment organizations. The size and diversity of the eligible set of assets available to life companies in any period are a function of past budgeting allocations to the investment department.

(4) The need for substantial investment organizations can be a source of inertia, inflexibility, and necessary compromise of short-term, expected yield maximization. The problem is most acute in mortgage departments and, within mortgage loan activity, in the residential loan sector. Because residential loan markets are essentially local markets, a large and proliferated field organization is required for a large company to produce and service a home loan portfolio. Overhead cost in branch office organization, the necessity of maintaining a loyal and efficient correspondent system, and contacts with large builders are all considerations demanding a substantial and reasonably steady flow of mortgage funds from life companies to the field. Life companies seem to be willing to sacrifice yield in the short run to maintain the mortgage operation in the long run when such a decision is forced upon them by market conditions.

(5) Within the securities department, some large life companies have remarkably small investment staffs to produce and review security investments. Small staffs tend to make companies dependent upon outside sources for generation, evaluation, and negotiation of prospective investment opportunities. They also tend to limit the diversity of areas in which a company invests. These circumstances result in production of a limited eligibility set from which the company can choose. Substantial expansion of the

opportunity set can be achieved by increasing the size and diversified skills of the department staff, and by maintaining close contacts with borrowing customers, brokers, and other lenders. Some short-run sacrifice of yield may sometimes be required to maintain these contacts, but the problem here appeared to be much less acute than in the mortgage organization. Development of a set of corporate lending specialities may have resulted in some competitive advantages to life companies. There seemed to be nothing inherent in industry specialization that prevents a company from responding quickly to a changing mix of opportunities. However, it takes good management to maintain a fluid and flexible organization.

(6) In large companies investment choice decisions are a product of a complex set of interactions among the finance committee, the top operating investment officers, and the staff analysts. Conflicts in tastes, preferences, backgrounds, evaluations of risks, and views about the ultimate investment objectives of life companies among these three groups often exist and can produce uncertain and sluggish responses in asset choices. The most flexible companies, therefore, are likely to be medium-sized companies with a single financial vice president, respected by the finance committee, making all basic allocation policy decisions and reviewing all loans generated by the investment organization.

(7) Diversification, income risk, and liquidity considerations play minor roles at most in influencing selection of investments in security departments. Concern for geographic diversification does have some influence on the allocation of residential mortgage funds. Its primary effect has been to restrain life company lending in California, and perhaps marginally in one or two other high growth areas. It is difficult to separate diversification motives from other factors influencing geographic diversity, however. The desire to maintain a nationwide field organization in the long run and the desire to sell insurance policies nationwide both tend to produce restraints on geographic concentration of mortgage funds. Some special risk features of the high growth areas may also enter in a marginal way. It is clear that some short and intermediate losses in yield are incurred as a result of life company geographic allocation policy.

(8) Some rough notions regarding loan priorities exist which do

result in nonprice rationing. In the securities department, customer, policyholder, and public service loans may receive some degree of preferential treatment. Usury complexes tend to result in nonprice rationing in high demand periods, although equity incentive financing is sometimes used to increase yield without showing "excessive" contract interest rates. Companies also ration by reducing the maximum and average size of loans in tight funds periods.

(9) Within mortgage departments, companies active in lending on residential properties will often give this sector priority status in a tight funds period in order to maintain the field organization. Within the residential sectors many companies expressed strong preferences for conventional as opposed to federally underwritten loans. In particular, there is pervasive reluctance to acquire deep discount FHA or VA loans. The usual sluggish adjustment of ceiling contract rates on these loans therefore results in their being rationed out of life company portfolios to a significant degree in high interest rate periods.

(10) It appeared that companies adjust residential mortgage flows, in particular, by varying downpayment, maturity, and borrower credit requirements more frequently than yields. This practice reflects the traditional sluggishness of mortgage yields. It also implies that the demand for mortgage funds is terms elastic.

It is difficult to obtain sound quantitative estimates from qualitative evidence. We do not know whether the conclusions summarized above refute a yield maximization hypothesis or whether their impact is limited to producing a little friction in the time rate of response. To evaluate the sensitivity of life company portfolio decisions to changes in relative asset yields, an empirical analysis of investment decisions is needed. However, to test aggregate life company responses to changing yields empirically, we need to separate life company responses to, from life company determination of, the structure of financial asset yields. In addition we must recognize the existence of competing motivations and the complexity of investment mechanics which also shape portfolio selections. It is to these problems that we now turn.

An Empirical Investigation of
Life Insurance Company Portfolio Choices

Objectives

The object of this investigation is to isolate the primary factors which have shaped life insurance companies' portfolio selections from a variety of available investments. Capital markets can be expected to allocate loanable funds efficiently among competing demands only if the principal lenders alter the composition of their investments reasonably quickly in response to changing market signals. In practice the set of market signals usually most clearly observed by participants is that represented in the structure of yields available in new and outstanding financial assets. As financial institutions go, life insurance companies control a large volume of investible funds and tend to purchase a relatively wide range of assets. Therefore, the degree of responsiveness in life companies' portfolio choice decisions to variations in the yield structure is of considerable importance to an evaluation of the performance of U.S. capital markets.

Abstracting from the mechanical details of the investment process, we have formulated a simple maximization of expected yield decision rule as a hypothesis about the way in which life companies' portfolio choices are made. We reinterpreted the hypothesis in the context in which life company asset allocation decisions have to be made, recognizing the difficulties involved in forecasting cash flow and the set of available assets. Next, we reviewed the process by which life company portfolio selections are made. We found that nonyield considerations and problems of investment costs and organization in some cases compromise an expected yield rule, and in others suggest the likelihood of a sluggish rate of response to variations in relative yields. The task before us now is to specify more precisely: (1) how yield responsiveness should be reflected in observable magnitudes; and (2) the way in which nonyield considerations affect life company portfolio composition decisions.

Determinants of the Corporate Bond/Residential Mortgage Mix

During the 1950s better than three-quarters of the dollar volume of life insurance companies' portfolio acquisitions consisted of corporate debt obligations and mortgage loans. Consequently, as a first approximation of the portfolio choice problem, we shall treat the allocation problem as one of choosing between corporate bonds and mortgage loans. Indeed, since nonresidential mortgage loans are a heterogeneous collection presenting some special problems, we shall narrow the choice further and consider residential mortgage loans as the alternative to corporate bonds. The objective of this section, then, is to explain the allocation of new investment decisions between the corporate and residential mortgage sectors.

From the results of our analysis of forward commitments in Chapter VI, and the interview evidence just summarized, we can isolate the many and diverse factors affecting the composition of new commitments under four headings:

(1) the going yields on corporate bonds and residential mortgages;
(2) the anticipated flow of available funds through life companies and their current stock of liquid assets;
(3) organizational restrictions inhibiting shifts in portfolio proportions;
(4) the demand for delayed takedown commitments.

In the remainder of this chapter we consider the manner in which each of these factors is expected to shape the corporate bond/residential mortgage loan commitment mix. Having translated these influences into empirically observable magnitudes, we shall report the results of the regression analysis in Chapter VIII.

RELATIVE YIELDS

How sensitive are life companies to relative yields on bonds and mortgages in their allocation of commitments? This is a difficult question to formulate with conceptual preciseness or to hope to answer empirically. Life insurance companies in the aggregate are not a negligible force in either the corporate or the mortgage markets. They influence as well as react to bond mortgage yield spreads. Nonetheless, if there are strong forces external to life companies' lending decisions and if enough richness of experience in terms of variations in yield differentials is available, it may be possible to estimate the direction and relative strength of life company responses to changes in yields.

Measurement problems

Measurement of asset yields presents many problems. These include making appropriate allowance for differences in the risk characteristics of various assets, estimating lending costs associated with particular asset types, dealing with geographic variations in yields, interpreting the meaning of externally imposed controls upon interest rates, evaluating the reliability of market quotations, and distinguishing between yields on newly issued and seasoned assets of the same type.

The quality of credit is an elusive concept.[26] Many terms in a loan contract and many characteristics of the borrower can influence a lender's appraisal of the loan's quality in the context of the lender's portfolio objectives. It may be the case in some markets that market adjustments are made largely through loan terms other than yields.[27] In general tightness in loan terms is positively correlated over the business cycle with the level of yields, although some complications exist where contract terms impinge upon the risk characteristics of a loan in more than one way.[28] Thus, although temporal deterioration of credit is commonly identified with liberalization of credit terms, these are not necessarily always equivalent concepts.[29] In sum, the relations among mort-

---

[26] For a recent discussion of the meaning of credit quality and its measurement, see the U.S. Savings and Loan League, Conference on Savings and Residential Financing, 1964 *Proceedings*, pp. 58–96.

[27] It is suggested above (p. 430) that this is true of the residential mortgage market. Also see Guttentag, "The Short Cycle in Residential Construction, 1946–59," p. 283. High intercorrelation of mortgage yields and other loan terms has made empirical separation of the effect of yields, maturities, downpayments, etc., upon the demand for funds and for housing very difficult, however. For example, see Break, *The Economic Impact of Federal Loan Insurance*, p. 242.

[28] For some examples, see Guttentag's discussion of the relation of loan maturity and loan size to risk and yield in the U.S. Savings and Loan League Conference on Savings and Residential Financing, 1964, *Proceedings*, pp. 134–136.

[29] See Kendall, "The Quality of Credit," in *ibid.*, pp. 58–73.

gage loan yields, other terms, and risk are quite complex and relatively little is known about the nature of the interrelations.[30]

Estimation of effective yields obtained by lenders is also particularly difficult for mortgage loans because of substantial origination, servicing, and legal costs which are sensitive to loan size and the volume of mortgage activity engaged in by the lender. Geographic variations in yields are also primarily a problem in the mortgage market. Finally, the existence of administered ceiling rates on VA-guaranteed and FHA-insured mortgages complicates the selection of an appropriate yield index for these loans.

Measurement of corporate bond yields presents fewer critical problems, but is not without difficulties. Quality grading of corporate bond issues makes allowance for risk less of a problem. There are bothersome differences between new issue and seasoned issue bond yields, however, and between yields on publicly as opposed to privately placed bond issues.

We shall return to measurement problems below. First, however, in order to formulate a meaningful net yield spread hypothesis, we must be able to place life insurance companies' supply response in the context of a corporate bond–residential mortgage model in which yields and loan volumes are determined. There is a fairly substantial bloc of literature concerned with the impact of monetary policy on residential mortgage and construction markets, which depicts mortgage lenders in general and life insurance companies in particular as passively responding to changes in mortgage–bond yield spreads generated by shifts in the corporate sector's demand for external financing.[31] In this literature the roughly countercyclical movements in residential financing and construction activity have been attributed to fluctuations in the supply of mortgage credit about a presumed stable demand for mortgage credit schedule. The orientation of most of these writers

---

[30] Break has experimented with a composite credit-terms variable, including interest rate, loan-to-value, and maturity components in estimating demand elasticity. See Break, *op. cit.*, Appendix A.

[31] See, for example, Guttentag, "The Short Cycle in Residential Construction"; Break, *The Economic Impact of Federal Loan Insurance*, Chapter 5; Alberts, "Business Cycles, Residential Construction Cycles and the Mortgage Market"; Brimmer, *Life Insurance Companies in the Capital Market*; Klaman, *The Postwar Residential Mortgage Market*; and the papers contributed by James J. O'Leary and Warren L. Smith to the U.S. Senate Subcommittee on Housing, *Study of Mortgage Credit*, 1958, pp. 209–264.

is well summarized in an observation of Goldsmith's appearing in his foreword to Klaman's *The Postwar Residential Mortgage Market*. Goldsmith wrote:

> . . . we know very little about the demand for mortgage loans. Klaman's book, as virtually all literature in the field, concentrates on the supply side, partly because, as he suggests, it has been supply rather than demand that has determined volume and price in the postwar residential mortgage market.[32]

Unfortunately, the authors of these credit supply oriented studies have produced largely impressionistic and sketchy models. In most cases the relevant demand and supply schedules are only vaguely specified. Nonetheless, since most of these writers do clearly regard life insurance companies as lenders responsive to yield differentials, their works provide a useful starting place for us.

A descriptive model

Reading some specifics into this literature, we can spell out the relevant interrelationships as follows. Imagine a capital markets model with a corporate long-term debt sector and a residential mortgage loan sector. The corporate sector's demand for long-term external funds as a function of bond yields is assumed to be quite inelastic and highly volatile over the general business cycle. Presumably, this assumption is made with a demand for external funds schedule in mind that is derived from a modified accelerator theory of investment demand. Taking an eclectic position, we might postulate the corporate demand for long-term funds via bond issues to be a function of the sector's:

(1) capacity utilization;
(2) rate of internal funds (depreciation plus retained earnings) flow;
(3) outstanding debt and stock of liquid assets;
(4) direct borrowing costs.

With the demand schedule formulated as a function of interest costs, the other variables listed are shift variables. The existence of a general business cycle is assumed. The cyclical fluctuations in overall economic activity generate changes in capacity pressure

---

[32] P. xxiv.

and in the cash flow and balance sheet variables. Consequently, cyclical patterns on the demand for external funds are created. Given the supply of funds to the corporate sector (to be discussed below), volatility in the demand schedule produces variations in corporate debt contract terms in general and bond yields in particular.

By way of contrast, the demand for funds in the residential mortgage loan market is presumed to be quite elastic with respect to loan yields (or an index of loan terms) and to possess a high degree of stability over the general business cycle. The demand for mortgage funds is assumed to derive from the final demand for housing space.[33] Demand for housing is theoretically quite complex.[34] A staggering list of variables that have been considered as relevant demand determinants in published studies of residential construction can be found in the Commission on Money and Credit paper prepared by Grebler and Maisel.[35] Further, many of these variables are thought to be interrelated in quite complicated ways.[36]

Following Maisel, the proximate determinants of demand for housing units can be identified as:[37]

   (a) household formation
   (b) changes in desired vacancy rates and
   (c) net removals from the housing stock

---

[33] The closeness of the link between demand for housing and demand for mortgage funds seems to be taken for granted. Its plausibility derives from the fact that a high proportion of housing investment is externally financed. It is true that residential mortgage credit extension during the 1950s was approximately equal to the value of new residential construction. There has never been any reason, however, to think this near-equivalence was anything but accidental. Recently, in the early 1960s, mortgage financing has increased relative to residential construction, and any illusion of the existence of a systematic relation between loan and construction activity has been empirically quashed. See Sommers and Rhine, "The New Dimension in Mortgage Debt." Given this caveat, however, it is no doubt true that the demand for housing space is the dominant determinant of the demand for mortgage funds.

[34] See Duesenberry, *Business Cycles and Economic Growth,* Chapter 7; Lewis, *Business Conditions Analysis,* Chapter 20; and Maisel, "A Theory of Fluctuations in Residential Construction Starts."

[35] Grebler and Maisel, "Determinants of Residential Construction: A Review of Present Knowledge," pp. 476–477.

[36] *Ibid.*

[37] Maisel, "A Theory of Fluctuations," pp. 362–371.

These immediately influential factors can, in turn, be affected by a variety of potential variables including:

(a) demographic characteristics
(b) household disposable income
(c) household assets (liquid and housing)
(d) housing prices and rents
(e) credit terms
(f) consumer tastes
(g) builders' and promoters' profit expectations

Demographic and taste variables presumably shape the long-run equilibrium demand for housing. Around this "real" demand trend, short-run fluctuations in final demand occur.[38] The impact of the general business cycle on household disposable income and liquid assets may generate some shifts in housing demand, but the moderate nature of postwar economic fluctuations is thought to have rendered this effect of secondary importance quantitatively.[39] Builders are assumed to respond reasonably quickly to profit opportunities created by excess demand whether this condition is reflected to them in rising house prices (rents), lower vacancy rates, or more rapid sale of completed units. The crucial short-run factor shaping housing and mortgage credit demand, most authors argue, is the cost and availability of credit.

There is no unanimity among mortgage market students with regard to the question of whether mortgage interest rates represent the cost of capital to potential homeowners or whether other loan terms dominate. For those demanders of housing space who are

---

[38] This is where Maisel (*ibid.*) breaks with the credit-oriented studies. Maisel finds no convincing theoretical rationale or empirical evidence of systematic short-run shifts in final demand. He believes that deviations from an equilibrium trend path are an inventory cycle phenomenon with real — not financial — roots.

[39] The essentially countercyclical pattern of the postwar residential construction cycle seems to have been enough to convince most analysts that changes in disposable income have not been responsible for the cyclical variations in housing activity. See Grebler, *Housing Issues in Economic Stabilization Policy*, pp. 16–21, and Guttentag, "The Short Cycle in Residential Construction," pp. 286–287. Estimates of the income elasticity of housing demand show generally small coefficients (about 0.5), see Grebler and Maisel, "Determinants of Residential Construction," p. 605. A low short-run demand elasticity is not necessarily inconsistent with a relatively income-elastic long-term function. See Reid, *Housing and Income*, p. 6, who obtained housing demand income elasticity coefficients of 1.5 to 2.0 using a permanent income measurement.

seeking to purchase their first home, it has often been suggested that downpayment requirements play a critical role in determining the point in time at which these households enter the market.[40] Monthly payments, which are a function of loan maturities as well as interest rates and the loan/value ratio, and the ancillary costs of home ownership may also influence the decision to form a new household, to shift from rental to home ownership, or to upgrade housing. Only new household formation obviously increases the demand for new housing units, but upgrading and normally the rental-to-ownership shift increase the average expenditure per unit.[41]

If a move toward credit ease does stimulate an increase in the number of housing units demanded and/or the demand for upgraded housing, there may be some cumulative effect resulting from increased activity in real estate markets. This will be true to the extent that increased activity makes it easier for those households contemplating moves to sell the homes they currently occupy. Some upward pressure on prices may develop which may in turn induce more sales of existing homes and reinvestment of the gains in upgraded housing. This effect will be dampened, of course, by the influence of rising house prices on demand.

It is conceivable that a reshuffling of the housing stock might itself have some influence on the total number of units demanded as households find it easier to acquire the particular type of housing desired. This movement could result in shortages of some types of housing accompanied by increases in vacancy rates for housing with less desirable characteristics. Thus a stimulus to

---

[40] See, for example, Duesenberry, *op. cit.*, p. 139. Implicit in the credit-oriented explanations is the notion that lenders consciously ration credit by changing acceptable loan/value ratios over the business cycle. If lenders were always willing to make any size loan, relative to the appraised value of the property, at a price (interest rate), then it would be the going interest rate that rationed demand. For a view that a contract terms rationing assumption is neither plausible nor necessary to explain postwar mortgage market activity, see Muth, "Interest Rates, Contract Terms, and the Allocation of Mortgage Funds."

[41] It seems to be an empirical truth that home owners spend more on housing than rental households in equivalent income classes. (Grebler and Maisel, *op. cit.*, p. 610.) It is useful theoretically and necessary statistically to separate demand for housing units from average expenditure per unit. (*Ibid.*, p. 548.) We are, of course, concerned with the sum of both elements of housing demand.

new construction might result from a redistribution of a given stock. Further, it is possible that an active market would stimulate new household formation derived from undoubling. Finally, an active market may lead to greater buoyancy in builders' sales and profit expectations, inducing them to increase starts and housing inventories. However, very little is known about the quantitative significance of any of these possibilities.[42]

The lack of agreement regarding the route by which credit terms affect residential construction is reflected in discussions of the role of a backlog in basic housing demand in producing credit-induced cyclical waves. It has been suggested that a prerequisite to the credit sensitive postwar housing demand was a depression-war backlogging of housing needs, which could be quickly translated into effective demand by easing the availability or cost of credit.[43] Guttentag, however, has argued that a credit-based short cycle can be self-sustaining even though the housing stock is in equilibrium with respect to the basic long-run demand for housing.[44] Credit terms are viewed as affecting the timing of demand within a year or two. Thus the short-term response to easier credit derives from those who were forced to postpone effective market action during the preceding tight credit period. This presumably means that the housing upswing would tend to lose some of its force after having existed for a couple of years even though no credit tightening takes place.

On the supply side it must be assumed that residential construction starts, in fact, respond to changes in the demand stimuli. Builders are expected to respond to changes in housing prices or rents (relative to construction costs) or to an excess demand for housing at going prices.[45]

Finally, lenders are assumed to be sensitive to changes in the relative attractiveness of competing corporate and residential

---

[42] See Maisel's discussion of the effect of credit terms on builders' desired inventories, "A Theory of Fluctuations," p. 378. Break does find that the timing of household formation is affected by credit terms and availability and implicitly by real estate market activity. Break, *op. cit.*, pp. 63–65.

[43] Grebler and Maisel, *op. cit.*, pp. 492–493.

[44] Guttentag, "Determinants of Residential Construction," esp. pp. 290–298.

[45] Alberts explicitly postulates an elastic supply schedule of new houses with respect to house prices: "Business Cycles, Residential Construction Cycles, and the Mortgage Market." Also, see Duesenberry's discussion in *Business Cycles and Economic Growth*, pp. 145–149.

mortgage debt obligations. Specifically, it is assumed that a significant bloc of lenders exists in the residential mortgage market whose supply of mortgage funds schedule is highly elastic with respect to the differential between mortgage yields and the yields on corporate instruments. The larger life insurance companies, mutual savings banks, and some commercial banks are considered to make up this group of responsive lenders.[46]

We can now summarize the foregoing discussion. For simplicity, we suppose that suppliers of funds to the corporate debt and residential mortgage sectors are not active in supplying other markets. Further, we assume away the existence of secondary markets; all portfolio acquisitions are of new issues. For any period, let

D_B = demand for funds by the corporate sector through new bond issues

D_M = demand for funds by households via mortgage loans on residential property

S_B = lender supply of funds to the corporate sector

S_M = lender supply of funds to the residential mortgage market

K_U = an index of capacity utilization in the corporate sector

PD = the retained profits and depreciation flow available to the corporate sector during the period

L_C = liquid assets held by the corporate sector

D_C = corporate term debt outstanding

r_B = yield on new corporate bond issues

Y_D = households' disposable income

A_H = household assets available for expenditure on housing

F = the flow of investible funds available to lenders during the period

r_M = yield on new residential mortgage loans

Behavioral equations:

$$D_B = f_1(\overline{K_U}, \overline{PD}, \overline{L_C}, \overline{D_C}, r_B)$$

---

[46] Most savings banks and savings and loan associations will find that variations in the amount of mortgage funds supplied will be determined for them by fluctuations in net savings inflow, particularly in response to variations in the level of interest rates. Here it is depositors, rather than the institutional intermediaries, who are sensitive to variations in the bond-mortgage yield spread.

$$D_M = f_2 \left(\overline{Y_D}, \overline{A_H}, r_M \right)$$
$$S_B = f_3 \left(\overline{F}, r_B, r_M \right)$$
$$S_M = f_4 \left(\overline{F}, r_M, r_B \right)$$

Equilibrium conditions:

$$S_B = D_B$$
$$S_M = D_M$$

Budget Equation:

$$\overline{F} = S_B + S_M$$

Excepting bond and mortgage yields, all variables are assumed to be exogeneous or predetermined. The general business cycle is taken as given. During the cyclical expansion rising profits and pressure on capacity produce a demand for capital goods in excess of the internally generated cash flow available for capital financing. Thus D_B shifts to the right, producing upward pressure on bond yields. As lenders respond, mortgage yields also rise. Lender supply schedules are not sufficiently elastic to prevent a rise in the bond-mortgage yield spread. Eventually, as capital goods are put in place, the growth of aggregate demand slows and corporate debt ratios rise, D_B shifts back to the left. Consequently bond yields fall, and as lenders respond, mortgage yields also fall, but not as much. As aggregate demand declines this process is accentuated. The demand for mortgage loans is responsive to reduced mortgage yields so the volume of mortgage loan activity increases to offset the decline in bond issues.

What does this tell us about life insurance allocation of funds between corporate bonds and residential mortgage loans? Is it possible to identify statistically the life insurance sector's supply of funds schedules for the mortgage and bond markets? If the story we have related is empirically viable, then we ought to observe a high positive correlation between life companies' bond/mortgage allocation decisions and the ratio of, or spread between, going bond and mortgage yields. There does seem to be an observable cyclical pattern in bond-mortgage yield differentials during the postwar period (see Table VI-B-1). The above account explains the major movements and changes in direction of this yield spread in terms of shifts in the corporate demand for funds schedules. Supply of funds and demand for mortgage funds schedules are assumed to be relatively quite stable over the observed cycles. However, the extent to which yield differentials move in response to shifts in corporate demand does depend on the interest rate elasticity of each of the remaining schedules. If life company allocation decisions are essentially unaffected in the short run (short cycle) by variables other than yield spreads,[47] then as a first approximation it is reasonable to formulate and estimate life company supply of funds schedules in the form shown above.

Forward commitments in the model

We have attempted to capture the essence of the credit-oriented residential construction literature at the risk of some oversimplification. The above description is static in the sense of assuming that a given volume of funds is allocated among the various demands for funds with bond and mortgage yields determined by the current demand and supply schedules and the budget constraint. However, a strict budget equation need not be imposed. Indeed we have suggested that the relevant measure of life companies' allocation decisions must be new loan and investment commitments. If lending decisions are represented by forward commitments, then the relation between commitment decisions and current funds flows can be quite loose.[48] Some of the short-run adjustment process may take place through slack in the relation of total loan commitments to lender cash flow. When dealing with a period as short as a quarter or less, it may be more reasonable to consider all the independent variables predetermined. Then the demand and supply schedules are functions of past yields and current decisions affect future asset yields.

---

[47] It is assumed either that lenders and borrowers are responsive to yields alone or that variations in yields are a good proxy for the changes in the mix of loan terms that in fact occur to equilibrate demand and supply.

[48] It may be that life companies aim at keeping the stock of commitments in line with expected future cash flow (see Chapter VI). In this case a fairly strict budget constraint may be definable in terms of forecast available funds. As noted below, the yield spread thesis must assume that the adjustment of commitments to future cash flow is neutral with respect to the composition of new commitments.

In this sense recognition of the existence of forward commitment activity may be at least partial justification for assuming current bond and mortgage yields are determined independently of current life company portfolio decisions. This interpretation is valid if forward commitment decisions are made on the basis of current, not expected future, yields. As we have seen from interview evidence (Chapter VI), this is a reasonable assumption.

All the above argument is based on the assumption that the flow of investible funds through life companies does not vary systematically over the business cycle in any way that affects the allocation of portfolio decisions between bonds and mortgages. For the sake of simplicity, in the model above we assumed the total supply of funds to be invariant during the period of analysis. Where the supply decisions are interpreted to be new forward commitment decisions, the funds variable must be interpreted as the forecast of available funds flow over some designated future period. Assuming that it is proportions of funds flows that are allocated to the competing sectors on the basis of relative yields, then it is possible to treat as the dependent variables S_B/F and S_M/F, where $S_B/F + S_M/F = 1$. The supply schedules have finite elasticity, i.e., investment flows are always diversified because of nonyield portfolio objectives or organization inflexibilities. This approach does assume, however, that variations in F do not influence the desired allocation of F among competing assets, that is, the proportions S_B/F and S_M/F are independent of F.

Next we consider whether it is, in fact, appropriate to treat changes in future funds flows as neutral with respect to decisions about portfolio proportions at the margin. Subsequently we shall consider whether other variables that shape the life insurance supply of funds function can be regarded as stable over the business cycle.

CASH FLOW AND LIQUID ASSETS

From our analysis of the time sequence of total new commitments (Chapter VI), we concluded that life companies were strongly influenced by a desire to achieve and maintain a fully invested position. Life companies seemed to be consciously adjusting their stock of forward commitments in line with their anticipated flow of investible funds. By the same logic commitment decisions should be responsive to any gap between actual and target liquid asset holdings although the case for a liquid asset effect was empirically inconclusive. The question here is whether pursuit of the loaned-up objective influences the corporate bond/residential mortgage composition of new commitments.

It is conceivable that attempts to fulfill a fully invested goal will be nonneutral with respect to the composition of commitment decisions. Such an effect may be a consequence of differences among the major asset categories in terms of the anticipated time distribution of payments from new commitments and the predictability of the payout distribution. In addition, alternative investment outlets may differ in terms of the ease of adjusting the flow of funds into particular assets. Matters of the loan mechanics, loan size, and demand for funds elasticities are relevant in determining the ability of life companies to control the volume and composition of commitment decisions.

The payout distribution

The time distribution of payouts from current loan commitments matters because the loaned-up objective focuses on adjusting loan decisions to anticipated funds inflow over the coming six months or so. Takedowns from residential mortgage loan commitments seem to be concentrated in a period two to eight months following finance committee voting, the early takedowns representing loans on existing properties and the later disbursements, loans on newly constructed single family homes. Longer disbursement periods are to be expected on new apartment and commercial construction.

Takedowns from corporate security commitments seem to be less concentrated in terms of elapsed time between voting and payout. In addition, we have seen (Chapter VI) that the shape of the disbursement distribution varies considerably over time. These differences between corporate and residential mortgage commitment-takedown lags are not very surprising when one considers the relative heterogeneity of the needs that trigger a corporation's search for external financing. These differences matter if they influence the mortgage/bond mix of new commitments when shifts in net future funds availability call for expansion or contraction of total commitment activity. Other things being equal, the greater concentration of residential mortgage loan disbursements in the relevant period suggests that adjustments in total votings prompted by loaned-up considerations may be effected disproportionately in residential mortgage loans.[49]

This judgment, however, is based on ex post voting-payout patterns observed for a large sample of loans over time. In order to achieve operating flexibility, loan officers must be able to predict future disbursements with reasonable accuracy. Klaman has asserted that a high degree of predictive accuracy has not been achieved by life companies in their mortgage commitment activity.[50] Instead, he finds the mortgage commitment process characterized by uncertain voting-payout lags and uncertain commitment attrition rates resulting from borrower cancellation of commitments. Such uncertainty is thought not to be characteristic of corporate security commitments. Klaman concludes, "The timing of acquisitions and hence of the actual need for ready funds in the mortgage market is far less certain than in the market for corporate securities." [51]

It is difficult to uncover any hard evidence on the relative predictability of commitment-disbursement lags between the corporate bond and residential mortgage sectors. Klaman's comparison apparently is an impression derived from interviews with life insurance company investment officers. He suggests, for example, that while the typical lag on new residential construction may be anywhere between six and twelve months, direct placement commitments for corporate bonds ". . . are quite definite as to dates so that the time of acquisition can be carefully planned." [52] We were unable to acquire the data necessary to test this assertion, but our qualitative impressions from interviews do not corroborate Klaman's conclusion. It appeared to us that, particularly in the case of large companies making a substantial volume of corporate bond commitments for which expected takedown dates were a year or more in the future, the anticipated delivery dates were

---

[49] This is the conclusion reached by Roger F. Miller in a draft paper, "A Model of Life Insurance Company Investment Behavior" (ditto), pp. 10–11.

[50] Klaman, *The Postwar Residential Mortgage Market*, p. 144.

[51] *Ibid.*

[52] *Ibid.*

often quite vague. More relevant for evaluating the impact of the "fully invested" goal is the predictability of takedowns from new commitments expected to be disbursed within six or eight months. Even in this range, we did not obtain the impression that delivery dates for corporate bonds were nearly so predictable as Klaman indicates.[53] This is quite a complex question, however, and in large companies where different people are involved in residential mortgage lending from those active in the securities department, it proved very difficult to elicit meaningful comparisons of the success in predicting payouts from mortgage as opposed to bond commitments.

Two ancillary observations are relevant here, however. Flexibility with respect to mortgage loan deliveries from mortgage company originators is available where loans are ready in advance of prediction or of the actual investible cash flow by asking the mortgage company temporarily to inventory the completed loans. This is not difficult so long as working capital financing is readily available to the mortgage company. Second, even if the ability of predicting the disbursement of funds for individual commitments is somewhat inferior for mortgage compared with bond votings, larger life companies, in particular, may nonetheless have better success predicting timing of takedowns for a bloc of mortgage commitments than for an equivalent dollar volume of corporate security votings. Ten million dollars of commitments may be accounted for by a handful of corporate bond votings but will represent hundreds of separate loan commitments to the mortgage department.

Klaman's evidence on commitment attrition consists of the experience of one large life insurance company. He reports that the cancellation rate for this company during the 1950s had averaged one-fifth of its mortgage commitments and had varied widely

---

[53] As noted in Chapter VI, we did secure a complete list of new commitments for corporate securities for one large life insurance company over a considerable portion of the 1950s. In general, we found that the longer the commitment, the more vague the expected takedown date. However, even for relatively short commitments, the anticipated delivery date was often represented as a range of two or three months. Indeed this vagueness regarding forecast disbursements proved troublesome in trying to estimate the time distribution frequency of anticipated takedowns for various subperiods. Since we were unable to obtain the record of actual delivery dates, we could not evaluate the accuracy of the forecasts which were made.

over time from less than 10% to 40%. It is not clear whether this rate is computed for all the company's mortgage activity, but it apparently does include some nonresidential loan commitments. The LIAA began collecting data on borrower cancellation of commitments in 1957. For the period which overlaps most of our regression analysis of new commitments (January 1957–March 1960), we computed the ratio of commitment cancellations to total disposals of outstanding commitments, i.e., acquisitions plus cancellations. The quarterly attrition ratios by major loan category are displayed for this period in Table VII-1.

TABLE VII-1. Commitment Cancellation Ratios:* Quarterly, 1957/I–1960/I

Asset Type: Quarter	Corporate Bonds	Residential Mortgages	Business & Industrial Mortgages	All Assets†
1957/I	.066	.138	.062	.084
II	.099	.153	.115	.114
III	.041	.100	.100	.076
IV	.038	.095	.192	.095
1958/I	.071	.130	.108	.102
II	.067	.131	.287	.115
III	.081	.114	.266	.117
IV	.066	.102	.195	.106
1959/I	.078	.104	.208	.097
II	.056	.105	.174	.082
III	.218	.108	.143	.141
IV	.032	.102	.123	.076
1960/I	.069	.085	.174	.086
1957/I–1960/I	.076	.111	.165	.100

* Computed as cancellations/acquisitions plus cancellations. Acquisitions include loans made from commitments contracted during the same month as well as acquisitions from commitments outstanding at the beginning of the month.

† Includes asset types not shown separately.

SOURCE: LIAA *Forward Commitment Survey.*

The attrition rate is somewhat higher for mortgages than corporate bonds although the problem appears to be more acute in the commercial mortgage sector than in residential lending. In either case, Klaman's company seems to have had an exceptionally adverse cancellation record.[54] Also, for the aggregate data the range of attrition rates is narrower over time for residential loans than it is for corporate bonds, contrary to Klaman's presumption.

Control over commitments

Do life companies have better control over the origination of residential mortgage loan or corporate bond commitments? On this question also the evidence is mixed.

There are some reasons for thinking that the volume of funds allocated to the mortgage sector is under tighter control than are corporate security commitments. In part this is based on the considerations of loan size cited above in connection with predictability of commitment payouts. It is plausible to suggest that the time rate of funds flow into small home loans is easier to control than the flow into large, indivisible corporate obligations. In fact the time path of life company corporate bond votings (and acquisitions) is characterized by sharp discontinuities while the analogous pattern of home mortgage loan votings (and takedowns) is relatively smooth.[55] This presumably reflects, in good part, the lumpiness of investment activity in securities departments.

In turn life company portfolio preferences and cost considerations are being reflected. Life companies prefer relatively long-term obligations, and the demand for funds in this sector of the market comes in large chunks compared to borrowing for working capital purposes. In addition life companies like to lend in relatively large amounts for cost reasons — securities analysis is a complex and costly business — and total investigating costs are largely independent of loan size. In our interviews we found that most large life companies had a policy of trying to avoid loans to corporations in amounts under $250,000. Therefore direct placement activity, in particular, results in quite large loans by residential property standards and in loan originations that have a relatively long gestation period before bearing a new commitment.

---

[54] Barring a significant general reduction in attrition between the mid-1950s and the late 1950s.

[55] See Charts VI-7 and VI-9.

Another aspect of the question of control over investment flow is demand elasticity. As we have observed, it is generally believed that the demand for residential mortgage funds is substantially more price elastic than the demand from corporate borrowers. For this reason it is considered possible to regulate the flow of mortgage loan commitments through relatively small changes in loan terms whereas only a much cruder control over corporate bond commitments can be exercised in this manner.

There is, however, a contrary argument based on the mechanics of loan origination. Corporate bond commitments are generated largely through home office personnel; home mortgage loans are generated primarily through a network of mortgage correspondents and/or branch office personnel. There is some evidence that control over the inflow of new commitments diminishes with the distance of the originating agents from the home office. Although this may not be inevitable, many companies in fact reported difficulties maintaining control over the inflow of new mortgage loan proposals to the finance committee. Reports of unhappy experiences with mortgage overcommitments were frequent in the literature and in our interviews. As a consequence many companies found it necessary to impose dollar volume quotas on their mortgage originating agents as a supplemental or substitute device to regulation of the mortgage flow by varying acceptable terms. While use of dollar quotas may bring the rate of loan commitments under better control, their use dramatizes life companies' inflexibility in responding quickly to variations in the flow of available funds. Perhaps the appropriate conclusion to draw from these considerations about life companies' ability to regulate the volume of mortgage loan commitments is that home mortgage loan activity can be expanded quickly, but some time is required to implement a decision to reduce loan volume.[56] Doubts exist regarding their ability to control the rate of expansion, however.

Summary

Does life company pursuance of a fully invested objective have implications for the composition of commitment decisions? On balance there are reasons for expecting residential mortgage vot-

---

[56] This seems to be Klaman's conclusion. See *ibid.*, p. 143.

ings to be more responsive to variations in the future available funds flow than corporate bond votings. This conclusion is based on differences between mortgages and bonds in regard to the time sequence of payouts from loan commitments, average loan size, typical negotiation time, and the terms elasticity of final demand. The conclusion is somewhat clouded by a lack of knowledge regarding the relative predictability of funds disbursement dates for mortgages as opposed to bonds. More important, there exist some serious doubts about the ability of life companies with large field organizations to regulate the mortgage loan commitment volume.

It remains, therefore, an empirical question whether a fully invested goal compromises the relative yield objective in life company portfolio composition selections. In any case neutrality cannot be safely assumed *a priori*.

THE SERVICING HYPOTHESIS

In Chapter V we investigated the time rate of issuance of total new loan commitments by life insurance companies. We found that life companies' desire to invest their cash flow as it becomes available had a primary role in shaping the time pattern of total votings. However, the loaned-up objective seemed to apply with force only to new commitments which would be expected to produce loan takedowns within six or eight months. This left unexplained the time path of votings not anticipated to result in delivery within this period. To explain these delayed takedown commitments, we offered the servicing hypothesis. This thesis simply recognized that long-term loan commitments are of value to certain borrowers, and that the demand for delayed takedown commitments is therefore distinguishable from the demand for current funds. One reason life companies are in the forward commitment business is that they are peculiarly able to provide such a service and a demand for it exists.

As we observed in Chapter VI, these two hypotheses are essentially complementary; the loaned-up thesis is relevant for understanding the volume of loan votings generated over time that are expected to result in takedowns within a few months, and the servicing hypothesis applies particularly to longer delayed takedown votings. Empirically, then, the logical procedure was to separate loan votings into at least two groups classified by the anticipated voting–delivery lag and explain each set of votings separately. However, the LIAA *Forward Commitment Survey* did not provide this breakdown. Therefore we had to conduct the analysis on total votings and include variables representing each of the complementary hypotheses in the same multiple regression equations.

The servicing hypothesis reappears in this chapter as apparently competitive with the yield spread and loaned-up hypotheses for the same reason. We began the analysis of investment composition choices with a simple variant of the "maximize expected yield" portfolio selection rule. Applied to the life insurance company sequential investment problem, this involved life companies in making forecasts of (a) available funds, (b) their opportunity set of available financial assets, and (c) the structure of yields on these assets. On the basis of these forecasts, life company policymakers established minimally acceptable yields and terms on eligible assets. An arbitrarily designated investment period was considered; six months or a year seemed reasonable from discussions with life company officers. Given the policy guidelines, the investment organization proceeds to generate loan proposals which meet the current standards.

In order to perform an empirical analysis of the descriptive validity of this sort of yield-focused model of asset choice, we have to examine investment decisions. But investment decisions are commitment decisions, and for life insurance companies not all commitment decisions made in any period are relevant to the asset composition of funds actually invested during the period. Once again the desirable procedure would be to separate current investment decisions which determine the allocation of current cash flow from current decisions which commit future cash flow and analyze the former. But we do not have the breakdown of votings data that makes this separation possible.

Thus once more in conducting the empirical analysis of the composition of life company votings decisions we shall have to work with total votings in each asset category. If delayed take-down votings were made on the same criteria as votings affecting the cash flow allocation in the current period, this would not be a serious problem. It would only mean that it is not possible to define a budget restriction on total votings. Indeed we have concluded above (Chapter VI) that life companies do seem to negotiate direct placements on the basis of current market conditions regardless of the anticipated takedown date on the prospective loan. But the forward commitment servicing hypothesis introduces a specific nonreturn consideration into life companies' asset choice decisions, or perhaps better, alleges for a particular reason that observable interest rate indices are an imperfect measure of relative asset returns.

In the context of the bond/mortgage choice, the forward commitment servicing thesis applies strongly to corporate bonds, and, excepting large multifamily projects, essentially not at all to residential mortgage lending.[57] It predicts that total corporate bond votings depend not so much on the bond/residential mortgage yield spread, but on the corporate demand for delayed takedown forward commitments. Since we are empirically unable to identify corporate bond votings by their expected takedown dates, we shall have to consider the servicing phenomenon as a specific modification of the yield spread hypothesis and look for an adequate measure of shifts in the corporate demand for delayed forward commitments.

ORGANIZATIONAL CONSTRAINTS AND ASSET PREFERENCES

The elasticity of life companies' investment composition response to changing relative asset yields will depend upon the importance of organizational constraints and asset preferences which inhibit portfolio choice flexibility. These considerations will determine both the yield-elasticity of life company supply of funds schedules and the time rate of adjustment in the allocation mix when relative yields change. We have just completed discussion of the loaned-up and servicing objectives as qualifications to a simple yield-spread hypothesis. But our summation of life insurance company allocation mechanics and nonreturn motives constituted a warning that considerable additional inertia, inflexibility, and compromise with yield maximization may be evident.

In the context of the corporate bond/residential mortgage loan selection decision, the organizational requirements for production

---

[57] It may have applicability to life company relations with some large tract builders and promoters.

and servicing of home loans can lead to substantial compromises with yield objectives. This is a consequence of difficulties in maintaining control over the rate at which loan proposals come in from the field and also of a need to provide reasonably steady funds flows of a minimum volume to the field in order to reduce asset costs and/or maintain a loyal and efficient field organization. Devices intended to solve the inflow control problem, such as volume limits on field offices or correspondents, generally produce the secondary effect of reducing a life company's flexibility in changing the flows. The minimum total mortgage funds flow requirement, at times when mortgage yields are low relative to those on competing assets, can lead to a target investment mix which is biased toward mortgage loans when compared with an expected yield maximization norm. The practice of some companies in setting long-run mortgage/asset targets suggests that they may be relatively unresponsive to short-run variations in relative yields. We have caught the most important bias in corporate bond votings in the servicing objective.

Nonreturn portfolio objectives and peculiar asset preferences may also offset the corporate bond/residential mortgage selection mix. Diversification and other nonyield considerations seemed to lead to a geographic spreading of life company mortgage funds which results in some yield sacrifice. Thus, while the mortgage sector may get more than its share of life company funds at certain times in order to placate the field organization, it may receive less than its share because of constraints on loan concentration in specific high growth areas, especially California.[58] The proportion of cash flow placed in residential mortgage loans is also affected by life company attitudes toward the federally underwritten mortgage programs. We found adverse attitudes in a number of companies. In particular, most large life companies seem very reluctant to allot funds to deep discount FHA and VA loans.

Finally, evidence of use of nonyield rationing devices indicated that yields are not the sole concern of life companies. It appeared that the mortgage flow was more frequently altered by changes in nonyield loan terms and credit standards than by adjustments in acceptable yields. In corporate bond selections, evidence of usury

---

[58] Interpreting "its share" as the share which would result from concern with relative yields alone.

complexes, preferential treatment to customers, and adjustments in acceptable loan size provided indications of nonyield rationing.

Summary

We have argued that, with some qualification, life insurance companies allocate their cash flow among alternative eligible assets by selecting the assets carrying the highest yields. Their yield orientation is qualified by a desire to maintain a fully invested position and to take advantage of competitive devices available to them to secure and cultivate attractive customers. A particular competitive device which limitations in commitment data require us to recognize is life companies' utilization of forward commitments as a service designed to meet the needs of some corporate borrowers. Finally, the yield elasticity of life company funds supply schedules and the speed of their response to changes in the yield structure is conditioned by various other nonyield considerations and mechanical details of the allocation process.

In order to test the relative importance of these determinants of life companies' investment composition over time, we performed a least squares multiple regression analysis on life company commitment authorizations by broad investment categories. These results we now report in Chapter VIII.

ALLOCATION OF INVESTIBLE

FUNDS AMONG ALTERNATIVE ASSETS:

The Regression Evidence

In an attempt to separate and discriminate among the several forces which may have influenced the composition of life insurance company portfolio selections during the 1950s, we performed simple least squares regression analyses on life company commitment votings by sector. As before, we particularly focused upon the sensitivity of portfolio composition choices to relative asset yields. To the extent that this relationship is weak, we wish to isolate the specific nonyield objectives and mechanical inflexibilities of the allocation process which are responsible for the failure to observe a strong and reasonably prompt response to changes in yield spreads.

The bulk of this analysis is confined to an examination of the corporate bond-residential mortgage loan votings mix. Loan authorizations in these two categories accounted for a little better than 70% of total loan votings during the period for which we had commitment data (October 1952–June 1960). We also briefly examine two other areas in which life companies have been relatively active; namely, (1) nonfarm, commercial, and industrial mortgage loans, and (2) state and local government debt obligations. The nonfarm, nonresidential mortgage loan sector is potentially of considerable importance but the properties securing the loans included under this heading are quite heterogeneous, and the quality of available data including both the breakdown of commitments by type of property and yield information is very poor. Consequently our analysis of this sector is more limited than it ought to be. As we have seen, the 1959 tax reform cre-

Variable Symbol	*Meaning*
Dependent Variables:	
V_B	Total corporate bond votings (new commitments)
V_{MR}	Total residential mortgage loan votings
V_{MF}	Total federally underwritten mortgage loan votings
V_{MG}	VA-guaranteed mortgage loan votings
V_{MI}	FHA-insured mortgage loan votings
V_{RC}	Conventional residential mortgage loan votings
V_{MB}	Business mortgage loan votings
V_{IM}	Manufacturing bond votings
V_L	State and local bond votings
Independent Variables:	
r_U	New issue corporate bond yields (Bankers Trust Grade 2 Public Utility bond series)
r_F	Effective yield on federally underwritten mortgage loans (including discount)
$r_{I(G)}$	Effective yield on FHA loans (Guttentag series)
r_G	Effective yield on VA loans (*House and Home* data)
r_I	Effective yield on FHA loans (*House and Home* data)
r_{RC}	Yield on conventional residential mortgage loans (composite)
r_B	Yield on new issue corporate bonds, industrial sector (composite estimate)
$r_F{}^c$	Legal ceiling contract rate on federally underwritten loans
$r_U{}^n$	Twelve-month moving average of r_U
r_{MB}	Yield on business mortgage loans (based on loans on Manhattan real estate)
r_L	Moody's Baa municipal bond yield series, adjusted to tax-equivalent level
D_F	Price discount (below par) on federally underwritten loans
D_G	Price discount on VA loans
D_I	Price discount on FHA loans
D_T	Price discount on Treasury bonds
$AF_{m,m+5}$	Estimate of investible funds available for six months (net of expected loan takedown from loan commitments outstanding as of the beginning of $t = m$), where the dependent variable is observed at $m = 0$

TABLE VIII-1 (continued)

Variable Symbol	Meaning

Independent Variables:

$AF_{m,m+1}$	Estimate of six months' available funds where dependent variable is observed quarterly, $m = 0$
G_M	Gross mortgage loan acquisitions
G_{MC}	Gross conventional mortgage loan acquisitions
N_M	Net mortgage loan acquisitions
N_{MC}	Net conventional mortgage loan acquisitions
T_S	Stock of short-term Treasury obligations (due in less than one year) held by life companies
CT_S	Stock of cash plus short-term Treasury securities held by life companies
V_M	Total mortgage loan votings
C	Stock of total outstanding life company loan commitments
$E_{m,m+5}$	Loan commitments expected to be taken down during the six months indicated (dependent variable observed for month $t = 0$)
T	Stock of total Treasury securities held by life companies
S	Total life company assets
NB_M	New issues of manufacturing sector bonds (SEC reported)
ΔB_M	Change in outstanding stock of manufacturing bond issues
CAN	NICB new capital appropriations
R	New issues of revenue bonds by state and local governments (*Bond Buyer*)

ated the potential for greater life company interest in municipal issues, so a separate investigation of the qualities of municipal obligations which have attracted life companies seemed desirable.

The commitment data we have to work with are the same as those utilized in Chapter VI.[1] The meanings of the symbols used in this chapter are explained in Table VIII-1. The yield and price discount data utilized are displayed in Appendix VIII-A. We proceed now to the reporting of the regression results.

---

[1] The reader will recall that the forward commitment data are compiled monthly by the Life Insurance Association of America from a survey questionnaire covering about 65 or 66 companies representing approximately two-thirds of the industry's assets.

The Corporate Bond-Residential Mortgage Votings Mix

To begin, we test the proposition that the corporate bond/residential mortgage new commitment composition is responsive to the differential between bond and mortgage yields. Using quarterly observations, we regress the ratio of corporate bond to residential mortgage votings on the bond/residential mortgage yield spread. Bond yields were represented by the Bankers Trust Grade 2 New Issue Public Utility Bond series used in Chapter VI's total votings regressions. The mortgage yield series is based on reported effective yields on federally underwritten loans. To allow for the higher unit cost of home mortgage loan origination and servicing, we deducted 50 basis points from the reported gross effective yields.[2]

The results of regressing the bond/mortgage votings ratio on the bond/mortgage yield differential appear in equations (1) to (3) of Table VIII-2. Over the 31 quarters for which the commitment data were available, the relationship is positive as predicted but the fit is unimpressive.[3] We also ran separate regressions for two subperiods by dividing the original period at end-1956. From our analysis in Chapter IV we found that this point roughly separates the relatively flush funds, open-to-buy transition environment of the immediate post-Accord years from the relatively scarce funds circumstances prevailing later in the decade. Curiously enough, we find (equations 2 and 3) a rather strong sensi-

---

[2] This is inconsequential. It would be helpful in estimating elasticities of votings response to yields if the level of the bond yield series accurately reflected typical returns life companies were obtaining. In general, yields on Grade 2 utility bonds are too low for this purpose and are based on a sector which had declining importance in life company portfolios during the 1950s. As noted in Chapter VI, however, we wanted a series based on sufficient homogeneous observations and representing activity in new issues to obtain an accurate reflection of the cyclical pattern of bond yields. We did experiment with adjusting the Bankers Trust series to reflect the level of industrial bond yields and using data on yields obtained by a few life companies to reflect the level of yields relevant to life companies. Judging by equations in which this series was tried as an alternative to the Bankers Trust series, somewhat higher R^2s can be obtained by using the adjusted series where yields appeared to be relevant explanatory variables. However, in what follows most of the results reported are based on the Bankers Trust series.

[3] Lagging the yield spread one quarter does not improve the fit.

TABLE VIII-2. *Regression Analysis of the Corporate Bond–Residential Mortgage Votings Mix*

Quarterly
1952/IV–1960/II
$n = 31$

(1) $V_B/V_{MR} = 1.1408 + .3183\,(r_U - r_F)$
$\qquad\qquad\qquad (.1585)$
$R^2 = .1220 \qquad s = .2853$

Quarterly
1952/IV–1956/IV
$n = 17$

(2) $V_B/V_{MR} = 1.5802 + .8249\,(r_U - r_F)$
$\qquad\qquad\qquad (.1997)$
$R^2 = .532 \qquad s = .2448$

Quarterly
1957/I–1960/II
$n = 14$

(3) $V_B/V_{MR} = .8540 - .1283\,(r_U - r_F)$
$\qquad\qquad\qquad (.2263)$
$R^2 = .026 \qquad s = .2486$

Quarterly
1952/IV–1959/IV
$n = 29$

(4) $V_B/V_{MR} = 1.120 + .3234\,(r_U - r_F)$
$\qquad\qquad\qquad (.1506)$
$R^2 = .145 \qquad s = .2608$
$\overline{R}^2 = .114 \qquad \bar{s}^2 = .2703$

Quarterly
1952/IV–1959/IV
$n = 29$

(5) $V_B/V_{MR} = 1.259 + .2671\,(r_U - r_F)$
$\qquad\qquad\qquad (.1667)$
$\qquad\qquad - .0001603\,AF_{0,5}$
$\qquad\qquad\quad (.0001974)$
$R^2 = .166 \qquad s = .2576$
$\overline{R}^2 = .102 \qquad \bar{s} = .2720$

Quarterly
1952/IV–1959/IV
$n = 29$

(6) $V_B/V_{MR} = 1.341 + .1240\,(r_U - r_F)$
$\qquad\qquad\qquad (.2138)$
$\qquad\qquad - .0003220\,AF_{3,8}$
$\qquad\qquad\quad (.0002479)$
$R^2 = .197 \qquad s = .2528$
$\overline{R}^2 = .136 \qquad \bar{s} = .2669$

Quarterly
1952/IV–1960/I
$n = 30$

(7) $V_B/V_{MR} = 1.3036 - .0003419\,AF_{0,5}$
$\qquad\qquad\qquad\quad (.0001871)$
$R^2 = .105 \qquad s = .2932$

Quarterly
1957/I–1960/I
$n = 14$

(8) $V_B/V_{MR} = 1.2484 - .0003366\,AF_{0,5}$
$\qquad\qquad\qquad\quad (.0002249)$
$R^2 = .169 \qquad s = .2398$

Quarterly
1953/I–1959/IV
$n = 28$

(9) $V_B/V_{MR} = 1.231 - .0002919\,AF_{0,5}$
$\qquad\qquad\qquad\quad (.0001886)$
$R^2 = .084 \qquad s = .2748$
$\overline{R}^2 = .042 \qquad \bar{s} = .2852$

Quarterly
1953/I–1959/IV
$n = 28$

(10) $V_B/V_{MR} = 1.258 - .0001598\,AF_{0,5}$
$\qquad\qquad\qquad\quad (.0002018)$
$\qquad\qquad + .2672\,(r_U - r_F)$
$\qquad\qquad\quad (.1700)$
$R^2 = .166 \qquad s = .2621$
$\overline{R}^2 = .099 \qquad \bar{s} = .2774$

TABLE VIII-2 (continued)

Quarterly
1953/I–1959/IV
$n = 28$

(11) $V_B/V_{MR} = 1.739 - .0003561\, AF_{0,5}$
$(.0002514)$
$+ .3745\, (r_U - r_F) - .05710\, D_F$
$(.1877)$ $(.04462)$

$R^2 = .219$ $s = .2536$
$\overline{R}^2 = .122$ $\bar{s} = .2740$

Quarterly
1953/I–1959/IV
$n = 28$

(12) $V_B/V_{MR} = 1.414 - .0002292\, AF_{0,5}$
$(.0003060)$
$+ .3782\, (r_U - r_F)$
$(.1895)$
$- .04281\, D_F + .00006442\, CAN$
$(.04899)$ $(.00008679)$

$R^2 = .238$ $s = .2506$
$\overline{R}^2 = .105$ $\bar{s} = .2766$

Quarterly
1953/I–1959/IV
$n = 28$

(13) $V_B/V_{MR} = .9796 + .0001393\, AF_{0,5}$
$(.0002862)$
$+ .7012\, (r_U - r_F)$
$(.1918)$
$- .05645\, D_F + .00008037\, CAN$
$(.04195)$ $(.00007410)$
$+ .0008311\, \Delta BM_{(2)}$
$(.0002668)$

$R^2 = .471$ $s = .2088$
$\overline{R}^2 = .351$ $\bar{s} = .2356$ $d = 1.1171$

NOTE: $\overline{R}^2$ is the coefficient of determination adjusted for degrees of freedom. $\overline{S}$ is the standard error of estimate adjusted for degrees of freedom. d is the Durban-Watson coefficient.

tivity of the votings mix to the yield spread in the earlier subperiod but no response (the regression coefficient actually has a negative sign) during the tight funds years.

It is not obvious why such a difference in response should have existed. However, it is possible that the relatively liquid position in which life companies found themselves in the earlier years permitted greater responsiveness to variations in yield spreads. Life company sensitivity to yield differentials does not seem to have produced more narrow variations in spreads during these years, however. This may mean that the difference in life company reaction to movements in yield spreads between the two periods was not so great, or that life companies' ability to influence this particular spread is limited, or that much of the adjustment in the mortgage market takes place in other loan terms, and mortgage yields are at best an imperfect proxy for the relevant composite terms variable.

Lack of sensitivity to yields in the post-1956 era could reflect any number of considerations discussed in the preceding chapter. Organizational inertia, faulty control over issuance of commitments, concentration on keeping "fully invested" or on servicing repeat customers are some of the possibilities. Mistakes from the perspective of relative yields may appear more magnified and the adjustments may proceed more slowly when there is only a limited pot of liquid assets to draw upon as a source of funds.

In equations (4) to (8), Table VIII-2, we add available funds[4] to the picture in order to ascertain whether pursuance of the loaned-up goal produces a secondary effect on portfolio composition. Again the R^2s are low but the sign on the available funds variable is consistent whether it is used as the lone explanatory variable or in conjunction with the bond/mortgage yield spread, whether the funds measure overlaps or fully leads the quarter of voting decisions, and regardless of the period for which the regression is run. This is some, albeit weak, evidence that residential mortgage loans tend to be the preferred avenue for adjusting the stock of commitments to the available future funds inflow. The pull of the available funds flow in this direction appears to be somewhat, but not much, stronger in the later (post-1956) subperiod than in the period as a whole.

Some of the other considerations we have discussed may also compete with or impede the yield objective in determination of the votings mix. In equations (9) to (13) we add variables representing two of the factors which seemed important in prior analysis. Aversion to price discounts on federally underwritten mortgage loans may inhibit life companies' response to favorable mortgage yields. The size of the prevailing discount is added to the funds and yield spread variables in equation (11). The sign on the regression coefficient is consistent with the discount aver-

---

[4] The variable is the same used in Chapter VI. It is designed to measure the flow of investible funds available to life companies at any initial date, $t = 0$, net of the stock of commitments existing at $t = 0$ and due for delivery during the period of interest. See Chapter VI's discussion of the computation and weakness of the series.

sion hypothesis, but the coefficient is not significant and addition of this variable contributes little to the explained variance.

We have also suggested previously that corporate bond commitments may respond to customer demand independently of observable movements in market yield spreads. The difficulty lies in measuring these broad shifts in the corporate demand for loan commitments. As a rough means of ascertaining whether there might be something in this hypothesis we added two proxy measures of corporate demand for future long-term funds. These were the National Industrial Conference Board's New Capital Appropriations series and the net change in the stock of SEC-reported, long-term manufacturing debt outstanding two quarters in the future. Each of these is obviously quite crude for the purpose and there is some danger of circularity in using the SEC series. However, a clear negative result from introducing these variables would indicate that this line of reasoning is not worth following further. The actual results in equations (12) and (13) are mixed. Both have the right sign, but the appropriations variable is nonsignificant and contributes nothing to explaining the votings composition. The future change in manufacturing debt variable does make a statistical contribution, however. Its addition also increases the importance and significance of the yield spread variable, suggesting that some mix of relative yields and corporate customer demand has an important explanatory role to play here. To check the seriousness of the serial correlation problem we computed the Durbin-Watson test coefficient for the last equation. Its value is in the inconclusive range of the Durbin-Watson significance test.

On balance, these results are not very promising. Some indication of yield responsiveness is present but not consistently. The results do not reject the other determinants tested, namely, the investment composition impact of the loaned-up goal, the distaste of mortgage price discounts, and the corporate customer servicing theses. Neither do they clearly confirm the importance of any combination of these explanatory hypotheses. It may be that we attempt too much in seeking to explain the bond/mortgage votings composition directly by regression analysis. As we have seen previously, it is very possible that this particular mix is of no special consequence to life companies, and simply comes out in the wash as companies try to meet a number of more specific objectives. Also, since corporate bond and residential mortgage loan commitments add up to less than three-quarters of new commitment decisions, factors influencing votings in the residual categories may well affect the bond/mortgage votings mix.

It appears that we can reduce the complexities involved by breaking down the problem further and attempt to isolate the significance of various forces at work in each sector independently. Then we can put the pieces back together again. We proceed to analyze, first, residential mortgage votings and, second, new corporate bond commitments. After this we shall briefly examine nonresidential mortgage loan and municipal bond commitments.

Residential Mortgage Loan Votings

As we have seen, much has been made of the existence of a short cycle in residential construction and mortgage credit activity during the postwar years. Most literature on residential mortgage financing is supply oriented; it places considerable emphasis on the existence of some lenders, particularly in the life insurance industry, who are responsive to variations in the relative attractiveness between residential mortgage loans and competing assets. If the arguments underlying these explanations of cyclical activity in residential mortgage and construction markets are correct, then we ought to observe new home mortgage loan commitments responding to variations in the spread between mortgage and bond yields, assuming that the time path of yields is a reasonably accurate stand-in for movements in the whole complex of loan terms that are relevant to life companies' calculation of anticipated returns.

There is a question regarding the level of aggregation appropriate in explaining life company residential mortgage market activity. The main concern is whether life companies treat FHA-insured, VA-guaranteed, and conventional loans as different assets or whether they are essentially indifferent to the form a loan takes. This question has been raised and discussed above.[5] Here we are specifically faced with deciding what measure of mortgage yields

---

[5] Chapters IV and VII.

is relevant to the regression analysis and whether or not separate equations for each of these loan types is necessary or meaningful.[6]

A specific complication arising from the operation of federally underwritten mortgage loan programs has been the existence of legal ceiling contract loan rates chargeable on FHA and VA loans. This fact forces a choice between using the administered ceiling rate as an index of mortgage yields or, where discounting occurs, an effective yield series incorporating the price discount into the yield computation.[7] Presumably, if discounting is common, an effective yield series is the only appropriate measure. The problem is muddied, however, where legal, public relations, or psychic barriers to discounting exist. Judging from our interviews with life company officers, aversion to dealing in federally underwritten loans with significant price discounts is quite strong in a number of companies. Some companies may even be so sensitive that use of the ceiling rate would be justified. For the industry as a whole, however, or that part included in the commitment survey evidence, the qualitative evidence suggests that the appropriate method of handling this problem is to use effective yield data and to include price discount information as a separate variable.

Actually, in the regression analysis reported on in Table VIII-3, we have included the discounting phenomenon in two ways. Some equations include estimates of prevailing price discounts, consistent with estimates of current effective yields, as a separate variable — measured as price points below par. In other equations the mortgage/bond yield differential is split into two variables: (1) the spread between the federally underwritten mortgage ceiling rate and the corporate bond yield,[8] and (2) the excess of the effective mortgage loan yield over the ceiling rate.

---

[6] Another breakdown which would be most relevant for eventually fitting the mortgage financing results into a residential construction expenditures model is the distinction between loan commitments on existing as opposed to newly constructed structures. This distinction is unfortunately not available in the commitment statistics.

[7] Premiums seem to have been rare during the period under study, so for practical purposes effective yield on FHA-VA loans has never been less than the ceiling rate.

[8] As before, we have not attempted to adjust for any variations in lending costs which may have occurred over time. Where residential mortgage loan-bond yield spreads are used, 50 basis points have been deducted from the mortgage yield figures. This, of course, has no impact on significance tests.

TABLE VIII-3. *Regression Analysis of Residential Mortgage Votings: Results of Runs on Monthly Observations*

Runs: October 1952–January 1960 $n = 88$

A. Total Residential Mortgage Votings

(1) $V_{MR} = 135.8477 + 61.0862 \, (r_{I(G)} - r_U)$
(18.5148)

$R^2 = .112$ $s = 57.6558$
$\overline{R}^2 = .092$ $\bar{s} = 58.3477$

(2) $V_{MR} = 80.3291 + 104.4643 \, (r_{I(G)} - r_U)_{-3}$
(16.1435)

$R^2 = .328$ $s = 50.1859$
$\overline{R}^2 = .312$ $\bar{s} = 50.8383$

(3) $V_{MR} = 249.2719 + 25.3724 \, (r_{I(G)} - r_U) - 19.7803 \, D_F$
(15.9502) (2.9389)

$R^2 = .421$ $s = 46.5706$
$\overline{R}^2 = .401$ $\bar{s} = 47.4554$

(4) $V_{MR} = 198.8881 + 52.7737 \, (r_{I(G)} - r_U)_{-3} - 15.3050 \, D_F$
(18.6536) (3.9312)

$R^2 = .455$ $s = 45.1794$
$\overline{R}^2 = .436$ $\bar{s} = 46.0378$

B. Federally Underwritten Mortgage Votings

(5) $V_{MF} = 5.1683 + 85.0872 \, (r_F - r_U)$
(12.5051)

$R^2 = .350$ $s = 40.7274$
$\overline{R}^2 = .335$ $\bar{s} = 41.2569$

(6) $V_{MF} = 98.5634 + 45.6310 \, (r_F - r_U) - 14.0922 \, D_F$
(12.6602) (2.4397)

$R^2 = .533$ $s = 34.5156$
$\overline{R}^2 = .517$ $\bar{s} = 35.1714$

C. VA Mortgage Votings

(7) $V_{MG} = 41.5182 + 81.0018 \, (r_G - r_U)$
(11.9975)

$R^2 = .346$ $s = 40.9775$
$\overline{R}^2 = .331$ $\bar{s} = 41.5102$

(8) $V_{MG} = 62.0854 + 33.7294 \, (r_G - r_U) - 11.0551 \, D_F$
(11.0730) (1.4272)

$R^2 = .617$ $s = 31.3757$
$\overline{R}^2 = .603$ $\bar{s} = 31.9718$

D. FHA Mortgage Votings

(9) $V_{MI} = 34.3087 + 15.1168 \, (r_{I(G)} - r_U)$
(6.7165)

$R^2 = .056$ $s = 20.9155$
$\overline{R}^2 = .034$ $\bar{s} = 21.1874$

TABLE VIII-3 (continued)

(10) $V_{MI} = 32.2938 + 15.8204\,(r_{I(G)} - r_U) + .4484\,D_I$
$\qquad\qquad\quad (7.1923) \qquad\qquad\qquad (1.5782)$

$\underline{R^2} = .057 \qquad\qquad s = 20.9069$
$\overline{R}^2 = .023 \qquad\qquad \bar{s} = 21.3041$

E. Conventional Residential Mortgage Votings

(11) $V_{RC} = 121.2986 - 7.7582\,(r_{RC} - r_U)$
$\qquad\qquad\qquad\quad (5.8820)$

$\underline{R^2} = \quad .020 \qquad\qquad s = 20.7170$
$\overline{R}^2 = -.003 \qquad\qquad \bar{s} = 20.9863$

(12) $V_{RC} = 117.0553 - 23.8630\,(r_{RC} - r_U) + .2391\,V_{MF}$
$\qquad\qquad\qquad\quad (5.9309) \qquad\qquad\qquad (.0446)$

$\underline{R^2} = .268 \qquad\qquad s = 17.9093$
$\overline{R}^2 = .242 \qquad\qquad \bar{s} = 18.2496$

F. Available Funds Added to the Analysis

$\qquad$ Monthly: January 1953–December 1959 $\qquad$ $n = 84$

(13) $V_{MR} = 88.4099 + .1184\,AF_{1,6}$
$\qquad\qquad\qquad\quad (.0192)$

$\underline{R^2} = .317 \qquad\qquad s = 50.7234$
$\overline{R}^2 = .301 \qquad\qquad \bar{s} = 51.3828$

(14) $V_{MR} = 67.1496 + .1361\,AF_{-2,3}$
$\qquad\qquad\qquad\quad (.0181)$

$\underline{R^2} = .407 \qquad\qquad s = 47.2662$
$\overline{R}^2 = .393 \qquad\qquad \bar{s} = 47.8807$

(15) $V_{MR} = 220.6129 + .0516\,AF_{1,6} - 17.3862\,D_F$
$\qquad\qquad\qquad\quad (.0212) \qquad\qquad\quad (3.3666)$

$\underline{R^2} = .486 \qquad\qquad s = 43.9984$
$\overline{R}^2 = .467 \qquad\qquad \bar{s} = 44.8784$

(16) $V_{MR} = 128.3866 + .1050\,AF_{-2,3} - 8.1270\,D_{F(-3)}$
$\qquad\qquad\qquad\quad (.0221) \qquad\qquad\quad (3.4908)$

$\underline{R^2} = .444 \qquad\qquad s = 45.7634$
$\overline{R}^2 = .424 \qquad\qquad \bar{s} = 46.6787$

(17) $V_{MF} = -14.9468 + .1084\,AF_{-2,3}$
$\qquad\qquad\qquad\quad (.0155)$

$\underline{R^2} = .373 \qquad\qquad s = 40.4409$
$\overline{R}^2 = .358 \qquad\qquad \bar{s} = 40.9666$

(18) $V_{MF} = -11.5596 + .1068\,AF_{1,6}$
$\qquad\qquad\qquad\quad (.0153)$

$\underline{R^2} = .373 \qquad\qquad s = 40.4461$
$\overline{R}^2 = .358 \qquad\qquad \bar{s} = 40.9717$

(19) $V_{MF} = 102.5226 + .0492\,AF_{1,6} - 15.0021\,D_F$
$\qquad\qquad\qquad\quad (.0164) \qquad\qquad\quad (2.6078)$

$\underline{R^2} = .555 \qquad\qquad s = 34.0807$
$\overline{R}^2 = .539 \qquad\qquad \bar{s} = 34.7623$

TABLE VIII-3 (continued)

(20) $V_{RC} = 82.0811 + .0277 \, AF_{-2,3}$
$\qquad\qquad\qquad (.0074)$
$\qquad R^2 = .145 \qquad s = 19.3076$
$\qquad \overline{R}^2 = .125 \qquad \overline{s} = 19.5586$

Monthly: October 1956–January 1960 $\qquad n = 40$

(21) $V_{MR} = 162.5847 + 8.9764 \, (r_{I(G)} - r_U) - 12.5991 \, D_F$
$\qquad\qquad\qquad (16.0202) \qquad\qquad\qquad (3.5964)$
$\qquad\qquad + \ .0765 \, AF_{1,6}$
$\qquad\qquad\quad (.0241)$
$\qquad R^2 = .483 \qquad s = 44.0136$
$\qquad \overline{R}^2 = .458 \qquad \overline{s} = 45.1139$

(22) $V_{MF} = 36.2526 + 38.1148 \, (r_F - r_U) - 9.4534 \, D_F + .0506 \, AF_{1,6}$
$\qquad\qquad\qquad (12.4145) \qquad\qquad (2.8337) \qquad (.0174)$
$\qquad R^2 = .576 \qquad s = 32.9080$
$\qquad \overline{R}^2 = .556 \qquad \overline{s} = 33.7636$

(23) $V_{MG} = 54.5955 + 32.4648 \, (r_G - r_U) - 10.7444 \, D_G$
$\qquad\qquad\qquad (11.4657) \qquad\qquad\qquad (1.5877)$
$\qquad\qquad + \ .0069 \, AF_{1,6}$
$\qquad\qquad\quad (.0151)$
$\qquad R^2 = .618 \qquad s = 31.3391$
$\qquad \overline{R}^2 = .600 \qquad \overline{s} = 32.1539$

(24) $V_{MI} = 10.8423 - 6.9816 \, (r_I - r_U) + 3.1279 \, D_I + .0396 \, AF_{1,6}$
$\qquad\qquad\qquad (7.2458) \qquad\qquad (1.7957) \qquad (.0100)$
$\qquad R^2 = .161 \qquad s = 19.7140$
$\qquad \overline{R}^2 = .121 \qquad \overline{s} = 20.2266$

(25) $V_{RC} = 106.4001 - 28.0956 \, (r_{RC} - r_U) + .1804 \, V_{MF}$
$\qquad\qquad\qquad (6.1101) \qquad\qquad\qquad (.0511)$
$\qquad\qquad + \ .0203 \, AF_{1,6}$
$\qquad\qquad\quad (.0092)$
$\qquad R^2 = .308 \qquad s = 17.4139$
$\qquad \overline{R}^2 = .275 \qquad \overline{s} = 17.8667$

Monthly: January 1953–December 1959 $\qquad n = 84$

(26) $V_{MF} = 144.3251 + .0045 \, AF_{1,6} + 49.5339 \, (r_{F^c} - r_B)$
$\qquad\qquad\qquad\quad (.0175) \qquad\quad (10.9202)$
$\qquad\qquad - \ 144.5630 \, (r_F - r_{F^c})$
$\qquad\qquad\quad (39.2437)$
$\qquad R^2 = .647 \qquad s = 30.3814$
$\qquad \overline{R}^2 = .629 \qquad \overline{s} = 31.2017$

(27) $V_{MF} = 85.3602 + .0294 \, AF_{-2,3} + 58.3684 \, (r_{F^c} - r_B)_{-3}$
$\qquad\qquad\qquad (.0196) \qquad\qquad (12.1420)$
$\qquad\qquad - \ 33.3721 \, (r_F - r_{F^c})_{-3}$
$\qquad\qquad\quad (42.6946)$
$\qquad R^2 = .559 \qquad s = 33.9442$
$\qquad \overline{R}^2 = .537 \qquad \overline{s} = 34.8607$

TABLE VIII-3 (continued)

$$(28) \quad V_{RC} = 95.0154 + .0234\, AF_{-2,3} - 20.4122\, (r_{RC} - r_{F^c})_{-3}$$
$$\phantom{(28) \quad V_{RC} = 95.0154} (.0076) \phantom{+ .0234\, AF_{-2,3}} (10.5657)$$

$R^2 = .183 \qquad s = 18.8790$
$\overline{R}^2 = .153 \qquad \bar{s} = 19.2566$

Monthly: August 1953–November 1956 $\qquad n = 65$
December 1957–December 1959

$$(29) \quad V_{MF} = 12.9209 + .0919\, AF_{0,5}$$
$$\phantom{(29) \quad V_{MF} = 12.9209} (.0199)$$

$R^2 = .253 \qquad s = 41.6365$
$\overline{R}^2 = .229 \qquad \bar{s} = 42.3860$

$$(30) \quad V_{MF} = 83.7224 + .0261\, AF_{0,5} + 79.4810\, (r_{F^c} - r_B)$$
$$\phantom{(30) \quad V_{MF} = 83.7224} (.0187) \phantom{+ .0261\, AF_{0,5}} (12.4975)$$

$R^2 = .548 \qquad s = 32.3949$
$\overline{R}^2 = .526 \qquad \bar{s} = 33.3020$

$$(31) \quad V_{MF} = 153.5438 - .0025\, AF_{0,5} + 57.8184\, (r_{F^c} - r_B)$$
$$\phantom{(31) \quad V_{MF} = 153.5438} (.0206) \phantom{- .0025\, AF_{0,5}} (14.2697)$$
$$\phantom{(31) \quad V_{MF} = 153.5438} - 139.2248\, (r_F - r_{F^c})$$
$$\phantom{(31) \quad V_{MF} = 153.543} (50.7361)$$

$R^2 = .598 \qquad s = 30.5673$
$\overline{R}^2 = .571 \qquad \bar{s} = 31.6066$

Monthly: July 1956–January 1960 $\qquad n = 43$

$$(32) \quad V_{MR} = 115.3551 + .0732\, AF_{0,5}$$
$$\phantom{(32) \quad V_{MR} = 115.3551} (.0169)$$

$R^2 = .313 \qquad s = 32.1411$
$\overline{R}^2 = .279 \qquad \bar{s} = 33.0411$

$$(33) \quad V_{MR} = 115.8519 + .0729\, AF_{0,5} + .1761\, (G_M - N_M)$$
$$\phantom{(33) \quad V_{MR} = 115.8519} (.0236) \phantom{+ .0729\, AF_{0,5}} (.1301)$$
$$\phantom{(33) \quad V_{MR} = 115.8519} - 31.6123\, (r_{RC} - r_U) - 3.6476\, D_F$$
$$\phantom{(33) \quad V_{MR} = 115.85} (14.8596) \phantom{(r_{RC} - r_U) -} (4.6962)$$

$R^2 = .426 \qquad s = 29.4101$
$\overline{R}^2 = .350 \qquad \bar{s} = 31.3218$

$$(34) \quad V_{RC} = 88.3743 + .0374\, AF_{0,5} + .0505\, (G_M - N_M)$$
$$\phantom{(34) \quad V_{RC} = 88.3743} (.0106) \phantom{+ .0374\, AF_{0,5}} (.0717)$$
$$\phantom{(34) \quad V_{RC} = 88.3743} - 29.0091\, (r_{RC} - r_U)$$
$$\phantom{(34) \quad V_{RC} = 88.374} (8.1921)$$

$R^2 = .343 \qquad s = 16.4628$
$\overline{R}^2 = .276 \qquad \bar{s} = 17.3353$

$$(35) \quad V_{MF} = 28.6623 + .0497\, AF_{0,5}$$
$$\phantom{(35) \quad V_{MF} = 28.6623} (.0100)$$

$R^2 = .376 \qquad s = 18.9532$
$\overline{R}^2 = .346 \qquad \bar{s} = 19.4839$

$$(36) \quad V_{MF} = 33.5778 + .0540\, AF_{0,5} - 9.5411\, (r_F - r_U)$$
$$\phantom{(36) \quad V_{MF} = 33.5778} (.0110) \phantom{+ .0540\, AF_{0,5}} (10.1814)$$

$R^2 = .390 \qquad s = 18.7541$
$\overline{R}^2 = .344 \qquad \bar{s} = 19.4855$

TABLE VIII-3 (continued)

$$(37) \quad V_{MF} = 63.4545 + .0425\, AF_{0,5} - 8.4960\, (r_F - r_U) - 4.0518\, D_F$$
$$\quad\quad\quad\quad\quad (.0136) \quad\quad\quad (10.0863) \quad\quad\quad\quad (2.8799)$$

$$\quad R^2 = .419 \quad\quad\quad s = 18.3013$$
$$\quad \bar{R}^2 = .359 \quad\quad\quad \bar{s} = 19.2713$$

$$(38) \quad V_{MF} = 3.1883 + .1118\, AF_{0,2} + .0251\, AF_{3,6} + .0570\, T_S$$
$$\quad\quad\quad\quad\quad (.0255) \quad\quad\quad (.0126) \quad\quad\quad (.0219)$$

$$\quad R^2 = .459 \quad\quad\quad s = 18.5893$$
$$\quad \bar{R}^2 = .372 \quad\quad\quad \bar{s} = 20.0950$$

Finally, we added the available funds measure into the analysis to see whether we find any further confirmation of the suggestion that residential mortgage lending plays a special role in life companies' use of forward commitment mechanics as a device to keep fully invested.

Yield Spreads

In Parts A to E of Table VIII-3 are displayed the main regression results derived from exploring the yield-spread hypothesis. This evidence indicates that yield differentials between residential mortgage loans and corporate bonds were a significant force in shaping the time path of life company new residential mortgage loan commitments during the 1950s.[9] The price discount on federally underwritten loans required to obtain the prevailing effective yield also enters strongly as a deterrent to residential mortgage activity.[10]

The strength of the discount variable in the total residential mortgage equation (Part A) suggests that variations in federally underwritten mortgage loan activity dominated the behavior of total residential lending. This presumption is confirmed by a comparison of results splitting total residential loans into two

---

[9] It makes no significant difference to the results reported in Parts A to E whether one of the FHA-VA effective yield series or the conventional residential yield series is used as the mortgage yield.

[10] There is evidence of serious serial correlation of the residuals in many of the reported regressions. We computed the Durbin-Watson test coefficient for the last equation in each set of regressions run in which independent variables were added stepwise. To keep the reporting manageable, we have not listed all these equations and therefore no 'd' coefficients appear in Table VIII-3. The equations for which 'd' was computed are similar to the ones reported except that quarterly seasonal dummy variables were included and in a number of equations a variable measuring mortgage loan turnover is

categories: (1) federally underwritten, and (2) conventional (Parts B and E). The yield spread and discount variables do perform strongly in the federally underwritten loan regressions. However, the spread between the conventional residential mortgage yield series and the corporate bond yield has the wrong sign. The discount variable is irrelevant for explaining conventional loan votings except to the extent that conventionals can be substituted for VA or FHA loan commitments when discounts are a deterrent. To measure this substitution effect directly, we introduced current federally underwritten loan votings as an independent variable (Equation 12). If conventional and federally underwritten loans were essentially alternatives within a given total permissible volume of mortgage commitments, the sign on V_{MF} in (12) ought to be negative. However, its coefficient turns out to be positive. Thus variations in conventional loan commitments tend to be in the same direction as federally underwritten loans, although the common force influencing both is apparently something other than a simple mortgage/bond yield spread.

Separation of federally underwritten loan commitments into its VA and FHA components reveals strikingly disparate patterns.

---

also included. The results obtained from adding these variables to the ones reported are summarized below.

For the runs on the period October 1952–January 1960 (Parts A to E) the range of 'd' coefficients were:

Part A .90–1.03
B .67– .84
C .44– .48
D .91– .92
E 1.40–1.95.

Since at the 5% significance level a 'd' ratio of less than about 1.48 is indicative of positively autocorrelated residuals, autocorrelation is a serious problem in all except the conventional residential loan votings equations. Most of the coefficients for the latter set (Part E) are either in the inconclusive range or permit rejection of the null hypotheses. Very similar coefficients resulted for sets of equations run on a slightly shorter period, January 1953 to December 1959 (Part F).

The discussion in the text is conducted on the assumption that this degree of serial correlation does not impair comparisons involving rough orders of magnitude of R^2 and standard errors. Obviously a good deal of caution is warranted, however. In particular, these results may exaggerate the difference between the fits on the federally underwritten loan equations compared to those on conventional loans. The validity of the general conclusions in the text is further tested below by an analysis of split time periods and of quarterly data where the more serious autocorrelation problems are alleviated.

(See Parts C and D.) It appears that life company VA loan activity totally dominated the federally underwritten commitment behavior. The R^2 for the FHA equations are insignificant and the sign on the discount variable is wrong. By way of contrast, the yield spread and discount variables appear to explain 60% of the variance in VA commitments over the period. This apparent insignificance of FHA lending is deceiving. Broadly, the pattern of life company total residential mortgage commitment (and federally underwritten) activity during the period under study appears as two complete cyclical movements with troughs in 1953, 1957, and 1960. The first cycle is much more prominent (in amplitude), particularly for FHA-VA loans. Within the federally underwritten loan category the bulk of commitments during the first of the two cycles occurred in VA-guaranteed loans, but in the second cycle FHAs composed most of a diminished total of federal loan commitments. In general the lower level of activity during the latter (1957–1960) period is due in part (as indicated by the regression results) to a narrower mortgage/bond yield spread and higher price discounts implied by the prevailing effective FHA and VA yields. We do not want to digress further into an explanation of the composition of federal credit program loans here. It will suffice for the moment to observe that discounts were smaller on FHAs than on VAs (i.e., the legal ceiling rate was higher for FHAs) during the late 1950s. Given the apparent significance of the discount factor, this fact must have borne strongly on the change in the FHA-VA composition. Other factors were relevant, however, including particularly changes in housing legislation which affected the relative attractiveness of the two broad programs and, of course, the specific eligibility requirement in the VA program (i.e., veteran status).

In all the loan categories included in Parts A to E in Table VIII-3, we also ran regressions similar to the ones reported with the yield spread and discount variables lagged three months. In most cases there was little to choose between the lagged and unlagged results. Where there was a significant difference, it is recorded in Table VIII-3. The rationale of using lagged independent variables is, of course, that it recognizes that companies may take some time to adjust policy in response to changes in yields, etc. Even very quick responses may not be reflected in votings for two or three months. It might well be that three months' allowance is insufficient to reflect the inertia in company policy decisions and loan mechanics. In the absence of reasonably clear *a priori* knowledge of the appropriate lag structure, however, there is little profit in experimenting with numerous varieties.

In sum, it appears that yield spreads and price discounts on FHA-VA loans together played a significant role in determining the time pattern of federally underwritten and total residential mortgage loan commitments of life insurance companies during the 1950s. As can be seen from the equations in Table VIII-3, introduction of a second independent variable generally has a significant impact on the regression coefficient of the first, indicating the presence of colinearity. Thus the relative importance of the yield spread and discount effects cannot be determined from these results. Very substantial positive serial correlation of the residuals is also present in many of the above regressions. This is especially troublesome in the total federally underwritten and VA loan regressions.

Available Funds

The next variable we have added (Table VIII-3, Part F) is the available funds flow measure, introduced to test the postulated discriminatory impact of pursuance of the fully invested goal on the composition of new commitments. The regression results displayed in Table VIII-3, Part F, equations (13) to (20) are composed of equations relating residential mortgage votings to the available funds variable.[11] Yield spreads are reintroduced below. The price discount variable was added to the available funds influence in some equations in the first set of regressions.

It appears that the response of residential mortgage votings to the available future funds flow was quite strong. In interpreting the relationships, it should be recalled that the subscripts on the available funds variable refer to the first and last month included in the six months' net funds inflow where the dependent variable

---

[11] Because of the manner in which the available funds variable is computed, the period of coverage is slightly narrower for these equations than for the yield spread regressions.

is understood to be observed in $t = 0$. In some equations we used $AF_{-2,3}$ as an independent variable. This may appear odd since the logic of the loaned-up hypothesis was that companies adjust their stock of loan commitments to the anticipated rate of future funds inflow. If, however, there is a lag between the decision to change the rate of mortgage votings on the basis of a six months' cash flow forecast, it may be two or three months before this decision is reflected in votings. If, as suggested earlier, the loaned-up proposition implies a particular sensitivity to relatively short-range cash flow predictions, then $AF_{-2,3}$ may be a more relevant variable than $AF_{1,6}$. It does seem to perform somewhat better than $AF_{1,6}$ in explaining variations in total residential mortgage votings.

As in the yield spread regressions, substantial discounts on federally underwritten loans seem to have a significant dampening effect on residential mortgage votings. Thus in equation (19) it appears that an increase of $130 million in available funds over the coming six months can be offset in its impact on VA-FHA loan votings by a one point decline in the market price of federally underwritten loans. Even allowing for the presence of colinearity between the available funds and discount variables, life companies' aversion to discounts appears to be real.

We have not included separate VA and FHA equations in this section, since the above summary of their respective time patterns suggested it made more sense to work with total federally underwritten loans. When separated, FHA votings appear more responsive to the funds flow and VAs to discounts as would be expected. As was true with yield spreads, federally underwritten loan votings appear more sensitive to variations in available funds than conventional loans. However, the response of conventional loan votings to available funds is positive and the regression coefficient is significant. In the conventional loan regressions, $AF_{-2,3}$ performed slightly better than $AF_{1,6}$.

As might be expected, there is some seasonality in mortgage loan commitments. We chose, however, not to run the regression analysis with seasonally adjusted data because such adjustments often hide more than they illuminate. We did estimate the importance of the seasonal pattern on votings by including quarterly seasonal dummies as variables in some equations. The effect of adding such dummies to equation (15) was to raise the adjusted R^2 from .467 to .552 and reduce the adjusted standard error of estimate from 44.89 to 41.15. Adding seasonal dummies to equation (19) raises $\overline{R}^2$ from .539 to .615 and reduces $\overline{s}$ from 34.76 to 31.73. As before, substantial positive serial correlation of the residuals is present in most of these regressions. It is most serious in the federally underwritten loan equations (e.g., the Durbin-Watson ratio for equation (19) with quarterly seasonal dummies is .9368, indicating significant positive autocorrelation of the residuals).

Thus, on the basis of the evidence discussed to this point, the version of the loaned-up hypothesis which asserts that the loaned-up objective is achieved particularly through residential mortgage commitment activity has about an equal claim to validity as the yield spread hypothesis. The available funds and yield spread variables are combined in a multiple regression analysis in the remaining equations recorded in Table VIII-3, (21) to (38).

Yield Spreads and Available Funds

Turning to this set of equations, interpretation of the relative significance of the yield spread, discount, and available funds variables is rendered difficult by the degree of multicolinearity present. Nonetheless an overview of all the regression evidence presented here suggests that all three variables are jointly relevant and significant in explaining the time path of life company residential mortgage loan votings during the period under study.

In most versions of total residential mortgage multivariate regressions run, the coefficient of the yield spread variable appears nonsignificant, but the overall evidence suggests the yield spread explanation cannot be discarded. Both yield and available funds considerations contribute significantly in the federally underwritten loan regressions. The aversion to discounts also continues to come through strongly. As before, apparently much better fits are obtained in the federal loan equations as compared to conventional votings, but the federal loan estimates continue to be plagued with strong positive autocorrelation of the residuals. Conventional votings still appear negatively related to the mortgage/bond yield spread even after introduction of the available funds variable into the regressions.

Nonetheless there is an overriding pull of conventional and federal loan votings in the same direction. Partly this reflects the common influence of available funds, but consistent directional movements appear to exist even with available funds partialed out. This is reflected in equation (25) where federal loan votings are included as an independent variable in a conventional loan votings equation and draws a positive (significant) sign. Also in equation (28) we included the spread between the going yield on conventional loans and the ceiling rate on federal loans as an explanatory variable. The reason for introducing this variable is to test the strength of the substitution effect between conventional and federally underwritten loans. The common influence of available funds on both types of loans and the disparate influence of the mortgage/bond yield spread suggested to us the following pattern of reaction to changes in available funds: (1) an increase in funds available in the near future triggers more residential loan votings; (2) if the mortgage/bond yield spread is favorable and the associated discounts low, then federal loan votings are particularly affected because it is in this form that new loans can be generated in volume most quickly; (3) if discounts are high and therefore a deterrent to heavy federal loan votings, conventional loan activity responds disproportionately. If this sort of substitution effect, dependent on prevailing discounts, was quite strong, then we might expect to see conventional loan votings positively related to the spread of the conventional loan rate over the ceiling federal loan contract rate, the impact of available funds having been allowed for. However, the conventional yield-ceiling rate spread variable draws a negative sign in equation (28), indicating that the substitution effect is not so strong as to control the absolute level of conventional votings. The above story may still be true, of course, as stated in terms of proportions.

In equations (26) and (27) we have handled the price discount problem by splitting the mortgage/bond yield spread into two variables, the split being made at the prevailing ceiling rate on federal loans. Again the discount deterrent is evident, as federal loan votings turn out to be positively related to the ceiling rate/bond yield differential, but negatively affected by the spread of the effective mortgage rate over the ceiling rate. It appears that the discount aversion may have been so strong that life company mortgage lending was reduced when discounts at the prevailing effective mortgage yield were high even though mortgage lending at lower yields still would have been attractive relative to securities investment. In these equations colinearity results in the appearance that the available funds variable is insignificant.

Of the principal internal constraints to short-run flexibility in the mortgage/bond votings composition, perhaps the most significant is the need to supply a minimum flow of funds to the high overhead mortgage departments. During most of the 1950s, an examination of yield spreads suggested, and interviews with life company loan officers confirmed, that mortgage loans were quite attractive relative to corporate debt opportunities on a net yield basis. Indeed, we saw that some companies had formulated mortgage/asset target ratios substantially in excess of prevailing proportions in mid-decade in recognition of the relative attractiveness of mortgages. Nonetheless, during the tight money phases in 1953 and 1957, the mortgage/bond yield spread was substantially reduced, and it is possible that life companies had minimum mortgage flow rules in force during these periods. Some indication of this sort of phenomenon appeared in examining residuals from federally underwritten loan voting equations. These residuals tended to be highly autocorrelated; in particular, actual votings exceed those predicted from the regression equation persistently during the tight money phases. Consequently, we ran a set of federal loan regressions dropping observations from the tight 1953 and 1957 phases to see if this resulted in greater observed sensitivity to yield and funds variables and reduced serial correlation. Samples from these results are reported in equations (29) to (31). Serial correlation is reduced slightly[12] but otherwise the results are essentially the same as the analogous regression run over the whole period. Thus, it does not appear that imposition of a minimum mortgage flow constraint on regression estimation would have any statistical payoff.

Logically, if the funds flow available in the near future influences mortgage loan votings, then fluctuations in companies' liquid asset

---

[12] The 'd' coefficients were computed for two equations in this set (ones including the quarterly seasonal dummies). For both 'd' was 1.32, higher than for federal loan equations run for the complete period but still indicative of significant positive serial correlation.

position, assuming desired levels are relatively stable, should have a similar impact. We argued, from an examination of the pattern of life company liquid asset variations in Chapter V, that life companies did seem to have rather stable target holdings and fluctuations resulted primarily from forecasting mistakes and to some extent, from taking advantage of available opportunities to dispose of securities. However, since all the explanatory variables we have been investigating have a rather strong cyclical element in their time pattern and liquid asset holdings are also dominated by a cyclical movement, addition of liquid asset holdings after available funds, yield spread, and discount effects have been partialed out does not contribute significantly to explaining the votings variance. Addition of total life company Treasury security holdings, or the excess over an assumed target of the Treasury obligations/total assets proportion, contributed nothing to an explanation of mortgage votings. The Treasury securities variable in any form is almost a pure trend variable, but apparently there is not much residual trend in mortgage votings even after the influence of the cyclical variables has been accounted for.

There is a question of causal relationship which needs to be aired before we conclude this section. This involves the assumption that it is variations in available funds that influence voting decisions. Part of the problem is one we discussed in Chapter VI, to wit, that the available funds series used is not actually an anticipatory series but is based on funds that in fact became available and portfolio acquisitions that were in fact made. This was a necessary expedient because anticipatory cash flow data were available only for the last part of the 1950s. In future studies cash flow data should be available for a sufficient period that it will not be necessary to risk accusations of regressing a partial identity.

A second problem of interpretation will arise even with use of anticipatory cash flow data, however. Voting decisions must be functionally related to gross cash flow, not simply net new inflow, for changes in the rate of portfolio rollover necessitate loan decisions as surely as changes in net new money flows through life companies. A problem of causality arises if it is possible to conceive of loan voting decisions leading to changes in the rate of portfolio turnover. If variations in mortgage loan activity result primarily from the supply of funds side of the market, and if increased mortgage lending tends to activate real estate markets, leading to more transfers of existing houses and to turnover of mortgage loans and refinancing of loans on different houses, then it could be that the relation between loan votings and mortgage portfolio turnover is essentially the reverse of that assumed. To test the importance of this possibility, we computed an estimate of mortgage rollover per period, gross acquisitions less net acquisitions, for the covered companies, and deducted this time series from available funds. Fortunately, substituting the resulting net available funds variable for the original made essentially no difference in the regressions sampled. This was done in all categories of regression equations reported on in Table VIII-3. The mortgage rollover, gross minus net acquisitions, was included as a separate variable in some equations. Its coefficient always had a positive sign but generally nonsignificant, and it made little additional contribution toward the R^2. Thus the available funds variable seems to survive as a meaningful and significant influence on votings decisions.

Mortgage Votings in the Scarce Funds Period

The remaining equations in Table VIII-3 to be discussed are those, (32) to (38), run for the post-open-to-buy period only. We ran some regressions with the open-to-buy cutoff placed at mid-1956 and the others beginning with January 1957. It did not seem to matter much which starting date was employed. The primary conclusion derived from these runs is that the available funds variable seems to be stronger and the yield spread influence weaker than seemed to be true for the period as a whole. This comes through particularly in the federally underwritten loan votings equations. In terms of the above discussion of the conventional, VA, and FHA breakdown, it reflects the fact that FHA loans dominated all federal program loans during the late 1950s. Results for conventional loan votings are no different than they were for the period as a whole. The yield spread and discount variables perform somewhat less well in the total residential mortgage loan regressions for the post-open-to-buy months.

Statistical analysis is somewhat easier for the late 1950s, and it probably will be also for the 1960s when the data become available, because the leading candidates as explanatory variables

are less colinear than over the 1952–1960 period as a whole.[13]
Thus, in the July 1956–January 1960 regressions the coefficient
for the available funds variable is not much affected by the
introduction of additional variables in a multiple regression
analysis. In equations (33) and (34) the mortgage turnover variable, gross less net mortgage acquisitions, appears but contributes
little to R^2 in either equation. It will be observed that the yield
spread variable draws the wrong sign in all the equations displayed.
While this result did not hold in all forms of mortgage regressions
run for the post-open-to-buy period, it was consistently true that
both yield spread and discount variables contributed far less to
explaining votings in this subperiod than they had in the regression
estimates for the entire period. An example of a federal mortgage
loan regression with just funds variables in it is displayed as
equation (38). The short-term cash flow and liquidity position
appear to have considerable power in shaping federal loan votings
in this result.

In sum, we tentatively conclude that life companies' residential
mortgage votings responded reasonably quickly and strongly to
variations in the mortgage/bond yield spread during the immediate post-Accord years when the companies possessed substantial
liquidity in the form of excessive Treasury securities that could
be liquidated at prices not far below par. As the environment
changed, however, their stock of Treasuries diminished and falling
bond prices drove many companies into the locked-in range.
Their mortgage votings became less responsive to yield spreads
and were shaped more by the loaned-up objective and institutional
constraints on portfolio choice flexibility. A negative way of
phrasing the fully invested proposition in the post-open-to-buy
years is that scarcity of funds sources forced life companies to
improve cash flow forecasts and to place controls on the lending
activity of mortgage departments. Such procedures enabled life
companies to keep their stock of commitments due in six months
in line with variations in cash flow which occurred, but probably

---

[13] The autocorrelation problem is reduced somewhat as well. The 'd' coefficients computed for total residential loan and federal loan votings equations
confined to the late 1950s were all in the "inconclusive" range of the Durbin-
Watson test. We are able to reject the positive serial correlation hypothesis
in the conventional loan equations.

at some cost in terms of flexibility in selecting the composition of new commitments.

Regressions on Quarterly Data

To conclude our regression analysis of new residential mortgage loan commitments, we ran a set of total residential mortgage regressions using quarterly observations on the same variables that appeared most relevant in the monthly regression analysis. In this way we hoped to reduce the amount of "noise" in the votings series that results from observing quite short time periods, and to reduce the seriousness of the residual autocorrelation problem in some regressions. Results of the quarterly regressions are displayed in Table VIII-4.

Equations (1) to (17), Part A, are the results of regressions run over 29 quarters from fourth quarter 1952 through 1959. We attempt to explain total new residential mortgage commitments by the available cash flow, the bond/mortgage yield spread, and the size of prevailing discounts on federally underwritten mortgage loans. Also in equations (15) to (17) we added the stock of liquid assets at the end of the previous quarter as a separate funds source variable. Liquid assets for this purpose include cash and Treasury obligations due to mature in less than one year.

On the whole the results are encouraging. The noise level is somewhat reduced and generally higher corrected R^2s are obtained. The available funds, yield spread, and discount variables again appear to jointly explain a substantial portion of the variance in residential mortgage votings. However, since there is still considerable colinearity present and the relative importance of these three factors varies with the specific formulation, we are not able to separate the relative contribution of each independent variable. Addition of the liquid assets variable was not helpful. As we have seen from Chapter V's analysis of the cyclical play in life companies' liquid assets, the magnitude of the variation is probably just too small to have much of an impact upon commitment decisions.

In reference to the available funds variable, it will be noted that the six-month flow measure used in Table VIII-4's reported regressions overlaps in the first three months with the votings being explained. As before, this is the "right" timing for this measure

TABLE VIII-4. Regression Analysis of Residential Mortgage Votings: Results of Runs on Quarterly Data

A. 1952/IV–1959/IV $\qquad n = 29$

(1) $V_{MR} = 193.1 + .4128\, AF_{0,1}$
$\qquad\qquad\qquad (.0815)$

$\qquad R^2 = .487 \qquad s = 119.1$
$\qquad \overline{R}^2 = .468 \qquad \bar{s} = 123.4$

(2) $V_{MR} = 178.0 + .3425\, AF_{0,1} - 142.6\,(r_U - r_F)$
$\qquad\qquad\qquad (.0851) \qquad\qquad (71.86)$

$\qquad R^2 = .554 \qquad s = 111.0$
$\qquad \overline{R}^2 = .520 \qquad \bar{s} = 117.2$

(3) $V_{MR} = 428.1 + .2413\, AF_{0,1} - 85.30\,(r_U - r_F) - 30.19\, D_F$
$\qquad\qquad\qquad (.1015) \qquad\qquad (77.20) \qquad\qquad (17.79)$

$\qquad R^2 = .600 \qquad s = 105.1$
$\qquad \overline{R}^2 = .552 \qquad \bar{s} = 113.2$

(4) $V_{MR} = 251.5 + .2215\, AF_{0,1} - 231.0\,(r_U - r_F)_{-1}$
$\qquad\qquad\qquad (.1051) \qquad\qquad (90.01)$

$\qquad R^2 = .590 \qquad s = 106.4$
$\qquad \overline{R}^2 = .559 \qquad \bar{s} = 112.4$

(5) $V_{MR} = 357.7 + .2120\, AF_{0,1} - 180.0\,(r_U - r_F)_{-1} - 19.03\, D_{F(-1)}$
$\qquad\qquad\qquad (.1036) \qquad\qquad (96.08) \qquad\qquad (13.91)$

$\qquad R^2 = .619 \qquad s = 102.6$
$\qquad \overline{R}^2 = .573 \qquad \bar{s} = 110.5$

(6) $V_{MR} = 506.8 + .2463\, AF_{0,1} - 38.81\, D_F$
$\qquad\qquad\qquad (.1018) \qquad\qquad (16.06)$

$\qquad R^2 = .581 \qquad s = 107.6$
$\qquad \overline{R}^2 = .549 \qquad \bar{s} = 113.7$

(7) $V_{MR} = 474.9 - 263.0\,(r_U - r_F)$
$\qquad\qquad\qquad (81.70)$

$\qquad R^2 = .277 \qquad s = 141.4$
$\qquad \overline{R}^2 = .250 \qquad \bar{s} = 146.6$

(8) $V_{MR} = 771.0 - 93.60\,(r_U - r_F) - 55.04\, D_F$
$\qquad\qquad\qquad (83.73) \qquad\qquad (15.63)$

$\qquad R^2 = .510 \qquad s = 116.4$
$\qquad \overline{R}^2 = .473 \qquad \bar{s} = 122.9$

(9) $V_{MR} = 406.0 - 365.4\,(r_U - r_F)$
$\qquad\qquad\qquad (67.41)$

$\qquad R^2 = .521 \qquad s = 115.1$
$\qquad \overline{R}^2 = .503 \qquad \bar{s} = 119.3$

(10) $V_{MR} = 515.5 - 303.0\,(r_U - r_F)_{-1} - 20.92\, D_{F(-1)}$
$\qquad\qquad\qquad (79.37) \qquad\qquad (14.71)$

$\qquad R^2 = .555 \qquad s = 110.9$
$\qquad \overline{R}^2 = .521 \qquad \bar{s} = 117.1$

(11) $V_{MR} = 625.8 + .2052\, AF_{0,1} - 722.4\,(r_F - r_F{}^c)$
$\qquad\qquad\qquad (.0933) \qquad\qquad (216.6)$

$\qquad R^2 = .640 \qquad s = 99.72$
$\qquad \overline{R}^2 = .613 \qquad \bar{s} = 105.3$

TABLE VIII-4 (continued)

(12) $V_{MR} = 610.8 + .1706 \, AF_{0,1} - 512.0 \, (r_F - r_F{}^c)$
$\qquad\qquad (.0945) \qquad\qquad (257.0)$
$\qquad\quad + 91.94 \, (r_F{}^c - r_B)$
$\qquad\qquad (63.41)$

$R^2 = .668 \qquad\qquad s = 95.77$
$\overline{R}^2 = .629 \qquad\qquad \bar{s} = 103.1 \qquad\qquad d = 1.2065^{**}$

(13) $V_{MR} = 565.4 + .2464 \, AF_{0,1} - 668.9 \, (r_F - r_F{}^c)$
$\qquad\qquad (.0846) \qquad\qquad (196.3)$

$R^2 = .645 \qquad\qquad s = 99.07$
$\overline{R}^2 = .618 \qquad\qquad \bar{s} = 104.6$

(14) $V_{MR} = 583.2 + .1691 \, AF_{0,1} - 405.9 \, (r_F - r_F{}^c)$
$\qquad\qquad (.0885) \qquad\qquad (226.3)$
$\qquad\quad + 130.2 \, (r_F{}^c - r_B)$
$\qquad\qquad (64.20)$

$R^2 = .695 \qquad\qquad s = 91.81$
$\overline{R}^2 = .659 \qquad\qquad \bar{s} = 98.88 \qquad\qquad d = .8979^{*}$

(15) $V_{MR} = 227.7 + .2554 \, AF_{0,1} + .1143 \, (CT_s)_{-1} - 79.07 \, (r_U - r_F)$
$\qquad\qquad (.1029) \qquad\quad (.1217) \qquad\qquad (77.66)$
$\qquad\quad - 28.52 \, D_F$
$\qquad\qquad (17.93)$

$R^2 = .614 \qquad\qquad s = 103.2$
$\overline{R}^2 = .550 \qquad\qquad \bar{s} = 113.5 \qquad\qquad d = .9117^{*}$

(16) $V_{MR} = 453.8 + .1848 \, AF_{0,1} + .0916 \, (CT_s)_{-1} - 535.7 \, (r_F - r_F{}^c)$
$\qquad\qquad (.0969) \qquad\quad (.1166) \qquad\qquad (260.8)$
$\qquad\quad + 74.60 \, (r_F{}^c - r_B)$
$\qquad\qquad (67.61)$

$R^2 = .677 \qquad\qquad s = 94.56$
$\overline{R}^2 = .623 \qquad\qquad \bar{s} = 103.9 \qquad\qquad d = 1.2816^{**}$

(17) $V_{MR} = 479.8 + .1801 \, AF_{0,1} + .0565 \, (CT_s)_{-1}$
$\qquad\qquad (.0924) \qquad\quad (.1107)$
$\qquad\quad - 404.9 \, (r_F - r_F{}^c)_{-1} + 122.1 \, (r_F{}^c - r_B)$
$\qquad\qquad (229.7) \qquad\qquad (67.1)$

$R^2 = .698 \qquad\qquad s = 91.31$
$\overline{R}^2 = .648 \qquad\qquad \bar{s} = 100.3 \qquad\qquad d = .7987^{*}$

B. 1952/IV–1956/II $\qquad\qquad n = 15$

(18) $V_{MR} = 135.3 + .4910 \, AF_{0,1}$
$\qquad\qquad (.1573)$

$R^2 = .428 \qquad\qquad s = 134.9$
$\overline{R}^2 = .384 \qquad\qquad \bar{s} = 145.0$

(19) $V_{MR} = -118.0 + .4514 \, AF_{0,1} - 364.0 \, (r_U - r_F)$
$\qquad\qquad (.1159) \qquad\qquad (104.3)$

$R^2 = .716 \qquad\qquad s = 95.11$
$\overline{R}^2 = .668 \qquad\qquad \bar{s} = 106.3$

TABLE VIII-4 (continued)

(20) $V_{MR} = 280.4 + .2767\ AF_{0,1} - 314.1\ (r_U - r_F) - 73.30\ D_F$
$\qquad\qquad\quad (.1354) \qquad\quad (96.5) \qquad\qquad (36.59)$
$\quad R^2 = .792 \qquad s = 81.41$
$\quad \overline{R}^2 = .735 \qquad \bar{s} = 95.07 \qquad\qquad d = 1.7563$***

(21) $V_{MR} = 127.4 + .0542\ AF_{0,1} - .3926\ (CT_s)_{-1}$
$\qquad\qquad\quad (.1751) \qquad\quad (.2188)$
$\qquad\quad - 358.3\ (r_U - r_F) - 138.5\ D_F$
$\qquad\qquad (91.4) \qquad\qquad (49.4)$
$\quad R^2 = .842 \qquad s = 70.81$
$\quad \overline{R}^2 = .779 \qquad \bar{s} = 86.73 \qquad\qquad d = 2.0908$***

(22) $V_{MR} = 152.0 + .2263\ AF_{0,1} - 427.1\ (r_U - r_F) - 25.67\ D_{F(-1)}$
$\qquad\qquad\quad (.1290) \qquad\qquad (110.4) \qquad\qquad (30.87)$
$\quad R^2 = .769 \qquad s = 85.71$
$\quad \overline{R}^2 = .706 \qquad \bar{s} = 100.0 \qquad\qquad d = 1.4010$**

(23) $V_{MR} = 368.7 + .1823\ AF_{0,1} - .1090\ (CT_s)_{-1}$
$\qquad\qquad\quad (.1565) \qquad\quad (.2032)$
$\qquad\quad - 459.9\ (r_U - r_F)_{-1} - 33.34\ D_{F(-1)}$
$\qquad\qquad (129.4) \qquad\qquad\qquad (34.97)$
$\quad R^2 = .776 \qquad s = 84.51$
$\quad \overline{R}^2 = .686 \qquad \bar{s} = 103.5 \qquad\qquad d = 1.4363$**

(24) $V_{MR} = 654.2 + .1833\ AF_{0,1} - 857.2\ (r_F - r_F{}^c)$
$\qquad\qquad\quad (.1217) \qquad\qquad (400.1)$
$\qquad\quad + 172.8\ (r_F{}^c - r_B)$
$\qquad\qquad (148.7)$
$\quad R^2 = .841 \qquad s = 71.10$
$\quad \overline{R}^2 = .798 \qquad \bar{s} = 83.02 \qquad\qquad d = 1.8023$***

(25) $V_{MR} = 912.8 + .1426\ AF_{0,1} - .1321\ (CT_s)_{-1}$
$\qquad\qquad\quad (.1327) \qquad\quad (.1578)$
$\qquad\quad - 888.4\ (r_F - r_F{}^c) + 209.6\ (r_F{}^c - r_B)$
$\qquad\qquad (407.3) \qquad\qquad\qquad (157.0)$
$\quad R^2 = .851 \qquad s = 68.73$
$\quad \overline{R}^2 = .792 \qquad \bar{s} = 84.18 \qquad\qquad d = 2.0324$***
$\qquad\qquad (.1403) \qquad\qquad (.1866)$

(26) $V_{MR} = 771.8 + .1330\ AF_{0,1} - .2029\ (CT_s)_{-1}$
$\qquad\qquad\quad (.1403) \qquad\quad (.1866)$
$\qquad\quad - 138.2\ (r_F - r_F{}^c)_{-1} + 533.9\ (r_F{}^c - r_B)_{-1}$
$\qquad\qquad (364.8) \qquad\qquad\qquad (187.5)$
$\quad R^2 = .815 \qquad s = 76.64$
$\quad \overline{R}^2 = .742 \qquad \bar{s} = 93.87 \qquad\qquad d = 1.2796$**

C. 1956/III–1959/IV $\qquad\qquad n = 14$

(27) $V_{MR} = 314.4 + .2504\ AF_{0,1}$
$\qquad\qquad\quad (.0692)$
$\quad R^2 = .521 \qquad s = 67.66$
$\quad \overline{R}^2 = .481 \qquad \bar{s} = 73.08$

TABLE VIII-4 (continued)

(28) $V_{MR} = 321.1 + .3072\ AF_{0,1} + 139.3\ (r_U - r_F)$
　　　　　　　　(.0666)　　　　　　(65.7)

　　$R^2 = .660$　　　　　$s = 57.00$
　　$\overline{R}^2 = .598$　　　　　$\overline{s} = 64.31$

(29) $V_{MR} = 344.2 + .2982\ AF_{0,1} + 138.9\ (r_U - r_F) - 2.95\ D_F$
　　　　　　　　(.0928)　　　　　　(68.9)　　　　　　　(19.92)

　　$R^2 = .661$　　　　　$s = 56.94$
　　$\overline{R}^2 = .559$　　　　　$\overline{s} = 67.37$　　　　$d = 1.9127$***

(30) $V_{MR} = 251.4 + .2770\ AF_{0,1} + .0849\ (CT_s)_{-1}$
　　　　　　　　(.0980)　　　　　(.1047)
　　　　　$+ 129.9\ (r_U - r_F) - 8.24\ D_F$
　　　　　　(71.0)　　　　　　　(21.30)

　　$R^2 = .684$　　　　　$s = 54.97$
　　$\overline{R}^2 = .543$　　　　　$\overline{s} = 68.56$　　　$d = 2.1412$***

(31) $V_{MR} = 371.9 + .4105\ AF_{0,1} + 222.4\ (r_U - r_F)_{-1}$
　　　　　　　　(.0946)　　　　　　(95.4)
　　　　　$- 23.51\ D_{F(-1)}$
　　　　　　(12.43)

　　$R^2 = .721$　　　　　$s = 51.62$
　　$\overline{R}^2 = .638$　　　　　$\overline{s} = 61.07$　　　$d = 2.4985$***

(32) $V_{MR} = 381.6 + .4133\ AF_{0,1} - .0064\ (CT_s)_{-1}$
　　　　　　　　(.1101)　　　　　(.1068)
　　　　　$+ 225.9\ (r_U - r_F) - 23.63\ D_{F(-1)}$
　　　　　　(115.7)　　　　　　　(13.27)

　　$R^2 = .721$　　　　　$s = 51.60$
　　$\overline{R}^2 = .598$　　　　　$\overline{s} = 64.36$　　　$d = 2.4915$***

(33) $V_{MR} = 193.8 + .2989\ AF_{0,1} + 210.3\ (r_F - r_F{}^c) - 2.8\ (r_F{}^c - r_B)$
　　　　　　　　(.1167)　　　　　　(275.3)　　　　　　(111.2)

　　$R^2 = .552$　　　　　$s = 65.43$
　　$\overline{R}^2 = .418$　　　　　$\overline{s} = 77.42$　　　$d = 1.7060$**

(34) $V_{MR} = 51.38 + .3070\ AF_{0,1} + .0955\ (CT_s)_{-1}$
　　　　　　　　(.1202)　　　　　(.1338)
　　　　　$+ 105.1\ (r_F - r_F{}^c) - 41.9\ (r_F{}^c - r_B)$
　　　　　　(318.5)　　　　　　(126.6)

　　$R^2 = .576$　　　　　$s = 63.65$
　　$\overline{R}^2 = .388$　　　　　$\overline{s} = 79.39$　　　$d = 1.9413$**

(35) $V_{MR} = 304.3 + .1642\ AF_{0,1} + .1261\ (CT_s)_{-1}$
　　　　　　　　(.0998)　　　　　(.1148)
　　　　　$- 282.8\ (r_F - r_F{}^c)_{-1} + 27.57\ (r_F{}^c - r_B)_{-1}$
　　　　　　(280.4)　　　　　　(96.64)

　　$R^2 = .634$　　　　　$s = 59.17$
　　$\overline{R}^2 = .471$　　　　　$\overline{s} = 73.80$　　　$d = 1.6443$**

* Positive serial correlation significant at the 5% level.
** Inconclusive range of Durbin-Watson test.
*** Not significant at 5% level.

if an average lag of two to three months existed between a decision based on an upcoming six months' cash flow forecast and the decision's impact on votings. We had no clear rationale for lagging the funds variable further, so where other variables are lagged a quarter in Table VIII-4's results, the funds variable is not. We did run the same set of equations with $AF_{1,2}$, i.e., six months' funds flow following the current (votings) quarter, substituted for $AF_{0,1}$. The results are qualitatively the same, but the lead form of the funds variable is consistently less strong than $AF_{0,1}$. This is consistent with our earlier finding that votings are most responsive to the near-term funds flow.

Unfortunately confidence in these fits is undermined to some extent by the continued persistence of positively autocorrelated residuals in most of the regression equations. However, although short on degrees of freedom, we ran some residential mortgage regressions for the separate subperiods: 1952/IV–1956/II, and 1956/III–1959/IV (Table VIII-4, Parts B and C). One consequence of splitting the 1952–1959 period was that a substantial lessening of the serial correlation problem was effected.

Also, for the earlier transition open-to-buy subperiod higher corrected R^2s were obtained than were on similar equations run for the period as a whole. Again the available cash flow, yield spread, and discount variables appeared jointly relevant, although the yield spread and discount variables contribute somewhat more to the explained variance than they do for the period as a whole. The equations in which the yield spread and discount variables are measured currently are somewhat more satisfactory than those in which these variables are lagged. Somewhat disturbing, however, is the fact that the highest $\overline{R}^2$ is obtained in an equation (24) in which the coefficient of only one of the three independent variables is significant at the 5% level. Addition of the liquid assets variable is not only not helpful, but it seriously disturbs the coefficients in some of the other independent variables.

Less satisfactory fits are obtained on residential mortgage votings regressions run for the "scarce funds" subperiod (1956/III–1959/IV), largely because the discount effect is negligible in most equations. The available funds variable still contributes strongly to the explanation of the votings pattern, and new commitments still appear to respond, although not quite as strongly as in the earlier subperiod, to variations in the bond/mortgage yield spread.

A much higher proportion of life companies' mortgage commitments are conventional loans in the latter period than was true during 1952 — mid-1956. In general, with the exception of two quarters, mortgages were much less attractive on a relative yield basis after mid-1956 than they had been previously. Responding to this change in yield spreads, life companies reduced the proportion of funds allocated to this market and were able to meet their needs more completely than earlier in the conventional loan submarket. Therefore their residential mortgage votings became less responsive to variations in going discounts on federal loans than before. This fact also shows up in the regressions as reduced responsiveness to the differential between the ceiling rate on FHA-VA loans and bond yields. Thus administrative variations in ceiling rates apparently had a lesser impact on life companies after the 1954–1956 mortgage and residential construction boom was exhausted.

In sum then, the quarterly regression results lend strength to the conclusion that the time path of life company new residential mortgage loan commitments during the 1950s was determined primarily by (1) use of mortgage commitments to pursue an overall desired commitment stock/cash flow position and (2) responsiveness to the yield spread between residential mortgage loan and corporate bond opportunities. The desire to remain fully invested made life companies' mortgage commitment decisions especially sensitive to changes in their short-term uncommitted cash flow position. Finally, in the early and mid-1950s at least, life companies' distaste for discounting, and their dependence upon the VA-FHA market as an outlet for their desired volume of mortgage investment, resulted in the time path of their home loan commitments also being quite sensitive to the level of price discounts prevailing. Thus available cash flow, yield differentials, and VA-FHA price discounts jointly seemed capable of explaining a substantial portion of the marked variations observed in life company new residential mortgage commitments during the 1950s.

New Corporate Bond Commitments

The time sequence of residential mortgage votings during the 1950s seems to have been dominated by broad cyclical swings. By way of contrast, no systematic pattern emerges from an examination of the corporate bond votings time series (see Charts VI-7, VI-9). The corporate bond time profile appears frighteningly erratic. Thus, it was with some considerable trepidation that we approached the explanation of this time path through multiple regression analysis.

Paralleling our investigation of residential mortgage votings, we began analysis of the corporate sector by testing for sensitivity of corporate bond votings to yields and available funds. Using monthly data, we ran regressions over the period October 1952 to January 1960 with yields, available funds, liquid assets, and other independent variables. In a number of regressions the level of bond yields was used as an independent variable. If mortgage terms are relatively sticky as often asserted, then an index of corporate bond yields by itself should serve as a measure of investment opportunities in the corporate sector. To allow for cyclical and secular changes in evaluation of the attractiveness of a given bond yield, we also used the spread between the current yield and a moving average of past yields as an explanatory variable. These are the same bond yield measures used in the aggregate votings analysis of Chapter VI.

Our fears regarding our ability to explain the erratic and volatile corporate bond votings series by regression analysis proved fully justified. The monthly regression results were negative and discouraging. A sample regression is displayed in Table VIII-5.

As examination of the sample result will show, neither the level of bond yields nor the six months' available funds flow explain the time sequence of corporate bond votings. Most of the time the bond yield coefficient, r_U, draws a negative sign. The same is true when the spread between the current yield and the moving average of past yields is used instead. The bond/mortgage yield spread fares only slightly better.

As we have seen previously, corporate bond votings need not be closely tied to funds availability since commitments for rather

TABLE VIII-5. Regression Analysis of Corporate Bond Votings: Monthly Observations, October 1952–January 1960, Sample Result

r_U	$AF_{1,6}$	V_M	$C-E_{1,6}$	T_S	T/S	D_T	Constant	s	R^2	$\bar{R}^2$
-20.5049 (11.3636)							267.8830	74.65	.037	.014
-12.6669 (13.1540)	.0382 (.0325)						195.7385	74.06	.052	.018
-9.3107 (12.9121)	-.0088 (.0376)	.2940 (.1272)					128.6299	71.81	.109	.066
-27.8246 (12.9502)	.0319 (.0355)	.1189 (.1269)	.1133 (.0299)				52.5962	66.31	.240	.194
-27.8810 (13.1096)	.0141 (.0359)	.1177 (.1311)	.1138 (.0321)	.0022 (.0568)			51.2622	66.32	.240	.185
13.5783 (20.5220)	.0243 (.0349)	.1918 (.1301)	.1627 (.0365)	.0191 (.0553)	1554.7360 (605.0043)		-370.4885	63.77	.297	.237
-84.2785 (34.8857)	.0496 (.0337)	.0955 (.1258)	.1503 (.0345)	-.0427 (.0552)	949.1924 (597.5742)	19.3348 (5.738)	9.0758	59.68	.385	.323

long delayed takedown of funds are common. Nonetheless available funds are permissive of corporate bond votings, and it is conceivable that achievement of the loaned-up objective could be dependent upon responsiveness of life companies' securities departments to variations in anticipated cash inflow. It will be recalled that this may well be the case if corporate sector votings are, in fact, under closer control of life companies than their mortgage lending operations. Again referring to Table VIII-5, however, we find that although the available funds coefficient generally draws the right sign (positive), it is not significantly different from zero and contributes negligibly to explaining the variance in bond votings. No improvement is obtained by slight changes in the timing of the funds variable. In one set of regressions we deducted from available funds an estimate of the current month's mortgage votings expected to be delivered in six months — this based on the thesis that mortgage loan propositions flowing in from outside correspondents have priority on the use of available funds. This variable performed no better than the simple available funds measure.

In the particular equations reported on in Table VIII-5, we included current mortgage votings as a separate variable on the same sort of logic; i.e., mortgage and corporate bond lending are alternatives. On this basis a negative sign on the V_M coefficient is expected. A significant result in this direction would not in any meaningful sense explain bond votings, but it would tell us that mortgage and bond votings are essentially substitutes and thereby help point toward an explanation. The sign on V_M is positive, however, indicating that if bond and mortgage votings tend to move systematically relative to one another, it is in the same direction. There is evidence from the introduction of V_M into the equation that mortgage votings are colinear with available funds which is not surprising in view of the results of our analysis of residential mortgage votings.

As suggested in Chapter VI, one of the reasons the time profile of votings is so erratic is that flexibility with respect to commitment-delivery lags permits the votings sequence to diverge considerably from cash flow. This is particularly the case with corporate bond commitments. We had indicated therefore that it might be fruitful, if not necessary, to disaggregate votings by length of the expected votings-takedown lag. The data are not available to do this, however.

As a measure of life company willingness to make delayed take-down commitments, we did introduce the stock of commitments due for takedown beyond six months as an additional independent variable. The presumption is that a "large" stock discourages delayed delivery commitments; a "small" stock permits them. Assuming that this commitment stock influence is reflected in total corporate bond votings, the relationship should be negative. Inclusion of this variable picks up R^2 more and reduces the standard error of estimate more than any other variable used in the regression displayed in Table VIII-5. But although the partial regression coefficient is significant, it is positive, not negative. Bond votings are high when the delayed takedown commitment stock is high. This perverse result suggests that the customer servicing hypothesis may, as suggested in Chapter VI, be relevant in explaining bond votings activity. We shall proceed to investigate this possibility as soon as the liquid asset variables used in Table VIII-5's regression result are disposed of.

Two measures of life companies' liquid reserves are introduced as independent variables in Table VIII-5. The first is companies' holdings of short-term Treasury obligations due to mature within one year, and the second is the ratio of companies' total Treasury security holdings to total ledger assets. Finally, since life companies appeared to have some considerable aversion to realizing book losses on security sales, the encouragement Treasury security holdings offered to votings must have been dampened by bond prices significantly below par. Thus we included the prevailing price discount below par on the bulk of life company Treasury bond holdings as an additional variable. We expect, then, to observe positive partial regression coefficients on the two Treasury holdings variables and a negative sign on the discount variable. The results showed the coefficient on the short-term Treasuries variable to be essentially zero in all equations. The total Treasury security holdings/total asset ratio turned out positive, but its significance is diminished by the fact that the bond price discount variable also unexpectedly turns up positive and significant. It again may be picking up some generalized corporate demand for funds, or commitments.

Thus, we are left with a regression bag of negative results. Measures of bond yields, mortgage yields, liquid assets, outstanding commitments, and mortgage activity prove unable, separately or jointly, to produce a consistent and significant explanation of corporate bond votings. The only light this empirical exercise seems to offer is a suggestion that some corporate demand factors, not reflected in the time pattern of bond yields, may play a significant role in shaping life company corporate sector commitment decisions.

We have such a hypothesis embodied in the so-called forward commitment servicing motivation. This thesis postulates the existence of a corporate demand for the forward commitment service to which life companies find it profitable to cater. The difficulty with testing this proposition is that we have no measure for such a demand. As a means of seeing whether this sort of demand factor is empirically plausible, we introduced several very crude measures of corporate demand in the regression analysis reported on below. Proxies used include the National Industrial Conference Board's new capital appropriations series and SEC-reported new manufacturing bond issues and the net change in the stock of long-term manufacturing debt outstanding. These are all obviously very crude variables and can only measure very generally variations in the manufacturing sector's demand for long term external debt financing.

The NICB capital appropriations series is reported on a quarterly basis. For this reason, and because in the monthly corporate bond votings series it appeared that the "static" dominated any systematic elements, we ran a set of regressions including the demand proxies on the basis of quarterly observations. A sample of the results are recorded in Table VIII-6.

In equations (1) to (5) we were testing once again the explanatory power of yields, available funds, and liquid assets. Some slight improvement over monthly data regressions is visible. In the quarterly equations the signs on the partial regression coefficients are right most of the time. But the coefficient values do not consistently exceed their standard errors, and the fits are little better than before. We still do not get much mileage from these variables separately or jointly.

In the remaining equations we have introduced the corporate

TABLE VIII-6. Corporate Bond Votings: Regression Results, Quarterly Observations

A. 1952/IV–1959/IV $n = 29$

(1) $V_B = 383.9 + .1627\, AF_{0,1}$
             $(.0992)$

   $R^2 = .090$ $s = 145.1$
   $\overline{R}^2 = .056$ $\bar{s} = 150.3$

(2) $V_B = 630.9 + .1113\, AF_{0,1} - 48.99\, r_U$
             $(.1094)$ (44.73)

   $R^2 = .130$ $s = 141.8$
   $\overline{R}^2 = .063$ $\bar{s} = 149.8$

(3) $V_B = 1243 + .1443\, AF_{0,1} + 117.0\, r_U - 256.8\, r_F$
             $(.1045)$ (91.4) (125.4)

   $R^2 = .255$ $s = 131.2$
   $\overline{R}^2 = .166$ $\bar{s} = 141.4$

(4) $V_B = 389.2 + .1875\, AF_{0,1} + 50.37\, (r_U - r_F)$
             $(.1105)$ (93.39)

   $R^2 = .100$ $s = 144.3$
   $\overline{R}^2 = .031$ $\bar{s} = 152.3$

(5) $V_B = 247.3 + .1824\, AF_{0,1} + 78.97\, (r_U - r_F) + .02135\, T$
             $(.1115)$ (100.30) $(.02628)$

   $R^2 = .123$ $s = 142.4$
   $\overline{R}^2 = .018$ $\bar{s} = 153.4$

(6) $V_B = 267.2 + .1356\, AF_{0,1} + 8.450\, (r_U - r_F) + .2528\, NB_M$
             $(.1087)$ (9.161) $(.1321)$

   $R^2 = .215$ $s = 134.7$
   $\overline{R}^2 = .121$ $\bar{s} = 145.1$

(7) $V_B = 150.6 + .3761\, AF_{0,1} + 186.9\, (r_U - r_F) + .3894\, \Delta B_{M(2)}$
             $(.1247)$ (100.3) $(.1527)$

   $R^2 = .286$ $s = 128.5$
   $\overline{R}^2 = .200$ $\bar{s} = 138.4$

B. 1953/I–1959/IV $n = 28$

(8) $V_B = -48.24 + .3539\, AF_{0,1} + 113.50\, (r_U - r_U{}^n)$
             $(.1415)$ (88.61)
    $+ .08744\, CAN$
       $(.04211)$

   $R^2 = .241$ $s = 133.6$
   $\overline{R}^2 = .147$ $\bar{s} = 144.3$

(9) $V_B = -20.20 + .2293\, AF_{0,1} + 36.41\, (r_U - r_U{}^n)$
             $(.1483)$ (92.66)
    $+ .07490\, CAN + .2725\, NB_M$
       $(.04036)$ $(.1325)$

   $R^2 = .349$ $s = 123.8$
   $\overline{R}^2 = .236$ $\bar{s} = 136.6$

TABLE VIII-6 (continued)

(10) $V_B = -546.6 + .2401 \, AF_{0,1} + 101.50 \, (r_U - r_U{}^n)$
$\qquad\qquad\quad (.1356) \qquad\quad (89.04)$
$\qquad + .08691 \, CAN + .3347 \, NB_M + .05603 \, T$
$\qquad\quad (.03722) \qquad\quad (.1301) \qquad\quad (.02377)$
$R^2 = .480 \qquad\quad s = 110.6$
$\overline{R}^2 = .362 \qquad\quad \bar{s} = 124.8$

(11) $V_B = -853.6 + .5802 \, AF_{0,1} + 260.9 \, (r_U - r_U{}^n)$
$\qquad\qquad\quad (.1355) \qquad\quad (85.4)$
$\qquad + .1074 \, CAN + .3601 \, \Delta B_{M(2)} + .04649 \, T$
$\qquad\quad (.0356) \qquad\quad (.1203) \qquad\quad (.02240)$
$R^2 = .520 \qquad\quad s = 106.3$
$\overline{R}^2 = .410 \qquad\quad \bar{s} = 120.0 \qquad\quad d = 1.5591^*$

(12) $V_B = -574.4 + .5372 \, AF_{0,1} + 341.8 \ \ (r_U - r_F)$
$\qquad\qquad\quad (.1114) \qquad\quad (91.4)$
$\qquad + .1087 \, CAN + .5034 \, \Delta B_{M(2)} + .04985 \, T$
$\qquad\quad (.0330) \qquad\quad (.1274) \qquad\quad (.02085)$
$R^2 = .582 \qquad\quad s = 99.27$
$\overline{R}^2 = .487 \qquad\quad \bar{s} = 111.9 \qquad\quad d = 1.4543^*$

C. 1953/I–1959/IV $\qquad\quad n = 28$

(13) $V_B/AF_6 = .2800 + .0001220 \, CAN$
$\qquad\qquad\qquad\qquad (.0000436)$
$R^2 = .230 \qquad\quad s = .1620$
$\overline{R}^2 = .200 \qquad\quad \bar{s} = .1681$

(14) $V_B/AF_6 = .2108 + .0001038 \, CAN + .0003588 \, \Delta B_{M(2)}$
$\qquad\qquad\qquad\qquad (.0000398) \qquad\quad (.0001323)$
$R^2 = .405 \qquad\quad s = .1424$
$\overline{R}^2 = .357 \qquad\quad \bar{s} = .1507$

(15) $V_B/AF_6 = .3526 + .0001008 \, CAN + .0004765 \, \Delta B_{M(2)}$
$\qquad\qquad\qquad\qquad (.0000323) \qquad\quad (.0001120)$
$\qquad\qquad + .2650 \, (r_U - r_F)$
$\qquad\qquad\quad (.0712)$
$R^2 = .623 \qquad\quad s = .1134$
$\overline{R}^2 = .575 \qquad\quad \bar{s} = .1224$

(16) $V_B/AF_6 = .02804 + .0001099 \, CAN + .0005037 \, \Delta B_{M(2)}$
$\qquad\qquad\qquad\qquad (.0000306) \qquad\quad (.0001058)$
$\qquad\qquad + .3340 \, (r_U - r_F) + .00004433 \, T$
$\qquad\qquad\quad (.0745) \qquad\qquad (.00002130)$
$R^2 = .682 \qquad\quad s = .1040$
$\overline{R}^2 = .627 \qquad\quad \bar{s} = .1147 \qquad\quad d = 1.1377^*$

(17) $V_B/AF_6 = .5490 + .0001165 \, CAN + .0004175 \, \Delta B_{M(2)}$
$\qquad\qquad\qquad\qquad (.0000376) \qquad\quad (.0001332)$
$\qquad\qquad + .2472 \, (r_U - r_F) - .0001401 \, (CT_s)_{-1}$
$\qquad\qquad\quad (.0748) \qquad\qquad (.0001684)$
$R^2 = .634 \qquad\quad s = .1117$
$\overline{R}^2 = .570 \qquad\quad \bar{s} = .1232$

TABLE VIII-6 (continued)

$$(18) \quad V_B/AF_6 = .1302 + .0001164 \, CAN + .0004764 \, \Delta B_{M(2)}$$
$$ (.0000357) (.0001302)$$
$$+ .3228 \, (r_U - r_F) - .0000618 \, (CT_s)_{-1}$$
$$ (.0816) (.0001651)$$
$$+ .00004221 \, T$$
$$ (.00002245)$$

$$\overline{R}^2 = .684 \qquad s = .1037$$
$$\overline{R}^2 = .613 \qquad \overline{s} = .1170 \qquad d = 1.1902*$$

* Inconclusive range of Durbin-Watson test for serial correlation.

demand indicators. Also, in addition to using the dollar volume of new corporate bond commitments as the dependent variable, we experimented with the ratio of bond commitments to available funds over the six months covering the current and succeeding quarters. The particular demand variables used are indices of the manufacturing sector's demand for investment funds, given the implicit assumption that this demand is not significantly elastic with respect to bond yields. It is in the manufacturing sector that volatility of demand seems especially important, and it appears that the life company manufacturing sector bond votings display particular instability. Statistically, introduction of these proxies does pick up a good deal of the variance in corporate bond votings. Specifically, current new capital appropriations by NICB surveyed manufacturing concerns and the net change in manufacturing sector bond issues outstanding two quarters hence seem to provide the best statistical performances. These variables are not highly colinear, so the highest R^2s are obtained where more than one demand indicator appears. There is no clear economic justification for doing this, however. Also, explaining today's life company bond votings by future observed reported total bond issues is a dubious procedure.

Nonetheless, finding a handle to explain corporate bond commitments has proved so frustrating that no clues can be left unexplored. However crude, these results do suggest that life company corporate sector votings are triggered by investment opportunities not reflected in the level of reported bond yields or bond/mortgage yield spreads. Bond votings do not seem to be used primarily to adjust the total stock of commitments to anticipated cash flow.[14]   One hypothesis, which explains how corporate demand for life company funds goes unreflected in yields, is based on the distinction between the demand for forward commitments and the demand for current funds.   While it is dangerous to adopt an explanation because no other seems available, we do have some corroborating evidence of the commitment servicing proposition in the evidence of one company's pattern of delayed takedown commitment votings reported in Chapter VI, and in the interview evidence emphasizing the function of forward commitments in the corporate sector as a customer servicing device.   If it is true that the commitment process in the corporate sector does not serve as a means for maintaining a fully invested position, and that it does not permit life companies to manipulate interperiod allocation of funds to improve their rate of return over time, then the rationalization for forward commitments must rest with the proposition that they provide a service borrowing customers desire.   An encouraging aspect of the regression results reported in Table VIII-6 is that introduction of the demand proxies improves significantly the performance of the available funds, yield, and total Government security holdings variables.   With the variations in demand for commitments, per se, netted out, the level of bond yields, the bond/mortgage yield spread and funds availability come into their own in at least a modest fashion.

Since the demand proxies which appear to supply the key to corporate bond votings are all variables based in the manufacturing sector, confidence in them as indicators would be strengthened if they turn out to explain particularly well variations in manufacturing sector bond votings.   To test this we ran a set of regressions on quarterly data using manufacturing sector votings as the dependent variable.   Sample results are reported in Table VIII-7. The results are rather disappointing.   Unfortunately the time profile of manufacturing sector votings appears more erratic and unsystematic than votings of corporate bonds as a whole.   Thus, the regression fits are even less impressive than the total corporate

---

[14] Also the beginning period stock of short-term liquid assets was included in several equations including some (e.g. (17) and (18)), in which V_B/AF_6 was the dependent variable.   As in the examples shown, the liquid asset variable consistently contributed nothing.   The total stock of Treasury obligations (T) is significant in equations containing the demand indices.

TABLE VIII-7. *Manufacturing Sector Bond Votings: Regression Results,*
Quarterly Data

1953/I–1959/IV $\qquad$ $n = 28$

(1) $V_{IM} = -79.85 + .05675 \, CAN + .1754 \, \Delta B_M + .1426 \, AF_{0,1}$
$\qquad\qquad\quad (.03519) \qquad\quad (.1156) \qquad\quad (.0890)$
$R^2 = .201 \qquad\qquad s = 114.5$
$\overline{R}^2 = .101 \qquad\qquad \bar{s} = 123.7$

(2) $V_{IM} = -185.2 + .04762 \, CAN + .2683 \, \Delta B_{M(2)} + .2361 \, AF_{0,1}$
$\qquad\qquad\quad (.03261) \qquad\quad (.1093) \qquad\qquad (.0891)$
$R^2 = .300 \qquad\qquad s = 107.2$
$\overline{R}^2 = .212 \qquad\qquad \bar{s} = 115.8$

(3) $V_{IM} = -317.7 + .06501 \, CAN + .4177 \, \Delta B_{M(2)} + 182.1 \, (r_U - r_F)$
$\qquad\qquad\quad (.03106) \qquad\quad (.1204) \qquad\qquad (80.2)$
$\qquad + .3885 \, AF_{0,1}$
$\qquad\quad (.1016)$
$R^2 = .428 \qquad\qquad s = 96.89$
$\overline{R}^2 = .329 \qquad\qquad \bar{s} = 106.9$

bond votings regressions. Nevertheless the demand proxies "explain" far more of the variation in manufacturing sector votings than any other combination of variables tried. And, with the effect of the demand indicators partialed out, yield spreads and future cash flow assume their proper roles in these regressions.

Thus, it appears, there is a demand factor at work shaping life company corporate bond commitment behavior. This demand factor is not reflected in available bond yield series.[15] The forward commitment servicing proposition is consistent with this finding. Therefore our somewhat tentative conclusion with respect to corporate bond votings is that their time pattern during the 1950s was shaped most importantly by variations in corporate demand for the forward commitment service. This having been allowed for, votings were responsive at the margin to changes in future cash inflow and bond/mortgage yield spreads.

Commercial, Industrial, and Institutional Mortgage Loan Votings

Life insurance companies have been quite active in mortgage lending on nonresidential properties. The loan category consid-

[15] This includes some bond yield information on (1) commitments and (2) acquisitions by individual life companies.

ered in this section covers all nonresidential, nonfarm mortgage lending. Most of the loans generated in this area consist of loans on commercial properties, especially retail stores and office buildings. Some loans to industrial enterprises are made on the basis of mortgaged real property, and life companies place a limited amount of funds on secured property of nonprofit institutions. Except for the corporate bond and residential mortgage sectors, the commercial, industrial, and institutional mortgage loan sector has been the most important outlet for life company funds during the postwar period. Unfortunately data on financing in this sector are sparse, and published analyses of the determinants of the supply of and demand for funds in nonresidential, nonfarm mortgage markets are virtually nonexistent.

Most reliable balance sheet, acquisitions, and recordings data on mortgage lending lump multifamily residential property loans with nonresidential property loans. During the seven years 1953–1959 on which our empirical analysis is mostly focused, life companies were the most important financial institutions lending in this area, acquiring about a third of the increase in outstanding nonfarm, non-1–4 family property mortgage loans. These loan acquisitions amounted to 15% of the growth in life company assets.[16] The LIAA forward commitment data does segregate "real estate mortgage loans to business and industrial concerns" from loans on residential properties. New commitments for business and industrial mortgage loans were nearly 17% of all new investment commitments reported by the surveyed life insurance companies during the period October 1952–June 1960.

Judging from a survey of life insurance company loan authorizations during the four years 1953–1956,[17] loans on retail trade establishments and general office buildings accounted for nearly two-thirds of life company commercial and industrial mortgage loan

---

[16] Computed from data in the *Federal Reserve Bulletin,* ILI *Life Insurance Fact Book,* and the Housing and Home Finance Agency, *Housing Statistics,* Historical Supplement, October 1961.

[17] The survey was conducted by the Life Insurance Association of America at the request of Representative Wright Patman, Chairman of the Select Committee on Small Business of the House of Representatives. The survey covered 67 life companies, who held 77% of all life insurance company assets at end-1956. The figures in the text are computed from survey data in the ALC-LIAA *Joint Investment Bulletin,* No. 321, Table C-5.

commitments during the 1950s. Loans on other commercial properties (hotels, garages, theaters) accounted for another 9% of business mortgage loans. About 9% of life company business loans also were made on manufacturing and nonrail transportation facilities. The remaining 16% of business and industrial mortgage loans was not classified. The regular LIAA *Forward Commitment Survey* did classify business mortgage commitment data into "trade," "manufacturing," "finance company," and "all other" categories until 1959, but we found the reporting by these subsectors unreliable.

What we have here, then, is an important but heterogeneous collection of markets about which little is known. Since there seems to be no reason to expect the demand for mortgage funds to finance existing or new retail stores, office buildings, manufacturing plants and warehouses, hospitals, churches, and schools to be explained by the same set of determinants, save perhaps for the common pull of some broad aggregate variables, it seems necessary to distinguish three or four separate categories for analysis. Although the breakdown provided in the forward commitment data is not fully adequate, we began our analysis of life company votings by working with these subsectors. As indicated above, however, we discovered in the process that company reporting on the detail of their business and industrial mortgage commitments was often inaccurate and generally unreliable.[18] Therefore we had to drop this attempt at a disaggregated analysis.

In principle, it seems that the demand for mortgage funds to finance commercial enterprises ought to be reasonably elastic with

---

[18] We checked through the records of three large companies in some detail and found substantial inconsistencies between loan types reported in commitment data and independent acquisitions and balance sheet statements. For two companies we had voting lists of individual loans for portions of the 1952–1960 period, and could check directly the accuracy of new commitment composition reported in the survey forms. A common source of error seemed to be simply reporting all loans in the "all other" category if no one had classified votings by the time the survey forms were being filled out. We know independently that many life companies do not keep records on this basis as a matter of course. In the LIAA survey for the Patman Committee (see note 17 above), nine companies accounting for 39% of the assets of the responding companies failed to report mortgage data on an authorizations (commitment) basis. The LIAA *Forward Commitment Survey* discontinued reporting on subsectors of business and industrial mortgage loans in 1959, perhaps because they were not receiving meaningful data.

respect to interest costs and other loan terms. This should be particularly true of new office buildings and shopping centers built by speculative promoters for their own account. In this case the promoter must be concerned about longer-term mortgage financing as well as financing construction. However, some analysts have argued that financing costs can reasonably be ignored in formulating a first approximation explanation of the pattern of retail store and office building construction. For example, Joseph Bower asserts that retail store construction has developed along a pattern explained by an accelerator theory modified to allow for important technological innovation.[19]

Life insurance company loans to commercial and industrial concerns take the mortgage form where inadequate evidence on the earnings potential of the borrower exists or where the principal income-producing asset of the borrower is real property. Statutory requirements governing unsecured loans by life companies often necessitate using the mortgage route to extend credit to certain types of business enterprises. As an alternative, direct real estate investment or purchase and leaseback contracts are sometimes employed by life companies.

In our interviews with life insurance company investment officers, we attempted to discover whether there existed any significant organizational or portfolio preference barriers to pursuance of a yield maximization objective in this area, beyond those already discussed in regard to the corporate bond and residential mortgage sectors. Organizationally, commercial, industrial, and institutional mortgage lending is carried out via the same channels that are used in residential loans. Loans are originated through home office personnel, branch office personnel, and mortgage correspondents. Loans are also sometimes obtained through independent mortgage brokers. In general, the income-property mortgage organizations are much smaller and less geographically diverse than the corresponding residential mortgage organizations. Often, even in large companies, substantial proportions of loans are originated through the home office. Loan servicing is performed at all levels, but much higher proportions are serviced by the home office than is true in residential operations. Large multifamily

---

[19] Bower, *The Rate of Commercial Construction in a Cross-Section of American Cities, 1957–1958,* p. 5.

residential mortgage loans are sometimes generated and serviced by the commercial and industrial mortgage organization. Most of the companies referred to above as being essentially out of the home loan market have been active in apartment loans as well as other types of mortgage lending. Sometimes retail store mortgage financing will be included in an apartment project package.

The need for mortgage originating and servicing organizations in this field is based on the same considerations which underlie the necessity for strong residential mortgage organizations. This requirement is accompanied by a similar emphasis on maintenance of reasonably steady funds flows to this sector. The officers interviewed did have notions of minimum flows required for the maintenance of an effective organization. Some minimum flow rules were quite explicitly formulated. Most officers felt that substantial minimum funds flows would be maintained to commercial and industrial mortgage loans so long as gross yields (before costs) were equivalent to those on corporate bonds. On the basis of lending cost data (summarized below), this implies a willingness to sacrifice 25 to 30 basis points on the average before seriously considering reducing the allotment of funds to this sector. This organizational commitment is less strong than the analogous commitment to maintain the home loan organization. Business loan correspondents are less likely to be dependent on life company funds than home loan originators. We found no cases of life companies' making any explicit funds guarantees to commercial and industrial loan correspondents. As might be expected, the organizational commitment seemed stronger in companies who were not active in the home loan field. There appeared to be some element of customer relationship in the business mortgage sector, largely through the field organization (correspondents or branch offices), but there was no indication of a significant constraint here.

In general, life company officers interviewed seemed less concerned about geographic diversity in their commercial and industrial mortgage lending than were officers with residential mortgage responsibilities. Typically, companies interviewed had concentrated their business mortgage activity in (1) the home office region and (2) the high growth-high yield areas. Geographic yield differentials persist in this sector but they are apparently smaller than corresponding spreads among residential loan markets. Some geographic diversification is, of course, desired,[20] but is probably obtainable at little cost in expected yield. Companies do tend to place limits on certain types of loans, but often they reflect situations that are not regarded as particularly attractive loans anyway (e.g., finance companies, hotels, manufacturing plants). Loans are made on manufacturing plants only in special cases (e.g., light plants, such as a soft drink bottling plant of a national manufacturer). Loans on ancillary facilities, such as warehouses, are more common. Two officers interviewed indicated there was probably some limit to the proportion of their portfolio they would want in apartments loans, but did not know quite where the limit was and did not think they were close to it. Some officers regard apartment lending outside the largest cities, where substantial proportions of the population are accustomed to apartment living, as quite a risky venture.

The traditional emphasis on a single criterion in evaluating prospective commercial property loans, i.e. location, has yielded somewhat in the postwar years to a second requirement — strong tenancy. In interview discussions we did not find life companies employing rigid rules in this respect; in large shopping centers or office buildings, a lease with a "national" tenant for the length of the loan is highly desirable but not a minimum requirement. Strong tenancy, in terms of long leases with high credit tenants covering a large proportion of the project space, is more important the more remote the location of the property. Many commercial mortgage loan officers still consider location risk as comparable in importance to industry risk in the corporate securities sector. For retailing establishments location is a function of purchasing power in the region, traffic accessibility, and parking facilities. Evaluating the quality of large general purpose office space locations is a somewhat more complex analytical problem.

In loans on manufacturing property, life companies look for relatively unspecialized properties. Loan limits in this area tend to be relatively conservative in terms of both loan/appraisal value ratios and loan amounts per square foot of usable space. In

---

[20] Although in the past there have been reported examples of extreme geographical concentration. For two examples see the testimony of J. G. McLaughton (Mutual Life Insurance Company) and George W. Smith (New England Mutual Life Insurance Company) in the TNEC *Hearings*, pp. 15052–53 and 15087, respectively.

transportation, various forms of shipping have been popular life company investments. Credit extensions occur both in the form of mortgage loans and purchase and leaseback deals. In institutional loans, something beyond the region's buying power is expected, e.g., a financially strong church or success in a community's general hospital fund drive. We found quite divergent views among officers interviewed regarding investment preferences with respect to newly constructed as opposed to older buildings. This disparity of views arose in regard to retail stores, office buildings, and apartments. It seemed to result in several cases in strong polarization — concentration of loans almost exclusively in new construction, on the one hand, or buildings 15 to 30 years old, on the other. These differences reflect varying opinions with regard to the impact of changing construction quality and costs on the profitability of owning and operating these sorts of properties, and with respect to the significance of technological changes in the design and use of space.

Business mortgage loans have been made over a wide range of loan size, but the bulk of loans seem to fall within a range of $100,000 to $5,000,000. Better than two-thirds of the loan amounts authorized by respondents to the LIAA-Patman survey during 1953–1956 fell within this range. During the four years 22 loans of over $10,000,000 were authorized by the reporting companies. Joint participation loans are practically nonexistent in this area since mortgaged property does not lend itself to creditor shares. The largest loans seem to be made on large downtown office buildings and regional shopping centers. The companies we interviewed, all of whom were quite sizable, all reported they had set $50,000 as a desirable minimum loan size in this field. Exceptions to this limit were not uncommon, however.[21] Most companies reported that they reduced both very large and very small loans in tight funds periods and tried to ration funds to loans in the $100,000 to $5,000,000 size range.[22] Loan

---

[21] During the four years covered by the LIAA-Patman survey, the amount lent by the responding companies in loans of less than $50,000 declined steadily from 6.4% in 1953 to 3.9% in 1956. ALC-LIAA *Joint Investment Bulletin*, No. 321, Table C-1.

[22] As we have seen, some companies consciously compromise yield objectives by reducing funds allotments to income-property mortgage activity in tight periods in order to maintain flows to the home loan field organization.

to value ratios on income-property loans seem, typically, to fall between ½ and ⅔. A ⅔ statutory limit has been common in many states. Although a ⅔ limit on conventional residential loans did seem to pose an obstacle to many life companies, we found less evidence that companies wished to exceed the ⅔ rule on commercial and industrial property.[23]

The cost of business mortgage lending operations has been significantly less than the unit cost of acquiring and servicing residential mortgage loans, but more than costs incurred in corporate security investments. In terms of basis points, portfolio costs for the large life insurance companies interviewed ran about 45 to 60 points for the residential loan portfolio, 25 to 30 points for business mortgage loans, and, perhaps, 4 or 5 basis points for corporate bond investments. The cost differences reflect variations in average loan size among these three categories, differences in the organizational overhead required to operate in these sectors, and relative differences in the volume of loans generated in each area during the 1950s. Since mortgage lending is a relatively high overhead operation, unit costs on mortgage portfolios are particularly sensitive to loan volume.[24]

Effective maturities on business mortgage loans appear comparable to those on corporate bonds — somewhat longer than residential mortgage loan maturities. Interview responses placed the

---

[23] This was true, at least, at the time of our interviews with life company officers (1960). In 1963 industry representatives did urge the New York state legislature to raise the maximum loan/value ratio on all conventional real estate loans from ⅔ to ¾. See the *Report* of the Joint Legislative Committee on Insurance Rates and Regulation, 1964, p. 48. In testimony before the Joint Legislative Committee, James J. O'Leary of the LIAA indicated that life companies were most interested in increasing their nonfirm, nonresidential mortgage loans (*ibid.*, p. 50).

[24] The interview estimates seem to be in line with other evidence. The LIAA has conducted an annual survey of mortgage lending income and costs. The survey results for 1958 include a breakdown of companies whose mortgage portfolios were predominantly in conventional loans (over 60% of their loan portfolio in conventionals). Forty-five of 90 companies responding were in this category. Of these 45, 5 had portfolios "largely" (over 60%) in business and commercial loans and 9 had portfolios "largely" (over 60%) in conventional residential loans. Total portfolio costs as a percent of their monthly average investment amounted to 0.32% for the largely commercial mortgage companies and 0.62% for the residential loan companies. Total portfolio costs include originating fees and premiums, servicing fees, branch office expenses, and home office expenses allocable to the mortgage operation.

effective life of commercial and industrial loans in the range of 15 to 18 years. However, it is apparently not uncommon to write the initial loan for a shorter period, say 10 to 15 years, and then to extend the loan to the full term after several years earnings experience.

To sum up, it appears that within life companies' attitudes regarding eligible income-property mortgage loans, it is reasonable to suppose that the primary objective is yield. The minimum net yield requirements were reported to be the same (6%) for corporate bonds, residential mortgages, and commercial and industrial mortgages for companies we interviewed in 1960. Diversification considerations did not seem to provide a significantly competing objective in this sector. The geographic concentration of business mortgage loans is less than that for residential loans, with more willingness to lend in growth areas with relatively high yields. No evidence of significant diversification constraints on loan types was found. The need to maintain a home office and field organization does put a premium on maintaining minimum funds flows into business mortgages although the magnitude of this constraint seemed to be less than in the residential loan sector. This means that a rough priority ranking may exist in a tight funds period in many companies with home loans in a preferred position, income property mortgage loans next, and corporate bonds last. Some sacrifice of the yield objective is implied. Within the business mortgage sector, rationing takes two forms:

(1) Reduction or elimination of types of loans in which the company is only marginally active. In the aggregate this may mean loans on manufacturing or institutional property are discriminated against in a tight period.
(2) Narrowing of the acceptable size range for loans. This may mean a reluctance to enter into large office building or regional shopping center loans in order to spread limited funds over more correspondents and borrowers.

There was some suggestion that companies might also restrict the number of small loans (say, under $50,000 or under $100,000) they would be willing to make. Since it appears that the gross yield spread between large and small loans narrows as the level of interest rates rise,[25] perhaps due to prevailing usurious rate or

---

[25] See the LIAA-Patman Survey, Table C-3.

"just price" concepts applicable to small loans, this behavior can be regarded as reflecting a yield motivation, if the rate stickiness is taken as institutionally given.

Regression Analysis of Business Mortgage Votings

Although we were unable to conduct an analysis of the primary subsectors in the commercial, industrial, and institutional mortgage loan grab-bag, we did examine the time series of total new commitments in this area, looking particularly for evidence of responsiveness to relative yields among the major asset categories. Since the future available funds flow appeared to be of major importance in explaining the pattern of residential loan votings, we also included it as an independent variable in this analysis. Barring any special reason to the contrary — such as an analogue to the corporate bond forward commitment service hypothesis — this sector is important enough to expect votings to have a positive relation to future available funds.[26] On the basis of what we know of the frequency distribution of votings-delivery lags for residential loan, business mortgage loan, and corporate bond commitments, we would expect the available funds variable to exert most influence in home loan votings, least on corporate bond votings, with business mortgages somewhere in between.

The major data problem that arises in attempting to examine the responsiveness of business mortgage votings to yield spreads is finding a suitable index of business mortgage loan yields. This problem exists not only because business mortgage loans are composed of a very heterogeneous collection of loans on quite different properties, but also because very little yield information exists for any of the business loan subsectors. Saul Klaman obtained some interest rate data on conventional loans from several life insurance companies. He presents a quarterly series on income-

---

[26] There may very well be a commitment servicing function operating here. Life companies presumably have some competitive advantage in bidding for mortgage loans on large new construction projects, e.g., office buildings and regional shopping centers, which require long-term forward commitments. However, in the aggregate, this sort of commitment seems less important in the business mortgage total than it is in corporate bonds. The percentage of outstanding commitments expected to be taken down in six months runs consistently and significantly higher for business mortgage loans than it does for corporate bonds. The proportion of residential loan commitments due for takedown in six months is still much higher, of course.

property mortgage loans closed by two life companies for the period, 1951–1956.[27] Average annual gross contract rates obtained by life companies during the years 1953–1956 are reported in the LIAA-Patman survey summary for each of the subsectors discussed above.[28] These rates are reported on loan commitments rather than closings.[29] From individual life insurance companies we secured scattered data on rates obtained on new business mortgage loan commitments (from four companies) and on loan closings (from three companies). The LIAA survey of city mortgage lending income and costs reports average gross contract rates on new loan acquisitions for nonresidential conventional loans on an annual basis. All these data together were not adequate to piece together a suitable quarterly, let along monthly, yield series for use in business mortgage votings regressions.

From outside the life insurance industry we obtained a complete listing of loans entered into by a large New England food retailing chain, with data on loan amount and rate paid for the period from mid-1953 through 1960. Within its home state, this chain financed all its new construction, additions, and remodeling with loans from savings banks. The chain reported that the rate charged by life insurance companies generally exceeded the savings bank rate by a quarter of an interest point. The chain also reported that it bargained for "the constant" (interest plus amortization payments). Finally, we obtained a yield series based on mortgage loans made on Manhattan real estate.[30] This series was available on a monthly basis for the period 1949–1960, except that rates for the months April–July were reported only as an average for these four months.

None of these series is really satisfactory for our purpose. However, to obtain an impression of the forces at work, we decided to run one round of a regression analysis on business mortgage votings. After comparing all the available scattered data

---

[27] The data are a weighted average of contract interest rates on loans closed by the companies. Klaman reports the series represents "chiefly loans on large-scale apartment buildings and high-quality commercial properties." See *The Postwar Residential Mortgage Market*, p. 81, and Table A-5, p. 286.

[28] See the ALC-LIAA *Joint Investment Bulletin*, No. 321, Table C-6.

[29] With some exceptions noted above.

[30] This series was prepared by James Felt and Company, Inc., New York City. It includes loans over $10,000. See Table VI-B-1.

on business mortgage yields, we concluded that the Manhattan real estate loan series seemed to reflect all the significant movements in yields visible in the other partial series. Therefore it seemed preferable to use this series simply as a proxy for business mortgage yields rather than a hybrid blended from all available information. As might be expected, the Manhattan series runs somewhat below the Klaman life company income-property loan rate series for the period in which they overlap. Because of relatively erratic month-to-month movements in the Manhattan series, and because independent observations were not available for the April–July months, we converted the monthly data into quarterly averages before using the series.

The regression results are reported in Table VIII-8. As expected, they do not provide very conclusive results. The primary explanatory variables used were yield spreads between business mortgage and (1) residential mortgage and (2) corporate bond, yields, and the future available funds flow. In the regressions on monthly observations the strongest explanatory variable seems to be the spread between business mortgage and residential mortgage loan yields. The business mortgage-corporate bond yield differential makes no useful contribution. This sort of result is consistent with the proposition that the allocation of new loan commitments between the corporate and mortgage departments is affected by some important nonyield considerations — servicing corporate customers, maintaining funds flows to mortgage organizations, etc. — but that within the mortgage department, funds allocation is dominated by yield considerations. In the monthly regressions, the level of business mortgage votings appears to be modestly influenced by future available funds. The sign in the available funds partial regression coefficient is always right and the coefficient exceeds its standard error, but is generally nonsignificant.[31]

In running the quarterly regressions we took out the influence of the available funds variable first. The funds influence appears

---

[31] In these regressions the available funds variable is used in a form in which 80% of the current month's residential mortgage votings is subtracted from the six months' available funds. This was done on the supposition that high current home loan votings might reduce a life company's willingness to make new business loan commitments. It turned out to make little difference, however, whether or not the adjustment is made.

TABLE VIII-8. *Business and Commercial Mortgage Loan Votings:*
Regression Results

A. Monthly Observations, October 1952–January 1960 $n = 88$

   (1) $V_{MB} = 84.0490 + 11.4567 \ (r_{MB} - r_U)$
$$(7.0632)$$
      $R^2 = .0297$ $s = 24.9934$
      $\overline{R}^2 = .0071$ $\bar{s} = 25.3183$

   (2) $V_{MB} = 114.2930 + 5.6542 \ (r_{MB} - r_U) + 91.7617 \ (r_{MB} - r_{RC})$
$$(6.3757) \qquad\qquad (18.6252)$$
      $R^2 = .2452$ $s = 22.0049$
      $\overline{R}^2 = .2186$ $\bar{s} = 22.4638$

   (3) $V_{MB} = 94.4934 - 7.7097 \ (r_{MB} - r_U) + 86.7828 \ (r_{MB} - r_{RC})$
$$(7.3589) \qquad\qquad (17.7592)$$
        $+ .0347 \ (AF_{1-6} - .8 \ V_{MR})$
$$(.0108)$$
      $R^2 = .3271$ $s = 20.8168$
      $\overline{R}^2 = .2951$ $\bar{s} = 21.3580$

   (4) $V_{MB} = 205.8640 - 58.3369 \ (r_{MB} - r_U^n) + 127.0224 \ (r_{MB} - r_{RC})$
$$(14.2389) \qquad\qquad (18.5527)$$
      $R^2 = .3639$ $s = 20.2384$
      $\overline{R}^2 = .3414$ $\bar{s} = 20.6229$

   (5) $V_{MB} = 71.5914 + 20.5586 \ (r_{MB} - r_U)_{-3} + 56.1195 \ (r_{MB} - r_{RC})_{-3}$
$$(8.5670) \qquad\qquad (18.4297)$$
        $+ .0197 \ (AF_{1,6} - .8 \ V_{MR})$
$$(.0123)$$
      $R^2 = .3005$ $s = 21.2243$
      $\overline{R}^2 = .2672$ $\bar{s} = 21.7761$

   (6) $V_{MB} = 108.2147 - 23.2677 \ (r_U - r_U^n)_{-3}$
$$(7.4887)$$
        $+ 63.9205 \ (r_{MB} - r_{RC})_{-3} + .0125 \ (AF_{1,6} - .8 \ V_{MR})$
$$(17.4804) \qquad\qquad (.0124)$$
      $R^2 = .3296$ $s = 20.7782$
      $\overline{R}^2 = .2977$ $\bar{s} = 21.3184$

B. Quarterly Observations, 1952/IV–1959/IV $n = 29$

   (7) $V_{MB} = 160.4 + .1157 \ AF_{0,1}$
$$(.0343)$$
      $R^2 = .297$ $s = 50.08$
      $\overline{R}^2 = .271$ $\bar{s} = 51.91$

   (8) $V_{MB} = 62.73 + .1226 \ AF_{0,1} + 18.42 \ r_{MB}$
$$(.0356) \qquad (23.25)$$
      $R^2 = .313$ $s = 49.49$
      $\overline{R}^2 = .261$ $\bar{s} = 52.27$

   (9) $V_{MB} = 65.08 + .1083 \ AF_{0,1} + 113.4 \ r_{MB} - 89.63 \ r_F$
$$(.0388) \qquad (104.2) \qquad (95.85)$$
      $R^2 = .337$ $s = 48.65$
      $\overline{R}^2 = .257$ $\bar{s} = 52.39$

TABLE VIII-8 (continued)

(10) $V_{MB} = 83.80 + .1129\,AF_{0,1} + 104.4\,r_{MB} - 92.53\,r_F + 9.072\,r_U$
$\qquad\qquad\quad (.0435) \qquad\quad (112.4) \qquad (98.40) \quad (36.57)$

$\quad R^2 = .338 \qquad\qquad s = 48.58$
$\quad \overline{R}^2 = .228 \qquad\qquad \bar{s} = 53.41$

(11) $V_{MB} = 183.5 + .1063\,AF_{0,1} + 66.70\,(r_{MB} - r_F)$
$\qquad\qquad\quad (.0385) \qquad\quad (93.00)$

$\quad R^2 = .310 \qquad\qquad s = 49.60$
$\quad \overline{R}^2 = .257 \qquad\qquad \bar{s} = 52.38 \qquad\quad d = 1.0577^*$

(12) $V_{MB} = 241.5 + .1044\,AF_{0,1} - .0378\,(CT_s)_{-1} + 55.45\,(r_{MB} - r_F)$
$\qquad\qquad\quad (.0389) \qquad\quad (.0569) \qquad\qquad (95.53)$

$\quad R^2 = .322 \qquad\qquad s = 49.16$
$\quad \overline{R}^2 = .241 \qquad\qquad \bar{s} = 52.95 \qquad\quad d = .9653^*$

(13) $V_{MB} = 193.6 + .1157\,AF_{0,1} + 80.14\,(r_{MB} - r_F)$
$\qquad\qquad\quad (.0431) \qquad\quad (96.26)$
$\qquad\qquad\quad\; - 21.41\,(r_{MB} - r_U)$
$\qquad\qquad\quad\;\; (32.71)$

$\quad R^2 = .322 \qquad\qquad s = 49.18$
$\quad \overline{R}^2 = .241 \qquad\qquad \bar{s} = 52.97$

(14) $V_{MB} = 231.9 + .1143\,AF_{0,1} - .04361\,(CT_s)_{-1}$
$\qquad\qquad\quad (.0345) \qquad\quad (.05523)$

$\quad R^2 = .313 \qquad\qquad s = 49.49$
$\quad \overline{R}^2 = .261 \qquad\qquad \bar{s} = 52.27$

(15) $V_{MB} = 219.0 + .09425\,AF_{0,1} + .02099\,(CT_s)_{-1} + 261.1\,r_{RC}$
$\qquad\qquad\qquad\; (.02834) \qquad\quad (.04757) \qquad\quad (67.5)$

$\quad R^2 = .570 \qquad\qquad s = 39.15$
$\quad \overline{R}^2 = .519 \qquad\qquad \bar{s} = 42.16 \qquad\quad d = 1.6733^{***}$

(16) $V_{MB} = 255.6 + .1186\,AF_{0,1} - .03153\,(CT_s)_{-1} + 179.9\,(r_{RC})_{-1}$
$\qquad\qquad\quad (.0312) \qquad\quad (.04994) \qquad\qquad (67.7)$

$\quad R^2 = .464 \qquad\qquad s = 43.71$
$\quad \overline{R}^2 = .400 \qquad\qquad \bar{s} = 47.07 \qquad\quad d = 1.5071^{**}$

(17) $V_{MB} = 145.5 + .2098\,(G_M - N_M)$
$\qquad\qquad\quad (.1424)$

$\quad R^2 = .149 \qquad\qquad s = 55.12$
$\quad \overline{R}^2 = .117 \qquad\qquad \bar{s} = 57.12$

(18) $V_{MB} = 157.3 + .3498\,(G_M - N_M) + 204.8\,(r_{MB} - r_F)$
$\qquad\qquad\quad (.1321) \qquad\qquad\qquad (84.49)$

$\quad R^2 = .305 \qquad\qquad s = 49.78$
$\quad \overline{R}^2 = .252 \qquad\qquad \bar{s} = 52.57$

(19) $V_{MB} = 102.3 + .3826\,(G_M - N_M) + 165.2\,(r_{MB} - r_F)$
$\qquad\qquad\quad (.1344) \qquad\qquad\qquad (90.73)$
$\qquad\qquad\quad\; + 34.33\,(r_{MB} - r_F)$
$\qquad\qquad\quad\;\; (29.82)$

$\quad R^2 = .340 \qquad\qquad s = 48.51$
$\quad \overline{R}^2 = .261 \qquad\qquad \bar{s} = 52.25$

TABLE VIII-8 (continued)

(20) $V_{MB} = 253.8 + .03054\ AF_{1,2}$
$\qquad\qquad\quad (.03959)$
$\qquad R^2 = .021 \qquad\qquad s = 59.10$
$\qquad \overline{R}^2 = -.014 \qquad\quad \bar{s} = 61.25$

C. Quarterly Observations 1956/III–1959/IV $\qquad n = 14$

(21) $V_{MB} = 139.7 + .1435\ AF_{0,1}$
$\qquad\qquad\quad (.0367)$
$\qquad R^2 = .560 \qquad\qquad s = 35.88$
$\qquad \overline{R}^2 = .523 \qquad\qquad \bar{s} = 38.76$

(22) $V_{MB} = 268.3 + .1450\ AF_{0,1} - .08162\ (CT_s)_{-1}$
$\qquad\qquad\quad (.0348) \qquad\quad (.05288)$
$\qquad R^2 = .638 \qquad\qquad s = 32.53$
$\qquad \overline{R}^2 = .572 \qquad\qquad \bar{s} = 36.70$

(23) $V_{MB} = 271.6 + .1476\ AF_{0,1} - .08696\ (CT_s)_{-1}$
$\qquad\qquad\quad (.1024) \qquad\quad (.07163)$
$\qquad\qquad - 15.11\ (r_{MB} - r_F)$
$\qquad\qquad\quad (128.6)$
$\qquad R^2 = .638 \qquad\qquad s = 32.51$
$\qquad \overline{R}^2 = .530 \qquad\qquad \bar{s} = 38.47 \qquad\qquad d = 1.7925$***

(24) $V_{MB} = 212.0 + .1336\ AF_{0,1} - .02191\ (CT_s)_{-1} + 117.9\ r_{RC}$
$\qquad\qquad\quad (.0389) \qquad\quad (.09766) \qquad\quad (160.7)$
$\qquad R^2 = .656 \qquad\qquad s = 31.69$
$\qquad \overline{R}^2 = .554 \qquad\qquad \bar{s} = 37.50 \qquad\qquad d = 1.9637$***

(25) $V_{MB} = 271.0 + .1446\ AF_{0,1} - .08612\ (CT_s)_{-1} - 22.7\ (r_{RC})_{-1}$
$\qquad\qquad\quad (.0364) \qquad\quad (.05909) \qquad\quad (104.7)$
$\qquad R^2 = .640 \qquad\qquad s = 32.45$
$\qquad \overline{R}^2 = .532 \qquad\qquad \bar{s} = 38.40 \qquad\qquad d = 1.7682$**

(26) $V_{MB} = 252.9 + .1597\ AF_{0,1} - .09286\ (CT_s)_{-1} - 120.8\ (r_F)_{-1}$
$\qquad\qquad\quad (.0363) \qquad\quad (.05278) \qquad\quad (101.8)$
$\qquad R^2 = .683 \qquad\qquad s = 30.46$
$\qquad \overline{R}^2 = .588 \qquad\qquad \bar{s} = 36.04 \qquad\qquad d = 1.6628$**

* Positive serial correlation significant at the 5% level.
** Inconclusive range of Durbin-Watson test.
*** Not significant at 5% level.

much stronger in this set of equations. The relationship is sensitive to the period over which the six months' funds variable is measured, however. (See equation (20).) With available funds picking up most of the variance in votings the regressions are able to explain, the yield spread hypothesis fares more poorly than in the monthly regressions. In some equations we substituted the total mortgage portfolio rollover for the available funds measure. Mortgage turnover affects total votings if allocations among departments proceed on a rollover plus a share of net funds inflow basis. Assuming intermortgage department allocations are made on a yield basis, then the business mortgage sector benefits in terms of funds available by a high turnover rate of residential as well as business loans. In the business mortgage sector there is much less likelihood of there being a reverse causal effect at work. The short-term liquid assets variable was added in a few equations as a separate variable. As in the analysis of residential and corporate bond sectors, the liquid assets measure does not contribute to explaining the votings pattern.

In addition to using the various combinations of yield spreads, the relevant yield series are introduced by themselves in some equations. Where this is done, we expect existence of yield responsiveness to produce a positive sign on the business mortgage yield variable and a negative coefficient for the other yield variables. The business mortgage yield coefficient is consistently positive but often not significant. The signs on coefficients of the other yield variables are mixed. Curiously, the conventional residential mortgage interest rate series draws a significant positive sign and contributes strongly to the R^2. Possibly this series is a better index of the pattern of nonresidential mortgage yields than the series we used, but we have no basis for asserting this.

Finally, we ran some business mortgage loan voting regressions for the post-open-to-buy period (Part C). The available funds variable appears to be a much stronger influence in this limited period. The liquid assets variable consistently draws the wrong sign, as do the yield and yield spread variables most of the time. Introduction of the conventional residential mortgage yield series no longer contributes to the regression explanation. Thus the one striking result of this set of regressions is that available funds alone is capable of explaining over half of the variance in business mortgage votings during the late 1950s.

In summary, we tentatively conclude that business mortgage loan votings were significantly influenced by the near-term available cash flow. This influence is not so strong as it was on residential mortgage votings, but the nature of the relationship is probably quite similar. We have not been able to analyze individual life company commitments in this manner but an implication of the aggregative analysis is that we should expect to find business mortgage votings particularly sensitive to the available funds flow in life companies which are inactive in the home loan sector. It appeared from the regressions run on monthly data that yield differentials among mortgage loan alternatives also had a significant role in determining the time path of business mortgage votings, but the results of the quarterly regression analysis do not confirm this conclusion.

Thus we tentatively conclude that future available funds and yield differentials among mortgage loan alternatives probably played a significant role in influencing the time pattern of business mortgage votings during the 1950s. But the fits are not good and the results inconclusive. From our qualitative evidence we have not found any single overriding constraint that prevents pursuance of a yield-oriented portfolio selection policy in the business mortgage sectors, but several secondary constraints may at times be additive and produce compromise of a yield objective. Adequate estimation of supply of funds determinants to this sector depends upon further analyses of the determinants of the demand for funds in the major subsectors, and development of satisfactory estimates of yields on the primary types of commercial and industrial mortgage loans.

State and Local Government Securities

Obligations issued by political units at the state and local level have not been a primary investment outlet for life insurance company funds during the postwar years. Neither have life company purchases of these issues had a substantial impact on the overall market for state and local government securities. During the eight years 1953–1960 life companies added (net) $2.3 billion of municipals to their portfolios. This amounted to 5.6% of the net gain in life company assets. Holdings of U.S. municipal bonds accounted for 3.8% of life insurance company assets at the end of 1960.[32] Life company net acquisitions of $2.3 billion represented 7.4% of net issues by state and local governments during the eight years.[33]

Life companies played a more significant role in the revenue

---

[32] Data from the ILI, *Life Insurance Fact Book*, annual.

[33] Federal Reserve Board, *Flow of Funds Accounts*, 1963 Supplement.

bond subsector of the municipal securities market, however. Data are not available on the composition of life companies' municipal bond portfolios prior to 1959, but as of the end of 1959 revenue bonds accounted for 73% of life company state and local bond holdings.[34] Large life companies which dominate the forward commitment data apparently have higher proportions of revenue bonds in their municipal bond portfolios. A number of the companies we interviewed indicated they rarely acquired general obligation issues.[35] At the end of the 1950s life companies held perhaps 13% of revenue bonds outstanding, although their holdings of all types of municipal obligations accounted for only 5% of total issues outstanding.[36]

The explanation of life companies' concentration in revenue issues seems quite simple; namely, yield. This came through in our interviews as a single-minded motivation for investing in municipal bonds. Brimmer obtained similar responses from his questionnaire survey.[37] Because of their risk features, revenue bonds have typically carried yields nearly comparable to those obtainable from corporate bonds with the same quality rating. In contrast, guaranteed or general obligation issues have been priced by the market at substantially lower yields.[38]

Acquisition of new revenue bond issues requires the same sort

---

[34] Computed from data provided in the ILI, *Tally of Life Insurance Statistics*, monthly. During the first four years that a breakdown of life companies' municipal bond holdings was provided (January 1959–January 1963), three-quarters of life company net acquisitions were revenue bonds. The *Tally* data cover companies holding about 94% of the industry's assets.

[35] Brimmer reports on a survey of 62 life companies conducted in 1959. His results indicate that about 70% of these companies' holdings of state and local obligations consisted of revenue bonds. However, for a sample of 16 large companies (asset sizes from $540 million to $3,900 million), the proportion of revenue bonds was nearly 80%. See Brimmer, *Life Insurance Companies in the Capital Market*, Table VII-10, p. 309.

[36] *Ibid.*, p. 321.

[37] For large companies responding to Brimmer's questionnaire, return was clearly the dominant objective sought by companies investing in state and local obligations. Small companies (assets under $112 million) reported portfolio diversification as a significant secondary consideration in acquiring municipals. Cf. Brimmer, Table VIII-1, p. 288. Several of the companies we interviewed did mention long maturities in connection with competitively attractive yields as a favorable characteristic of revenue bonds.

[38] Much of toll road financing was accomplished only with a yield differential over high grade tax-exempts of about 2 percentage points. See Robinson, *Postwar Market for State and Local Securities*, p. 210.

of security analysis which life company staffs are accustomed to performing on corporate issues. Since past experience of the issuing authority does not always exist and past earnings experience on the specific project being financed never exists, appraisals are heavily dependent on engineering estimates. As some toll road experiences have dramatically demonstrated, engineering estimates are subject to considerable error. Because of these risk considerations, most revenue bonds are not rated by Moody's or other agencies at the time of issue. Risk, together with the lack of a standardized rating, means revenue issues have limited marketability during the first years following issue. After several years of demonstrated earning capacity, the issue may be rated. Thus, it is common for such issues to appreciate in price with seasoning.[39]

As a consequence of these risk and marketability characteristics of revenue bonds, they have been priced at yields attractive to investors with little interest in the tax-exempt income feature of municipals. It happens that the principal buyers of state and local obligations — wealthy individuals, commercial banks, and fire and casualty insurance companies — have portfolio tastes which put a high premium on quality and are attracted to the municipals market by the prospect of tax-free income. Being risk averters and unequipped to perform detailed security analysis, these investors have concentrated on bonds with high ratings. Therefore lower rated and unrated obligations have to be sold to investors willing and able to accept the greater risks, and generally less attracted by tax-exempt features.[40] During most of the 1950s the marginal federal income tax rate on life insurance companies' investment income was of the order of 6.5% to 8%. Thus, at prevailing yields, the tax-exemption feature of municipals could not have been worth more than 25 or 30 basis points to them.[41]

It appears, then, that we ought to expect the time path of life

---

[39] *Ibid.*

[40] See *ibid.*, pp. 12–16, 70–93.

[41] Some companies may have correctly anticipated an increase in federal income tax liability, since life companies operated under temporary tax legislation throughout the 1950s until passage of the Life Insurance Company Tax Act of 1959. On the other side, it should be noted that the legal status of tax freedom from income earned on revenue issues has never been as clearly defined as it is on general obligations. There is a body of opinion which considers many revenue bonds taxable under existing laws. See Ratchford, "Revenue Bonds and Tax Immunity."

company new state and local bond commitments to be shaped primarily by the prevailing yields on new issues of lower rated (A-Baa) general obligation and revenue bond issues relative to yields obtainable by the securities departments on comparable quality new corporate bond issues. Secondarily, we might expect the available funds flow to have a permissive influence on municipal bond votings. A tight funds position may restrict votings for municipals independent of relative yields if customer and organizational priorities dominate votings.

Given life company preferences in this sector, the relevant municipal bond yield series for an empirical test of life companies' yield sensitivity would be a new issue revenue bond yield index. However, no satisfactory yield series of this sort was available to us for the period covered by the commitment data. Therefore we used Moody's Baa seasoned municipal bond yield series adjusted for the changing marginal federal income tax rate for life companies during the 1950s.[42] The differential between new issue corporate bond yields and this municipal bond series was employed as an independent variable in a multiple regression analysis of life company new commitments for state and local obligations.

To take account of the apparent strong life company preference for new revenue bond issues, and recognizing that new revenue issues have tended to be bunched in time, we introduced as an explanatory variable the monthly estimates of new revenue bond sales compiled by *The Bond Buyer*.[43] Finally, we included the six months available funds measure as an independent variable.

The regression results are summarized in Table VIII-9.[44] Sales

[42] We adjusted Moody's series to a taxable-yield equivalent by assuming life companies' marginal federal income tax rate was 6.5% during 1953–1955, 7.8% for 1956–1958, and 15% in 1959–1960. See Chapter II for a discussion of life companies' tax position during the 1950s.

[43] It should be noted that revenue financing takes many forms, and the distinction between revenue and other issues is not always clear. There probably exist some differences in definition and inclusion among *The Bond Buyer*, the Investment Bankers Association, the Bureau of the Census, and the Institute of Life Insurance in their compilations of revenue bonds. See Robinson, *Postwar Market for State and Local Securities*, p. 202.

[44] The regression analysis begins in mid-1953 because we did not have monthly data on revenue bond sales for the earlier period. The life company votings series contains some commitments for Canadian provincial issues in the earlier period through October 1956. It was not possible to separate these issues out of the total. Balance sheet data indicate the problem is

TABLE VIII-9.   *Regression Analysis of State and Local Government Bond Votings*

I   Monthly Observations, July 1953–January 1960 $n = 79$

(1) $V_L = 17.50 - 30.4826 \, (r_U - r_L)$
          (10.7082)

$R^2 = .0952$ $s = 15.7854$
$\overline{R}^2 = .0717$ $\bar{s} = 16.0064$

(2) $V_L = 1.8211 - 7.7418 \, (r_U - r_L) + .0988 \, R$
          (8.0646) $(.0114)$

$R^2 = .5467$ $s = 11.1742$
$\overline{R}^2 = .5288$ $\bar{s} = 11.3977$

(3) $V_L = 1.3594 - 7.4884 \, (r_U - r_L) + .0988 \, R + .0004 \, AF_{1,6}$
          (8.5223) $(.0114)$ $(.0045)$

$R^2 = .5467$ $s = 11.1745$
$\overline{R}^2 = .5225$ $\bar{s} = 11.4874$

II Quarterly Observations, 1953/III–1960/I $n = 27$

(4) $V_L = 29.67 + .02772 \, AF_{0,1}$
          $(.01780)$

$R^2 = .051$ $s = 35.05$
$\overline{R}^2 = .013$ $\bar{s} = 36.42$

(5) $V_L = 2.101 + .00241 \, AF_{0,1} + .1041 \, R$
          $(.01780)$ $(.0210)$

$R^2 = .531$ $s = 24.62$
$\overline{R}^2 = .492$ $\bar{s} = 26.12$

(6) $V_L = 7.378 - .00158 \, AF_{0,1} + .09602 \, R - .4143 \, (r_U - r_L)$
          $(.01808)$ $(.02211)$ $(.3735)$

$R^2 = .555$ $s = 23.99$
$\overline{R}^2 = .497$ $\bar{s} = 25.99$

(7) $V_L = 4.262 + .1049 \, R$
          $(.0197)$

$R^2 = .531$ $s = 24.63$
$\overline{R}^2 = .512$ $\bar{s} = 25.60$

(8) $V_L = 5.929 + .09564 \, R - .4078 \, (r_U - r_L)$
          $(.02121)$ $(.3584)$

$R^2 = .555$ $s = 23.99$
$\overline{R}^2 = .518$ $\bar{s} = 25.45$

of revenue bonds by state and local governments have a strong
impact on new life company commitments to acquire municipal

---

not serious.   The net increase in life company holdings of foreign municipal
bond issues between end-1953 and end-1956 was only $46 million.   Beginning
with November 1956, the votings data include only issues of U.S. political
units.   The commitment data do not distinguish between revenue bonds and
other issues.

obligations.[45]   Although the signs on the partial regression coefficients are always right for the corporate bond/municipal bond yield spread, and in all but one case for the available funds variable, neither of these variables contribute much to an explanation of life companies' municipal bond votings.   There is no significant colinearity among the independent variables in these equations, nor are we troubled with serial correlation problems.

In sum, life companies' interest in municipal bonds was largely confined to revenue issues during the 1950s.   Authorizations from life company finance committees to buy municipals are strongly associated with the availability of opportunities as represented by new revenue bond financing.

The qualitative evidence suggests life companies' allocation of funds to the municipal debt sector should vary inversely with the size of the spread between yields obtainable on new issue corporate bonds and going yields on state and local government obligations. For this purpose yields on bonds of about Baa quality seemed most appropriate.   Our regression results are broadly consistent with this view, with perhaps some qualification for rationing of funds allocated to governments in tight credit periods in order that corporate customer needs can be satisfied.   The yield spread measure used as an independent variable did not contribute much explanatory power, but it seems reasonable to regard life companies' sensitivity to revenue bond issues as reflecting primarily a yield objective.

Summary

In this chapter we have employed single equation least squares regression analysis as a means of empirically sorting out some of the potential determinants of life insurance companies' investment composition decisions.   In particular, we have been concerned with discovering whether or not life company funds allocation

---

[45] Since these issues are generally public offerings, the commitment-takedown time lag is typically short.   Thus the pattern of commitments and acquisitions is little different, and very similar results would be obtained from using acquisitions of municipals as the dependent variable.

decisions during the 1950s were responsive to changes in the structure of yields among alternative assets. Because for many investments funds flows lag considerably behind portfolio decisions, the analysis was conducted on investment commitments rather than on acquisitions.

Since the major categories in which life companies invested during the 1950s were corporate bonds and residential mortgage loans, we began the empirical analysis with an examination of the time path of the ratio of new corporate bond commitments to new residential mortgage loan commitments. Using quarterly observations over 1952 to 1960, we found some positive responsiveness of this portfolio authorizations ratio to the differential in yields between corporate bonds and residential mortgage loans. However, the fits obtained were unimpressive.

Splitting the period in two at the end of 1956, we found a strong yield spread response in the early years but none during the post-1956 period. This result suggested that life companies found it possible to alter the proportion of new commitments made in these two sectors quickly when their liquidity position was reasonably strong, but that their flexibility was impeded once the open-to-buy environment had clearly ended. The regression results were somewhat improved by adding available (uncommitted) funds as an additional explanatory variable, and consistent with the above result, the funds variable performed somewhat more strongly after 1956. Inclusion of the price discounts prevailing on FHA and VA loans as an independent variable produced a partial regression coefficient which had the right sign (positive) but was nonsignificant.

An indirect test of the hypothesis that many corporate bond commitments are made in response to the demand of corporate borrowing customers for this service was made by adding two proxies for corporate commitment demand in some regression equations. There variables showed promise but overall the fits obtained using the new commitments ratio as the dependent variable were not satisfactory. Because of the variance in the distribution of new commitments by the commitment-to-delivery lag, it appeared that composition of votings simply was not a matter of concern to investment officers but rather a by-product of other decisions. Consequently we attempted regression analysis on the residential mortgage loan and corporate bond commitment components separately.

In conducting the analysis on residential mortgage votings we experienced considerable difficulty with serial correlation and multicolinearity. Nonetheless it did appear that the variance in new residential mortgage loan commitments was quite adequately explained by a combination of (1) the short-term uncommitted funds flow available for investment; (2) the yield spread between residential loans and corporate bonds; and (3) prevailing price discounts on federally underwritten loans. Splitting the 1952–1960 period into two portions at year-end 1956 (or alternatively, at the middle of 1956), we found a strong contribution being made by the price discount variable in the first period but not in the second. The yield spread variable explained more in the earlier period, and available funds proved more important during the later years. These results seemed to be consistent with the notion that the passing of the open-to-buy environment made the desire of life companies to remain fully invested a more dominant goal in shaping commitment policy, and suggested that the need to control commitments and commitment stock-funds flow relationships reduced the ability of life companies to respond quickly to temporal variations in yield spreads.

The time path of corporate bond commitments authorized by life companies during the 1950s was quite erratic, and we experienced only limited success in rationalizing it. The primary difficulty seemed to be the wide variety of prospective takedown dates associated with bond commitments made in any period. We did not possess data on the breakdown of bond votings by anticipated time to takedown which would have made it possible to test the hypothesis that delayed takedown commitments are determined primarily by customer demand whereas short-term commitments are determined by life companies' attempting to meet specific loaned-up, yield, or other goals.

Nonetheless our results did suggests that this hypothesis remains a useful approach to explaining life companies' willingness to supply bond commitments. Regressing new corporate bond commitments on various combinations of bond yield, mortgage yields, short-term uncommitted funds, liquid assets, outstanding commitments, and measures of mortgage activity did not produce any positive results. We put the stock of delayed takedown commitments (delivery not expected in the next six months) into the analysis to see what retarding effect it might exercise on new corporate bond authorizations and found that it entered with a *positive* regression coefficient. Thus bunching of new commitments seemed to occur for some reason not simply related to anticipated funds inflows or asset yields.

Use of our proxy variables for customer demand for commitments did improve the statistical results very significantly. Of particular importance was the fact that the bond/mortgage yield spread contributed strongly to an explanation of the votings pattern when introduced into equations with the customer commitment demand proxies. To a lesser extent this was also true of the short-term available funds variable. Thus there appeared to be substantial validity to the notion that corporations' desire for the forward commitment service played a critical role in shaping the time path of life insurance companies' commitment authorizations. The pattern is consistent with the assumption that corporate borrowers demanded commitments when anticipating increases in interest rates. Alternative explanations of the timing are also plausible, however. In any case, our conclusions with regard to the significance of this demand remain tentative because of the difficulty of measuring it.

If the above conclusions are proximately valid, then we have isolated several specific nonyield considerations which impinge importantly upon commitment allocation decisions. These include the practice of servicing corporate borrower requests for forward commitments and maintaining minimum funds flows to a widespread mortgage organization. The loaned-up goal appeared to be pursued through commitment policy by a policy of keeping commitments in line with anticipated funds flows, and permitting asset composition decisions to serve this objective. Reluctance to make federally underwritten mortgage loans at large price discounts showed up as a very real phenomenon in the regression analysis.

Within the mortgage market, excepting some constraints upon the geographical distribution of funds to existing branch offices or agents, there seemed every reason to expect that yields would direct the allocation of commitments. This presumably should apply when mortgage lending on commercial and industrial as well as residential properties is considered. This proved difficult to confirm, however, because of the great heterogeneity of mortgage loans aggregated under the commercial and industrial rubric, and because consistent time series data on yields on this type of loan was unavailable. In our regression analysis of commercial and industrial mortgage loan commitments, the short-term available funds variable did contribute strongly, especially in the post-1956 period. We would expect the funds pull to be particularly strong in life companies which were relatively inactive in the residential mortgage market, but we were unable to test this assumption.

There were compelling qualitative reasons for expecting life companies to respond strongly to loan opportunities on commercial and industrial properties. Attractive features included prospective yields, the size of loans and possibilities of generating substantial loan packages, the ability to generate large dollar volumes through a relatively small number of agents or branch offices, and the comparative advantage larger life companies possess over savings depositories in being able to afford the expertise and lending skills required in the nonresidential loan market.

The regression analysis conducted upon life company commitments to acquire obligations of state and local governments tended to confirm expectations that yields primarily determined life companies' activity in this sector. In the analysis of the 1950s, this relationship was picked up statistically by the time path of municipal revenue bond issues better than by yield measures *per se*. Passage of the 1959 Tax Act generated expectations of increased life insurance company participation in the municipal bond market, but these expectations were not borne out as the resurgence of commercial bank asset growth, particularly in time deposits, resulted in a decline in the relative yield attractiveness of municipal issues.

APPENDIX VIII — A

Table VIII-A-1 presents the data used in the regression analysis reported on in Chapter VIII for those variables which have not been described elsewhere in the study. A complete listing of the variables utilized in Chapter VIII is provided in Table VIII-1.

TABLE VIII-A-1. *Yield and Price Discount Data Utilized in the Regression Results Reported in Chapter VIII*

Month	(1) $r_{I(G)}$	(2) r_G	(3) r_I	(4) r_B	(5) D_F	(6) D_G	(7) D_I	(8) D_T
1952/10	4.44%	4.35%	4.35%	3.43%	$2.10	$3.60	$1.10	$2.91
11	4.44	4.35	4.35	3.45	2.10	3.60	1.10	3.18
12	4.45	4.36	4.36	3.41	2.17	3.67	1.17	4.00
1953/ 1	4.46	4.37	4.37	3.39	2.25	3.75	1.25	4.00
2	4.46	4.37	4.37	3.47	2.25	3.75	1.25	5.27
3	4.47	4.37	4.37	3.54	2.30	3.80	1.30	5.91
4	4.48	4.38	4.38	3.71	2.67	3.83	1.67	7.27
5	4.52	4.39	4.39	3.87	2.56	4.06	1.56	8.91
6	4.62	4.46	4.46	4.00	3.17	4.67	2.17	7.24
7	4.71	4.80	4.80	3.96	3.00	3.00	3.00	4.78
8	4.84	4.90	5.01	3.96	4.00	4.00	5.00	4.85
9	4.97	4.82	4.90	4.00	3.25	3.25	4.00	3.50
10	5.01	4.82	4.90	3.83	3.25	3.25	4.00	3.43
11	4.93	4.80	5.01	3.73	3.00	3.00	5.00	2.79
12	4.92	4.85	4.90	3.66	3.50	3.50	4.00	2.18
1954/ 1	4.89	4.80	4.85	3.69	3.00	3.00	3.50	1.00
2	4.85	4.80	4.75	3.48	3.00	3.00	2.50	0.77
3	4.76	4.75	4.75	3.40	2.50	2.50	2.50	0.50
4	4.68	4.75	4.70	3.37	2.50	2.50	2.00	0.12
5	4.66	4.70	4.65	3.43	2.00	2.00	1.50	0.91
6	4.62	4.65	4.60	3.43	2.50	2.50	1.00	0.30
7	4.61	4.60	4.60	3.46	1.00	1.00	1.00	0.24
8	4.60	4.55	4.50	3.47	0.50	0.50	0	0.24
9	4.59	4.55	4.50	3.48	0.50	0.50	0	0.60
10	4.59	4.55	4.50	3.42	0.50	0.50	0	1.50
11	4.59	4.55	4.50	3.42	0.50	0.50	0	1.77
12	4.59	4.55	4.50	3.44	0.50	0.50	0	2.00
1955/ 1	4.59	4.55	4.50	3.50	0.50	0.50	0	2.43
2	4.60	4.55	4.50	3.52	0.50	0.50	0	3.00
3	4.60	4.55	4.55	3.57	0.50	0.50	0.50	3.08

TABLE VIII-A-1 (continued)

Month	(1) $r_{I(G)}$	(2) r_G	(3) r_I	(4) r_B	(5) D_F	(6) D_G	(7) D_I	(8) D_T
4	4.63%	4.60%	4.55%	3.55%	$1.00	$1.00	$0.50	$3.77
5	4.64	4.60	4.55	3.61	1.00	1.00	0.50	3.60
6	4.67	4.65	4.55	3.56	1.50	1.50	0.50	4.00
7	4.67	4.65	4.55	3.64	1.50	1.50	0.50	4.37
8	4.69	4.70	4.65	3.66	2.00	2.00	1.50	4.50
9	4.72	4.70	4.65	3.65	2.00	2.00	1.50	4.91
10	4.78	4.75	4.65	3.60	2.50	2.50	1.50	4.24
11	4.81	4.70	4.65	3.64	2.00	2.00	1.50	4.67
12	4.85	4.70	4.65	3.70	2.00	2.00	1.50	4.67
1956/ 1	4.81	4.70	4.65	3.63	2.00	2.00	1.50	4.30
2	4.81	4.70	4.65	3.59	2.00	2.00	1.50	4.24
3	4.78	4.70	4.65	3.67	2.00	2.00	1.50	4.60
4	4.74	4.75	4.65	3.95	2.50	2.50	1.50	6.54
5	4.80	4.75	4.80	3.99	2.50	2.50	3.00	5.86
6	4.88	4.75	4.80	3.92	2.50	2.50	3.00	5.50
7	4.92	4.80	4.75	4.03	3.00	3.00	2.50	6.12
8	4.92	4.80	4.75	4.54	3.00	3.00	2.50	7.24
9	5.00	4.85	4.90	4.53	3.50	3.50	4.00	7.50
10	5.07	4.90	5.01	4.60	4.00	4.00	5.00	7.73
11	5.11	4.96	5.12	4.76	4.50	4.50	6.00	8.56
12	5.20	5.12	5.20	4.93	4.00	6.00	2.00	8.00
1957/ 1	5.42	5.22	5.31	5.26	5.00	7.00	3.00	7.12
2	5.47	5.33	5.31	5.08	5.50	8.00	3.00	7.43
3	5.49	5.33	5.31	5.08	5.50	8.00	3.00	7.30
4	5.47	5.33	5.31	5.15	5.50	8.00	3.00	8.43
5	5.47	5.33	5.31	5.40	5.50	8.00	3.00	8.74
6	5.44	5.33	5.31	5.75	5.50	8.00	3.00	9.60
7	5.47	5.33	5.41	5.56	6.00	8.00	4.00	9.50
8	5.51	5.39	5.52	5.56	6.75	8.50	5.00	9.30
9	5.75	5.50	5.52	5.53	7.25	9.50	5.00	9.12
10	5.87	5.56	5.63	5.63	8.00	10.00	6.00	9.60
11	5.95	5.56	5.61	5.59	6.00	10.00	3.50	6.80
12	6.01	5.68	5.61	5.35	6.50	11.00	3.50	5.00
1958/ 1	5.93	5.62	5.59	4.77	6.25	10.50	3.25	4.60
2	5.90	5.39	5.56	4.78	6.00	8.50	3.00	3.55
3	5.86	5.39	5.51	5.01	5.50	8.50	2.50	4.00
4	5.79	5.24	5.45	4.73	3.25	4.75	2.00	3.00
5	5.68	5.21	5.40	4.78	2.75	4.50	1.50	3.50
6	5.63	5.39	5.40	4.68	2.75	4.75	1.50	4.24
7	5.59	5.39	5.35	4.63	2.25	4.75	1.00	5.36
8	5.58	5.39	5.35	4.88	2.25	4.75	1.00	8.05
9	5.59	5.37	5.45	5.15	3.25	6.00	2.00	9.60
10	5.77	5.48	5.56	4.96	4.25	7.00	3.00	9.00

TABLE VIII-A-1 *(continued)*

Month	(1) $r_{I(G)}$	(2) r_G	(3) r_I	(4) r_B	(5) D_F	(6) D_G	(7) D_I	(8) D_T
11	5.88%	5.54%	5.56%	4.97%	$4.50	$7.50	$3.00	$7.67
12	5.92	5.54	5.61	5.09	5.00	7.50	3.50	8.35
1959/ 1	5.92	5.54	5.61	5.14	5.00	7.50	3.50	8.50
2	5.92	5.54	5.61	5.01	5.00	7.50	3.50	8.11
3	5.90	5.57	5.61	4.91	5.00	7.75	3.50	8.92
4	5.88	5.57	5.61	5.04	5.00	7.75	3.50	10.50
5	5.90	5.54	5.66	5.19	5.25	7.50	4.00	10.42
6	5.97	5.59	5.66	5.16	5.50	8.00	4.00	11.32
7	6.06	5.77	5.72	5.21	4.75	5.00	4.50	10.50
8	6.11	5.77	5.77	5.31	5.00	5.00	5.00	11.55
9	6.19	5.89	5.83	5.62	5.75	6.00	5.50	13.67
10	6.26	6.00	6.07	5.50	4.75	7.00	3.00	11.17
11	6.33	6.11	6.07	5.62	5.00	8.00	3.00	12.24
12	6.40	6.11	6.12	5.69	5.25	8.00	3.50	12.00
1960/ 1	6.40	6.17	6.18	5.41	5.50	8.00	4.00	11.86
2	6.42	6.23	6.18	5.61	5.50	8.50	4.00	11.67
3	6.40	6.23	6.18	5.40	5.75	9.00	4.00	9.35

DESCRIPTION AND SOURCES:

Col. (1): Effective yields on FHA insured home loans. This series was prepared by and obtained from Jack M. Guttentag. Data through 1957 and a description of the raw data and computational assumptions can be found in Guttentag, "Some Studies of the Post-World War II Residential Construction and Mortgage Markets." For most of the period shown, the raw data are price quotations on FHA Section 203 loans compiled by the FHA from monthly surveys of FHA field offices. Price quotations are converted into yields by assuming that loans have maturities of 20 years and are prepaid after 8 years.

Col. (2): Effective yields on VA guaranteed home loans. Yields are based on commitments for future delivery loans on "typical" houses with 25-year maturities requiring down-payments of 5% or more. The yields have been computed from price quotations on a yield to maturity basis. Data are obtained for various cities monthly, from *House and Home*.

Col. (3): Effective yields on FHA insured home loans. Based on the same type of loans and obtained from the same source as the VA yields in Col. (2).

Col. (4): Estimated new issue yields on Baa quality industrial bonds. Obtained by adding to the Moody's seasoned Industrial Baa corporate bond yield series, the spread between the yield on new issue Grade 2 public utility bond yields (Bankers Trust Company, Table VI-B-1, col. (1)) and the yield on Moody's Aa seasoned public utility bond yields.

Col. (5): Price discount below par (equals $100) prevailing on FHA-VA home loans. Price quotations obtained from the same opinion survey sources for the same loans cited in col. (2) above and in Table VI-B-1, col. (3). The yield series in Table VI-B-1 matches the price quotations reported here.

Col. (6): Price discount below par (equals $100) on VA guaranteed home loans. Source: same as Col. (2) above.

TABLE VIII-A-1 *(continued)*

Col. (7): Price discount below par (equals $100) on FHA insured home loans. Source: same as Col. (3) above.

Col. (8): Price discount below par (equals $100) on U.S. Treasury bonds. Computed by the author from price data in the Treasury *Bulletin* for the Treasury bond issues which dominated life insurance company portfolios.

NOTES: The yields reported in Cols. (1)–(4) above are gross; i.e., no deduction for lending costs has been made. In the regression analysis reported in Chapter VIII, 50 basis points were deducted from mortgage yields wherever a mortgage loan-bond yield spread was utilized as an independent variable. No deduction was made from bond yields. Where use is made of the administered ceiling interest on FHA-VA loans the following composite ceiling rate was utilized.

1952/10–1953/6	4.00%
1953/ 7–1956/12	4.50
1957/ 1–1957/9	5.00
1957/10–1959/8	5.25
1959/ 9–1960/3	5.75

Chapter IX | SOME CONCLUSIONS AND

IMPLICATIONS

In this study we have probed life insurance company portfolio practices to discover how effectively these companies perform their role of financial intermediation. Our primary objective has been to examine systematically the process by which supplies and demands are balanced in the capital markets, and thereby contribute to an evaluation of the operating efficiency of financial institutions and the allocative efficiency of the markets in which they intermediate. The rationale for this particular effort lay in the assumption that intensive studies of the major participants are an important prerequisite to the serious development of flow-of-funds capital market models which can eventually be integrated into real expenditure models.

This ultimate objective then dictated the shape and limits of our study. Specifically, it was responsible for our treating life companies as an essentially homogeneous group of lenders and for conducting the empirical analysis upon aggregated industry data and data representative only of the larger companies in the industry. Our approach has been old-fashioned in a sense; it has proceeded through hypothesis sorting, hypothesis formation, and hypothesis testing. The statistical investigations have thereby been directed at distinguishing among competing behavioral hypotheses rather than estimating parameters in a highly specified take-it-or-leave-it model. Finally, in the process of narrowing the range of plausible hypotheses useful for explaining major life company portfolio decisions, we attempted to retain as much richness of institutional detail as seemed relevant to our broad purpose.

A single elemental question has occupied us throughout this study: Do prices, here asset yields, play the primary role in directing life insurance companies' investment decisions; if not, why not; and if not, what specific considerations do govern their portfolio choices? The investigation was carried out in three stages. First we examined the setting in which life insurance company portfolio decisions are made by exploring (a) life companies' basic investment objectives, and (b) the major aspects of the external environment which impinge upon their selections. Second, we focused upon those portfolio decisions made by life companies which specifically affect the allocation of funds flows over time. Finally, attention was devoted to the composition of life company investment selections. Summaries of our findings in these areas are supplied liberally throughout the previous chapters. In this chapter we shall simply highlight the broad conclusions which are relevant to the objectives outlined above and draw some specific implications from these conclusions.

The Setting

An analysis of the process by which funds are allocated through capital markets which focuses upon interest rates as the prime rationing device presupposes that high portfolio return is a major goal of lenders and that borrowers' cost of capital is affected significantly by movements in market interest rates. There has been some resurgence in recent years of the notion that market interest rates do matter to potential borrowers. On the funds supply side of the market we found reason to expect that competitive pressures within the insurance industry ought to have made life insurance companies investment-return conscious. However, this expectation was somewhat diluted by the difficulty of showing that portfolio return over time is, in fact, positively correlated with overall measures of success for companies in the industry, and by the qualitative observation that many large companies have treated their investment operations quite casually and devoted very little in the way of resources to investment departments.

Furthermore, it was clear that significant competing objectives exist. The overriding objective of a life insurance company must be maintenance of financial solvency. Operating through a concern for capital certainty and income certainty, the solvency objective has been responsible for much of life companies' interest in nonyield asset and portfolio characteristics such as liquidity, maturity, credit quality, and diversification. The solvency concern has been reinforced, and indeed redefined, by externally imposed restrictions designed (although not always well-designed) to insure investment safety and protect policyholders from unwise and/or fraudulent investment practices. These restrictions have taken the form of statutory investment regulations and rules governing the valuation of assets for statement purposes. Additionally, the federal income tax structure has impinged upon life company portfolio decisions by altering the yield and risk characteristics of some potential investments.

The primary consequence of these competing investment goals and the externally applied constraints has been to restrict significantly the range and variety of investment opportunities open to serious consideration by life company investment departments. Broadly, these factors have tended to restrict life company asset acquisitions to medium-term and long-term private, investment-grade, debt obligations.

Within this restricted set of eligible financial assets, it appeared that asset yields could be a major factor determining portfolio selections. In approaching the analysis of life companies' investment responsiveness to interest rates, we explicitly recognized a number of problems which seriously affected our ability to observe, measure, and interpret portfolio responses. Among these difficulties were the long time horizon of life insurance companies, their inability to trade a substantial portion of their asset holdings, the sequential nature of the investment process, and the development of the forward commitment technique to the point of wide and significant use. All these problems raised questions with respect to the role of expectations about future investment opportunities, interest rate levels, and cash flows in shaping life company investment policy. They also influenced the manner in which we formulated problems for analysis. Two particular decisions affecting our analytical approach are of sufficient importance to be noted here. One of these was concerned with whether analysis of portfolio selections should be framed in stock or flow terms; the second involves the effect of the forward commitment process upon the analysis of investment choices.

The Analytical Approach

The Stock/Flow Problem

Should investment choices be analyzed as flow decisions or stock decisions or some combination of both? Traditional portfolio theory as well as much of monetary and financial theory suggests that financial asset selection should be treated as a part of the general theory of wealth holding, and thereby places primary emphasis upon stocks. Decision units are assumed to care about balance sheet composition, and flows are produced by wealth holders adjusting their balance sheets in response to changes in the structure of interest rates and other relevant variables. On the other hand, much descriptive analysis of capital market activity is couched in flow terms, and the manner in which the social accounts in this area, the "flow of funds accounts," have been constructed suggests that it is financial flows in their own right which are of first importance.

In this study we have found that for many purposes analysis of life insurance companies' investment activity can best proceed on the basis that it is flows alone which count. This is partly due to the fact that life companies have specialized in acquiring financial assets which are relatively long term and essentially nonmarketable. Thus typically something less than one-fifth of life company portfolios have been made up of tradable assets. More important, within broad ranges life companies did not appear to be concerned about portfolio proportions. As we have noted above, portfolio liquidity, maturity, quality, and diversification targets were satisfied by limiting the range of acceptable investments, but within these limits nonyield objectives imposed very little restriction upon portfolio proportions. Thus, by and large, life companies could be characterized as making decisions to allocate a flow of current and anticipated funds (determined independently of current investment policy) among alternative assets in response to targets determined independently of the composition of their inherited balance sheets. The primary determinants of this flow allocation appeared to be: (1) relative yields; (2) the desire to invest funds quickly as they became available; and (3) the desire to maintain good customer, brokerage, and agency relations so as to insure a flow of attractive investment opportunities. There may be some portfolio stock targets lurking behind the last objective, but these channels are kept productive primarily through the provision of regular flows.

Some qualification to this emphasis on flows is in order, however. Statutory restrictions have imposed portfolio composition boundaries on some companies, most commonly on their investments in equities, and in a few cases on company holdings of conventional mortgage loans. Portfolio proportion limits have been imposed by life company finance committees occasionally on selected types of investments (e.g., below investment grade securities, finance company obligations). Some companies acted as if they treated federally underwritten mortgage loans as a special risk category and either limited them as a percentage of the portfolio or made acceptable yields on these loans a function of the proportion held. Mostly, however, we found that portfolio proportion targets were used as an administrative expedient employed to achieve a favorable rate of return over time.

The most important qualifications to the flow approach occurred in examining investment activity in those portions of the portfolio where assets were easily shiftable, i.e., marketable securities. Thus we dealt with the large Treasury security holdings of life companies after World War II as a problem in adjusting a stock to a target proportion of total assets. Even here, however, we found it appropriate to represent this stock adjustment in a simple capital markets model in which flows predominated. Abstracting from the special problem of the depression-war inheritance of extraordinary holdings of marketable securities, we also analyzed the pattern of intertemporal shifts of funds within a cyclical context under more normal circumstances. This investigation was carried out by analyzing changes in balance sheet items, namely liquid assets and indebtedness. However, this procedure was adopted primarily for data reasons; the balance sheet items were available over a longer period than were reliable cash inflow estimates. Furthermore, we concluded that much of the cyclical pattern of adjustment in stock items which occurred did not reflect adjustments to changing stock targets, but were produced by mechanical problems associated with operations on flows.

Forward Commitments and Investment Choices

Having determined that most life insurance company portfolio behavior could be appropriately analyzed in terms of flow decisions unconstrained by stock targets, our central objective was to explore the yield responsiveness of these flow decisions. The major analytical problem faced here was that the widespread use by life companies of the forward commitment technique resulted in funds flows being separated in time from investment decisions. It was clear that the time lag between decision and funds delivery was of substantial duration in a high percentage of life company portfolio acquisitions. Thus the allocation of funds in any time period proved to be the product of decisions made at various points of time in the past. Evaluation of yield responsiveness then clearly required analysis of investment selections at the time decisions were made; i.e., a focus upon loan commitments, not loan acquisitions.

In focusing on commitments one is confronted with the problem of explaining to what interest rates, current or anticipated, life companies are expected to respond. Examination of the available evidence convinced us that commitments are nearly always negotiated on the basis of current market interest rates, even where the delivery of funds is expected to be delayed a year or more. This does not preclude the possibility that lenders and/or borrowers may be speculating upon the future course of interest rates in setting the terms in a commitment contract (e.g., takedown date, commitment fees) and in deciding whether or not to enter into a forward commitment at all. Consequently, we explicitly conducted the analysis of the time path of life company commitments with expectations in the forefront.

Responsiveness of Life Insurance Company Portfolio Decisions to Changes in Asset Yields

Our conclusion with respect to the influence of interest rates upon life company portfolio behavior varied considerably among the several contexts in which their investment responses were examined. These conclusions can briefly be summarized as follows.

Disposal of Government Securities

Perhaps the strongest evidence of life insurance company concern with investment return was contained in their liquidation of Treasury securities after World War II. Particularly from the end of the war to the 1951 monetary-debt management policy Accord, the liquidation pattern was consistent with the hypothesis that life companies were open to buy any eligible investments on which the yield exceeded the current yield on Treasury bonds by a minimum risk allowance. As an indication of the strength and uniformity of life companies' reactions to yield differentials, however, this performance was somewhat illusory. Because of the extraordinary magnitude of Government bonds held by life companies in the early postwar years it was necessary that only a portion of the companies follow an aggressive open-to-buy policy in order for the hypothesis to appear confirmed for the industry as a whole.

After 1951 the differences among companies showed up more clearly. Some companies seemed to be locked in to their Government bond holdings by relatively modest declines in bond prices, largely for vague public relations reasons; some companies had liquidated bonds at a much slower pace than the industry as a consequence of either a more conservative estimate of secondary liquidity needs or inattention to the opportunities present. For some companies bond sales diminished because from a yield maximization standpoint they had liquidated at an excessively fast pace during the late 1940s, accepting yields on risk assets that were hardly distinguishable from prevailing yields on comparable maturity Treasury obligations.

Overall, however, the abrupt decline in the rate of Government bonds marketed by life companies after 1951 was more consistent with yield maximization behavior than most explanations of the liquidation phenomenon have recognized. If one allows that life companies' reluctance to accept significant price discounts on federally unwritten loans was rational and consistent with yield sensitive behavior under the prevailing institutional circumstances, then it follows that life company funds available for investment in other risk assets were considerably augmented after 1951 and reduced disposals of Governments were consistent with continuance of the policy of pegging the risk asset-Treasury bond yield spread.

The open-to-buy hypothesis remained at least a good first approximation to an explanation of life companies' disposal of Governments for several years after 1951. As the years passed, however, bond prices declined further, especially after 1955, and the locked-in impact increased. Furthermore as time passed a larger proportion of the industry's Government bond holdings were necessarily left in the portfolios of the less aggressive, more conservative companies. Finally as the aggressive companies neared their ultimate target Treasury bond holdings, it became rational for them to widen the spread between yields on risk assets and Treasury bond yields required for a switch to be made.

Interest Rate Expectations and Investment Decisions

Abstracting from the peculiar problem of life company post-World War II Treasury bond holdings, we looked for evidence that life companies' portfolio decisions were timed in response to expectations about future movements in interest rates. In this connection we examined decisions respecting: (1) asset maturity, (2) borrowing, (3) liquidity, and (4) the use of forward commitments. In these areas of intertemporal allocation, we found very little evidence that speculation on secular or cyclical movements in interest rates played a significant role in life company decisions.

MATURITY SELECTIONS

If life companies had adjusted the maturity distribution of their portfolios in response to the secular uptrend in interest rates since World War II, the average maturity would have been lengthening. However, no significant changes in overall effective maturity composition appear to have taken place; if anything, portfolio maturity has probably shortened for the industry as a whole.

In a cyclical context, responsiveness of asset maturity selection to interest rates means choosing short-term investments when yields are low and acquiring long-term assets during the boom, or high yield, phase of the business cycle. The shape of the yield to maturity schedule for high grade marketable securities might be used as an indicator of the expected movement of interest rates.

To the extent that securities acquired by most life companies have somewhat longer maturities on the average than mortgage loans made, the changes in the composition of funds allocated to these two sectors over the cycle are broadly consistent with this hypothesis. Furthermore there was some evidence of portfolio switching–selling longer-term securities to acquire short-term assets–in the relatively low interest rate portion of cycles observed. However, the pattern of mortgage/security acquisition seemed to be best explained by factors unrelated to the maturity consideration, and the limited trading observed in bond portfolios appeared to be triggered more by high bond prices *per se* rather than by a speculative judgment that interest rates were "low."

Also, within the bond portfolio life company acquisitions of municipal and public utility obligations, generally with longer maturities than industrial debentures, seemed to be concentrated in the lower interest rate phase of the cycle. The highly publicized very long-term industrial bond and governmental revenue bond issues acquired by life companies were purchased for the most part in lower interest rate portions of the cycle. Comparisons of expected maturities by asset type are hindered by differing prepayment provisions, however, and life companies' heightened concern with call protection on corporate bond investments during higher interest rate periods illustrated action taken to lock-in attractive yields for as long as possible. On balance, however, there is very little evidence of maturity selection responding to expectations about trend or cyclical interest rate movements.

BORROWING

Similarly, there is no real evidence that life companies have borrowed funds on the basis of their anticipations regarding future changes in interest rates. So far as can be observed, most life company borrowing has taken the form of mortgage warehousing. From the point of view of playing the interest rate cycle, the warehousing record appeared to be perverse, shifting funds from higher interest rate to lower interest rate phases of the cycle. Furthermore, the substantial warehousing activity which occurred in 1954–1955 appeared to be a unique experience, reflecting problems of forecasting cash flows and controlling loan commitments.

Any borrowing which is undertaken as a part of a cyclical interest rate strategy must be quite insignificant in amount.

LIQUIDITY

The main findings which emerged from an analysis of the cyclical behavior of life company liquid asset holdings were: (1) a clear, but quantitatively modest, cyclical pattern has existed in life company liquidity holdings; and (2) the pattern does not appear explainable by the cyclical interest rate hypothesis. Instead, the pattern seems to be a product of systematic errors in forecasting the cyclical path of cash inflow, systematic errors in forecasting loan commitment takedowns, imperfect control over new commitments (particularly in the mortgage sector), and a tendency of life companies to take advantage of high bond prices by selling longer-term securities. Life companies have experienced a cyclical element in their temporal cash flow pattern with roughly the same timing as that experienced by the savings depository institutions. The cyclical swings have been of a much lower order of magnitude for the life insurance industry, however. The pattern is produced in all major contributors to the flow of available investment funds; i.e., change in ledger assets, involuntary portfolio rollover, and voluntary asset liquidation. This characteristic of the cash flow record appears to be proximately explainable in terms of cyclical movements in disposable personal income, interest rates, and activity in real estate markets.

COMMITMENTS

The practice of issuing forward commitments appears to have been an inescapable part of the mechanics of mortgage lending for any substantial life company which wished to place a significant portion of its funds flow into mortgage instruments. The willingness of life companies to issue forward commitments in the corporate debt sector undoubtedly contributed greatly to the predominant position life companies have occupied among investors in corporate bonds. In analyzing the forward commitment process as a device to separate investment decisions from funds flows, however, we found that the possibilities for utilizing this device to speculate on future (essentially cyclical) interest rate movements were quite limited. At any rate it was clear that life companies have not successfully employed forward commitments to this purpose.

Although we did not possess sufficient data to test the conclusion fully, we did tentatively conclude that the time path of new commitments was determined by essentially two variables: (1) the net cash flow available for investment over the upcoming six months or so, and (2) the demand for long-term forward commitments by substantial corporate borrowers. Thus we viewed forward commitments as a useful device to enable life companies to invest funds "permanently" as they become available. The scheduling of delivery of funds was often a matter of negotiation, with the life company's cash flow position one of the considerations. By way of contrast, long delayed takedown commitments (one year or more), normally were made to accommodate the borrower.

Asset Yield Spreads and the Composition of Life Companies' Investment Decisions

As we have seen, the opportunity set of investments eligible for life company portfolios is severely constrained by statutory restrictions, asset valuation rules, tax law, and life companies' traditional concern about solvency. Within this restricted number of eligible assets, life companies are free to respond to variations in yields among the several broad types of assets. Variations in the mix of investment acquisitions primarily meant shifts in the allocation of funds between the corporate bond and mortgage loan sectors. In order to detect responsiveness to yield spreads we carried out the empirical analysis on investment commitment decisions.

Variation in yield spreads did clearly appear to have an impact on the mix of forward commitment votings. However, the impact was reduced by life companies' use of mortgage loan commitments to keep asset acquisitions in line with the cash flow available for investment, their willingness to make long-term commitments to corporate customers, and their aversion to substantial price discounts on federally underwritten loans.

Life company commitments to acquire state and local security issues appeared to be almost entirely prompted by yield considerations. Investment officer appraisals and choices of equity investments, including corporate preferred, and common shares and real property seemed to be based on income yield calculations, not on prospective capital gains.

Life Insurance Companies as Financial Intermediaries: A Capsule Summary

Unlike the savings depository institutions, life insurance companies are not inevitably financial intermediaries. It is conceivable that life companies could carry out their primary mission without exerting influence in the capital markets. The savings generated through life company insurance and annuity contracts can be viewed as a by-product of contractual arrangements designed primarily to sell protection.

Because life companies are primarily oriented toward the insurance business, they appear to treat portfolio decisions with a casualness which disturbs some observers concerned with capital market efficiency. For most companies the labor, capital, and material resources employed in making investment decisions represent a negligible portion of total resources utilized by the companies. Although not unknown, it is quite rare for the chief executive officer of a life insurance company to have had experience in the investment side of the business. Also, given the characteristic of their liabilities, life companies must be judged to have been quite conservative investors. Risk averters are purchasers of insurance and commonly are heavily dependent upon the insurance (retirement) protection they possess. In this circumstance life companies have judged it desirable to adopt a prudent image and pursue portfolio policies appropriate to strong risk averters.

Thus even where life companies appear concerned with portfolio rate of return, they have typically pursued this goal by cautious means. We have found that over the long run companies achieve a satisfactory yield performance more by keeping fully invested and maintaining close contacts with brokers and potential customers than by speculating against the future in their liquidity, borrowing, and forward commitment policy, or "reaching for yield" in their asset mix selections. Whether or not this sort of policy benefits companies over the long haul, it does serve to temper their temporal and investment composition responses and thereby to create some friction in the capital market adjustment process. Nonetheless life companies are not locked into any given sector of the capital markets irrevocably, portfolio responses are observable, and the responses are broadly consistent with variations in asset yields.

Some Implications

Monetary Policy and Life Insurance Companies

Monetary policy may in principle impinge upon life insurance companies in a number of ways, including affecting: (a) their willingness to trade in secondary markets; (b) their cash inflow from the insurance business and portfolio repayments; (c) their liquidity needs and willingness to incur debt; (d) the volume of forward commitments they will issue; and (e) the composition of their investment decisions. The conclusions of this study are relevant for an evaluation of the impact and efficiency of monetary policy as it operates through each of these channels.

During the 1950s much of the literature dealing with financial intermediation was oriented toward a concern with monetary policy. A much discussed facet of this problem revolved around the issue of whether substantial liquid asset holdings (particularly Treasury obligations) of intermediaries impeded or assisted the actions taken by the monetary authorities. It is not clear that this issue was ever fully resolved, but there did seem to be a reasonably strong consensus that these liquidity positions provided a mechanism via which the linkage between the money supply (or interest rates) and GNP was weakened. Conversely, monetary policy has been viewed as more potent in the 1960s because these liquid cushions have receded and lending institutions have been forced to tap sources of funds which are under closer control of the monetary authorities, or confine themselves to allocation of the current savings flow.

However, we have seen that during the period in which life companies held substantial amounts of Treasury obligations, relatively small changes in monetary policy had quite important effects upon life companies. In particular the tightening which followed the 1951 Accord played a significant role in dramatically reducing the rate at which life companies sold Governments. This reduction resulted in part from life companies' aversion to realizing capital losses on Treasury bond sales, although this restraint worked primarily through actual losses, not through expectations as assumed in the credit availability doctrine. More importantly, in an open-to-buy environment rising interest rates reduced life company lending in sectors in which yields were sticky. This was particularly obvious in the mortgage sector and was accentuated by the administrative ceiling rates enforced on federally underwritten loans. Price discounts were not considered a legitimate device for avoiding the ceiling by most life companies at this time. Because companies were already making all loans which satisfied their minimum requirements, loan reductions achieved in any sector represented a net reduction in total credit extended to the private sector by the life insurance industry. Monetary policy had a significant impact upon life companies in this manner for several years following the Accord.

Since the mid-1950s monetary policy has continued to exert some, but diminishing, influence on the timing of life company bond sales. We did, however, find cyclical elements in life companies' cash inflow experience, their borrowing activity, liquidity accumulation and decumulation, forward commitments issued, and the composition of their investment selections. Changes in the level of interest rates were partially responsible for these cyclical patterns. To this extent life company portfolio behavior is affected by monetary policy. In particular, the more monetary policy is relied upon as a stabilization tool instead of fiscal policy, the stronger the impact of a given cyclical fluctuation in national income will be upon life companies.

In the time period analyzed in this study, variations in the level of interest rates primarily affected cash inflow and the composition of assets. The observable variance in liquid asset positions and borrowing seemed to reflect passive adjustments to changing flows of investible funds, not active speculation on the future course of interest rates. Except to the extent that better procedures for forecasting and controlling cash inflows and loan takedowns are devised, wider cyclical swings in interest rates can be expected to produce, *ceteris paribus*, wider swings in life company liquid asset and debt positions.

Furthermore, since we have observed that some play in liquidity holdings is permitted and borrowing is not disallowed, it could be argued that wider swings in interest rates might convert passive acceptance of liquidity swings and occasional borrowing into a conscious, cyclically oriented policy. The potential for any quantitatively significant destabilizing actions on the part of life insurance companies developing in this fashion, however, is diminished by our persistent finding that the objective to "permanently" invest funds as they become available is very strong. This objective appeared to be playing a central role both in shaping the time path of forward commitment contracts issued and in influencing the composition of commitments made.

To the extent that we found the composition of commitment decisions responsive to yield spreads among alternative assets, then wider cyclical variation in interest rates together with sticky yields on some asset categories would produce greater cyclical variance in the mix of life company investments. This variance is constrained by the problem of maintaining high overhead lending organizations; for life companies, this has meant mortgage originating and servicing organizations. Life companies have more flexibility than most of the savings depository institutions, however, to abandon lending efforts in a major sector of the capital markets. Thus, for example, if a high level employment economy was maintained over a period of years and home mortgage loans remained uncompetitive, we would expect to observe a number of sizable life companies disbanding their home mortgage lending organizations. Given the market mechanics which have prevailed in the postwar years, re-entry into this market would be a long and costly process.

Finally, with reference to any conscious cyclical policies pursued by life insurance companies, the cash flow pattern is clearly not shaped by a cyclical policy of varying the terms on new (or outstanding) liabilities issued by life companies. There is no evidence that this sort of policy exists, and, in contrast to the savings depositories, variations in the rate at which new liabilities are issued have very limited impact upon net cash inflow for a year or so. Life insurance policies are certainly not significant substitutes for money in most (potential) policyholder portfolios, and when life insurance companies are recognized as a significant class of financial intermediaries, it is difficult to regard without suspicion any assertion that the cross-elasticity with respect to return is greater among "indirect" assets than between "indirect" and "direct" assets. In general, although we have found life insurance company portfolio behavior vulnerable to criticism on a number of grounds, it does not appear that accusations of cyclically destabilizing behavior have much merit.

Market Mechanics

The efficiency with which funds are allocated through capital markets depends not only upon the behavioral responsiveness of lenders but also upon the existence of an efficient market mechanism in the form of underwriters, brokers, and secondary market facilities. We found that part of the apparent sluggishness in life company responses to the changing level and structure of yields was attributable to imperfect market mechanisms. The organization problem appeared greatest in mortgage lending, where either a large salaried organization or a complex network of loan originating and servicing agents was required. In either case a substantial volume of funds had to be allocated to this market regardless of the attractiveness of alternative loan opportunities.

Mortgage markets have remained segmented local markets to a significant degree. Some ongoing reforms may improve the flow of funds into these markets and attract other lenders (e.g., pension funds, households) into the market. The federally underwritten loan programs were an advance in this regard; private guarantee systems, participation loans, and the development of a true secondary market should further remove impediments to funds flows in this sector. Progress in this area may prove quite critical in terms of the economy's ability to finance the long anticipated housing boom of the late 1960s and early 1970s.

There are several implications of more sophisticated and flexible markets for life insurance companies. As mortgage markets become more regional and national in character, the need for branch offices or contracted agencies as loan originators should decline; widespread servicing facilities may continue to be necessary, but by themselves would be less of a constraint on funds allocations. It is quite possible, of course, that as underwriting and brokerage facilities make mortgage loans attractive to a wider group of lenders, life companies will tend to withdraw from at least the single family loan market. Because of the size of companies which dominate the industry from the perspective of investment policy, life companies have tended to specialize in areas where markets are thin, underwriting and brokerage facilities exist in only a primitive state or can be bypassed, and consequently high returns are available from the application of investment expertise to risk appraisal. This partly explains life companies' specialization in privately placed corporate debt rather than public issues, state and local revenue bond issues rather than general obligations, large mortgage financing projects rather than corporate shares, and forward commitment contracts rather than secondary market trading.

A particular element of the market environment which we found quite significant at several points in this study was the government-imposed contractual ceiling interest rate on federally underwritten mortgage loans. In a period of rising or high interest rates, these ceilings were an effective restraint on life company FHA-VA lending. In addition, loan insurance and guarantees did not appear to be highly valued by life companies which have a strong aversion toward loan defaults regardless of whether or not any loss is directly incurred as a consequence of the default. Life companies' attitudes toward price discounts on these loans and toward the value of guarantees are, of course, shaped by their concern with their public image as insurers.

Our analysis of life company attitudes on these points is not simply interesting history, but is also relevant to any appraisal of the role they are likely to play in financing the upcoming housing boom. Although the relative importance of federally underwritten loans has sharply declined since the mid-1950s, the FHA program has continued to grow in absolute terms and, as of this writing, it appears that a revived veterans' program may play a significant role in financing residential construction during the next few years.

It is not valid, of course, to conclude that removal of the administrative ceilings on contract rates for FHA and VA loans would necessarily reduce the amplitude of the residential construction cycle. Mortgage rates will probably still remain sticky, and as long as monetary policy is heavily relied upon as a stabilization tool, housing will bear the brunt of a restrictive policy. More flexible rates together with improved market mechanics may attract households directly into the guaranteed loan market in a tight money period. Modification of ceiling rate policy will also affect the extent to which life companies are active in this segment of the mortgage market, and will have some influence on who gets the mortgage funds in a tight credit period.

Regulation of Life Insurance Companies

During the last decade there has developed a good deal of concern and some action with respect to the question of whether financial intermediaries are over-regulated and consequently over-specialized. There seems to exist a general belief that capital markets would allocate funds more efficiently and the selective impact of monetary policy could be partially dissipated by granting institutional lenders greater investment flexibility. Attention has been directed primarily to the savings depositories, but there is also a case for less regulation of life insurance companies' portfolio decisions.

The primary effect of statutory investment regulations and the rules governing asset valuation has been to restrict life companies willing to accept more investment risk from doing so. These restrictions have had significant impact on life companies' ability to take risk in the corporate debt, noncorporate business debt, and conventional mortgage loan sectors. Probably the most dramatic difference in life company portfolio acquisitions over the last two decades, had these restrictions not existed, would have occurred in their purchases of corporate equity issues. In this case the resulting difference in portfolio return would have been significant for life company policyholders and stockholders, and would probably have influenced the relative position of life companies in competing for the savings flow. It may be questionable whether or not this particular consequence of a hypothesized liberalization of regulations would have yielded positive social benefits. However, greater life insurance company participation in higher risk debt instruments would undoubtedly have had desirable public policy consequences.

BIBLIOGRAPHY

Alberts, William, "Business Cycles, Residential Construction Cycles, and the Mortgage Market," *Journal of Political Economy*, June 1962

American Bankers Association, *The Commercial Banking Industry*. Englewood Cliffs: Commission on Money and Credit Monograph, Prentice-Hall, 1962

American Life Convention, *General Proceedings*, annually

American Life Convention-Life Insurance Association of America (ALC-LIAA) Joint Investment Bulletin, *The Investment Experience of Eighteen Major United States Life Insurance Companies in Bonds and Stocks*, annually

Report of the Joint Committee on Economic Policy, annually

Report of the Joint Industry Committee, 1951

Report of the Joint Committee on the Valuation of Assets, April 10, 1951

Report in Support of Proposed Amendments to Article 5, Section 81, of the New York Insurance Law, 1951

Anderson, W. H. Locke, *Corporate Finance and Fixed Investment*. Boston: Division of Research, Harvard Business School, 1964

Anderson, W. M., "The Long View of Life Insurance Investment," American Life Convention, *General Proceedings*, 1954

Andrews, V. L., "Noninsured Corporate and State and Local Government Retirement Funds in the Financial Structure," in *Private Capital Markets*. Englewood Cliffs: Commission on Money and Credit Monograph, Prentice-Hall, 1964

———, "Pension Funds in the Securities Markets," *Harvard Business Review*, November–December 1959

Arnold, H. B., "The Investment of Policyholders' Legal Reserve Funds," American Life Convention, *General Proceedings*, 1929

Badger, R. E. and H. G. Guthman, *Investment Principles and Practices*. New York: Prentice-Hall, 4th edition, 1956

Badger, Sherwin C., "Unusual Features of Life Insurance Investing," *Journal of Finance*, June 1951

———. "The Valuation of Assets," in David McCahan, editor, *Invest-*

ment of Life Insurance Funds. Philadelphia: University of Pennsylvania Press, 1953

Bailey, A. H., "On the Principles on Which Funds of Life Assurance Societies Should Be Invested," *The Journal of the Institute of Actuaries*, Cambridge, England, Volume 10, 1862

Bankers Trust Company, *The Investment Outlook*, annually

Beard, Winston C., *The Effects of State Investment Requirements for Life Insurance Companies*. Prepared for the Arkansas Insurance Commissioner by the University of Arkansas College of Business Administration, Industrial Research and Extension Center, in Cooperation with the Arkansas Industrial Development Commission, October 1958

Bell, Houghton, "Asset Reserves of Life Insurance Companies," American Life Convention, *General Proceedings*, Legal Section, 1953

——— and Harold G. Fraine, "Legal Framework, Trends, and Developments in Investment Practices of Life Insurance Companies," *Law and Contemporary Problems*, Winter 1952

Bernstein, M. C., *The Future of Private Pensions*. New York: The Free Press of Glencoe, 1964

Biegel, H. C. et al., *Pensions and Profit Sharing*. Washington: Bureau of National Affairs, 3rd edition, 1964

Bower, Joseph L., *The Rate of Commercial Construction in a Cross-Section of American Cities*, The Rand Corporation, Memorandum RM-3094-RC, December 1963

Break, George F., *The Economic Impact of Federal Loan Insurance*. Washington: National Planning Association, 1961

Brimmer, Andrew F., *Life Insurance Companies in the Capital Market*. East Lansing: Michigan State University Business Studies, 1962

———, "Monetary Policy, Interest Rates and Life Insurance Company Investment," unpublished Ph.D. dissertation, Harvard University, 1957

Burnett, T. W., "Some Aspects of Portfolio Management," American Life Convention, *General Proceedings*, 1957

Cary, William L., "Corporate Financing Through the Sale and Leaseback of Property: Business Tax and Policy Considerations," *Harvard Law Review*, November 1948

Clayton, G., "Role of the British Life Assurance Companies in the Capital Market," *Economic Journal*, March 1951

——— and W. T. Osborn, "Insurance Companies and the Finance of Industry," *Oxford Economic Papers*, N. S. Vol. 10, No. 1, February 1958

——— and ———, "Insurance Companies and the Capital Market," *The Three Banks Review*, March 1958

―――― and ――――, *Insurance Company Investment, Principles and Policies*. London: George Allen and Unwin, Ltd., 1965

Cleary, M. J., "The Response of Life Insurance Funds to American Needs," Life Insurance Association of America, *Proceedings*, 1937

Cohan, Avery B., *Yields on Corporate Debt Directly Placed*. New York: National Bureau of Economic Research, 1967

Colean, Miles, *Impact of Government on Real Estate Finance in the United States*. New York: National Bureau of Economic Research, 1950

Conklin, George T., Jr., "Some Fundamental Considerations of Investment Policy," American Life Convention, *General Proceedings*, Financial Section, October 8, 1954

―――――, "Factors Determining the Investment Policy of Life Insurance Companies," *Journal of the American Society of Chartered Life Underwriters*, Winter 1956

Duesenberry, James S., *Business Cycles and Economic Growth*. New York: McGraw-Hill, 1958

Edmunds, Stahrl, "Outlets for Life Insurance Investments," *Harvard Business Review*, Summer 1947

Ernst and Ernst, *Guide to the Life Insurance Income Tax Act of 1959*, Cleveland, 1960

Farrell, M. J., "On the Structure of the Capital Market," *Economic Journal*, December 1962

Federal Reserve Bank of Boston, "Broader Investment Channels for Life Insurance Companies," *Monthly Review*, November 1949

Federal Reserve Bank of New York, "Commercial Banks in the Mortgage Market," *Monthly Review*, April 1956

―――――, "Savings and Loan Associations in the Mortgage Market," *Monthly Review*, July 1956

―――――, "Private Pension Plans," *Monthly Review*, December 1953

Federal Reserve Board, *Flow of Funds Accounts*, annually

Fisher, Lawrence and James H. Lorie, "Rates of Return on Investments in Common Stocks," *Journal of Business*, January 1964

Fraine, Harold G., *Valuation of Securities Holdings of Life Insurance Companies*. Homewood: Richard D. Irwin, 1962

Friend, Irwin and Vito Natrella, *Individual Savings: Volume and Composition*. New York: John Wiley & Sons, 1954

Gerard, Victor, "More Call Price Protection Is Vital," American Life Convention, *General Proceedings*, 1953

Goldsmith, Raymond W., *The Flow of Capital Funds in the Postwar Economy*. New York: National Bureau of Economic Research, Columbia University Press, 1965

———, *A Study of Savings in the United States*, Volume II. Princeton: National Bureau of Economic Research, Princeton University Press, 1955

Grebler, Leo, *Housing Issues in Economic Stabilization Policy*. New York: National Bureau of Economic Research, Occasional Paper 72, 1960

——— and Sherman J. Maisel, "Determinants of Residential Construction: A Review of Present Knowledge," in *Impacts of Monetary Policy*. Englewood Cliffs: Commission on Money and Credit Monograph, Prentice-Hall, 1962

Guertin, Alfred N., "Life Insurance Company Income Tax Act of 1959," *Eastern Underwriter,* October 2, 1959

Gurley, J. G., "Financial Institutions in the Saving-Investment Process," *Proceedings* of the Second Annual Conference on Savings and Loan League, 1959. Reprinted in M. D. Ketchum and L. T. Kendall, editors, *Readings in Financial Institutions.* Boston: Houghton Mifflin Company, 1965

———, *Liquidity and Financial Institutions in the Postwar Economy*, Study Paper No. 14, Joint Economic Committee, 86th Cong., 2d Sess., Washington, 1960

——— and E. S. Shaw, "Financial Intermediaries and the Savings-Investment Process," *Journal of Finance,* May 1956

——— and ———. *Money in a Theory of Finance*. Washington: The Brookings Institution, 1960

Guttentag, Jack, "Commercial Banks in the Mortgage Market," Federal Reserve Bank of New York, *Monthly Review,* April 1956

———, "The Federal National Mortgage Association," in *Federal Credit Agencies*. Englewood Cliffs: Commission on Money and Credit Monograph, Prentice-Hall, 1963

———, "Mortgage Interest Rates: Trends and Structure," United States Savings and Loan League, Conference on Savings and Residential Financing, *Proceedings*, Chicago, 1964

———, "Mortgage Warehousing," *Journal of Finance,* December 1957

———, "The Short Cycle in Residential Construction, 1946–56," *American Economic Review,* June 1961

———, "Some Studies of the Post-World War II Residential Construction and Mortgage Markets," unpublished Ph.D. dissertation, Columbia University, 1958

Haines, Charles C., "Pension Fund Investing," *Trusts and Estates,* December 1965

Hansen, Alvin H., *The American Economy*. New York: McGraw-Hill, 1957

Hart, Orson H., "Life Insurance Companies and the Equity Capital Markets," *Journal of Finance,* May 1965

Hickman, W. Braddock, *Corporate Bond Quality and Investor Experience.* Princeton: National Bureau of Economic Research, Princeton University Press, 1958

Hodgman, D., "The Deposit Relationship and Commercial Bank Investment Behavior," *Review of Economics and Statistics,* August 1961

Hoffman, G. Wright, "Preferred and Common Stocks," in David McCahan, editor, *Investment of Life Insurance Funds.* Philadelphia: University of Pennsylvania Press, 1953

Hood, W. C., *The Financing of Economic Activity in Canada.* Ottawa: Royal Commission on Canada's Economic Prospects, 1958

——— and O. W. Main, "The Role of Canadian Life Insurance Companies in the Postwar Capital Market," *Canadian Journal of Economics,* November 1956

Housing and Home Finance Agency, *Housing Statistics,* monthly

Howell, Paul L., "A Re-examination of Pension Fund Investment Policies," *Journal of Finance,* May 1958

Hubbell, F. W., "Investment Indicators," American Life Convention, *General Proceedings,* 1943

Huston, F. Edward, "Actuarial Developments of 1942," American Life Convention, *General Proceedings,* 1942

Institute of Life Insurance, *Life Insurance Fact Book,* annually

———, *Tally of Life Insurance Statistics,* monthly

Jewett, John G., "Real Estate and Other Property," in David McCahan, editor, *Investment of Life Insurance Funds.* Philadelphia: University of Pennsylvania Press, 1953

Johnson, Harry G., "Monetary Theory and Policy," *American Economic Review,* June 1962

Jones, Lawrence D., "Portfolio Objectives, External Constraints, and the Postwar Investment Behavior of Life Insurance Companies," unpublished Ph.D. dissertation, Harvard University, September 1959

Kaplan, Mortimer, "Yields on Recently Issued Corporate Bonds: A New Index," *Journal of Finance,* March 1962

Karaken, John H., "Lenders' Preferences, Credit Rationing and the Effectiveness of Monetary Policy," *Review of Economics and Statistics,* August 1957

Kaufman, Stephen M., "The Life Insurance Company Income Tax Act of 1959," *National Tax Journal,* Part I, December 1963, and Part II, March 1964

———, "The Life Insurance Company Income Tax Act of 1959," unpublished senior thesis, Harvard College, 1962

Keir, Jack G., "The Liquidity Structure of Life Insurance Companies," unpublished Ph.D. dissertation, University of Pennsylvania, 1956

Kendall, Leon T., "Anatomy of the Residential Mortgage," Occasional Paper No. 2, United States Savings and Loan League, Chicago, 1964

——, "The Quality of Credit: Part I," United States Savings and Loan League, Conference on Savings and Residential Financing, *Proceedings*, Chicago, 1964

——, *The Savings and Loan Business: Its Purposes, Functions, and Justification*, Englewood Cliffs: Commission on Money and Credit Monograph, Prentice-Hall, 1962

Klaman, Saul B., "Effects of Credit and Monetary Policy on Real Estate Markets: 1952–1954," *Land Economics*, Vol. 32, August 1956

——, *The Postwar Residential Mortgage Market*. Princeton: National Bureau of Economic Research, Princeton University Press, 1961

——, "The Postwar Rise of Mortgage Companies." New York: National Bureau of Economic Research, Occasional Paper No. 60, 1959

——, "The Volume of Mortgage Debt in the Postwar Decade." New York: National Bureau of Economic Research, Technical Paper No. 13, 1958

Lewis, John P., *Business Conditions Analysis*. New York: McGraw-Hill, 1959

Life Insurance Association of America, *Cash Flow Survey*, quarterly

——, *City Mortgage Lending Income and Cost Survey*, 1958

——, *Direct Placement Survey*, monthly

——, *Forward Commitment Survey*, monthly

——, *Instructions and Definitions*, "Report on Direct Placement Yields," 1960

——, *Life Insurance Companies as Financial Institutions*. Englewood Cliffs: Commission on Money and Credit Monograph, Prentice-Hall, 1962 (LIAA-CMC Monograph)

——, *Record of Life Insurance Investments*, annually

Life Office Management Association, *Readings in Life Insurance: A Compendium*, Vols. I, II, 1934

Lindbeck, Assar, *The "New" Theory of Credit Control in the United States*, Stockholm Economic Studies, Pamphlet Series, I, 2nd edition, 1962

Lintner, John, *Mutual Savings Banks in the Savings and Mortgage Markets*. Boston: Division of Research, Harvard Business School, 1948

Linton, M. A., "Panics and Cash Values," *Transactions* of the Actuarial Society of America, Vol. XXXIII, Part 2, No. 88, 1932

Loewy, Harris, "Net Cash Money Flows Through Life Insurance Companies," *Journal of Finance*, December 1956

McDiarmid, F. J., "Life Insurance Company Investments and the Capital Market," *Journal of the American Statistical Association*, June 1948

———, *Investments of Life Insurance Companies in the United States and Canada.* New York: Life Office Management Association, 1953

McGill, Dan M., *Fundamentals of Private Pensions.* Homewood: Richard D. Irwin, 2nd edition, 1964

McLean, Alexander T., "Present Day Problems in Investment of Life Insurance Funds," *Journal of the American Society of Chartered Life Underwriters*, December 1948

Maisel, Sherman J., "A Theory of Fluctuations in Residential Construction Starts," *American Economic Review*, June 1963

Markowitz, Harry M., "Portfolio Selection," *Journal of Finance*, March 1952

———, *Portfolio Selection*, Cowles Foundation Monograph No. 16. New York: John Wiley & Sons, 1959

Marples, W. F., *Actuarial Aspects of Pension Security.* Homewood: Richard D. Irwin, 1965.

Matz, J. Edwin, *Transactions*, Society of Actuaries, November 3, 1960

Meader, J. W., "Diversification: A Sound Principle Often Carried to Unwarranted Extremes," *The Annalist*, Vol. 44, No. 1125, August 10, 1934

Melone, J. J. and E. T. Allen, Jr., *Pension Planning.* Homewood: Richard D. Irwin, 1966

Metropolitan Life Insurance Company, *A Study on the Necessity and Desirability of Amending Section 81 of the New York State Insurance Law to Provide More Adequately for Loans to Small Business*, New York, 1950

Moore, Geoffrey H., *Business Cycle Indicators.* Princeton: National Bureau of Economic Research, Princeton University Press, Volume I, 1961

———, "The Quality of Credit in Booms and Depressions," *Journal of Finance*, May 1956

Muth, Richard F., "Interest Rates, Contract Terms, and the Allocation of Mortgage Funds," *Journal of Finance*, March 1962

Nash, Thomas G., Jr., *Federal Taxation of Life Insurance Companies.* New York: Mathew Bender & Co., 1965

National Association of Mutual Savings Banks, *Mutual Savings Banking: Basic Characteristics and Role in the National Economy.*

Englewood Cliffs: Commission on Money and Credit Monograph, Prentice-Hall, 1962

National Association of Insurance Commissioners, Committee on Valuation of Securities, *Final Report to Insurance Companies, Societies and Associations re: Annual Statements as of December 31, 1957*, June 17, 1957

———, *Valuation Procedures and Instructions for Bonds and Stocks*, Section II, Procedures for Valuing Preferred Stocks; Section III, Procedures for Valuing Bonds, 1961

National Industrial Conference Board, *Investment Statistics*, New Capital Appropriations Series, quarterly

Natrella, Vito, "Implications of Pension Fund Accumulations," *Proceedings* of the American Statistical Association, Business and Economic Statistics Section, 1957

Nerlove, S. H., "Common Stocks as Investments for American Life Insurance Companies: A Non-Academic View," *Journal of Finance*, October 1948

New York Insurance Report, Vol. I, *Life*, annually

New York Joint Legislative Committee on Insurance Rates and Regulations, *Report*, 1950, 1951, 1952

New York, *Report* of the Joint Committee of the Senate and Assembly of the State of New York Appointed to Investigate the Affairs of Life Insurance Companies, 1906 (Armstrong Committee *Report*)

New York State Bankers Convention, Trust Division, *Report* of the Trust and Investment Study Committee, 1950

New York State, Joint Legislative Committee on Insurance Rates and Regulation, *Report*, 1964

O'Leary, James J., "Forward Investment Commitments of Life Insurance Companies," *The Quality and Economic Significance of Anticipations Data*, Universities–National Bureau of Economic Research Conference Series, Princeton: Princeton University Press, 1960

———, "The Institutional Savings-Investment Process and Current Economic Theory," *Papers and Proceedings* of the American Economic Association, May 1954

———, *A Review of the New York Law Governing Life Insurance Company Investments:* A Report to the Superintendent of Insurance of the State of New York, February 13, 1964

Patrick, R. B., "Management of the Life Insurance Investment Portfolio," in David McCahan, editor, *Investment of Life Insurance Funds*. Philadelphia: University of Pennsylvania Press, 1953

Penman, W., "A Review of Investment Principles and Practices," *The Journal of the Institute of Actuaries*, Vol. 64, 1933

Pizer, Leroy M., *Government Bond Market Analysis:* New York Institute of Finance, 1952

Ratchford, B. U., "Revenue Bonds and Tax Immunity," *National Tax Journal,* March 1954

Reid, Margaret G., *Housing and Income.* Chicago: University of Chicago Press, 1962

Robinson, Roland I., *The Management of Bank Funds.* New York: McGraw-Hill, 2nd edition, 1962

————, *Money and Capital Markets.* New York: McGraw-Hill, 1964

————, *Postwar Market for State and Local Securities.* Princeton: National Bureau of Economic Research, Princeton University Press, 1960

Roosa, Robert V., "Federal Reserve Operations in the Money and Government Securities Markets," Federal Reserve Bank of New York, 1956

————, "Interest Rates and the Central Bank," in *Money, Trade and Economic Growth, Essays in Honor of John H. Williams.* New York: Macmillan, 1951

————, "Monetary Policy Again: Comments," Oxford Symposium on Monetary Policy, *Oxford University Bulletin of the Institute of Statistics,* Vol. 14, August 1952

Rydgren, A. A., "An Investment Policy for a Life Insurance Company," in *Readings in Life Insurance: A Compendium,* Vol. II. New York: Life Office Management Association, 1934

Saulnier, R. J., *Urban Mortgage Lending by Life Insurance Companies.* New York: National Bureau of Economic Research, 1950

Scott, Ira O., Jr., *Government Securities Market.* New York: McGraw-Hill, 1965

Securities and Exchange Commission, *Cost of Flotation of Directly Placed Corporate Securities,* 1955

————, *Statistical Bulletin,* Survey of Corporate Pension Funds, 1951–1954

Shands, William R., "Investment Laws — Changes During the Last Decade," *Papers Presented to the Association of Life Insurance Counsel,* Vol. IX, 1946

Shiskin, Julius, "Electronic Computers and Business Indicators," Occasional Paper No. 57. New York: National Bureau of Business Research, 1957

Smith, Warren L., "On the Effectiveness of Monetary Policy," *American Economic Review,* September 1956

Smutney, Rudolf, "Investments of Retirement Funds," paper delivered before the 50th Annual Conference of the Committee on Public

Employment Retirement Administration of the Municipal Finance Officers Association, 1956

Soldofsky, Robert M., "The Size and Maturity of Direct Placement Loans," *Journal of Finance,* March 1960

Sommers, Albert T. and Shirley H. Rhine, "The New Dimension in Mortgage Debt," Technical Paper No. 15. New York: National Industrial Conference Board, 1964

Souvain, H. C., "Some Economic Considerations Affecting Investment Policy," American Life Convention, *General Proceedings,* 1949

Sproul, Allan, "Central Banking and the Private Economy," an address before the Annual Meeting of the Life Insurance Association of America, New York, December 1951. Reprinted in The Federal Reserve Bank of New York, *Monthly Review,* January 1952

Tatlock, John, "On the Proper Method of Valuation of Fixed Term Securities Owned by Life Insurance Companies," *Proceedings* of the Association of Life Insurance Company Presidents, 1907

Temporary National Economic Committee, *Hearings, Part 28, Life Insurance Operating Results and Investment,* 76th Cong., 2d Sess., February–March 1940

———, *Study of Legal Reserve Life Insurance Companies,* Monograph No. 28, 76th Cong., 3d Sess., 1940

Tobin, James, "Monetary Policy and the Management of the Public Debt; The Patman Inquiry," *Review of Economics and Statistics,* May 1953

Travis, Frank J., "Life Insurance Company Investments in Preferred Stocks," *Journal of the American Society of Chartered Life Underwriters,* Winter 1957

U.S. Congress, House

Committee on Banking and Currency, Subcommittee on Domestic Finance, *Comparative Regulations of Financial Institutions,* 88th Cong., 1st Sess., November 22, 1963

———, ———, Subcommittee on Housing, *Hearings, Investigation of Housing,* 84th Cong., 1st Sess., Part 1, October 1955

———, ———, ———, *Mortgage Credit and FHA Multifamily Housing,* Report No. 2, January 31, 1956

Committee on Ways and Means, Subcommittee on Internal Revenue Taxation, *Hearings,* 85th Cong., 2d Sess., November 1958

———, Subcommittee on the Taxation of Life Insurance Companies, *A Preliminary Statement of the Facts and Issues,* November 1953

U.S. Congress, Joint Committee on the Economic Report, *Hearings on the Volume and Stability of Private Investment,* 81st Cong., 1st Sess., Part 2, December 1949

———, ———, Subcommittee on General Credit Control and Debt Management, *Hearings on Monetary Policy and Management of the Public Debt, Their Role in Achieving Price Stability and High Level Employment* (the Patman *Hearings*), 82nd Cong., 2d Sess., March 1952

———, ———, ———, *Replies to Questions and Other Material for the Use of the Subcommittee* (the Patman *Replies*), 82d Cong., 2d Sess., Part 2, March 1952

U.S. Congress, Senate

    Committee on Banking and Currency, Subcommittee on Housing, *Study of Mortgage Credit,* 85th Cong., 2d Sess., December 22, 1958

    Committee on Finance, *Hearings on the Taxation of Life Insurance Income,* 85th Cong., 2d Sess., March 5 and 6, 1958

    Senate Finance Committee, *Hearings on H.R. 8245,* 67th Cong., 1st Sess., 1921

United States Savings and Loan League, Conference on Savings and Residential Financing, *Proceedings,* Chicago, 1964

United States v. *Southeastern Underwriters Association,* 322 U.S. 533 (1944)

Walter, James E., *The Investment Process as Characterized by Leading Life Insurance Companies.* Boston: Division of Research, Harvard Business School, 1962

Wehrle, Leroy S., "Life Insurance Investment — The Experience of Four Companies," *Yale Economic Essays,* Vol. I, No. 1, Spring 1961

———, "A Theory of Life Insurance Company Portfolio Selection," Cowles Discussion Paper No. 60, December 1, 1958

Williams, C. A. and H. A. Williams, "Incentive Financing — A New Opportunity," *Harvard Business Review,* March–April 1960

Winn, Willis J., "Factors Influencing Life Insurance Company Investments," *Journal of the American Society of Chartered Life Underwriters,* Spring 1958

Wood, Arthur D., "The Permanence of Life Insurance," American Life Convention, *General Proceedings,* 1934

Wood, J. Harry, "What the Life Insurance Underwriter Should Know About Investments," *Journal of the American Society of Chartered Life Underwriters,* Summer 1958

Wright, Kenneth M., "Gross Flow of Funds Through Life Insurance Companies," *Journal of Finance,* May 1960

Zartman, Lester W., *The Investments of Life Insurance Companies.* New York: Henry Holt & Co., 1906

INDEX

of assets; quality of assets; solvency

rate of return, 16, 21–22, 33, 62–72, 183–184, 225–228, 332, 334–347, 450, 527, 537

see also forward commitments; rate of return; yield maximization

portfolio policy defined, 15, 73

portfolio rollover

and the business cycle, 314–316

defined, 307

in flow of funds, 25, 65, 305, 307–310, 322, 360–361, 422, 477

in regression analysis of votings, 478

portfolios, "efficient," defined, 14–15

preferred stock

investment restrictions on, 78, 85–88, 103–104, 108

taxation of, 164

valuation of, 129, 131, 133–134, 136, 138–141, 144

Prudential Life Insurance Company

liquidity position of, 286–287n

mortgage commitments, 386–387

warehousing loan, 273, 286

quality of assets

attitude toward, 31–34, 37, 180–183

and holdings of Government securities, 180–181, 204, 226

mortgage bonds, 36–37, 43, 45, 169, 521

as objective, 30–45, 51, 169, 514, 527–528

rating of corporate bonds, 34–36, 127–128, 169

statutory requirements for, 30–31, 81–86, 88–90, 94–95

rate of return

calculation of, from interest rates, 340–344, 394–397

effect on net cost of policies, 62–63

and forward commitments, 332, 334–347, 368–372, 387–389

as investment motive, 111–112, 183–184

and investment process, 68–70

and maturity of assets, 50–53, 55, 59, 398, 533–534

see also yield

real estate

attitude toward investing in, 119–123

housing developments, 79, 91, 119

investment restrictions on, 78–80, 89–92, 117, 119–120, 122, 169

investments in, 92, 118–120, 168, 170, 499

lease-back purchases of, 120–121, 123, 166–168, 170–171, 499

redevelopment companies, 91

and taxation, 151, 158, 166–168

valuation of holdings, 126, 142–143

refunding, attitude toward, 55–56, 58

regulation of investment

effect of, 169–172, 528, 530, 536, 543

federal, 74

purpose of, 74–76, 121, 528

regulation of investment by states

company attitude toward, 94–95, 101–110, 113

for corporate bonds, 82–84

for corporate stock, 85–88, 98–99

effect on portfolio acquisitions, 94–99, 108–114, 123, 165, 169–172, 398

history of, 76–80

insurance departments, 76, 108

"leeway provisions," 80, 84, 92–93, 96

for mortgage loans, 88–89, 96, 171

for real estate, 89–92, 169–170

summary by type of asset, 80–93

summary of laws, 1928–1951, 77–80

for U.S. Government bonds, 81–82, 94

see also state regulatory laws

regulation of operation, reserves, 17

rejection rates on investments, 413

risk

of default, 20–22, 31, 36, 52, 71, 249–250, 425, 542

and Government underwritten mortgages, 37, 249–250, 268, 425

income, 22, 33, 52–59, 401, 429

and liquidity, 23–24

and maturity, 22, 52–57

reduction of, 22, 45–46

risk-bearing yields, 30–33, 542

A

I